Middle School 3-2
학교시험 완벽대비

2학기 전과정
적중 100 plus

영어 **기출문제집**

중 **3**

시사 | 박준언

Best Collection

구성과 특징

교과서의 주요 학습 내용을 중심으로 학습 영역별 특성에 맞춰 단계별로 다양한 학습 기회를 제공하여
단원별 학습능력 평가는 물론 중간 및 기말고사 시험 등에 완벽하게 대비할 수 있도록 내용을 구성

Words & Expressions

Step1 Key Words 단원별 핵심 단어 설명 및 풀이
Key Expression 단원별 핵심 숙어 및 관용어 설명
Word Power 반대 또는 비슷한 뜻 단어 배우기
English Dictionary 영어로 배우는 영어 단어

Step2 실력평가 단원별 수시평가 대비 주관식, 객관식 문제풀이

Step3 서술형 대비 학업성취도 및 수행능력평가 대비 서술형 문제풀이

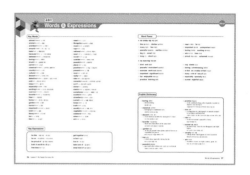

Conversation

Step1 핵심 의사소통 소통에 필요한 주요 표현 방법 요약
핵심 Check 기본적인 표현 방법 및 활용능력 확인

Step2 대화문 익히기 교과서 대화문 심층 분석 및 확인

Step3 교과서 확인학습 빈칸 채우기를 통한 문장 완성 능력 확인

Step4 기본평가 시험대비 기초 학습 능력 평가

Step5 실력평가 단원별 수시평가 대비 주관식, 객관식 문제풀이

Step6 서술형 대비 학업성취도 및 수행능력평가 대비 서술형 문제풀이

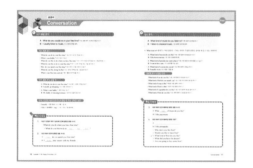

Grammar

Step1 주요 문법 단원별 주요 문법 사항과 예문을 알기 쉽게 설명
핵심 Check 기본 문법사항에 대한 이해 여부 확인

Step2 기본평가 시험대비 기초 학습 능력 평가

Step3 실력평가 단원별 수시평가 대비 주관식, 객관식 문제풀이

Step4 서술형 대비 학업성취도 및 수행능력평가 대비 서술형 문제풀이

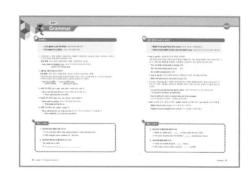

Reading

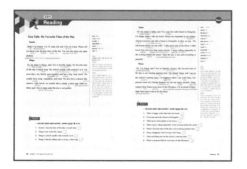

Step1 구문 분석 단원별로 제시된 문장에 대한 구문별 분석과 내용 설명
확인문제 문장에 대한 기본적인 이해와 인지능력 확인

Step2 확인학습A 빈칸 채우기를 통한 문장 완성 능력 확인

Step3 확인학습B 제시된 우리말을 영어로 완성하여 작문 능력 키우기

Step4 실력평가 단원별 수시평가 대비 주관식, 객관식 문제풀이

Step5 서술형 대비 학업성취도 및 수행능력평가 대비 서술형 문제풀이
교과서 구석구석 교과서에 나오는 기타 문장까지 완벽 학습

Composition

|영역별 핵심문제|
단어 및 어휘, 대화문, 문법, 독해 등 각 영역별 기출문제의 출제 유형을 분석하여 실전에 대비하고 연습할 수 있도록 문제를 배열

|단원별 예상문제|
기출문제를 분석한 후 새로운 시험 출제 경향을 더하여 새롭게 출제될 수 있는 문제를 포함하여 시험에 완벽하게 대비할 수 있도록 준비

|서술형 실전 및 창의사고력 문제|
학교 시험에서 점차 늘어나는 서술형 시험에 집중 대비하고 고득점을 취득하는데 만전을 기하기 위한 학습 코너

|단원별 모의고사|
영역별, 단계별 학습을 모두 마친 후 실전 연습을 위한 모의고사

교과서 파헤치기

- **단어 Test1~3** 영어 단어 우리말 쓰기, 우리말을 영어 단어로 쓰기, 영영풀이에 해당하는 단어와 우리말 쓰기
- **대화문 Test1~2** 대화문 빈칸 완성 및 전체 대화문 쓰기
- **본문 Test1~5** 빈칸 완성, 우리말 쓰기, 문장 배열연습, 영어 작문하기 복습 등 단계별 반복 학습을 통해 교과서 지문에 대한 완벽한 습득
- **구석구석지문 Test1~2** 지문 빈칸 완성 및 전문 영어로 쓰기

Lesson 6

Meet the World

의사소통 기능

- 주제 소개하기
  Let's talk about food.
- 제안하기 · 권유하기
  I suggest you visit Independence Hall.

언어 형식

- '계속적 용법'의 관계대명사 which/who
  Someone uses the word kiwi, **which** has several meanings.
- '부사적 용법'의 to부정사
  If you say "kia ora" to the villagers, they will be **glad to hear** it.

Words & Expressions

Key Words

- **abroad** [əbrɔ́ːd] 부 해외에(서), 해외로
- **achieve** [ətʃíːv] 동 달성하다, 성취하다
- **activity** [æktívəti] 명 활동
- **amaze** [əméiz] 동 (대단히) 놀라게 하다
- **appreciate** [əpríːʃièit] 동 진가를 알아보다, 인정하다
- **carry** [kǽri] 동 가지고 가다
- **clearly** [klíərli] 부 명확하게
- **color** [kʌ́lər] 동 칠하다
- **common** [kámən] 형 흔한
- **confused** [kənfjúːzd] 형 (사람이) 혼란스러워 하는
- **culture** [kʌ́ltʃər] 명 문화
- **European** [jùərəpíən] 명 유럽인
- **experience** [ikspíəriəns] 동 겪다, 경험하다
- **hill** [hil] 명 언덕
- **hot spring** 온천
- **information** [ìnfərméiʃən] 명 정보
- **kiwi** [kíːwi] 명 키위, 키위새, 뉴질랜드인
- **landscape** [lǽndskeip] 명 풍경
- **main** [mein] 형 주요한, 주된
- **Maori** [máuri] 명 마오리인(뉴질랜드 원주민), 마오리어
- **match** [mætʃ] 명 경기, 시합
- **native** [néitiv] 형 (특정한 곳의) 토박이의
- **natural** [nǽtʃərəl] 형 자연의, 천연의
- **New Zealander** 뉴질랜드 사람
- **nickname** [níknèim] 명 별명
- **people** [píːpl] 명 (특정 국가 지역의) 국민[민족/종족]
- **plaid** [plæd] 명 격자무늬, 격자무늬 천
- **potluck** [pátlək] 명 각자 준비한 음식을 나눠먹는 식사
- **recommend** [rèkəménd] 동 추천하다
- **return** [ritə́ːrn] 동 돌아오다[가다]
- **rival** [ráivəl] 명 경쟁자, 경쟁 상대
- **rugby** [rʌ́gbi] 명 럭비
- **several** [sévərəl] 형 몇몇의
- **society** [səsáiəti] 명 (공동체를 이루는 일반적인) 사회
- **someday** [sʌ́mdei] 부 언젠가, 언제든, 훗날
- **station** [stéiʃən] 명 [흔히 합성어에서] 방송국
- **success** [səksés] 명 성공, 성과
- **suggest** [səgdʒést] 동 제안하다
- **surely** [ʃúərli] 부 확실히, 분명히
- **symbol** [símbəl] 명 상징, 상징물
- **throughout** [θruːáut] 전 도처에
- **traditional** [trədíʃənl] 형 전통적인
- **trail** [treil] 명 자취, 오솔길
- **twin** [twin] 형 쌍둥이의 명 쌍둥이 (중의 한 명)
- **view** [vjuː] 명 (특히 아름다운 시골) 경관, 전망
- **village** [vílidʒ] 명 마을, 부락, 촌락
- **waterfall** [wɔ́ːtərfɔl] 명 폭포
- **wedding** [wédiŋ] 명 결혼(식)
- **wildly** [wáildli] 부 걷잡을 수 없이, 극도로

Key Expressions

- **a couple of** 두서너 개의, 몇 개의
- **all year round** 일 년 내내
- **be covered with** ~으로 덮이다
- **be famous for** ~로 유명하다
- **be glad to** ~하게 되어 기쁘다
- **be known as** ~로 알려져 있다
- **come to one's mind** 생각이 나다, 생각이 떠오르다
- **filled with** ~로 가득 찬
- **long before** 훨씬 이전에
- **look forward to** ~을 기대하다
- **look like** ~처럼 보이다
- **prepare for** ~을 준비하다
- **take a bike tour** 자전거 여행을 하다
- **take a photo of** ~의 사진을 찍다
- **try on** (옷을) 입어보다
- **with the help of** ~의 도움을 받아서

Word Power

※ 서로 비슷한 뜻을 가진 어휘

- □ **abroad** 해외에(서), 해외로 – **overseas** 해외에
- □ **achieve** 달성하다 – **accomplish** 성취하다
- □ **amaze** 놀라게 하다 – **astonish** 놀라게 하다
- □ **clearly** 명확하게 – **certainly** 확실하게
- □ **landscape** 풍경 – **scenery** 경치

- □ **main** 주요한, 주된 – **major** 주된
- □ **rival** 경쟁자, 경쟁 상대 – **competitor** 경쟁자
- □ **suggest** 제안하다 – **propose** 제안하다
- □ **surely** 확실히 – **clearly** 명확하게
- □ **wildly** 걷잡을 수 없이 – **madly** 격렬하게

※ 서로 반대되는 뜻을 가진 어휘

- □ **common** 흔한 ↔ **uncommon** 흔치 않은
- □ **natural** 자연의, 천연의 ↔ **artificial** 인위적인

- □ **confused** 혼란스러워 하는 ↔ **calm** 침착한, 냉정한
- □ **success** 성공, 성과 ↔ **failure** 실패

※ 형용사 – 명사

- □ **confused** 혼란스러워 하는 – **confusion** 혼란
- □ **natural** 자연의, 천연의 – **nature** 자연
- □ **successful** 성공적인 – **success** 성공, 성과

- □ **symbolic** 상징적인 – **symbol** 상징, 상징물
- □ **traditional** 전통적인 – **tradition** 전통

※ 동사 – 명사

- □ **achieve** 성취하다 – **achievement** 성취
- □ **act** 행동하다 – **activity** 활동
- □ **appreciate** 진가를 알아보다 – **appreciation** 평가

- □ **inform** 알려주다 – **information** 정보
- □ **recommend** 추천하다 – **recommendation** 추천
- □ **succeed** 성공하다 – **success** 성공, 성과

English Dictionary

- □ **abroad** 해외에(서), 해외로
  → in or to a foreign country
  외국에 있거나 외국으로 가는

- □ **achieve** 달성하다, 성취하다
  → to successfully complete something or get a good result
  성공적으로 일을 완수하거나 좋은 결과를 얻다

- □ **common** 흔한
  → happening often and to many people or in many places
  많은 사람에게 또는 많은 장소에서 자주 일어나는

- □ **kiwi** 키위새
  → a New Zealand bird that cannot fly
  날 수 없는 뉴질랜드의 새

- □ **Maori** 마오리인
  → someone who belongs to the race of people that first lived in New Zealand
  뉴질랜드에 처음 살았던 종족에 속하는 사람

- □ **plaid** 격자무늬
  → a pattern of crossed of lines and squares
  십자 모양의 선과 사각형으로 된 무늬

- □ **potluck** 각자 준비한 음식을 나눠먹는 식사
  → a meal in which everyone who is invited brings something to eat
  초대받은 모든 사람들이 먹을 무언가를 가지고 오는 식사

- □ **rugby** 럭비
  → an outdoor game played by two teams with an oval(= egg-shaped) ball
  타원형의 공을 가지고 두 팀이 하는 야외 경기

- □ **symbol** 상징, 상징물
  → a picture or shape that has a particular meaning or represents a particular organization or idea
  의미를 가지거나 조직, 사상을 나타내는 그림이나 모양

- □ **trail** 오솔길
  → a rough path across countryside or through a forest
  시골을 가로지르거나 숲을 지나가는 거친 길

01 다음 문장의 빈칸에 공통으로 들어갈 말로 알맞은 것은?

- This cloth is made from _____ fibers.
- Mt. Bugak impresses visitors with both its stunning _____ beauty and cultural assets.

① exhibition　　② entrance
③ natural　　④ poem
⑤ specialist

서답형
02 〈영영풀이〉를 읽고 빈칸에 알맞은 단어를 쓰시오.

Wearing safety gear, including helmets and _____ pads, is also advised.

┌─영영풀이─┐
the joint where your leg bends

[03~04] 다음 설명에 해당하는 단어를 고르시오.

03

in or to a foreign country

① aboard　　② broad
③ station　　④ abroad
⑤ board

04

happening often and to many people or in many places

① main　　② common
③ sure　　④ confused
⑤ traditional

서답형
05 다음 우리말에 맞게 빈칸에 세 단어를 쓰시오.

푸른 잔디로 뒤덮였던 서울 광장이 붉은색 테니스 코트로 변했다.

➡ Seoul Plaza, which used to _____ _____ _____ green lawn, has turned into a tennis court in red.

06 다음 빈칸에 들어갈 말이 바르게 짝지어진 것은?

(A) She _____ the four judges and got a YES from all of them.
(B) They _____ music composed by Johann Bach, George Handel, and Antonio Vivaldi.

	(A)	(B)
①	amazed	recommend
②	amazed	color
③	achieved	experience
④	achieved	recommend
⑤	returned	suggest

서답형
07 다음 짝지어진 단어의 관계가 같도록 빈칸에 알맞은 말을 쓰시오.

landscape – scenery : propose – _____

08 다음 빈칸에 들어갈 가장 알맞은 말은?

I will _____ receiving a nice birthday present from you!

① look like　　② carry on
③ be famous for　　④ belong to
⑤ look forward to

01 다음 빈칸에 들어갈 말을 〈보기〉에서 찾아 쓰시오. (필요하면 어형을 변화시키고, 동사는 현재형으로 쓸 것)

┌─ 보기 ┐
landscape   fill   suggest   appreciate
└─────────────────────────┘

(1) He hopes to make the world a better place _____ with healthy people.

(2) Professor Achor _____ that you see the good, positive things in your life.

(3) The event teaches children to _____ all types of art.

(4) New Zealand is a country well-known for its breathtaking _____ and abundant wildlife.

02 다음 문장의 빈칸에 들어갈 알맞은 단어를 쓰시오.

┌─────────────────────────┐
The Niagara Falls is the most popular _____ in North America.
└─────────────────────────┘

03 다음 우리말과 같은 표현이 되도록 문장의 빈칸을 채우시오.

(1) 이제, 서울 도처에 추위를 피할 수 있는 도피처들이 생겨나고 있다.
➡ Now, some refuges from the cold are popping up _____ Seoul.

(2) 주의 깊은 설명을 들은 후에도, 우리는 여전히 혼란스럽다.
➡ Even after some careful explanation, we are still left _____.

(3) 그 경기는 독일의 골로 거칠게 시작되었다.
➡ The match started _____ with a goal from Germany.

(4) 그들은 온천에서 목욕을 하면서 눈을 감고 있습니다.
➡ They are closing their eyes while bathing in a _____.

04 다음 영영풀이에 해당하는 단어를 〈보기〉에서 찾아 첫 번째 빈칸에 쓰고, 두 번째 빈칸에는 우리말 뜻을 쓰시오.

┌─ 보기 ┐
rival   length   north   wedding
└─────────────────────────┘

(1) _____ : the measurement of something from one end to the other end: _____

(2) _____ : the direction on your left when you are looking at the sunrise: _____

(3) _____ : a person who is competing for the same object or goal as another: _____

(4) _____ : a marriage ceremony and any celebrations such as a meal or a party that follow it: _____

05 빈칸에 'tradition'을 이용하여 알맞은 형태를 쓰시오.

┌─────────────────────────┐
• Korea is a beautiful country with a wonderful culture and unique _____s.
• It's the _____ way to "fight the heat with heat."
└─────────────────────────┘

Conversation

① 주제 소개하기

- **Let's talk about food.** 음식에 관해 이야기해 봅시다.

■ 'Let's talk about ~.(~에 대하여 이야기해 봅시다.)'는 주제를 소개하는 표현이다. 이야기하고 싶은 주제를 소개할 때는 'I'd like to talk about ~.(~에 대하여 이야기하고 싶어요.)'라고 할 수도 있지만 'would like to' 대신에 'will', 'want to' 등을 사용하여 'Today, I will talk about ~.', 'I want to talk about ~.'라고 할 수도 있다.

■ 원하는 무엇인가를 하려고 할 때 'I'd like to ~.'라고 한다. 지금부터 상대에게 새로운 주제를 소개하려고 할 때는 '~에 대하여 말씀드리겠습니다.'라는 의미로 'I'd like to talk about ~.', 'I'd like to say something about ~.', 'I'd like to tell you ~.'라고 한다. 그 외에 주제를 소개하는 다른 표현으로 'I'm going to talk about ~.', 'Let me tell you about ~.', 'May I tell you about ~?', 'I'd like to introduce ~.' 등이 있다.

■ 상대에게 격식을 차려서 주제를 소개할 때는 'I'd like to give a presentation about ~.' 또는 'I'd like to give you an introduction about ~.'라고 할 수도 있다. '~에 대해서 말하자면 ~'이라는 뜻으로 'Speaking of ~, 주어+동사 ~.', 'Talking of ~, 주어+동사 ~.'와 같은 표현을 사용하기도 한다.

주제 소개하기

- Let's talk about ~.   ~에 대하여 이야기해 봅시다.
- I'd like to say something about ~.   ~에 대하여 이야기하고 싶어요.
- I'd like to talk about ~.   ~에 대하여 말씀드리겠습니다.
- I'd like to tell you ~.   ~에 대하여 말씀드리겠습니다.
- I want to talk about ~.   ~에 대하여 말씀드리고 싶습니다.

핵심 Check

1. 밑줄 친 우리말과 일치하도록 주어진 단어를 포함하여 영작하시오.

> G: Brian, <u>세계 음식 축제를 위해서 우리가 무엇을 준비할지 이야기해 봅시다.</u> (let's, prepare, the World Food Festival, talk)
>
> B: I will make a meat pie. It is famous in Australia. How about you, Sera?
>
> G: I want to make a popular English dish, fish and chips.
>
> B: Fish and chips? What does it look like?
>
> G: It's fried fish with hot potato chips.
>
> B: That sounds interesting. Let's prepare them.

➡ _____

❷ 제안하기 · 권유하기

> • **I suggest (that) we learn yoga.** 나는 요가를 배우자고 제안합니다.

■ 'I suggest we ~.'는 상대방에게 무언가를 같이 하자고 제안하거나 권유할 때 쓰는 표현이다. 동사 'suggest(제안하다)' 다음에는 명사절을 이끄는 접속사 'that'이 생략되고 'that'절에서는 조동사 'should' 를 쓰는데, 이를 생략하고 동사원형을 사용하여 'I suggest (that)+주어+(should)+동사원형 ~.'의 구문 으로 나타낸다.

■ 'suggest'를 이용한 표현은 'suggest+that (should)절' 이외에도 'suggest+-ing', 'suggest+wh-절', 'suggest+wh- to do' 등으로 나타내기도 한다. 한편 'suggest'가 '암시하다, 시사하다, 말하다' 등의 의미 로 제안의 의미가 아닌 경우에는 that절에 should를 사용하지 않는다.

■ 제안이나 권유를 나타내는 유사한 표현으로 'Let's ~.(~하자.)', 'had better(~하는 편이 낫다)', 'Why don't you/we ~?(~하는 것이 어때?)', 'May I suggest that ~?(~하는 것이 어떠세요?)' 등이 있다. 'How about'과 'What about'은 'How about 명사/~ing?(~는 어때?)', 'What about 명사/~ing?(~하는 것이 어때?)'의 형태로 쓰며 상대에게 제안이나 권유하는 의미와 함께 상대의 의견을 물어보는 의미로도 사용한다.

제안이나 권유하기

• I suggest (that) 주어+(should)+동사원형 ~.	(~하자고 제안한다.)
• You had better+동사원형 ~.	(~하는 편이 낫다.)
• (I think) You should/ought to+동사원형 ~.	(~해야 한다고 생각해.)
• Why don't you/we ~?	(~하는 것이 어때?)
• Would you like (me) to ~?	(~하기를 원하세요?)

제안이나 권유에 답하기

〈긍정〉 (That) Sounds good. / No problem.
〈부정〉 I'm afraid I can't (learn yoga). / Thank you, but I don't want to (learn yoga).

✎ 핵심 Check

2. 다음 빈칸에 주어진 단어를 적절한 형태로 쓰시오.

> B: Wow, we finally arrived in Hong Kong, Mom.
> W: I'm looking forward to our visit. What should we do today, Mike?
> B: I suggest we _____ (visit) Victoria Peak.

Listen & Speak 1 A-1

B: ❶Let's talk about traditional clothing from other countries.

G: Hmm... Do you know ❷what a kilt is?

B: No, I don't. What is it?

G: It is traditional clothing from Scotland. ❸It looks like a knee-length skirt and has a plaid pattern.

B: A skirt of knee length with a plaid pattern?

G: Yes. It is unique because it is a skirt for men.

B: ❹That sounds interesting. I want to try one on.

B: 다른 나라의 전통 의상에 대해 이야기해 보자.
G: 흠… 너는 킬트가 뭔지 아니?
B: 아니, 몰라. 그게 뭐야?
G: 킬트는 스코틀랜드의 전통 의상이야. 그건 무릎길이의 치마 같이 생겼고, 체크무늬가 있어.
B: 무릎길이의 체크무늬 치마라고?
G: 응. 킬트는 남자를 위한 치마이기 때문에 특이해.
B: 흥미롭게 들린다. 나는 킬트를 입어보고 싶어.

❶ 'Let's talk about ∼.(∼에 대하여 이야기해 봅시다.)'는 주제를 소개하는 표현이다.
❷ 동사 'know'의 목적어로 '의문사(what)+주어(a kilt)+동사(is)' 어순의 간접의문문이다.
❸ 'look like+명사'는 '∼처럼 보이다'라는 뜻이고, and 뒤의 has는 단수동사 'looks'와 병렬 관계이다.
❹ 'sound+형용사' 형태로 '∼하게 들리다'로 해석한다.

Check(√) True or False

(1) They are talking about a kilt.   T ☐ F ☐

(2) A kilt is a skirt for women.   T ☐ F ☐

Listen & Speak 2 A-1

B: Wow, we finally arrived in Hong Kong, Mom.

W: ❶I'm looking forward to our visit. What should we do today, Mike?

B: ❷I suggest we visit Victoria Peak.

W: Victoria Peak?

B: It is the highest mountain in Hong Kong and is in a lot of movies. We can enjoy the fantastic view.

W: That sounds good. Let's go.

B: 와, 엄마, 우리가 마침내 홍콩에 도착했어요.
W: 우리가 방문할 곳들이 기대된다. 오늘 우리는 무엇을 해야 하니, Mike?
B: 저는 우리가 빅토리아 피크에 가는 것을 제안해요.
W: 빅토리아 피크?
B: 빅토리아 피크는 홍콩에서 가장 높은 산이고, 영화에도 많이 나왔어요. 우리는 환상적인 경관을 즐길 수 있어요.
W: 그거 좋겠구나. 가 보자.

❶ 'look forward to+명사/동명사'는 '∼을 기대하고 있다'라는 의미이다.
❷ 'I suggest we ∼.'는 상대방에게 무언가를 같이 하자고 제안하거나 권유할 때 쓰는 표현이다. 동사 'suggest(제안하다)' 다음에는 명사절을 이끄는 접속사 'that'이 생략되고 'that'절에서는 조동사 'should'를 쓰는데, 이를 생략하고 동사원형을 사용하여 'I suggest (that)+주어+(should)+동사원형 ∼.'의 구문으로 나타낸다.

Check(√) True or False

(3) Mike and his mother are traveling to Hong Kong.   T ☐ F ☐

(4) Victoria Peak is the highest mountain in Hong Kong. T ☐ F ☐

Listen & Speak 1 A-2

G: Brian, let's talk about ❶what we will prepare for the World Food Festival.

B: I will make a meat pie. It is famous in Australia. How about you, Sera?

G: ❷I want to make a popular English dish, fish and chips.

B: Fish and chips? ❸What does it look like?

G: It's fried fish with hot potato chips.

B: That sounds interesting. Let's prepare them.

❶ 전치사 'about'의 목적어로 '의문사+주어+동사' 어순의 간접의문문이다.

❷ 'want'는 to부정사를 목적어로 취하고, 'English dish'와 'fish and chips'는 동격 관계이다.

❸ '어떻게 생겼니?'의 의미로 '사물의 모습'이나 '사람의 외모'를 물어볼 때 사용하는 표현이다.

 Listen & Speak 2 A-2

G: My American friend invited me to a potluck dinner next Friday.

B: You know, you should take food ❶to share at the dinner.

G: What would you recommend ❷that I take?

B: ❸I suggest you take some Korean food. How about Gimbap, Suji?

G: Yes. It's not spicy and it's easy ❹to carry.

B: I think it'll be good for dinner.

❶ to부정사의 형용사적 용법으로 명사 'food'를 수식한다.

❷ 'that I take'는 동사 'recommend'의 목적어로 사용되었고, 'take' 앞에는 'should'가 생략되어 있다. What은 의문대명사로 take의 목적어이다.

❸ 'suggest' 뒤에 접속사 'that'이 생략되어 있고 'that'절의 해석이 '~해야 한다'일 때 '주어+should+동사원형'을 사용한다. 이때 'should'는 생략 가능하다.

❹ 형용사 'easy'를 수식하는 '부사적 용법'으로 '~하기에'로 해석한다.

 Real Life Talk

Seho: Good morning.

Jessie, Andy: Hi, Seho.

Seho: I will visit my uncle in Philadelphia this winter. Can you tell me about the city?

Jessie: Sure. I was there a few years ago. First, ❶let's talk about food.

Seho: Okay. What food is Philadelphia famous for?

Jessie: ❷The most famous food in Philadelphia is the cheese steak sandwich. It is a big sandwich ❸filled with beef and melted cheese.

Seho: Good suggestion. I will try it. Are there any places ❹that are popular with tourists?

Andy: ❺I suggest you visit Independence Hall. It is very important in American history.

Seho: Wonderful. Thank you for the information.

Andy: My pleasure.

❶ 주제를 소개하는 표현이다. 이야기하고 싶은 주제를 소개할 때는 'I'd like to talk about ~.(~에 대하여 이야기하고 싶어요.)'라고 할 수도 있지만 'would like to' 대신에 'will', 'want to' 등을 사용하여 'Today, I will talk about ~.', 'I want to talk about ~.'라고 할 수도 있다.

❷ 'famous'의 최상급 형태로 'the most'를 사용한다.

❸ 'filled with beef and melted cheese.'는 명사 'a big sandwich'를 수식하는 과거분사 구문이다. 'sandwich'와 'filled' 사이에는 '주격 관계대명사 (which+)be동사(is)'가 생략되어 있다.

❹ 주격 관계대명사절로 선행사 'places'를 수식한다. 선행사가 복수명사인 'places'이기 때문에 주격 관계대명사 뒤의 동사는 복수동사 'are'를 사용한다.

❺ 'suggest' 뒤에 접속사 'that'이 생략되어 있고 'visit' 앞에는 조동사 'should'가 생략되어 있다.

 Wrap Up

M: Welcome to Australia. The capital of Australia is Canberra. People speak English. Meat pie is a popular dish in Australia. Every year, ❶lots of tourists visit the Sydney Opera House and the beautiful beaches in Melbourne.

❶ 'lots of'는 'a lot of', 'plenty of'와 같은 의미로 '많은'의 뜻이다.

● 다음 우리말과 일치하도록 빈칸에 알맞은 말을 쓰시오.

Listen & Speak 1 A

1. B: _____ _____ about traditional clothing from _____ countries.

   G: Hmm... Do you know _____ _____ _____ _____?

   B: No, I don't. What is it?

   G: It is _____ _____ from Scotland. It _____ _____ a _____ skirt and has a _____ _____.

   B: A skirt of knee length _____ a plaid pattern?

   G: Yes. It is _____ _____ it is a skirt for men.

   B: That sounds _____. I want _____ _____ one _____.

2. G: Brian, let's talk _____ what we will _____ for the World Food Festival.

   B: I will make a meat pie. It is _____ in Australia. How about you, Sera?

   G: I want to make a _____ English _____, fish and chips.

   B: Fish and chips? _____ does it _____ _____?

   G: It's _____ fish _____ hot potato chips.

   B: That sounds _____. _____ _____ them.

Listen & Speak 2 A

1. B: Wow, we finally _____ _____ Hong Kong, Mom.

   W: I'm _____ _____ _____ our visit. What should we do today, Mike?

   B: I _____ we _____ Victoria Peak.

   W: Victoria Peak?

   B: It is _____ _____ mountain in Hong Kong and is _____ _____ _____ _____ movies. We can enjoy the _____ _____.

   W: That _____ good. Let's go.

해석

1. B: 다른 나라의 전통 의상에 대해 이야기해 보자.
   G: 흠… 너는 킬트가 뭔지 아니?
   B: 아니, 몰라. 그게 뭐야?
   G: 킬트는 스코틀랜드의 전통 의상이야. 그건 무릎길이의 치마같이 생겼고, 체크무늬가 있어.
   B: 무릎길이의 체크무늬 치마라고?
   G: 응. 킬트는 남자를 위한 치마이기 때문에 특이해.
   B: 흥미롭게 들린다. 나는 킬트를 입어보고 싶어.

2. G: Brian, 우리 세계 음식 축제에 무엇을 준비할 것인지 이야기해 보자.
   B: 나는 미트 파이를 만들 거야. 그건 호주에서 유명해. 너는 어때, 세라야?
   G: 나는 영국의 유명한 요리인 피시앤칩스를 만들고 싶어.
   B: 피시앤칩스? 그건 어떻게 생겼어?
   G: 그건 뜨거운 감자튀김이 곁들여진 튀긴 생선이야.
   B: 그거 흥미롭다. 우리 함께 그것들을 준비하자.

1. B: 와, 엄마, 우리가 마침내 홍콩에 도착했어요.
   W: 우리가 방문할 곳들이 기대된다. 오늘 우리는 무엇을 해야 하니, Mike?
   B: 저는 우리가 빅토리아 피크에 가는 것을 제안해요.
   W: 빅토리아 피크?
   B: 빅토리아 피크는 홍콩에서 가장 높은 산이고, 영화에도 많이 나왔어요. 우리는 환상적인 경관을 즐길 수 있어요.
   W: 그거 좋겠구나. 가 보자.

2. **G:** My American friend _____ me to a _____ dinner next Friday.

   B: You _____, you should take food to _____ at the dinner.

   G: What would you _____ _____ I take?

   B: I _____ you _____ some Korean food. _____ about Gimbap, Suji?

   G: Yes. It's not _____ and it's easy _____ _____.

   B: I think it'll be good _____ dinner.

2. G: 나의 미국인 친구가 다음 주 금요일에 있을 포틀럭 저녁 식사에 나를 초대했어.
   B: 네가 알다시피, 너는 저녁 식사에 함께 나눠 먹을 음식을 가지고 가야 해.
   G: 무엇을 가져갈지 추천해 줄래?
   B: 나는 네가 한국 음식을 가져가는 것을 추천해. 수지야, 김밥 어때?
   G: 그래. 김밥은 맵지도 않고, 들고 가기도 쉽겠다.
   B: 내 생각에는 김밥이 저녁 식사에 좋을 것 같아.

Real Life Talk

Seho: Good morning.

Jessie, Andy: Hi, Seho.

Seho: I will visit my uncle in Philadelphia this winter. _____ _____ _____ _____ _____ the city?

Jessie: Sure. I was there _____ _____ _____ _____. _____, _____ talk about food.

Seho: Okay. _____ _____ is Philadelphia _____?

Jessie: _____ _____ _____ food in Philadelphia is the cheese steak sandwich. It is a big sandwich _____ _____ beef and _____ cheese.

Seho: Good _____. I will try it. Are there any places _____ _____ _____ with tourists?

Andy: I _____ you visit _____ Hall. It is very important in American _____.

Seho: Wonderful. Thank you for the _____.

Andy: My _____.

세호: 안녕.
Jessie, Andy: 안녕, 세호야.
세호: 나 이번 겨울에 필라델피아에 계신 삼촌을 뵈러 가. 너희들 나한테 그 도시에 대해 알려줄 수 있니?
Jessie: 물론이지. 난 몇 년 전에 거기에 갔었어. 먼저 음식에 대해 이야기해 보자.
세호: 좋아. 필라델피아는 어떤 음식이 유명해?
Jessie: 필라델피아에서 가장 유명한 음식은 치즈 스테이크 샌드위치야. 소고기와 녹인 치즈로 채워진 큰 샌드위치지.
세호: 멋진 제안이다. 먹어 볼게. 여행자들에게 인기 있는 장소가 있니?
Andy: 나는 네가 독립 기념관에 방문하는 것을 제안해. 그곳은 미국 역사에서 아주 중요해.
세호: 멋지겠다. 정보 고마워.
Andy: 천만에.

Wrap Up

M: _____ to Australia. The _____ of Australia is Canberra. People speak English. Meat pie is a _____ _____ in Australia. Every year, _____ _____ tourists visit the Sydney Opera House and the beautiful _____ in Melbourne.

M: 호주에 온 것을 환영한다. 호주의 수도는 캔버라다. 사람들은 영어로 말한다. 고기 파이는 호주에서 인기 있는 음식이다. 매년 많은 관광객들이 시드니 오페라 하우스와 멜버른의 아름다운 해변을 방문한다.

01 우리말에 맞도록 문장의 빈칸에 알맞은 말을 쓰시오.

> 나는 네가 독립 기념관에 방문하는 것을 제안해.
>
> ➡ I _____ you _____ Independence Hall.

02 다음 대화의 빈칸에 들어갈 말로 알맞은 것은?

> A: _____
>
> B: I went to Jejudo with my family.

① I suggest we learn more about Jejudo.

② I'd like to talk about my experiences.

③ I'm not quite sure if you know about Jejudo.

④ Let's talk about travel experiences.

⑤ I'd like to tell you what this island is.

03 다음 대화의 빈칸에 들어갈 말로 <u>어색한</u> 것은?

> A: What can we do if we visit India?
>
> B: _____
>
> A: That's a good idea.

① I suggest we visit the Taj Mahal.

② I suggest we visit there.

③ I suggest we eat different kinds of curry.

④ I suggest we try on some traditional clothing.

⑤ I suggest we learn yoga.

04 다음 대화의 밑줄 친 부분의 의도로 알맞은 것은?

> A: <u>Let's talk about school life in Canada.</u>
>
> B: Students start a new school year in September.

① 권유하기　　　　② 알고 있는지 묻기

③ 관심 표현하기　　④ 의도 묻기

⑤ 주제 소개하기

[01~02] 다음 대화를 읽고 물음에 답하시오.

Seho: Good morning.

Jessie, Andy: Hi, Seho.

Seho: I will visit my uncle in Philadelphia this winter. (A)_____

Jessie: Sure. I was there a few years ago. First, let's talk about food.

Seho: Okay. What food is Philadelphia famous for?

Jessie: The most famous food in Philadelphia is the cheese steak sandwich. It is a big sandwich filled with beef and melted cheese.

Seho: Good suggestion. I will try it. Are there any places that are popular with tourists?

Andy: I suggest you visit Independence Hall. It is very important in American history.

Seho: Wonderful. Thank you for the information.

Andy: My pleasure.

01 위 대화의 빈칸 (A)에 들어갈 말로 알맞은 것은?

① Are you going to visit there, too?
② Let's talk about food in the UK.
③ What should we do in Philadelphia?
④ What would you recommend that I take?
⑤ Can you tell me about the city?

02 위 대화의 내용과 일치하지 <u>않는</u> 것은?

① Seho will visit his uncle in Philadelphia.
② The cheese steak sandwich is the most famous food in Philadelphia.
③ They are talking about Philadelphia.
④ Independence Hall is Andy's favorite place.
⑤ Seho will probably eat the cheese steak sandwich in Philadelphia.

03 다음 대화의 (A)~(D)를 알맞은 순서로 배열한 것은?

G: My American friend invited me to a potluck dinner next Friday.

(A) I suggest you take some Korean food. How about Gimbap, Suji?
(B) What would you recommend that I take?
(C) You know, you should take food to share at the dinner.
(D) Yes. It's not spicy and it's easy to carry.

B: I think it'll be good for dinner.

① (A)–(C)–(B)–(D)   ② (B)–(A)–(D)–(C)
③ (C)–(B)–(A)–(D)   ④ (C)–(D)–(A)–(B)
⑤ (D)–(C)–(A)–(B)

04 다음 대화의 빈칸에 들어갈 말로 알맞은 것은?

A: _____
B: Students go to school at the age of five.

① I'm looking forward to going to school next week.
② Let's talk about school life in the UK.
③ I'd like to say something about students.
④ What time do students in the UK go to school?
⑤ I suggest that we go to school wearing a school uniform.

[05~06] 다음 대화를 읽고 물음에 답하시오.

> B: Let's talk about traditional clothing from other countries.
> G: Hmm... Do you know (a)what a kilt is?
> B: No, I don't. What is it?
> G: It is traditional clothing from Scotland. It looks like a knee-length skirt and (b)have a plaid pattern.
> B: A skirt of knee length (c)with a plaid pattern?
> G: Yes. It is unique (d)because it is a skirt for men.
> B: That sounds interesting. I want to (e)try one on.

05 위 대화를 읽고 다음 물음에 영어로 답하시오.

> Q: Why is a kilt unique?

➡ Because ＿＿＿＿＿＿＿＿＿＿ .

06 위 대화의 밑줄 친 (a)~(e) 중 어법상 어색한 것은?

① (a)　② (b)　③ (c)　④ (d)　⑤ (e)

[07~08] 다음 대화를 읽고 물음에 답하시오.

> B: Wow, we finally arrived in Hong Kong, Mom.
> W: I'm looking forward to our visit. What should we do today, Mike?
> B: I suggest we visit Victoria Peak.
> W: Victoria Peak?
> B: (A)빅토리아 피크는 홍콩에서 가장 높은 산이고, 영화에 많이 나왔어요. We can enjoy the fantastic view.
> W: That sounds good. Let's go.

07 위 대화의 밑줄 친 (A)의 우리말에 맞게 주어진 단어를 알맞은 순서로 배열하여 쓰시오. (단어 하나를 추가하고, 필요시 변형하시오.)

> high / in / in Hong Kong / and / is / a lot of / mountain / movies

➡ It is ＿＿＿＿＿＿＿＿＿＿＿＿＿

＿＿＿＿＿＿＿＿＿＿＿＿＿＿ .

08 What will Mike and his mother do? Fill in the blanks with suitable words.

➡ They will ＿＿＿＿＿＿＿＿ and ＿＿＿＿＿＿＿＿ of Hong Kong.

09 다음 짝지어진 대화 중 어색한 것은?

① A: Let's talk about the pose we will make for our picture.
　 B: I think it will be good to show our teamwork in the pose.

② A: Let's talk about school life in Korea.
　 B: Okay. What do you want to say about it?

③ A: The window is not clean.
　 B: I suggest we should clean the window every Thursday.

④ A: Let's talk about which country we are going to look into.
　 B: I'd love to, but I'm looking forward to visiting there.

⑤ A: What do you know about Australia?
　 B: It is a big island on the southern part of the world.

[01~02] 다음 대화를 읽고 물음에 답하시오.

Seho: Good morning.

Jessie, Andy: Hi, Seho.

Seho: I will visit my uncle in Philadelphia this winter. Can you tell me about the city?

Jessie: Sure. I was there a few years ago. First, let's talk about food.

Seho: Okay. What food is Philadelphia famous for?

Jessie: The most famous food in Philadelphia is the cheese steak sandwich. It is a big sandwich filled with beef and melted cheese.

Seho: Good suggestion. I will try it. Are there any places that are popular with tourists?

Andy: (A)I suggest you visit Independence Hall. It is very important in American history.

Seho: Wonderful. Thank you for the information.

Andy: My pleasure.

01 What place is popular with tourists in Philadelphia? Answer in English with a full sentence.

➡ _____

02 위 대화의 밑줄 친 (A)를 관계대명사의 계속적 용법을 이용하여 한 문장으로 바꾸어 쓰시오.

➡ _____
_____

03 다음 대화의 빈칸 (A)에 들어갈 말을 〈조건〉에 맞게 쓰시오.

G: My American friend invited me to a potluck dinner next Friday.

B: You know, you should take food to share at the dinner.

G: What would you recommend that I take?

B: (A)_____ How about Gimbap, Suji?

G: Yes. It's not spicy and it's easy to carry.

B: I think it'll be good for dinner.

┌── 조건 ──┐
• 제안하는 표현을 사용할 것.
• 'suggest', 'some Korean food'를 사용할 것. (7 words)

➡ _____

04 밑줄 친 (A)의 우리말에 맞게 주어진 단어를 활용하여 영어로 쓰시오.

B: (A)다른 나라의 전통 의상에 대해 이야기해 보자. (let's / about / from / clothing)

G: Hmm... Do you know what a kilt is?

B: No, I don't. What is it?

G: It is traditional clothing from Scotland. It looks like a knee length skirt and has a plaid pattern.

B: A skirt of knee-length with a plaid pattern?

G: Yes. It is unique because it is a skirt for men.

B: That sounds interesting. I want to try one on.

➡ _____

Grammar

1 '계속적 용법'의 관계대명사 which / who

- Someone uses the word kiwi, **which** has several meanings.
  어떤 사람은 키위라는 단어를 사용하는데, 그것은 여러 가지 의미가 있다.
- My uncle Roger, **who** was in the movie *Best Friends*, is a famous actor.
  나의 삼촌 Roger는 영화 '절친한 친구'에 나왔고, 유명한 배우이다.

■ 계속적 용법은 형태상으로 콤마(,)를 쓰며, '선행사의 범위'가 비교적 자유롭다.

- Mike helped me with my work, **which** was too hard. (Mike는 내 일을 도와줬는데, 그 일은 너무 힘들었다.) − 선행사가 my work
- Mike helped me with my work, **which** helped me save some time. (Mike가 내 일을 도와줬는데, 그것은 내가 시간을 좀 절약하도록 도움이 되었다.) − 선행사가 앞 문장
- My baby puppy tried to feed herself, **which** I was proud of.
  = My baby puppy tried to feed herself, **and** I was proud of **that**. (나의 아기 강아지는 스스로 먹으려고 노력했는데, 나는 그것을 자랑스럽게 여겼다.) → 선행사는 앞 문장 전체(강아지가 스스로 노력한 일)이며, '접속사 and와 대명사 it/that'으로 받을 수 있다.

■ 계속적 용법의 관계대명사는 '접속사+대명사'로 전환 가능하다. (and, but, for, though 등)

- Sam bought a laptop, **which** was broken.
  = Sam bought a laptop, **but it** was broken. (Sam은 노트북 한 대를 구매했지만, 그것은 고장났다.)
  cf. Sam bought a laptop **which** was broken. (제한적: Sam은 고장 난 노트북 한 대를 구매했다.)
- Mom has been collecting a lot of used coins, **some of which** are rare and precious.
  = Mom has been collecting a lot of used coins, **and some of them** are rare and precious. (엄마는 많은 중고 동전들을 수집해 오고 계신데, 그 중에 어떤 것들은 진귀하다.)

■ that, what은 계속적 용법으로 쓸 수 없고, '전치사+관계대명사'는 관계부사로 바꿀 수 있다.

- Christine saw the house, **and** Van Gogh once lived **in it**. (Christine은 그 집을 봤는데, Van Gogh가 한 때 거기에서 살았다.)
  = Christine saw the house, **which** Van Gogh once lived **in**.
  = Christine saw the house, **in which** Van Gogh once lived.
  = Christine saw the house, **where** Van Gogh once lived.
  = Christine saw the house, **and** Van Gogh once lived **there**.

핵심 Check

1. 괄호 안에서 알맞은 단어를 고르시오.

(1) Sumi studied hard, (that / which) helped her pass the test.

(2) The teachers praised only Robert, (which / who) made his classmates jealous.

(3) My family had lunch in a restaurant, (which / that) we liked very much.

② '부사적 용법'의 to부정사

- If you say "kia ora" to the villagers, they will be glad **to hear** it.

  네가 만약 마을 사람들에게 "kia ora"라고 말한다면, 그들은 그것을 듣고 기뻐할 것이다.

- Jane was pleased **to meet** her old friends. Jane은 오랜 친구들을 만나 기뻤다.

■ to부정사가 문장에서 주어, 목적어, 보어 등의 역할을 하면 명사적 용법, 명사를 수식하거나 be동사 뒤에서 보어 역할을 하면 형용사적 용법이다. 그 외의 to부정사는 부사적 용법으로 이해하면 된다.

- **To meet** her old friend is not possible. 그녀의 옛 친구를 만나는 것: 주어(명사적 용법)
- It is not possible for Jane **to meet** her old friend. 진주어(명사적 용법)
- Jane wants **to meet** her old friend. 목적어(명사적 용법)
- Jane's hope is **to meet** her old friend. 보어(명사적 용법)
- Jane told me a plan **to meet** her old friend. 명사 수식(형용사적 용법)
- Jane is **to meet** her old friend this evening. 보어(형용사적 용법)
- Jane wants to know **how to meet** her old friend. 의문사+to부정사(명사적 용법)

■ to부정사의 부사적 용법은 보통 해석에 따라 분류한다.

- 목적: Jane came **to meet** her old friend. (Jane은 그녀의 오랜 친구를 만나러 왔다.)
- 결과: Jane grew up **to meet** her old friend. (Jane은 자라서 그녀의 옛 친구를 만나게 되었다.)
- 원인, 이유: Jane was pleased **to meet** her old friend. (Jane은 그녀의 오랜 친구를 만나게 되어 기뻤다.)
- 판단의 근거: Jane must be pleased **to meet** her old friend. (Jane은 그녀의 오랜 친구를 만나서 기쁜 것임에 틀림없다.)
- 조건: Jane will be pleased **to meet** her old friend. (Jane이 그녀의 오랜 친구를 만난다면 기뻐할 것이다.)
- 형용사 수식: Jane's old friend is hard **to meet**. (Jane의 옛 친구는 만나기 어렵다.)
  cf. It is hard **to meet** Jane's old friend. (진주어, 명사적 용법)
- 부사 수식: Jane is not healthy enough **to meet** her old friend. (Jane은 옛 친구를 만날 수 있을 만큼 충분히 건강하지 않다.)

■ 숙어처럼 자주 쓰이는 to부정사의 부사적 용법 표현들

- be able to V: ~할 수 있다
- be willing to V: 기꺼이 ~하다
- be sure to V: 확실히 ~하다
- be eager to V: 몹시 ~하고 싶다
- be ready to V: ~할 준비가 되어 있다
- be reluctant to V: ~하기를 꺼리다
- be likely to V: ~할 것 같다
- be about to V: ~하려는 참이다

핵심 Check

2. 다음 우리말과 같은 뜻이 되도록 주어진 어구를 알맞게 배열하시오.

> 그는 파티에 초대되지 않아 슬펐다. (sad, to the party, be, not, was, he, invited, to)

➡ _____

01 다음 문장을 바꿔 쓸 때 빈칸에 들어갈 말로 어법상 가장 적절한 것은?

> Mom bought Jane those books, and they influenced her so much.
> ➡ Mom bought Jane those books, _____ influenced her so much.

① who   ② whom   ③ which
④ that   ⑤ what

02 다음 중 밑줄 친 부분이 어법상 다른 하나는?

① Someone from Tokyo came here to see Robert.
② Tommy learned magic to make his wife pleased.
③ Sarah was happy to see the author of the book tonight.
④ My uncle must be a genius to solve the problem.
⑤ Jason wanted to see Ms. Smith yesterday.

03 다음 밑줄 친 부분을 바꿔 쓸 때 가장 알맞은 것은?

> Elizabeth likes the boy, who has recently changed his hair style.

① and it   ② for she   ③ him but
④ and he   ⑤ with him

04 다음 중 〈보기〉의 밑줄 친 부분과 같은 용법으로 쓰인 것을 고르시오.

> ─┤ 보기 ├─
> Minsu was glad to learn the culture of the Maori.

① Andrew woke up early not to be late for school.
② Bonita went to the clinic to meet the doctor.
③ Harley planned to visit New Zealand for filming his movie.
④ Lucy can't be a fool to solve such a difficult problem.
⑤ Chris got nervous to think of meeting her father.

서답형

01 다음 중 어법상 어색한 것을 모두 골라 기호를 쓰고 알맞게 고치시오.

> ⓐ A lot of kiwi fruit is grown in New Zealand, which is known as the land of kiwi.
> ⓑ Many students like the lecture of the professor Potter, that will never be boring.
> ⓒ My aunt Mary, which was in the movie *Killers*, is a famous actress.
> ⓓ Anne bought a parrot, which speak French.
> ⓔ Everyone wants to know the way which Alice got employed by Google.
> ⓕ That is the house, where Schubert lived in.

➡ _____

_____

_____

02 다음 중 밑줄 친 to부정사의 용법이 나머지 넷과 다른 것은?

① We spoke Maori <u>to please</u> the villagers.
② <u>To say</u> that he agreed with them, the Maori chief nodded.
③ Yesterday I planned <u>to invite</u> Maori friends to our base camp.
④ The Maori girl cannot be a fool <u>to say</u> so.
⑤ My family went to New Zealand <u>to visit</u> the Maori village.

서답형

03 다음 우리말에 맞게 주어진 단어를 빈칸에 알맞게 배열하시오.

> 마오리인들은, 그들에 대해 당신이 이미 들은 적이 있겠지만, 전쟁 춤으로 하카를 추기 시작했다.
> ➡ The Maori people, _____
> _____, started doing the haka as a war dance.(have, about, who, heard, you, already)

04 다음 문장의 빈칸 (A)~(C)에 들어갈 말로 가장 적절한 것은?

> • New Zealand is known for its natural beauty, __(A)__ has allowed a lot of famous movies to be made there.
> • Sam's grandparents live in Wellington, __(B)__ is the capital of New Zealand.
> • Don't become confused when someone uses the word kiwi, __(C)__ may want to mean some other things.

	(A)	(B)	(C)
①	which	who	which
②	who	who	who
③	that	who	which
④	that	which	who
⑤	which	which	who

중요

05 다음 중 어법상 옳은 문장은?

① It is raining, that makes me stay all day long.
② The CEO announced that she would resign, who was shocking.
③ There is a closet by the door, of which is made of wood.
④ The books, which I borrowed from the library, were so touching.
⑤ Michael is a famous actor, who often come to eat Korean food.

[06~07] 다음 우리말을 영어로 바르게 옮긴 것은?

06 민주는 그 잔인한 장면을 보지 않기 위해 고개를 돌렸다.

① Minju didn't turn her head to see the cruel scene.

② Minju was turned her head to not see the cruel scene.

③ Minju turned her head to see not the cruel scene.

④ Minju turned her head to not see the cruel scene.

⑤ Minju turned her head not to see the cruel scene.

07 마을 사람들은 "키아 오라"라는 인사말을 들으면, 기뻐할 것이다.

① The villagers were glad to hear the word "kia ora."

② The villagers will be heard to say the word "kia ora."

③ The villagers do feel glad to hear the word "kia ora."

④ The villagers will be glad to hear the word "kia ora."

⑤ The villagers will be glad to be heard the word "kia ora."

[08~09] 다음 중 어법상 <u>어색한</u> 문장은?

08 ① I had my car fixed by my uncle, who saved me a lot of money.

② My students helped the blind cross the street, who had trouble walking fast.

③ The audience gave the singer a big hand, which was impressive.

④ There was an airplane crash yesterday, which killed 93 people on board.

⑤ Sumi doesn't know where her phone is, which was on my table an hour ago.

09 ① Susan's uncle likes the hotel, which is widely known for the special service.

② Bell invented the telephone, which made the people around the world comfortable to communicate.

③ The producer called the show's host, who didn't answer immediately.

④ I met my husband at the basketball court in 2019, which corona pandemic broke out.

⑤ The famous actor is going to move to Jeju island, where his first movie was filmed.

서답형

10 다음 그림을 보고 아래의 대화가 자연스럽게 이뤄지도록 주어진 단어를 모두 활용하여 문장을 완성하시오. (주어진 단어들 중 1 단어만 변형할 것.)

Mom: Do you know why Mina goes to the park every day?

Miju: _____

(feed, she, to, the cats, there, go)

[11~12] 다음 문장의 밑줄 친 부분과 쓰임이 같은 것을 고르시오.

11

> Haka dancers shout and move their bodies wildly <u>to threaten</u> their enemy.

① Please, don't forget <u>to take</u> an umbrella with you today!

② Robert woke up <u>to find</u> himself in a strange room.

③ New Zealanders felt happy <u>to be</u> called as kiwi.

④ Hojung went to Italy <u>to study</u> classical music.

⑤ It is not easy for me <u>to master</u> swimming as I don't have much time.

12

> The enemy must be scared <u>to watch</u> the haka moves of the Maori warriors.

① Bob went to Egypt <u>to see</u> the Sphinx.

② Sunny grew up <u>to be</u> a famous singer.

③ Everyone was delighted <u>to talk</u> with the author of the popular books.

④ I think you are smart <u>to solve</u> the problem so easily and quickly.

⑤ We needed something <u>to cover</u> the baby cats.

[13~14] 다음 문장의 밑줄 친 부분과 쓰임이 **다른** 하나를 고르시오.

13

> I searched the Internet <u>to learn</u> more about the kiwi birds.

① Susan stopped <u>to watch</u> who was following her.

② What does David do <u>to be</u> a robot engineer?

③ My sister went to the library <u>to borrow</u> a book.

④ Minsu was proud <u>to meet</u> his old friend who won the prize.

⑤ Plants need sunlight and water <u>to live</u> healthily.

14

> The Maori people do the haka <u>to scare</u> the rival teams.

① There are a lot of beautiful places <u>to visit</u> in New Zealand.

② Jenny went to the playground <u>to play</u> badminton with her father.

③ Japanese businessmen came to my village <u>to buy</u> some furniture.

④ Kate met the researchers from UK <u>to discuss</u> the international cooperation.

⑤ My younger brother sang the songs <u>to please</u> the guests.

 다음 중 어법상 올바른 문장의 개수는?

> ⓐ The students helped the old man to cross the street, which was a rare thing nowadays.
>
> ⓑ Mary purchased a scarf, who was very soft to touch.
>
> ⓒ Susan met the lady living next door, and who had the washing machine fixed.
>
> ⓓ Mike advised his sister to clean her desk, who was messy with books and pens.
>
> ⓔ Hojun got hurt in the ankle, which was the reason he was late for the meeting.

① 1개 ② 2개 ③ 3개 ④ 4개 ⑤ 5개

01 다음 주어진 단어와 to부정사의 부사적 용법을 이용하여 우리 말에 맞게 영작하시오.

(1) 마오리인들은 적에게 겁을 주기 위해서 춤을 춘다. (scare, the Maori people, enemy)

➡ _____

(2) 돌고래들은 숨을 쉬기 위해 수면으로 올라온다. (come up, breathe, the surface)

➡ _____

(3) 그녀가 그 말을 믿다니 지혜롭지 않은 것임에 틀림없다. (the word, unwise, must)

➡ _____

(4) 뉴질랜드 원주민들이 그 말을 들으면, 기뻐할 것이다. (the native people, glad, hear)

➡ _____
_____

(5) 지호의 방은 청소하기가 쉽지 않다. (easy, clean, not)

➡ _____

(6) 심청은 아버지를 다시 만나게 되어 기뻤다. (Simcheong, see, again, pleased, her father)

➡ _____

02 다음 문장을 관계대명사의 계속적 용법을 이용하여 한 문장으로 만드시오.

(1) • George Washington is widely known for the episode of his honesty.
• But it was not true.

➡ _____
_____

(2) • Sumin fell in love with Brian.
• Brian met her only twice.

➡ _____
_____

(3) • The Maori people were so good at haka dancing.
• It made the visitors also dance with excitement.

➡ _____
_____

(4) • I added some more hot sauce into the food.
• It made my mom upset.

➡ _____
_____

03 다음 두 문장을 각각의 조건에 맞게, to부정사의 부사적 용법을 이용하여 한 문장으로 만드시오.

(1) • Jack walked to school.
• He had to save some money. (8 단어로)

➡ _____

(2) • Caroline exercises hard every day.
• She wants to lose weight. (8 단어로)

➡ _____

(3) • Potter was surprised.
• He watched the news. (7 단어로)

➡ _____

(4) • Angela woke up.
• She found herself alone in the dark. (10 단어로)

➡ _____

(5) • I am sure that Sam is happy.
• Sam meets her old friend. (조동사 must를 반드시 사용, 9 단어로)

➡ _____

04 다음 그림을 보고, 우리말에 맞게 괄호 안의 단어를 활용하여 영작하시오.

지수의 부모님이 점심 시간에 급식 자원봉사를 해주셨는데, 그것이 그녀를 자랑스럽게 느끼도록 만들었다.
(Jisoo, her, to serve, feel, the meal, proud, make, volunteer, which 등을 사용할 것, 동사는 변형 가능, 총 14 단어)

➡ _____

_____

05 다음 주어진 문장을 to부정사의 부사적 용법을 사용하여 바꾸시오.

(1) My grandma exercises every day in order that she can keep healthy.
➡ _____

(2) She was pleased because she received thank-you notes from her neighbors.
➡ _____
_____

(3) Sandra went to the river so that she could catch some fish.
➡ _____

(4) The stone was so heavy that I could not lift it.
➡ _____

(5) You need ice and sugar so that you can make Bingsu.
➡ _____

(6) It was impossible for Peter to solve the problem in an hour.
➡ _____
_____

(7) A lot of firefighters ran into the woods so that they could rescue the koalas.
➡ _____
_____

06 다음 각 문장에서 어법상 어색한 부분을 한 곳씩 찾아 모두 고치시오.

(1) My parents ordered my sister to meet the rich old man, that made her so depressed.
➡ _____

(2) The math teacher punished Tom for not paying attention, who made him feel sad.
➡ _____

(3) Amy made her first goal in soccer, who was very important to her.
➡ _____

07 다음 우리말을 조건에 맞게 영작하여 빈칸을 채우시오.

어제, 우리는 kiwi라는 단어를 배웠는데, 그 단어는 여러 가지 의미를 갖고 있다.
(the word kiwi, several, learn 사용, Yesterday를 포함, 10 단어로 영작할 것)

➡ Yesterday, _____
_____.

Reading

Hello! New Zealand

New Zealand is a place of natural beauty. It has many beautiful lakes and waterfalls. New Zealand has two main islands, the South Island and the North Island. In the South Island, there are mountains that are covered with snow all year round. You will be amazed by the fantastic views.

In the North Island, there are many hot springs, lakes, and areas with green grass. Because of its natural beauty, many famous movies have been made in New Zealand. If you visit New Zealand, you will surely appreciate its nature.

When you hear the word kiwi, what comes to your mind? Maybe a fruit, but, in New Zealand the word kiwi has a couple of meanings. First, kiwi is the name of a delicious, green fruit. A lot of kiwi fruit is grown there, so New Zealand is known as the land of kiwi fruit.

Kiwi is also the name of one of New Zealand's native birds. The kiwi is special to New Zealanders because it is the symbol of the nation. Also, kiwi is a nickname for people from New Zealand. Today, New Zealanders are sometimes called Kiwis throughout the world.

natural: 자연의, 천연의
waterfall: 폭포
main: 주요한, 주된
amaze: (대단히) 놀라게 하다
view: 경관, 전망
be covered with: ~으로 덮이다
all year round: 일 년 내내
surely: 확실히, 분명히
appreciate: 진가를 알아보다, 인정하다
kiwi: 키위, 키위새, 뉴질랜드인
hot spring: 온천
a couple of: 두 서너 개의, 몇 개의
symbol: 상징, 상징물
throughout: 도처에
several: 몇몇의

 확인문제

● 다음 문장이 본문의 내용과 일치하면 T, 일치하지 <u>않으면</u> F를 쓰시오.

1 We can enjoy the natural beauty when we visit New Zealand. ☐

2 There are many areas with green grass in the South Island. ☐

3 Kiwi is the only bird which is native to New Zealand. ☐

4 People know New Zealand as the land of kiwi fruit. ☐

Now, you know that kiwi is the name of a fruit, a bird, and also a
명사절 접속사(know의 목적어를 이끎)
people. Next time, don't become confused when someone uses the
부정관사와 함께 쓰일 때는 '국민, 민족'이라는 의미   혼란을 느끼는 것이므로 과거분사
word kiwi, which has several meanings.
관계대명사의 계속적 용법(앞 문장이나 단어에 대한 부연 설명)
   Now, let's talk about the Maori. They are the native people of New

Zealand. They went to live on the islands long before Europeans
     The Maori 지칭   시간을 나타내는 접속사
arrived. The Maori culture is an important part of today's New Zealand

society. The Maori language is taught at some schools and there are
                  언어는 가르쳐 지는 것이므로 수동태
Maori language radio and TV stations. There are Maori villages in

many parts of the country. You can visit Maori villages and experience
               가능을 나타내는 조동사   visit에 병렬 연결
Maori culture. If you say "kia ora" to the villagers, they will be glad to
        조건의 부사절에서 현재시제로 미래를 대신함
hear it. It means "hi" in English.
to부정사의 부사적 용법 중 감정의 원인
   Have you ever watched the haka? The haka may look scary because
     경험을 묻는 현재완료   감각동사의 보어로 형용사
haka dancers shout and move their bodies wildly. The Maori people,

who you've already heard about, started doing the haka as a war
관계대명사의 계속적 용법   = to do 자격이나 기능을 나타내는 전치사(~으로)
dance. Today, however, New Zealanders do the haka at sport matches,
weddings, or other important events. For example, New Zealand's
national rugby team members do the haka before every match. It is
                              every+단수 명사
famous all over the world. If you see the haka, you will probably agree
that the rival team must be scared.
       확실한 추측을 나타낼 때 쓰는 조동사(~임에 틀림없다)
   Like the kiwi bird, the haka is a national symbol.
전치사(~처럼)

Maori: 마오리인
European: 유럽인
society: 사회
station: 방송국
village: 마을, 부락, 촌락
experience: 겪다, 경험하다
long before: 훨씬 이전에

확인문제

● 다음 문장이 본문의 내용과 일치하면 T, 일치하지 않으면 F를 쓰시오.

1 The word kiwi has three meanings in New Zealand. ☐

2 European people brought the Maori people to New Zealand. ☐

3 The Maori culture is considered to be important in New Zealand. ☐

4 It is possible to experience the Maori culture in their villages. ☐

5 People move their bodies wildly when they do the haka. ☐

6 Today, New Zealanders do the haka only at sport matches. ☐

● 우리말을 참고하여 빈칸에 알맞은 말을 쓰시오.

Hello! New Zealand

1 New Zealand is _____ _____ _____ _____ _____.
   It has many beautiful _____ and _____.

2 New Zealand has _____ _____ _____, the South Island
   and the North Island.

3 In the South Island, there _____ _____ that _____
   _____ _____ snow all year round.

4 You will _____ _____ _____ the fantastic views.

5 In the North Island, there are _____ _____ _____, lakes,
   and areas _____ green grass.

6 _____ _____ its natural beauty, many famous movies
   _____ _____ _____ in New Zealand.

7 If you visit New Zealand, you _____ _____ _____ its
   nature.

8 When you _____ the word kiwi, what _____ _____ your
   mind?

9 Maybe a fruit, but, in New Zealand the word kiwi has _____
   _____ _____ _____.

10 First, kiwi is _____ _____ of a _____, green fruit.

11 A lot of kiwi fruit _____ _____ there, so New Zealand
    _____ _____ _____ the land of kiwi fruit.

12 Kiwi is also the name of _____ of _____ _____
    _____ _____.

13 The kiwi is _____ _____ New Zealanders _____ it is
    the _____ of the nation.

14 Also, kiwi is _____ _____ _____ people _____ New
    Zealand.

15 Today, New Zealanders _____ _____ _____ Kiwis
    throughout the world.

16 Now, you know _____ kiwi is _____ _____ _____ a
    fruit, a bird, and also a people.

안녕! 뉴질랜드

1 뉴질랜드는 자연의 아름다움이
   가득한 곳이다. 뉴질랜드는 아름
   다운 호수와 폭포들이 많다.

2 뉴질랜드에는 남섬과 북섬, 두 개
   의 본섬이 있다.

3 남섬에는 일 년 내내 눈으로 덮인
   산들이 있다.

4 당신은 굉장히 멋진 경관에 놀랄
   것이다.

5 북섬에는 많은 온천과 호수, 초원
   지역이 있다.

6 뉴질랜드 자연의 아름다움 때문
   에 많은 유명한 영화들이 뉴질랜
   드에서 촬영되었다.

7 뉴질랜드를 방문하면, 분명히 그
   자연의 진가를 인정할 것이다.

8 키위라는 단어를 들을 때, 무엇이
   떠오르는가?

9 아마도 과일이 떠오르겠지만, 뉴
   질랜드에서 키위는 몇 가지 뜻이
   있다.

10 먼저, 키위는 맛있는 초록색 과일
    의 이름이다.

11 많은 키위가 그곳에서 자라기 때
    문에 뉴질랜드는 키위의 나라로
    알려져 있다.

12 키위는 뉴질랜드 토종 새의 이름
    이기도 하다.

13 키위 새는 국가의 상징이기 때문
    에, 뉴질랜드 사람들에게 특별하
    다.

14 또한, 키위는 뉴질랜드 출신의 사
    람들을 부르는 별명이기도 하다.

15 오늘날 뉴질랜드인들은 전 세계
    적으로 키위라고 불리기도 한다.

16 이제, 당신은 키위가 과일과 새,
    그리고 국민의 명칭이라는 것을
    알았다.

17 Next time, don't become _____ when someone _____ the word kiwi, _____ _____ several meanings.

18 Now, _____ _____ about the Maori. _____ are _____ _____ _____ of New Zealand.

19 They went to _____ _____ the islands _____ _____ Europeans _____.

20 The Maori culture is _____ _____ _____ of _____ New Zealand society.

21 The Maori language _____ _____ at some schools and _____ _____ Maori language radio and TV stations.

22 There are Maori villages _____ _____ _____ _____ the country.

23 You can _____ Maori _____ and _____ Maori _____.

24 If you _____ "kia ora" _____ the villagers, they _____ _____ _____ _____ _____ it. It _____ "hi" in English.

25 _____ you ever _____ the haka?

26 The haka may _____ _____ _____ haka dancers _____ and _____ their bodies _____.

27 The Maori people, _____ you've already _____ _____, started _____ the haka _____ a war dance.

28 Today, _____, New Zealanders _____ the haka _____ _____ _____, weddings, or other important events.

29 _____ _____, New Zealand's _____ _____ _____ do the haka _____ every match.

30 It is _____ _____ _____ the world.

31 If you see the haka, you _____ probably _____ the rival team _____ _____ _____.

32 _____ the kiwi bird, the haka is _____ _____ _____.

---

17 다음에는 누군가가 키위라는 단어를 사용할 때 혼동하지 마라. 그 단어는 여러 뜻을 가지고 있기 때문이다.

18 이제, 마오리족에 대해 이야기해 보자. 마오리족은 뉴질랜드의 원주민이다.

19 그들은 유럽인들이 도착하기 오래 전에 이 섬에 와서 살았다.

20 마오리족의 문화는 오늘날 뉴질랜드 사회의 중요한 부분이다.

21 몇몇 학교에서 마오리어를 가르치고 있으며, 마오리어의 라디오와 TV 방송국이 있다.

22 나라의 여러 곳에 마오리 마을이 있다.

23 당신은 마오리 마을을 방문해 마오리 문화를 경험할 수 있다.

24 당신이 마을 사람들에게 "kia ora"라고 말한다면 그들은 그것을 듣고 좋아할 것이다. 그것은 영어로 "안녕"이라는 뜻이다.

25 하카를 본 적이 있는가?

26 하카 춤을 추는 사람들이 소리 지르고, 그들의 몸을 사납게 움직이기 때문에 하카는 무서워 보일 수도 있다.

27 당신이 이미 그들에 대해 들은 적이 있겠지만, 마오리인들은 전쟁 춤으로 하카를 추기 시작했다.

28 하지만, 오늘날 뉴질랜드 사람들은 하카를 운동 경기, 결혼식 또는 다른 중요한 행사가 있을 때 한다.

29 예를 들어, 뉴질랜드의 럭비 국가 대표 팀 선수들은 모든 경기 전에 하카를 춘다.

30 그것은 전 세계적으로 유명하다.

31 당신이 하카를 본다면, 상대 팀이 틀림없이 겁을 먹을 것이라는 것에 아마 동의할 것이다.

32 키위와 마찬가지로 하카는 나라의 상징이다.

● 우리말을 참고하여 본문을 영작하시오.

1 뉴질랜드는 자연의 아름다움이 가득한 곳이다. 뉴질랜드는 아름다운 호수와 폭포들이 많다.
➡ _____

2 뉴질랜드에는 남섬과 북섬, 두 개의 본섬이 있다.
➡ _____

3 남섬에는 일 년 내내 눈으로 덮인 산들이 있다.
➡ _____

4 당신은 굉장히 멋진 경관에 놀랄 것이다.
➡ _____

5 북섬에는 많은 온천과 호수, 초원 지역이 있다.
➡ _____

6 뉴질랜드 자연의 아름다움 때문에 많은 유명한 영화들이 뉴질랜드에서 촬영되었다.
➡ _____

7 뉴질랜드를 방문하면, 분명히 그 자연의 진가를 인정할 것이다.
➡ _____

8 키위라는 단어를 들을 때, 무엇이 떠오르는가?
➡ _____

9 아마도 과일이 떠오르겠지만, 뉴질랜드에서 키위는 몇 가지 뜻이 있다.
➡ _____

10 먼저, 키위는 맛있는 초록색 과일의 이름이다.
➡ _____

11 많은 키위가 그곳에서 자라기 때문에 뉴질랜드는 키위의 나라로 알려져 있다.
➡ _____

12 키위는 뉴질랜드 토종 새의 이름이기도 하다.
➡ _____

13 키위 새는 국가의 상징이기 때문에, 뉴질랜드 사람들에게 특별하다.
➡ _____

14 또한, 키위는 뉴질랜드 출신의 사람들을 부르는 별명이기도 하다.
➡ _____

15 오늘날 뉴질랜드인들은 전 세계적으로 키위라고 불리기도 한다.
➡ _____

16 이제, 당신은 키위가 과일과 새, 그리고 국민의 명칭이라는 것을 알았다.
➡ _____

17 다음에는 누군가가 키위라는 단어를 사용할 때 혼동하지 마라. 그 단어는 여러 뜻을 가지고 있기 때문이다.

➡ _____

18 이제, 마오리족에 대해 이야기해 보자. 마오리족은 뉴질랜드의 원주민이다.

➡ _____

19 그들은 유럽인들이 도착하기 오래 전에 이 섬에 와서 살았다.

➡ _____

20 마오리족의 문화는 오늘날 뉴질랜드 사회의 중요한 부분이다.

➡ _____

21 몇몇 학교에서 마오리어를 가르치고 있으며, 마오리어의 라디오와 TV 방송국이 있다.

➡ _____

_____

22 나라의 여러 곳에 마오리 마을이 있다.

➡ _____

23 당신은 마오리 마을을 방문해 마오리 문화를 경험할 수 있다.

➡ _____

24 당신이 마을 사람들에게 "kia ora"라고 말한다면 그들은 그것을 듣고 좋아할 것이다. 그것은 영어로 "안녕"이라는 뜻이다.

➡ _____

25 하카를 본 적이 있는가?

➡ _____

26 하카 춤을 추는 사람들이 소리 지르고, 그들의 몸을 사납게 움직이기 때문에 하카는 무서워 보일 수도 있다.

➡ _____

27 당신이 이미 그들에 대해 들은 적이 있겠지만, 마오리인들은 전쟁 춤으로 하카를 추기 시작했다.

➡ _____

28 하지만, 오늘날 뉴질랜드 사람들은 하카를 운동 경기, 결혼식 또는 다른 중요한 행사가 있을 때 한다.

➡ _____

29 예를 들어, 뉴질랜드의 럭비 국가 대표 팀 선수들은 모든 경기 전에 하카를 춘다.

➡ _____

30 그것은 전 세계적으로 유명하다.

➡ _____

31 당신이 하카를 본다면, 상대 팀이 틀림없이 겁을 먹을 것이라는 것에 아마 동의할 것이다.

➡ _____

32 키위와 마찬가지로 하카는 나라의 상징이다.

➡ _____

[01~03] 다음 글을 읽고 물음에 답하시오.

New Zealand is a place of ⓐ_____ . It has many beautiful lakes and waterfalls. New Zealand has two main islands, the South Island and the North Island. In the South Island, there are mountains that are covered with snow ⓑall year round. You will be amazed by the fantastic views.

In the North Island, there are many hot springs, lakes, and areas with green grass. Because of its ⓒ_____ , many famous movies have been made in New Zealand. If you visit New Zealand, you will surely appreciate its nature.

01 다음 중 빈칸 ⓐ와 ⓒ에 공통으로 들어갈 말로 가장 적절한 것은?

① beautiful minds of people
② the famous tradition
③ lots of water
④ natural beauty
⑤ natural life style

02 다음 중 밑줄 친 ⓑ의 의미로 가장 적절한 것은?

① from time to time
② all of a sudden
③ throughout the year
④ once in a while
⑤ here and there

03 서답형 What is New Zealand made up with? Answer in English.

➡ _____

_____

[04~06] 다음 글을 읽고 물음에 답하시오.

When you hear the word kiwi, what comes to your mind? Maybe a fruit, but, in New Zealand the word kiwi has a couple of meanings. First, kiwi is the name of a delicious, green fruit. A lot of kiwi fruit is grown there, so New Zealand is known as the land of kiwi fruit.

Kiwi is also the name of one of New Zealand's native birds. The kiwi is special to New Zealanders because it is the symbol of the nation. Also, kiwi is a nickname for people from New Zealand. Today, New Zealanders are sometimes called Kiwis throughout the world. Now, you know that kiwi is the name of a fruit, a bird, and also a people. Next time, don't become confused when someone uses the word kiwi, which has several meanings.

04 서답형 Write the reason why the kiwi is special to New Zealanders. Use the phrase 'It's because.'

➡ _____

05 다음 중 위 글의 내용과 일치하는 것은?

① The word kiwi has one meaning in New Zealand.
② It is hard to find kiwi fruit grown in New Zealand.
③ A kiwi bird is one of foreign birds in New Zealand.
④ Kiwi is a word to refer to people who came from New Zealand.
⑤ New Zealanders don't have any special nickname.

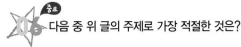 다음 중 위 글의 주제로 가장 적절한 것은?

① the world's largest producer of kiwi

② various meanings the word kiwi has in New Zealand

③ the most popular fruit in the world

④ the reason lots of kiwi fruit is grown in New Zealand

⑤ many words to refer to kiwi in New Zealand

07 다음 글을 읽고 답할 수 있는 것은?

> Now, let's talk about the Maori. They are the native people of New Zealand. They went to live on the islands long before Europeans arrived. The Maori culture is an important part of today's New Zealand society. The Maori language is taught at some schools and there are Maori language radio and TV stations. There are Maori villages in many parts of the country. You can visit Maori villages and experience Maori culture. If you say "kia ora" to the villagers, they will be glad to hear it. It means "hi" in English.

① What is the population of New Zealand?

② When did the Maori start to live in New Zealand?

③ When did Europeans arrive in New Zealand?

④ Where is the Maori language taught?

⑤ Why did the Maori settle in New Zealand?

[08~11] 다음 글을 읽고 물음에 답하시오.

> Have you ever watched the haka? The haka may look scary because haka dancers shout and move their bodies wildly. The Maori people, who you've already heard about, started doing the haka as a war dance. Today, (A)_____, New Zealanders do the haka at sport matches, weddings, or other important events. For example, New Zealand's national rugby team members do the haka before every match. It is famous all over the world. If you see the haka, you will probably agree that (B)상대 팀이 틀림없이 겁을 먹을 것이다. Like the kiwi bird, the haka is a national symbol.

 다음 중 빈칸 (A)에 들어갈 말로 가장 적절한 것은?

① for example   ② that is

③ however   ④ what's worse

⑤ unfortunately

09 위 글의 내용을 바르게 이해한 사람은?

① Jane: The haka danced by the Maori must be really relaxing.

② Paul: It is interesting that the Maori did the haka during weddings.

③ Carl: I'm so sorry that the haka isn't danced anymore.

④ David: The haka is known to only New Zealanders.

⑤ Zach: I want to see the Maori move their bodies wildly when doing the haka.

서답형

10 When do New Zealand's national rugby team members do the haka? Answer in English with seven words.

➡ _____

서답형

11 주어진 단어를 활용하여 밑줄 친 우리말 (B)를 영어로 쓰시오.

> (rival, must)

➡ _____

[12~15] 다음 글을 읽고 물음에 답하시오.

Have you ever ①watched the haka? The haka may look ②scary because haka dancers (A)_____. The Maori people, who you've already heard ③about, started doing the haka as a war dance. Today, however, New Zealanders do the haka at sport matches, weddings, or other important events. For example, New Zealand's national rugby team members do the haka before every ④matches. It is famous all over the world. If you see the haka, you will probably agree that the rival team must be ⑤scared. Like the kiwi bird, the haka is a national symbol.

12 다음 중 빈칸 (A)에 들어갈 말로 가장 적절한 것은?

① move their bodies like swans
② make some funny faces on purpose
③ shout and move their bodies wildly
④ make loud noises to wake people up
⑤ shout but dance with joy

13 다음 중 위 글의 내용과 일치하는 것은?

① The Maori learned how to do the haka from New Zealanders.
② The Maori don't know what the haka is.
③ The haka is the only national symbol.
④ People don't want to do the haka at all.
⑤ The haka still makes people scared.

서답형
14 At what events do New Zealanders do the haka today? Answer in English.

➡ _____

_____

15 밑줄 친 ①~⑤ 중 어법상 어색한 것은?

①   ②   ③   ④   ⑤

[16~18] 다음 글을 읽고 물음에 답하시오.

When you hear the word kiwi, what comes to your mind? Maybe a fruit, but, in New Zealand the word kiwi has a couple of meanings. ① First, kiwi is the name of a delicious, green fruit. A lot of kiwi fruit is grown there, so New Zealand is known as the land of kiwi fruit. ② Kiwi is also the name of one of New Zealand's native birds. ③ The kiwi is special to New Zealanders because it is the symbol of the nation. ④ Today, New Zealanders are sometimes called Kiwis throughout the world. Now, you know that kiwi is the name of a fruit, a bird, and also a people. ⑤ Next time, don't become (A)_____ when someone uses the word kiwi, which has several meanings.

16 빈칸 (A)에 들어갈 말로 가장 적절한 것은?

① amazed   ② confused   ③ upset
④ nervous   ⑤ bored

17 다음 중 주어진 문장이 들어가기에 가장 적절한 곳은?

Also, kiwi is a nickname for people from New Zealand.

①   ②   ③   ④   ⑤

서답형
18 Write the reason why New Zealand is known as the land of kiwi fruit. Use the phrase 'It's because.'

➡ _____

_____

[19~21] 다음 글을 읽고 물음에 답하시오.

Now, let's talk about the Maori.

(A) You can visit Maori villages and experience Maori culture. If you say "kia ora" to the villagers, they will be glad ⓐto hear it. It means "hi" in English.

(B) The Maori language is taught at some schools and there are Maori language radio and TV stations. There are Maori villages in many parts of the country.

(C) They are the native people of New Zealand. They went to live on the islands long before Europeans arrived. The Maori culture is an important part of today's New Zealand society.

19 자연스러운 글이 되도록 (A)~(C)를 바르게 나열한 것은?

① (A)–(C)–(B)　　② (B)–(A)–(C)
③ (B)–(C)–(A)　　④ (C)–(A)–(B)
⑤ (C)–(B)–(A)

서답형

20 What can we do when we visit Maori villages? Answer in English with five words.

➡ _____

21 다음 중 밑줄 친 ⓐ와 쓰임이 같은 것은?

① He must be generous to lend you money.
② It was my job to take care of the employees.
③ Do you have paper to write on?
④ She was upset to see him using her computer without asking.
⑤ They tried hard to get the first prize.

[22~24] 다음 글을 읽고 물음에 답하시오.

New Zealand is a place of natural beauty. It has many beautiful lakes and waterfalls. New Zealand has two main islands, the South Island and the North Island. In the South Island, there are mountains (A)that are covered with snow all year round. You will be amazed by the fantastic views.

In the North Island, there are many hot springs, lakes, and areas with green grass. Because of its natural beauty, many famous movies have been made in New Zealand. If you visit New Zealand, you will surely appreciate its nature.

서답형

22 다음과 같이 풀이되는 말을 위 글에서 찾아 쓰시오.

> to like something because you recognize its good qualitie.

➡ _____

23 다음 중 밑줄 친 (A)를 대신하여 쓸 수 있는 것은?

① who　　② whom　　③ which
④ whose　　⑤ what

24 다음 중 위 글의 내용과 일치하는 것은?

① New Zealand is famous for its cities.
② The view of the South Island is similar to that of the North Island.
③ The writer is sure that the fantastic view of New Zealand will make people amazed.
④ It is hard to find mountains covered with snow in New Zealand.
⑤ We can find many lakes and waterfalls in many countries except New Zealand.

Reading　**37**

[01~04] 다음 글을 읽고 물음에 답하시오.

New Zealand is a place of natural beauty. It has many beautiful lakes and waterfalls. New Zealand has two main islands, the South Island and the North Island. In the South Island, there are mountains that are covered with snow all year round. You will be amazed by the fantastic views.

In the North Island, there are many hot springs, lakes, and areas with green grass. Because of its natural beauty, many famous movies have been made in New Zealand. (A)If you will visit New Zealand, you will surely appreciate its nature.

01 What are there in the South Island of New Zealand? Answer in English.

➡ _____

_____

02 If you want to enjoy hot springs in New Zealand, where should you go? Answer in English.

➡ _____

03 밑줄 친 (A)를 어법에 맞게 바르게 고쳐 쓰시오.

➡ _____

_____

04 According to the passage, what is New Zealand famous for? Answer in English.

➡ _____

[05~08] 다음 글을 읽고 물음에 답하시오.

When you hear the word kiwi, what comes to your mind? Maybe a fruit, but, in New Zealand the word kiwi has a couple of meanings. First, kiwi is the name of a delicious, green fruit. A lot of kiwi fruit is grown there, so New Zealand is known as the land of kiwi fruit.

Kiwi is also the name of one of New Zealand's native birds. The kiwi is special to New Zealanders because it is the symbol of the nation. Also, kiwi is a nickname for people from New Zealand. Today, New Zealanders are sometimes called Kiwis throughout the world. Now, you know that kiwi is the name of (A)_____. Next time, don't become confused when someone uses the word kiwi, ___(B)___ has several meanings.

05 빈칸 (A)에 들어갈 말을 위 글을 읽고 바르게 유추하여 쓰시오.

➡ _____

06 빈칸 (B)에 들어갈 알맞은 말을 쓰시오.

➡ _____

07 Where is a lot of kiwi fruit grown? Answer in English with a full sentence.

➡ _____

08 위 글의 내용에 맞게 빈칸에 알맞은 말을 쓰시오. 한 칸에 하나의 단어만 쓰시오.

Unless you understand _____ _____ _____ _____, you will become confused.

[09~12] 다음 글을 읽고 물음에 답하시오.

Now, let's talk about the Maori. They are the native people of New Zealand. They went to live on the islands long before Europeans arrived. The Maori culture is an important part of today's New Zealand society. The Maori language is taught at some schools and there are Maori language radio and TV stations. There are Maori villages in many parts of the country. You can visit Maori villages and experience Maori culture. If you say "kia ora" to the villagers, they will be glad to hear it. It means "hi" in English.

09 Before Europeans arrived in New Zealand, who went to live on there?

➡ _____

_____

10 What can we find in many parts of New Zealand? Answer in English.

➡ _____

_____

11 If you want to say "hi" to the villagers in the Maori language, what should you say?

➡ _____

12 다음 중 위 글의 내용과 일치하지 <u>않는</u> 것을 두 군데 찾아 바르게 고쳐 쓰시오.

> The Maori people are the native people of Canada. Their food is an important part of today's New Zealand society.

➡ _____

_____

[13~16] 다음 글을 읽고 물음에 답하시오.

(A)<u>하카를 본 적이 있는가?</u> The haka may look scary because haka dancers shout and move their bodies wildly. The Maori people, who you've already heard about, started doing the haka as a war dance. Today, however, New Zealanders do the haka at sport matches, weddings, or other important events. For example, New Zealand's national rugby team members do the haka before every match. It is famous all over the world. If you see the haka, you will probably agree that the rival team must be scared. Like the kiwi bird, the haka is a national symbol.

13 주어진 단어를 활용하여 밑줄 친 우리말 (A)를 영어로 쓰시오. (6 words)

> (watch)

➡ _____

14 Write the reason why the haka may look scary. Use the phrase 'it's because.'

➡ _____

_____

15 According to the passage, what are we likely to see the rugby players do before their match? Answer in English and use the word 'them.'

➡ _____

_____

16 위 글의 내용에 맞게 빈칸에 알맞은 말을 쓰시오.

> _____ as well as _____ is a national symbol.

구석구석

Before You Read

Rugby is a popular sport in New Zealand.
넓은 장소에 쓰는 전치사

New Zealand is in the southern part of the world.
방향을 나타내는 말 앞에 정관사 the

The Maori people are the native people of New Zealand and have their
원주민   동사 are와 병렬 연결

culture.

구문해설 • popular: 인기 있는 • southern: 남쪽의 • native: 토박이의, ~ 태생인 • culture: 문화

럭비는 뉴질랜드에서 인기 있는 운동이다.
뉴질랜드는 남반구에 있다.
마오리족은 뉴질랜드의 원주민이고, 그들의 문화가 있다.

Enjoy Writing

We Invite You

Do you know about New Zealand? It has two main islands and 600 smaller

islands. Its capital is Wellington. The kiwi, which is a bird native to New
소유격 It's(X)   관계대명사 계속적 용법(주어)

Zealand, is one of the symbols of the country. If you come to New Zealand,
one of+복수 명사   조건의 부사절(현재시제)

you should visit a Maori village, which shows the native culture of New
관계대명사의 계속적 용법

Zealand. We suggest you try a traditional dish of the Maori people. They cook
suggest(제안)+that+주어+should+원형동사: should 생략 가능

meat and vegetables in the ground with heated rocks. It is great. Many people
수동의 의미(과거분사)

visit New Zealand to enjoy the beautiful nature. We are happy to invite you to
to부정사의 부사적 용법(목적)   to부정사의 부사적 용법(감정의 원인.)

this beautiful country.

구문해설 • capital: 수도 • native to: ~ 태생의, 원산지의 • traditional dish: 전통 요리 • heated rock: 가열된 돌

우리는 당신을 초대합니다
당신은 뉴질랜드에 대해 아는가? 그곳은 두 개의 본섬과 600개의 작은 섬들로 되어 있다. 그곳의 수도는 웰링턴이다. 키위는 뉴질랜드 태생의 새인데, 그 나라의 상징 중 하나이다. 뉴질랜드에 온다면 마오리 마을을 반드시 방문해야 하는데, 왜냐하면 그 마을이 뉴질랜드 원주민들의 문화를 보여 주기 때문이다. 우리는 당신이 마오리족의 전통 요리를 먹어 보는 것을 제안한다. 그들은 열을 가한 돌로 땅 속에서 고기와 채소를 요리한다. 그것은 훌륭하다. 많은 사람들은 아름다운 자연을 즐기기 위해 뉴질랜드를 방문한다. 우리는 당신을 이 아름다운 나라에 초대하게 되어 기쁘다.

Project Step 1

A: Let's talk about which country we are going to look into.
전치사 about의 목적어 역할로 '의문사(which country)+주어(we)+동사(are going~)' 형태의 간접의문문이다.

B: Which country do you prefer, Australia or the UK?
'Which+명사+do you prefer. A or B?' 형태의 선택의문문이다.

C: I suggest we search for information on the UK.
'suggest (that)+주어+(should)+동사원형'으로 '~할 것을 제안한다'라는 의미이다.

There is a lot of information to work with.
information을 수식하는 형용사 용법이다.

D: Okay.

구문해설 • look into: ~을 조사하다 • prefer: 선호하다 • suggest: 제안하다 • search for: ~을 조사하다
• information: 정보

A: 어느 나라를 조사할 것인지 이야기해 보자.
B: 호주와 영국 중에서 어느 나라를 선호하니?
C: 나는 영국에 관한 정보를 찾아볼 것을 제안해. 우리가 작업해야 할 많은 정보들이 있잖아.
D: 그래.

영역별 핵심문제

01 다음 주어진 두 단어의 관계가 같도록 빈칸에 알맞은 단어를 쓰시오. (주어진 철자로 시작할 것)

abroad – overseas : accomplish – a _____

02 다음 문장의 빈칸 (A)와 (B)에 들어갈 단어가 바르게 짝지어진 것은?

• The Chinese consider a panda as a (A)_____ of bravery.
• The Maori people are the (B)_____ people of New Zealand.

① harmony – several
② statue – dependent
③ sign – desirable
④ symbol – native
⑤ organization – traditional

[03~04] 다음 영영풀이에 해당하는 것을 고르시오.

03

a pattern of crossed lines and squares

① hall   ② confusion
③ flag   ④ trail
⑤ plaid

04

a meal in which everyone who is invited brings something to eat

① potluck   ② dinner
③ lunch   ④ breakfast
⑤ snack

05 다음 우리말에 맞게 주어진 문장의 빈칸을 네 단어로 채우시오.

유명인들의 도움으로 그러한 정치인들은 대중에 더 쉽게 다가갈 수 있다.

➡ _____ celebrities such politicians can easily approach the public.

06 다음 중 밑줄 친 부분의 뜻이 <u>잘못된</u> 것은?

① Of course, you have to commit to your goal until you <u>achieve</u> it! (달성하다)
② She is not only my best friend but also a strong <u>rival</u>! (경쟁자)
③ I <u>recommend</u> this dictionary to you. (빌려주다)
④ He has made cameo appearances in <u>several</u> Indian movies, too. (몇몇의)
⑤ The <u>main</u> reason is that the food here is so delicious! (주요한)

07 다음 대화의 빈칸에 들어갈 말로 알맞은 것은?

A: _____
    What do you think about it?
B: I think Group 1's picture is very nice.

① Let's talk about the pose we will make for our picture.
② Let's talk about places in the UK.
③ I saw Group 1 in the National Museum.
④ Let's talk about the picture of Group 1.
⑤ How much do you know about the picture?

08 다음 그림을 보고, 대화의 빈칸에 주어진 단어를 이용하여 제안하는 표현을 쓰시오.

> A: Let's talk about activities we can enjoy in the UK. What should we do in the UK?
> B: _____
> (suggest, watch, soccer game) (7 words)

[09~11] 다음 대화를 읽고 물음에 답하시오.

> Seho: Good morning.
> Jessie, Andy: Hi, Seho.
> Seho: I will visit my uncle in Philadelphia this winter. Can you tell me about the city?
> Jessie: Sure. (①) I was there a few years ago. First, let's talk about food.
> Seho: Okay. (②) What food is Philadelphia famous for?
> Jessie: The most famous food in Philadelphia is the cheese steak sandwich. (③) It is a big sandwich filled with beef and melted cheese.
> Seho: (④) Are there any places that are popular with tourists?
> Andy: I suggest you visit Independence Hall. It is very important in American history. (⑤)
> Seho: Wonderful. Thank you for the information.
> Andy: My pleasure..

09 위 대화의 (①)~(⑤) 중 주어진 문장이 들어갈 위치로 알맞은 것은?

> Good suggestion. I will try it.

①   ②   ③   ④   ⑤

10 What is a cheese steak sandwich like?

➡ _____

_____

11 위 대화를 읽고 답할 수 <u>없는</u> 질문은?

① When will Seho visit his uncle in Philadelphia?

② What food is Philadelphia famous for?

③ What is Independence Hall for?

④ What place is popular with tourists in Philadelphia?

⑤ Why does Andy suggest to Seho that he visit Independence Hall?

Grammar

12 다음 중 어법상 올바른 문장을 <u>모두</u> 고르면?

① Taylor recently attended Mr. Robert's lecture, that was boring.

② James visited a traditional market in Mokpo, which sell fresh seafood.

③ Mom read the letter from Daddy before he died, which made all of us cry.

④ Dave is proud of the works of his brother, who are helpful for the blind.

⑤ I respect Father Lee, who devoted his whole life to helping poor people in Southern Africa.

13 다음 중 문장의 의미가 나머지 넷과 <u>다른</u> 것은?

① My older sister gets up early not to be late for work.

② My older sister gets up early so that she may not be late for work.

③ My older sister gets up early in order not to be late for work.

④ My older sister gets up early but she isn't late for work.

⑤ My older sister gets up early so as not to be late for work.

[14~15] 다음 중 밑줄 친 부분의 쓰임이 주어진 문장과 <u>다른</u> 것은?

14

> The kiwi birds poke the ground with their beak <u>to find</u> their food.

① The Maori people waved their hands <u>to welcome</u> the visitors from Korea.

② I went to New Zealand <u>to study</u> the species of kiwi birds.

③ My ex-girlfriend just called <u>to say</u> she missed me much.

④ Sarah doesn't like <u>to make</u> the same mistakes again.

⑤ What do your family members do <u>to keep</u> healthy?

15

> A lot of movie directors go to New Zealand <u>to film</u>.

① The Maori warriors danced <u>to scare</u> their enemy.

② Alex was disappointed <u>to receive</u> his grade report card.

③ Laura lived <u>to be</u> 103, which was surprising.

④ The people of New Zealand do their best not <u>to lose</u> the endangered species.

⑤ Sally promised not <u>to smoke</u> again in front of her kids.

16 다음 주어진 세 문장을 관계대명사의 계속적 용법과 제한적 용법을 활용하여, 〈조건〉에 맞게 한 문장으로 표현하시오.

> • The public library introduced a new system.
> • The new system would help the people to easily borrow the audio books.
> • The audio books had always been difficult to borrow.

┤ 조건 ├
that과 which를 반드시 사용할 것. 본문에 있는 표현만을 활용할 것. (변형불가)

➡ _____

_____

_____

17 다음 중 어법상 <u>어색한</u> 문장은?

① We were surprised to hear the sound, which was from across the street.

② The children in my class like David's P.E. class, which are fun.

③ Everybody voted for Sarah, which was good for her future.

④ These are Jamie's books published a year ago, which I've read three times.

⑤ Andrew was talking about New Zealand, which is his home country.

18 주어진 우리말에 맞게 영작할 때 어법상 <u>어색한</u> 문장을 하나 고르시오.

> Clara가 가방을 샀는데, 내가 어제 삼촌으로부터 받은 것과 비슷하다.

① Clara bought a bag, and it is very similar to the one what I received from my uncle yesterday.

② Clara bought a bag, which is very similar to the one that I received from my uncle yesterday.

③ Clara bought a bag, which is very similar to what I received from my uncle yesterday.

④ Clara bought a bag, and it is very similar to the one which I received from my uncle yesterday.

⑤ Clara bought a bag, and it is very similar to what I received from my uncle yesterday.

19 다음 사진을 보고 우리말과 조건에 맞게 영작하여 빈칸을 채우시오.

> 뉴질랜드 축구 선수들은 상대를 겁먹게 하기 위해 하카를 춘다.
>
> (the haka, their opponents, do, scare 활용, 7 단어)

➡ New Zealand soccer players _____
_____ .

[20~22] 다음 글을 읽고 물음에 답하시오.

New Zealand is a place of natural ①beauty. It has many beautiful lakes and waterfalls. New Zealand has two main islands, the South Island and the North Island. In the South Island, there ②are mountains that ③<u>are covered</u> (A)_____ snow all year round. You will be amazed ④<u>by</u> the fantastic views.

In the North Island, there are many hot springs, lakes, and areas with green grass. ⑤Because its natural beauty, many famous movies have been made in New Zealand. If you visit New Zealand, you will surely appreciate its nature.

20 What are there in the North Island of New Zealand? Answer in English with a full sentence.

➡ _____
_____

21 다음 중 빈칸 (A)에 들어갈 말과 같은 말이 들어가는 것은?

① David was anxious _____ his test results.

② The restaurant was crowded _____ many people.

③ You must devote yourself _____ learning English.

④ Did you apply _____ the job that you wanted to get?

⑤ She is not accustomed _____ riding a bike.

22 밑줄 친 ①~⑤ 중 문맥상 바르지 <u>않은</u> 것은?

①   ②   ③   ④   ⑤

[23~25] 다음 글을 읽고 물음에 답하시오.

Have you ever watched the haka? ① The haka may look scary because haka dancers shout and move their bodies wildly. ② The Maori people, who you've already heard about, started doing the haka as a war dance. ③ For example, New Zealand's national rugby team members do the haka before every match. ④ It is famous all over the world. If you see the haka, you will probably agree that the rival team must be scared. ⑤ Like the kiwi bird, the haka is a national symbol.

23 ①~⑤ 중 주어진 문장이 들어가기에 가장 적절한 곳은?

> Today, however, New Zealanders do the haka at sport matches, weddings, or other important events.

①   ②   ③   ④   ⑤

24 본문의 단어를 활용하여 빈칸에 알맞은 말을 쓰시오.

> New Zealand's national rugby team members do the haka before every match in order to _____ the rival team.

25 다음 중 위 글을 읽고 답할 수 있는 것은?

① When was the haka invented?
② How long have the Maori people done the haka?
③ How many people do you need to do the haka?
④ Why did the kiwi bird become a national symbol?
⑤ Why does the haka look scary?

[26~29] 다음 글을 읽고 물음에 답하시오.

We Invite You

(A) They cook meat and vegetables in the ground with heated rocks. It is delicious. Many people visit New Zealand to enjoy the beautiful nature. We are happy to invite you to this beautiful country.

(B) If you come to New Zealand, you should visit a Maori village, which shows the native culture of New Zealand. We suggest you try a traditional dish of the Maori people.

(C) Do you know about New Zealand? It has two main islands and 600 smaller islands. Its capital is Wellington. The kiwi, which is a bird native to New Zealand, is one of the symbols of the country.

26 자연스러운 글이 되도록 (A)~(C)를 바르게 나열하시오.

➡ _____

27 If you want to see the native culture of New Zealand, where should you visit? Answer in English with six words.

➡ _____

28 According to the passage, why do many people visit New Zealand?

➡ _____

29 다음 중 위 글의 내용과 일치하는 것은?

① The Maori people cook meat and vegetables with cold rocks.
② The food that the Maori people make is not tasty.
③ The writer recommends us not to try a traditional food of the Maori people.
④ New Zealand is made up of many islands.
⑤ The kiwi is the only national symbol of New Zealand.

출제율 95%

01 다음 짝지어진 단어의 관계가 같도록 빈칸에 알맞은 말을 쓰시오.

> confused – calm : artificial – _____

출제율 90%

02 다음 영영풀이에 해당하는 단어는?

> a rough path across countryside or through a forest

① society　　② street　　③ trail
④ station　　⑤ hall

[03~04] 다음 대화를 읽고 물음에 답하시오.

B: Wow, we finally arrived in Hong Kong, Mom.
W: (A)우리가 방문할 곳들이 기대된다. (I'm / our / looking / to / visit / forward) What should we do today, Mike?
B: I suggest we visit Victoria Peak.
W: Victoria Peak?
B: It is the highest mountain in Hong Kong and is in a lot of movies. We can enjoy the fantastic view.
W: That sounds good. Let's go.

출제율 100%

03 위 대화의 밑줄 친 (A)의 우리말에 맞게 주어진 단어를 알맞은 순서로 배열하시오.

　➡ _____

출제율 95%

04 위 대화의 내용과 일치하지 <u>않는</u> 것은?

① Mike and his mother is in Hong Kong.
② They will first visit Victoria Peak.
③ Victoria Peak is the highest mountain in China.
④ Victoria Peak is in a lot of movies.
⑤ They will enjoy the fantastic view in Victoria Peak.

[05~06] 다음 대화를 읽고 물음에 답하시오.

B: Let's talk about (a)traditional clothing from other countries.
G: Hmm... Do you know what a kilt is?
B: No, I don't. What is it?
G: It is traditional clothing from Scotland. It looks like a knee-length (b)skirt and has a (c)plaid pattern.
B: A skirt of knee-length with a plaid pattern?
G: Yes. It is (d)common because it is a skirt for men.
B: That sounds (e)interesting. I want to try one on.

출제율 95%

05 위 대화의 밑줄 친 (a)~(e) 중 어휘의 쓰임이 <u>어색한</u> 것은?

① (a)　② (b)　③ (c)　④ (d)　⑤ (e)

출제율 90%

06 위 대화에서 다음 〈영영풀이〉가 설명하는 단어를 찾아 쓰시오.

> following the customs or ways of behaving that have continued in a group of people for a long time

　➡ _____

[07~08] 다음 대화를 읽고 물음에 답하시오.

G: Brian, let's talk about what we will prepare for the World Food Festival.
B: I will make a meat pie. It is famous in Australia. How about you, Sera?
G: I want to make a popular English dish, fish and chips.
B: Fish and chips? (A)_____
G: It's fried fish with hot potato chips.
B: That sounds interesting. Let's prepare them.

07 위 대화의 빈칸 (A)에 들어갈 말로 알맞은 것은?

① What do you do?

② How can we make fish and chips?

③ What does it look like?

④ How much do you like it?

⑤ What kind of food do you like?

08 위 대화를 읽고 답할 수 없는 질문은?

① What kind of festival will Brian and Sera participate in?

② What dish is popular in England?

③ What dish is famous in Australia?

④ What does fish and chips look like?

⑤ What does a meat pie look like?

09 다음 글에서 문법적으로 틀린 부분 두 곳을 찾아 바르게 고쳐 쓰시오.

> Welcome to Australia. The capital of Australia is Canberra. People are spoken English. Meat pie is a popular dish in Australia. Every year, lots of tourists visits the Sydney Opera House and the beautiful beaches in Melbourne.

➡ _____

10 다음 중 어법상 어색한 문장은?

① My father bought me a watch, that I don't like very much.

② Ms. Johnson moved her daughter to new school, who had trouble adjusting.

③ Gloria always wore the shirt, which her aunt bought for her.

④ I got my umbrella stolen, which I had put next to James' desk.

⑤ The clients urged the clerk to bring them chairs, which were for VIP.

11 다음 각 문장의 밑줄 친 to부정사의 용법을 〈보기〉에서 기호를 골라 각각의 괄호 안에 써 넣으시오.

┌─ 보기 ┐
ⓐ 명사적 용법
ⓑ 형용사적 용법
ⓒ 부사적 용법 '목적'
ⓓ 부사적 용법 '감정의 원인, 이유'
ⓔ 부사적 용법 '판단의 근거'
ⓕ 부사적 용법 '결과'
ⓖ 부사적 용법 '형용사/부사 수식'
└──────────┘

(1) I would like to drink zero calorie soda not to gain weight. (_____)

(2) Mina practiced the drum solo 8 hours a day to make her parents proud. (_____)

(3) Hermione hurried to the station only to miss the train. (_____)

(4) They were disappointed to find out the dark side of the organization. (_____)

(5) My parents were quite relieved to know that I wasn't hurt at the accident. (_____)

(6) David must have been so upset to accept the offer. (_____)

(7) The math problem is too difficult for Robert to solve in 10 minutes. (_____)

(8) We have a lot of friends to support us. (_____)

(9) Alicia grew up to be a world wide super star in fashion industry. (_____)

(10) Ms. Baek has learned to cook Italian food to open her own restaurant. (_____)

(11) Mina can't be lonely to have such friends like you. (_____)

(12) Jake is very rich enough to buy all the houses in this city. (_____)

(13) It is impossible for Natalie to move the furniture to the next room. (_____)

12 다음 중 밑줄 친 관계대명사가 가리키는 것으로 바르지 않은 것은?

① Karen is a doctor at the hospital, which is her second work place.
   (➡ the hospital)
② The reporter forgot the singer's name, which started with the letter C.
   (➡ the singer's name)
③ Mr. Brett was not afraid of sea water, which let him be a professional diver.
   (➡ sea water)
④ Alice is a teacher at Yujin middle school, which is located in Incheon.
   (➡ Yujin middle school)
⑤ The foreign visitors should take the subway line 2, which circulates Seoul.
   (➡ the subway line 2)

13 다음 중 밑줄 친 부분의 쓰임이 같은 것끼리 연결된 것은?

ⓐ All the employees went to the public health center to check their condition.
ⓑ During my visit to London, I need to see the tower and bridge.
ⓒ Sumi and her friends went to the street to watch the live performance of the band.
ⓓ The actor went outside to run in the park.
ⓔ Yoyo practices the piano hard to do well on the school festival.
ⓕ I'd like to play basketball this afternoon.
ⓖ It's important for her to keep promises.

① ⓑ, ⓓ, ⓔ, ⓖ   ② ⓐ, ⓒ, ⓓ, ⓔ
③ ⓐ, ⓑ, ⓔ, ⓕ   ④ ⓐ, ⓒ, ⓓ, ⓖ
⑤ ⓑ, ⓔ, ⓕ, ⓖ

14 다음 문장의 밑줄 친 부분과 쓰임이 같은 것은?

If you say "kia ora" to the villagers, they will be glad to hear it. It means "hi" in English.

① The Maori boy grew up to be a world famous athlete.
② It was not easy for the Maori villagers to learn Korean Fan dance.
③ I'd like to go to New Zealand to study the animals only living there.
④ The New Zealanders were satisfied to hear the news of their winning.
⑤ Please don't forget to visit New Zealand.

[15~16] 다음 글을 읽고 물음에 답하시오.

Now, let's talk about the Maori. They are the native people of New Zealand. They went to live on the islands long before Europeans arrived. The Maori culture is (A)_____. The Maori language is taught at some schools and there are Maori language radio and TV stations. There are Maori villages in many parts of the country. You can visit Maori villages and experience Maori culture. If you say "kia ora" to the villagers, they will be glad to hear it. It means "hi" in English.

15 다음 중 빈칸 (A)에 들어갈 말로 가장 적절한 것은?

① hard to find in New Zealand
② protected in an small island of New Zealand
③ paid no attention to by people in New Zealand
④ destroying an important part of New Zealand society
⑤ an important part of today's New Zealand society

16 다음 중 위 글의 내용과 일치하지 <u>않는</u> 것은?

① The Maori people are native to New Zealand.
② There are some schools teaching the Maori language.
③ The Maori villages are concentrated on one place.
④ We can hear radio broadcast in the Maori language.
⑤ Before Europeans arrived in New Zealand, the Maori people had lived there.

[17~18] 다음 글을 읽고 물음에 답하시오.

New Zealand is a place of natural beauty. It has many beautiful lakes and waterfalls. New Zealand has two main islands, the South Island and the North Island. In the South Island, there are mountains that are covered with snow all year round. You will be amazed by the fantastic views.

In the North Island, there are many hot springs, lakes, and areas with green grass. Because of its natural beauty, many famous movies have been made in New Zealand. If you visit New Zealand, you will surely appreciate its nature.

17 Write the reason why many famous movies have been made in New Zealand. Answer in English with five words.

➡ _____

18 다음 중 위 글의 내용과 일치하지 <u>않는</u> 곳을 두 군데 찾아 바르게 고쳐 쓰시오.

In the South Island, there are hills that are covered with snow all year round. Many hot springs, and areas with tall trees are in the North Island.

➡ _____
_____

[19~20] 다음 글을 읽고 물음에 답하시오.

Do you know about New Zealand? It has two main islands and 600 smaller islands. Its capital is Wellington. The kiwi, ①which is a bird native to New Zealand, ②is one of the symbols of the country. If you come to New Zealand, you should visit a Maori village, which ③show the native culture of New Zealand. We suggest you try a traditional dish of the Maori people. They cook meat and vegetables in the ground with ④heated rocks. It is delicious. Many people visit New Zealand ⑤to enjoy the beautiful nature. We are happy to invite you to this beautiful country.

19 밑줄 친 ①~⑤ 중 어법상 바르지 <u>않은</u> 것은?

①   ②   ③   ④   ⑤

20 위 글을 읽고 뉴질랜드에 관하여 답할 수 <u>없는</u> 것은?

① How many main islands does it have?
② What is its capital?
③ How many symbols does it have?
④ Why do many people visit there?
⑤ Where should you visit when you go there?

서술형 실전문제

01 Read the dialogue and answer the question in English.

> G: Brian, let's talk about what we will prepare for the World Food Festival.
> B: I will make a meat pie. It is famous in Australia. How about you, Sera?
> G: I want to make a popular English dish, fish and chips.
> B: Fish and chips? What does it look like?
> G: It's fried fish with hot potato chips.
> B: That sounds interesting. Let's prepare them.
>
> Q: What do you think Sera will prepare for the festival?
>
> ➡ _____

02 다음 대화의 밑줄 친 (A)와 같은 의미가 되도록 주어진 단어를 사용하여 바꿔 쓰시오.

> B: Wow, we finally arrived in Hong Kong, Mom.
> W: I'm looking forward to our visit. What should we do today, Mike?
> B: (A)I suggest we visit Victoria Peak. (why / we)
> W: Victoria Peak?
> B: It is the highest mountain in Hong Kong and is in a lot of movies. We can enjoy the fantastic view.
> W: That sounds good. Let's go.
>
> ➡ _____

03 다음 〈보기〉와 같이 두 문장이 같은 의미가 되도록 관계대명사나 관계부사를 활용하여 영작하시오.

> ┤ 보기 ├
> We met the Maori people and they showed us haka dance.
> → We met the Maori people, who showed us haka dance.

(1) New Zealand is known as the land of kiwi fruit, and a lot of kiwi fruit is grown there.

➡ _____
_____

(2) I won't get confused when somebody uses the word kiwi, and it has several meanings.

➡ _____

(3) Janet received a letter of invitation from her friend, but she didn't read it.

➡ _____

(4) All the employees in the company stop working at noon, and they go out for lunch then.

➡ _____

(5) The boss praised Sean, though he didn't mean to do well this time.

➡ _____
_____

04 다음 그림을 보고 우리말과 조건에 맞게 영작하여 빈칸을 채우시오.

> 나는 베트남의 아름다운 밤 풍경 사진을 찍기 위해 카메라를 가져갔다.
> (night scenery, take pictures 활용, 8단어)

➡ I took a camera _____ _____ of Vietnam.

[05~07] 다음 글을 읽고 물음에 답하시오.

Have you ever watched the haka? The haka may look scary because haka dancers shout and move their bodies wildly. The Maori people, who you've already heard about, started doing the haka as a war dance. Today, however, New Zealanders do the haka at sport matches, weddings, or other important events. For example, New Zealand's national rugby team members do the haka before every match. It is famous all over the world. If you see the haka, (A)상대팀이 틀림없이 겁을 먹을 것이라는 것에 아마 동의할 것이다. Like the kiwi bird, the haka is a national symbol.

05 주어진 단어를 활용하여 밑줄 친 우리말 (A)를 영어로 쓰시오.

(probably / that / team, 11단어)

➡ _____

_____

06 위 글의 내용과 맞지 않는 부분을 두 군데 찾아 바르게 고쳐 쓰시오.

Haka dancers sing and move their bodies wildly, so the haka may look happy. New Zealanders do the haka at many kinds of important events.

➡ _____

_____

07 As what did the Maori people start doing the haka? Answer in English.

➡ _____

_____

[08~09] 다음 글을 읽고 물음에 답하시오.

Do you know about New Zealand? It has two main islands and 600 smaller islands. Its capital is Wellington. The kiwi, (A)_____, is one of the symbols of the country. If you come to New Zealand, you should visit a Maori village, which shows the native culture of New Zealand. We suggest you try a traditional dish of the Maori people. They cook meat and vegetables in the ground with heated rocks. It is delicious. Many people visit New Zealand to enjoy the beautiful nature. We are happy to invite you to this beautiful country.

08 주어진 어구를 바르게 나열하여 빈칸 (A)에 들어갈 말을 완성하시오.

(a bird / which / to / New Zealand / native / is)

➡ _____

09 위 글의 내용에 맞게 빈칸에 알맞은 말을 쓰시오.

New Zealand has _____ besides two main islands.

창의사고력 서술형 문제

01 주어진 그림과 문장을 참고하여 〈보기〉와 같이 주제를 소개하는 표현을 쓰시오.

• learn the Maori language
• start a new school year in September

• go to school at the age of five
• change the classroom for each subject

보기

A: Let's talk about school life in the USA.
B: Students change the classroom for each subject.

02 다음 Yujin에 대해 설명하는 글을 읽고, 관계대명사나 관계부사의 계속적 용법을 사용하여 빈칸에 알맞은 내용을 자유롭게 영작하시오.

• Yujin usually listens to the international radio channels online from various countries.
• Yujin enjoys talking to the foreigner about each other's life and culture.
• Yujin makes the club in her school to study various languages and cultures.
• Yujin wants to go to a foreign language high school, _____.

03 주어진 정보를 이용하여 아일랜드를 홍보하는 글을 완성하시오.

land: the third largest island in Europe
capital: Dublin
the symbol of the country: the color green – It stands for the green land.
the place to visit: the Cliffs of Moher – They show the beautiful nature of Ireland.
the traditional dish: bread boiled in milk with some sugar
the reason people visit Ireland: to get refreshed

We Invite You
Do you know about Ireland? It is _____. Its capital is _____.
The color green, _____, is one of the symbols of the country. If
you come to Ireland, you should visit _____
_____. We suggest you try _____ in Ireland. It is _____
_____. It is very delicious. Many people visit Ireland to _____.

단원별 모의고사

01 다음 단어에 대한 영어 설명이 <u>어색한</u> 것은?

① a couple of: approximately two or three

② appreciate: to feel thanks about something

③ chip: very thinly sliced potato snacks that is sold in a plastic bag

④ native: relating to the place where someone or something grows naturally

⑤ rival: a person who works together with others for a special purpose

02 다음 짝지어진 단어의 관계가 같도록 빈칸에 알맞은 말을 쓰시오.

achieve – achievement : act – _____

03 다음 영영풀이에 해당하는 어구를 고르시오.

to think of an idea suddenly

① be covered with

② look forward to

③ come to one's mind

④ be known as

⑤ take care of

04 다음 중 짝지어진 대화가 <u>어색한</u> 것은?

① A: What can we do if we visit India?
   B: I suggest we learn yoga.

② A: Let's talk about places in the UK. Where should we visit in the UK?
   B: I suggest we visit Big Ben.

③ A: Let's talk about activities we can enjoy in Canada. What should we do in Canada?
   B: I suggest we go skiing.

④ A: When you hear the word kiwi, what comes to your mind?
   B: I prefer kiwis to apples.

⑤ A: Some students use their cellphones during class.
   B: I suggest we promise to turn off our cellphones before the class.

[05~07] 다음 대화를 읽고 물음에 답하시오.

Seho: Good morning.

Jessie, Andy: Hi, Seho.

Seho: (a)I will visit my uncle in Philadelphia this winter. Can you tell me about the city?

Jessie: Sure. I was there a few years ago. First, (A)let's talk about food.

Seho: Okay. What food is Philadelphia famous for?

Jessie: (b)The most famous food in Philadelphia is the cheese steak sandwich. (c)It is a big sandwich filled with beef and melted cheese.

Seho: Good suggestion. I will try it. (d)Are there any places that are popular with tourists?

Andy: (e)I suggest you visit Independence Hall. It is very important in American history.

Seho: Wonderful. Thank you for the information.

Andy: My pleasure.

05 위 대화의 밑줄 (A)와 같은 의미로 사용된 표현이 <u>아닌</u> 것은?

① I'd like to say something about food.

② let me tell you about food.

③ I want to talk about food.

④ may I tell you about food?

⑤ can you tell me about food?

06 위 대화의 밑줄 친 (a)~(e)에 대한 설명 중 잘못된 것은?

① (a) 이번 겨울에 필라델피아를 방문할 것이라는 미래 계획을 말하는 표현으로, 'I'm going to visit'으로 바꾸어 쓸 수 있다.

② (b) 'famous'의 최상급 형태로 'the most famous'를 사용했다.

③ (c) 'filled'는 'sandwich'가 소고기와 녹인 치즈로 채워져 있다는 의미로 현재분사 'filling'으로 고치는 것이 올바르다.

④ (d) 'that are popular with tourists'는 명사 'any places'를 수식하는 주격 관계대명사절로 'that are'는 생략 가능하다.

⑤ (e) 제안하는 표현으로 'you should visit'에서 'should'가 생략된 형태이다.

07 위 대화의 내용과 일치하지 <u>않는</u> 것은?

① Both Jessie and Andy know well about Philadelphia.

② Jessie has been to Philadelphia before.

③ Many people in Philadelphia like to eat the cheese steak sandwich.

④ Seho decides to eat the cheese steak sandwich.

⑤ Andy suggests Seho visit Independence Hall because it is a popular place for Americans.

08 다음 대화의 밑줄 친 우리말에 맞게 주어진 단어를 알맞은 순서로 배열하시오.

> G: My American friend invited me to a potluck dinner next Friday.
>
> B: You know, you should take food to share at the dinner.
>
> G: <u>무엇을 가져갈지 추천해 줄래?</u>(that / recommend / what / you / I / would / take / ?)

B: I suggest you take some Korean food. How about Gimbap, Suji?

G: Yes. It's not spicy and it's easy to carry.

B: I think it'll be good for dinner.

➡ _____

09 다음 그림의 빈칸에 주어진 어구를 이용하여 제안이나 권유하는 말을 영어로 쓰시오.

G: _____

crossing the street. (we, look to the right)

10 다음 대화의 빈칸 (A)에 들어갈 말로 나머지와 성격이 <u>다른</u> 하나는?

> B: Wow, we finally arrived in Hong Kong, Mom.
>
> W: I'm looking forward to our visit. What should we do today, Mike?
>
> B: (A)_____
>
> W: Victoria Peak?
>
> B: It is the highest mountain in Hong Kong and is in a lot of movies. We can enjoy the fantastic view.
>
> W: That sounds good. Let's go.

① I suggest we visit Victoria Peak.

② We'd better visit Victoria Peak.

③ I'd like to say something about visiting Victoria Peak.

④ I think we should visit Victoria Peak.

⑤ Why don't we visit Victoria Peak?

11 다음 내용을 읽고, 질문에 대한 답을 조건에 맞게 영작하시오.

> • Nowadays, people are afraid of the corona virus.
> • The virus causes the critical disease.
> • People hope the cure will come out soon so that they may not worry any longer.

(1) What are people afraid of and why are they afraid of it? (계속적 용법의 관계대명사를 반드시 사용할 것, 12 단어)

➡ _____

_____

(2) What do people hope? (to부정사의 '부사적' 용법을 반드시 사용할 것, 13 단어)

➡ _____

_____

12 다음 중 밑줄 친 부분이 나머지와 <u>다른</u> 용법으로 사용되었고, 어법상으로도 <u>어색한</u> 것을 찾으시오.

① All my school students will go to New Zealand <u>to learn</u> its nature and culture.
② The Maori people practice the haka dance <u>to keep</u> their tradition.
③ The native people of New Zealand like <u>to call</u> 'Kiwis' by the people of other countries.
④ The people of New Zealand do many things <u>to protect</u> the kiwi birds.
⑤ I was sad not <u>to be</u> invited to the festival at the Maori village.

13 다음 중 밑줄 친 to부정사의 용법이 '부사적 용법'으로 쓰인 것은?

① Remember <u>to protect</u> kiwi birds.
② There are many places <u>to see</u> in New Zealand.

③ I was pleased <u>to learn</u> several meanings of the word kiwi.
④ Many people in my country would like <u>to visit</u> New Zealand.
⑤ It's important <u>to save</u> the kiwi birds.

14 다음 그림과 우리말 설명을 보고 괄호 안에 주어진 단어를 모두 활용하여 조건에 맞게 배열하시오.

> 사다리는 이상한 믿음과 관련되어 있는데, 그것은 그 아래로 지나가는 것은 불운을 가져온다는 것이다.
> (a strange belief / linked with / passing / bad luck / ladders are / brings / under them / is that)

(1) 접속사와 대명사를 추가하여 배열하시오.

➡ _____

(2) 계속적 용법의 관계대명사를 추가하여 배열하시오.

➡ _____

[15~16] 다음 밑줄 친 부분과 어법상 쓰임이 같은 것은?

15

> • The students chose to go on a field trip to New Zealand, <u>which</u> is well known for its natural beauty.

① The captain announced <u>which</u> of the players his team would accept.

② Suji has been doing volunteer work, <u>which</u> is doing laundries for the people in need.

③ This is the hospital in <u>which</u> Janet's first daughter was born.

④ If there are only two pens for you to use in the world, <u>which</u> will you choose?

⑤ What she told me didn't bother me but the way in <u>which</u> she said made me totally upset.

16

• Tiffany hurried to the subway station not <u>to be</u> late for the meeting.

① My pet dog likes <u>to ring</u> the bell to say something to me.

② It is not always easy for me <u>to memorize</u> all the guests' names.

③ The judge looked at her watch <u>to check</u> the time.

④ Please don't forget <u>to come</u> a little earlier than we agreed.

⑤ <u>To master</u> swimming skills is too difficult for the little kids.

17 다음 그림을 보고 우리말과 조건에 맞게 영작하시오.

내가 잔디밭에서 네잎 클로버를 발견했는데, 그것이 나에게 행운을 가져올 것이다.
(good luck, would, me, bring 등을 활용, 6단어)

➡ I found a four-leaf clover among the grass, _____.

[18~21] 다음 글을 읽고 물음에 답하시오.

When you hear the word kiwi, what comes to your mind? Maybe a fruit, but, in New Zealand the word kiwi has a couple of meanings. First, kiwi is the name of a delicious, green fruit. A lot of kiwi fruit is grown there, so New Zealand is known (A)_____ the land of kiwi fruit.

Kiwi is also the name of one of New Zealand's native birds. The kiwi is special to New Zealanders because it is the symbol of the nation. Also, kiwi is a nickname for people from New Zealand. Today, New Zealanders are sometimes called Kiwis throughout the world. Now, you know that kiwi is the name of (B)_____, (C)_____, and also (D)_____. Next time, don't become confused when someone uses the word kiwi, which has several meanings.

18 다음 중 빈칸 (A)에 들어갈 말과 같은 말이 들어가는 것은?

① Let me introduce myself _____ you.

② She is worried _____ her test results.

③ He thought of the place _____ his home.

④ The detective promised to look _____ the matter.

⑤ Some people are very difficult to deal _____.

19 빈칸 (B)~(D)에 들어갈 말을 위 글에서 찾아 쓰시오.

➡ (B)_____ (C)_____ (D)_____

20 According to the passage, what can you call people from New Zealand? Answer in English with five words.

➡ _____

21 다음 중 위 글의 내용과 일치하지 <u>않는</u> 것은?

① Kiwi has various meanings in New Zealand.

② New Zealand is known as the land of kiwi fruit.

③ Kiwi is the most popular fruit in New Zealand.

④ New Zealanders think the bird kiwi to be special.

⑤ It can be confusing to understand what kiwi means unless you know its several meanings.

[22~23] 다음 글을 읽고 물음에 답하시오.

New Zealand is a place of natural beauty. It has many beautiful lakes and waterfalls. ① In the South Island, there are mountains that are covered with snow all year round. ② You will be amazed by the fantastic views. ③

In the North Island, there are many hot springs, lakes, and areas with green grass. ④ Because of its natural beauty, many famous movies have been made in New Zealand. ⑤ If you visit New Zealand, you will surely appreciate its nature.

22 ①~⑤ 중 주어진 문장이 들어가기에 가장 적절한 곳은?

New Zealand has two main islands, the South Island and the North Island.

①   ②   ③   ④   ⑤

23 다음 중 위 글을 읽고 답할 수 <u>없는</u> 것은?

① What is New Zealand famous for?

② What are there in the North Island?

③ How many main islands does New Zealand have?

④ How many movies have been made in New Zealand?

⑤ What will we appreciate when we visit New Zealand?

[24~25] 다음 글을 읽고 물음에 답하시오.

Now, let's talk about the Maori. They are the native people of New Zealand. They went to live on the islands long before Europeans arrived. (A)The Maori culture is an important part of today's New Zealand society. The Maori language is taught at some schools and there are Maori language radio and TV stations. There are Maori villages in many parts of the country. You can visit Maori villages and experience Maori culture. If you say "kia ora" to the villagers, they will be glad to hear it. It means "hi" in English.

24 According to the passage, what does "kia ora" mean in English?

➡ _____

25 글쓴이가 밑줄 친 (A)와 같이 말한 이유로 가장 적절한 것은?

① New Zealanders don't care about the Maori people.

② People in New Zealand maintain the Maori language and culture.

③ It is easy to find people speaking only the Maori language.

④ There live only the Maori people in New Zealand.

⑤ The Maori people have built many schools in New Zealand.

MEMO

Lesson 7

How to Get Along with People

 의사소통 기능

- 요청하기
  Do you mind helping me?

- 감사하기
  I really appreciate your advice.

 언어 형식

- 관계부사 'how'
  June didn't like **how** Mike had acted.

- The + 비교급 ~, the + 비교급 …
  The more sincere your apology is, **the better** it will be received.

Words & Expressions

Key Words

- **accidentally** [æksədéntəli] 부 우연히, 뜻하지 않게
- **apologize** [əpálədʒàiz] 동 사과하다
- **apology** [əpálədʒi] 명 사과
- **appreciate** [əprí:ʃièit] 동 고마워하다, 감사하다
- **borrow** [bárou] 동 빌리다
- **brave** [breiv] 형 용감한
- **break** [breik] 동 (관계를) 끝내다, 끊다
- **cafeteria** [kæfətíəriə] 명 구내식당
- **case** [keis] 명 사례, 경우
- **casual** [kǽʒuəl] 형 대충하는, 건성의
- **cheerful** [tʃíərfəl] 형 발랄한, 쾌활한
- **delete** [dilí:t] 동 삭제하다
- **dislike** [disláik] 동 싫어하다
- **elementary school** 초등학교
- **emotional** [imóuʃəul] 형 감정적인
- **especially** [ispéʃəli] 부 특히, 유난히
- **feeling** [fí:liŋ] 명 느낌, 감정
- **generous** [dʒénərəs] 형 너그러운
- **helpful** [hélpfəl] 형 도움이 되는, 유용한
- **humorous** [hjú:mərəs] 형 재미있는, 유머러스한
- **hurry** [hə́:ri] 동 서두르다, 급히 가다
- **hurt** [hə:rt] 명 상처 형 기분이 상한, 상처를 입은 동 마음을 아프게 하다, 감정을 상하게 하다
- **ignore** [ignɔ́:r] 동 무시하다
- **include** [inklú:d] 동 포함하다
- **intend** [inténd] 동 의도하다
- **let** [let] 동 (~하게) 놓아두다, (~을 하도록) 허락하다
- **loud** [laud] 형 소리가 큰, 시끄러운
- **mind** [maind] 동 꺼리다, 싫어하다 명 마음
- **mistake** [mistéik] 명 실수, 잘못
- **necessary** [nésəsèri] 형 필요한
- **nervous** [nə́:rvəs] 형 긴장하는, 초조해 하는
- **prepare** [pripɛ́ər] 동 ~을 준비하다 (for)
- **proper** [prápər] 형 적절한, 제대로 된
- **receive** [risí:v] 동 받다, 받아들이다
- **regret** [rigrét] 동 후회하다
- **relationship** [riléiʃənʃip] 명 관계
- **relaxed** [rilǽkst] 형 느긋한, 여유 있는
- **responsibility** [rispànsəbíləti] 명 책임
- **right** [rait] 부 바르게, 정확하게
- **seem** [si:m] 동 (~인 것처럼) 보이다, ~인 것 같다
- **serious** [síəriəs] 형 심각한, 진지한
- **sincere** [sinsíər] 형 진정한, 진심 어린
- **sincerely** [sinsíərli] 부 진심으로
- **solve** [sɑlv] 동 해결하다
- **suggestion** [səgdʒéstʃən] 명 의견, 제안
- **thoughtful** [θɔ́:tfəl] 형 사려 깊은, 생각에 잠긴
- **tray** [trei] 명 식판, 쟁반
- **treat** [tri:t] 동 처리하다, 대우하다
- **wound** [wu:nd] 명 상처, 부상

Key Expressions

- **add up to** (결과가) ~가 되다, ~임을 보여 주다
- **after all** (설명·이유를 덧붙일 때) 어쨌든, (예상과는 달리) 결국에는
- **at once** 즉시
- **be busy –ing** ~하느라 바쁘다
- **bump into** ~에 부딪히다
- **care about** ~에 마음을 쓰다, ~에 관심을 가지다
- **get along with** ~와 잘 지내다
- **get into the rhythm** 리듬을 타다
- **laugh off** ~을 웃어넘기려 하다
- **make a mistake** 실수를 하다
- **pass by** 지나가다
- **pick out** 선택하다, 고르다
- **seem to+동사원형** ~인 것처럼 보이다
- **take responsibility for** ~에 책임을 지다
- **think nothing of** ~을 아무렇지 않게 여기다
- **trip over** ~에 걸려 넘어지다
- **turn down** (소리를) 줄이다
- **with all one's heart** 진심으로

Word Power

※ 서로 비슷한 뜻을 가진 어휘

- □ **thoughtful** 사려 깊은 – **considerate** 배려하는
- □ **accidentally** 우연히 – **by chance** 우연히
- □ **delete** 삭제하다 – **cancel** 삭제하다, 지우다
- □ **dislike** 싫어하다 – **hate** 싫어[혐오]하다
- □ **generous** 너그러운, 후한 – **lavish** 아끼지 않는
- □ **helpful** 유용한, 도움이 되는 – **useful** 유용한

- □ **ignore** 무시하다 – **disregard** 무시하다
- □ **regret** 후회하다 – **repent** 후회하다
- □ **nervous** 긴장하는 – **anxious** 초조한
- □ **proper** 적절한 – **appropriate** 적절한
- □ **sincere** 진심어린 – **serious** 진지한, 진정인
- □ **prepare** 준비하다 – **arrange** 정하다, 준비하다

※ 서로 반대되는 뜻을 가진 어휘

- □ **emotional** 감정적인 ↔ **emotionless** 감정이 없는
- □ **necessary** 필요한 ↔ **unnecessary** 불필요한
- □ **generous** 후한, 너그러운 ↔ **stingy**, **mean** 인색한
- □ **brave** 용감한 ↔ **timid** 겁 많은, 소심한

- □ **receive** 받다 ↔ **give** 주다
- □ **right** 바르게 ↔ **wrong** 틀리게
- □ **cheerful** 즐거운, 쾌활한 ↔ **gloomy** 우울한

※ 형용사 – 명사

- □ **generous** 너그러운, 후한 – **generosity** 관대함
- □ **nervous** 긴장하는 – **nerve** 신경, 긴장

- □ **helpful** 도움이 되는 – **help** 도움
- □ **proper** 적절한 – **propriety** 적절, 적당함

※ 동사 – 명사

- □ **ignore** 무시하다 – **ignorance** 무지, 무식
- □ **include** 포함하다 – **inclusion** 포함

- □ **solve** 해결하다 – **solution** 해결책, 해법
- □ **intend** 의도하다 – **intention** 의도

English Dictionary

- □ **accidentally** 우연히
  → in a way that was not planned or intended
  계획되거나 의도되지 않은 방식으로

- □ **apology** 사과
  → an act of saying that you are sorry for something wrong you have done
  당신이 저지른 잘못된 일에 미안하다고 말하는 행위

- □ **appreciate** 감사하다
  → to be grateful for something
  무언가에 고마워하다

- □ **brave** 용감한
  → showing no fear of dangerous or difficult things
  위험하거나 어려운 일에 대해 어떠한 두려움도 보이지 않는

- □ **delete** 삭제하다
  → to remove part or all of a written or electronic text
  서면이나 전자 텍스트의 일부 또는 전부를 제거하다

- □ **generous** 관대한, 너그러운
  → willing to give money, help, kindness, etc., especially more than is usual or expected
  평소 또는 예상했던 것보다 더 많이 돈, 도움, 친절을 기꺼이 주는

- □ **ignore** 무시하다
  → to intentionally not listen or give attention to
  의도적으로 듣지 않거나 주의를 기울이지 않다

- □ **prepare** 준비하다
  → to make or get something or someone ready for something that will happen in the future
  어떤 일이나 사람이 미래에 일어날 일에 준비가 되도록 하다

- □ **relationship** 관계
  → the way in which two things are connected
  두 가지가 연결되는 방식

- □ **responsibility** 책임
  → something that it is your job or duty to deal with
  당신이 처리해야 할 일이나 의무인 것

- □ **sincere** 진정한, 진심어린
  → honest and true, and based on what you really feel and believe
  정직하고 진실하며, 당신이 정말로 느끼고 믿는 것에 근거하는

- □ **suggestion** 제안
  → an idea, plan, or action that is suggested or the act of suggesting it
  제안되는 아이디어, 계획 또는 행동 또는 제안하는 행위

- □ **thoughtful** 사려 깊은
  → always thinking of the things you can do to make people happy or comfortable
  사람들을 행복하게 하거나 편안하게 하기 위해 할 수 있는 일들을 항상 생각하는

01 중요 다음 문장의 빈칸에 공통으로 들어갈 말로 알맞은 것은?

- Those are not _____ clothes for an interview.
- Their goal is to promote _____ Korean language usage among Koreans.

① nervous ② gloomy
③ proper ④ generous
⑤ casual

02 서답형 빈칸에 주어진 〈영영풀이〉를 읽고 알맞은 단어를 쓰시오.

The high school principal was touched by such a _____ gesture.

┤영영풀이├

always thinking of the things you can do to make people happy or comfortable

[03~04] 다음 설명에 해당하는 단어를 고르시오.

03

honest and true, and based on what you really feel and believe

① repair ② proper
③ anxious ④ cheerful
⑤ sincere

04

to make or get something or someone ready for something that will happen in the future

① repair ② prepare
③ proper ④ promote
⑤ solve

05 서답형 다음 우리말에 맞게 빈칸에 알맞은 말을 쓰시오.

야생 동물들은 보통 다른 종들과는 잘 어울리지 않습니다.

➡ Wild animals usually don't _____ _____ well _____ other species.

06 중요 다음 빈칸에 들어갈 말이 바르게 짝지어진 것은?

(A) Remember that anything you post on the Internet will stay there forever, even if you _____ it.
(B) If you are interested in this program, you should _____ because only 100 lucky students will be able to attend this school.

	(A)	(B)
①	store	recommend
②	store	apologize
③	post	receive
④	delete	hurry
⑤	delete	appreciate

07 다음 짝지어진 단어의 관계가 나머지와 다른 하나는?

① generous – generosity
② nervous – nerve
③ proper – propriety
④ helpful – help
⑤ intend – intention

01 다음 빈칸에 들어갈 말을 〈보기〉에서 찾아 쓰시오. (필요하면 어형을 변화시키고, 동사는 현재형으로 쓸 것.)

┌─ 보기 ─┐
emotion   relax   suggest   appreciate
└────────┘

(1) Do you have any _____ or ideas to improve education and your school?

(2) Some people believe that pets may help patients recover faster with _____ support.

(3) Stretching is a good way to stay fit and feel _____.

(4) We _____ someone's listening to us, because it shows that the person cares.

02 다음 문장의 빈칸에 공통으로 들어갈 단어를 주어진 철자로 시작하여 쓰시오.

┌─────────────────────────────┐
• If you feel n_____, try standing straight with your shoulders back.

• Try to act confidently, even if you feel n_____.

• I thought I would remain calm, but when I was confronted with the TV camera, I became very n_____.
└─────────────────────────────┘

03 다음 우리말과 같은 표현이 되도록 문장의 빈칸을 채우시오.

(1) 운전자들은 가끔 속도를 내고, 신호를 무시하고 달리며, 도로의 규칙들을 무시한다.
➡ Divers often speed, run lights, and _____ the rules of the road.

(2) 그는 일을 그만두기로 한 자신의 결정을 조금도 후회하지 않는다.
➡ He does not _____ his decision to quit his job one bit.

(3) 화장실을 쓰려고 줄을 서서 기다리고 있었는데, 한 아이가 우연히 내 신발에 침을 뱉었어.
➡ I waited in line to use the bathroom, and a kid _____ spat on my shoes.

(4) 거주자들은 관광객 또는 고양이들을 꺼리는 것 같지 않습니다.
➡ The residents do not seem to _____ the tourists or the cats.

04 영영풀이에 해당하는 단어를 〈보기〉에서 찾아 첫 번째 빈칸에 쓰고, 두 번째 빈칸에는 우리말 뜻을 쓰시오.

┌─ 보기 ─┐
relationship   generous   responsibility
apology
└────────┘

(1) _____: something that it is your job or duty to deal with: _____

(2) _____: an act of saying that you are sorry for something wrong you have done: _____

(3) _____: the way in which two things are connected: _____

(4) _____: willing to give money, help, kindness, etc., especially more than is usual or expected: _____

Conversation

1 요청하기

Do you mind helping me? 나를 도와 줄 수 있나요?

- 'Do you mind ~ing?'는 '당신은 ~하는 것이 괜찮으신가요?'라는 뜻으로 상대방에게 무엇인가를 조심스럽고 정중하게 요청할 때 사용하는 표현이다. mind는 동명사를 목적어로 취하기 때문에 동사 뒤에 ~ing를 붙인 형태를 사용한다. 동명사 대신 if절을 사용하여 'Do you mind if ~?'로 좀 더 정중하게 물을 수 있으며 'Would you mind ~?'로 물을 수도 있다.

- 요청에 답하는 표현
  - 요청을 승낙할 때 mind는 '꺼리다'의 뜻이므로 부정어(not)를 써서 승낙을 표현한다.
    Of course not. / Not at all. / Surely not. / Certainly not. / No, I don't (mind).
  - 요청을 거절할 때 Sorry라고 말하면서 거절하는 이유를 덧붙여 말하며, Yes라고 답하면 '꺼린다'라는 거절의 표현이 된다.
    (I'm) Sorry, but I can't ~. / Yes, I do[would]. / Sure. / Of course.
    - **A:** Do you mind opening the door? 문을 열어 주시겠어요?
      B: Not at all (= Of course not. / No problem.) 물론입니다.
    - **A:** Do you mind turning off your cell phone? 네 휴대전화를 꺼 줄 수 있니?
      B: Of course not. 물론이야.

요청하기의 다른 표현들

- (Please) Help me.
- Can you help me(, please)?
- Could I ask you to help me?
- Is it okay if I ~?
  - 제안, 권유, 요청에 답하기
    (긍정) Yes. / Okay. / Sure. / All right. / No problem.
    (부정) (I'm) Sorry, but I can't. / I'm afraid I can't. / Thank you, but ~. / No, thank you.

핵심 Check

1. 다음 우리말과 일치하도록 빈칸에 알맞은 말은?

> **A:** Do you mind taking a picture with us? 우리랑 사진 찍을래?
> **B:** _____ Let's use my phone. 물론이야. 내 전화기를 사용하자.

① Of course.　　② Certainly.　　③ Of course not.

④ Yes, I do.　　⑤ Sure.

2 감사하기

I really appreciate your advice. 당신의 충고에 정말 감사드립니다.

■ 감사하기 표현
감사하는 표현은 아주 간단히 'Thank you.'로 할 수 있지만 좀 더 정중하게 표현할 때는 '감사하다'는 의미를 가지는 동사 appreciate를 사용하여 'I appreciate ~.'로 표현할 수 있다. 이때 appreciate 뒤에는 감사의 내용이 오면 된다.
예를 들어 너의 친절이 감사하다고 할 때는 'I appreciate your kindness.'라고 쓰면 된다. '네가 ~해주면 감사하겠다.'고 상대방에게 정중히 부탁할 때에는 'I would appreciate it if you ~.'라고 표현한다.
• **A:** I really appreciate your advice. 당신의 충고에 정말 감사드립니다.
  B: Not at all. I'm glad that I could help you. 천만에요. 당신을 도울 수 있어서 기쁩니다.

■ 감사하기 표현에 대한 응답 표현
'I appreciate ~.'에 대한 대답은 'You're welcome.', 'No problem.', 'Not at all.', '(It was) My pleasure.', 'Don't mention it.' 등을 사용하면 된다.
• **A:** I appreciate your help.
  B: You're welcome.

■ 감사하기의 다른 표현
  − Thanks for your advice.
  − Thanks (a lot). / Thank you (very / so) much.

핵심 Check

2. 다음 빈칸에 들어갈 말로 어색한 것은?

> **B:** Irene, what are you doing?
>
> **G:** Well, I've lost my favorite cap. I can't find it.
>
> **B:** Let me help you. What does it look like?
>
> **G:** It's red. My name is written in black on the side.
>
> **B:** Oh, is this yours? It was under the table.
>
> **G:** Yes, it is. Thank you, Jim. I appreciate your help.
>
> **B:** _____

① It's my pleasure. ② Don't mention it. ③ You're welcome.
④ Not at all. ⑤ You're right.

Listen & Speak 1 A-1

B: Judy, ❶do you mind turning down the volume?

G: ❷No, I don't. Is it too loud?

B: Yes, it is. I can hear it in my room.

G: I'm sorry. I'll ❸turn it down.

B: Thanks a lot.

> B: Judy, 볼륨을 좀 낮춰 줄래?
> G: 그래. 소리가 너무 크니?
> B: 응, 소리가 커. 내 방에서도 소리가 들려.
> G: 미안해. 내가 볼륨을 낮출게.
> B: 정말 고마워.

❶ Do you mind ~ing?는 '당신은 ~하는 것이 괜찮으신가요?'라는 뜻으로 상대방에게 무엇인가를 조심스럽고 정중하게 요청할 때 사용하는 표현이다. mind는 동명사를 목적어로 취하기 때문에 동사 뒤에 ~ing를 붙인 동명사 형태를 사용한다.

❷ 요청을 승낙하는 표현으로, mind는 '꺼리다'의 뜻이므로 부정어(not)를 써서 승낙을 표현한다. Of course not. / Not at all. / Surely not. / Certainly not. / No, I don't (mind). 등으로 바꾸어 말할 수 있다.

❸ '동사(turn)+부사(down)' 형태의 '이어동사'로 목적어가 인칭대명사일 때는 반드시 '동사+대명사+부사' 어순을 취한다.

Check(√) True or False

(1) Judy asks the boy for a favor politely.   T ☐ F ☐

(2) Judy is going to turn down the volume.   T ☐ F ☐

Listen & Speak 2 A-1

G: You ❶seem to be busy, Minsu. Can I come in?

B: Sure. I'm preparing for the dance contest, but it's not easy.

G: I can help you. I was in the contest last year.

B: Really? That would be great, Amy.

G: You ❷are good at getting into the rhythm. But ❸one thing you need to do is to be more relaxed. You are too nervous.

B: Your advice is very helpful. ❹I really appreciate your advice.

G: ❺It's my pleasure.

> G: 민수야, 너 바빠 보인다. 나 들어가도 되니?
> B: 물론. 나 춤 경연대회를 준비하고 있는데 쉽지 않아.
> G: 내가 도와줄게. 나 작년에 대회에 참가 했었거든.
> B: 정말? Amy, 그거 정말 좋을 거 같아.
> G: 너는 리듬을 타는 건 잘하는 편이야. 하지만 네가 해야 할 한 가지는 긴장을 더 푸는 것이야. 너는 너무 긴장을 해.
> B: 네 조언이 정말 도움이 된다. 너의 조언 정말 고마워.
> G: 도움이 됐다니 기뻐.

❶ 'seem+ 부정사'는 '~처럼 보인다'라는 의미로, 의견을 제시하는 표현이다. 'It seems (to me) that you are busy, Minsu.'로 바꾸어 쓸 수 있다.

❷ be good at은 '~을 잘한다'라는 의미로, 전치사 'at' 다음에는 '동명사 getting'이 와야 한다.

❸ 'you need to do'는 주어인 'one thing'을 수식하는 관계대명사절로 목적격 관계대명사 'that/which'가 생략되어 있다. 주어가 단수 명사(one thing)이므로 단수동사 'is'가 사용되었다. 'to be ~'는 보어 자리에 사용된 to부정사의 명사적 용법이다.

❹ 'I appreciate ~.'는 감사를 나타내는 표현으로 appreciate 뒤에는 감사의 내용이 오면 된다.

❺ I appreciate ~.에 대한 대답으로 You're welcome. No problem., Not at all., Don't mention it. 등으로 바꾸어 사용할 수 있다.

Check(√) True or False

(3) Minsu is preparing for the singing contest.   T ☐ F ☐

(4) Amy advised Minsu to be more relaxed.   T ☐ F ☐

Listen & Speak 1 A-3

> B: Karen, do you mind coming to my house tomorrow at 7 a.m.?
> G: That's very early.
> B: I know, but I need the book ❶that you borrowed before class.
> G: I see. Then ❷let's meet at seven.
> B: See you then.

B: Karen, 내일 오전 7시에 우리 집에 와 줄래?
G: 그건 너무 이른데.
B: 그건 알지만, 수업 시작하기 전에 네가 빌려 간 책이 필요하거든.
G: 알겠어. 그럼 7시에 보자.
B: 그때 보자.

❶ 목적격 관계대명사절로 선행사 'the book'을 수식한다. 이때 'that'은 생략 가능하다.
❷ '~하자'는 뜻으로 제안을 할 때 사용한다.

Check(√) True or False

(5) Karen won't go to the boy's house tomorrow at 7 a.m.　　　　T ☐ F ☐

(6) The boy needs the book that Karen borrowed before class.　　　T ☐ F ☐

Listen & Speak 2 A-2

> B: Irene, what are you doing?
> G: Well, I've lost my favorite cap. I can't find it.
> B: ❶Let me help you. ❷What does it look like?
> G: It's red. My name ❸is written in black on the side.
> B: Oh, is this yours? It was under the table.
> G: Yes, it is. Thank you, Jim. I appreciate your help.
> B: ❹No problem.

B: Irene, 너 뭐 하고 있어?
G: 음, 내가 제일 좋아하는 모자를 잃어버렸어. 그 모자를 못 찾겠어.
B: 내가 도와줄게. 그것은 어떻게 생겼어?
G: 그건 빨간색이야. 모자 옆 부분에 내 이름이 검은색으로 쓰여 있어.
B: 오, 이거 네 것이니? 이거 탁자 아래에 있었어.
G: 응, 맞아. 고마워, Jim. 도와줘서 고마워.
B: 천만에.

❶ 'Let+목적어+목적보어(원형부정사)' 형태로 '…가 ~하도록 하게 하다'라는 뜻이다.
❷ 사람이나 사물의 외모나 모습을 물어보는 표현이다.
❸ 'be+과거분사'의 수동태로 '이름이 쓰여 있다'라는 의미이다.
❹ 감사를 표현하는 말에 대한 대답으로 '천만에.'라고 해석한다. 'You're welcome., Not at all., Don't mention it.' 등으로 바꾸어 사용할 수 있다.

Check(√) True or False

(7) Irene has found her favorite cap.　　　　T ☐ F ☐

(8) Irene's cap was under the table.　　　　T ☐ F ☐

Listen & Speak 1 A-2

G: I ❶accidentally broke my mom's favorite plate.

B: ❷That's too bad, Mina.

G: ❸Do you mind telling me how to say sorry to her?

B: No, not at all. You should apologize sincerely.

G: I see. I'll talk to her with all my heart.

❶ 'accidentally'는 '우연히'라는 뜻으로, 'by chance', 'by accident'로 바꾸어 쓸 수 있다.

❷ 상대방의 좋지 않은 일에 대한 반응으로 '안됐구나.'라는 뜻이다.

❸ 상대방에게 요청하는 표현으로 'Is it OK if I ask you to tell me how to say sorry to her?'로 바꾸어 쓸 수 있다.

 Real Life Talk

Jessie: Hi, Andy. What's up?

Andy: Hi, Jessie. I'm going to buy a present for Amy. ❶You've been friends with her for a long time, haven't you?

Jessie: Yes, since first grade in elementary school.

Andy: Well, I know ❷you're really busy studying, but do you mind helping me? I am sure you could ❸help me pick out something nice.

Jessie: No problem. What's the present for? It's not her birthday.

Andy: Well, two months ago, when my leg was broken, she carried my backpack to school.

Jessie: That was nice of her.

Andy: Yes, it was. What should I get for her?

Jessie: Well, ❹how about a case for her smartphone? She broke her case recently.

Andy: Really? Thank you for your suggestion.

❶ 현재완료 형태로 부사구 'for a long time'과 호응하여 과거부터 현재까지의 상태를 나타낸다. 'haven't you?'는 부가의문문으로 평서문의 긍정문 조동사 'have'를 부정으로 바꾸어 사용한다.

❷ 'be busy+-ing'는 '~하느라 바쁘다'라는 표현이다.

❸ 'help+목적어+목적보어(원형부정사)' 구문이다. 목적보어 자리에는 'to부정사'를 사용할 수도 있다.

❹ 'how about+명사/동명사 ~?'는 상대방에게 제안하는 표현으로 '~는 어때?'라는 뜻이다.

 Wrap Up 1

G: ❶I am planning to go to Jejudo.

B: That's cool, Suhee. I ❷used to live there.

G: Do you mind telling me ❸what to do in Jejudo?

B: Not at all. Jejudo has many beautiful beaches. You should visit them.

G: Good. I will go swimming. What else can I do?

B: ❹Why don't you hike Halla Mountain? You can see the mountain from everywhere on the island.

G: Great. How about food?

B: If you like fish, on Jejudo raw fish is fresh and delicious.

G: I'll try everything. I appreciate your tips.

❶ 'be planning to+동사원형'은 '~할 계획이다, ~하려고 하다'라는 뜻으로 미래 계획을 말할 때 사용한다.

❷ 'used to+동사원형'은 '~하곤 했다'라는 과거의 습관을 나타내는 표현이다.

❸ '의문사+to부정사' 형태로 목적어 자리에 사용된 to부정사의 명사적 용법이다.

❹ 'Why don't you+동사원형?'은 제안할 때 사용하는 표현으로 '~하는 게 어때?'라는 의미이다.

 Wrap Up 2

W: Mike does not feel very well. He ❶might have caught a cold. He needs to see a doctor, but he has a meeting with Jane in an hour. He wants to meet her tomorrow instead. What should he say to her?

❶ 'might have+과거분사'는 과거의 추측을 나타내는 표현으로 '~이었을지 몰라'라는 뜻이다.

다음 우리말과 일치하도록 빈칸에 알맞은 말을 쓰시오.

Listen & Speak 1 A-1

B: Judy, do you _____ _____ down the volume?

G: _____, _____ _____ . Is it too _____?

B: Yes, it is. I can _____ it in my room.

G: I'm sorry. I'll _____ _____ _____.

B: _____ a lot.

Listen & Speak 1 A-2

G: I _____ broke my mom's _____ _____ .

B: _____ _____ _____ , Mina.

G: _____ _____ _____ _____ m e _____ _____ _____ sorry to her?

B: No, _____ _____ _____ . You should _____ _____ .

G: I see. I'll talk to her _____ _____ _____ _____ .

G: 내가 실수로 엄마가 제일 좋아하는 접시를 깼어.
B: 그것 참 안됐구나, 미나야.
G: 엄마한테 미안하다고 어떻게 말해야 하는지 말해 줄래?
B: 응, 물론이지. 너는 진심으로 사과해야 해.
G: 알겠어. 엄마에게 진심으로 이야기해야겠어.

Listen & Speak 1 A-3

B: Karen, do you mind _____ to my house tomorrow at 7 a.m.?

G: That's very _____ .

B: I know, but I need the book _____ you _____ before class.

G: I see. Then _____ meet at seven.

B: See you _____ .

B: Karen, 내일 오전 7시에 우리 집에 와 줄래?
G 그건 너무 이른데.
B: 그건 알지만, 수업 시작하기 전에 네가 빌려 간 책이 필요하거든.
G: 알겠어. 그럼 7시에 보자.
B: 그때 보자.

Listen & Speak 1 B

A: Hellen, do you mind _____ _____ ?

B: No, I don't. / Sorry _____ I can't.

A: Hellen, do you mind _____ _____ _____ ?

B: No, I don't. / Sorry but I _____ .

A: Hellen, 조용히 좀 해 줄래?
B: 알았어. / 미안하지만 그럴 수 없어.

A: Hellen, 쓰레기 좀 주워 줄래?
B: 알았어. / 미안하지만 그럴 수 없어.

Listen & Speak 2 A-1

G: You _____ _____ be busy, Minsu. Can I come in?

B: Sure. I'm _____ for the dance _____, but it's not easy.

G: I can help you. I was in the _____ last year.

B: Really? That would be _____, Amy.

G: You _____ _____ _____ _____ into the _____. But one thing you need to do is to be more _____. You are too _____.

B: Your _____ is very _____. I really _____ your advice.

G: It's my _____.

Listen & Speak 2 A-2

B: Irene, what are you doing?

G: Well, I've _____ my favorite cap. I can't find it.

B: _____ _____ _____ you. _____ does it look _____?

G: It's red. My name _____ _____ in black on the side.

B: Oh, is this _____? It was under the table.

G: Yes, it is. Thank you, Jim. I _____ your help.

B: _____ _____.

Listen & Speak 2 B

A: _____ me _____ you the way.

B: I _____ your time.

A: _____ _____ _____ your backpack.

B: I _____ _____ _____.

Real Life Talk

Jessie: Hi, Andy. _____ _____?

Andy: Hi, Jessie. I'm going to buy a present for Amy. You'_____ _____ friends with her for a long time, _____ you?

Jessie: Yes, _____ first grade in _____ school.

Andy: Well, I know you're really _____ _____, but _____ _____ _____ _____ me? I am sure you could _____ _____ _____ _____ something nice.

G: 민수야, 너 바빠 보인다. 나 들어가도 되니?

B: 물론. 나 춤 경연대회를 준비하고 있는데 쉽지 않아.

G: 내가 도와줄게. 나 작년에 대회에 참가했었거든.

B: 정말? Amy, 그거 정말 좋을 거 같아.

G: 너는 리듬을 타는 건 잘하는 편이야. 하지만 네가 해야 할 한 가지는 긴장을 더 푸는 것이야. 너는 너무 긴장을 해.

B: 네 조언이 정말 도움이 된다. 너의 조언 정말 고마워.

G: 도움이 됐다니 기뻐.

B: Irene, 너 뭐 하고 있어?

G: 음, 내가 제일 좋아하는 모자를 잃어버렸어. 그 모자를 못 찾겠어.

B: 내가 도와줄게. 그것은 어떻게 생겼어?

G: 그건 빨간색이야. 모자 옆 부분에 내 이름이 검은색으로 쓰여 있어.

B: 오, 이거 네 것이니? 이거 탁자 아래에 있었어.

G: 응, 맞아. 고마워, Jim. 도와줘서 고마워.

B: 천만에.

A: 제가 길을 알려 줄게요.

B: 시간 내 줘서 감사합니다.

A: 내가 너의 가방을 들어 줄게.

B: 도와 줘서 고마워.

Jessie: 안녕, Andy. 무슨 일이니?

Andy: 안녕, Jessie. 나는 Amy한테 줄 선물을 사려고 해. 너는 그 애와 오랫동안 친구로 지냈지, 그렇지 않니?

Jessie: 응, 초등학교 1학년 때부터.

Andy: 음, 네가 공부하느라 바쁘다는 것을 알지만, 나를 좀 도와줄 수 있니? 괜찮은 것을 고르도록 네가 도와줄 수 있을 것이라고 확신해.

Jessie: No _____. What's the present _____? It's not her birthday.

Andy: Well, two months ago, when my leg _____ _____, she carried my backpack to school.

Jessie: That was nice _____ _____.

Andy: Yes, it was. What should I get for her?

Jessie: Well, _____ _____ a case for her smartphone? She broke her case _____.

Andy: Really? Thank you for your _____.

Jessie: 좋아. 무엇을 위한 선물이니? 그 애의 생일은 아닌데.

Andy: 음, 두 달 전에 내 다리가 부러졌을 때, 그 애가 학교까지 내 가방을 들어줬어.

Jessie: 그 애는 정말 친절했구나.

Andy: 응, 그랬어. 그 애를 위해 무엇을 사야 할까?

Jessie: 음, 스마트폰 케이스는 어떠니? 그 애는 최근에 케이스를 깨뜨렸어.

Andy: 정말? 제안해 줘서 고마워.

Wrap Up 1

G: I _____ _____ _____ _____ to Jejudo.

B: That's _____, Suhee. I _____ _____ _____ there.

G: _____ _____ _____ me _____ _____ _____ in Jejudo?

B: _____ _____ _____. Jejudo has many beautiful _____. You should visit them.

G: Good. I will go _____. What _____ can I do?

B: Why _____ _____ hike Halla Mountain? You can see the mountain from _____ on the island.

G: Great. _____ _____ food?

B: If you like fish, on Jejudo _____ _____ is _____ and _____.

G: I'll try everything. I _____ your _____.

G: 나는 제주도에 갈 계획이야.

B: 그거 멋지다, 수희야. 나 예전에 제주도에 살았어.

G: 내가 제주도에서 뭘 해야 하는지 말해 줄래?

B: 물론. 제주도에는 아름다운 해변들이 많아. 그 해변들을 꼭 가봐야 해.

G: 좋아. 나는 수영하러 갈 거야. 그 밖에 내가 할 수 있는 것은 무엇이니?

B: 한라산을 등반해 보는 건 어때? 섬의 모든 곳에서 그 산을 볼 수 있어.

G: 좋아. 음식은 어때?

B: 네가 생선을 좋아한다면, 제주도에서는 회가 신선하고 맛있어.

G: 나는 모든 걸 다 해 볼 거야. 조언해 줘서 고마워.

Wrap Up 2

W: Mike does not feel very _____. He _____ _____ _____ _____ a cold. He _____ _____ see a doctor, but he has a meeting with Jane in an hour. He wants _____ _____ her tomorrow _____. What should he say to her?

W: Mike는 몸이 별로 좋지 않아. 그는 감기에 걸렸을지도 몰라. 그는 병원에 가야 하지만, 한 시간 후에 Jane과 회의가 있어. 그는 대신 내일 그녀를 만나기를 원해. 그는 그녀에게 뭐라고 말해야 할까?

Conversation 시험대비 기본평가

01 우리말에 맞도록 문장의 빈칸에 알맞은 말을 쓰시오.

Do you _____ _____ me? (나를 도와 줄 수 있나요?)

02 대화의 빈칸에 들어갈 말로 알맞은 것을 <u>모두</u> 고르시오.

A: Let me carry your backpack.
B: _____

① I appreciate your kindness.
② I appreciate your advice.
③ I'm not quite sure if you can carry my backpack.
④ I appreciate your help.
⑤ I appreciate your consideration.

03 다음 대화의 빈칸에 들어갈 말로 <u>어색한</u> 표현은?

G: I accidentally broke my mom's favorite plate.
B: That's too bad, Mina.
G: Do you mind telling me how to say sorry to her?
B: _____ You should apologize sincerely.
G: I see. I'll talk to her with all my heart.

① No, not at all.   ② Of course.
③ Surely not.   ④ Certainly not.
⑤ No, I don't.

04 다음 대화의 밑줄 친 부분의 의도로 알맞은 것은?

A: <u>I really appreciate your advice.</u>
B: Not at all. I'm glad that I could help you.

① 권유하기   ② 요청하기
③ 관심 표현하기   ④ 능력 말하기
⑤ 감사하기

[01~02] 다음 대화를 읽고 물음에 답하시오.

Jessie: Hi, Andy. What's up?

Andy: Hi, Jessie. I'm going to buy a present for Amy. You've been friends with her for a long time, haven't you?

Jessie: Yes, since first grade in elementary school.

Andy: Well, I know you're really busy studying, but (A)_____ I am sure you could help me pick out something nice.

Jessie: No problem. What's the present for? It's not her birthday.

Andy: Well, two months ago, when my leg was broken, she carried my backpack to school.

Jessie: That was nice of her.

Andy: Yes, it was. What should I get for her?

Jessie: Well, how about a case for her smartphone? She broke her case recently.

Andy: Really? Thank you for your suggestion.

01 위 대화의 빈칸 (A)에 들어갈 말로 알맞은 것은?

① do you mind picking up the present?

② do you mind closing the window?

③ do you mind putting the books back in the right places?

④ do you mind helping me?

⑤ do you mind studying with me?

02 위 대화의 내용과 일치하지 <u>않는</u> 것은?

① Andy and Jessie have been friends since first grade in elementary school.

② Jessie is busy studying.

③ Amy carried Andy's backpack to school two months ago.

④ Andy really appreciates Amy's help.

⑤ Amy broke her smartphone case recently.

03 다음 대화의 (A)~(D)를 알맞은 순서로 배열한 것은?

B: Irene, what are you doing?

(A) It's red. My name is written in black on the side.

(B) Oh, is this yours? It was under the table.

(C) Well, I've lost my favorite cap. I can't find it.

(D) Let me help you. What does it look like?

G: Yes, it is. Thank you, Jim. I appreciate your help.

B: No problem.

① (A) – (C) – (B) – (D)

② (B) – (A) – (D) – (C)

③ (C) – (B) – (A) – (D)

④ (C) – (D) – (A) – (B)

⑤ (D) – (C) – (A) – (B)

04 다음 대화의 빈칸에 들어갈 말로 알맞은 것은?

A: Sue, _____

B: Of course not. We don't have enough fresh air in the room.

① can you help me open the window?

② do you mind opening the window?

③ could I ask you to help me close the window?

④ can you open the door, please?

⑤ is it OK if I open the door?

[05~06] 다음 대화를 읽고 물음에 답하시오.

G: You (a)seem to be busy, Minsu. Can I come in?
B: Sure. I'm preparing for the dance contest, but it's not easy.
G: I can help you. I (b)was in the contest last year.
B: Really? That would be great, Amy.
G: You are good at (c)getting into the rhythm. But one thing you need to do (d)are to be more (e)relaxed. You are too nervous.
B: Your advice is very helpful. I really appreciate your advice.
G: It's my pleasure.

서답형

05 위 대화를 읽고 다음 물음에 영어로 답하시오.

Q: What is Minsu good at according to Amy? (8 단어로 답하시오.)

➡ _____

06 위 대화의 밑줄 친 (a)~(e) 중 어법상 어색한 것은?

① (a) ② (b) ③ (c) ④ (d) ⑤ (e)

중요

07 다음 중 두 사람의 대화가 어색한 것은?

① A: Let me read the directions for you.
   B: I appreciate your time.
② A: Mike, do you mind putting the books back in the right places?
   B: No, I don't.
③ A: Do you mind closing the window?
   B: Of course. Go ahead.
④ A: Let me set the table.
   B: I appreciate your kindness.
⑤ A: Happy birthday! This is for you.
   B: Thank you for your present.

[08~09] 다음 대화를 읽고 물음에 답하시오.

B: Karen, do you mind coming to my house tomorrow at 7 a.m.?
G: That's very early.
B: I know, but (A)수업 시작하기 전에 네가 빌려 간 책이 필요하거든.
G: I see. Then let's meet at seven.
B: See you then.

서답형

08 위 대화의 밑줄 친 (A)의 우리말에 맞게 주어진 단어를 알맞은 순서로 배열하여 쓰시오. (단어 하나를 추가하고, 필요시 변형하시오.)

I / need / class / you / book / before / the / borrowed

➡ _____
_____

서답형

09 위 대화를 읽고 다음 물음에 괄호 안의 주어진 단어를 활용하여 영어로 답하시오.

Q: Why is Karen going to meet the boy at 7 a.m.? (have to / return / borrow)

➡ Because she _____ _____ _____ the _____ book to the boy.

서답형

10 다음 글의 마지막 물음에 대한 답을 주어진 어구를 활용하여 영작하시오.

W: Mike does not feel very well. He might have caught a cold. He needs to see a doctor, but he has a meeting with Jane in an hour. So he wants to meet her tomorrow. What should he say to her?

(mind / put off / until tomorrow)

➡ _____

[01~02] 다음 대화를 읽고 물음에 답하시오.

Jessie: Hi, Andy. What's up?

Andy: Hi, Jessie. I'm going to buy a present for Amy. (A)You were friends with her for a long time, weren't you?

Jessie: Yes, (a)since first grade in elementary school.

Andy: Well, I know you're really busy studying, but do you mind helping me? I am sure you could help me pick out something nice.

Jessie: No problem. What's the present for? It's not her birthday.

Andy: Well, two months ago, when my leg was broken, she carried my backpack to school.

Jessie: That was nice of her.

Andy: Yes, it was. What should I get for her?

Jessie: Well, how about a case for her smartphone? She broke her case recently.

Andy: Really? Thank you for your suggestion.

01 다음 질문에 대한 답을 'Because'로 시작하여 쓰시오.

Q: Two months ago, why did Amy carry Andy's backpack to school?

➡ _____

02 위 대화의 밑줄 친 (A)는 문법적으로 틀린 문장이다. 밑줄 친 (a) 문장을 참고하여 바르게 고치시오.

➡ _____
_____

03 다음 대화의 밑줄 친 (A)를 〈조건〉에 맞게 영어로 쓰시오.

G: I am planning to go to Jejudo.

B: That's cool, Suhee. I used to live there.

G: (A)내가 제주도에서 뭘 해야 하는지 말해 줄래?

B: Not at all. Jejudo has many beautiful beaches. You should visit them.

G: Good. I will go swimming. What else can I do?

B: Why don't you hike Halla Mountain? You can see the mountain from everywhere on the island.

G: Great.

┤ 조건 ├
- 'mind'를 이용하여 요청하는 표현을 사용할 것
- '의문사+to부정사'를 사용할 것.

➡ _____

04 빈칸 (A)에 들어갈 말을 주어진 단어를 이용하여 쓰시오.

B: Irene, what are you doing?

G: Well, I've lost my favorite cap. I can't find it.

B: Let me help you. (A)_____

G: It's red. My name is written in black on the side.

B: Oh, is this yours? It was under the table.

G: Yes, it is. Thank you, Jim. I appreciate your help.

B: No problem.

(what / look like)

➡ _____

Grammar

교과서

① 관계부사 how

> • June didn't like **how** Mike had acted. June은 Mike의 행동 방식이 마음에 들지 않았다.
> • That is **how** I solved the difficult problem. 그것이 내가 그 어려운 문제를 풀었던 방법이다.

■ 관계부사는 접속사와 부사의 역할을 동시에 하는 것으로 선행사를 수식한다.

  • I want to know **the way**. He became the leader **in the way**.
  = I want to know **the way (how)** he became the leader. 나는 그가 리더가 된 방법을 알고 싶다. (선행사 the way와 관계부사 how는 같이 쓰지 않는다.)

■ 선행사가 장소, 시간, 이유, 방법 등의 명사일 때 전치사와 관계대명사로 표현 가능하며, 생략 등 각각의 용례도 조금씩 다르다.

  (1) 장소(where): This is **the house**. Mozart was born **in the house**.
   → This is **the house which**[**that**] Mozart was born **in**.
   → This is **the house in which** Mozart was born. (in that 불가)
   → This is **the house where** Mozart was born. 이곳이 Mozart가 태어난 집이다.
  (2) 시간(when): This is **the day**. Mozart was born **on the day**.
   → This is **the day which**[**that**] Mozart was born **on**.
   → This is **the day on which** Mozart was born. (on that 불가)
   → This is **the day when** Mozart was born. 이 날이 Mozart가 탄생한 날이다.
  (3) 이유(why): This is **the reason**. Mozart is a genius **for the reason**.
   → This is **the reason which**[**that**] Mozart is a genius **for**.
   → This is **the reason for which** Mozart is a genius. (for that 불가)
   → This is **the reason why** Mozart is a genius. 이것이 Mozart가 천재인 이유이다.
   → This is **why** Mozart is a genius. : the reason 또는 why 둘 중 하나 생략 가능
  (4) 방법(how): This is **the way**. Mozart composed music **in the way**.
   → This is **the way which**[**that**] Mozart composed music **in**.
   → This is **the way in which** Mozart composed music. (in that 불가)
   → This is **the way how** Mozart composed music. (×) (the way와 how 동시 불가)
   → This is **the way** Mozart composed music. : the way / how 둘 중 하나만 쓴다.
   → This is **how** Mozart composed music. 이것이 Mozart가 음악을 작곡한 방법이다.

■ 선행사가 'the place, the time, the reason'과 같은 일반적 의미일 경우 생략 가능하다.

  • This is (the place) **where** children can play. 이곳은 아이들이 놀 수 있는 장소이다.

핵심 Check

1. 괄호 안에서 알맞은 말을 고르시오.

  (1) This manual shows (how / which) we can use the machine.
  (2) I don't know the reason (how / why) she is late.

② The+비교급 ~, the+비교급 … 구문

- **The more sincere** your apology is, **the better** it will be received. 당신의 사과가 더 진실할수록 그것은 더 잘 받아들여질 것이다.

- **The faster** you walk, **the earlier** you will arrive. 당신이 더 빨리 걸을수록, 더 일찍 도착할 것이다.

■ 'The+비교급+주어+동사 ~, the+비교급+주어+동사 …'는 '~하면 할수록 더 …하다'의 의미로, 상응하는 두 절의 형용사나 부사, 형용사를 포함한 명사절의 비교급 형태를 'the'와 함께 주어 앞으로 이동하여 만든다.

(1) 형용사
- You are good at something. + You should be careful when doing it.
  → **The better** you are at something, **the more careful** you should be when doing it. 당신이 어떤 일을 더 잘하게 될수록, 그것을 할 때 더욱 주의해야 한다.
- **The older** we get, **the wiser** we become. 우리는 나이를 먹을수록 더 지혜로워진다.

(2) 부사
- They get up early. + They will get there soon.
  → **The earlier** they get up, **the sooner** they will get there.
  그들이 더 일찍 일어날수록, 그곳에 더 빨리 도착할 것이다.
- **The higher** you go up the mountain, **the better** you can see the lake below.
  당신이 그 산에 더 높이 올라갈수록, 아래의 호수를 더 잘 볼 수 있다.

(3) 형용사를 포함한 명사절
- People eat healthy food. + People can live a healthy life.
  → **The healthier food** people eat, **the healthier life** people can live.
  사람들이 더 건강한 음식을 먹을수록, 더욱 건강한 삶을 살 수 있다.

(4) 의미가 통할 경우, '동사' 또는 '주어+동사' 생략 가능
- **The warmer** the weather, **the lighter** the air. 날씨가 더 따뜻할수록, 공기가 더 가볍다.
- **The more**, **the better**. 많으면 많을수록 좋다.

■ 'The+비교급 ~, the+비교급 …' 구문은 접속사 If 또는 As를 사용해서 전환할 수 있다.

- **The earlier** you finish the report, **the better grade** you will get.
  = **If** you finish the report earlier, you will get a better grade.
  = **As** you finish the report earlier, you will get a better grade.

핵심 Check

2. 다음 우리말에 맞게 괄호 안의 어구를 바르게 배열하시오.

> 그들에게 숙제가 많을수록 학생들은 더 피곤하게 느낀다. (the students, homework, tired, the more, the more, feel, have, they)

➡ _____

01 다음 빈칸에 들어갈 말로 알맞은 것은?

> The greater the risk of virus is, the _____ people meet.

① often ② most often ③ less often
④ more oftener ⑤ less oftener

02 다음 두 문장을 한 문장으로 연결할 때, 각각의 빈칸에 들어갈 알맞은 말을 써 넣으시오. (반드시 관계사가 포함되도록 할 것)

(1) They learned the way. The researcher found it in the way.
➡ They learned the way _____ _____ the researcher found it.
➡ They learned _____ the researcher found it.

(2) Sam visited the house. The legendary singer lived in the house.
➡ Sam visited the house _____ _____ the legendary singer lived.
➡ Sam visited the house _____ the legendary singer lived.

03 다음 밑줄 친 부분 중 어법상 옳지 <u>않은</u> 것을 고르시오.

① I don't know the reason <u>why</u> she left me.
② I want to know the way <u>how</u> he earned so much money.
③ She was interested in the restaurant <u>where</u> the cook worked.
④ This is <u>how</u> the basketball player became the MVP of the year.
⑤ Let me know the way <u>in which</u> Paula got an A on the subject.

04 다음 〈보기〉에서 필요한 단어를 골라, 어법에 알맞은 형태로 빈칸에 써 넣으시오.

┌─── 보기 ───┐
flexible, much, climb, high, old, hot
└────────────┘

(1) _____ _____ the weather gets, the _____ water we drink.
(2) The _____ the mountain is, the harder it is _____ _____.
(3) The _____ you get, the _____ _____ you become.

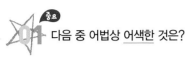

01 다음 중 어법상 <u>어색한</u> 것은?

① This is the street where you can enjoy a lot of street foods.
② They wondered about the reason why Sam Smith was so mad at the officer.
③ Those are the buildings where this movie is going to be filmed.
④ I will show my students the way how I could be a teacher.
⑤ Can you remember the day when you first ate the blue berry?

[02~03] 다음 빈칸에 들어갈 말이 알맞게 짝지어진 것을 고르시오.

02

The _____ you work, the _____ money you can earn.

① much – much
② hard – better
③ more – most
④ harder – more
⑤ best – more

03

_____ they learn Korean history, _____ the visitors may feel.

① So much – as much interested
② The more well – more interested for
③ The more – the more interested
④ More as – the more interesting
⑤ The better – most interesting

[04~05] 다음 우리말을 어법상 알맞게 영작한 것을 고르시오.

04

그것이 경쟁이 치열한 연예계에서 Joseph이 성공한 이유이다.

① That is which Joseph succeeded in the world of competitive show business for.
② That is the reason which Joseph succeeded in the world of competitive show business.
③ That is the reason why Joseph succeeded in the world of competitive show business for.
④ That is why Joseph succeeded in the world of competitive show business.
⑤ That is the reason on which Joseph succeeded in the world of competitive show business.

05

그 발표가 열리는 장소를 그녀가 알고 있습니까?

① Does she know where will the presentation be held?
② Where does she know the place the presentation will be held?
③ Does she know the place at where the presentation will be held?
④ Does she know the place on which the presentation will be held in?
⑤ Does she know the place where the presentation will be held?

[06~07] 다음 주어진 문장의 의미가 자연스럽게 되도록 빈칸에 들어갈 말로 가장 적절한 것은?

06

> The less sincerely a close friend apologizes for his or her mistake, _____.

① the easier people feel

② the happier people get

③ the more pleased people become

④ the more easily people get hurt

⑤ the more easily people get along

07

> The more sincere your apologies are, _____.

① the more they will be necessary

② the better they will be received

③ the lighter they will be considered

④ the more casually they will be received

⑤ the more they will be ignored

[08~10] 다음 중 어법상 <u>어색한</u> 문장은?

08 ① Sumin's sister disliked the way that Sumin had treated her.

② Sumin's sister disliked how Sumin had treated her.

③ Sumin's sister disliked the way in which Sumin had treated her.

④ Sumin's sister disliked the way in how Sumin had treated her.

⑤ Sumin's sister disliked the way Sumin had treated her.

09 ① This was not the first time Jane hadn't apologized to her little sister.

② This was not the first time when Jane hadn't apologized to her little sister.

③ This was not the first time of which Jane hadn't apologized to her little sister.

④ This was not the first time that Jane hadn't apologized to her little sister.

⑤ This was not the first time for which Jane hadn't apologized to her little sister.

10 ① He wanted to know the reason Michelle didn't say anything about the problem.

② He wanted to know why Michelle didn't say anything about the problem.

③ He wanted to know the reason for which Michelle didn't say anything about the problem.

④ He wanted to know the reason which Michelle didn't say anything about the problem for.

⑤ He wanted to know why didn't Michelle say anything about the problem.

11 다음 〈보기〉의 문장과 가장 가까운 뜻을 가진 문장을 고르시오.

> **─┤ 보기 ├──**
>
> Quicker apology will show that you are more thoughtful and responsible.

① As the quicker your apology is, you look more thoughtful and responsible.

② The more quicker your apology is, the most thoughtful and responsible you will look.

③ The quicker your apology is, the more thoughtful and responsible you will look.

④ The quickest your apology is, the most thoughtful and responsible you will look.

⑤ If you apology quicker, the more thoughtful and responsible you look.

서답형

[12~13] 다음 두 문장을 한 문장으로 표현할 때, 빈칸에 들어갈 알맞은 한 단어를 쓰시오.

12

• Tom wants to know the way.
• Kate recovered from the disease in the way earlier than the doctor expected.

➡ Tom wants to know _____ Kate recovered from the disease earlier than the doctor expected.

13

• The famous composer was born on the day.
• Germany was unified on that day.

➡ The famous composer was born on the day _____ Germany was unified.

서답형

[14~15] 우리말과 일치하도록 괄호 안에 주어진 어구를 바르게 배열하시오.

14

당신이 뉴스를 많이 볼수록, 세상일이 어떻게 되는지 더 잘 알게 된다.
(the news, know, watch, you, the better, you, the more) what the world is like.

➡ _____

_____ what the world is like.

15

어떤 제품들은 가격이 비싸면 비쌀수록 더 많은 사람들이 사려고 한다.
→ (some products, buy, people, the more, the more, are, them, to, expensive, want).

➡ _____

_____

[16~17] 다음 빈칸 (A), (B), (C)에 들어갈 말로 가장 적절한 것은?

16

• The way (A)_____ she persuaded her parents is not known.
• The ladies have just come out of the building (B)_____ is next to my office.
• Mom remembers the day (C)_____ I was allowed to go to the college.

	(A)	(B)	(C)
①	which	which	on which
②	in which	where	when
③	that	which	when
④	how	where	that
⑤	how	which	on which

17

• Is there anyone to tell me (A)_____ Susan answered the impossible question?
• Mike wants to know the reason (B)_____ his wife is upset about him.
• Christina will never forget the name of the cafe (C)_____ she met the man.

	(A)	(B)	(C)
①	why	why	which
②	what	which	where
③	that	for which	which
④	how	why	where
⑤	when	for which	on which

⭐**1** 다음 우리말과 일치하도록 괄호 안에 주어진 어구를 바르게 배열하여 문장을 완성하시오.

(1) 당신이 실수에 대해 빨리 사과할수록, 사람들은 덜 상처받게 된다. (people, you, apologize for, hurt, the sooner, the less, get, the mistake)

➡ _____

_____

(2) 우리는 더 많이 가질수록, 더 많이 원한다. (we, we, the, the, more, more, want, have)

➡ _____

(3) 당신에게 선택사항들이 더 많을수록, 결정하는 일은 더 어려워진다. (it, you, decide, to, options, difficult, have, the more, the more, is)

➡ _____

_____

(4) 그 친구를 더 많이 알수록, 그녀를 향한 내 신뢰는 더 강해진다. (my trust, the more, the stronger, know, becomes, I, in, her, the friend)

➡ _____

_____

(5) 우리가 더 많이 줄수록, 우리는 더 많은 것을 보상으로 얻게 될 것이다. (in, we, we, the, the, more, more, return, get, give, will)

➡ _____

_____

(6) 그가 열심히 일할수록, 그의 미래는 더욱 밝을 것이다. (his future, works, the brighter, he, be, the harder, will)

➡ _____

_____

02 다음 그림을 보고 자연스러운 문장이 되도록 괄호 안에 주어진 단어를 바르게 배열하여 빈칸을 완성하시오.

(1)

➡ Ms. Kim didn't _____ _____ for the problem. (her son, the way, excuses, like, made)

(2)

➡ The animals wonder _____ _____. (his, has, the turtle, health, how, managed)

(3)

➡ That is the famous restaurant _____

_____.

(Bulgogi, people, line up, to eat, every morning, where)

03 다음 괄호 안에 주어진 단어를 이용하여 어법에 맞게 빈칸을 완성하시오.

(1) _____ _____(old) the student gets, _____ _____(much) he looks like his grandfather.

(2) _____ _____(many) books your kids read, _____ _____ _____ (intelligent) they will become.

(3) _____ _____(loud) you practice, _____ _____(well) you can speak a foreign language.

(4) _____ _____(far) the patient walks every day, _____ _____(healthy) she will get.

04 다음 학급 신문의 〈내 친구를 소개합니다〉 코너에 나온 글을 읽고, 어법상 불필요해서 삭제해야 하는 단어를 모두 찾아 쓰시오. (2개)

My Great Friend, Miso

 I'd like to introduce my friend, Miso. I have known her for ten years. She is always funny, generous, and cheerful. This is the way how she helped me. Two weeks ago, I forgot to take my lunch to school. Miso shared her lunch with me. I am lucky to have her as my friend. The more I know her, the more happier I am.

➡ (1) _____

 (2) _____

05 다음 (A)와 (B) 문장을 〈조건〉에 맞게 영작하시오.

┤ 조건 ├

 1. (A)와 (B)를 연결하여 (A)가 앞에 오는 한 문장으로 만들 것.
 2. 표의 위에서부터 순서대로 영작할 것.
 3. 가급적 '선행사+관계부사'로 영작할 것.
 4. 관계부사는 생략하지 말 것. (that은 사용할 수 없음.)

(A)	(B)
The researchers found the special planet.	He made his films in the way.
The director taught us the way.	She can enjoy white snow and skiing in the season.
Her favorite season is winter.	The President of Brazil stayed at the hotel.
Please let me know the reason.	My daughter walked for herself on the day.
This is the hotel.	My professor was mad at me for the reason.
I would never forget the day.	Life can live on the planet.

(1) _____
_____
(2) _____
(3) _____
_____
(4) _____
_____
(5) _____
(6) _____
_____

Three Things about a Proper Apology

Because we are human, we all make mistakes. It is not easy to get along with everyone all the time. Sometimes we hurt people's feelings without intending to. Sometimes, we do something wrong and regret it later. When that happens, what should we do? We should apologize. Read the following case studies and learn three things about a proper apology.

When June tripped over a backpack and fell, Mike found it funny and laughed. He took a picture and uploaded it on an SNS. June saw the picture and became angry. Mike said, with a laugh, "Sorry, June!" and deleted it. After that, June felt even more hurt because of Mike's casual apology. June didn't like how Mike had acted. Mike seemed to think it was nothing serious.

What did you learn from this case? Yes. You guessed right. You should be sincere when you apologize. Apologizing is necessary to build good friendships. Saying you're sorry is more than just words. You need to show that you respect the other person and care about his or her feelings. If you truly want to make things right, be sincere in your apology. The more sincere your apology is, the better it will be received.

Here is another case. While Kate was hurrying across the cafeteria, she accidentally bumped into Hojun. Some food on Hojun's tray fell on his jacket.

proper: 적절한
apology: 사과
mistake: 실수, 잘못
intend: 의도하다
regret: 후회하다
delete: 삭제하다
casual: 대충하는, 건성의
seem: ~인 것 같다
sincere: 진정한, 진심 어린
receive: 받다, 받아들이다
trip over: ~에 걸려 넘어지다
care about: ~에 마음을 쓰다, ~에 관심을 가지다
cafeteria: 구내식당
accidentally: 우연히
bump into: ~에 부딪히다
tray: 쟁반, 식판

확인문제

● 다음 문장이 본문의 내용과 일치하면 T, 일치하지 않으면 F를 쓰시오.

1 Although we don't intend to hurt other people, we often do. ☐

2 June was upset despite Mike's serious apology. ☐

3 Showing that you care about people's feelings is necessary when apologizing. ☐

Kate didn't apologize. Hojun felt bad. He thought, 'Why doesn't she say something? It would be nothing if she apologized right now.'

가정법 과거(Kate가 바로 사과하지 않은 것에 대한 호준이의 아쉬움을 나타냄)

This case shows that when an apology is necessary, you should

명사절 접속사

apologize at once. A quick apology shows that you are thoughtful and take responsibility for your action. All you need to do is to say, "I'm

단수 취급

sorry." Then, the hurt friend will think nothing of it and laugh it off.

Kate가 호준이와 부딪힌 일

Finally, apologies are necessary among family members and loved

사랑하는 사람들(나에게서 사랑을 받는 사람이라는 의미)

ones, too. One day, Sunmin borrowed her sister's favorite book.

역시(긍정에 대한 동의)

Later, she lost it. Sunmin didn't apologize because she thought it was

선민이가 잃어버린 책

not important. She thought, 'We're sisters, after all.' Sunmin's sister disliked how Sunmin had treated her. How could her own sister ignore

= the way Sunmin had treated her

her feelings? This was not the first time Sunmin hadn't apologized to

예전부터 선민이가 사과하지 않았다는 의미이므로 과거완료(had p.p.)

her little sister.

People need to apologize when they do something wrong. This includes family members and the people who are close to you. People

주격 관계대명사

get hurt more easily when the hurt comes from a family member or a friend. We may think that they will let it go because they are close to

명사절 접속사   사역동사+목적어+동사원형

us. Remember, however, that small mistakes and no apology add up to

명사절 접속사

big emotional wounds. This is especially true among family members and loved ones.

Have you ever heard of the saying, "No more apologies, no more

경험을 묻는 현재완료

chances"? People make mistakes, but don't let one mistake break a

사역동사+목적어+동사원형

beautiful relationship. Do you want to apologize to someone? Try to do it now. A quick and sincere "I'm sorry" can solve many problems.

thoughtful: 사려 깊은
at once: 즉시
take responsibility for: ~에 책임을 지다
think nothing of: ~을 아무렇지 않게 여기다
laugh off: ~을 웃어넘기려 하다
borrow: 빌리다
dislike: 싫어하다
treat: 대하다, 대우하다
ignore: 무시하다
after all: 결국에는
include: 포함하다
emotional: 감정적인
wound: 상처, 부상
especially: 특히, 유난히
relationship: 관계
break: (관계를) 끝내다, 끊다
add up to: (결과가) ~가 되다

 **확인문제**

● 다음 문장이 본문의 내용과 일치하면 T, 일치하지 않으면 F를 쓰시오.

1 It is good to apologize at once when an apology is necessary. ☐

2 It is not necessary to apologize family members or loved ones. ☐

3 Sunmin's sister thought her feelings were ignored by Sunmin. ☐

● 우리말을 참고하여 빈칸에 알맞은 말을 쓰시오.

1 _____ we are human, we all make mistakes. _____ _____ not easy _____ _____ _____ everyone all the time.

2 Sometimes we _____ people's feelings _____ _____ _____. Sometimes, we do _____ _____ and regret it later.

3 When _____ happens, what should we do? We _____ _____.

4 Read the _____ _____ studies and learn three things about _____ _____ _____.

5 When June _____ _____ a backpack and fell, Mike found _____ _____ _____ and _____. He _____ a picture and _____ it on an SNS.

6 June _____ the picture and _____ _____. Mike said, _____ a laugh, "Sorry, June!" and _____ _____.

7 After that, June felt _____ more hurt _____ Mike's casual apology.

8 June didn't like _____ _____ _____ _____ _____. Mike _____ _____ _____ it was _____ _____.

9 What did you learn from this case? Yes. You guessed right. You _____ _____ _____ when you apologize.

10 _____ is necessary _____ build good friendships. _____ you're sorry is _____ _____ just words.

11 You need to show _____ you _____ the other person and _____ _____ his or her _____.

12 If you truly want to _____ _____ _____, be _____ in your apology.

13 _____ _____ sincere your apology is, _____ _____ it will be _____.

14 Here is _____ case. While Kate was hurrying across the cafeteria, she _____ _____ _____ Hojun.

15 Some food _____ Hojun's tray _____ _____ his jacket. Kate didn't _____. Hojun _____ _____ _____.

1 우리는 인간이기 때문에 모두가 실수한다. 모든 사람과 항상 잘 지내기는 쉽지 않다.

2 때때로 우리는 의도하지 않게 다른 사람의 감정을 상하게 한다. 때때로 우리는 나쁜 일을 하고 나중에 그것을 후회한다.

3 이런 일이 생기면, 우리는 무엇을 해야 할까? 우리는 사과해야 한다.

4 다음 사례 연구들을 읽고 올바른 사과를 위한 세 가지를 알아보자.

5 June이 가방에 걸려 넘어졌을 때, Mike는 그것이 재미있다고 생각하고 웃었다. 그는 사진을 찍어서 SNS에 올렸다.

6 June은 그 사진을 보고 화가 났다. Mike는 웃으면서 "미안해, June!"이라고 말하고 사진을 삭제했다.

7 그 후, June은 Mike의 가벼운 사과에 한층 더 화가 났다.

8 June은 Mike의 행동 방식이 마음에 들지 않았다. Mike는 이 일이 심각한 일이 아니라고 생각하는 것처럼 보였다.

9 이 사례로부터 무엇을 배웠는가? 맞다. 당신은 바르게 추측했다. 당신은 사과할 때에 진실해야 한다.

10 사과하는 것은 좋은 교우 관계를 만들기 위해 필요하다. 미안하다고 말하는 것은 단지 말 이상이다.

11 당신이 타인을 존중하고, 타인의 감정에 관심을 갖고 있음을 보여 주어야 한다.

12 당신이 진실로 일을 바로잡기를 원한다면, 당신의 사과는 진실해야 한다.

13 당신의 사과가 진실할수록, 그것은 더 잘 받아들여질 것이다.

14 또 다른 사례가 있다. Kate가 급식실을 가로질러 급하게 뛰어갈 때, 호준이와 실수로 부딪쳤다.

15 호준이의 급식판에 있던 음식이 그의 재킷에 떨어졌다. Kate는 사과하지 않았다. 호준이는 기분이 나빴다.

16 He thought, '_____ _____ she _____ something? It would be nothing _____ she apologized _____ _____.'

17 This case shows _____ when an apology _____ _____, you should _____ _____ _____.

18 A quick apology _____ _____ you are _____ and take _____ for your action.

19 _____ you need _____ _____ is to say, "I'm sorry." Then, the hurt friend will _____ _____ of it and _____ _____ _____.

20 Finally, apologies _____ necessary _____ family _____ and _____ _____, too.

21 One day, Sunmin _____ her sister's _____ book. Later, she _____ it.

22 Sunmin didn't _____ because she thought it was _____ _____. She thought, 'We're sisters, after all.'

23 Sunmin's sister disliked how Sunmin had treated her. How could her own sister _____ her feelings?

24 This was not the first time Sunmin _____ _____ her little sister.

25 People need _____ _____ when they do _____ _____. This _____ family members and the people _____ _____ to you.

26 People _____ _____ _____ _____ when the hurt _____ _____ a family member or a friend.

27 We may think that they will _____ _____ _____ because they _____ _____ to us.

28 Remember, however, that _____ _____ and _____ _____ _____ _____ big emotional wounds.

29 This is especially true _____ family members and _____ _____.

30 Have you ever _____ _____ the saying, "_____ _____ apologies, _____ _____ _____"?

31 People _____ mistakes, but don't _____ one mistake _____ a beautiful relationship.

32 Do you want to _____ _____ someone? _____ _____ it now. A quick and sincere "I'm sorry" _____ _____ many problems.

16 그는 '왜 그녀는 아무 말도 하지 않지? 그녀가 즉시 사과한다면 아무 일도 아닐 텐데.' 라고 생각했다.

17 이 사례는 사과가 필요할 때는 사과를 즉시 해야 한다는 것을 보여준다.

18 신속한 사과는 당신이 사려 깊고, 당신의 행동에 책임을 진다는 것을 보여준다.

19 당신이 해야 할 행동은 "미안해."라고 말하는 것뿐이다. 그러면 상처받은 친구는 당신의 잘못을 아무렇지 않게 생각하고, 웃어넘길 것이다.

20 마지막으로 사과는 가족이나 사랑하는 사람들 사이에서도 필요하다.

21 어느 날, 선민이는 여동생이 가장 좋아하는 책을 빌렸다. 나중에 그녀는 그것을 잃어버렸다.

22 선민이는 그것이 중요하지 않다고 생각하여 사과하지 않았다. 그녀는 '우리는 어쨌든 자매니까.'라고 생각했다.

23 선민이의 여동생은 언니가 본인을 대했던 방식이 마음에 들지 않았다. 어떻게 자신의 언니가 그녀의 기분을 무시할 수 있는가?

24 선민이가 여동생에게 사과하지 않았던 것은 이번이 처음이 아니었다.

25 사람들은 잘못했을 때, 사과해야 한다. 이것은 가족이나 당신에게 가까운 사람도 포함한다.

26 사람들은 마음의 상처가 가족이나 친구에게서 올 때 더 쉽게 상처 받는다.

27 우리는 아마 그들이 가깝기 때문에 그냥 넘어갈 것이라고 생각할지 모른다.

28 하지만 작은 실수를 하고 사과하지 않는 것은 큰 감정적인 상처가 된다는 것을 기억하라.

29 이것은 가족과 사랑하는 사람들에게 특히 더 그러하다.

30 당신은 "더 이상 사과하지 않는다면 더 이상 기회가 없다."는 말을 들어본 적이 있는가?

31 사람들은 실수하지만, 그 실수가 아름다운 관계를 깨뜨리게 해서는 안 된다.

32 누군가에게 사과하고 싶은가? 지금 하려고 노력해라. 빠르고 진정한 "미안해."라는 말이 많은 문제를 해결해 줄 것이다.

● 우리말을 참고하여 본문을 영작하시오.

1 우리는 인간이기 때문에 모두가 실수한다. 모든 사람과 항상 잘 지내기는 쉽지 않다.

➡ _____

2 때때로 우리는 의도하지 않게 다른 사람의 감정을 상하게 한다. 때때로 우리는 나쁜 일을 하고 나중에 그것을 후회한

➡ _____

3 이런 일이 생기면, 우리는 무엇을 해야 할까? 우리는 사과해야 한다.

➡ _____

4 다음 사례 연구들을 읽고 올바른 사과를 위한 세 가지를 알아보자.

➡ _____

5 June이 가방에 걸려 넘어졌을 때, Mike는 그것이 재미있다고 생각하고 웃었다. 그는 사진을 찍어서 SNS에 올렸다.

➡ _____

6 June은 그 사진을 보고 화가 났다. Mike는 웃으면서 "미안해, June!"이라고 말하고 사진을 삭제했다.

➡ _____

7 그 후, June은 Mike의 가벼운 사과에 한층 더 화가 났다.

➡ _____

8 June은 Mike의 행동 방식이 마음에 들지 않았다. Mike는 이 일이 심각한 일이 아니라고 생각하는 것처럼 보였다.

➡ _____

9 이 사례로부터 무엇을 배웠는가? 맞다. 당신은 바르게 추측했다. 당신은 사과할 때에 진실해야 한다.

➡ _____

10 사과하는 것은 좋은 교우 관계를 만들기 위해 필요하다. 미안하다고 말하는 것은 단지 말 이상이다.

➡ _____

11 당신이 타인을 존중하고, 타인의 감정에 관심을 갖고 있음을 보여 주어야 한다.

➡ _____

12 당신이 진실로 일을 바로잡기를 원한다면, 당신의 사과는 진실해야 한다.

➡ _____

13 당신의 사과가 진실할수록, 그것은 더 잘 받아들여질 것이다.

➡ _____

14 또 다른 사례가 있다. Kate가 급식실을 가로질러 급하게 뛰어갈 때, 호준이와 실수로 부딪쳤다.

➡ _____

15 호준이의 급식판에 있던 음식이 그의 재킷에 떨어졌다. Kate는 사과하지 않았다. 호준이는 기분이 나빴다.

➡ _____

16 그는 '왜 그녀는 아무 말도 하지 않지? 그녀가 즉시 사과한다면 아무 일도 아닐 텐데.'라고 생각했다.
➡ _____

17 이 사례는 사과가 필요할 때는 사과를 즉시 해야 한다는 것을 보여준다.
➡ _____

18 신속한 사과는 당신이 사려 깊고, 당신의 행동에 책임을 진다는 것을 보여준다.
➡ _____

19 당신이 해야 할 행동은 "미안해."라고 말하는 것뿐이다. 그러면 상처받은 친구는 당신의 잘못을 아무렇지 않게 생각하고, 웃어넘길 것이다.
➡ _____

20 마지막으로 사과는 가족이나 사랑하는 사람들 사이에서도 필요하다.
➡ _____

21 어느 날, 선민이는 여동생이 가장 좋아하는 책을 빌렸다. 나중에 그녀는 그것을 잃어버렸다.
➡ _____

22 선민이는 그것이 중요하지 않다고 생각하여 사과하지 않았다. 그녀는 '우리는 어쨌든 자매니까.'라고 생각했다.
➡ _____

23 선민이의 여동생은 언니가 본인을 대했던 방식이 마음에 들지 않았다. 어떻게 자신의 언니가 그녀의 기분을 무시할 수 있는가?
➡ _____

24 선민이가 여동생에게 사과하지 않았던 것은 이번이 처음이 아니었다.
➡ _____

25 사람들은 잘못했을 때, 사과해야 한다. 이것은 가족이나 당신에게 가까운 사람도 포함한다.
➡ _____

26 사람들은 마음의 상처가 가족이나 친구에게서 올 때 더 쉽게 상처 받는다.
➡ _____

27 우리는 아마 그들이 가깝기 때문에 그냥 넘어갈 것이라고 생각할지 모른다.
➡ _____

28 하지만 작은 실수를 하고 사과하지 않는 것은 큰 감정적인 상처가 된다는 것을 기억하라.
➡ _____

29 이것은 가족과 사랑하는 사람들에게 특히 더 그러하다.
➡ _____

30 당신은 "더 이상 사과하지 않는다면 더 이상 기회가 없다."는 말을 들어본 적이 있는가?
➡ _____

31 사람들은 실수하지만, 그 실수가 아름다운 관계를 깨뜨리게 해서는 안 된다.
➡ _____

32 누군가에게 사과하고 싶은가? 지금 하려고 노력해라. 빠르고 진정한 "미안해."라는 말이 많은 문제를 해결해 줄 것이다.
➡ _____
_____

[01~03] 다음 글을 읽고 물음에 답하시오.

Because we are human, we all make mistakes. ① It is not easy to get along with everyone all the time. ② Sometimes we hurt people's feelings without intending to. ③ Sometimes, we do something wrong and regret it later. ④ When that happens, what should we do? ⑤ Read the following case studies and learn three things about a proper apology.

01 ①~⑤ 중 주어진 문장이 들어가기에 가장 적절한 곳은?

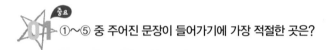

We should apologize.

①   ②   ③   ④   ⑤

서답형

02 다음과 같이 풀이되는 말을 위 글에서 찾아 쓰시오.

correct or most suitable

➡ _____

03 다음 중 위 글에 이어질 내용으로 가장 적절한 것은?

① when to do case studies
② how to apologize appropriately
③ why we make mistakes occasionally
④ the way you forgive your friends
⑤ some rules not to hurt your friends' feelings

[04~07] 다음 글을 읽고 물음에 답하시오.

When June tripped over a backpack and fell, Mike found it ①funny and laughed. He took a picture and uploaded it on an SNS. June saw the picture and became ②angry. Mike said, with a laugh, "Sorry, June!" and ③ deleted it. After that, June felt (A)_____ more hurt because of Mike's ④serious apology. June didn't like how Mike had acted. Mike seemed to think it was nothing ⑤serious.

What did you learn from this case? Yes. You guessed right. You should be sincere when you apologize. Apologizing is necessary to build good friendships. Saying you're sorry is more than just words. You need to show that you respect the other person and care about his or her feelings. If you truly want to make things right, be sincere in your apology. The more sincere your apology is, the better it will be received.

04 빈칸 (A)에 들어갈 말로 적절하지 않은 것은?

① far   ② still   ③ very
④ much   ⑤ even

05 ①~⑤ 중 글의 흐름상 어색한 것은?

①   ②   ③   ④   ⑤

06 위 글을 읽고 답할 수 있는 것은?

① What time did June fall?
② How many friends saw the picture?
③ How did friends feel about the picture?
④ What didn't June like?
⑤ Which SNS did Mike upload the picture?

서답형

07 When you apologize, how should you be? Answer in English with four words.

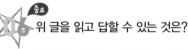

➡ _____

[08~10] 다음 글을 읽고 물음에 답하시오.

Here is another case. While Kate was hurrying across the cafeteria, she accidentally bumped into Hojun. Some food on Hojun's tray fell on his jacket. Kate didn't apologize. Hojun felt bad. He thought, 'Why doesn't she say something? It would be nothing if she apologized right now.'

This case shows that when an apology is necessary, you should apologize (A)_____. A quick apology shows that you are thoughtful and take responsibility for your action. All you need to do is to say, "I'm sorry." Then, the hurt friend will think nothing of it and laugh it off.

08 다음 중 빈칸 (A)에 들어갈 말로 가장 적절한 것은?

① later   ② for once

③ at once   ④ secretly

⑤ from time to time

서답형

09 위 글의 내용에 맞게 빈칸에 알맞은 말을 다섯 단어로 쓰시오.

> When Kate bumped into Hojun, he was holding _____. The bumping made it fall on his jacket.

중요

10 Choose one that is TRUE.

① Kate bumped into Hojun on purpose.

② Some food fell on Kate's jacket.

③ Kate wanted Hojun to apologize to her.

④ It is good to postpone apologizing.

⑤ Hojun felt bad because of Kate's attitude.

[11~12] 다음 글을 읽고 물음에 답하시오.

Finally, apologies are necessary among family members and loved ones, too.

One day, Sunmin borrowed ①her sister's favorite book. Later, ②she lost it. Sunmin didn't apologize because ③she thought (A) it was not important. She thought, 'We're sisters, after all.' Sunmin's sister disliked how Sunmin had treated her. How could her own sister ignore ④her feelings? This was not the first time Sunmin hadn't apologized to ⑤her little sister.

11 밑줄 친 (A)가 의미하는 것은?

① buying a new book

② having lost her sister's book

③ making an appointment

④ borrowing her sister's book

⑤ having apologized to her sister

중요

12 ①~⑤ 중 지칭하는 바가 다른 하나는?

①   ②   ③   ④   ⑤

[13~14] 다음 글을 읽고 물음에 답하시오.

People need to apologize when they do something wrong. This includes family members and the people who are close to you. People get hurt more easily when the hurt comes from a family member or a friend. We may think that they will let it go because they are close to us. Remember, (A)_____, that small mistakes and no apology add up to big emotional wounds. This is especially true among family members and loved ones.

13 빈칸 (A)에 들어갈 말로 가장 적절한 것은?

① nevertheless
② however
③ therefore
④ as a result
⑤ for instance

서답형

14 When do people need to apologize?

➡ _____

_____

[15~17] 다음 글을 읽고 물음에 답하시오.

(A) He took a picture and uploaded it on an SNS. June saw the picture and became angry.

(B) After that, June felt even more hurt because of Mike's casual apology. June didn't like how Mike had acted. Mike seemed to think it was nothing serious.

(C) When June tripped over a backpack and fell, Mike found it funny and laughed.

(D) Mike said, with a laugh, "Sorry, June!" and deleted it.

What did you learn from this case? Yes. You guessed right. You should be sincere when you apologize. Apologizing is necessary to build good friendships. Saying you're sorry is more than just words. You need to show that you respect the other person and care about his or her feelings. If you truly want to make things right, be sincere in your apology. The more sincere your apology is, the better it will be ⓐreceived.

서답형

15 자연스러운 글이 되도록 (A)~(D)를 바르게 나열하시오.

➡ _____

중요

16 다음 중 밑줄 친 ⓐ를 대신하여 쓸 수 있는 것은?

① recalled
② accepted
③ persuaded
④ followed
⑤ regretted

17 다음 중 위 글의 내용과 일치하는 것은?

① June tripped over Mike's leg.
② Mike didn't apologize to June at all.
③ Mike took the situation seriously.
④ Apologizing is related to good friendships.
⑤ Apology shows that the other person likes you.

[18~20] 다음 글을 읽고 물음에 답하시오.

Here is another case. While Kate was hurrying across the cafeteria, she accidentally bumped into Hojun. Some food on Hojun's tray fell on his jacket. Kate didn't apologize. Hojun felt bad. He thought, 'Why doesn't she say something? It would be nothing if (A)_____.'

This case shows that when an apology is necessary, you should apologize at once. A quick apology shows that you are thoughtful and take responsibility for your action. All you need to do is to say, "I'm sorry." Then, the hurt friend will think nothing of it and laugh it (B)_____.

18 빈칸 (A)에 들어갈 말로 가장 적절한 것은?

① I forgot about it
② she apologized right now
③ she kept behaving like that
④ I asked her to say sorry to me
⑤ she thanked me for forgiving her

중요

19 빈칸 (B)에 들어갈 말과 같은 말이 들어가는 것은?

① You'd better work _____ every day.
② I was surprised to come _____ Julie.
③ The book consists _____ several chapters.
④ He kept me _____ visiting his uncle.
⑤ The moon does not give _____ any light on its own.

서답형

20 According to the passage, what should you do when an apology is necessary? Answer in English.

➡ _____

_____

[21~22] 다음 글을 읽고 물음에 답하시오.

Finally, apologies are necessary among family members and loved ones, too. One day, Sunmin borrowed her sister's favorite book. Later, she lost it. Sunmin didn't apologize because she thought it was not important. She thought, 'We're sisters, after all.' Sunmin's sister disliked (A)how Sunmin had treated her. How could her own sister ignore her feelings? This was not the first time Sunmin hadn't apologized to her little sister.

서답형

21 What happened after Sunmin borrowed her sister's favorite book? (4 words)

➡ _____

중요

22 다음 중 밑줄 친 (A)의 의미로 가장 적절한 것은?

① Sunmin had been the best sister ever.

② Sunmin had shared everything with her sister.

③ Sumin hadn't cared about her sister's feelings.

④ Sunmin's sister had borrowed everything from Sunmin.

⑤ Sunmin and her sister hadn't talked with each other for a long time.

[23~25] 다음 글을 읽고 물음에 답하시오.

People need to apologize (A)_____. This includes family members and the people who are ①close to you. People get hurt more ②easily when the hurt comes from a family member or a friend. We may think that they will let it go because they are close to us. Remember, however, that small mistakes and no apology add up to ③big emotional wounds. This is especially true among family members and loved ones.

Have you ever heard of the saying, "No more apologies, no more chances"? People make mistakes, but don't let one mistake ④break a beautiful relationship. Do you want to apologize to someone? Try to do it ⑤later. A quick and sincere "I'm sorry" can solve many problems.

서답형

23 주어진 단어를 빈칸 (A)에 바르게 쓰시오.

(do / wrong / they / something / when)

➡ _____

중요

24 What is the above passage mainly talking about?

① how to accept one's apology

② the importance of making good friends

③ why we should not hurt family members

④ the importance of apologizing

⑤ what we should do to maintain a good relationship

서답형

25 ①~⑤ 중 글의 흐름상 어색한 것을 한 군데 찾아 바르게 고쳐 쓰시오.

➡ _____

[01~03] 다음 글을 읽고 물음에 답하시오.

Because we are human, we all make mistakes. It is not easy to get along with everyone all the time. Sometimes we hurt people's feelings without intending (A)to. Sometimes, we do something wrong and regret it later. When that happens, what should we do? We should apologize. Read the following case studies and learn three things about a proper apology.

01 밑줄 친 (A)가 의미하는 것을 위 글에서 찾아 쓰시오.

➡ _____

02 According to the passage, what is not easy to do? Answer in English with a full sentence.

➡ _____
_____

03 다음과 같이 풀이되는 말을 위 글에서 찾아 쓰시오.

something that you say or write in order to tell someone that you are sorry that you have hurt them or caused trouble for them

➡ _____

[04~07] 다음 글을 읽고 물음에 답하시오.

When June tripped over a backpack and fell, Mike found it funny and laughed. He took a picture and uploaded it on an SNS. June saw the picture and became angry. Mike said, with a laugh, "Sorry, June!" and deleted it. After that, June felt even more hurt because of Mike's casual apology. June didn't like how Mike had acted. Mike seemed to think it was nothing serious.

What did you learn from this case? Yes. You guessed right. You should be sincere when you apologize. Apologizing is necessary to build good friendships. Saying you're sorry is more than just words. You need to show that you respect the other person and care about his or her feelings. If you truly want to make things right, be sincere in your apology. (A)당신의 사과가 진실할수록, 그것은 더 잘 받아들여질 것이다.

04 주어진 단어를 바르게 나열하여 밑줄 친 우리말 (A)를 영어로 쓰시오. 필요하다면 어형을 바꾸시오.

(be / is / will / receive / the better / it / the more / your / sincere / apology)

➡ _____
_____

05 What did Mike do after he took a picture of June? Answer in English.

➡ _____

06 Write the reason why June felt even more hurt after Mike deleted the picture. Use the phrase 'It's because.'

➡ _____

07 위 글의 내용에 맞게 빈칸에 알맞은 말을 쓰시오.

According to the passage, what makes your apology sincere is to show that_____.

➡ _____
_____

Here is another case. While Kate was hurrying across the cafeteria, she accidentally bumped into Hojun. Some food on Hojun's tray fell on his jacket. Kate didn't apologize. Hojun felt bad. He thought, 'Why doesn't she say something? It would be nothing if she apologized right now.'

This case shows that when an apology is necessary, you should apologize at once. A quick apology shows that you are thoughtful and take responsibility for your action. All you need to do is to say, "I'm sorry." Then, the hurt friend will think nothing of it and laugh it off.

08 Write the reason why some food fell on Hojun's jacket. Use the word 'because.'

➡ _____

09 다음 중 위 글의 내용과 일치하지 않는 곳을 두 군데 찾아 바르게 고쳐 쓰시오.

> Kate bumped into Hojun by chance. Hojun was holding food on his tray and some of it fell on his jacket because of her. But she made an apology. Hojun felt good.

➡ _____

10 위 글의 내용에 맞게 빈칸에 알맞은 말을 쓰시오.

> When you want to take responsibility for your action, _____ as soon as possible.

[11~14] 다음 글을 읽고 물음에 답하시오.

Finally, apologies are ①necessary among family members and ②loved ones, too. One day, Sunmin ③borrowed her sister's favorite book. Later, she lost it. Sunmin didn't apologize because she thought it was not ④important. She thought, 'We're sisters, after all.' Sunmin's sister disliked how Sunmin had treated her. How could her own sister ⑤respect her feelings? This was not the first time Sunmin hadn't apologized to her little sister.

People need to apologize when they do something wrong. (A)This includes family members and the people who are close to you. People get hurt more easily when the hurt comes from a family member or a friend. We may think that they will let it go because they are close to us. Remember, however, that small mistakes and no apology add up to big emotional wounds. This is especially true among family members and loved ones.

11 ①~⑤ 중 글의 흐름상 어색한 것을 찾아 바르게 고쳐 쓰시오.

➡ _____

12 밑줄 친 (A)가 의미하는 것을 우리말로 쓰시오.

➡ _____

13 When do people get hurt more easily? Answer in English with a full sentence.

➡ _____
_____

14 다음 빈칸에 들어갈 말을 위 글에서 찾아 쓰시오.

> No matter how _____ the person is to you, you need to apologize to them when you do _____ _____.

After You Read C

Inho went to a store to buy shoes. He was hit by a woman's bag accidentally
<small>to부정사의 부사적 용법 중 목적(~하기 위해서)</small>

as she passed by. The woman said, "Sorry," and she walked away quickly.
<small>때를 나타내는 접속사(~할 때)</small>

Inho was angry because the woman did not make a sincere and proper
<small>원인을 나타내는 접속사</small>

apology. He thought that the woman should care about his feelings.
<small>명사절 접속사(+완전한 절)</small>

구문해설 • accidentally: 우연히 • pass by: 지나가다 • sincere: 진실한 • proper: 적절한

해석

인호는 신발을 사려고 가게에 갔다. 어떤 여자가 지나갈 때 그는 우연히 그 여자의 가방에 부딪혔다. 그 여자는 "미안해."라고 말하고는 빠르게 걸어갔다. 인호는 그녀가 진실되고 올바른 사과를 하지 않았다고 생각했기 때문에 화가 났다. 그는 그 여자가 그의 감정에 신경 써야 한다고 생각했다.

Enjoy Writing C

My Wonderful Friend, Jinsu

I'd like to introduce my friend, Jinsu. I have known him since elementary
<small>현재완료(계속) / 전치사(~ 이래로)</small>

school. He is always humorous, brave, and cheerful. This is how he helped
<small>형용사 병렬 구조 A, B, and C / 관계부사(= the way (in which))</small>

me. Last Friday I was sick and missed a math class. Jinsu showed me his class
<small>4형식</small>

notes. I am lucky to have him as my friend. The more I know him, the deeper
<small>to부정사(부사적 용법–원인) / The+비교급 ~, the+비교급 … 구문</small>

our friendship becomes.

구문해설 • elementary school: 초등학교 • cheerful: 발랄한

나의 훌륭한 친구, 진수

나는 나의 친구 진수를 소개하고 싶어. 나는 그를 초등학교 때부터 알았어. 그는 항상 재미있고, 용감하고, 발랄해. 이게 그가 나를 도와주었던 방법이야. 지난 금요일 나는 아파서 수학 수업을 못 들었어. 진수가 내게 자신의 수업 노트를 보여 줬어. 나는 그를 친구로 두어서 행운이야. 내가 그를 많이 알수록 우리의 우정은 더 깊어져.

Project Step 1

A: Do you know how we write a note of apology?
<small>know의 목적어로 '의문사+주어+동사'의 간접의문문이다.</small>

B: Yes. First, write about what we did.
<small>전치사 'about'의 목적어로 관계대명사 'what'이 사용되었고 'what'절은 불완전한 문장이 온다.</small>

C: Then write that we are sorry for it.
<small>동사 write의 목적어로 접속사 'that'절이 사용되었다. 'that'절은 완전한 문장이 온다.</small>

D: Do not make excuses for our actions.

A: Thank you for the tips. I really appreciate it.

구문해설 • note: 편지, 쪽지 • apology: 사과 • excuse: 변명 • tip: 조언 • appreciate: 감사하다

A: 너는 우리가 어떻게 사과 편지를 쓰는지 아니?

B: 응. 먼저, 우리가 뭘 했는지 써야 해.

C: 그리고 나서 그것에 대해 미안하다고 써야 해.

D: 우리 행동에 대해 변명을 하면 안 돼.

A: 조언해 줘서 고마워. 정말 고마워.

01 다음 주어진 두 단어의 관계가 같도록 빈칸에 알맞은 단어를 쓰시오.

> include – inclusion : _____ – solution

02 다음 빈칸 (A)와 (B)에 들어갈 어휘가 바르게 짝지어진 것은?

> • You (A)_____ your friends. Then you and they will get hurt.
> • Students do not have enough time to (B)_____ their clothes in the mornings.

① get into – pick up
② look into – turn down
③ put into – trip over
④ bump into – pick out
⑤ enter into – pass by

[03~04] 다음 영영풀이에 해당하는 것을 고르시오.

03
> in a way that was not planned or intended

① purposely   ② especially
③ sincerely   ④ friendly
⑤ accidentally

04
> to remove part or all of a written or electronic text

① delete   ② suggest
③ touch   ④ regret
⑤ treat

05 다음 우리말에 맞게 주어진 문장의 빈칸을 네 단어로 채우시오.

> 누군가를 진심으로 사랑할 수 있었기 때문에 그때가 제 인생에서 가장 행복했던 때 같아요.
> ➡ I think that was the best time in my life because I was able to love someone _____.

06 Sohee와 Minsu가 영화를 보러 갔을 때 그림과 같은 상황에서 Sohee가 여자에게 요청할 말을 주어진 단어를 이용하여 완성하시오.

No, not at all.

(mind / change seats / with me)

➡ _____

07 다음 대화의 빈칸에 들어갈 말을 주어진 단어를 알맞은 순서로 배열하여 완성하시오.

> G: I accidentally broke my mom's favorite plate.
> B: That's too bad, Mina.
> G: _____
> B: No, not at all. You should apologize sincerely.
> G: I see. I'll talk to her with all my heart.

(to / you / sorry / do / mind / say / telling / me / to / her / how / ?)

➡ _____

[08~10] 다음 대화를 읽고 물음에 답하시오.

Jessie: Hi, Andy. What's up?

Andy: Hi, Jessie. I'm going to buy a present for Amy. You've been friends with her for a long time, haven't you?

Jessie: Yes, since first grade in elementary school. (1)

Andy: Well, I know you're really busy studying, but do you mind helping me? (2)

Jessie: No problem. What's the present for? It's not her birthday. (3)

Andy: Well, two months ago, when my leg was broken, she carried my backpack to school. (4)

Jessie: That was nice of her.

Andy: Yes, it was. What should I get for her?

Jessie: Well, how about a case for her smartphone? She broke her case recently. (5)

Andy: Really? Thank you for your suggestion.

08 위 대화의 (1)~(5) 중 다음 문장이 들어갈 위치로 알맞은 것은?

I am sure you could help me pick out something nice.

① (1) ② (2) ③ (3) ④ (4) ⑤ (5)

09 다음 물음에 대한 답을 〈조건〉에 맞게 영어로 쓰시오.

Q: What does Jessie suggest Andy buy for Amy?

─┤ 조건 ├─
that절을 이용하고 조동사 should는 사용하지 말 것.

➡ _____

_____

10 위 대화를 읽고 답할 수 없는 질문은?

① What does Andy ask to Jessie?
② Why is Andy going to buy a present for Amy?
③ Does Jessie mind helping Andy?
④ Why did Andy break his leg two months ago?
⑤ Have Jessie and Amy been friends with each other for a long time?

Grammar

11 다음 중 주어진 문장과 의미가 가장 가까운 것을 고르시오.

As the weather gets colder, people tend to catch a cold more than before.

① The colder the weather gets, the more people catch a cold.
② Once the weather gets cold, the more cold people catch.
③ Because of the cold weather, a lot of people catch a cold.
④ The cold the weather gets, the much more people catch a cold.
⑤ When the much colder weather comes, most people catch a cold.

[12~14] 다음 중 어법상 어색한 문장을 고르시오.

12 ① This is how Miso helped me repair my smartphone.
② This is the way Miso helped me repair my smartphone.
③ This is the way in how Miso helped me repair my smartphone.
④ This is the way that Miso helped me repair my smartphone.
⑤ This is the way in which Miso helped me repair my smartphone.

13 ① Minsu can't forget the year when his aunt died of cancer.

② An aquarium is a glass container in which fish and other water creatures can be kept in.

③ Remember the time when you should take the medicine after every meal.

④ Can you guess the reason why James hasn't finished the work yet?

⑤ The town where the painter lived has a famous museum.

14 ① The higher we went up, the more it was difficult for us to breathe.

② The hotter the curry rice is, the harder it becomes to eat it.

③ The more you earn, the more you should save for the future.

④ The less people have, the more they want to receive.

⑤ The more promises we make, the harder it becomes to keep them.

15 다음 중 밑줄 친 부분을 생략할 수 <u>없는</u> 것은?

① I want to find out <u>the way</u> that Paul solved the difficult problem.

② Will you let me know <u>the time</u> when your uncle will arrive at the airport?

③ This Monday is <u>the day</u> when my kids first go to school.

④ She knows the way <u>in which</u> her mother supported all her kids.

⑤ Can you explain to me <u>the reason</u> why you didn't show up at the meeting?

[16~18] 다음 밑줄 친 부분 중 어법상 옳은 것을 고르시오.

16 ① This is the building <u>in which</u> my grandfather designed 30 years ago.

② The bed town <u>which</u> my neighbors are going to move is quite far from here.

③ This is the park <u>where</u> Smith picked up the ID card for the Olympic games.

④ I forgot the name of the store <u>where</u> I bought some groceries at.

⑤ The Netherlands is the country <u>where</u> is famous for growing tulips.

17 ① The longer the break time is, <u>the more relaxed the workers do.</u>

② <u>More the women eat, more</u> weight they will gain.

③ The heavier a safe is, <u>the more expensive it becomes.</u>

④ The sooner we start, <u>the more earlier we will reach the destination.</u>

⑤ The more you think, <u>the more you will be careful.</u>

18 ① He will show Jenny <u>the way how</u> the prisoner escaped from the jail.

② Does Tammy know <u>the reason why</u> her son came home late for?

③ Wendy can't forget <u>the day when</u> she first met the green fairy on.

④ That evening was <u>the moment at when</u> I fell in love with the princess.

⑤ I don't know <u>the exact time when</u> the train leaves.

Reading

[19~22] 다음 글을 읽고 물음에 답하시오.

When June tripped over a backpack and fell, Mike found it ①funny and laughed. He took a picture and uploaded it on an SNS. June ②saw the picture and became angry. Mike said, with a laugh, "Sorry, June!" and deleted it. After that, June felt even more ③hurt because of Mike's casual apology. June didn't like how Mike had acted. Mike seemed to think it was nothing ④casual.

What did you learn from this case? Yes. You guessed right. You should be sincere when you apologize. Apologizing is ⑤necessary (A)to build good friendships. Saying you're sorry is more than just words. You need to show that you respect the other person and care about his or her feelings. If you truly want to make things right, be sincere in your apology. The more sincere your apology is, the better it will be received.

19 위 글의 밑줄 친 ①~⑤ 중 글의 흐름상 어색한 것은?

① ② ③ ④ ⑤

20 위 글의 밑줄 친 (A)와 쓰임이 같은 것은?

① Is there anything to watch in this room?
② It is necessary to drink lots of water.
③ Tim went there to see his brother.
④ Jake wants to meet you again.
⑤ Jane decided to make more cookies.

21 위 글의 내용을 참고하여 다섯 단어로 이루어진 조언을 쓰시오.

Jessica slipped on the floor this afternoon. I thought it was a little funny, so I laughed out loud. However, Jessica looked embarrassed and upset because of me. I think I owed her an apology. How should I apologize to her?

➡ _____

22 위 글을 읽고 답할 수 없는 것은?

① Why did June fall?
② What did Mike find funny?
③ Why did June feel even more hurt?
④ How did June feel when he saw the picture?
⑤ What SNS did Mike use to upload the picture?

[23~25] 다음 글을 읽고 물음에 답하시오.

Finally, apologies are necessary among family members and loved ones, too. One day, Sunmin borrowed her sister's favorite book. Later, she lost it. Sunmin didn't apologize because she thought it was not important. She thought, 'We're sisters, after all.' Sunmin's sister disliked how Sunmin had treated her. How could her own sister ignore her feelings? This was not the first time Sunmin hadn't apologized to her little sister. ① People need to apologize when they do something wrong. ② People get hurt more easily when the hurt comes from a family member or a friend. ③ We may think that they will let it go because they are close to us. ④ Remember, however, that small mistakes and no apology add up to big emotional wounds. ⑤ This is especially true among family members and loved ones.

23 ①~⑤ 중 주어진 문장이 들어가기에 가장 적절한 곳은?

> This includes family members and the people who are close to you.

①   ②   ③   ④   ⑤

24 According to the passage, what results in big emotional wounds? Answer in English with a full sentence.

➡ _____

_____

25 다음 중 위 글의 내용과 일치하는 것은?

① Sunmin lost her sister's books several times.
② Sunmin didn't apologize because she thought she did the right thing.
③ Sunmin's sister thought Sunmin didn't care about her feelings.
④ This was the first time that Sunmin didn't apologize to her sister.
⑤ It is okay not to apologize to family members when you do something wrong.

[26~28] 다음 글을 읽고 물음에 답하시오.

I'd like to introduce my friend, Jinsu. I have known him since elementary school. He is always humorous, brave, and cheerful. This is how he helped me. Last Friday I was sick and missed a math class. Jinsu showed me his class notes. I am lucky to have him as my friend. The more I know him, the deeper our friendship becomes.

26 다음 중 위 글의 제목으로 가장 적절한 것은?

① The Hero in Our School, Jinsu
② My Wonderful Friend, Jinsu
③ The Most Popular Boy, Jinsu
④ The Smartest Boy, Jinsu
⑤ What Makes Jinsu Happy

27 What happened to the writer last Friday? Answer in English.

➡ _____

28 What is Jinsu like? Answer in English.

➡ _____

출제율 95%

01 다음 짝지어진 단어의 관계가 같도록 빈칸에 알맞은 말을 쓰시오.

> disregard – ignore : considerate – _____

출제율 90%

02 다음 영영풀이에 해당하는 단어는?

> showing no fear of dangerous or difficult things

① timid　　② hurt　　③ emotional

④ right　　⑤ brave

[03~04] 다음 대화를 읽고 물음에 답하시오.

Suhee: I am planning to go to Jejudo.

Minjun: That's cool, Suhee. I used to (a)living there.

Suhee: Do you mind (b)telling me what to do in Jejudo?

Minjun: Not at all. Jejudo has many beautiful beaches. You should visit them.

Suhee: Good. I will (c)go swimming. What else can I do?

Minjun: (d)Why don't you hike Halla Mountain? You can see the mountain from everywhere on the island.

Suhee: Great. How about food?

Minjun: (e)If you like fish, on Jejudo raw fish is fresh and delicious.

Suhee: I'll try everything. I appreciate your tips.

출제율 95%

03 위 대화의 밑줄 친 (a)~(e) 중 어법상 어색한 것은?

① (a)　② (b)　③ (c)　④ (d)　⑤ (e)

출제율 95%

04 위 대화의 내용과 일치하지 <u>않는</u> 것은?

① Suhee is planning to go to Jejudo.

② Minjun lived in Jejudo but he doesn't live there anymore.

③ Suhee asks Minjun to tell her what to do in Jejudo.

④ Minjun doesn't recommend climbing Halla Mountain.

⑤ Suhee is planning to do everything that Minjun recommends.

[05~06] 다음 대화를 읽고 물음에 답하시오.

G: You seem to be busy, Minsu. Can I come in?

B: Sure. I'm preparing for the dance contest, but it's not easy.

G: I can help you. I was in the contest last year.

B: Really? That would be great, Amy.

G: You are good at getting into the rhythm. But (A)네가 해야 할 한 가지는 더 긴장을 푸는 것이야.(one thing / you / more / to / need / is / be / relaxed / to do) You are too nervous.

B: Your advice is very helpful. I really appreciate your advice.

G: It's my pleasure.

출제율 95%

05 위 대화의 밑줄 친 우리말 (A)에 맞게 주어진 단어를 알맞은 순서로 배열하시오. (one thing으로 문장을 시작하시오.)

➡ _____

출제율 90%

06 위 대화에서 다음 〈영영풀이〉가 설명하는 단어를 찾아 쓰시오.

> to be grateful for something

➡ _____

B: Irene, what are you doing?
G: Well, I've lost my favorite cap. I can't find it.
B: Let me help you. What does it look like?
G: It's red. My name is written in black on the side.
B: Oh, is this yours? It was under the table.
G: Yes, it is. Thank you, Jim. I appreciate your help.
B: (A)_____

07 위 대화의 빈칸 (A)에 들어갈 말로 알맞지 <u>않은</u> 것은?

① Of course not.
② It's my pleasure.
③ No problem.
④ Don't mention it.
⑤ Not at all.

08 위 대화를 읽고 답할 수 <u>없는</u> 질문은?

① What is Irene doing?
② What is written on Irene's cap?
③ Where did Jim find Irene's cap?
④ Does Jim mind helping Irene?
⑤ Why did Irene lose her cap?

09 다음 글에서 문법적으로 <u>틀린</u> 부분을 찾아 바르게 고쳐 쓰시오.

W: Mike does not feel very well. He might catch a cold. He needs to see a doctor, but he has a meeting with Jane in an hour. He wants to meet her tomorrow instead. What should he say to her?

➡ _____

10 다음 대화의 밑줄 친 (a)~(e) 중 어법상 <u>어색한</u> 것은?

Jessie: Hi, Andy. What's up?
Andy: Hi, Jessie. I'm going to buy a present for Amy. You've been friends with her for a long time, (a)weren't you?
Jessie: Yes, (b)<u>since first grade in elementary school.</u>
Andy: Well, I know you're really busy (c)<u>studying</u>, but do you mind helping me? I am sure you could help me (d)<u>pick out</u> something nice.
Jessie: No problem. What's the present for? It's not her birthday.
Andy: Well, two months ago, when my leg (e)<u>was broken</u>, she carried my backpack to school.
Jessie: That was nice of her.
Andy: Yes, it was. What should I get for her?
Jessie: Well, how about a case for her smartphone? She broke her case recently.
Andy: Really? Thank you for your suggestion.

① (a) ② (b) ③ (c) ④ (d) ⑤ (e)

[11~12] 다음 밑줄 친 부분의 쓰임이 〈보기〉와 <u>다른</u> 것은?

11

June didn't like <u>how</u> Mike acted because of Mike's casual apology.

① That was <u>how</u> the king treated the poor people of the village.
② Show me <u>how</u> the researcher solved the problem so soon.
③ Let us see <u>how</u> you made the wild animals quiet like lambs.
④ I wonder <u>how</u> strong the bears will be in their mature state.
⑤ Everyone in this school likes <u>how</u> she laughed at what seemed so little.

12

출제율 100%

We visited the town <u>where</u> the legendary singer was born.

① This Friday is the day <u>when</u> my son will graduate from high school.

② The student saw her teacher enter the restaurant <u>where</u> she met David.

③ Steve went to the city <u>where</u> his uncle used to live.

④ Janet still misses the holiday <u>when</u> she went to Egypt and the Mediterranean Sea.

⑤ Franklin was taking a shower <u>when</u> someone rang the bell.

[13~14] 다음 주어진 우리말을 바르게 영작한 것을 고르면?

13

출제율 90%

사과를 늦게 하면 할수록 상대방과의 관계는 더 악화될 것이다.

① When you apologize the later, you are likely to be your relationship with the other the worse.

② As the later you apologize, the more your relationship with the other will be likely worse.

③ The later you apologize, the more worse the relationship with the other is to be.

④ The later you apologize, your relationship with the other will be the worse.

⑤ The later you apologize, the worse the relationship with the other will be.

14

출제율 95%

날씨가 더워지면 더워질수록, 우리는 더 많은 전기를 사용한다.

① The more hotter the weather, so much more electricity we use.

② The hotter the weather is, the more electricity we use.

③ The hotter the weather will be, the more electricity we have used.

④ The more hot the weather, we use the more electricity.

⑤ The hotter the weather is, the better electricity we will use.

[15~16] 다음 글을 읽고 물음에 답하시오.

Because we are human, we all make mistakes. It is not easy (A)<u>to get</u> along with everyone all the time. Sometimes we hurt people's feelings without intending to. Sometimes, we do something wrong and regret (B)<u>it</u> later. When that happens, what should we do? We should apologize. Read the following case studies and learn three things about a proper apology.

15

출제율 90%

밑줄 친 (A)와 쓰임이 같은 것은?

① I need someone <u>to depend</u> on.

② <u>To bake</u> cookies, you need flour.

③ The boy tried hard <u>to get</u> on the top.

④ Daisy woke up <u>to find</u> herself famous.

⑤ It was surprising <u>to see</u> her there.

16

출제율 95%

밑줄 친 (B)의 의미로 가장 적절한 것은?

① making other people happy

② doing something wrong

③ intending to hurt other people

④ getting along with friends

⑤ apologizing in the right way

[17~18] 다음 글을 읽고 물음에 답하시오.

People need to apologize when they do something wrong. This includes family members and the people who are close to you. People get hurt more easily when the hurt comes from a family member or a friend. We may think that they will let it go because they are close to us. Remember, however, that (A)_____ add up to big emotional wounds. This is especially true among family members and loved ones.

Have you ever heard of the saying, "No more apologies, no more chances"? People make mistakes, but don't let one mistake break a beautiful relationship. Do you want to apologize to someone? Try to do it now. A quick and sincere "I'm sorry" can solve many problems.

✏️ 출제율 90%

17 다음 중 빈칸 (A)에 들어갈 말로 가장 적절한 것은?

① some mistakes and proper apologies
② small troubles made by close people
③ small apologies with no mistakes
④ making beautiful relationship work
⑤ small mistakes and no apology

✏️ 출제율 100%

18 다음 빈칸에 들어갈 말이 바르게 짝지어진 것은?

> Unless you apologize for your mistakes _____, it can lead to _____ a beautiful relationship.

① honestly – maintaining
② immediately – breaking
③ suddenly – making
④ on purpose – breaking
⑤ easily – maintaining

[19~21] 다음 글을 읽고 물음에 답하시오.

When June tripped over a backpack and ① <u>fell</u>, Mike found it funny and laughed. He took a picture and uploaded ②<u>it</u> on an SNS. June saw the picture and ③<u>became angry</u>. Mike said, with a laugh, "Sorry, June!" and deleted it. After that, June felt even more hurt ④<u>because of</u> Mike's casual apology. June didn't like ⑤<u>how had Mike acted</u>. Mike seemed to think it was nothing serious.

What did you learn from this case? Yes. You guessed right. You should be sincere when you apologize. Apologizing is necessary to build good friendships. Saying you're sorry is more than just words. You need to show that you respect the other person and care about his or her feelings. If you truly want to make things right, be sincere in your apology. The more sincere your apology is, the better it will be received.

✏️ 출제율 95%

19 ①~⑤ 중 어법상 <u>어색한</u> 것의 번호를 적고 바르게 고쳐 쓰시오.

➡ _____

✏️ 출제율 100%

20 Choose one that is TRUE.

① Mike thought June's situation was embarrassing.
② June was satisfied with Mike's apology.
③ Apologizing is essential in building good friendships.
④ June felt the respect and care in Mike's apology.
⑤ You need to be sincere when you make friends with someone.

✏️ 출제율 90%

21 What do you need to show when we apologize to someone?

➡ _____
_____

01 다음 대화의 괄호 안의 동사를 알맞은 형태로 바꾸어 쓰시오.

Jessie: Hi, Andy. What's up?

Andy: Hi, Jessie. I'm going to buy a present for Amy. You've been friends with her for a long time, haven't you?

Jessie: Yes, since first grade in elementary school.

Andy: Well, I know you're really busy (A)(study), but do you mind (B)(help) me? I am sure you could help me (C)(pick) out something nice.

Jessie: No problem. What's the present for? It's not her birthday.

Andy: Well, two months ago, when my leg (D)(break), she carried my backpack to school.

Jessie: That was nice of her.

ndy: Yes, it was. What should I get for her?

Jessie: Well, how about a case for her smartphone? She broke her case recently.

Andy: Really? Thank you for your suggestion.

➡ (A) _____ , (B) _____
(C) _____ , (D) _____

02 다음 그림에서 여자의 말에 대해 집배원이 할 말을 2 단어를 추가하여 영어로 쓰시오.

Let me open the door for you.

Oh, _____ your help.

Q: What will the mail carrier say?

➡ _____ your help.

03 다음 대화의 (A)와 같은 의미가 되도록 주어진 단어를 사용하여 문장의 빈칸을 완성하시오.

G: (A)It seems that you are busy, Minsu. Can I come in?

B: Sure. I'm preparing for the dance contest, but it's not easy.

➡ _____ (seem to)

04 다음 주어진 문장의 밑줄 친 부분을 다시 쓰고자 한다. 빈칸에 알맞은 관계부사를 써 넣으시오.

(1) Can the rich woman tell the poor man the way in which she made a lot of money?
➡ Can the rich woman tell the poor man _____ she made a lot of money?

(2) The tired medical staff at the hospital need a place in which they can take a rest.
➡ The tired medical staff at the hospital need a place _____ they can take a rest.

(3) The book showed the reason for which the Japanese government interrupted the peace between two Koreas.
➡ The book showed _____ the Japanese government interrupted the peace between two Koreas.

05 다음 〈보기〉에 주어진 단어 조합들을 한 번씩만 사용해서 흐름에 알맞게 빈칸을 채워 넣으시오. (필요시 변형할 것)

┌─ 보기 ─┐
few–happy, hard–much,
clear–long, soon–good, old–smart
└─────┘

(1) The _____ you work, the _____ money you earn.

(2) The _____ the video quality is, the _____ it takes to download it.

(3) The _____ classes there are on a hot summer day, the _____ the students feel.

(4) The _____ the girl grew, the _____ she became.

(5) The _____ you finish the project, the _____ position you can get in the negotiation.

06 다음 두 문장을 가능하면 선행사와 관계부사를 모두 써서 한 문장으로 쓰시오. (단, 관계부사는 반드시 사용해야 함.)

(1) • Tell me the way.
   • Mary persuaded her parents to give her the car in that way.

   ➡ _____
   _____

(2) • No one knows the day.
   • Minju will marry the handsome guy of the idol group on the day.

   ➡ _____
   _____

(3) • Bucheon is the city.
   • International Fantastic Film Festival will take place in Bucheon.

   ➡ _____
   _____

[07~09] 다음 글을 읽고 물음에 답하시오.

Finally, apologies are necessary among family members and loved ones, too. One day, Sunmin borrowed her sister's favorite book. Later, she lost it. Sunmin didn't apologize because she thought it was not important. She thought, 'We're sisters, after all.' Sunmin's sister disliked how Sunmin had treated her. How could her own sister ignore her feelings? This was not the first time Sunmin hadn't apologized to her little sister.

People need to apologize when they do something wrong. This includes family members and the people who are close to you. People get hurt more easily when the hurt comes from a family member or a friend. We may think that they will let it go because they are close to us. Remember, however, that small mistakes and no apology add up to big emotional wounds. (A)This is especially true among family members and loved ones.

07 밑줄 친 (A)가 의미하는 것을 우리말로 쓰시오.

   ➡ _____
   _____

08 위 글의 내용에 맞도록 빈칸에 알맞은 말을 〈보기〉에서 골라 쓰시오.

┌─ 보기 ─────────────────────────┐
close / far / necessary / hated / loved /
forgiveness / hurt
└────────────────────────────────┘

┌────────────────────────────────┐
Apologies are _____ even for family members and _____ ones. People are more likely to get _____ when the hurt comes from their _____ friends or family members.
└────────────────────────────────┘

09 Write the reason why Sunmin didn't apologize to her little sister for having lost her book. Use the phrase 'It's because.'

   ➡ _____

창의사고력 서술형 문제

01 다음 그림을 보고 자유롭게 관계부사 how가 들어간 문장을 2개 만드시오. 단, 〈보기〉에 주어진 단어 중 하나는 반드시 포함하는 문장이어야 한다.

> 보기
>
> find, walk, set the table, read

(1) _____

(2) _____

(3) _____

(4) _____

02 나를 도와준 친구에 대한 질의 응답을 읽고 친구를 소개하는 글을 완성하시오.

> Q: What's the name of your friend who helped you?
> A: Her name is Miso.
> Q: How long have you known her?
> A: I have known her for ten years.
> Q: What kind of a person is she?
> A: She is funny, generous, and cheerful.
> Q: When did she help you?
> A: It was two weeks ago.
> Q: Why did you need her help?
> A: Because I forgot to take my lunch to school.
> Q: What did she do for you?
> A: She shared her lunch with me.

> **My Great Friend, Miso**
> I'd like to introduce my friend, Miso. I have known her _____. She is always _____. This is how _____. _____, _____ _____. Miso _____. I am lucky to have her as my friend. The more I know her, the happier I am.

단원별 모의고사

01 다음 단어에 대한 영어 설명이 <u>어색한</u> 것은?

① ignore: to intentionally not listen or give attention to

② appreciate: to feel thanks about something

③ suggestion: an idea, plan, or action that is suggested or the act of suggesting it

④ mistake: an action, decision, or judgment that produces an unwanted or unintentional result

⑤ borrow: to give something to someone for a short period of time, expecting it to be given back

02 다음 짝지어진 단어의 관계가 같도록 빈칸에 알맞은 말을 쓰시오.

right – wrong : generous – s_____

03 다음 영영풀이에 해당하는 어구를 고르시오.

to lose your balance after knocking your foot against something when you are walking or running, or to cause someone to do this

① turn down   ② look forward to

③ trip over   ④ give off

⑤ laugh off

04 다음 중 짝지어진 대화가 <u>어색한</u> 것은?

① A: Do you mind closing the window?
   B: No, not at all. Go ahead.

② A: I didn't bring my textbook.
   B: Let's share mine.
   A: I appreciate your kindness.

③ A: Do you know how we write a note of apology?
   B: Yes. First, we should write why we feel sorry.

④ A: Do you mind turning down the volume?
   B: Yes, I do. I'll turn it down.

⑤ A: I am planning to go to Jejudo.
   B: That's cool.

[05~06] 다음 대화를 읽고 물음에 답하시오.

G: I am planning to go to Jejudo.
B: That's cool, Suhee. I (a)used to live there.
G: (b)Do you mind telling me what to do in Jejudo?
B: (A)_____ Jejudo has many beautiful beaches. You should visit them.
G: Good. I will (c)go swimming. What else can I do?
B: (d)Why don't you hike Halla Mountain? You can see the mountain from everywhere on the island.
G: Great. How about food?
B: If you like fish, on Jejudo raw fish is fresh and delicious.
G: I'll try everything. (e)I appreciate your tips.

05 위 대화의 빈칸 (A)에 들어갈 말로 <u>어색한</u> 것은?

① Not at all.   ② No problem.

③ No, I don't.   ④ Of course not.

⑤ Yes, I do.

06 위 대화의 밑줄 친 (a)~(e)에 대한 설명 중 잘못된 것은?

① (a): '~했었다'라는 과거의 상태를 나타내는 표현이다.

② (b): 요청을 하는 표현으로 'mind'의 목적어 자리에 사용된 'telling'은 'to tell'로 바꾸어 쓸 수 있고, 'what to do'는 'what I should do'로 바꿀 수 있다.

③ (c): 'go+-ing' 형태로 '~하러 가다'라는 의미로 사용된다.

④ (d): '~하는 게 어때?'라는 의미로 제안할 때 사용하는 표현으로 'What about hiking Halla Mountain?'으로 바꾸어 쓸 수 있다.

⑤ (e): 감사하는 표현으로 'Thank you for your tips.'로 바꾸어 쓸 수 있다.

[07~08] 다음 대화를 읽고 물음에 답하시오.

Jessie: Hi, Andy. What's up?

Andy: Hi, Jessie. I'm going to buy a present for Amy. You've been friends with her for a long time, haven't you?

Jessie: Yes, since first grade in elementary school.

Andy: Well, (A)네가 공부하느라 바쁘다는 것을 알지만, 나를 좀 도와줄 수 있니?(you're / know / busy / study / really / I / but / mind / do / help / you / me) I am sure you could help me pick out something nice.

Jessie: No problem. What's the present for? It's not her birthday.

Andy: Well, two months ago, when my leg was broken, she carried my backpack to school.

Jessie: That was nice of her.

Andy: Yes, it was. What should I get for her?

Jessie: Well, how about a case for her smartphone? She broke her case recently.

Andy: Really? Thank you for your suggestion.

07 위 대화의 밑줄 친 (A)의 우리말에 맞게 주어진 단어를 알맞은 순서로 배열하시오. (2 단어를 반드시 변형할 것.)

➡ _____

_____

08 다음 물음에 주어진 단어를 이용하여 영어로 답하시오.

> Q: What does Andy ask Jessie to do?
> (ask / to help / pick out / nice / Amy)

➡ _____

_____

09 다음 대화를 읽고 답할 수 <u>없는</u> 질문은?

> G: You seem to be busy, Minsu. Can I come in?
> B: Sure. I'm preparing for the dance contest, but it's not easy.
> G: I can help you. I was in the contest last year.
> B: Really? That would be great, Amy.
> G: You are good at getting into the rhythm. But one thing you need to do is to be more relaxed. You are too nervous.
> B: Your advice is very helpful. I really appreciate your advice.
> G: It's my pleasure.

① What is Minsu preparing for?

② When did Amy participate in the dance contest?

③ According to Amy, what is Minsu good at?

④ What is Minsu going to do to be relaxed?

⑤ How does Minsu respond to Amy's advice?

10 다음 대화의 흐름상 빈칸 (A)에 들어갈 말로 가장 알맞은 것은?

> G: I accidentally broke my mom's favorite plate.
> B: That's too bad, Mina.
> G: Do you mind telling me how to say sorry to her?
> B: No, not at all. You should apologize sincerely.
> G: I see. (A)_____

① I think my mom will understand me.
② I'll be more careful not to make mistakes.
③ I'll talk to my mom with all my heart.
④ I think I should often talk with my mom.
⑤ I think there is no man that doesn't make mistakes.

[11~12] 다음 중 주어진 문장과 같은 의미로 쓰인 것을 고르시오.

11

> The higher you go up the mountain, the colder it becomes.

① As you go up the mountain higher, it becomes colder.
② If you go up the mountain higher, you should feel colder.
③ Since you go up the mountain higher, the climate becomes colder.
④ Though you go up the mountain higher, it becomes colder.
⑤ While the air goes up the mountain higher, you become colder.

12

> As we grow older, our muscles and bones become less flexible.

① We get the older, the less flexible our muscles and bones become.
② Older we get, less flexible our muscles and bones become.
③ The much older we get, less flexible the muscles and bones become.
④ The older we get, the less flexible our muscles and bones become.
⑤ The older get we, the less flexible become our muscles and bones.

13 다음 각 문장의 밑줄 친 '전치사+관계대명사'를 관계부사로 바꿀 때 어법상 어색한 것은?

① Ellen will tell her instructor the reason for which she failed the test.
  → Ellen will tell her instructor the reason why she failed the test.
② This is the theater in which my parents watched the film last year.
  → This is the theater where my parents watched the film last year.
③ I will remember the moment at which I participated in the historic event.
  → I will remember the moment when I participated in the historic event.
④ That's the way in which Sean solved the difficult questions.
  → That's the way how Sean solved the difficult questions.
⑤ Egypt is the country in which a number of people live.
  → Egypt is the country where a number of people live.

14 다음 각 문장의 밑줄 친 관계부사를 관계대명사를 이용해서 전환하고자 할 때, 빈칸에 알맞은 단어를 쓰시오.

(1) Do you know the reason <u>why</u> Jenny came late for the meeting?

➡ Do you know the reason _____ _____ Jenny came late for the meeting?

(2) All the neighbors visited the restaurant <u>where</u> my mother worked.

➡ All the neighbors visited the restaurant _____ _____ my mother worked.

(3) The famous cook showed us <u>how</u> he made the delicious food.

➡ The famous cook showed us the way _____ _____ he made the delicious food.

(4) The car accident took place on the day <u>when</u> Tommy was fired from work.

➡ The car accident took place on the day _____ _____ Tommy was fired from work.

15 다음 우리말을 주어진 〈조건〉에 맞게 영작하시오.

┌─ 조건 ─┐
1. 'the 비교급 ~, the 비교급 …' 구문을 사용할 것.
2. 주어와 시제에 유의하고, 괄호 안의 단어를 활용할 것. (내용과 어법에 맞게 변형 가능함.)
3. 글자 수에 맞게 영작할 것.

(1) 비가 많이 내릴수록, 그녀는 기분이 더 우울해졌다. (depress, much, it, feel, 9 단어)

➡ _____

(2) 그녀의 사과가 더욱 진실할수록, 그가 그것을 더 잘 받아들일 것이다. (sincere, well, accept, 12 단어)

➡ _____

[16~17] 다음 글을 읽고 물음에 답하시오.

Here is another case. While Kate was hurrying across the cafeteria, she accidentally bumped into Hojun. Some food on Hojun's tray ①fell on his jacket. Kate didn't apologize. Hojun felt bad. He thought, 'Why doesn't she say something? It would be ②nothing if she apologized ③right now.'

This case shows that when an apology is necessary, you should apologize at once. A ④quick apology shows that you are ⑤thoughtless and (A)_____ responsibility for your action. All you need to do is to say, "I'm sorry." Then, the hurt friend will think nothing of it and laugh it off.

16 다음 중 빈칸 (A)에 들어갈 동사와 <u>다른</u> 것이 들어가는 것은?

① It will _____ me half an hour to get there.
② You need to _____ up your mind to do it.
③ Don't _____ advantage of your friends.
④ You can _____ off your coat. It's warm inside.
⑤ Ken, _____ your feet off your seat.

17 밑줄 친 ①~⑤ 중 글의 흐름상 어색한 것은?

① ② ③ ④ ⑤

[18~19] 다음 글을 읽고 물음에 답하시오.

People need to apologize when they do something wrong. This includes family members and the people who are close to you. People get hurt more easily when the hurt comes from a family member or a friend.

We may think that they will let it go because they are close to us. Remember, however, that small mistakes and no apology add up to big emotional wounds. This is especially true among family members and loved ones.

① Have you ever heard of the saying, "No more apologies, no more chances"? ② People make mistakes, but don't let one mistake break a beautiful relationship. ③ Do you want to apologize to someone? ④ A quick and sincere "I'm sorry" can solve many problems. ⑤

18 위 글의 ①~⑤ 중 주어진 문장이 들어가기에 가장 적절한 곳은?

Try to do it now.

①   ②   ③   ④   ⑤

19 위 글의 내용과 일치하지 <u>않는</u> 것은?

① It is necessary to apologize to family members when you do something wrong.

② Making mistakes with no apology leads to big emotional wounds.

③ Family members let our mistakes go even though there are no apologies.

④ You can get more chances with more apologies.

⑤ Many problems can be solved by saying quick and sincere apologies.

[20~22] 다음 글을 읽고 물음에 답하시오.

When June tripped over a backpack and fell, Mike found it funny and laughed. He took a picture and uploaded it on an SNS. June saw the picture and became angry. Mike said, with a laugh, "Sorry, June!" and deleted it. After that, June felt even more (A)[hurt / relieved] because of Mike's casual apology. June didn't like how Mike had acted. Mike seemed to think it was nothing serious.

What did you learn from this case? Yes. You guessed right. You should be sincere when you apologize. Apologizing is necessary to build good friendships. Saying you're sorry is more than just words. You need to show that you (B)[respect / ignore] the other person and care about his or her feelings. If you truly want to make things right, be sincere in your apology. The more sincere your apology is, the better it will be (C)[rejected / received].

20 What did Mike seem to think about uploading June's picture on SNS? Answer in English with a full sentence.

➡ _____

21 (A)~(C)에서 글의 흐름상 자연스러운 것이 바르게 짝지어진 것은?

① hurt – respect – rejected

② hurt – ignore – rejected

③ hurt – respect – received

④ relieved – ignore – received

⑤ relieved – respect – received

22 위 글의 내용에 맞게 빈칸에 알맞은 말을 쓰시오.

Mike wasn't _____ in his apology. That's why June felt even more hurt.

MEMO

Lesson 8

Have Fun with Art!

 의사소통 기능

- 관심 표현하기
  I was fascinated by the colors in his paintings and his creativity.

- 만족이나 불만족에 대해 묻기
  How do you like this T-shirt?

언어 형식

- 분사구문
  Using common images, pop art looks plain.

- be동사+worth+동명사
  Pop art **is worth paying** attention to.

Words & Expressions

Key Words

- **ability** [əbíləti] 명 능력
- **advertising** [ǽdvərtàiziŋ] 명 광고
- **advice** [ædváis] 명 충고, 조언
- **amazing** [əméiziŋ] 형 놀라운
- **art museum** 미술관
- **art work** 예술 작품
- **artistic** [ɑːrtístik] 형 예술적인
- **backpack** [bǽkpæk] 명 가방, 배낭
- **boring** [bɔ́ːriŋ] 형 지루한, 지겨운
- **cartoon** [kɑːrtúːn] 명 만화
- **classical** [klǽsikəl] 형 클래식의, 고전적인
- **colorful** [kʌ́lərfəl] 형 화려한
- **common** [kámən] 형 흔한, 평범한, 공통의
- **cone** [koun] 명 원뿔, 원뿔형 물체
- **cool** [kuːl] 형 멋진
- **copy** [kápi] 명 복사본
- **create** [kriéit] 동 만들다, 창조하다
- **creative** [kriéitiv] 형 창의적인
- **creativity** [krìːeitívəti] 명 창의력
- **decoration** [dèkəréiʃən] 명 장식
- **exciting** [jksáitiŋ] 형 신나는, 흥미진진한
- **exhibition** [èksəbíʃən] 명 전시회
- **familiar** [fəmíljər] 형 친숙한
- **fantastic** [fæntǽstik] 형 환상적인, 멋진
- **favorite** [féivərit] 형 가장 좋아하는
- **fever** [fíːvər] 명 열, 발열
- **goods** [gudz] 명 상품, 제품
- **huge** [hjuːdʒ] 형 거대한, 큰
- **include** [inklúːd] 동 포함하다, 넣다
- **lesson** [lésn] 명 교훈
- **lively** [láivli] 형 활기 넘치는, 생생한
- **main character** 주인공
- **mean** [miːn] 동 의미하다
- **meaning** [míːniŋ] 명 의미
- **musician** [mjuːzíʃən] 명 음악가
- **object** [ábdʒikt] 명 물건, 물체, 대상
- **outdoor** [áutdɔr] 형 실외의
- **practice** [prǽktis] 동 연습하다
- **performance** [pərfɔ́rməns] 명 연기, 공연
- **plain** [plein] 형 보통의, 평범한
- **plate** [pleit] 명 접시
- **pop art** 팝 아트
- **popular** [pápjulər] 형 대중적인, 인기 있는
- **probably** [prábəbli] 부 아마
- **refreshing** [rifréʃiŋ] 형 신선한, 참신한
- **run** [rʌn] 동 운영하다
- **sculpture** [skʌ́lptʃər] 명 조각품
- **special effects** 특수효과
- **speech balloon** 말풍선
- **subject** [sʌ́bdʒikt] 명 주제, 과목, 실험대상자
- **toilet** [tɔ́ilit] 명 변기, 화장실
- **traditional** [trədíʃənl] 형 전통적인
- **truly** [trúːli] 부 진심으로, 정말로
- **worth** [wəːrθ] 형 ~의 가치가 있는

Key Expressions

- **as well** 또한, 역시
- **back then** 그 당시에
- **be able to** ~할 수 있다
- **be fascinated by** ~에 매료되다
- **be filled with** ~로 가득 차 있다
- **be made of** ~로 만들어지다
- **be made up of** ~로 구성되다
- **be regarded as** ~로 여겨지다
- **be short for** ~의 줄임말이다
- **be worth+동명사** ~할 가치가 있다
- **break down** ~을 부수다
- **by+—ing(동명사)** ~함으로써
- **change A into B** A를 B로 바꾸다
- **in other words** 다시 말해서, 즉
- **instead of** ~ 대신에
- **look like+명사(구)** ~처럼 보이다
- **no wonder** ~은 (별로) 놀랄 일이 아니다[~하는 것도 당연하다]
- **one of+복수 명사** ~ 중의 하나
- **pay attention to** ~에 주의를 기울이다
- **set up** 설치하다
- **the other day** 요전 날, 며칠 전
- **turn one's eyes to** ~로 눈길을 돌리다

Word Power

※ 서로 비슷한 뜻을 가진 어휘
- □ **familiar** 친숙한 – **intimate** 친숙한, 친밀한
- □ **as well** 또한 – **also** 또한
- □ **lively** 활기 넘치는 – **animated** 생기가 있는
- □ **common** 흔한, 평범한 – **ordinary** 평범한

- □ **create** 만들다 – **produce** 제작하다
- □ **advice** 조언, 충고 – **tip** 조언
- □ **run** 운영하다 – **operate** 운영하다
- □ **performance** 연기 – **acting** 연기

※ 서로 반대되는 뜻을 가진 어휘
- □ **familiar** 친숙한 ↔ **unfamiliar** 낯선
- □ **outdoor** 실외의 ↔ **indoor** 실내의
- □ **colorful** 화려한 ↔ **colorless** 무색의
- □ **huge** 거대한 ↔ **tiny** 아주 작은

- □ **include** 포함하다 ↔ **exclude** 제외하다
- □ **popular** 인기 있는 ↔ **unpopular** 인기 없는
- □ **lively** 활기 넘치는 ↔ **dull** 활기 없는
- □ **copy** 복사본 ↔ **original** 원형, 원본

※ 형용사 – 명사
- □ **creative** 창의적인 – **creativity** 창의력
- □ **traditional** 전통적인 – **tradition** 전통

- □ **popular** 인기 있는 – **popularity** 인기
- □ **familiar** 친밀한 – **familiarity** 친밀함

English Dictionary

- □ **ability** 능력
  → the physical or mental power or skill needed to do something
  원가를 하기 위해 필요한 신체적 또는 정신적 힘이나 기술

- □ **advice** 충고
  → an opinion that someone offers you about what you should do or how you should act in a particular situation
  어떤 사람이 특정한 상황에서 당신이 무엇을 해야 하는지 또는 어떻게 행동 해야 하는지에 대해 당신에게 제안하는 의견

- □ **boring** 지루한
  → not interesting or exciting
  재미있거나 흥미롭지 않은

- □ **classical** 클래식의, 고전적인
  → traditional in style or form, or based on methods developed over a long period of time, and considered to be of lasting value
  전통적 스타일이나 형식, 또는 오랜 기간에 걸쳐 개발된 방법에 기 초하고, 지속적인 가치가 있는 것으로 여겨지는

- □ **cone** 원뿔
  → a shape with a flat, round or oval base and a top that becomes narrower until it forms a point
  평평한, 둥근 또는 타원형의 기초와 점이 형성될 때까지 좁아지는 꼭대 기를 가진 형태

- □ **creativity** 창의력
  → the ability to produce or use original and unusual ideas
  독창적이고 특이한 아이디어를 생산하거나 사용하는 능력

- □ **exhibition** 전시회
  → an event at which objects such as paintings are

shown to the public, a situation in which someone shows a particular skill or quality to the public, or the act of showing these things
그림과 같은 사물들이 대중에게 보여지는 경우, 누군가가 대중에게 특정한 기술이나 자질을 보여주는 상황, 또는 이러한 것들을 보여주는 행위

- □ **familiar** 친숙한
  → easy to recognize because of being seen, met, heard, etc. before
  이전에 보고, 만나고, 들었기 때문에 알아차리기 쉬운

- □ **include** 포함하다
  → to contain something as a part of something else, or to make something part of something else
  무언가를 다른 어떤 것의 일부로 포함하거나 어떤 것을 다른 어떤 것 의 일부로 만들다

- □ **plain** 평범한
  → not decorated in any way; with nothing added
  어떤 식으로든 장식되지 않은; 아무것도 추가하지 않은

- □ **popular** 대중적인, 인기 있는
  → liked, enjoyed, or supported by many people
  많은 사람들이 좋아하거나, 즐기거나, 지지를 하는

- □ **practice** 연습하다
  → to do or play something regularly or repeatedly in order to become skilled at it
  어떤 것에 숙련되기 위해 그것을 규칙적으로 또는 반복적으로 하거나 연주하다

- □ **traditional** 전통적인
  → following or belonging to the customs or ways of behaving that have continued in a group of people or society for a long time without changing
  오랜 시간 동안 변화 없이 한 무리의 사람들 또는 사회에서 지속되어 온 관 습이나 행동 방식을 따르거나 속해 있는

 01 문장의 빈칸에 공통으로 들어갈 말로 가장 알맞은 것은?

- College is where we learn knowledge about a specific _____.
- Students had an argument for and against a given _____.

① object
② goods
③ sculpture
④ subject
⑤ musician

서답형
02 주어진 〈영영풀이〉를 읽고 빈칸에 메을 이용하여 3 단어로 쓰시오.

Interestingly, the library will _____ _____ _____ e-books instead of paper books.

┤영영풀이├
to put a substance into an empty space

문장의 빈칸에 들어갈 말로 가장 알맞은 것은?

(A) It's _____ Athens is the birthplace of democracy!
(B) The name "Bulgaria" is _____ as the oldest country name in Europe.

	(A)	(B)
①	as well	regarded
②	as well	fascinated
③	no wonder	regarded
④	no wonder	made
⑤	no wonder	fascinated

[04~05] 다음 설명에 해당하는 단어를 고르시오.

04

following or belonging to the customs or ways of behaving that have continued in a group of people or society for a long time without changing

① traditional
② lively
③ classical
④ popular
⑤ artistic

05

not decorated in any way; with nothing added

① personal
② plain
③ proper
④ familiar
⑤ huge

서답형
다음 빈칸에 우리말에 맞게 주어진 단어를 활용하여 세 단어를 쓰시오.

이 영화는 두 번 볼 만한 가치가 있다. (watch)

➡ This movie _____ _____ _____ twice.

07 다음 짝지어진 단어의 관계가 나머지 넷과 다른 것은?

① create – produce
② lively – animated
③ common – ordinary
④ run – operate
⑤ include – exclude

01 다음 빈칸에 들어갈 말을 〈보기〉에서 찾아 쓰시오. (필요하면 어형을 변화시킬 것.)

┌─ 보기 ┤
amaze   mean   create   goods
└──────────────────

(1) Prices are marked on the _____.

(2) There is so much history and _____ behind Taegeukgi.

(3) Horses are _____ animals. They are beautiful, strong, and smart.

(4) A _____ person has the ability to come up with interesting ideas.

02 다음 문장의 빈칸에 공통으로 들어갈 단어를 쓰시오.

┌────────────────────────────┐
│ • Our luggage is brown and _____. │
│ • _____s and deserts stretched to the │
│   wooded coastal ranges and the Pacific │
│   Ocean. │
│ • They like to look at beautiful faces │
│   rather than _____ faces. │
└────────────────────────────┘

03 다음 우리말과 같은 표현이 되도록 문장의 빈칸을 채우시오.

(1) 식이 시작되기 전, 여러 가지 문화 공연과 행사들이 있었습니다.

➡ Before the ceremony began, there were many cultural _____ and events.

(2) 그 당시만 해도 사람들은 지금보다 더 친환경적이지 않았다.

➡ _____ _____ people were not as environmentally conscious as they are now.

(3) 아이들은 컴퓨터가 있다면 선생님의 말에 귀를 기울이지 않을 것입니다.

➡ Kids will not _____ _____ _____ the teacher if they have a computer.

(4) 플라스틱 분자는 길고 단단한 탄소 골격으로 이루어져 있기 때문에 플라스틱 제품들은 시간이 지나도 쉽게 분해되지 않습니다.

➡ Plastic products don't _____ _____ easily over time because plastic molecules consist of long, sturdy carbon chains.

04 영영풀이에 해당하는 단어를 〈보기〉에서 찾아 첫 번째 빈칸에 쓰고, 두 번째 빈칸에는 우리말 뜻을 쓰시오.

┌─ 보기 ┤
cone   practice   include   boring
└──────────────────

(1) _____: not interesting or exciting: _____

(2) _____: to do or play something regularly or repeatedly in order to become skilled at it: _____

(3) _____: a shape with a flat, round or oval base and a top that becomes narrower until it forms a point: _____

Conversation

1 관심 표현하기

> **I was fascinated by the colors in his paintings and his creativity.** 나는 그의 작품에서 보이는 색감과 그의 창의성에 매료되었다.

- 'be fascinated by'는 '~에 매료되다'라는 의미로 어떤 것에 대해 깊은 관심이 있음을 나타낸다. by는 전치사이므로 뒤에 명사(구)나 동명사가 온다.

- 관심을 나타내는 다른 표현들
  상대방의 말에 관심을 나타낼 때 사용하는 표현으로는 'That interests me a lot.'이라고 표현한다. 이 표현은 '그것 참 재미있네요.' 또는 '그것 참 흥미롭네요.' 정도로 해석할 수 있다. 또는 I'm interested in ~.(나는 ~에 관심이 있다.) / I have an interest in ~.(나는 ~에 관심을 가지고 있다.) / I'm into ~.(나는 ~에 관심이 많다.) 등으로 나타낼 수 있다.
  - I'm fascinated by Korean traditional houses. 나는 한국의 전통 가옥에 매료되었다.
  - I'm into hip hop music. 나는 힙합 음악에 관심이 있다.
  - **A:** I'm really fascinated by musicals these days. 나는 요즘 뮤지컬에 정말 매료되었어.
    B: Are you sure? I have two tickets for the musical "*Cats*." 정말? 나에게 뮤지컬 'Cats' 표 두 장이 있어.
  - I am interested in K-pop. 저는 K-pop에 관심이 있습니다.
    = I have an interest in K-pop.
    = I am fascinated by K-pop.
    = I'm into K-pop.

핵심 Check

1. 다음 대화의 빈칸에 들어가기에 <u>어색한</u> 말은?

   > **A:** What movie do you like?
   > **B:** I like *Fly to the Moon*.
   > **A:** Why do you like it?
   > **B:** _____

   ① I'm fascinated by its special effects.
   ② Yes. I read it in an article.
   ③ I'm into its story.
   ④ I'm interested in its scenes.
   ⑤ I have an interest in its characters.

2 만족이나 불만족에 대해 묻기

How do you like this T-shirt? 이 티셔츠 어때?

- How do you like ~?'는 어떤 것에 대해 만족하는지 아니면 불만족하는지 묻는 표현이다.
  만족이나 불만족에 대해 묻는 표현으로 'Is this what you wanted?'나 'Do you like it?' 등으로 물을 수 있다.
  - **A:** Is this what you wanted? 이것 마음에 드시나요?
    B: Oh, no! That's not it at all. 오, 세상에! 그건 아니잖아요.
  - **A:** How do you like your new phone, Sejin? 세진아, 새로 산 네 전화기 어떠니?
    B: I love it. 정말 좋아.

- 만족이나 불만족을 나타내는 추가 표현
  - Are you satisfied with this T-shirt?
  - Are you happy with this T-shirt?
  - Is this T-shirt what you want(ed)/have[had] in mind?

- 만족 표현하기
  - Good! / Fine! / Excellent! 좋아! / 훌륭해!
  - I'm (very) satisfied. 나는 매우 만족해.
  - That'll do. 그거면 충분해.
- 불만족 표현하기
  - I'm not satisfied/happy (with ~). 나는 (~에) 만족하지 않아.
  - That won't do[work]. 그건 효과가 없을 거야.

핵심 Check

2. 다음 빈칸에 들어갈 말로 알맞은 것은?

> **A:** _____ this backpack?
> **B:** I like it. It's useful.

① Why do you like   ② When did you buy
③ Where did you get   ④ Do you have
⑤ How do you like

Listen & Speak 1 A-1

> B: Sandy, you can listen to ❶many kinds of music in this music library.
>
> G: That's cool, Bob. Can I listen to classical music?
>
> B: Sure. Do you like classical music?
>
> G: Yes, Beethoven is ❷one of my favorite musicians. How about you?
>
> B: ❸I like pop music more than classical music.
>
> G: I see. What do you like most about pop music?
>
> B: ❹I'm really fascinated by its exciting rhythms.

> B: Sandy, 너는 이 음악 도서관에서 많은 종류의 음악을 들을 수 있어.
>
> G: 그거 멋지다, Bob. 클래식 음악도 들을 수 있어?
>
> B: 물론이지. 너 클래식 음악 좋아하니?
>
> G: 응. 베토벤이 내가 가장 좋아하는 음악가 중의 하나야. 너는 어때?
>
> B: 나는 클래식보다는 대중음악이 더 좋아.
>
> G: 그렇구나. 너는 대중음악의 어떤 점이 가장 마음에 들어?
>
> B: 나는 대중음악의 신나는 리듬이 정말 좋아.

❶ 'many+복수 명사(kinds)'로 '많은 종류'라는 의미이다.
❷ 'one of the+복수명사' 형태로 '~ 중 하나'로 해석한다.
❸ '비교급 than' 구문으로 'I prefer pop music to classical music.'으로 바꾸어 쓸 수 있다. 'prefer A to B'는 'B보다 A를 더 좋아하다'라는 의미이다.
❹ 'be fascinated by'는 '~에 매료되다'라는 의미로 어떤 것에 대해 깊은 관심이 있음을 나타낸다. by는 전치사이므로 뒤에 명사(구)나 동명사가 온다.

Check(√) True or False

(1) Sandy likes classical music. T ☐ F ☐

(2) Bob prefers classical music to pop music. T ☐ F ☐

 Listen & Speak 2 A-1

> B: The other day I watched a play, *A Love Story in the War*.
>
> G: Oh, ❶how did you like the play?
>
> B: I liked the main characters. The actors' performances were fantastic.
>
> G: Was the story good ❷as well?
>
> B: No. It was a little boring, but the music was pretty good.
>
> G: So, do you think I should see it?
>
> B: ❸Only if you have a lot of time and money.

> B: 며칠 전에 '전쟁 속의 사랑 이야기'라는 연극을 봤어.
>
> G: 오, 그 연극 어땠어?
>
> B: 주인공들이 좋았어. 배우들의 연기가 끝내줬거든.
>
> G: 이야기도 좋았어?
>
> B: 아니. 이야기는 조금 지루했는데, 음악은 꽤 괜찮았어.
>
> G: 그럼, 너는 내가 그 연극을 보아야 한다고 생각하니?
>
> B: 네가 돈과 시간이 많을 경우에만.

❶ 'How do you like ~?'는 어떤 것에 대해 만족하는지 아니면 불만족하는지 묻는 표현이다. 'Is this what you wanted?'나 'Do you like it?' 등으로 물을 수 있다.
❷ 'as well'은 문장 끝에서 '또한'의 의미로 사용된다.
❸ 'only if+주어+동사 ~'는 어떤 일이 가능한 유일한 상황을 진술할 때 사용하는 표현으로 '~해야만'의 의미를 갖고 있다.

Check(√) True or False

(3) The boy was satisfied with the story of the play. T ☐ F ☐

(4) The girl will see the play if she has much time and money. T ☐ F ☐

Listen & Speak 1 A-2

G: Jim, did you finish your art homework?

B: Yes. I drew the face of my role model on a plate.

G: ❶Sounds interesting. Who is your role model?

B: My dad. He always ❷gives me good advice. Who did you draw, Amy?

G: Well, I drew myself surfing in the sea.

B: Wonderful! ❸I'm fascinated by your drawing.

G: Thank you.

❶ 'sound+형용사': '~하게 들리다'의 의미이다.
❷ 4형식 문장으로 '~에게(간접목적어) …을(직접목적어) 주다'로 해석한다.
❸ 관심을 나타낼 때 사용하는 표현으로 'I'm interested in your drawing.', 'I'm into your drawing.' 등으로 쓸 수 있다.

 Listen & Speak 2 A-2

B: Claire, ❶how do you like your art class?

G: It's great. I learn a lot in the class.

B: What do you like most about it?

G: I ❷enjoy learning different drawing skills. What about you, Allen?

B: I also like the class. I learn good painting skills. I love painting with many colors.

G: Oh, I saw your work last time. I thought it was very creative.

B: Thanks. I practice a lot.

❶ 'How do you like ~?'는 어떤 것에 대해 만족하는지 아니면 불만족하는지 묻는 표현으로, 'Are you satisfied with your art class?', 'Are you happy with your art class?' 등으로 바꾸어 쓸 수 있다.
❷ 동사 'enjoy'는 동명사를 목적어로 취하는 동사로 'learning' 형태가 온다.

 Real Life Talk

Bora: Andy, ❶you went to the art museum, didn't you?

Andy: Yes. They had a special Chagall exhibition.

Bora: How did you like it?

Andy: It was fantastic! ❷I was fascinated by the colors in his paintings and his creativity.

Bora: No wonder. He was ❸one of the greatest painters ever. What else did you see in the museum?

Andy: I went to a gift shop and saw things like umbrellas, cups, and backpacks. Famous works of art were printed on them.

Bora: Did you buy anything?

Andy: Yes. I bought this T-shirt. How do you like it?

Bora: ❹It looks great on you.

Andy: Thank you.

❶ 사실을 확인하는 표현으로 'didn't you?'는 부가의문문으로 '그렇지 않니?'라고 해석한다.
❷ 상대방의 말에 관심을 나타낼 때 사용하는 표현으로는 'The colors in his paintings and his creativity interested me a lot.'으로 바꾸어 표현할 수 있다.
❸ 'one of the+최상급+복수명사' 형태로 '가장 ~한 것 중 하나'로 해석한다.
❹ '너에게 매우 잘 어울려.'라는 의미로 전치사 'on'은 '착용'의 의미가 있다.

 Wrap Up 1

B: Cindy, you went to the music festival, didn't you?

G: Yes. A lot of famous musicians performed there.

B: How did you like the festival?

G: It was fantastic! I really liked the special guest. Do you know the band ❶called *the Brothers*?

B: Oh, I've heard about them. The singer is famous.

G: Yes. His performance was great.

B: ❷No wonder.

❶ 'called'는 '~라 불리는'의 수동 의미를 가지는 과거분사이다.
❷ 'No wonder.'는 '당연해. 놀랄 일도 아니야'라는 의미를 가지고 있다.

● 다음 우리말과 일치하도록 빈칸에 알맞은 말을 쓰시오.

Listen & Speak 1 A

1. B: Sandy, you can _____ _____ many _____ of music in this _____ _____.

   G: That's _____, Bob. Can I listen to _____ music?

   B: _____. Do you like classical music?

   G: Yes, Beethoven is _____ _____ _____ _____ _____. How about you?

   B: I like pop music _____ _____ classical music.

   G: I see. _____ _____ _____ _____ most about pop music?

   B: I'm really _____ by its _____ rhythms.

2. G: Jim, did you _____ your art homework?

   B: Yes. I _____ the face of my role model on a _____.

   G: _____ _____. Who is your role model?

   B: My dad. He always gives me good _____. Who did you draw, Amy?

   G: Well, I drew _____ _____ in the sea.

   B: Wonderful! I'm _____ _____ your drawing.

   G: Thank you.

Listen & Speak 2 A

1. B: _____ _____ _____ _____ I watched a _____, *A Love Story in the War*.

   G: Oh, _____ _____ _____ _____ the play?

   B: I liked the _____ _____. The actors' _____ were _____.

   G: Was the story good _____ _____?

   B: No. It was _____ _____ _____, but the music was pretty good.

   G: So, do you think I _____ _____ it?

   B: _____ _____ you have _____ _____ _____ time and money.

2. **B:** Caire, _____ _____ _____ your art class?

   G: It's great. I learn _____ _____ in the class.

   B: _____ _____ _____ _____ about it?

   G: I enjoy _____ _____ _____ _____. _____ about you, Allen?

   B: I also like the class. I learn good _____ _____. I love painting _____ many colors.

   G: Oh, I saw your _____ last time. I thought it was very _____.

   B: Thanks. I _____ _____ _____.

2. **B:** Claire, 미술 수업 어때?
   G: 훌륭해. 나는 그 수업에서 많은 것을 배워.
   B: 배우는 것 중에 어떤 것이 가장 좋아?
   G: 다양한 그림 기술 배우는 것이 재미있어. 너는 어때, Allen?
   B: 나도 미술 수업이 좋아. 괜찮은 색칠하기 기술들을 배우잖아. 나는 다양한 색깔을 사용해서 그림 그리는 것이 정말 좋아.
   G: 오, 지난번에 네 작품을 봤어. 나는 그게 굉장히 창의적이라고 생각했어.
   B: 고마워. 연습을 많이 했거든.

Real Life Talk

Bora: Andy, you went to the art museum, _____ _____?

Andy: Yes. They had a _____ Chagall exhibition.

Bora: _____ _____ _____ _____ it?

Andy: It was _____! I _____ _____ _____ the colors in his paintings and his _____.

Bora: _____ _____. He was _____ _____ _____ _____ _____ ever. _____ _____ did you see in the museum?

Andy: I went to _____ _____ _____ and saw things like umbrellas, cups, and backpacks. Famous works of art _____ _____ on them.

Bora: Did you buy _____?

Andy: Yes. I bought this T-shirt. _____ _____ _____ _____ it?

Bora: It _____ _____ _____ you.

Andy: Thank you.

보라: Andy야, 너 미술관에 갔었지, 그렇지 않니?
Andy: 응. 샤갈 특별 전시회가 있었어.
보라: 그거 어땠니?
Andy: 멋졌어! 나는 그의 그림에 쓰인 색깔과 그의 창의성에 매료됐어.
보라: 당연해. 그는 가장 위대한 화가 중 한 명이었잖아. 너는 미술관에서 또 무엇을 봤니?
Andy: 기념품점에 갔었는데 우산, 컵, 가방 같은 것들을 봤어. 유명 예술 작품들이 그것들에 그려져 있었어.
보라: 구입한 게 있니?
Andy: 응. 나 이 티셔츠 샀어. 어때?
보라: 네게 잘 어울린다.
Andy: 고마워.

Wrap Up 1

B: Cindy, you went to the music _____, _____ you?

G: Yes. A lot of famous musicians _____ there.

B: _____ _____ _____ _____ the festival?

G: It was fantastic! I really liked the _____ _____. Do you know the band _____ _the Brothers_?

B: Oh, I've _____ about them. The singer is famous.

G: Yes. His _____ was great.

B: _____ _____.

B: Cindy, 너 음악 축제에 갔었지, 그렇지 않니?
G: 응. 많은 유명 가수들이 거기서 공연을 했어.
B: 그 축제는 어땠어?
G: 아주 환상적이었어. 나는 특별 손님이 정말 좋았어. 너 '더 브라더스'라고 불리는 밴드를 아니?
B: 오, 들어본 적이 있어. 가수가 유명하잖아.
G: 맞아. 그의 공연은 굉장했어.
B: 놀랄 일도 아니지.

01 우리말에 맞도록 주어진 단어들을 이용하여 문장의 빈칸에 알맞은 말을 쓰시오.

이 재킷 어때? (how, do)

➡ _____ this jacket?

02 다음 대화의 빈칸에 들어갈 말로 알맞지 <u>않은</u> 것은?

A: What movie do you like?
B: I like *World Z.*
A: Why do you like it?
B: _____ its characters.

① I'm fascinated by　　② I'm into
③ I'm interested in　　④ I'm very satisfied
⑤ I have an interest in

03 다음 대화의 빈칸에 들어갈 말로 알맞은 표현은?

B: Cindy, you went to the music festival, didn't you?
G: Yes. A lot of famous musicians performed there.
B: _____
G: It was fantastic! I really liked the special guest.

① What about you?
② Which do you prefer, the music festival or the Chagall exhibition?
③ How did you like the festival?
④ Who is the special guest?
⑤ How do you like this song?

다음 대화의 밑줄 친 말의 의도로 알맞은 것은?

A: <u>How do you like these shoes?</u>
B: I like them. They are colorful.

① 권유하기　　　② 만족이나 불만족에 대해 묻기
③ 관심 표현하기　④ 제안하기
⑤ 안부 묻기

[01~02] 다음 대화를 읽고 물음에 답하시오.

> **Bora:** Andy, you went to the art museum, didn't you?
>
> **Andy:** Yes. They had a special Chagall exhibition.
>
> **Bora:** (A)_____
>
> **Andy:** It was fantastic! I was fascinated by the colors in his paintings and his creativity.
>
> **Bora:** No wonder. He was one of the greatest painters ever. What else did you see in the museum?
>
> **Andy:** I went to a gift shop and saw things like umbrellas, cups, and backpacks. Famous works of art were printed on them.
>
> **Bora:** Did you buy anything?
>
> **Andy:** Yes. I bought this T-shirt. How do you like it?
>
> **Bora:** It looks great on you.
>
> **Andy:** Thank you.

위 대화의 빈칸 (A)에 들어갈 말로 알맞은 것을 <u>모두</u> 고르시오.

① What are you interested in?
② Were you satisfied with it?
③ Why did you like it?
④ How did you like it?
⑤ Do you mind going to the art museum with me?

 위 대화의 내용과 일치하지 <u>않는</u> 것은?

① Andy went to the art museum with Bora.
② Andy was fascinated by the colors in Chagall's paintings and his creativity.
③ Andy bought a T-shirt at a gift shop.
④ Famous works of art were printed on things.
⑤ Chagall was one of the greatest painters ever.

 다음 대화의 (A)~(D)를 알맞은 순서로 배열한 것은?

> **B:** The other day I watched a play, *A Love Story in the War.*

> (A) Was the story good as well?
> (B) No. It was a little boring, but the music was pretty good.
> (C) Oh, how did you like the play?
> (D) I liked the main characters. The actors' performances were fantastic.

> **G:** So, do you think I should see it?
> **B:** Only if you have a lot of time and money.

① (A) – (C) – (B) – (D)
② (B) – (A) – (D) – (C)
③ (C) – (B) – (A) – (D)
④ (C) – (D) – (A) – (B)
⑤ (D) – (C) – (A) – (B)

04 다음 대화의 빈칸에 들어갈 말로 가장 알맞은 것은?

> **A:** How do you like this song?
> **B:** I love it. It sounds exciting.
> **A:** Yes, but I prefer this one, *The Phantom of the Opera.* _____
> **B:** I like it, too.

① I'm fascinated by your drawing.
② I'm fascinated by its rhythms and melody.
③ Are you happy with this T-shirt?
④ I liked the story of the movie.
⑤ I'm interested in its special effects.

[05~06] 다음 대화를 읽고 물음에 답하시오.

> B: Sandy, you can listen to many (a)kinds of music in this music library.
> G: That's cool, Bob. Can I listen to classical music?
> B: Sure. Do you like classical music?
> G: Yes, Beethoven is one of my favorite (b) musician. How about you?
> B: I like pop music (c)more than classical music.
> G: I see. What do you like most about pop music?
> B: I'm really (d)fascinated by its (e)exciting rhythms.

 서답형

05 위 대화를 읽고 다음 물음에 영어로 답하시오.

> Q: What kind of music does Sandy like? (4 단어로 답하시오.)

➡ _____

06 위 대화의 밑줄 친 (a)~(e) 중 어법상 어색한 것은?

① (a) ② (b) ③ (c) ④ (d) ⑤ (e)

중요

07 다음 두 사람의 대화가 어색한 것은?

① A: Why do you like the play?
   B: I'm fascinated by its characters.
② A: How do you like this song?
   B: I love it. It sounds exciting.
③ A: What do you want to make with these paper cups?
   B: I think we can make one of the world-famous bridges using paper cups.
④ A: How did you like the festival?
   B: Oh, I've heard about it. The singer is famous.
⑤ A: I bought this pencil case yesterday. How do you like it?
   B: It looks great. I like it.

[08~09] 다음 대화를 읽고 물음에 답하시오.

> B: Claire, (A)_____
> G: It's great. I learn a lot in the class.
> B: What do you like most about it?
> G: I enjoy learning different drawing skills. What about you, Allen?
> B: I also like the class. I learn good painting skills. I love painting with many colors.
> G: Oh, I saw your work last time. I thought it was very creative.
> B: Thanks. I practice a lot.

서답형

08 위 대화의 빈칸 (A)에 알맞은 말을 주어진 〈조건〉에 맞게 쓰시오. (단어 하나를 추가할 것.)

> ┌─ 조건 ┐
> • 어떤 것에 대해 만족하는지 아니면 불만족하는지 묻는 표현을 쓸 것.
> • you / like / your / do / ? / art class

➡ _____

서답형

09 위 대화를 읽고 다음 물음에 영어로 답하시오.

> Q: What did Claire think about Allen's work?

➡ _____

서답형

10 다음 글의 빈칸에 들어갈 말을 주어진 〈조건〉에 맞게 영작하시오.

> Our group liked the umbrella designed by Jinsu. He used the painting, *On White II*. We _____ its design. How do you like this umbrella?

> ┌─ 조건 ┐
> • 관심을 표현하는 문장을 쓸 것.
> • fascinate를 활용할 것.
> • 시제 일치를 맞출 것.

01 다음 대화를 읽고 밑줄 친 (A)를 구체적인 단어로 바꾸어 질문에 영어로 답하시오.

> G: Jim, did you finish your art homework?
> B: Yes. I drew the face of (A)my role model on a plate.
> G: Sounds interesting. Who is your role model?
> B: My dad. He always gives me good advice. Who did you draw, Amy?
> G: Well, I drew myself surfing in the sea.
> B: Wonderful! I'm fascinated by your drawing.
> G: Thank you.

> Q: What did Jim draw for his art homework?

➡ _____

[02~03] 다음 대화를 읽고 물음에 답하시오.

> Bora: Andy, you went to the art museum, didn't you?
> Andy: Yes. They had a special Chagall exhibition.
> Bora: (A)_____
> Andy: It was fantastic! I was fascinated by the colors in his paintings and his creativity.
> Bora: No wonder. He was one of the greatest painters ever. What else did you see in the museum?
> Andy: I went to a gift shop and saw things like umbrellas, cups, and backpacks. Famous works of art were printed on them.
> Bora: Did you buy anything?
> Andy: Yes. I bought this T-shirt. How do you like it?
> Bora: It looks great on you.

02 위 대화의 빈칸 (A)에 알맞은 말을 주어진 〈조건〉에 맞게 영어로 쓰시오.

┌─── 조건 ───┐
'how'와 대명사 'it'을 사용할 것

➡ _____

03 위 대화를 읽고 다음 질문에 대한 답을 본문에 있는 문장을 그대로 사용하여 3 단어로 쓰시오.

> Q: How did Andy like the Chagall exhibition?

➡ _____

[04~05] 다음 대화를 읽고 물음에 답하시오.

> B: The other day I watched a play, *A Love Story in the War*.
> G: Oh, how did you like the play?
> B: I liked the main characters. The actors' performances were fantastic.
> G: Was the story good as well?
> B: No. It was a little boring, but the music was pretty good.
> G: So, do you think I should see it?
> B: 네가 돈과 시간이 많을 경우에만. (only / a lot of)

04 위 대화의 밑줄 친 우리말에 맞게 주어진 단어를 이용하여 쓰시오.

➡ _____

05 다음 질문에 영어로 답하시오.

> Q: What is the title of the play the boy watched?

➡ _____

Grammar

1 분사구문

> - **Using** common images, pop art looks plain. 흔한 이미지를 사용하기 때문에 팝 아트는 평범해 보인다.
> - I did my math homework, **listening** to classical music. 나는 클래식 음악을 들으며, 수학 숙제를 했다.

■ 분사구문은 종속접속사가 이끄는 부사절을 분사를 이용하여 간략한 부사구로 바꾼 것이다.

- **When I arrived** home, I saw my sister crying.
  = **Arriving** home, I saw my sister crying. 집에 도착했을 때, 나는 내 여동생이 울고 있는 것을 보았다.

■ 부사구와 주절의 관계에 따라 양보, 동시동작, 이유, 시간, 조건 등의 의미로 쓰인다.

(1) 양보: **Although he is** short, the player always scored best in the game.
  = **Being** short, the player always scored best in the game. 키가 작지만, 그 선수는 항상 경기에서 최고 득점을 했다.
(2) 동시동작(부대상황): **While she ate** her sandwich, she walked to work.
  = **Eating** her sandwich, she walked to work. 샌드위치를 먹으며, 그녀는 직장으로 걸었다.
(3) 이유: **Because I felt** satisfied with the machine, I ordered another one online.
  = **Feeling** satisfied with the machine, I ordered another one online. 그 기계에 만족해서, 나는 인터넷으로 또 한 대를 주문했다.
(4) 시간: **When she cleans** the room, she uses the special tools.
  = **Cleaning** the room, she uses the special tools. 청소할 때, 그녀는 특별 도구를 쓴다.
(5) 조건: **If you turn** left, you'll see the city hall.
  = **Turning** left, you'll see the city hall. 좌회전하면, 시청이 보일 것이다.

■ 종속절의 시제가 주절보다 앞선 경우, 완료분사구문을 사용한다.

- **As she had watched** the film before, Susan knew the complex relationships.
  = **Having watched** the film before, (그 영화를 전에 봤기 때문에 Susan은 그 복잡한 관계를 알았다.)

■ 주절과 종속절의 주어가 다를 경우, 분사구문의 주어를 남겨 두는 것을 독립분사구문이라고 하며, 일반 인이 주어일 경우에는 생략이 가능하다. (비인칭 독립분사구문)

(1) 독립분사구문: **Since it is rainy**, we can't play baseball.
  = **It being** rainy, we can't play baseball. 비가 와서, 우리는 야구를 할 수 없다.
(2) 비인칭 독립분사구문: **generally speaking**(일반적으로 말해), **considering** ~(~를 고려하면)
(3) with+목적어+분사: The dog fell asleep **with its eyes closed**. (그 개는 눈을 감은 채로 잠이 들어 있었다.)

핵심 Check

1. 괄호 안에서 알맞은 말을 고르시오.
   (1) (Feeling / Felt) tired, the old man took a rest under the tree.
   (2) It (is / being) so snowy, the road got blocked with snow.

② be동사+worth+동명사

- Pop art **is worth paying** attention to. 팝 아트는 주목할 가치가 있다.
- Books about world history **are worth reading**. 세계사에 관한 책은 읽을 가치가 있다.

■ 'be동사+worth+동명사'는 동명사의 관용 표현으로 '~할 가치가 있다'는 뜻이다.
  - The East Sea **is worth going** to. 동해는 가 볼 만한 가치가 있다.

■ worth의 의미
  (1) 명사: '가치'
  - You don't know the true **worth** of the book. 너는 그 책의 진정한 가치를 모른다.
  (2) 형용사: '가치 있는, ~의 가치가 있는' (= worthy of)
  - These books are **worth** 1,000 dollars. 이 책들은 1,000달러의 가치가 있다.
  - These books are **worth** buying. 이 책들은 구매할 가치가 있다. 〈동명사 목적어〉

■ 의미는 '수동'이지만, '능동' 동명사를 쓴다.
  - The book **is worth** [**reading** / being read(×)]. 그 책은 읽을 가치가 있다.
  - The project **was worth** [**working** / being worked(×)] on. 그 프로젝트는 진행할 가치가 있었다.
  - The movie **is worth watching**. 그 영화는 볼 만한 가치가 있다.
    = **It** is **worth watching** the movie. → 동명사만 가능(능동)
    = The movie is **worthy of watching[being watched]**. → 동명사만 (수동형이 일반적)
    = The movie is **worthy to watch[to be watched]**. → to부정사 (to be p.p.가 자주 쓰임)
    = It is **worthwhile[worth while] watching[to watch]** the movie. → 둘 다 가능
    = It is **worth your while to watch** the movie. → to부정사만 가능(능동형만)

■ 그밖의 동명사의 관용적 표현들
  (1) can't help V-ing = can't but V '~하지 않을 수 없다'
  - I **couldn't help laughing** when I saw him. 그를 봤을 때, 웃지 않을 수 없었다.
  (2) spend 시간/돈 V-ing '~하느라 시간/돈을 쓰다'
  - He **spent her whole weekend watching** dramas. 그는 드라마를 보느라 주말을 다 썼다.
  (3) be busy V-ing '~하느라 바쁘다'
  - The teacher **is busy checking** my homework. 선생님은 내 숙제 검사를 하시느라 바쁘다.
  (4) feel like V-ing = feel inclined to V '~하고 싶다'
  - She **felt like eating** pizza. 그녀는 피자를 먹고 싶었다.
  (5) There is no V-ing = It is impossible to V '~하는 것은 불가능하다'
  - **There is no knowing** what will happen tomorrow. 내일 무슨 일이 일어날지 알 수 없다.
  (6) It is no use V-ing = It is useless[of no use] to V '~하는 것은 소용없다'
  - **It is no use waiting** for her there. 거기에서 그녀를 기다려 봐야 소용없다.

핵심 Check

2. 괄호 안에서 알맞은 말을 고르시오.

(1) The fish were worth (catching / being catched).

(2) It is worth (to read / reading) the science paper.

Grammar 시험대비 기본평가

01 다음 부사절을 분사구문으로 바꿔 쓸 때, 빈칸에 들어갈 말로 가장 적절한 것은?

When Tom arrived home, he saw his sister reading a book.
→ _____ home, Tom saw his sister reading a book.

① As Tom arriving
② Tom arriving
③ Being arrived
④ Being arriving
⑤ Arriving

02 다음 우리말을 바르게 영작한 것을 고르시오.

샌프란시스코는 두 번 방문할 가치가 있었다.

① San Francisco was worthwhile visited twice.
② San Francisco was worth to be visited twice.
③ San Francisco was worth to visit twice.
④ San Francisco was worth visiting twice.
⑤ It was worth to visiting San Francisco twice.

03 다음 두 문장을 한 문장으로 바르게 연결한 것을 고르시오.

• Billy watched the emotional scenes.
• She was moved.

① Watched the emotional scenes, Billy was moved.
② Watching the emotional scenes, Billy was moved.
③ Being watched the emotional scenes, Billy was moved.
④ While she watching the emotional scenes, Billy was moved.
⑤ Though watching the emotional scenes, Billy was moved.

04 다음 괄호 속 동사의 알맞은 형태를 빈칸에 써 넣으시오.

(1) The project was worth _____(work) on because I could experience many things.
(2) Pop art is worth _____. (pay attention to)
(3) It is no use _____(cry) over poor grades.

[01~02] 다음 중 어법상 알맞은 문장을 고르시오.

01
① Pop artists and their works are worth to be paid attention.
② Pop artists and their works have worth paying attention to.
③ Pop artists and their works are worthy being paid attention to.
④ Pop artists and their works are worth being paid attention to.
⑤ Pop artists and their works are worth paying attention to.

02
① I couldn't help falling in love with the beautiful song.
② I couldn't but falling in love with the beautiful song.
③ I couldn't help but falling in love with the beautiful song.
④ I couldn't but help falling in love with the beautiful song.
⑤ I couldn't help to falling in love with the beautiful song.

[03~04] 다음 주어진 우리말을 알맞게 영작한 것을 고르시오.

미술 전시회에서 친숙한 이미지들을 봤을 때 사람들은 그것들이 신선하다는 걸 알게 되었다.

① Seen familiar images in art exhibitions, people found them refreshing.
② Seeing familiar images in art exhibitions, people found them refreshing.
③ Being seen familiar images in art exhibitions, people found them refreshing.
④ When people seeing familiar images in art exhibitions, they found them refreshing.
⑤ Having seen familiar images in art exhibitions, people found them refreshing.

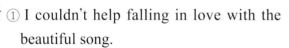
04
팝 아트가 평범해 보일지라도, 그것은 의미로 가득 차 있다.

① Pop art looking plain, it is filled with meaning.
② Being looked plain, pop art is filled with meaning.
③ Although pop art looking plain, it is filled with meaning.
④ Although looking plain, pop art is filled with meaning.
⑤ Although looked plain, pop art is filled with meaning.

05 다음 빈칸에 공통으로 들어갈 알맞은 말을 고르시오.

(1) Books about world history and culture development are _____ reading.
(2) The house must be _____ at least half a million dollars.

① value ② worth ③ price
④ expensive ⑤ cost

06 다음 문장에서 어법상 <u>어색한</u> 단어 한 개를 찾아서 고치시오.

Changed common objects into amazing art, the pop artists are creating the works of art for everyone in the world.

➡ _____

07 다음 밑줄 친 단어의 성격이 나머지 넷과 <u>다른</u> 하나를 고르시오.

① Those books written by the author are not worth <u>knowing</u>.
② There is no <u>knowing</u> what our lives in the future would be like.
③ Brian gave up the plan, <u>knowing</u> his friends were not going to join it.
④ We can't help <u>knowing</u> her since few Koreans live around here.
⑤ It was no use <u>knowing</u> that her problem came from anxiety

08 다음 밑줄 친 분사구문을 같은 의미의 부사절로 바꿔 쓸 때 적절하지 <u>않은</u> 것은?

① <u>Making a lot of copies</u>, Andy wanted to share arts with many people.
 → When he made a lot of copies,
② <u>Playing drums</u>, the member of the band sang the song.
 → While he was playing drums,
③ <u>Using common objects</u>, pop art looks plain.
 → Though they use common objects,
④ <u>Taking a shower</u>, Mr. Smith didn't receive the phone call.
 → As he was taking a shower,

⑤ <u>Cartoons not being regarded as an art form</u>, Roy Lichtenstein thought differently.
 → Though cartoons were not regarded as an art form,

09 다음 주어진 문장과 가장 가까운 의미의 문장으로 어법상 알맞은 것을 고르시오.

It is worth seeing and collecting the works of many pop artists .

① The works of many pop artists are worth to see and collect.
② The works of many pop artists are worth being seen and collected.
③ The works of many pop artists are worth seeing and collecting.
④ The works of many pop artists are worth to be seen and collected.
⑤ The works of many pop artists are worth for seeing and collecting.

10 다음 중 밑줄 친 분사구문의 용법이 〈보기〉와 같은 것은?

┌ 보기 ┐
Looking a little plain and common, pop art is filled with a lot of meaning.
└─────┘

① <u>Turning left at the next corner</u>, you can face the shopping mall.
② <u>Having lived in Madrid for 11 years</u>, Angella still can't speak Spanish well.
③ <u>Being honest</u>, Jack is trusted by everyone.
④ <u>Completing her team project</u>, Alice went out to have some snacks.
⑤ <u>Not knowing how rich David was</u>, Railey was surprised at his luxury car.

서답형

[11~12] 우리말과 일치하도록 괄호 안에 주어진 단어들을 바르게 배열하되, 한 단어만 어법에 맞게 형태를 바꾸시오.

11

그 당시에, 만화는 예술의 형태로 간주되지 않았지만, Roy Lichtenstein은 다르게 생각했다.
→ (regard, cartoons, an art form, being, as, not, at that time), Roy Lichtenstein thought differently.

➡ _____

_____, Roy Lichtenstein thought differently.

12

모든 사람들이 그의 예술을 즐기기를 원해서, Oldenburg는 자신의 작품들을 옥외에 설치했다.
→ (everyone, to, his, want, art, enjoy), Oldenburg set up his works in outdoor places.

➡ _____,

Oldenburg set up his works in outdoor places.

[13~14] 다음 중 어법상 <u>어색한</u> 것을 고르시오.

13 ① Pop art is worth paying attention.
② The city is worth visiting.
③ The idea was worth considering.
④ The works of pop artists were worth looking at.
⑤ The medicine was worth taking.

14 ① Sean couldn't help falling in love with the girl he met yesterday.
② She felt like sleeping after swimming.
③ Mom spent all the money buying the jacket.
④ It is of no use crying over spilt milk.
⑤ Dad is busy preparing for the party.

[15~16] 다음의 같은 의미를 표현하는 문장들 중에서 어법 또는 의미상 <u>틀린</u> 것은?

15 ① The bag made by the great craftsman is worth buying immediately.
② The bag made by the great craftsman is worthy of buying immediately.
③ The bag made by the great craftsman is worth to be bought immediately.
④ It is worth buying the bag immediately made by the great craftsman.
⑤ The bag made by the great craftsman is worth while buying immediately.

16 ① It is worth reading what my favorite poet writes three times.
② It is worth while to read what my favorite poet writes three times.
③ What is written by my favorite poet is worth reading three times.
④ What my favorite poet writes is worth while to read three times.
⑤ My favorite poem is worth being read three times.

Grammar **135**

01 다음 문장의 괄호 안의 단어를 어법상 알맞은 형태로 바꿔 빈칸에 쓰시오.

(1) A lot of small towns in the area are definitely worth _____ (visit).

(2) It's worth _____ (check) the details of the contract before you sign it.

(3) The film is worth _____ (see).

(4) It's not worth _____ (buy) a new phone as the one you have is just fine.

(5) Sammy couldn't help _____ (laugh) at my face.

(6) Sammy couldn't but _____ (laugh) at my face.

(7) Sammy couldn't help but _____ (laugh) when she saw my face.

(8) Sammy had no choice but _____ (laugh) when she saw my face.

(9) The cosmetic company spent 12 million dollars _____ (advertise) its new product.

(10) There is no _____ (know) what my teacher is thinking.

(11) It is impossible _____ (know) what my teacher is thinking.

(12) The ants were busy _____ (carry) food to their hill to store for the winter.

(13) It is of no use to _____ (prepare) for the final exam.

(14) It is no use _____ (prepare) for the final exam.

02 다음 우리말과 일치하도록 괄호 안에 주어진 단어들을 바르게 배열하여 빈칸에 넣으시오.

(1) 평범한 사물을 놀라운 예술로 변모시킬 수 있게 되면서 팝 아티스트들은 예술에 대한 고정관념을 바꿔왔다. (turn, amazing, to, being, common, art, into, able, objects)

➡ _____

_____, pop artists have changed the stereotype of the art.

(2) 팝 아티스트들은 예술이 쉬워야 한다고 믿었기 때문에, 고급 예술과 대중문화 사이의 벽을 허물었다. (art, artists, that, should, believing, be, pop, broke, easy)

➡ _____

_____ the wall between high art and popular culture.

(3) 여기 주변에 남은 친구들이 없었기 때문에, 그 개는 외로움을 느꼈다. (friends, around, there, any, here, not, being, left)

➡ _____,

the dog felt lonely.

(4) 잡지와 상점에서 그의 주제를 찾으면서, Andy Warhol은 팝 아트 작품들을 만들었다. (magazines, stores, subjects, finding, in, his, and)

➡ _____,

Andy Warhol made a lot of pop art works.

03 다음 〈보기〉와 같이 각 문장의 밑줄 친 부분을 동명사로 바꿔서, 같은 의미를 표현할 수 있는 가장 짧은 형태의 문장을 영작하시오.

┌─── 보기 ────
It is worth reading this book.
→ The book is worth reading.
└─────────────

(1) Gloria's mom had no choice but to drink the sour beverage to save her.

➡ _____

_____

(2) It was worth while to pay for the expensive TV set.

➡ _____

(3) It was of no use to fix the ceiling unless the water problem is resolved.

➡ _____

_____

(4) Those men were busy because they were preparing for the awards ceremony.

➡ _____

_____

(5) It is worthwhile to pay attention to pop art.

➡ _____

04 다음 중 각 문장에서 어법상 어색한 단어를 한 개씩 찾아, 다른 한 단어로 고치거나 생략 또는 이동하여 옳은 문장으로 다시 쓰시오.

(1) As Andy Warhol wanting to show that art is something you see every day, he made many copies of his works.

➡ _____

_____

(2) Use daily images in a creative way, you can make a work of art for everyone.

➡ _____

_____

(3) When seen familiar images in art exhibitions, people found them refreshing.

➡ _____

_____

(4) Used common images and everyday items, pop art looks plain.

➡ _____

_____

(5) Because looking plain, pop art is filled with meaning that art should be easy to understand.

➡ _____

_____

_____

(6) Wanting everyone to enjoy his art, a pop artist setting up his works in outdoor places.

➡ _____

_____

(7) Though cartoons being not regarded as an art form at that time, Roy Lichtenstein used them in making his works.

➡ _____

_____

_____

Grammar **137**

Pop Art: Art for Everyone

Welcome to the Pop Art Exhibition! What do you see? Paintings of soup cans? Big cartoons? Do they look like art works? Probably not,

look like+명사: ~처럼 보이다

but think again. They are all famous works of pop art. Pop is short for popular. So pop art means popular art, or art for people. It began in the 1950s in America. Pop artists at that time wanted to create something

in the (연도)s: ~년대에   전치사구: pop artists 수식

fun and easy. Instead of difficult traditional art works, they turned their

–thing으로 끝나는 부정대명사는 형용사의 수식을 뒤에서 받음   pop artists 지칭

eyes to popular culture. They used images from TV, comic books, magazines, and advertising. When people saw familiar images in art exhibitions, they found them refreshing.

신선함을 유발하므로 현재분사

Since then, pop art has become truly popular. People thought that

사람들이 친숙한 이미지의 팝아트를 보며 신선하다고 생각할 무렵

art was too difficult to understand. By using daily images and bright

= People thought that art was so difficult that they couldn't understand it.

colors, pop artists changed that thought.

Using common images, pop art looks plain. In other words, it doesn't

= As[Because] it uses common images.

look artistic. But it is still worth paying attention to. Although it looks

be worth Ving: V 할 가치가 있다   양보절을 이끄는 접속사

plain, it is filled with meaning. Let's learn about some famous pop artists. They became famous for their special artistic ability. They

some famous pop artists

some famous pop artists were able to change common objects into

change A into B: A를 B로 바꾸다

amazing art.

Andy Warhol is called the King of Pop Art. He found his subjects in

= People call Andy Warhol the King of Pop Art.

magazines and stores.

cartoon: 만화
pop art: 팝 아트
art work: 예술 작품
advertising: 광고
familiar: 친숙한
refreshing: 신선한, 참신한
turn one's eyes to: ~로 눈길을 돌리다
plain: 평범한
artistic: 예술적인
worth: ~의 가치가 있는
ability: 능력
object: 물건, 대상
in other words: 다시 말해서

 확인문제

● 다음 문장이 본문의 내용과 일치하면 T, 일치하지 않으면 F를 쓰시오.

1 Pop art is art for people. ☐

2 Pop artists want art to be fun and easy. ☐

3 People thought pop art was refreshing because of unfamiliar images. ☐

4 Andy Warhol went to stores to copy works of art. ☐

One of his famous works is made up of pictures of Marilyn Monroe,
<u>One of his famous works</u> <u>is</u>
　　one of 복수명사: 단수 취급
the American actor. <u>Another work</u> shows cans of soup. He made many
　Marilyn Monroe와 동격　　another+단수명사
copies of these works. Why did he make copies of his works? He

wanted to show <u>that</u> art is <u>something you see</u> every day.
　　　　　　　명사절 접속사　　　something (that) you see ~ : 목적격 관계대명사 생략
　Claes Oldenburg is another pop artist who <u>made art fun</u>. He made
　　　　　　　　　　　　　　　　　　　make+목적어+목적격보어(5형식)
sculptures of everyday items, <u>such as</u> a hamburger, cookies, and a
　　　　　　　　　　　　　　　　 ~와 같은
brush. In the beginning, he created soft sculptures. <u>They</u> were made of
　　　　　　　　　　　　　　　　　　　　　　 soft sculptures 지칭
plastic, paper, and other soft materials. For example, he used cloth <u>to</u>

<u>make</u> toilets. Later, he made huge sculptures of daily items, such as an
to부정사의 부사적 용법 중 목적(~하기 위해서)
ice cream cone. <u>Wanting everyone to enjoy his art</u>, he set up his works
　　　　　　= As[Because] he wanted everyone to enjoy his art
in outdoor places. He also ran a store inside his studio <u>to sell</u> his works.
　　　　　　　　　　　　　　　　　　　　　to부정사의 부사적 용법 중 목적(~하기 위해서)
For him, artistic works were fun goods for people.

　Roy Lichtenstein used cartoons in his works. <u>They</u> were large and
　　　　　　　　　　　　　　　　　　　　　cartoons 지칭
painted in <u>lively</u> colors. He even included speech balloons in his
　　　　　 명사+ly: 형용사
paintings. Back then, cartoons <u>were not regarded as</u> an art form.
　　　　　　　　　　　be regarded as: ~로 여겨지다
　However, Roy Lichtenstein thought differently. He asked <u>himself</u>,
　　　　　　　　　　　　　　　　　　　　　재귀대명사의 재귀적 용법
'Why are they not?' Then Roy Lichtenstein broke down the wall

between high art and popular culture <u>by adding</u> cartoons to art.
　　　　　　　　　　　　　　　　 by Ving: V함으로써
　Pop artists <u>believed</u> art should be easy. Anyone can create and enjoy
　　　　　 believed (that) ~: 명사절 접속사 that 생략
art. How about creating a work of pop art today? By using daily images

in a creative way, you can make a work of art for everyone. <u>This</u> is the
　　　　　　　　　　　'By using daily images in a creative way, you can make a work of art for everyone.'을 가리킴
most important lesson from pop art.

be made up of: ~으로 구성되다
sculpture: 조각품
toilet: 변기, 화장실
cone: 원뿔, 원뿔형 물체
goods: 상품, 제품
set up: 설치하다
lively: 활기 넘치는, 생생한
speech balloon: 말풍선
break down: ~을 부수다

📎 **확인문제**

● 다음 문장이 본문의 내용과 일치하면 T, 일치하지 <u>않으면</u> F를 쓰시오.

1　Marilyn Monroe's pictures were used as art works by Andy Warhol. ☐

2　Claes Oldenburg made toilets with clothes. ☐

3　Claes Oldenburg sold his works at a store inside his studio. ☐

4　Roy Lichtenstein set up the wall between hight art and popular culture. ☐

● 우리말을 참고하여 빈칸에 알맞은 말을 쓰시오.

Pop Art: Art for Everyone

1 _____ _____ the Pop Art Exhibition! _____ do you see? Paintings of soup cans? Big _____?

2 Do they _____ _____ art works? _____ not, but _____ again. They _____ all _____ _____ of pop art.

3 Pop _____ _____ _____ popular. So pop art means _____ _____, or art for people.

4 _____ _____ _____ the 1950s in America. Pop artists at that time _____ _____ create something fun and easy.

5 _____ _____ difficult _____ art works, they _____ their eyes _____ popular culture.

6 They _____ images _____ TV, comic books, magazines, and _____.

7 When people saw _____ _____ in art exhibitions, they found _____ _____.

8 Since then, pop art has _____ _____ _____.

9 People thought _____ art was _____ difficult _____ _____.

10 _____ _____ daily images and bright colors, pop artists _____ _____ _____.

11 _____ common images, pop art _____ _____. _____ _____ _____, it doesn't look _____.

12 But it is still _____ _____ _____ _____. Although it looks plain, it _____ _____ _____ meaning.

13 Let's learn about some _____ _____ _____.

14 They became _____ _____ their special artistic _____. They were _____ _____ _____ common objects _____ _____ art.

15 Andy Warhol _____ _____ the King of Pop Art. He _____ his _____ _____ magazines and stores.

---

1 팝 아트 전시회에 온 것을 환영한다! 무엇이 보이는가? 수프 통조림들을 모아 놓은 그림? 커다란 만화 그림?

2 그것들이 예술 작품처럼 보이는가? 아마 그렇게 보이지 않겠지만, 다시 생각해 봐라. 그것들은 모두 유명한 팝 아트 작품들이다.

3 'pop'은 'popular(대중적인)'의 줄임말이다. 그래서 팝 아트는 대중 예술 또는 사람들을 위한 예술이라는 뜻이다.

4 팝 아트는 1950년대 미국에서 시작됐다. 그 당시 팝 아트 작가들은 재미있고 쉬운 것을 만들고 싶어 했다.

5 어려운 전통 예술 작품 대신 그들은 대중문화로 눈을 돌렸다.

6 그들은 텔레비전, 만화책, 잡지 및 광고에 나오는 이미지들을 사용했다.

7 미술 전시회에서 친숙한 이미지들을 봤을 때 사람들은 그것들이 신선하다는 걸 알게 되었다.

8 그때부터 팝 아트는 정말 유명해졌다.

9 사람들은 예술이 너무 어려워서 이해할 수 없는 것으로 생각했다.

10 일상적인 이미지와 밝은 색을 씀으로써, 팝 아트 작가들은 그러한 관점을 바꿨다.

11 흔한 이미지를 사용하기 때문에 팝 아트는 평범해 보인다. 즉, 팝 아트는 예술적으로 보이지 않는다.

12 하지만 여전히 주목할 만한 가치가 있다. 평범해 보일지라도 그것은 의미로 가득 차 있다.

13 몇 명의 유명한 팝 아트 작가들에 대해 알아보자.

14 그들은 특별한 예술적인 능력으로 유명해졌다. 그들은 흔한 대상을 놀라운 예술로 바꿀 수 있었다.

15 Andy Warhol은 팝 아트의 왕이라 불린다. 그는 잡지와 상점에서 주제를 찾았다.

16 One of his famous works _____ _____ _____ of pictures of Marilyn Monroe, the American actor.

17 _____ _____ _____ cans of soup. He _____ many _____ of these works.

18 Why did he make _____ _____ _____ _____? He wanted _____ _____ _____ art is something _____ _____ every day.

19 Claes Oldenburg is _____ pop artist _____ _____ art _____.

20 He made _____ _____ _____ _____, such as a hamburger, cookies, and a brush.

21 _____ _____ _____, he _____ soft sculptures. They were _____ _____ plastic, paper, and other _____ _____.

22 _____ _____, he used _____ _____ _____ toilets. Later, he made _____ _____ of daily items, _____ _____ an ice cream cone.

23 _____ everyone _____ _____ his art, he _____ his works in _____ places.

24 He also _____ a store _____ his studio _____ his works. For him, artistic works _____ _____ for people.

25 Roy Lichtenstein _____ cartoons _____ _____ _____. They _____ large and _____ in _____ _____.

26 He even _____ speech balloons in his paintings. Back then, cartoons _____ not _____ _____ an art form.

27 _____, Roy Lichtenstein thought _____. He asked _____, '_____ are _____ _____?'

28 Then Roy Lichtenstein _____ _____ the wall high art _____ popular culture _____ _____ cartoons to art.

29 Pop artists _____ art _____ _____ easy. _____ can _____ and _____ art.

30 How about _____ a work of _____ _____ today?

31 _____ _____ daily images _____ a creative way, you can _____ a work of art _____ everyone. This is _____ _____ _____ _____ from pop art.

16 그의 유명 작품들 중 하나는 미국 배우인 Marilyn Monroe의 사진으로 구성되어 있다.

17 또 다른 작품은 수프 통조림들을 보여준다. 그는 이 작품들의 사본을 많이 만들었다.

18 그는 왜 작품의 복사본을 만들었나? 그는 예술은 여러분이 매일 보는 것임을 보여 주고 싶어 했다.

19 Claes Oldenburg는 예술을 재미있게 만들었던 또 다른 팝 아트 작가이다.

20 그는 햄버거와 쿠키, 붓 같은 일상적인 물품들의 조각품을 만들었다.

21 초기에 그는 부드러운 조각품을 만들었다. 그것들은 플라스틱, 종이, 그리고 다른 부드러운 재료들로 만들어졌다.

22 예를 들어서 그는 변기를 만들기 위해 천을 사용했다. 나중에 그는 아이스크림콘 같은 일상 물품의 거대한 조각품을 만들었다.

23 그는 모든 사람이 그의 작품을 보고 즐기기를 원했기 때문에 그의 작품들을 실외에 설치했다.

24 그는 작품 판매를 위해 그의 작업실 안에 상점을 운영하기도 했다. 그에게 예술적인 작품들은 사람들을 위한 재미있는 제품이었다.

25 Roy Lichtenstein은 그의 작품에 만화를 사용했다. 그것들은 크고 생기 넘치는 색들로 그려졌다.

26 그는 심지어 그의 작품에 말풍선을 넣었다. 그 당시에 만화는 예술 형식으로 여겨지지 않았다.

27 하지만 Roy Lichtenstein은 다르게 생각했다. 그는 스스로에게 '왜 만화는 예술로 간주되지 않을까?'라고 물었다.

28 만화를 예술에 첨가함으로써 Roy Lichtenstein은 순수 예술과 대중문화 사이의 벽을 허물었다.

29 팝 아트 작가들은 예술은 쉬워야 한다고 믿었다. 누구나 예술을 만들 수 있고, 즐길 수 있다.

30 오늘 팝 아트 작품 하나를 만들어 보는 것은 어떤가?

31 일상적인 이미지를 창의적인 방식으로 사용함으로써, 모든 사람을 위한 예술 작품을 만들 수 있다. 이것이 팝 아트의 가장 중요한 교훈이다.

● 우리말을 참고하여 본문을 영작하시오.

Pop Art: Art for Everyone

▶ 팝 아트 전시회에 온 것을 환영한다! 무엇이 보이는가? 수프 통조림들을 모아 놓은 그림? 커다란 만화 그림?

➡ _____

2▸ 그것들이 예술 작품처럼 보이는가? 아마 그렇게 보이지 않겠지만, 다시 생각해 봐라. 그것들은 모두 유명한 팝 아트 작품들이다.

➡ _____

3▸ 'pop'은 'popular(대중적인)'의 줄임말이다. 그래서 팝 아트는 대중 예술 또는 사람들을 위한 예술이라는 뜻이다.

➡ _____

4▸ 팝 아트는 1950년대 미국에서 시작됐다. 그 당시 팝 아트 작가들은 재미있고 쉬운 것을 만들고 싶어 했다.

➡ _____

5▸ 어려운 전통 예술 작품 대신 그들은 대중문화로 눈을 돌렸다.

➡ _____

6▸ 그들은 텔레비전, 만화책, 잡지 및 광고에 나오는 이미지들을 사용했다.

➡ _____

7▸ 미술 전시회에서 친숙한 이미지들을 봤을 때 사람들은 그것들이 신선하다는 걸 알게 되었다.

➡ _____

8▸ 그때부터 팝 아트는 정말 유명해졌다.

➡ _____

9▸ 사람들은 예술이 너무 어려워서 이해할 수 없는 것으로 생각했었다.

➡ _____

10▸ 일상적인 이미지와 밝은 색을 씀으로써, 팝 아트 작가들은 그러한 관점을 바꿨다.

➡ _____

11▸ 흔한 이미지를 사용하기 때문에 팝 아트는 평범해 보인다. 즉, 팝 아트는 예술적으로 보이지 않는다.

➡ _____

12▸ 하지만 여전히 주목할 만한 가치가 있다. 평범해 보일지라도 그것은 의미로 가득 차 있다.

➡ _____

13▸ 몇 명의 유명한 팝 아트 작가들에 대해 알아보자.

➡ _____

14▸ 그들은 특별한 예술적인 능력으로 유명해졌다. 그들은 흔한 대상을 놀라운 예술로 바꿀 수 있었다.

➡ _____

_____

15▸ Andy Warhol은 팝 아트의 왕이라 불린다. 그는 잡지와 상점에서 주제를 찾았다.

➡ _____

16▸ 그의 유명 작품들 중 하나는 미국 배우인 Marilyn Monroe의 사진으로 구성되어 있다.

➡ _____

17 또 다른 작품은 수프 통조림들을 보여준다. 그는 이 작품들의 사본을 많이 만들었다.

➡ _____

18 그는 왜 작품의 복사본을 만들었나? 그는 예술은 여러분이 매일 보는 것임을 보여 주고 싶어 했다.

➡ _____

19 Claes Oldenburg는 예술을 재미있게 만들었던 또 다른 팝 아트 작가이다.

➡ _____

20 그는 햄버거와 쿠키, 붓 같은 일상적인 물품들의 조각품을 만들었다.

➡ _____

21 초기에 그는 부드러운 조각품을 만들었다. 그것들은 플라스틱, 종이, 그리고 다른 부드러운 재료들로 만들어졌다.

➡ _____

22 예를 들어서 그는 변기를 만들기 위해 천을 사용했다. 나중에 그는 아이스크림콘 같은 일상 물품의
거대한 조각품을 만들었다.

➡ _____
_____

23 그는 모든 사람이 그의 작품을 보고 즐기기를 원했기 때문에 그의 작품들을 실외에 설치했다.

➡ _____

24 그는 작품 판매를 위해 그의 작업실 안에 상점을 운영하기도 했다. 그에게 예술적인 작품들은 사람들을 위
한 재미있는 제품이었다.

➡ _____

25 Roy Lichtenstein은 그의 작품에 만화를 사용했다. 그것들은 크고 생기 넘치는 색들로 그려졌다.

➡ _____

26 그는 심지어 그의 작품에 말풍선을 넣었다. 그 당시에 만화는 예술 형식으로 여겨지지 않았다.

➡ _____
_____

하지만 Roy Lichtenstein은 다르게 생각했다. 그는 스스로에게 '왜 만화는 예술로 간주되지 않을까?'라고 물
었다.

➡ _____

28 만화를 예술에 첨가함으로써 Roy Lichtenstein은 순수 예술과 대중문화 사이의 벽을 허물었다.

➡ _____

29 팝 아트 작가들은 예술은 쉬워야 한다고 믿었다. 누구나 예술을 만들 수 있고, 즐길 수 있다.

➡ _____

30 오늘 팝 아트 작품 하나를 만들어 보는 것은 어떤가?

➡ _____

31 일상적인 이미지를 창의적인 방식으로 사용함으로써, 모든 사람을 위한 예술 작품을 만들 수 있다. 이것이
팝 아트의 가장 중요한 교훈이다.

➡ _____
_____

[01~03] 다음 글을 읽고 물음에 답하시오.

Welcome to the Pop Art Exhibition! What do you see? Paintings of soup cans? Big cartoons? Do they look like art works? Probably not, but think again. They are all famous works of pop art.

Pop is short for popular. So pop art means popular art, or art for people. It began in the 1950s in America. Pop artists at that time wanted to create something fun and easy. Instead of difficult traditional art works, they turned their eyes to popular culture. They used images from TV, comic books, magazines, and advertising. When people saw familiar images in art exhibitions, they found them refreshing. Since then, pop art has become truly popular. People thought that art was too difficult to understand. By using daily images and bright colors, pop artists changed that thought.

서답형

01 다음과 같이 풀이되는 말을 위 글에서 찾아 쓰시오.

a humorous drawing or series of drawings in a newspaper or magazine.

➡ _____

서답형

02 What images did pop artists use? Answer in English.

➡ _____

_____

중요

03 위 글을 읽고 답할 수 있는 것은?

① Who is the most famous pop artist?
② How many pop artists are there?
③ What did people think about art?
④ Why didn't pop artists use dark colors?
⑤ How many art exhibitions were held?

[04~06] 다음 글을 읽고 물음에 답하시오.

Using common images, pop art looks plain. In other words, it doesn't look artistic. But it is still worth paying attention to. Although it looks plain, it is filled with meaning. Let's learn about some famous pop artists. They became famous for their special artistic ability. They were able to change common objects into amazing art.

Andy Warhol is called the King of Pop Art. ① He found his subjects in magazines and stores. ② One of his famous works is made up of pictures of Marilyn Monroe, the American actor. ③ Another work shows cans of soup. ④ Why did he make copies of his works? ⑤ He wanted to show that art is something you see every day.

04 ①~⑤ 중 주어진 문장이 들어가기에 가장 적절한 곳은?

He made many copies of these works.

①　　　　②　　　　③　　　　④　　　　⑤

서답형

05 What is Andy Warhol called? Answer in English with a full sentence.

➡ _____

중요

06 위 글의 내용과 일치하는 것은?

① Pop art looks very special.
② Pop artists used uncommon images.
③ Pop art doesn't have any special meanings.
④ It is worth paying attention to works of pop artists.
⑤ Andy Warhol used to cooperate with Marilyn Monroe who was also an artist.

[07~09] 다음 글을 읽고 물음에 답하시오.

Claes Oldenburg is another pop artist who made art fun. He made sculptures of everyday items, such as a hamburger, cookies, and a brush. In the beginning, he created soft sculptures. They were made of plastic, paper, and other soft materials. (A)_____, he used cloth to make toilets. Later, he made huge sculptures of daily items, such as an ice cream cone. Wanting everyone to enjoy his art, he set up his works in outdoor places. He also ran a store inside his studio to sell his works. For him, artistic works were fun goods for people.

07 다음 중 빈칸 (A)에 들어갈 말로 가장 적절한 것은?

① On the other hand ② For example
③ In other words ④ Nevertheless
⑤ However

서답형
08 What did Claes Oldenburg want everyone to do? Answer in English.

➡ _____

중요
09 다음 중 Claes Oldenburg의 작품에 해당할 수 있는 것은?

① a detailed portrait of a king
② an expensive dish made with silver
③ a sandwich made with soft material
④ a huge spaceship made of iron, and plastic
⑤ the smallest doll which can be seen with a microscope

[10~13] 다음 글을 읽고 물음에 답하시오.

Roy Lichtenstein used cartoons in his works. They were large and painted in lively colors.
[A] Then Roy Lichtenstein broke down the wall between high art and popular culture by adding cartoons to art.
[B] However, Roy Lichtenstein thought differently. He asked himself, 'Why are they not?'
[C] He even included speech balloons in his paintings. Back then, cartoons were not regarded ⓐ_____ an art form.
Pop artists believed art should be easy. Anyone can ⓑ_____. How about creating a work of pop art today? By using daily images in a creative way, you can make a work of art for everyone. This is the most important lesson from pop art.

서답형
10 자연스러운 글이 되도록 [A]~[C]를 바르게 나열하시오.

➡ _____

11 빈칸 ⓐ에 들어갈 말로 가장 적절한 것은?

① to ② in ③ as ④ for ⑤ at

중요
12 빈칸 ⓑ에 들어갈 말로 가장 적절한 것은?

① express their emotions
② create and enjoy art
③ appreciate and judge art
④ talk about how they feel
⑤ understand what an art means

서답형
13 According to the passage, what did pop artists believe? Answer in English.

➡ _____

[14~17] 다음 글을 읽고 물음에 답하시오.

Welcome to the Pop Art Exhibition! What do you see? Paintings of soup cans? Big cartoons? Do they look like art works? Probably not, but think again. They are all famous (A)works of pop art.

Pop is short for popular. So pop art means popular art, or art for people. It began in the 1950s in America. Pop artists at that time wanted to create something fun and easy. Instead of difficult traditional art works, they turned their eyes to popular culture. They used images from TV, comic books, magazines, and advertising. When people saw familiar images in art exhibitions, they found them refreshing. Since then, pop art has become truly popular. People thought that art was too difficult to understand. By using daily images and bright colors, pop artists changed that thought.

14 밑줄 친 (A)와 그 의미가 같은 것은?

① I can't underline{work} if I catch a cold.

② The phone doesn't underline{work} at all.

③ She has been out of underline{work} for a year.

④ I think this is Picasso's greatest underline{work}.

⑤ The pill the doctor gave me underline{works}.

15 다음 중 위 글의 내용과 일치하는 것은?

① Pop art means art for geniuses.

② Pop artist used images only from books.

③ People thought that pop art was too difficult to understand.

④ Pop artists focused on examining traditional art works.

⑤ Daily images were used by pop artists.

서답형
16 When did pop art begin? Answer in English with a full sentence.

➡ _____

17 다음 중 팝 아트의 특징으로 알맞은 것을 <u>모두</u> 고르시오.

① dark images　　　② daily items

③ unique images　　④ bright colors

⑤ few people enjoying it

[18~20] 다음 글을 읽고 물음에 답하시오.

Using common images, pop art looks plain. In other words, it doesn't look ①artistic. But it is still worth paying attention to. Although it looks ②plain, it is filled with meaning. Let's learn about some famous pop artists. They became famous for their ③special artistic ability. They were able to change ④special objects into amazing art.

Andy Warhol is called the King of Pop Art. He found his subjects in magazines and stores. One of his famous works is made up of pictures of Marilyn Monroe, the American actor. Another work shows cans of soup. He made many copies of these works. Why did he make copies of his works? He wanted to show that art is something you see ⑤every day.

18 ①~⑤ 중 글의 흐름상 어색한 것은?

①　　　②　　　③　　　④　　　⑤

19 위 글의 내용을 바르게 이해한 사람은?

① A: Pop art looks really special.

② B: I'm so sorry that pop art has no meaning.

③ C: I didn't know that Marilyn Monroe was one of pop artists.

④ D: It is surprising that cans of soup were turned into works of art.

⑤ E: It's so sorry that Andy Warhol always made only one work of art.

서답형

20 Where did Andy Warhol find his subjects? Answer in English.

➡ _____

[21~23] 다음 글을 읽고 물음에 답하시오.

Claes Oldenburg is another pop artist who made art fun. He made sculptures of (A)_____, such as a hamburger, cookies, and a brush. In the beginning, he created soft sculptures. They were made of plastic, paper, and other soft materials. For example, he used cloth to make toilets. Later, he made huge sculptures of daily items, such as an ice cream cone. Wanting everyone to enjoy his art, he set up his works in outdoor places. He also ran a store inside his studio to sell his works. For him, artistic works were fun goods for people.

 중요

21 빈칸 (A)에 들어갈 말로 가장 적절한 것은?

① something uncommon ② various foods
③ everyday items ④ great works
⑤ people around the world

서답형

22 What did Claes Oldenburg create in the beginning?

➡ _____

23 위 글을 읽고 답할 수 있는 것은?

① When was Claes Oldenburg born?
② When did Claes Oldenburg start pop art?
③ How huge were the sculptures?
④ What did Claes Oldenburg use to make toilets?
⑤ How many works did Claes Oldenburg set up in outdoor places?

[24~27] 다음 글을 읽고 물음에 답하시오.

Roy Lichtenstein used cartoons in his works. They were large and painted in lively colors. He even included speech balloons in his paintings. Back then, cartoons were not regarded as an art form. However, Roy Lichtenstein thought differently. He asked (A)himself, 'Why are (B) they not?' Then Roy Lichtenstein broke down the wall between high art and popular culture by adding cartoons to art.

Pop artists believed art should be easy. Anyone can create and enjoy art. How about creating a work of pop art today? By using daily images in a creative way, you can make a work of art for everyone. This is the most important lesson from pop art.

 중요

24 밑줄 친 (A)와 쓰임이 다른 하나는?

① She enjoyed herself very much.
② Karl made himself famous.
③ The door opened in itself.
④ They got themselves ready.
⑤ Tom cooked the food himself.

서답형

25 밑줄 친 (B)가 가리키는 것을 위 글에서 찾아 쓰시오.

➡ _____

서답형

26 What did Roy Lichtenstein add to art? Answer in English with a full sentence.

➡ _____

서답형

27 ①~⑤ 중 위 글의 내용과 일치하지 않는 것은?

Roy Lichtenstein was one of ①pop artists who thought that cartoons could be ②an art form. So he used them in his works with ③lively colors and ④speech balloons. In this way, he ⑤built the huge wall between high art and popular culture.

[01~04] 다음 글을 읽고 물음에 답하시오.

Welcome to the Pop Art Exhibition! What do you see? Paintings of soup cans? Big cartoons? Do they look like art works? Probably not, but think again. They are all famous works of pop art.

Pop is short for popular. So pop art means popular art, or art for people. It began in the 1950s in America. Pop artists at that time wanted to create something fun and easy. Instead of difficult traditional art works, they turned their eyes to popular culture. They used images from TV, comic books, magazines, and advertising. When people saw familiar images in art exhibitions, they found them refreshing. Since (A)then, pop art has become truly popular. People thought that art was too difficult to understand. By using daily images and bright colors, pop artists changed that thought.

01 What does pop art mean? Answer in English with a full sentence.

➡ _____

02 위 글의 내용에 맞게 빈칸에 알맞은 말을 쓰시오.

In 1950s, pop artists in America were interested in _____ _____ rather than _____ _____ _____ _____ .

03 밑줄 친 (A)가 의미하는 것을 우리말로 쓰시오.

➡ _____
_____

04 How did pop artists changed people's thought toward art? Answer in English with a full sentence.

➡ _____
_____

[05~07] 다음 글을 읽고 물음에 답하시오.

Using common images, pop art looks plain. In other words, it doesn't look artistic. But it is still worth paying attention to. Although it looks plain, it is filled with meaning. Let's learn about some famous pop artists. They became famous for their special artistic ability. They were able to change common objects into amazing art.

Andy Warhol is called the King of Pop Art. He found his subjects in magazines and stores. One of his famous works is made up of pictures of Marilyn Monroe, the American actor. Another work shows cans of soup. He made many copies of these works. Why did he make copies of his works? He wanted to show that art is something you see every day.

05 Write the reason why pop art looks plain. Use the phrase 'It's because.'

➡ _____

06 What were some famous pop artists able to do? Answer in English with ten words.

➡ _____
_____

07 위 글의 내용에 맞게 빈칸에 알맞은 말을 위 글에서 찾아 쓰시오.

> One of Andy Warhol's famous works is composed of ________ of Marilyn Monroe, who was ________ ________ ________. Besides the work, he produced many art works using ________ ________ which he could get with ease.

[08~10] 다음 글을 읽고 물음에 답하시오.

Claes Oldenburg is (A)예술을 재미있게 만들었던 또 다른 팝 아트 작가. He made sculptures of everyday items, such as a hamburger, cookies, and a brush. In the beginning, he created soft sculptures. They were made of plastic, paper, and other soft materials. For example, he used cloth to make toilets. Later, he made huge sculptures of daily items, such as an ice cream cone. (B)Wanting everyone to enjoy his art, he set up his works in outdoor places. He also ran a store inside his studio to sell his works. For him, artistic works were fun goods for people.

중요
08 주어진 단어를 활용하여 밑줄 친 우리말 (A)를 영어로 쓰시오.

(another / made / fun)

➡ ______________________________

09 접속사를 이용하여 밑줄 친 (B)와 같은 의미의 절을 쓰시오.

➡ ______________________________

10 What did Claes Oldenburg use to create soft sculptures? Answer in English.

➡ ______________________________

[11~13] 다음 글을 읽고 물음에 답하시오.

Roy Lichtenstein used cartoons in his works. They were large and painted in lively colors. He even included speech balloons in his paintings. Back then, cartoons were not regarded as an art form. However, Roy Lichtenstein thought differently. He asked himself, '(A)Why are they not?' Then Roy Lichtenstein broke down the wall between high art and popular culture by adding cartoons to art.

Pop artists believed art should be easy. Anyone can create and enjoy art. How about creating a work of pop art today? By using daily images in a creative way, you can make a work of art for everyone. (B)This is the most important lesson from pop art.

11 How was Roy Lichtenstein's works painted? Answer in English with a full sentence.

➡ ______________________________

중요
12 밑줄 친 (A)의 의미를 일곱 단어로 이루어진 한 문장으로 쓰시오.

➡ ______________________________

13 밑줄 친 (B)가 의미하는 것을 우리말로 쓰시오.

➡ ______________________________

____

Project Step 1

A: What do you want to make with these paper cups?
  want는 목적어로 to부정사를 취한다.

B: Why don't we make a tower?
  '~하는 게 어때?'라고 제안을 하는 표현으로 'How[What] about making a tower?'로 바꿀 수 있다.

C: Wonderful! Let's build a tower like the Leaning Tower of Pisa.
  ~와 같은, 전치사

D: How about drawing something on the cups?
  '~하는 게 어때?'라는 제안을 하는 표현이다.

B: Sounds great. First, let's give everyone some paper cups.

구문해설 • tower: 탑 • build: 만들다 • like: ~와 같은

해석

A: 이 종이컵들로 무엇을 만들고 싶어?
B: 탑을 만드는 게 어때?
C: 훌륭해! 피사의 사탑과 같은 탑을 만들어 보자.
D: 종이컵에 뭔가를 그리는 게 어때?
B: 좋은 생각이야. 먼저 모두에게 종이컵을 몇 개 나누어 주자.

Enjoy Writing B

The Best Musical of My Life

Last Saturday I went to the concert hall to watch a musical. The title of
  to부정사-부사적 용법(목적)
the musical was *You and Me*. I watched it because my favorite actor was in
it. I liked the songs and dances of the musical. The story was about a girl
  = the musical
who invited her best friends to her birthday party. They talked about their
  관계대명사(주격)
friendship. The main character was Sophie. She sang many beautiful songs.
It was fantastic. Singing along to the songs during the performance, I was
  분사구문(= As I sang)
excited. The musical was really worth watching.
  과거분사 exciting(X)   형용사   동명사

구문해설 • main character: 주연, 주인공 • be worth V-ing: ~할 가치가 있다.

내 생애 최고의 뮤지컬
지난 토요일 나는 뮤지컬을 보러 콘서트홀에 갔다. 뮤지컬 제목은 '너와 나'였다. 내가 가장 좋아하는 배우가 그 뮤지컬에 나왔기 때문에 그것을 보았다. 나는 공연의 노래와 춤이 좋았다. 뮤지컬의 내용은 가장 친한 친구들을 자신의 생일 파티에 초대했던 여자 아이에 관한 것이었다. 그들은 자신들의 우정에 대해 이야기했다. 주인공은 Sophie였다. 그녀는 많은 아름다운 노래들을 불렀다. 그것은 환상적이었다. 공연 중에 노래를 따라 부르며 매우 신났었다. 그 뮤지컬은 정말 볼 가치가 있었다.

Enjoy Writing B

A Movie That Moved Me

Last Saturday I went to my friend's house to watch a movie. The title of the
  to부정사의 부사적 용법 중 목적(~하기 위해서)
movie was *My Son*. I watched it because my friend recommended it. I liked the
  이유를 이끄는 접속사
story of the movie. The story was about a brave man who tried to find his lost
  주격 관계대명사   아들을 잃어버린 것이므로 과거분사
son. The main character was John. He was played by the actor Roy Jones, who
  관계대명사의 계속적 용법
was fantastic. It was touching. Watching the emotional scenes, I was moved.
  감동을 유발하므로 현재분사   감동을 느낀 것이므로 과거분사
The movie was really worth watching.

구문해설 • title: 제목 • recommend: 추천하다 • brave: 용감한 • main character: 주인공
• fantastic: 멋진 • emotional: 감동적인 • scene: 장면 • be worth Ving: V할 가치가 있다

나에게 감동을 준 영화
지난 토요일 나는 영화를 보러 친구 집에 갔다. 영화의 제목은 '나의 아들'이었다. 나는 내 친구가 그 영화를 추천해서 봤다. 나는 그 영화의 이야기가 마음에 들었다. 그것은 잃어버린 아들을 찾으려 했던 용감한 남자에 관한 이야기였다. 주인공은 John이었다. 그 역은 배우 Roy Jones가 연기했는데 아주 멋졌다. 그 영화는 감동적이었다. 나는 감동적인 장면들을 보며 감동받았다. 그 영화는 정말 볼 가치가 있었다.

영역별 핵심문제

01 다음 주어진 두 단어의 관계가 같도록 빈칸에 알맞은 단어를 쓰시오.

> dull – lively : familiar – _____

02 다음 문장의 빈칸 (A)와 (B)에 들어갈 단어로 바르게 짝지어진 것은?

> • I know a good spot to (A)_____ the tent.
> • They asked me to leave. (B)_____, I got fired.

① get into – For example
② look into – However
③ put into – On the other hand
④ set up – In other words
⑤ set for – Moreover

[03~04] 다음 영영풀이에 해당하는 것을 고르시오.

03

> the ability to produce or use original and unusual ideas

① purpose   ② creativity
③ advice   ④ performance
⑤ accident

04

> traditional in style or form, or based on methods developed over a long period of time, and considered to be of lasting value

① modern   ② familiar
③ popular   ④ refreshing
⑤ classical

05 다음 우리말에 맞게 주어진 문장의 빈칸을 네 단어로 채우시오.

> 그 위원회는 5명의 위원으로 구성될 것이다.
> The committee will _____ five members.

06 다음 밑줄 친 부분의 뜻이 잘못된 것은?

① His new work is a wooden sculpture. (조각품)
② I cleaned the toilet in the bathroom. (변기)
③ He had the ability to explain things clearly. (능력)
④ I went to an exhibition called *The World of Eric Carle*. (출구)
⑤ Computers can be expensive, but I think they are worth the money. (가치 있는)

07 다음 대화의 빈칸 (A)에 들어갈 말로 알맞은 것은?

> B: Do you like classical music?
> G: Yes, Beethoven is one of my favorite musicians. How about you?
> B: I like pop music more than classical music.
> G: I see. (A)_____
> B: I'm really fascinated by its exciting rhythms.

① Do you like pop music?
② How do you like classical music?
③ What do you like most about pop music?
④ How do you like this song?
⑤ Are you satisfied with classical music?

08 다음 그림에서 요리사가 할 말을 주어진 단어를 이용하여 영작하시오.

(how / your food)

➡ _____

[09~10] 다음 대화를 읽고 물음에 답하시오.

Bora: Andy, you went to the art museum, didn't you?

Andy: Yes. They had a special Chagall exhibition. (①)

Bora: How did you like it?

Andy: It was fantastic! I was fascinated by the colors in his paintings and his creativity. (②)

Bora: No wonder. He was one of the greatest painters ever. (③)

Andy: I went to a gift shop and saw things like umbrellas, cups, and backpacks. Famous works of art were printed on them. (④)

Bora: Did you buy anything?

Andy: Yes. I bought this T-shirt. How do you like it? (⑤)

Bora: It looks great on you.

Andy: Thank you.

09 위 대화의 (①)~(⑤) 중 주어진 문장이 들어갈 위치로 알맞은 것은?

What else did you see in the museum?

①   ②   ③   ④   ⑤

---

10 위 대화를 읽고 답할 수 없는 질문은?

① What was Andy fascinated by?

② What did Andy buy at the gift shop?

③ How did Andy like the Chagall exhibition?

④ Why did Andy buy a T-shirt?

⑤ What did Andy see at the gift shop?

11 다음 대화의 (A)~(E)를 알맞은 순서로 나열한 것은?

A: This is my treasure.

(A) That's amazing.

(B) Yes. I made it seven years ago. I've been using it every day since then.

(C) How do you like it?

(D) It's a mug, isn't it?

(E) It looks great. I like the drawing of a little bear.

① (A) – (C) – (B) – (E) – (D)

② (B) – (C) – (D) – (A) – (E)

③ (C) – (E) – (D) – (B) – (A)

④ (D) – (B) – (A) – (C) – (E)

⑤ (D) – (A) – (E) – (C) – (B)

12 다음 대화의 밑줄 친 (A)와 같은 의미가 되도록 주어진 단어를 이용하여 쓰시오.

G: Jim, did you finish your art homework?

B: Yes. I drew the face of my role model on a plate.

G: Sounds interesting. Who is your role model?

B: My dad. He always gives me good advice. Who did you draw, Amy?

G: Well, I drew myself surfing in the sea.

B: Wonderful! (A)I'm fascinated by your drawing. (an interest)

G: Thank you.

➡ _____

13 다음 각 문장의 밑줄 친 부분이 나머지와 쓰임이 <u>다른</u> 하나를 고르시오.

① It was worth <u>meeting</u> your family.
② Jessica couldn't help <u>meeting</u> the strange man because her mother had arranged her schedule.
③ Don't you see the president <u>meeting</u> a lot of citizens without a minute's rest?
④ My parents were so busy <u>meeting</u> the teachers that I wanted to go out.
⑤ It was no use <u>meeting</u> Tom and Jack, as they couldn't help us.

14 다음 문장의 밑줄 친 분사구문을 부사절로 옳게 바꾼 것은?

> There being a misconception that cartoons wouldn't belong to art, some pop artists made great works of art by using them.

① As a misconception was there that cartoons wouldn't belong to art,
② If there was a misconception that cartoons wouldn't belong to art,
③ Unless there was a misconception that cartoons wouldn't belong to art,
④ Though there was a misconception that cartoons wouldn't belong to art,
⑤ Because there was a misconception that cartoons wouldn't belong to art,

15 다음 그림을 보고 괄호 안의 단어를 배열하여 빈칸을 알맞게 채우되, 필요하다면 동사의 형태는 어법에 맞게 고치시오.

(1) (worth, see, works)

➡ The world famous pop artist Florentijn Hofman's _____.

(2) (busy, was, that, the show, so, watch)

➡ Minjun _____ he couldn't answer the phone.

16 다음 문장의 밑줄 친 부사절을 분사구문으로 알맞게 바꾼 것을 고르시오.

> <u>As they didn't want people to think art should be difficult,</u> pop artists tried to change it by using daily images and bright colors.

① As they wanting people to think art shouldn't be difficult,
② There being people thinking that art shouldn't be difficult,
③ Wanting not people to think art should be difficult,
④ As wanting people to think art should be difficult,
⑤ Not wanting people to think that art should be difficult,

17 다음은 아래 주어진 문장의 내용과 같은 문장들이다. 어법상 틀린 문장 하나를 고르시오.

> The exhibition of Andy Warhol's Works of Art in New York last year was worth visiting.

① It was worth while to visit the exhibition of Andy Warhol's Works of Art in New York last year.

② The exhibition of Andy Warhol's Works of Art in New York last year was worthy of visiting.

③ The exhibition of Andy Warhol's Works of Art in New York last year was worth visiting it.

④ It was worthwhile visiting the exhibition of Andy Warhol's Works of Art in New York last year.

⑤ The exhibition of Andy Warhol's Works of Art in New York last year was worth visiting.

Reading

[18~21] 다음 글을 읽고 물음에 답하시오.

Pop is short for popular. So pop art means popular art, or art for people. It began in the 1950s in America. Pop artists at that time wanted to create something fun and easy. Instead of difficult traditional art works, ①they turned ②their eyes to popular culture. ③They used images from TV, comic books, magazines, and advertising. When people saw familiar images in art exhibitions, ④they found them refreshing. Since then, pop art has become truly popular. People thought that art was too difficult to understand. By using daily images and bright colors, ⑤pop artists changed that thought.

18 ①~⑤ 중 지칭하는 것이 다른 하나는?

①   ②   ③   ④   ⑤

19 What is pop short for? Answer in English with a full sentence.

➡ _____

20 위 글의 내용과 일치하는 것은?

① People in 1950s didn't like pop arts.

② Pop artists tried to stick to traditional art works.

③ Pop arts were created to be fun and easy.

④ There weren't any pop art exhibitions.

⑤ Pop artists were fond of using only one color.

21 What did people think about art? Answer in English.

➡ _____

_____

[22~24] 다음 글을 읽고 물음에 답하시오.

Roy Lichtenstein used cartoons in his works. ① They were large and painted in lively colors. ② He even included speech balloons in his paintings. ③ Back then, cartoons were not regarded as an art form. ④ He asked himself, 'Why are they not?' ⑤ Then Roy Lichtenstein broke down the wall between high art and popular culture by adding cartoons to art.

Pop artists believed art should be easy. Anyone can create and enjoy art. How about creating a work of pop art today? By using daily images in a creative way, you can make a work of art for everyone. This is the most important lesson from pop art.

22 ①~⑤ 중 주어진 문장이 들어가기에 가장 적절한 곳은?

> However, Roy Lichtenstein thought differently.

① ② ③ ④ ⑤

23 According to the passage, what is the most important lesson from pop art?

① making people in the world happy
② spreading American art works
③ using daily images as little as possible
④ building strong walls for pure art
⑤ employing everyday items creatively

24 What did Roy Lichtenstein include in his paintings? Answer in English.

➡ _____

[25~27] 다음 글을 읽고 물음에 답하시오.

A Movie That Moved Me

Last Saturday I went to my friend's house to watch a movie. The title of the movie was *My Son*. I watched it ①because my friend recommended it. I liked the story of the movie. The story was about a brave man ②who tried to find his lost son. The main character was John. He was played by the actor Roy Jones, ③that was fantastic. It was touching. ④Watching the emotional scenes, I was moved. The movie was really worth ⑤watching.

25 ①~⑤ 중 어법상 바르지 않은 것은?

① ② ③ ④ ⑤

26 What did the writer like about the movie? Answer in English.

➡ _____

27 다음 중 위 글을 읽고 답할 수 없는 것은?

① When did the writer go to the friend's house?
② What was the title of the movie?
③ Who recommended the movie?
④ Who played the main character?
⑤ How long did it take to watch the movie?

01 출제율 95%

다음 짝지어진 단어의 관계가 같도록 빈칸에 알맞은 말을 쓰시오.

> creative – creativity : popular – _____

02 출제율 90%

다음 영영풀이에 해당하는 단어는?

> an opinion that someone offers you about what you should do or how you should act in a particular situation

① suggestion   ② lesson
③ emotion   ④ advice
⑤ cartoon

[03~04] 다음 대화를 읽고 물음에 답하시오.

Bora: Andy, you went to the art museum, didn't you?
Andy: Yes. They had a special Chagall exhibition.
Bora: (a)What did you like it?
Andy: It was fantastic! (b)I was fascinated by the colors in his paintings and his creativity.
Bora: (c)No wonder. He was one of the greatest painters ever. What else did you see in the museum?
Andy: I went to a gift shop and saw things like umbrellas, cups, and backpacks. Famous works of art were printed on them.
Bora: Did you buy anything?
Andy: Yes. I bought this T-shirt. (d)How do you like it?
Bora: (d)It looks great on you.
Andy: Thank you.

03 출제율 95%

위 대화의 밑줄 친 (a)~(e) 중 표현이 어색한 것은?

① (a)   ② (b)   ③ (c)   ④ (d)   ⑤ (e)

04 출제율 100%

위 대화의 내용과 일치하지 않는 것은?

① The art museum had a special Chagall exhibition.
② Bora and Andy are talking in the art museum.
③ Andy also went to a gift shop and saw things like umbrellas, cups, and backpacks.
④ Bora acknowledges Chagall as one of the greatest painters.
⑤ The T-shirt Andy bought looks great on him.

[05~06] 다음 대화를 읽고 물음에 답하시오.

B: The other day I watched a play, *A Love Story in the War*.
G: Oh, how did you like the play?
B: I liked the main characters. The actors' performances were fantastic.
G: 이야기도 좋았어?
B: No. It was a little boring, but the music was pretty good.
G: So, do you think I should see it?
B: Only if you have a lot of time and money.

05 출제율 95%

위 대화의 밑줄 친 우리말에 맞게 주어진 단어를 이용하여 영어로 쓰시오.

> good, well

➡ _____

06 출제율 90%

위 대화에서 다음 〈영영풀이〉가 설명하는 단어를 찾아 쓰시오.

> not interesting or exciting

➡ _____

B: Sandy, you can listen to many kinds of music in this music library.

G: That's cool, Bob. Can I listen to classical music?

B: Sure. Do you like classical music?

G: Yes, Beethoven is one of my favorite musicians. How about you?

B: (A)I like pop music more than classical music. (prefer / to)

G: I see. What do you like most about pop music?

B: I'm really fascinated by its exciting rhythms.

출제율 100%

07 위 대화를 읽고 답할 수 없는 질문은?

① Where are Bob and Sandy now?

② What kind of music does Sandy like?

③ Who is one of Sandy's favorite musicians?

④ What kind of music does Bob like?

⑤ How many kinds of music can they hear in this music library?

출제율 95%

08 위 대화의 밑줄 (A)와 같은 의미를 가진 문장이 되도록 주어진 단어를 활용하여 영작하시오.

➡ _____

출제율 90%

09 다음 대화의 밑줄 친 (a)~(e) 중 어법상 어색한 것은?

G: Jim, did you finish your art homework?

B: Yes. I (a)drew the face of my role model on a plate.

G: Sounds (b)interesting. Who is your role model?

B: My dad. He (c)always gives me good advice. Who did you draw, Amy?

G: Well, I drew (d)me surfing in the sea.

B: Wonderful! I'm (e)fascinated by your drawing.

G: Thank you.

① (a)　② (b)　③ (c)　④ (d)　⑤ (e)

출제율 95%

10 다음 주어진 문장의 부사절을 분사구문으로 적절히 전환한 문장을 고르시오.

Since he had not been invited to the awards ceremony, the actor watched it thorough the TV program.

① Having not been invited to the awards ceremony, the actor watched it thorough the TV program.

② As the actor not being invited to the awards ceremony, he watched it thorough the TV program.

③ As he being not invited to the awards ceremony, the actor watched it thorough the TV program.

④ Not having been invited to the awards ceremony, the actor watched it thorough the TV program.

⑤ Not having invited to the awards ceremony, the actor watched it thorough the TV program.

[11~12] 다음 주어진 우리말을 영작했을 때, 어법상 알맞지 않은 것을 고르시오.

출제율 95%

11

그 고대 유적지를 찾아가기 위해 우리가 썼던 돈은 낼 만한 가치가 있었다.

① The money we spent visiting the ancient site was worth being paid for.

② The money that we spent visiting the ancient site was worth paying for.

③ The money that we spent visiting the ancient site was worthy of being paid for.

④ It was worth paying for the money that we spent visiting the ancient site.

⑤ It was worthwhile to pay for the money that we spent visiting the ancient site.

12 출제율 100%

> 그 부부는 그들의 잃어버린 강아지를 발견하고 울지 않을 수 없었다.

① The couple couldn't help crying to find their lost puppy.
② The couple couldn't help but crying to find their lost puppy.
③ The couple couldn't but cry to find their lost puppy.
④ The couple had no choice but to cry when they found their lost puppy.
⑤ The couple couldn't help but cry when they found their lost puppy.

13 출제율 95%

다음 중 어법상 어색한 문장을 모두 고르면? (정답 2개)

① Have you ever felt like going swimming on a cold day?
② The expensive jewelry she wore tonight was worth to buy.
③ The people attending the meeting were busy discussing the sensitive issues.
④ Incheon International Airport is worth of being visited.
⑤ The audience could not help laughing at the story the comedian told them.

[14~17] 다음 글을 읽고 물음에 답하시오.

Using common images, pop art looks plain. (A)_____, it doesn't look artistic. But it is still worth paying attention to. Although it looks plain, it is filled with meaning. Let's learn about some famous pop artists. They became famous for their special artistic ability. They were able to change common objects into amazing art.

Andy Warhol is called the King of Pop Art. He found his (B)subjects in magazines and stores. One of his famous works is made up of pictures of Marilyn Monroe, the American actor. Another work shows cans of soup. He made many copies of these works. Why did he make copies of his works? He wanted to show that art is something you see every day.

14 출제율 100%

다음 중 빈칸 (A)에 들어갈 말로 적절한 것을 모두 고르시오.

① In other words   ② However
③ On the other hand   ④ That is
⑤ Nevertheless

15 출제율 95%

다음 중 밑줄 친 (B)와 쓰임이 같은 것은?

① Biology is my favorite subject.
② We need male subjects who are healthy.
③ The chapter deals with serious subjects.
④ Flights are subject to delay because of the fog.
⑤ 'She' is the subject of the sentence.

16 출제율 90%

What are some pop artists famous for? Answer in English.

➡ _____

17 Which is right about Andy Warhol?

① He went out with Marilyn Monroe.

② He was famous for making common things.

③ He made an artwork with his friends.

④ He wanted art to be scarce and hard to see.

⑤ He made an artwork by using cans of soup.

[18~19] 다음 글을 읽고 물음에 답하시오.

Claes Oldenburg is another pop artist who made art fun. He made sculptures of everyday items, such as a hamburger, cookies, and a brush. In the beginning, he created soft sculptures. They were made of plastic, paper, and other soft materials. For example, he used cloth to make toilets. Later, he made huge sculptures of daily items, such as an ice cream cone. Wanting everyone to enjoy his art, he set up his works in outdoor places. He also ran a store inside his studio to sell his works. For him, artistic works were fun goods for people.

18 다음 중 Claes Oldenburg가 주제로 삼을 만한 소재가 <u>아닌</u> 것은?

① cake
② a bottle
③ a knife
④ a spoon
⑤ a waterfall

19 Where did Claes Oldenburg set up his works?

➡ _____

[20~21] 다음 글을 읽고 물음에 답하시오.

Q: (A)_____

A: Pop art means art for people. It began in the 1950s in America. Pop artists used daily images and bright colors.

Q: What did these pop artists create?

A: Andy Warhol found his subjects in magazines and stores. He made many copies of his works. In the beginning, Claes Oldenburg created soft sculptures. Later, he made huge sculptures and set up his works in outdoor places. Roy Lichtenstein used cartoons in his works and even included speech balloons in his paintings.

20 빈칸 (A)에 들어갈 말로 가장 적절한 것은?

① What kind of art do people like?

② What do you know about art?

③ What is pop art?

④ What kinds of art are there around us?

⑤ Why does pop art become famous?

21 위 글의 내용에 맞게 빈칸에 알맞은 말을 쓰시오.

Each pop artist has their own artistic ability. Andy Warhol liked to find his subjects in _____, Claes Oldenburg was an excellent _____, and Roy Lichtenstein was famous for using _____ in his paintings.

01 다음 대화의 괄호 안의 단어를 알맞은 형태로 바꾸어 쓰시오.

> Bora: Andy, you went to the art museum, didn't you?
>
> Andy: Yes. They had a special Chagall exhibition.
>
> Bora: How did you like it?
>
> Andy: It was fantastic! I was (A)(fascinate) by the colors in his paintings and his creativity.
>
> Bora: No wonder. He was one of the greatest (B)(painter) ever. What else did you see in the museum?
>
> Andy: I went to a gift shop and saw things like umbrellas, cups, and backpacks. Famous works of art (C)(be) printed on them.
>
> Bora: Did you buy anything?
>
> Andy: Yes. I bought this T-shirt. How do you like it?
>
> Bora: It looks great on you.
>
> Andy: Thank you.

➡ (A) _____ (B) _____ (C) _____

02 다음은 아래 왼쪽의 명화와 이를 이용해 디자인한 우산을 소개한 글이다. 이 글을 바탕으로 어색한 문장을 찾아 올바른 문장으로 고쳐 쓰시오.

On White II

> Our group liked the umbrella designed by Jinsu. He used the painting, *On White II*. He was fascinated by its design.

A: Which painting did you choose?

B: (1)I chose *On White II*.

C: What did you like most about the painting?

B: (2)I was fascinated by the bright colors.

D: What did you design with the painting?

B: (3)I designed an umbrella. (4)How do you like my umbrella?

D: (5)I think it's beautiful.

➡ _____

03 다음 우리말에 맞도록 괄호 안에 주어진 어휘를 알맞게 배열하여 빈칸을 채우시오.

(1) 다른 사람들이 만화를 비웃고 있었지만, 팝 아티스트들은 그것들이 예술로 인정받도록 만들었다. (laughing, though, cartoons, at, people, other)

➡ _____
pop artists made them recognized as art.

(2) 흔한 일상적 사물과 이미지를 사용했기 때문에, 팝 아트는 정말 유명해졌다. (and, using, images, objects, everyday, common)

➡ _____
pop art has become really famous.

[04~05] 다음 우리말에 맞게 주어진 어구들을 알맞게 배열하여 빈칸을 채우시오.

04
> 동해의 섬, 독도는 우리가 일본으로부터 지켜야할 가치가 있다. (the island, is, in, protecting, the East Sea, worth)

➡ Dokdo, _____
from Japan.

05

> 지진이 얼마나 지속될지 아는 것은 불가능하다.
> (the, no, how, knowing, there, long, is)

➡ _____ earthquake will last.

06 다음 각 밑줄 친 부분 중 어법상 어색한 것을 고쳐 다시 쓰시오.

(1) Having rained heavily the day before, some of the streets got flooded.

➡ _____

(2) People strictly speaking, you can buy the condition of happiness but you can't buy happiness.

➡ _____

(3) Exhausting from a series of overtime work, I slept right away without even having dinner.

➡ _____

(4) Found the kitty the old lady had lost, Bentley told her to come quickly.

➡ _____

[07~09] 다음 글을 읽고 물음에 답하시오.

Pop is short for popular. So pop art means popular art, or art for people. It began in the 1950s in America. (A)그 당시 팝 아트 작가들은 재미있고 쉬운 것을 만들고 싶어 했다. Instead of difficult traditional art works, they turned their eyes to popular culture. They used images from TV, comic books, magazines, and advertising. When people saw familiar images in art exhibitions, they found (B)them refreshing.

07 Where did pop art begin? Answer in English with a full sentence.

➡ _____

08 주어진 단어를 활용하여 밑줄 친 우리말 (A)를 영어로 쓰시오.

> (at that time / something)

➡ _____
_____

09 밑줄 친 (B)가 가리키는 것을 위 글에서 찾아 쓰시오.

➡ _____

[10~11] 다음 글을 읽고 물음에 답하시오.

A Movie That Moved Me

Last Saturday I went to my friend's house to watch a movie. The title of the movie was My Son. I watched it because my friend recommended it. I liked the story of the movie. The story was about a brave man who tried to find his lost son. The main character was John. He was played by the actor Roy Jones, who was fantastic. It was (A)_____. (B)_____ the emotional scenes, I was (C)_____. The movie was really worth watching.

10 주어진 단어를 내용과 어법에 맞게 빈칸 (A)~(C)에 쓰시오.

> (touch / move / watch)

➡ (A)_____ (B)_____ (C)_____

11 Write the reason why the writer went to his friend's house. Answer in English.

➡ _____

01 다음 그림을 보고, 그림의 내용에 맞게 〈보기〉와 같이 분사구문이 포함된 문장을 자유롭게 영작하시오.

─ 보기 ─

- Sitting on the chair, she is playing the guitar.
- Having a fever, she stayed home.

① _____ ② _____
③ _____ ④ _____

02 다음 질의응답을 참고하여 감상문을 완성하시오.

Title: You and Me / Type: musical / When and Where: last Saturday, a concert hall

Q: Why did you watch the musical?

A: Because my favorite actor was in it.

Q: What did you like about it?

A: Songs and dances.

Q: What was it about?

A: It was about a girl who invited her best friends to her birthday party. They talked about their friendship.

Q: Talk about the main character.

A: The main character was Sophie. She sang many beautiful songs.

Q: How did you like it?

A: It was fantastic. Singing along to the songs during the performance, I was excited.

The Best Musical of My Life

_____ I went to _____ to watch _____. The title of the musical was _____. I watched it because _____. I liked _____ of the musical. The story was _____ _____. They talked _____. _____ Sophie. She _____. It was _____. _____ _____, I was _____. The musical was really worth watching.

단원별 모의고사

01 다음 단어에 대한 영어 설명이 <u>어색한</u> 것은?

① exhibition: an event at which objects such as paintings are shown to the public, a situation in which someone shows a particular skill or quality to the public, or the act of showing these things

② familiar: easy to recognize because of being seen, met, heard, etc. before

③ include: to contain something as a part of something else, or to make something part of something else

④ popular: liked, enjoyed, or supported by many people

⑤ copy: the first that a person made

02 다음 짝지어진 단어의 관계가 같도록 빈칸에 알맞은 말을 쓰시오.

> advice – tip : intimate – _____

03 다음 영영풀이에 해당하는 어구를 고르시오.

> in place of someone or something

① in spite of
② moreover
③ instead of
④ in other words
⑤ in the end

04 다음 중 짝지어진 대화가 <u>어색한</u> 것은?

① A: How do you like these shoes?
   B: I don't like them. They are too small.

② A: How do you like this movie?
   B: It looks great.

③ A: What was the story about?
   B: It was about the friendship between two friends.

④ A: I read the book, *The Wisdom*.
   B: I watched it alone.

⑤ A: What do you want to make with these paper cups?
   B: I think we can make one of the world-famous bridges using paper cups.

[05~06] 다음 대화를 읽고 물음에 답하시오.

Bora: Andy, you went to the art museum, didn't you?

Andy: Yes. They had a special Chagall exhibition.

Bora: (a)How did you like it?

Andy: It was fantastic! (b)I was fascinated by the colors in his paintings and his creativity.

Bora: (A)_____ He was (c)one of the greatest painters ever. What else did you see in the museum?

Andy: I went to a gift shop and saw things like umbrellas, cups, and backpacks. Famous works of art (d)were printed on them.

Bora: Did you buy anything?

Andy: Yes. I bought this T-shirt. How do you like it?

Bora: (e)It looks great on you.

Andy: Thank you.

05 위 대화의 빈칸 (A)에 들어갈 말로 알맞은 것은?

① Not at all.
② No problem.
③ No wonder.
④ Of course not.
⑤ Yes, I do.

06 위 대화의 밑줄 친 (a)~(e)에 대한 설명 중 잘못된 것은?

① (a): 어떤 것에 대해 만족하는지 아니면 불만족하는지 묻는 표현이다.

② (b): '~에 매료되었다'라는 의미로 어떤 것에 대해 깊은 관심이 있음을 나타내는 표현으로, I was into the colors로 바꾸어 표현할 수 있다.

③ (c): 'one of the 최상급+복수 명사' 형태로 '가장 ~한 것들 중 하나'의 뜻이다.

④ (d): 예술 작품들이 그려져 있다는 수동의 의미로 수동태를 사용하였고, them은 'gift shop'을 가리키는 대명사다.

⑤ (e): '너에게 잘 어울린다'라는 의미로 'It'은 'this T-shirt'를 가리킨다.

[07~08] 다음 대화를 읽고 물음에 답하시오.

G: Jim, did you finish your art homework?
B: Yes. I drew the face of my role model on a plate.
G: Sounds interesting. Who is your role model?
B: My dad. He always gives me good advice. Who did you draw, Amy?
G: Well, (a)나는 내가 바다에서 서핑하는 것을 그렸어.
B: Wonderful! (A)_____
G: Thank you.

07 위 대화의 빈칸 (A)에 들어갈 말로 알맞은 것은?

① I'm fascinated by its story.
② I'm fascinated by its characters.
③ I like its special effects.
④ I'm fascinated by your drawing.
⑤ I'm fascinated by its rhythms and melody.

08 위 대화의 밑줄 친 (a)의 우리말에 맞게 주어진 단어를 알맞은 순서로 배열하시오. (한 단어를 반드시 변형할 것.)

(I / in / the / surfing / sea / drew / me)

➡ _____

09 다음 대화의 빈칸에 들어갈 알맞은 말은?

B: The other day I watched a play, *A Love Story in the War*.
G: Oh, _____?
B: I liked the main characters. The actors' performances were fantastic.
G: Was the story good as well?
B: No. It was a little boring, but the music was pretty good.
G: So, do you think I should see it?
B: Only if you have a lot of time and money.

① is this what you wanted
② how did you like the play
③ did you have fun
④ how did you like the song
⑤ how did you respond to the play

10 다음 대화의 밑줄 친 우리말에 맞게 주어진 단어를 이용하여 영작하시오.

A: I watched the musical, *Mom, You're My Angel*.
B: How did you like it?
A: It was fantastic. Watching the musical, 눈을 뗄 수가 없었어. (take / off / it)

➡ _____

11 다음 각 문장의 밑줄 친 부사절을 분사구문으로 바꾼 것 중 옳은 것은?

① While my sister was drawing some pop art pictures, the dogs fell asleep.
→ Drawing some pop art pictures,

② If you use daily images in a creative way, you can make a work of art for everyone.
→ Using daily images in a creative way,

③ When the structures are observed from a little higher position, they may look like a butterfly.
→ The structures observed from a little higher position,

④ If it doesn't snow next week, you can't go to ski school this year.
→ Not snowing next week,

⑤ As Maggy memorized the lines of the play, she went to bed as happily as ever.
→ Maggy memorizing the lines of the play,

[12~14] 다음 중 어법상 어색한 문장은?

12 ① What the professor wrote was not worth reading.

② The clothes and machines are worthy of being recycled.

③ The studio where the painter lived is worth being visited someday.

④ The time I shared with the girl was worth investing in.

⑤ It is worth while going to the concert.

13 ① I couldn't help being upset with her.

② Since my favorite actor shot the film, I cannot help going to watch the movie.

③ Robert could not help but crying when he saw his mom walking again.

④ The villagers couldn't help making smiles to see the missing baby coming back.

⑤ The prince couldn't help falling in love with the girl with long hair.

14 ① Being sensitive to the feedback, the pop artist was carefully making her works of cartoon art.

② Developed carelessly, the machine has been criticized as the worst of the 20th century.

③ It being hot and humid, all the outdoor games had to be cancelled.

④ Being no coins left, Mr. Collins gave up throwing them into the fountain.

⑤ Wanting to create something fun and easy, pop artists used familiar images and bright colors.

15 다음 각 분사구문을 접속사가 이끄는 부사절로 만들 때, 빈칸에 알맞은 말을 써 넣으시오.

(1) Using everyday items such as a hamburger, cookies, and a brush, Claes Oldenburg made pop art sculptures.
➡ As he_____ _____ _____
such as a hamburger, cookies, and a brush, Claes Oldenburg made pop art sculptures.

(2) Watching the pop artist making the painting, they will understand the art is not difficult.

➡ _____ _____ _____ _____
_____ _____ _____ the
painting, they will understand the art is not difficult.

(3) Getting interested in the film, she bought the movie ticket.

➡ Since _____ _____ _____
_____ _____ _____, she
bought the movie ticket.

(4) Being unhealthy, the woman helped me carry the heavy boxes.

➡ _____ _____ _____ _____,
the woman helped me carry the heavy boxes.

[16~19] 다음 글을 읽고 물음에 답하시오.

Pop is short for popular. So pop art means popular art, or art for people. It began in the 1950s in America.

(A) Since then, pop art has become truly popular. People thought that art was too difficult to understand. By using daily images and bright colors, pop artists changed that thought.

(B) They used images from TV, comic books, magazines, and advertising. When people saw familiar images in art exhibitions, they found them refreshing.

(C) Pop artists at that time wanted to create something fun and easy. Instead of difficult traditional art works, they turned their eyes to popular culture.

Using common images, pop art looks plain. In other words, it doesn't look artistic. (D)하지만 여전히 주목할 만한 가치가 있다. Although it looks plain,

it is filled with meaning. Let's learn about some famous pop artists. They became famous for their special artistic ability. They were able to change common objects into amazing art.

16 다음 중 위 글의 제목으로 가장 적절한 것은?

① Pop Art: Unpopular Form of Art
② Pop Art: Art for Everyone
③ Unfortunate Art: Pop Art
④ Pop Art: Never Known to People
⑤ Enjoy the Bright Color of Art

17 자연스러운 글이 되도록 박스 안의 (A)~(C)를 바르게 나열하시오.

➡ _____

18 주어진 단어를 활용하여 밑줄 친 우리말 (D)를 영어로 쓰시오.

(but / still / worth / pay)

➡ _____

19 Choose one that is NOT true.

① Pop art is art for people.
② Pop artists wanted their works to be fun.
③ It is easy to say that pop art doesn't look artistic.
④ Pop art is meaningless because it looks plain.
⑤ People thought that it was refreshing to see familiar images in art exhibitions.

[20~21] 다음 글을 읽고 물음에 답하시오.

Andy Warhol is called the King of Pop Art. ①He found his subjects in magazines and stores. ②One of his famous works is made up of pictures of Marilyn Monroe, the American actor. ③She was the most beloved actor in America at that time but died young. ④Another work shows cans of soup. ⑤He made many copies of these works. Why did he make copies of his works? He wanted to show that art is something you see every day.

20 밑줄 친 ①~⑤ 중 글의 흐름상 어색한 문장은?

①   ②   ③   ④   ⑤

21 Write the reason why Andy Warhol made many copies of his works. Use the phrase 'It's because.'

➡ _____

_____

[22~25] 다음 글을 읽고 물음에 답하시오.

ⓐClaes Oldenburg is other pop artist who made art fun. He made sculptures of everyday items, such as a hamburger, cookies, and a brush. In the beginning, he created soft sculptures. They were made of plastic, paper, and other soft materials. ____ⓑ____, he used cloth (A)to make toilets. Later, he made huge sculptures of daily items, such as an ice cream cone. Wanting everyone to enjoy his art, he set up his works in outdoor places. He also ran a store inside his studio to sell his works. For him, artistic works were fun goods for people.

22 위 글의 밑줄 친 ⓐ에서 어법상 어색한 곳을 올바르게 고치시오.

_____ ➡ _____

23 위 글의 빈칸 ⓑ에 알맞은 것은?

① However   ② Therefore
③ That is   ④ For example
⑤ In the end

24 밑줄 친 (A)와 쓰임이 같은 것은?

① Is there someone to depend on?
② It is amazing to make her laugh.
③ There was no chance to get back the money.
④ I perfer to stay at home.
⑤ Jane waited there to visit me again.

25 Why did Claes Oldenburg run a store inside his studio? Answer in English.

➡ _____

_____

MEMO

Lesson 9

You Can Do It, Too

🎙 의사소통 기능

- 가능성 정도 묻기
  A: Is it possible for you to read ten books in a month?
  B: Yes. I think it's possible.

- 바람·소원 말하기
  A: I wish I could have matches.
  B: What would you do with matches?

🎙 언어 형식

- I wish 가정법 과거
  I wish she **had** a better robotic hand.

- 의문사가 없는 의문문의 간접의문문
  I wondered **if I could do something for those girls**.

Words & Expressions
교과서

Key Words

- **afford** [əfɔ́:rd] 동 ~할 여유가 되다
- **business** [bíznis] 명 사업
- **coin** [kɔin] 명 동전
- **collect** [kəlékt] 동 수집하다
- **control** [kəntróul] 동 통제하다, 조절하다, 조정하다
- **corn** [kɔ:rn] 명 옥수수
- **corn cob** 옥수수 속대
- **cost** [kɔ:st] 동 값이 들다
- **countryside** [kʌ́ntrisaid] 명 시골
- **entrance fee** 입장료
- **failure** [féiljər] 명 실패
- **fair** [fɛər] 명 박람회
- **fee** [fi:] 명 요금
- **filter** [fíltər] 명 여과장치, 필터 동 여과하다, 거르다
- **headband** [hédbænd] 명 머리띠
- **invention** [invénʃən] 명 발명(품)
- **inventor** [invéntər] 명 발명가
- **knife** [naif] 명 칼
- **leaf** [li:f] 명 나뭇잎
- **match** [mætʃ] 명 성냥
- **pollute** [pəlú:t] 동 오염시키다
- **pollution** [pəlú:ʃən] 명 오염
- **possible** [pásəbl] 형 가능한
- **president** [prézədənt] 명 대통령, 회장, 총재
- **raise** [reiz] 동 (자금을) 모으다

- **realize** [rí:əlàiz] 동 깨닫다, 인식하다
- **recommend** [rèkəménd] 동 추천하다
- **remove** [rimú:v] 동 제거하다
- **relaxed** [riláekst] 형 편안한, 여유 있는
- **robotic** [roubátik] 형 로봇식의
- **sew** [sou] 동 꿰매다, 바느질하다
- **sewing machine** 재봉틀
- **software** [sɔ́:ftweər] 명 소프트웨어
- **solve** [sɑlv] 동 풀다, 해결하다
- **space** [speis] 명 우주
- **stay** [stei] 동 머무르다
- **step** [step] 명 단계
- **success** [səksés] 명 성공
- **surprised** [sərpráizd] 형 놀란
- **system** [sístəm] 명 체계, 장치
- **teenager** [tí:nèidʒer] 명 십 대(= **teen**)
- **town** [taun] 명 마을
- **triangle** [tráiæŋgl] 명 삼각형
- **useful** [jú:sfəl] 형 유용한
- **useless** [jú:slis] 형 쓸모없는, 소용없는
- **wish** [wiʃ] 명 소원 동 ~이면 좋겠다고 생각하다
- **whether** [hwéðər] 접 ~인지 (아닌지)
- **wonder** [wʌ́ndər] 동 궁금하다
- **wonderful** [wʌ́ndərfəl] 형 훌륭한

Key Expressions

- **by Ving** V함으로써
- **change A into B** A를 B로 바꾸다
- **come across** 우연히 마주치다
- **for free** 무료로
- **for oneself** 스스로
- **get together** 만나다

- **hit on** ~을 생각해 내다
- **look forward to Ving** V하기를 고대하다
- **not only A but also B** A 뿐만 아니라 B도
- **pay for** 지불하다
- **thanks to** ~ 덕분에
- **think to oneself** 마음속으로 생각하다

Word Power

※ 서로 비슷한 뜻을 가진 어휘

□ **control** 조종하다 – **manage** 조종하다
□ **fee** 요금 – **charge** 청구 금액, 요금
□ **pollute** 오염시키다 – **contaminate** 오염시키다

□ **remove** 제거하다 – **eliminate** 제거하다
□ **useful** 유용한 – **helpful** 도움이 되는, 유용한
□ **realize** 깨닫다 – **understand** 깨닫다

※ 서로 반대되는 뜻을 가진 어휘

□ **failure** 실패 ↔ **success** 성공
□ **useful** 유용한 ↔ **useless** 쓸모없는

□ **possible** 가능한 ↔ **impossible** 불가능한
□ **wonderful** 훌륭한 ↔ **terrible** 끔찍한

※ 접미사 -ful → 명사+-ful

□ **beauty** 아름다움 – **beautiful** 아름다운
□ **harm** 해, 피해 – **harmful** 해로운
□ **help** 도움 – **helpful** 도움이 되는

□ **success** 성공 – **successful** 성공적인
□ **use** 사용 – **useful** 유용한
□ **wonder** 경이 – **wonderful** 훌륭한

※ 접미사 -tion → 동사+-tion

□ **communicate** 의사소통하다 – **communication** 의사소통
□ **illuminate** 빛나다 – **illumination** 빛
□ **invent** 발명하다 – **invention** 발명
□ **invite** 초대하다 – **invitation** 초대

□ **limit** 제한하다 – **limitation** 제한
□ **pollute** 오염시키다 – **pollution** 오염
□ **realize** 깨닫다 – **realization** 깨달음
□ **transport** 수송하다 – **transportation** 운송, 수송

English Dictionary

□ **afford** ~할 여유가 되다
→ to be able to do something
어떤 것을 할 수 있다

□ **business** 사업
→ a work of producing, buying, and selling of goods and services
상품과 서비스를 생산하고 구매하고 파는 일

□ **coin** 동전
→ a round piece of metal used as money
돈으로 사용되는 동그란 금속 조각

□ **come across** 우연히 마주치다
→ to meet or find by chance
우연히 만나거나 발견하다

□ **control** 통제하다, 조정하다
→ to make an organization, person, or system do what you want or have in the way you want
조직, 사람 혹은 시스템을 당신이 원하는 대로 하거나 원하는 방식대로 하다

□ **cost** 값이 들다
→ to be obtained at the price of
어떠한 가격으로 얻어지다

□ **fair** 박람회
→ a large public event where goods are bought and sold, usually from tables that have been specially arranged for the event
주로 행사를 위해 특별히 배열된 테이블에서 물건들이 구매되고 팔리는 큰 공공 행사

□ **for free** 무료로
→ without having to pay
지불할 필요가 없는

□ **headband** 머리띠
→ a narrow strip of material worn around the head, usually to keep your hair or sweat out of your eyes
머리에 두르는 좁은 재질의 줄로 주로 머리카락이나 땀이 눈으로 들어 가지 않게 하는 것

□ **hit on** ~을 생각해 내다
→ to think of a plan, a solution, etc. suddenly or by chance
계획, 해결책 등을 갑자기 혹은 우연히 생각하다

□ **pollute** 오염시키다
→ to damage the water, air, land, etc. by using harmful chemicals
유해한 화학물질을 이용함으로써 물, 공기, 땅을 손상시키다

□ **robotic** 로봇식의
→ relating to or like a robot
로봇과 같거나 혹은 로봇과 관련된

□ **sew** 꿰매다, 바느질하다
→ to stitch with thread
실로 꿰매다

□ **software** 소프트웨어
→ the operating applications programs that are used in a computer system
컴퓨터 시스템 내에서 사용되는 운영 응용 프로그램

□ **success** 성공
→ the achievement of an aim or purpose
목적 또는 목표의 성취

01 다음 짝지어진 단어의 관계가 같도록 빈칸에 알맞은 말은?

> useful – useless : valuable – _____

① invaluable   ② precious
③ valueless   ④ priceless
⑤ expensive

서답형
02 주어진 영어 설명에 맞게 문장의 빈칸에 알맞은 말을 쓰시오.

> My parents didn't _____ a new refrigerator.

┤영어 설명├
to be able to do something

03 밑줄 친 부분의 의미로 알맞지 <u>않은</u> 것은?

① The speaker ended <u>by suggesting</u> some serious topics for discussion. (제안함으로써)
② He <u>hit on</u> a new way of making people's lives more comfortable. (~을 명중하다)
③ <u>Thanks to</u> your effort, we could manage to finish this project. (~ 덕분에)
④ Every week they <u>get together</u> to make songs and perform together. (만나다)
⑤ You can hardly expect her to do it <u>for free</u>. (공짜로)

04 다음 〈보기〉의 단어를 사용하여 자연스러운 문장을 만들 수 <u>없</u>는 것은?

┤ 보기 ├
useless   control   whether   remove

① It is _____ for us to keep these things in the house.
② The government attempts to _____ immigration.
③ People _____ the environment with garbage.
④ Filters do not _____ all contaminants from water.
⑤ We don't know _____ he's alive or dead.

05 다음 빈칸에 공통으로 들어갈 말로 알맞은 것을 고르시오.

> • Thanks _____ your advice, the problem can be solved with ease.
> • We are looking forward _____ making another appointment with you.

① at   ② in   ③ by
④ with   ⑤ to

06 다음 중 두 단어의 관계가 <u>어색한</u> 것은?

① limit – limitation
② recommend – recommendation
③ invent – invention
④ consider – consideration
⑤ attempt – attemption

01 자연스러운 문장이 되도록 〈보기〉의 어구를 빈칸에 알맞게 쓰시오.

> ─ 보기 ─
> business / coin / for free / cost / control

(1) I have a _____ from China.

(2) You need to learn how to _____ your spending.

(3) She wants to have her own _____ someday.

(4) I can't believe it only _____ 5 dollars in total.

(5) You cannot expect people to work _____.

02 다음은 하나의 단어가 갖는 여러 가지 의미 중 일부이다. 해당하는 단어를 쓰시오.

> • a large public event where goods are bought and sold, usually from tables that have been specially arranged for the event
> • reasonable, right, and just

➡ _____

03 다음 짝지어진 두 단어의 관계가 같도록 빈칸에 알맞은 말을 쓰시오.

(1) inform – information : pollute – _____

(2) converse – conversation : limit – _____

(3) help – helpful : beauty – _____

04 우리말에 맞게 한 단어를 추가하여 주어진 어구를 알맞게 배열하시오.

(1) 우리는 사람들이 더 이상 필요로 하지 않는 신발과 옷 같은 것들을 모을 수 있습니다.
(we / things / no longer / can / shoes and clothes / that / need / like / people)

➡ _____
_____

(2) 어른들의 입장료는 10달러이다.
(for / the entrance / is / adults / $10)

➡ _____

(3) Sam은 공기를 오염시키지 않기 위해서 자전거를 탄다.
(the air / rides / Sam / to / not / a bike)

➡ _____

05 빈칸 (A)~(C)에 각각 공통으로 들어가는 전치사를 쓰시오.

> (A) We are looking forward _____ seeing you again.
> 'It can't be true,' he thought _____ himself.
> (B) She became very smart _____ reading a lot of books.
> David made the cookies _____ himself.
> (C) They lacked the money to pay _____ the repairs.
> Jennifer blamed me _____ being late for the meeting.

06 다음과 같이 풀이되는 말을 쓰시오.

> the achievement of an aim or purpose

➡ _____

Conversation

① **가능성 정도 묻기**

> **A:** Is it possible for you to read ten books in a month? 네가 한 달에 책 열 권을 읽는 것이 가능하니?
>
> **B:** Yes. I think it's possible. 응. 나는 가능하다고 생각해.

■ 어떤 일이 가능한지를 물을 때 'Is it possible ~?', 'Can you ~?', 'Are you likely to ~?' 등으로 물을 수 있다. 가주어 it에 진주어 to부정사를 쓸 경우 'for+목적격'을 이용하여 to부정사의 행위 주체를 나타낼 수 있다.

■ 이에 대한 대답으로 possible과 impossible을 이용하여 'Yes, I think it's possible.' 혹은 'No, I don't think it's possible.', 'No. I think it's impossible.'로 가능과 불가능에 대해 답할 수 있다.
(I'm) Sorry, but I can't ~. / Yes, I do[would]. / Sure. / Of course.

가능성 정도 묻기

- Is it possible for ~ to V …? (~가 V하는 것이 가능하니?) • Can S V …? (S가 V할 수 있니?)
- Is S likely to V …? (S가 V할 것 같니?) • Is it probable/likely that S can V …? (S가 V할 가능성이 있니?)
- Is it okay if I ~? (내가 ~한다면 괜찮겠니?)

가능성 정도 답하기

- Yes, I think it's possible. (응. 가능할 것 같아.) • No, I don't think it's possible. (아니. 가능할 것 같지 않아.)
- I'm not sure if I can. (내가 할 수 있는지 확신할 수 없어.) • Maybe you can. (아마도 넌 할 수 있을 거야.)

핵심 Check

1. 다음 괄호 안의 단어들을 이용해 밑줄 친 우리말을 영어로 쓰시오.

> **A:** 그녀가 그것들을 통제하는 것도 가능하니? (too / control / possible / it / them / is / for / to / her)
> **B:** Yes. I think it's possible.

➡ _____

2. 자연스러운 대화가 되도록 다음 빈칸에 알맞은 말을 쓰시오.

> **A:** Is it probable that _____?
> **B:** Yes. I think she can drive the truck.

② 바람 · 소원 말하기

A: I wish I could have matches. 나는 성냥을 가졌으면 좋겠어.

B: What would you do with matches? 성냥으로 무엇을 할 거야?

■ 'I wish I could ~.'는 현재의 바람이나 소원을 나타내는 표현으로 'I wish' 가정법 과거이다. 이와 같은 표현으로는 'I want to V ~.', 'I'd like to V ~.', 'I look forward to Ving ~.', 'I'm looking forward to Ving ~.' 등이 있다.

* I wish she loved me. 그녀가 나를 사랑한다면 좋을 텐데.

■ 'I wish+주어+동사의 과거형'의 형태로 현재 사실을 말하지만 반드시 동사의 과거형을 써야 한다. 원칙적으로 가정법 과거에서 be동사는 'were'를 쓰지만 현대 영어에서는 1, 3인칭 단수일 때는 'was'를 쓰기도 한다.

* I wish Sam spoke Korean. Sam이 한국말을 한다면 좋을 텐데. (실제 Sam은 한국말을 하지 못함)
* I wish she were[was] a doctor. 그녀가 의사이면 좋을 텐데. (실제 그녀는 의사가 아님)
* I wish I had my own room. 내가 내 방을 가진다면 좋을 텐데. (실제 내 방을 가지고 있지 않음)

■ 'I wish I could ~.' 뒤에는 사실과 반대되거나 가능성이 거의 없는 일이 오고, 만약 가능성이 있거나 결과를 아직 모르는 것을 희망할 때는 'I hope ~'를 쓴다.

* I wish I could live up to 200 years old. 내가 200살까지 살 수 있으면 좋을 텐데.
* I hope I will be able to buy that car some day. 나는 언젠가 그 차를 살 수 있길 바라.

바람 · 소원 말하기

* I wish I could ~.: 내가 ~하면 좋겠어.
* I want to ~ .: 나는 ~하고 싶어.
* I'd like to ~.: 나는 ~하고 싶어.
* I look forward to Ving ~.: 나는 ~하는 것을 기대해.
* I am looking forward to Ving ~.: 나는 ~하는 것을 기대하고 있어.

핵심 Check

3. 주어진 단어를 이용하여 다음 대화의 밑줄 친 우리말을 영어로 쓰시오.

> **A:** 내가 대도시에 살면 좋을 텐데. (wish)
> **B:** Right. Living in a big city would be fantastic.

➡ _____

Listen & Speak 1 A-1

G: ❶Can you draw this on the paper?

B: Sure. From the middle point, I draw two triangles. Then I draw the circle, like this.

G: Good. Now, is it possible ❷for you to draw it without taking your pencil off the paper?

B: I'll try. Hmm... No, how is that possible?

G: Well, start at ❸one of the four red points.

B: Do you mean any of the red points?

G: Yes. Draw the circle first and then the two triangles like this. Or you can draw the triangles first, like this.

B: Oh, now ❹I get it.

G: 너 이걸 종이에 그릴 수 있겠니?

B: 물론이지. 가운데 지점으로부터 두 개의 삼각형을 그리면 돼. 그러고 나서 이렇게 원을 그리면 되지.

G: 좋아. 그럼 종이에서 연필을 떼지 않고 그것을 그리는 것이 가능하니?

B: 시도해 볼게. 흠… 아니, 그게 어떻게 가능하니?

G: 음, 네 개의 빨간 점 중 한 곳에서 시작하면 돼.

B: 빨간 점 중에 아무 점이나 말하는 거야?

G: 응. 원을 먼저 그리고, 그 다음에 삼각형 두 개를 이렇게 그려. 아니면 이렇게 삼각형을 먼저 그릴 수도 있어.

B: 오, 이제 알겠어.

❶ 가능한지 묻는 표현(= Is it possible for you to draw this on the paper?)

❷ to부정사의 의미상 주어는 'for+목적격' 형태로 to부정사 앞에서 의미상의 행위 주체를 나타낼 때 쓰인다.

❸ one of+복수명사: ~들 중 하나

❹ '이해한다'는 표현으로 'I understand it.'과 같다.

Check(√) True or False

(1) It is impossible for the girl to draw the picture without taking her pencil off the paper.　　T ☐ F ☐

(2) The picture has two triangles and a circle.　　T ☐ F ☐

 Listen & Speak 2 A-1

B: Wendy, you ❶have been late for school a lot lately. What's wrong?

G: I want to wake up early, but I just can't.

B: Doesn't your mom ❷wake you up?

G: She does, but I don't get up right away. ❸I wish I could have an AI robot.

B: An AI robot?

G: Yes. I mean one that could make sure I got up and gave me breakfast in the morning.

B: That sounds great.

B: Wendy, 너 요즘 계속 지각하네. 무슨 일 있어?

G: 일찍 일어나고 싶은데, 그게 안돼.

B: 네 엄마가 널 깨워 주시지 않니?

G: 엄마가 깨워주시긴 하는데, 바로 일어나지 않아. 인공지능 로봇이 있으면 좋겠어.

B: 인공지능 로봇?

G: 응. 내가 아침에 꼭 일어나도록 확인해 주고, 아침밥을 가져다주는 그런 로봇 말이야.

B: 그거 좋은 생각이야.

❶ 현재완료 시제를 이용하여 최근의 상황을 표현한다.

❷ '타동사+부사'는 대명사 인칭목적어를 취할 때 '타동사+목적어+부사'의 어순을 취한다.

❸ 'I want to have an AI robot.'과 같은 의미이다.

Check(√) True or False

(3) Wendy has been late for school because her mom doesn't wake her up.　　T ☐ F ☐

(4) Wendy wants AI robot to make sure she did her homework.　　T ☐ F ☐

Listen & Speak 1 A-2

W: Hi. ❶I'm looking for a backpack for my son.

M: How old is your son?

W: He is five years old.

M: I want to recommend this ❷one.

W: Oh, it's so cute.

M: Yes, isn't it? It has a cap ❸that looks like a penguin, so kids love it.

W: ❹Is it possible for me to take the cap off for washing?

M: Sure. You can easily take it off and ❺put it back on.

W: That's wonderful. I'll take it.

❶ be looking for: ~을 찾는 중이다
❷ 정해지지 않은 하나를 가리킬 때 쓰는 부정대명사
❸ 주격 관계대명사
❹ 'Can I take the cap off for washing?'과 같은 뜻
❺ put A back on: A를 도로 끼다

Listen & Speak 2 A-2

B: ❶I'm planning to visit my uncle in Mexico.

G: What are you going to do there, Mike?

B: I'll spend most of my time at his house because he has a big swimming pool.

G: That's great. ❷Can you swim well?

B: No, ❸I wish I could, but I can't. So I'll have fun with a water walking ball instead.

G: A water walking ball? What is that?

B: It's a large ball. We go inside ❹it and walk on the water.

G: That ❺must be fun.

❶ be planning to V: ~할 계획이다
❷ 'Is it likely that you can swim well?'과 같은 뜻
❸ 소망을 나타내는 말(수영을 잘하고 싶지만 그렇지 못함)
❹ a water walking ball 지칭
❺ '~임에 틀림없다'는 확신을 나타내는 표현

Real Life Talk

Bora: What are you doing, Jessie?

Jessie: I'm drawing Dr. Rebecca, my favorite superhero.

Bora: Wow, that's great.

Jessie: Thanks. ❶I wish I could read people's minds like her.

Bora: Is it possible for her to control ❷them, too?

Jessie: Yes. She can control your mind ❸if she wants to.

Bora: That's very cool.

Jessie: What about you? Do you also have any favorite superheroes?

Bora: Sure. I love Sky X. I wish I could fly ❹like him.

Jessie: I like him, too. He can even breathe in space.

Bora: Yes. He can do ❺anything in space.

❶ 'I want to read people's minds like her.'와 같은 표현
❷ people's minds 지칭   ❸ 조건의 부사절을 이끄는 접속사(~라면)
❹ 전치사(~처럼)   ❺ 긍정문에서 쓰일 때 '무엇이든'으로 해석

Wrap Up 1

W: Hi, Tom. What are you doing?

B: I'm flying my drone.

W: Cool! ❶Are you good at it?

B: No, I'm not very good right now, but I'm practicing ❷hard.

W: ❸As you know, I run a sandwich restaurant. Is it possible for you to deliver orders with your drone?

B: No, ❹it isn't. But I think it will be possible ❺in one or two years.

W: That will be great.

❶ be good at: ~을 잘하다   ❷ 부사(열심히)   ❸ 너도 알다시피
❹ it is not possible for me to deliver orders with my drone
❺ 시간을 나타낼 때 '~ 후에'

● 다음 우리말과 일치하도록 빈칸에 알맞은 말을 쓰시오.

Listen & Speak 1 A-1

G: _____ _____ _____ this on the paper?

B: Sure. _____ the middle point, I draw _____ _____. Then I draw the circle, _____ _____.

G: Good. Now, is it _____ _____ _____ to draw it _____ _____ your pencil _____ the paper?

B: I'll try. Hmm... No, _____ _____ possible?

G: Well, start _____ one of the _____ _____ _____.

B: Do you mean _____ _____?

G: Yes. Draw the circle _____ and then _____ _____ _____ _____. Or you can draw the _____, like this.

B: Oh, now _____ _____ _____.

Listen & Speak 1 A-2

W: Hi. I'm _____ _____ a backpack _____ my son.

M: _____ _____ is your son?

W: He is _____ _____ _____.

M: I want _____ _____ this one.

W: Oh, it's _____ cute.

M: Yes, _____ _____? It has a cap _____ _____ _____ a penguin, so kids _____ _____.

W: Is it possible _____ _____ _____ the cap _____ for washing?

M: Sure. You can easily _____ _____ _____ and _____ _____ _____ on.

W: That's _____. I'll _____ _____.

Listen & Speak 2 A-1

B: Wendy, _____ _____ _____ _____ school a lot lately. What's _____?

G: I want to _____ _____ _____, but I just _____.

B: Doesn't your mom _____ _____ _____?

G: She _____, but I don't get up _____ _____. _____ I _____ have an AI robot.

B: _____ _____ _____?

G: Yes. I mean one _____ _____ _____ I got up and _____ _____ in the morning.

B: That sounds _____.

해석

G: 너 이걸 종이에 그릴 수 있겠니?

B: 물론이지. 가운데 지점으로부터 두 개의 삼각형을 그리면 돼. 그러고 나서 이렇게 원을 그리면 되지.

G: 좋아. 그럼 종이에서 연필을 떼지 않고 그것을 그리는 것이 가능하니?

B: 시도해 볼게. 흠… 아니, 그게 어떻게 가능하니?

G: 음, 네 개의 빨간 점 중 한 곳에서 시작하면 돼.

B: 빨간 점 중에 아무 점이나 말하는 거야?

G: 응. 원을 먼저 그리고, 그 다음에 삼각형 두 개를 이렇게 그려. 아니면 이렇게 삼각형을 먼저 그릴 수도 있어.

B: 오, 이제 알겠어.

W: 안녕하세요. 아들을 위한 배낭을 찾고 있어요.

M: 아들이 몇 살인가요?

W: 아들은 다섯 살이에요.

M: 이것을 추천하고 싶네요.

W: 오, 이거 정말 귀엽네요.

M: 네, 그렇지 않나요? 펭귄과 같이 생긴 모자가 있어서 아이들이 좋아하죠.

W: 제가 세탁을 위해 모자를 분리하는 것도 가능한가요?

M: 물론이죠. 모자를 쉽게 분리했다가 다시 붙일 수도 있어요.

W: 훌륭해요. 이걸 살게요.

B: Wendy, 너 요즘 계속 지각하네. 무슨 일 있어?

G: 일찍 일어나고 싶은데, 그게 안 돼.

B: 네 엄마가 널 깨워 주시지 않니?

G: 엄마가 깨워주시긴 하는데, 바로 일어나지 않아. 인공지능 로봇이 있으면 좋겠어.

B: 인공지능 로봇?

G: 응. 내가 아침에 꼭 일어나도록 확인해 주고, 아침밥을 가져다주는 그런 로봇 말이야.

B: 그거 좋은 생각이야.

Listen & Talk 2 A-2

B: I'm _____ _____ _____ my uncle in Mexico.

G: What are you _____ _____ _____ _____, Mike?

B: I'll _____ _____ _____ _____ at his house _____ he has a big _____ _____.

G: That's great. _____ you _____ _____?

B: No, _____ _____ _____ _____, but I can't. So I'll _____ _____ _____ a water walking ball _____.

G: A water walking ball? _____ _____ _____?

B: _____ a large ball. We _____ _____ it and _____ _____ the water.

G: That _____ _____ fun.

Real Life Talk

Bora: What _____ you _____, Jessie?

Jessie: I'm _____ Dr. Rebecca, _____ _____ _____.

Bora: Wow, that's _____.

Jessie: Thanks. I wish I _____ _____ _____ _____ _____ like her.

Bora: Is it possible _____ _____ _____ _____ them, too?

Jessie: Yes. She can control your mind _____ _____ _____ _____.

Bora: That's very _____.

Jessie: What about you? Do you also _____ _____ _____ _____?

Bora: Sure. I love Sky X. I wish I _____ _____ _____ _____ _____.

Jessie: I like him, too. He can _____ _____ _____ space.

Bora: Yes. He _____ _____ _____ in space.

Wrap Up 1

W: Hi, Tom. _____ _____ _____ _____ _____?

B: I'm _____ my drone.

W: Cool! _____ you _____ _____ it?

B: No, I'm not very good _____ _____, but I'm _____ _____.

W: _____ _____ _____, I _____ a sandwich restaurant. Is it possible _____ _____ _____ _____ _____ _____ with your drone?

B: No, it _____. But I think _____ _____ _____ _____ _____ one or two years.

W: _____ will _____ _____.

B: 나는 멕시코에 있는 삼촌을 방문할 계획이야.

G: 거기서 뭐 할 거야, Mike?

B: 삼촌이 큰 수영장을 가지고 계셔서 난 대부분의 시간을 삼촌 집에서 보낼 거야.

G: 멋지다. 너 수영 잘하니?

B: 아니, 잘했으면 좋겠는데, 못해. 그래서 대신 나는 물 위를 걷는 공을 가지고 놀 거야.

G: 물 위를 걷는 공? 그게 뭐야?

B: 그건 큰 공이야. 그 안에 들어가서 물 위를 걸으면 돼.

G: 그거 분명 재밌겠다.

Bora: Jessie야, 뭐 하고 있어?

Jessie: 내가 제일 좋아하는 슈퍼 영웅인 닥터 레베카를 그리고 있어.

Bora: 와, 훌륭해.

Jessie: 고마워. 나는 그녀처럼 사람들의 마음을 읽을 수 있으면 좋겠어.

Bora: 그녀가 사람들의 마음을 통제하는 것도 가능하니?

Jessie: 응. 그녀가 원하면 네 마음을 통제할 수 있어.

Bora: 그거 정말 멋지다.

Jessie: 너는 어때? 너도 좋아하는 슈퍼 영웅이 있니?

Bora: 물론. 나는 스카이 X를 좋아해. 스카이 X처럼 하늘을 날 수 있으면 좋겠어.

Jessie: 나도 그가 좋아. 그는 우주에서 숨을 쉴 수도 있잖아.

Bora: 응. 그는 우주에서 뭐든 할 수 있어.

W: 안녕, Tom. 무엇을 하는 중이니?

B: 지금 드론을 날리고 있어요.

W: 멋지구나! 드론 조종을 잘하니?

B: 아니요, 전 지금은 별로 잘하지 못하지만 열심히 연습하고 있어요.

W: 네가 알다시피, 내가 샌드위치 가게를 운영하고 있잖아. 너는 네 드론으로 주문한 음식을 배달하는 것이 가능하니?

B: 아니요, 불가능해요. 하지만 1~2년 후에는 가능할 거라 생각해요.

W: 그러면 좋겠구나.

01 다음 대화의 빈칸 (A)와 (B)에 공통으로 들어갈 말을 쓰시오. (가주어 it을 쓸 것.)

> A: I'm Sky X. I can fly.
> B: Hi, Sky X. Nice to meet you.
> C: I wish I could fly like you. (A)_____ to fly to the moon?
> A: Sure.
> D: Then (B)_____ to travel to the sun?
> A: No. That's impossible.

02 다음 대화의 밑줄 친 부분과 바꾸어 쓸 수 있는 것은?

> A: <u>Is it possible for us to arrive in 20 minutes?</u>
> B: No. I don't think it's possible.

① Is it possible that you arrive in 20 minutes?
② Do you make sure you can arrive in 20 minutes?
③ Is it likely that we can arrive in 20 minutes?
④ Do you want us to arrive in 20 minutes?
⑤ Can you tell me how to get there in 20 minutes?

[03~04] 다음 대화를 읽고 물음에 답하시오.

> B: Wendy, you have been ①<u>late</u> for school a lot lately. What's wrong?
> G: I want to wake up ②<u>early</u>, but I just ③<u>can</u>.
> B: Doesn't your mom wake you up?
> G: She ④<u>does</u>, but I don't get up right away. I wish (A)_____
> B: An AI robot?
> G: Yes. I mean one that could make sure I got up and gave me breakfast in the morning.
> B: That sounds ⑤<u>great</u>.

03 밑줄 친 ①~⑤ 중 대화의 흐름상 어색한 것은?

①   ②   ③   ④   ⑤

04 빈칸 (A)에 알맞은 말을 쓰시오. (6 words)

➡ _____

[01~02] 다음 대화를 읽고 물음에 답하시오.

G: Can you draw this on the paper?

B: (A)Sure. From the middle point, I draw two triangles. Then I draw the circle, like this.

G: Good. Now, is it possible for you to draw it without taking your pencil off the paper?

B: I'll try. Hmm... No, how is that possible?

G: Well, start at one of the four red points.

B: Do you mean any of the red points?

G: Yes. Draw the circle first and then the two triangles like this. Or you can draw the triangles first, like this.

B: Oh, now I get it.

01 밑줄 친 (A)를 대신하여 쓸 수 있는 것은?

① I'm not certain.

② That depends on you.

③ Yes. I think it's possible.

④ Don't be so negative.

⑤ Of course not.

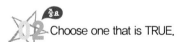

02 Choose one that is TRUE.

① They are making something with paper.

② There are five red points on the paper.

③ The boy doesn't know how to draw the picture at all.

④ It doesn't matter which red point you choose.

⑤ It is impossible for them to draw the picture without taking a pencil off the paper.

[03~05] 다음 대화를 읽고 물음에 답하시오.

B: Wendy, you have been late for school a lot ⓐlately. What's wrong?

G: I want to wake up early, but I just can't.

(A) She does, but I don't get up right away. I wish I could have an AI robot.

(B) That sounds great.

(C) An AI robot?

(D) Doesn't your mom wake you up?

(E) Yes. I mean one that could make sure I got up and gave me breakfast in the morning.

서답형

03 자연스러운 대화가 되도록 (A)~(E)를 바르게 나열하시오.

➡ _____

04 밑줄 친 ⓐ를 대신할 수 있는 것은?

① for a long time ② recently

③ hardly ④ behind time

⑤ frankly

서답형

05 Write the reason why Wendy has been late for school. Use the phrase 'It is because.'

➡ _____

서답형

06 주어진 단어를 활용하여 빈칸에 들어갈 말을 완성하시오.

A: _____

(wish / invent)

B: A time machine? What would you do with it?

07 다음 대화의 빈칸에 들어갈 말로 가장 적절한 것은?

> A: _____
>
> B: What would you do with it?
>
> A: I would send messages to my friends.

① I wish I had many friends.

② I want to have a watch.

③ I wish you could have a computer.

④ I'd like to have something to write.

⑤ I wish I could have a smartphone.

08 다음 대화의 밑줄 친 부분의 목적으로 가장 적절한 것은?

> A: Is it possible for you to make a classmate laugh in 10 seconds?
>
> B: Sure.

① asking for an opinion

② asking for possibility

③ saying hello to friends

④ making some suggestions

⑤ asking for help

09 다음 짝지어진 대화 중 어색한 것은?

① A: I wish I could fly like a bird.
   B: Why do you say so?

② A: Is it possible to visit the park on our second day?
   B: Sure. That sounds exciting.

③ A: Can we exchange this hat for a bigger one?
   B: Absolutely. It's not likely.

④ A: Is it likely that we can survive in Mars?
   B: No. I don't think it's possible.

⑤ A: I wish I could live on the water.
   B: Living on the water sounds interesting.

[10~12] 다음 대화를 읽고 물음에 답하시오.

> W: Hi, Tom. ①무엇을 하는 중이니?
>
> B: I'm flying my drone.
>
> W: Cool! ②드론 조종을 잘하니?
>
> B: No, I'm not very good right now, but ③열심히 연습하고 있어요.
>
> W: As you know, I run a sandwich restaurant. (A)Is it possible for you to deliver orders with your drone?
>
> B: ④아니요, 불가능해요. But I think it will be possible ⑤1~2년 후에는.
>
> W: That will be great.

10 밑줄 친 ①~⑤ 중 영어로 바르게 옮겨지지 않은 것은?

① What are you doing?

② Are you good at it?

③ I'm practicing hardly

④ No, it isn't.

⑤ in one or two years

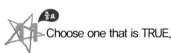
Choose one that is TRUE.

① Tom is not interested in flying his drone.

② Tom doesn't know that the woman runs a restaurant.

③ Tom thinks he is skillful enough to deliver orders.

④ The woman wants Tom to deliver orders with his drone.

⑤ The woman wonders if Tom wants to work with his friends.

서답형

12 주어진 단어를 활용하여 밑줄 친 (A)와 같은 의미의 말을 쓰시오.

> (can)

➡ _____

[01~03] 다음 대화를 읽고 물음에 답하시오.

G: (A)Can you draw this on the paper?
B: Sure. From the middle point, I draw two triangles. Then I draw the circle, like this.
G: Good. Now, is it possible for you to draw it without taking your pencil off the paper?
B: I'll try. Hmm... No, how is (B)that possible?
G: Well, start at one of the four red points.
B: Do you mean any of the red points?
G: Yes. Draw the circle first and then the two triangles like this. Or you can draw the triangles first, like this.
B: Oh, now I get it.

01 위 대화에 나오는 표현을 이용하여 밑줄 친 (A)와 같은 의미의 문장을 쓰시오.

➡ _____

02 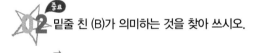 밑줄 친 (B)가 의미하는 것을 찾아 쓰시오.

➡ _____

03 Write the two ways how to draw the picture without taking off the pencil. Answer in Korean.

➡ _____
_____

04 다음은 Jane이 무인도에 홀로 남겨진다면 꼭 해야 할 일이라고 생각하는 것이다. 'I wish'를 이용하여 표현하시오.

- keep calm and pass the time
- create a shelter
- wait for help
- find food

➡ _____
_____
_____
_____

[05~06] 다음 대화를 읽고 물음에 답하시오.

Bora: What are you doing, Jessie?
Jessie: I'm drawing Dr. Rebecca, my favorite superhero.
Bora: Wow, that's great.
Jessie: Thanks. I wish I could read people's minds like her.
Bora: Is it possible for her to control them, too?
Jessie: Yes. She can control your mind if she wants to.
Bora: That's very cool.
Jessie: What about you? Do you also have any favorite superheroes?
Bora: Sure. I love Sky X. I wish I could fly like him.
Jessie: I like him, too. He can even breathe in space.
Bora: Yes. He can do anything in space.

05 According to the dialogue, what is it possible for Dr. Rebecca to do? Answer in English.

➡ _____
_____

06 Who is Bora's favorite superhero?

➡ _____

Grammar

1 **I wish 가정법 과거**

> • **I wish** she had a better robotic hand. 그녀가 더 좋은 로봇 손을 가지면 좋을 텐데.
>
> • **I wish** Tony could live in this town so that we could easily get together. Tony가 이 마을에 살아서 우리가 쉽게 만날 수 있으면 좋을 텐데.

■ 'I wish' 가정법 과거는 현재 사실에 반대되는 소망 또는 현재 사실에 대한 유감을 나타낸다.

  • **I wish** I **were** a great inventor like Edison. 내가 에디슨 같은 훌륭한 발명가라면 좋을 텐데.
    = In fact, I**'m not** a great inventor like Edison. (현재 사실 반대)
    = **I'm sorry that** I'm not a great inventor like Edison. (유감)

■ 가정법 과거: 현재 사실을 반대로 또는 실현 가능성이 없는 일을 가정. '**If**+주어+**동사 과거형** ~, 주어 +**would/could**+**동사원형** ….'의 형태, '만약 ~라면 …할 텐데.'의 뜻.

  • **If** she **had** a car, she **would take** me to the airport. 그녀가 차가 있다면, 나를 공항까지 데려다 줄 텐데. (가정법 과거, 현재 사실의 반대 가정)
    = **As** she **doesn't have** a car, she **won't take** me to the airport.
  cf. **If** she **has** a car, she **will take** me to the airport. 조건문(현재 또는 미래의 가능성)

■ 가정법 과거완료: 이미 일어난 과거 사실을 반대로 가정. '**If**+주어+**had**+**과거분사** ~, 주어+**would/ could**+**have**+**과거분사** ….'의 형태, '만약 ~했었더라면 …했을 텐데.'의 뜻.

  • **If** they **had stopped** at the gas station, **they would not have run** out of gas. 그들이 주유소에 들렀더라면 기름이 떨어지지 않았을 텐데.

■ 'I wish' 가정법 과거완료: 과거 사실에 반대되는 소망 또는 과거 사실에 대한 유감을 나타낸다.

  • **I wish** he **had not gone** there alone. 그가 그곳에 혼자 가지 않았더라면 좋을 텐데.
    = **I'm sorry that** he **went** there alone. (그가 혼자 갔던 것이 안타깝다.)

■ 가정법의 다양한 표현들

  • **As** he **is** weak, he **can't** lift the box. 그는 약해서, 그 상자를 들 수 없다. (직설법)
    → **If** he **were not** weak, he **could** lift the box. 그가 약하지 않으면, 그 상자를 들 수 있을 텐데. (가정법)
    → **Were** he **not** weak, he **could** lift the box. (If 생략 후 be동사와 주어 도치)
    → **Without** his being weak, he **could** lift the box. (without 표현)
    → **If it were not for** his being weak, he **could** lift the box.
    → **Were it not for** his being weak, he **could** lift the box. (If 생략 후 be동사와 주어 도치)

핵심 Check

1. 다음 괄호 안의 단어를 활용하여 빈칸에 알맞은 단어를 써 넣으시오.

  (1) I wish my uncle _____ with us. (live)

  (2) I wish I _____ a doctor. (be) I want to cure my mom's heart.

  (3) I wish Janet _____ sing well. (can) I can't stand it any more.

② 의문사가 없는 의문문의 간접의문문

- I wondered **if I could do something for those girls.** 나는 내가 그 소녀들을 위해서 어떤 것을 할 수 있을까 생각했다.

- I am not sure **whether the baby is hungry or sad.** 나는 그 아기가 배가 고픈 것인지 슬픈 것인지 모르겠다.

■ 간접의문문 만들기

(1) 의문사가 있을 때: '의문사+주어+동사' 어순
- She doesn't care. + Who is he? → She doesn't care **who he is.**
- Can he tell her? + What am I doing? → Can he tell her **what I am doing**?
- Nobody knows. + How did she come here? → Nobody knows **how she came here.**

cf. 주절의 동사가 think, believe, guess, suppose, imagine 등일 때, 의문사는 문두로 간다.
- Do you think? + Why is she upset? → **Why** do you <u>think</u> **she is upset**?
- Do you guess? + Who will be late? → **Who** do you <u>guess</u> **will be late**?

(2) 의문사가 없을 때: 'whether/if+주어+동사' 어순
- Does he know? + Is she upset? → Does he **know if she is upset**?
- I wonder. + Did she eat the cake? → I wonder **whether she ate the cake.**
- I'm not sure. + Is it going to rain? → I'm not sure **if it's going to rain.**
- I don't know. + Can anyone drink this? → I don't know **if anyone can drink this.**
- Do you know? + Does Paul speak Korean? → Do you know **whether Paul speaks Korean**?

■ whether와 if의 차이

(1) whether는 문두에서 주절을 이끌 수 있다. (if는 불가능)
- **Whether** he will join us (or not) is not certain. (그가 우리와 함께할지는 확실하지 않다.)

(2) whether는 전치사 뒤에서 명사절 목적어 가능. (if는 불가능)
- There is an argument **about whether** cell phone use should be allowed in school. (학교에서 휴대전화 사용이 허용되어야 할지에 대한 논란이 있다.)

(3) whether는 to부정사와 붙여 쓸 수 있다. (if는 불가능)
- How can you decide **whether to use** 'that' or 'which'? (that을 쓸지, which를 쓸지 당신은 어떻게 결정합니까?)

(4) 'whether or not' 가능 (if는 불가능. 단, 'or not'을 뒤에 따로 쓰면 가능)
- I wonder **whether or not** it was true. (나는 그것이 사실이었는지 아닌지 궁금하다.)
- No one knows **whether[if]** she'll die **or not**. (아무도 그녀가 죽을 지 안 죽을지를 모른다.)

핵심 Check

2. 다음 괄호 안에서 알맞은 말을 고르시오.

(1) They wonder (if / that) Mike is sleeping on a sofa.

(2) Irene asked the expert (that / whether) her dog could be nice again.

01 다음 각 가정법 문장에서 어법상 <u>어색한</u> 단어를 한 개씩만 찾아 고치시오.

(1) I wish I can pay for the school fees for the African girls.

_____ ➡ _____

(2) I wish the girl has a better robotic hand.

_____ ➡ _____

(3) If we work together, we could build a better world.

_____ ➡ _____

(4) If the girl were not poor, she may go to school.

_____　_____

02 다음 각 문장의 빈칸에 공통으로 들어갈 말로 알맞은 것은? (대 · 소문자 구분 없음)

> • I wondered _____ I could solve the problem.
> • _____ it will rain tomorrow or not depends on the wind.
> • They asked _____ she could predict the result of the experiment.

① if　　　　　　② that　　　　　　③ what
④ whether　　　⑤ which

03 다음 빈칸에 들어갈 말로 알맞은 것은?

> I wish the small holes in the corn cobs _____ dirty matter.

① filter　　　　　② will filter　　　　③ has filtered
④ could filter　　⑤ are filtered

04 다음 중 밑줄 친 부분의 쓰임이 〈보기〉와 같은 것을 고르시오.

> ┤ 보기 ├
> I'm not sure <u>if</u> we could win the first prize.

① Why don't we take a taxi <u>if</u> your babies feel too tired?
② You will never miss the train <u>if</u> you leave now.
③ All the students wondered <u>if</u> what she said was true.
④ Nicole can use her phone <u>if</u> she finishes the math homework.
⑤ Mike will be in trouble <u>if</u> he keeps eating junk food.

[01~03] 다음 중 어법상 어색한 문장은?

01
① I wish many girls in Africa could go to school.
② I wish my mom weren't sick from food poisoning.
③ I wish his invention could clean up all the lakes in my village.
④ I wish someone will make her a better robotic hand.
⑤ I wish they made much cheaper and better tools for the poor people.

02
① If I were in California, I would never be safe from the disease.
② If her father were very rich, she might be allowed a car.
③ If it were not for his help, I would not be able to use the system.
④ If the boy knew the answer to the quiz, he would tell me.
⑤ If I pushed the doors hard, they can be broken.

03
① I wonder whether or not Brian heard of my broken heart.
② I wonder whether Brian heard of my broken heart or not.
③ I wonder if or not Brian heard of my broken heart.
④ I wonder if Brian heard of my broken heart.
⑤ I wonder if Brian heard of my broken heart or not.

서답형
[04~07] 다음 우리말과 일치하도록 괄호 안에 주어진 어구를 바르게 배열하시오.

04
> 당신이 나를 도와줄 수 있을지 모르겠지만, 그럴 수 있기를 바란다.
> (help, I, me, you, know, if, don't, can), but I hope you can.

➡ _____

05
> 내가 미국의 대통령이라면 좋을 텐데.
> (the President, I, I, of, were, wish, the United States).

➡ _____

06
> David은 그 집에 화장실이 있는지 나에게 물어봤다.
> (there, whether, asked, was, me, a bathroom, David) in the house.

➡ _____

07
> 내가 그 소녀라면, 포기할 텐데.
> (give up, the girl, I, I, if, would, were).

➡ _____

[08~10] 다음 중 밑줄 친 부분의 쓰임이 나머지 넷과 다른 것은?

08 ① I was wondering if the man would lend me some money.

② I wonder if the kids dancing under the sun ate lunch today.

③ Please tell me if your teacher will read the invitation card or not.

④ Let's go swimming in the sea if it is fine this weekend.

⑤ The queen of the tribe wanted to know if the visitor could help her.

09 ① I wish the boy who I met yesterday could eat Kimchi.

② I could not help but laugh at the funny dress my dad wore.

③ If my uncle were not ill, he could take me to the amusement park.

④ If Sandy got an A in the math test, her mom would buy her a new laptop.

⑤ If I had some money, I could buy you the mask you need.

10 ① I'm wondering if Julie could help the kids in need.

② Karen was not sure if Jimin would come to the party.

③ Focus on the inner voice if you want to listen to your true self.

④ Do you know if she is going to study abroad or get married?

⑤ I'd like to know if my online fashion business will succeed.

11 다음 우리말을 영작할 때, 어법상 어색한 문장을 고르시오.

> 공기가 없다면, 지구에 생명체가 살 수 없을 것이다.

① Without air, lives on Earth would not be able to live.

② If there is no air, lives on Earth would not be able to live.

③ Were it not for air, lives on Earth would not be able to live.

④ If it were not for air, lives on Earth would not be able to live.

⑤ If there were no air, lives on Earth would not be able to live.

12 다음 짝지어진 두 문장의 의미가 다른 것은?

① I wish my best friend Saya were a great musical actor.

= In fact, my best friend Saya is not a great musical actor.

② If the boys studied harder, they could get good grades.

= As the boys don't study harder, they can't get good grades.

③ I wish I could play all the musical instruments in the museum.

= I am sorry that I can't play all the musical instruments in the museum.

④ If Susan told lies more often than now, I would not believe her.

= As Susan doesn't tell lies more often than now, I believe her.

⑤ I wish I could make a much cheaper and better robotic hand.

= I'm sorry that I couldn't make a much cheaper and better robotic hand.

13 다음 중 같은 뜻을 가진 문장으로 바르게 연결된 것은?

① Vannessa's sister doesn't have a cell phone, so she wants to get one.
= Vannessa's sister would get a cell phone if she wanted to have one.

② Nicky doesn't practice hard, so she can't show her parents what she wants.
= If Nicky practiced hard, she could show her parents what she wants.

③ Paul didn't have time, so he couldn't drive his daughter home.
= If Paul had time, he would drive his daughter home.

④ Grandma can't write a letter to my aunt as she doesn't know her address.
= Grandma couldn't write a letter to my aunt if she didn't know her address.

⑤ It rained cats and dogs, so all my family members stayed home.
= If it rained cats and dogs, all my family members wouldn't stay home.

[14~15] 다음 우리말을 어법상 알맞게 영작한 것을 고르시오.

14

그 어린 소녀는 그가 로봇 손을 만들 수 있는지 물었다.

① The little girl asked him to make the robotic hand.

② The little girl asked that he could make the robotic hand.

③ The little girl asked him that he could make the robotic hand.

④ The little girl asked him if he could make the robotic hand.

⑤ The little girl asked him whether he made the robotic hand.

15

나는 그가 수질 오염 문제를 해결할 수 있을지 궁금했다.

① I was wondering whether he can solve the problem of polluted water.

② I wondered whether the problem of polluted water can be solved by him.

③ I was curious about whether he will solve the problem of polluted water.

④ I wondered whether or not the problem of polluted water is solved by him.

⑤ I wondered whether he could solve the problem of polluted water.

16 다음 문장의 빈칸 (A)~(C)에 들어갈 말로 가장 적절한 것은?

• I wish I (A)_____ a mentor who could give me advice on my future job.

• Were it not for the sacrifice of the medical staff in our country, we (B)_____ be in trouble by the disease.

• I wish the girl (C)_____ a better and cheaper robotic hand and leg.

	(A)	(B)	(C)
①	had	will	has had
②	have	would	has
③	have	could	had
④	had	would	had
⑤	have had	will	has

01 다음 우리말과 일치하도록 괄호 안에 주어진 어구를 빈칸에 알맞게 배열하시오.

(1) 많은 가난한 소녀들이 학교에 갈 수 있도록 내가 수업료를 지불할 수 있으면 좋을 텐데.

➡ _____
_____ go to school. (could, I, pay, many, to, wish, the school fees, I, poor girls, for)

(2) 옥수수 속대 안의 작은 구멍들이 오염된 물로부터 더러운 물질을 걸러낼 수 있으면 좋을 텐데.

➡ _____
_____ dirty matter out of the polluted water. (the small holes, could, in, wish, the corn cobs, filter, I)

(3) 과학 박람회에서 만났던 그 소녀가 더 나은 로봇 손을 가지면 좋을 텐데.

➡ _____
a better robotic hand. (met, had, a science fair, wish, I, I, at, the girl)

(4) 마을 사람들이 나를 도와주면, 여과 장치를 만들 수 있을 텐데.

➡ If _____
a filtering system. (me, could, the villagers, build, I, helped)

02 다음 문장에서 어법상 어색한 단어를 하나만 찾아 바르게 고쳐 다시 쓰시오.

(1) I asked myself that night if I can solve the problem of the polluted water.

➡ _____
_____

(2) Tony wasn't sure that he could make it but he decided to try.

➡ _____
_____

(3) If Jane will follow her heart or not is important in her life.

➡ _____
_____

(4) Even her closest friends doubted whether could she do something for the girls in Africa.

➡ _____
_____

(5) Most people in my town are wondering if it rains next week.

➡ _____
_____

(6) Sean couldn't decide if to reject the job offer or not.

➡ _____
_____

(7) The researchers want to know that my filtering system can clean up all the lakes not only in my village but also in other areas.

➡ _____
_____
_____

03 다음 〈보기〉의 문장과 같은 뜻이 되도록 괄호 안에 주어진 조건에 맞게 빈칸을 채우시오.

| 보기 |
Without her invention, the town would suffer from the problem of polluted water.

(1) _____ her invention, the town would suffer from the problem of polluted water. (2 단어)

(2) _____ her invention, the town would suffer from the problem of polluted water. (it, be동사 활용, 5 단어)

(3) _____ her invention, the town would suffer from the problem of polluted water. (it, be동사 활용, 4 단어)

(4) _____ not suffer from the problem of polluted water. (직설법, there, 접속사 as 활용, 8 단어)

04 다음 그림과 대화를 보고 우리말에 맞게 괄호 안의 어구를 알맞게 배열하시오.

Mrs. Forestier: What's the matter?

Matilda: Can I borrow something from you?

Mrs. Forestier: Sure. Choose whatever.

Matilda: This diamond necklace is beautiful! Will you lend me this?

Mrs. Forestier: Certainly! Go enjoy the ball!

(1) Matilda는 Mrs. Forestier로부터 뭔가를 빌릴 수 있을지 궁금해했다.
(if, Mrs. Forestier, borrow, Matilda, she, could, something, wondered, from)

➡ _____
_____

(2) Matilda는 Mrs. Forestier에게 그 다이아몬드 목걸이를 빌려줄 것인지 물어봤다.
(if, Matilda, Mrs. Forestier, her, she, lend, would, that, asked, diamond necklace)

➡ _____
_____

[05~06] 다음 주어진 문장과 같은 뜻이 되도록 가정법을 이용하되, 글자 수 조건에 맞게 빈칸을 채우시오.

05
As the poor girls in Africa can't go to school, I feel sorry for it.

➡ I _____ to school. (8 단어)

06
I am sorry that I don't sing well like my grandfather who is a singer.

➡ I _____ my grandfather who is a singer. (5 단어)

[07~08] 다음 우리말을 if가 포함된 간접의문문을 사용하여 괄호 안에 주어진 조건과 글자 수에 맞게 영작하시오.

07
Susan이 한국말을 하는지 Mike에게 물어보아라.
(speak 활용, 변형 가능, 총 6 단어)

➡ _____

08
Gloria는 자신의 아기가 배가 고픈 것인지 슬픈 것인지 확신할 수 없었다.
(be sure 활용, 변형 가능, 축약형 불가, 총 11 단어)

➡ _____

Great Help with a Beautiful Mind

Who are the people who change the world? Do you think you are too
young to be one of these people? In the following stories you will meet
three teenagers who used their ideas to make the world a better place.

A Robotic Hand from a Helpful Mind (Easton LaChappelle)

One day, when I was fourteen, I came across a little girl at a science
fair. She had a robotic hand that could only open and close. I was
surprised that the hand had cost her 80,000 dollars! 'I wish she had a
better robotic hand,' I thought to myself. With that, I started to make a
much cheaper and better robotic hand.

After many failures, finally, by using 3D printing technology, I was
able to make a useful robotic hand for the price of only 300 dollars.
I decided to share the designs and software for my 3D robotic hand
with others for free. Maybe someone can take what I have done and do
something useful with it. No one person can change the world, but we
can build a better world by working together.

Headbands for Girls' Education (Mary Grace Henry)

'Why can't many girls in Africa go to school as I can? I wish they
could go to school, too.' I had this thought when I was twelve. I
realized that their families couldn't afford it. I wondered if I could do
something for those girls.

---

teenager: 십 대
robotic: 로봇식의
fair: 박람회
software: 소프트웨어
failure: 실패
come across: (우연히) 만나다
headband: 머리띠
realize: 깨닫다, 인식하다
afford: ~할 (금전적인) 여유가 되다

확인문제

● 다음 문장이 본문의 내용과 일치하면 T, 일치하지 않으면 F를 쓰시오.

1   At a science fair, Easton came across a girl who had a robotic hand. ☐

2   Easton succeeded in making a better robotic hand after many failures. ☐

3   The 3D printed robotic hand costs 80,000 dollars. ☐

Then I had an idea. For my birthday, I asked my parents to buy me a sewing machine. They bought me one, and I learned how to make headbands for myself. I created ten headbands and sold them at my school. Soon, I raised enough money to send one girl in Africa to school. I couldn't stop there.

I started a business to help girls in Africa who couldn't go to school. Thanks to the success of my business, I can pay the school fees for many poor girls in countries like Kenya and Uganda to go to school. I also pay for their textbooks, uniforms, and pencils.

Isn't it amazing? My advice to you is to just do something. When you see a need, act. Start small, taking little steps. Your warm heart can change lives.

Useless Corn Cobs as Useful Water Filters (Lalita Prasida)

As a young girl living in the countryside in India, I often found that the water around us was seriously polluted. I wondered how I could solve this problem. Then I hit on the idea to use corn cobs.

Useless corn cobs were everywhere in my village. I thought that the small holes in the corn cobs could filter dirty matter out of the polluted water.

One day, I picked up some dried cobs along the road, washed them, and placed them in a bowl of dirty water. After a while, I checked the water, and it looked much clearer. Then, using corn cobs that I had collected from farmers, I built a filtering system.

My system removed 70 to 80 percent of the dirty matter from the water. I hope my filtering system can clean up all the lakes not only in my village but also in other areas.

raise: (자금을) 모으다
sewing machine: 재봉틀
business: 사업
success: 성공
fee: 요금
thanks to: ~ 덕분에
useless: 쓸모없는, 소용없는
filter: 필터, 여과 장치
countryside: 시골
pollute: 오염시키다
corn cob: 옥수수 속대
hit on: 불현듯 ~을 생각해 내다

확인문제

- 다음 문장이 본문의 내용과 일치하면 T, 일치하지 않으면 F를 쓰시오.

1   Mary made headbands for her friends with the sewing machine. ☐

2   Mary believes people's lives can be changed by warm heart. ☐

3   Lalita wants the filtering system to be used only in her town. ☐

● 우리말을 참고하여 빈칸에 알맞은 말을 쓰시오.

1 Who are the people _____ _____ the world? Do you think you are _____ _____ _____ _____ one of these people?

2 In the following stories you _____ _____ three teenagers who used their ideas _____ _____ the world a better place.

A Robotic Hand from a Helpful Mind (Easton LaChappelle)

3 One day, _____ I was fourteen, I _____ _____ a little girl _____ a science _____ .

4 She had a _____ hand _____ could only _____ and _____ .

5 I was _____ _____ the hand _____ _____ _____ 80,000 dollars!

6 'I _____ she _____ a better robotic hand,' I thought _____ _____ .

7 With that, I started to make _____ _____ _____ and _____ robotic hand.

8 After many _____ , finally, _____ _____ 3D printing technology, I _____ _____ _____ make a useful robotic hand _____ the price _____ only 300 dollars.

9 I decided _____ _____ the designs and software _____ my 3D robotic hand _____ _____ _____ _____ _____ .

10 Maybe someone can _____ _____ _____ _____ _____ and do _____ _____ with it.

11 _____ _____ person can _____ the world, but we can _____ a better world _____ _____ together.

Headbands for Girls' Education (Mary Grace Henry)

12 'Why _____ many girls in Africa _____ _____ _____ as I can? I wish they _____ _____ to school, too.'

13 I _____ _____ _____ when I was twelve. I _____ _____ their families couldn't _____ it.

14 I wondered _____ _____ _____ _____ _____ _____ for those girls. Then I _____ an idea.

1 세상을 바꾸는 사람들은 누구인 가? 여러분은 너무 어려서 이런 사람들 중 하나가 될 수 없다고 생각하나요?

2 다음 이야기에서 여러분은 세상 을 더 나은 곳으로 만들기 위해 자신들의 아이디어를 사용한 세 명의 십 대들을 만날 겁니다.

돕는 마음으로부터 탄생한 로봇 손 (Easton LaChappelle)

3 내가 열네 살이었을 때, 어느 날 한 과학 박람회에서 어린 소녀를 우연히 만났다.

4 그녀는 겨우 접었다 펴지기만 하 는 로봇 손을 가지고 있었다.

5 나는 그녀가 그 손에 8만 달러를 지불했다는 데 놀랐다!

6 '나는 그녀가 더 나은 로봇 손을 가질 수 있으면 좋겠어.'라고 마음 속으로 생각했다.

7 나는 이런 생각을 가지고 더 싸고 좋은 로봇 손을 만들기 시작했다.

8 많은 실패 뒤 마침내 3D 프린트 기술을 사용해서 나는 단 300달 러짜리의 유용한 로봇 손을 만들 수 있었다.

9 나는 내 3D 로봇 손의 디자인과 소프트웨어를 다른 사람들과 무 료로 공유하기로 결심했다.

10 아마도 누군가는 내가 만든 것을 이용해 다른 유용한 것을 할 수 있을 것이다.

11 혼자 세상을 바꿀 수는 없지만, 함께 일 하면서 더 나은 세상을 만들 수 있다.

여학생 교육을 위한 머리띠 (Mary Grace Henry)

12 '아프리카의 많은 소녀들은 왜 나 처럼 학교에 갈 수 없지? 나는 그 들도 학교에 갈 수 있으면 좋을 텐데.'

13 내가 12살 때, 이런 생각을 했었 다. 나는 그들의 가족이 그럴 금 전적 여유가 없다는 것을 깨달았 다.

14 나는 내가 그 소녀들을 위해서 어 떤 것을 할 수 있을까 생각했다. 그때 아이디어가 떠올랐다.

15 For my birthday, I _____ my parents to _____ _____ _____ _____.

16 They _____ _____ _____, and I learned _____ _____ _____ headbands for myself.

17 I created _____ _____ and sold _____ at my school.

18 Soon, I _____ _____ _____ _____ to send one girl in Africa to school. I couldn't _____ there.

19 I started _____ _____ to help girls in Africa _____ couldn't _____ to school.

20 Thanks _____ _____ _____ _____ of my business, I can pay the school _____ _____ many poor girls in countries _____ Kenya and Uganda _____ _____ _____ _____.

21 I also _____ _____ their _____, _____, and pencils. Isn't it _____?

22 My _____ to you _____ to just _____ _____. When you see _____ _____, _____.

23 Start _____, _____ little steps. Your warm heart can change _____.

Useless Corn Cobs as Useful Water Filters (Lalita Prasida)

24 _____ a young girl _____ in the countryside in India, I _____ _____ _____ _____ the water around us was _____ _____.

25 I wondered _____ _____ _____ _____ this problem. Then I _____ _____ the idea _____ corn cobs.

26 _____ corn cobs _____ everywhere _____ my village.

27 I thought that _____ _____ _____ in the corn cobs _____ _____ _____ _____ out of the _____ water.

28 One day, I _____ up some dried cobs along the road, _____ _____ _____, and _____ them _____ _____ _____ dirty water.

29 _____ _____ _____ _____, I checked the water, and _____ looked _____ _____.

30 Then, _____ corn cobs _____ I had _____ _____ farmers, I built a _____ system.

31 My system _____ 70 to 80 percent of _____ _____ from the water.

32 I hope my _____ _____ can _____ _____ all the lakes _____ _____ in my village _____ _____ in other areas.

15 나는 내 생일에 부모님께 재봉틀을 사 달라고 부탁드렸다.

16 그들은 재봉틀을 사 주셨고 나는 머리띠 만드는 법을 혼자 배웠다.

17 10개의 머리띠를 만들어 학교에서 팔았다.

18 나는 곧 아프리카에 있는 한 명의 소녀를 학교에 보낼 수 있는 충분한 자금을 모았다. 나는 거기서 멈출 수 없었다.

19 나는 학교에 갈 수 없는 아프리카의 소녀들을 돕기 위해 사업을 시작했다.

20 내 사업의 성공 덕분에 나는 케냐와 우간다 같은 나라에 있는 많은 가난한 소녀들이 학교에 갈 수 있게 수업료를 지불할 수 있다.

21 나는 또한 그들의 교과서와 교복, 연필을 위한 비용도 지불한다. 놀랍지 않은가?

22 나의 조언은 그냥 무엇이든 하라는 것이다. 필요성이 보인다면 행동하라.

23 작은 단계를 밟아가면서 작은 것부터 시작하라. 너의 따뜻한 마음이 삶을 바꿀 수 있다.

유용한 물 여과 장치로 쓰인 쓸모없는 옥수수 속대 (Lalita Prasida)

24 인도의 시골에 살고 있었던 어린 소녀인 나는 종종 내 주변에 있는 물이 심각하게 오염되어 있는 것을 발견했다.

25 나는 이 문제를 어떻게 해결할 수 있을지 궁금했다. 그때 나는 옥수수 속대를 이용해야겠다는 생각이 불현듯 떠올랐다.

26 내가 사는 마을에는 쓸모없는 옥수수 속대가 곳곳에 널려 있다.

27 나는 옥수수 속대의 작은 구멍들이 더러운 물질을 오염된 물 밖으로 걸러 낼 수 있을 거라고 생각했다.

28 어느 날 나는 길을 따라 마른 옥수수 속대를 주운 뒤, 그것들을 씻어서 더러운 물이 담긴 그릇에 넣었다.

29 잠시 뒤 물을 확인했는데 훨씬 더 맑게 보였다.

30 그리고 나서 나는 농부들로부터 모은 옥수수 속대를 이용하여 여과 장치를 만들었다.

31 내 장치는 물에서 70~80%의 더러운 물질을 제거했다.

32 나는 내 여과 장치가 내 마을뿐만 아니라 다른 지역에 있는 모든 호수를 깨끗하게 해 줄 수 있기를 희망한다.

● 우리말을 참고하여 본문을 영작하시오.

1 세상을 바꾸는 사람들은 누구인가? 여러분은 너무 어려서 이런 사람들 중 하나가 될 수 없다고 생각하나요?

➡ _____

_____

2 다음 이야기에서 여러분은 세상을 더 나은 곳으로 만들기 위해 자신들의 아이디어를 사용한 세 명의 십 대들을 만날 겁니다

➡ _____

_____

A Robotic Hand from a Helpful Mind (Easton LaChappelle)

3 내가 열네 살이었을 때, 어느 날 한 과학 박람회에서 어린 소녀를 우연히 만났다.

➡ _____

4 그녀는 겨우 접었다 펴지기만 하는 로봇 손을 가지고 있었다.

➡ _____

5 나는 그녀가 그 손에 8만 달러를 지불했다는 데 놀랐다!

➡ _____

6 '나는 그녀가 더 나은 로봇 손을 가질 수 있으면 좋겠어.'라고 마음속으로 생각했다.

➡ _____

7 나는 이런 생각을 가지고 더 싸고 좋은 로봇 손을 만들기 시작했다.

➡ _____

8 많은 실패 뒤 마침내 3D 프린트 기술을 사용해서 나는 단 300달러짜리의 유용한 로봇 손을 만들 수 있었다.

➡ _____

_____

9 나는 내 3D 로봇 손의 디자인과 소프트웨어를 다른 사람들과 무료로 공유하기로 결심했다.

➡ _____

10 아마도 누군가는 내가 만든 것을 이용해 다른 유용한 것을 할 수 있을 것이다.

➡ _____

11 혼자 세상을 바꿀 수는 없지만, 함께 일 하면서 더 나은 세상을 만들 수 있다.

➡ _____

Headbands for Girls' Education (Mary Grace Henry)

12 '아프리카의 많은 소녀들은 왜 나처럼 학교에 갈 수 없지? 나는 그들도 학교에 갈 수 있으면 좋을 텐데.'

➡ _____

13 내가 12살 때, 이런 생각을 했었다. 나는 그들의 가족이 그럴 금전적 여유가 없다는 것을 깨달았다.

➡ _____

14 나는 내가 그 소녀들을 위해서 어떤 것을 할 수 있을까 생각했다. 그때 아이디어가 떠올랐다.

➡ _____

15 나는 내 생일에 부모님께 재봉틀을 사 달라고 부탁드렸다.

➡ _____

16 그들은 재봉틀을 사 주셨고 나는 머리띠 만드는 법을 혼자 배웠다.

➡ _____

17 10개의 머리띠를 만들어 학교에서 팔았다.

➡ _____

18 나는 곧 아프리카에 있는 한 명의 소녀를 학교에 보낼 수 있는 충분한 자금을 모았다. 나는 거기서 멈출 수 없었다.

➡ _____

19 나는 학교에 갈 수 없는 아프리카의 소녀들을 돕기 위해 사업을 시작했다.

➡ _____

20 내 사업의 성공 덕분에 나는 케냐와 우간다 같은 나라에 있는 많은 가난한 소녀들이 학교에 갈 수 있게 수업료를 지불할 수 있다.

➡ _____

_____

21 나는 또한 그들의 교과서와 교복, 연필을 위한 비용도 지불한다. 놀랍지 않은가?

➡ _____

22 나의 조언은 그냥 무엇이든 하라는 것이다. 필요성이 보인다면 행동하라.

➡ _____

23 작은 단계를 밟아가면서 작은 것부터 시작하라. 너의 따뜻한 마음이 삶을 바꿀 수 있다.

➡ _____

Useless Corn Cobs as Useful Water Filters (Lalita Prasida)

24 인도의 시골에 살고 있었던 어린 소녀인 나는 종종 내 주변에 있는 물이 심각하게 오염되어 있는 것을 발견했다.

➡ _____

_____

25 나는 이 문제를 어떻게 해결할 수 있을지 궁금했다. 그때 나는 옥수수 속대를 이용해야겠다는 생각이 불현듯 떠올랐다.

➡ _____

26 내가 사는 마을에는 쓸모없는 옥수수 속대가 곳곳에 널려 있다.

➡ _____

27 나는 옥수수 속대의 작은 구멍들이 더러운 물질을 오염된 물 밖으로 걸러 낼 수 있을 거라고 생각했다.

➡ _____

28 어느 날 나는 길을 따라 마른 옥수수 속대를 주운 뒤, 그것들을 씻어서 더러운 물이 담긴 그릇에 넣었다.

➡ _____

_____

29 잠시 뒤 물을 확인했는데 훨씬 더 맑게 보였다.

➡ _____

30 그리고 나서 나는 농부들로부터 모은 옥수수 속대를 이용하여 여과 장치를 만들었다.

➡ _____

31 내 장치는 물에서 70~80%의 더러운 물질을 제거했다.

➡ _____

32 나는 내 여과 장치가 내 마을뿐만 아니라 다른 지역에 있는 모든 호수를 깨끗하게 해 줄 수 있기를 희망한다.

➡ _____

[01~02] 다음 글을 읽고 물음에 답하시오.

Who are the people who change the world? Do you think you are too young to be one of (A)these people? In the following stories you will meet three teenagers who used their ideas to make the world a better place.

서답형

01 밑줄 친 (A)가 의미하는 것을 위 글에서 찾아 쓰시오.

➡ _____

중요

02 다음 중 위 글에 이어질 내용으로 가장 적절한 것은?

① some great ideas for teenagers
② some teens who helped the world with their ideas
③ people who are good at telling stories
④ some creative people who get their ideas from teenagers
⑤ tips for making the world a better place to live in

[03~05] 다음 글을 읽고 물음에 답하시오.

A Robotic Hand from a Helpful Mind (Easton LaChappelle)

One day, when I was fourteen, I came across a little girl at a science fair. She had ①a robotic hand that could only open and close. I was ②surprised that the hand had cost her 80,000 dollars! 'I wish she had a better robotic hand,' I thought to myself. With that, I started to make a much ③cheaper and better robotic hand. After many ④failures, finally, by using 3D printing technology, I was able to make a ⑤useless robotic hand for the price of only 300 dollars. I decided

to share the designs and software for my 3D robotic hand with others for free. Maybe someone can take what I have done and do something useful with it. No one person can change the world, but we can build a better world by (A)_____.

03 빈칸 (A)에 들어갈 말로 가장 적절한 것은?

① living alone
② working on our own
③ being careful
④ working together
⑤ being creative

중요

04 밑줄 친 ①~⑤ 중 글의 흐름상 어색한 것은?

①   ②   ③   ④   ⑤

서답형

05 What did the writer use to make the robotic hand? Answer in English.

➡ _____

[06~09] 다음 글을 읽고 물음에 답하시오.

Headbands for Girls' Education (Mary Grace Henry)

'Why can't many girls in Africa go to school as I can? I wish they could go to school, too.' (①) I had this thought when I was twelve. I realized that their families couldn't afford it. (②) I wondered if I could do something for those girls. Then I had an idea. (③) They bought me one, and I learned how to make headbands for myself. (④) I created ten headbands and sold them at my school. (⑤) Soon, I raised enough money to send one girl in Africa to school. I couldn't stop there.

I started a business to help girls in Africa who couldn't go to school. Thanks to the success of my business, I can pay the school fees for many poor girls in countries like Kenya and Uganda to go to school. I also pay for their textbooks, uniforms, and pencils.

Isn't it amazing? My advice to you is to just do something. When you see a need, act. Start small, taking little steps. Your warm heart can change lives.

06 (①)~(⑤) 중 주어진 문장이 들어가기에 가장 적절한 곳은?

> For my birthday, I asked my parents to buy me a sewing machine.

①　　　②　　　③　　　④　　　⑤

07 Write the reason why many girls in Africa couldn't go to school. Answer in English. (6 words)

➡ _____

08 다음과 같이 풀이되는 말을 위 글에서 찾아 쓰시오.

> to have enough money to pay for something

➡ _____

09 위 글을 읽고 답할 수 있는 것은?

① How many African girls can't go to school?
② How much did the writer charge for a headband?
③ When did the writer start the business to help girls in Africa?
④ How do the writer's friends think about her business?
⑤ Where did the writer sell ten headbands?

[10~12] 다음 글을 읽고 물음에 답하시오.

(A)_____(Lalita Prasida)

As a young girl living in the countryside in India, I often found ①that the water around us was seriously ②polluted. I wondered how I could solve this problem. Then I hit on the idea ③to use corn cobs. Useless corn cobs were everywhere in my village. I thought that the small holes in the corn cobs could filter dirty matter out of the polluted water.

One day, I picked up some dried cobs along the road, washed them, and ④place them in a bowl of dirty water. After a while, I checked the water, and it looked ⑤much clearer. Then, using corn cobs that I had collected from farmers, I built a filtering system. My system removed 70 to 80 percent of the dirty matter from the water. I hope my filtering system can clean up all the lakes not only in my village but also in other areas.

10 주어진 단어를 바르게 나열하여 빈칸 (A)에 들어갈 위 글의 제목을 쓰시오.

> (Useful / Useless / Filters / Corn Cobs / Water / as)

➡ _____

11 밑줄 친 ①~⑤ 중 어법상 바르지 않은 것은?

①　　　②　　　③　　　④　　　⑤

12 위 글의 내용과 일치하는 것은?

① Lalita lived in a city in India.
② No small holes can be found in corn cobs.
③ The filtering system that Lalita made can make 100 percent pure water.
④ Lalita got corn cobs from farmers.
⑤ Lalita saw someone using corn cobs to filter polluted water.

[13~16] 다음 글을 읽고 물음에 답하시오.

A Robotic Hand from a Helpful Mind (Easton LaChappelle)

One day, when I was fourteen, I came across a little girl at a science fair. She had a robotic hand that could only open and close. I was surprised that the hand had cost her 80,000 dollars! 'I wish she had a better robotic hand,' I thought to myself. With that, I started to make a (A)_____ cheaper and better robotic hand.

After many failures, finally, by using 3D printing technology, I was able to make a useful robotic hand for the price of only 300 dollars. I decided to share the designs and software for my 3D robotic hand with others for free. Maybe someone can take (B)what I have done and do something useful with it. No one person can change the world, but we can build a better world by working together.

13 다음 중 빈칸 (A)에 알맞지 <u>않은</u> 것은?

① much   ② a lot   ③ far
④ still   ⑤ very

14 밑줄 친 (B)의 의미로 가장 적절한 것은?

① the software of the 3D printer
② the designs and software for the robotic hand
③ the designs and software that the robotic hand made
④ the free product of 3D printing technology
⑤ making useful hands for a low price

서답형
15 Write the reason why Easton was surprised. Use the phrase 'It's because.'

➡ _____

_____

16 위 글을 읽고 답할 수 있는 것은?

① With whom did Easton go to the fair?
② How old was Easton when he invented the robotic hand?
③ How long did it take for the little girl to make a robotic hand?
④ Why did Easton start to make a robotic hand?
⑤ What did the little girl think about what Easton invented?

[17~20] 다음 글을 읽고 물음에 답하시오.

Headbands for Girls' Education (Mary Grace Henry)

(A) They bought me one, and I learned how to make headbands for myself. I created ten headbands and sold them at my school. Soon, I raised enough money to send one girl in Africa to school. I couldn't stop there.

(B) I realized that their families couldn't afford it. I wondered if I could do something for those girls. Then I had an idea. For my birthday, I asked my parents to buy me a sewing machine.

(C) I started a business to help girls in Africa who couldn't go to school. Thanks to the success of my business, I can pay the school fees for many poor girls in countries like Kenya and Uganda ⓐ_____ to school. I also pay for their textbooks, uniforms, and pencils.

(D) 'Why can't many girls in Africa go to school as I can? I wish they could go to school, too.' I had this thought when I was twelve.

Isn't it amazing? My advice to you is to just do something. When you see a need, ⓑ_____. Start small, taking little steps. Your warm heart can change lives.

서답형
17 동사 go를 어법에 맞게 빈칸 ⓐ에 쓰시오.

➡ _____

18 빈칸 ⓑ에 들어갈 말로 가장 적절한 것은?

① wait   ② act

③ calm down   ④ ignore it

⑤ pay attention to it

19 자연스러운 글이 되도록 (A)~(D)를 바르게 나열하시오.

➡ _____

20 위 글의 내용과 일치하는 것은?

① Mary bought headbands to collect them.

② Mary's parents gave her headbands as her birthday present.

③ Mary didn't succeed in sending one girl in Africa to school.

④ Mary started a business to make money to spend on her clothes.

⑤ Mary came up with an idea to help poor girls in Africa.

[21~25] 다음 글을 읽고 물음에 답하시오.

Useless Corn Cobs as Useful Water Filters (Lalita Prasida)

(A)As a young girl living in the countryside in India, I often found that the water around us was seriously polluted. (①) I wondered how I could solve (B)this problem. Then I hit on the idea to use corn cobs. (②) Useless corn cobs were everywhere in my village. I thought that the small holes in the corn cobs could filter dirty matter out of the polluted water. (③) One day, I picked up some dried cobs along the road, washed them, and placed them in a bowl of dirty water. (④) Then, using corn cobs that I had collected from farmers, I built a filtering system. My system removed 70 to 80 percent of the dirty matter from the water. (⑤) I hope my filtering system can clean up all the lakes not only in my village but also in other areas.

21 (①)~(⑤) 중 주어진 문장이 들어가기에 가장 적절한 곳은?

> After a while, I checked the water, and it looked much clearer.

①   ②   ③   ④   ⑤

22 What could filter dirty matter out of the polluted water? Answer in English.

➡ _____

_____

23 밑줄 친 (A)와 쓰임이 같은 것은?

① As you were out, I waited for a while.

② They were all dressed as clowns.

③ He works as a counselor.

④ We did as they told us to do.

⑤ As you know, I don't like her.

24 밑줄 친 (B)가 의미하는 것을 우리말로 쓰시오.

➡ _____

25 Choose one that is NOT true.

① Lalita tried to clean the polluted water.

② Corn cobs could be easily found in the village.

③ Corn cobs have a narrow hole.

④ Lalita made a filtering system by herself.

⑤ The filtering system is made of corn cobs.

[01~05] 다음 글을 읽고 물음에 답하시오.

A Robotic Hand from a Helpful Mind (Easton LaChappelle)

One day, when I was fourteen, I came across a little girl at a science fair. She had a robotic hand that could only open and close. I was surprised that the hand had cost her 80,000 dollars! 'I wish she had a better robotic hand,' I thought to myself. With (A)that, I started to make a much cheaper and better robotic hand.

After many failures, finally, by using 3D printing technology, I was able to make a useful robotic hand for the price of only 300 dollars. I decided to share the designs and software for my 3D robotic hand with others for free. Maybe someone can take what I have done and do something useful with it. No one person can change the world, but we can build a better world by working together.

01 Where did Easton meet the little girl? Answer in English with a full sentence.

➡ _____

02 밑줄 친 (A)가 의미하는 것을 우리말로 쓰시오.

➡ _____

03 What was Easton able to do by using 3D printing technology? Answer in English.

➡ _____

_____

04 According to Easton, how can we build a better world? Answer in English.

➡ _____

05 다음 중 위 글의 내용과 일치하지 않는 부분을 세 군데 찾아 바르게 고쳐 쓰시오.

Easton was surprised at a girl's cheap robotic foot and wanted to make a cheaper and better one. Finally he made one and decided to sell his designs and software for free.

➡ _____

[06~08] 다음 글을 읽고 물음에 답하시오.

Headbands for Girls' Education (Mary Grace Henry)

'Why can't many girls in Africa go to school as I can? I wish they could go to school, too.' I had this thought when I was twelve. I realized that their families couldn't afford it. I wondered if I could do something for those girls. Then I had an idea. For my birthday, I asked my parents to buy me a sewing machine. They bought me one, and I learned how to make headbands for myself. I created ten headbands and sold them at my school. Soon, I raised enough money to send one girl in Africa to school. I couldn't stop there.

I started a business to help girls in Africa who couldn't go to school. Thanks to the success of my business, I can pay the school fees for many poor girls in countries like Kenya and Uganda to go to school. I also pay for their textbooks, uniforms, and pencils.

Isn't it amazing? (A)나의 조언은 그냥 무엇이든 하라는 것이다. When you see a need, act. Start small, taking little steps. Your warm heart can change lives.

06 What did Mary ask her parents to do for her birthday? Answer in English with a full sentence.

➡ _____

_____

07 위 글의 내용에 맞게 빈칸에 알맞은 말을 쓰시오.

> Thanks to the success of her business, Mary can pay for not only _____ _____ _____ but also _____ _____, _____, _____ _____ for many poor girls in countries like Kenya and Uganda _____ _____ _____ _____.

08 주어진 단어를 바르게 배열하여 밑줄 친 우리말 (A)를 영어로 쓰시오. 하나의 단어를 두 번 사용하시오.

> (do / is / advice / something / to / my / just / you)

➡ _____

[09~12] 다음 글을 읽고 물음에 답하시오.

Useless Corn Cobs as Useful Water Filters (Lalita Prasida)

As a young girl living in the countryside in India, I often found that the water around us was seriously polluted. I wondered how I could solve this problem. Then I hit on the idea to use corn cobs. Useless corn cobs were everywhere in my village. I thought that the small holes in the corn cobs could filter dirty matter out of the polluted water.

One day, I picked up some dried cobs along the road, washed them, and placed them in a bowl of dirty water. After a while, I checked the water, and it looked much (A)_____. Then, using corn cobs that I had collected from farmers, I built a filtering system. My system removed 70 to 80 percent of the dirty matter from the water. I hope my filtering system can clean up all the lakes not only in my village but also in other areas.

09 위 글의 흐름상 빈칸 (A)에 들어갈 말로 가장 적절한 것을 쓰시오.

➡ _____

10 Where did Lalita Prasida live? Answer in English.

➡ _____

11 What did Lalita decide to use to filter water? Answer in English.

➡ _____

12 How much dirty matter did Lalita's system remove from the water? Answer in English with a full sentence.

➡ _____

_____

Communication Task

A: I'm Sky X. I can fly.

B: Hi, Sky X. Nice to meet you.

C: I wish I could fly like you. Is it possible for you to fly to the moon?
  소망을 나타내는 표현(I wish+주어+과거동사)   to부정사의 의미상 주어

A: Sure.

D: Then is it possible for you to travel to the sun?
  가능성을 묻는 표현(= can you travel to the sun?)

A: No. That's impossible.
  to travel to the sun

구문해설 • **possible**: 가능한 • **travel**: 여행하다, 이동하다

Enjoy Writing

To Genie,

I have three wishes. I wonder if you can make my wishes come true. First, I
  명사절 접속사(~인지 아닌지) = whether   make+목적어+동사원형

wish I lived in Hawaii. Then I could swim at a beautiful beach. Second, I wish
  I wish 가정법(~이라면 좋을 텐데)   조동사 과거(가정법 과거시제의 주절)   가정법

every Wednesday were a holiday. Then, I could be more relaxed. Finally, I
  과거형 is(X)   조동사 과거   보어(과거분사)

wish I were the president of Korea. Then I would try hard to make my country
  가정법 과거   조동사 과거   부사   5형식

a happier place to live in. I don't know if you can help me, but I hope you can.
  to부정사의 형용사적 용법   (= whether)   can (help me)

Best Wishes,
Sohee

구문해설 • **come true**: 실현되다 • **relaxed**: 편안한 • **president**: 대통령 • **Best Wishes**: 행운을 빌며
(편지의 끝 인사말)

After You Read

Creative Teens!

Easton was surprised at a girl's expensive robotic hand and wanted to make a
  ~에 놀랐다

cheaper and better one. Finally he made one for only 300 dollars and decided
  a cheaper and better robotic hand

to share his designs and software for free.

Mary wished she could send girls in Africa to school. She made and sold
  현재의 사실과 반대되는 상황을 가정할 때(wish+주어+과거동사)

headbands. Now she pays for the school fees, textbooks, uniforms, and pencils
of many poor school girls in Africa.

Lalita wondered how she could clean the water. Using corn cobs, she made
  간접의문문(의문사+주어+동사)   분사구문

a filtering system. It removed 70 to 80 percent of the dirty matter from the
water.

구문해설 • **surprised**: 놀란 • **expensive**: 비싼 • **decide**: 결정하다 • **for free**: 무료로 • **headband**: 머리띠
• **remove**: 없애다 • **matter**: 물질

해석

A: 나는 스카이 X야. 나는 하늘을 날 수 있어.

B: 안녕, 스카이 X. 만나서 반가워.

C: 나는 너처럼 하늘을 날 수 있으면 좋겠어. 너는 달까지 날아가는 것이 가능하니?

A: 물론이지.

D: 그럼 너는 태양으로 여행하는 것이 가능하니?

A: 아니. 그건 불가능해.

Genie에게

나는 세 가지 소원이 있다. 네가 나의 소원들을 모두 이루어 줄 수 있을지 궁금하다. 첫 번째로, 나는 하와이에 살았으면 좋겠다. 그럼 하와이의 아름다운 해변에서 수영할 수 있을 것이다. 두 번째로, 나는 모든 수요일이 휴일이었으면 좋겠다. 그럼 나는 더 편히 쉴 수 있을 것이다. 마지막으로, 나는 한국의 대통령이었으면 좋겠다. 그럼 나는 이 나라를 살기에 더 행복한 곳으로 만들기 위해 열심히 노력할 것이다. 나는 네가 나를 도와줄 수 있을지 모르겠지만, 네가 할 수 있길 바란다. 행운을 빌며, 소희가

창의적인 십 대들!

Easton은 어떤 소녀의 비싼 로봇 손을 보고 놀라서, 더 싸고 좋은 로봇 손을 만들고 싶었다. 마침내 그는 단 300달러짜리 로봇 손을 만들었고 그의 디자인과 소프트웨어를 무료로 나누기로 결심했다.

Mary는 아프리카 소녀들을 학교에 보낼 수 있기를 바랐다. 그녀는 머리띠를 만들어 팔았다. 이제 그녀는 아프리카의 많은 가난한 소녀들의 학비와 교과서, 교복 그리고 연필의 비용을 지불한다.

Lalita는 어떻게 물을 깨끗하게 할 수 있을지 궁금했다. 그녀는 옥수수 속대를 이용해서 정수 장치를 만들었다. 그 정수 장치는 오염된 물에서 70~80퍼센트의 더러운 물질을 제거했다.

01 다음 중 짝지어진 단어들의 관계가 나머지와 <u>다른</u> 것은?

① participate – participation
② sense – sensation
③ illuminate – illumination
④ inform – information
⑤ ment – mention

02 다음 빈칸에 들어갈 말로 가장 적절한 것은?

I can't _____ to buy a new air conditioner.
(나는 새 에어컨을 살 여유가 없어.)

① control   ② manage   ③ use
④ afford   ⑤ spend

03 다음 빈칸 (A)~(C)에 들어갈 말이 바르게 짝지어진 것은?

- She hits (A)_____ a new idea for her cafe.
- I came (B)_____ one of my friends in the restaurant. It made me really surprised.
- (C)_____ visiting schools, the actors hope to inspire children to realize their dream.

① by – across – On   ② on – across – By
③ upon – up – By   ④ on – with – In
⑤ by – across – About

04 〈보기〉의 밑줄 친 단어와 같은 의미로 쓰인 것은?

보기
The <u>fair</u> includes works by Impressionists.

① It was a pretty <u>fair</u> election.
② A <u>fair</u> number of people came along.
③ It is not <u>fair</u> to ask for the money.
④ I visited a world trade <u>fair</u> last weekend.
⑤ It is a <u>fair</u> and breezy day today.

05 다음 대화의 빈칸에 들어갈 말로 적절하지 <u>않은</u> 것은?

A: _____
B: Why not? You can be anything you want.

① Can I become a world-famous singer?
② Is it possible for me to be a dentist?
③ Is it likely that I can be a super model?
④ Is it okay if you become a doctor?
⑤ Is it probable that I can be a dancer?

06 다음 중 어색한 대화를 고르시오.

① A: I wish I could float around like an astronaut.
   B: Really? I don't. It looks uncomfortable.
② A: Is it possible for us to make delicious pie?
   B: Sure, why not?
③ A: I wish I could travel abroad alone.
   B: I'm with you. I'm sure that's every teenager's wish.
④ A: Can you speak French well?
   B: No. I don't think I can, but I'm practicing really hard.
⑤ A: I wish I could live in the desert.
   B: Me, too. It seems very dangerous.

[07~10] 다음 대화를 읽고 물음에 답하시오.

B: I'm planning to visit my uncle in Mexico.
G: What are you going to do there, Mike? (①)
B: I'll spend most of my time at his house because he has a big swimming pool. (②)
G: That's great. (A)Can you swim well?
B: No, I wish I could, but I can't. (③)
G: A water walking ball? What is that? (④)
B: It's a large ball. (⑤) We go inside it and walk on the water.
G: That must be fun.

07 단어 possible을 이용하여 밑줄 친 (A)와 같은 의미의 문장을 쓰시오.

➡ _____

08 Write the reason why Mike will spend most of his time at his uncle's house. Use the word 'Because.'

➡ _____

09 (①)~(⑤) 중 주어진 말이 들어가기에 가장 적절한 곳은?

So I'll have fun with a water walking ball instead.

①   ②   ③   ④   ⑤

10 다음 중 위 대화를 읽고 답할 수 없는 것은?

① Where does Mike's uncle live?
② What does Mike's uncle have in his house?
③ How can Mike enjoy the pool with a water walking ball?
④ How long is Mike going to stay in his uncle's house?
⑤ What is Mike planning to do?

11 주어진 문장에서 어법상 어색한 부분을 찾아, 바르게 고친 것을 고르시오.

Mom asked me that or not I could succeed in making the filter with corn cobs.

① Mom asked me if or not I could succeed in making the filter with corn cobs.
② Mom asked me however I could succeed in making the filter with corn cobs.
③ Mom asked me whether or not I could succeed in making the filter with corn cobs.
④ Mom asked me if could I succeed in making the filter with corn cobs.
⑤ Mom asked me whether I succeeded in making the filter with corn cobs or not.

12 다음 빈칸에 들어갈 말로 알맞은 것은?

_____ the student gets an A doesn't matter. How hard he prepared for the test is much more important.

① Though   ② As   ③ If
④ Whether   ⑤ Whatever

13 다음 〈보기〉와 같이 직설법 문장을 가정법으로 고치시오.

┤ 보기 ├
As he is not rich, he can't buy the boat.
➡ If he were rich, he could buy the boat.

(1) As I am not an inventor, I can't make cheaper and more convenient robotic arms.

➡ _____
_____

(2) Since Jake is wearing the skirt, he looks like a school girl.

➡ _____

_____

(3) As there is no pen, I can't write or draw a thing right now.

➡ _____

_____

(4) Because Henry doesn't have the violin, it is not easy for him to perform the songs.

➡ _____

_____

14 다음 그림을 보고 괄호 안의 단어를 배열하여 빈칸을 알맞게 채우시오.

➡ Yunho couldn't decide _____

_____.

(Canada, England, study, to, in, whether, or)

15 다음 중 밑줄 친 단어의 쓰임이 나머지와 <u>다른</u> 하나는?

① Any boy can use my bat and balls <u>if</u> he wants to play softball.
② Dave's mom asked me <u>if</u> he had done my homework for me.
③ The police will ask Robert <u>if</u> it's all right to live as before.
④ Kevin was wondering <u>if</u> his sister had breakfast that morning.
⑤ Kathy asked me <u>if</u> I had been to Spain.

[16~17] 다음 주어진 우리말을 어법에 맞게 바르게 영작한 것은?

16

옥수수 속대를 오염된 물에 대한 여과기로 쓸 수 있으면 좋을 텐데.

① I wished I could use corn cobs as a filter for the polluted water.
② I wish I could use corn cobs as a filter for the polluted water.
③ I wish could I use as a filter through corn cobs for the polluted water.
④ I wish I can use corn cobs as a filter for the polluted water.
⑤ I wish I could use the filter as corn cobs for the polluted water.

17

비가 충분히 온다면 곡식들이 전보다 더 잘 자랄 수 있을 텐데.

① If it didn't rain enough, the crops would grow better than before.
② If it had rained enough, the crops would have grown better than before.
③ Had it rained enough, the crops would grow better than before.
④ Did it rain enough, the crops will grow better than before.
⑤ If it rained enough, the crops would grow better than before.

18 다음 주어진 문장의 밑줄 친 if와 같은 용법으로 쓰인 문장은?

> I would be a dead person if it were not for my brother.

① Newton used to wonder if all the things would pull each other.

② They don't know if the game will be put off because of the rain.

③ My friends are wondering if my wife is going to her mother's house today.

④ The African girls would be happy if there were helping hands somewhere.

⑤ The reporter asked the medical staff if she was in good condition.

Reading

[19~22] 다음 글을 읽고 물음에 답하시오.

Who are the people who change the world? ⓐDo you think you are too young to be one of these people? In the following stories you will meet three teenagers who used their ideas to make the world a better place.

A Robotic Hand from a Helpful Mind (Easton LaChappelle)

(A) 'I wish she had a better robotic hand,' I thought to myself. With that, I started to make a much cheaper and better robotic hand. After many failures, finally, by using 3D printing technology, I was able to make a useful robotic hand for the price of only 300 dollars.

(B) One day, when I was fourteen, I came across a little girl at a science fair. She had a robotic hand that could only open and close. I was surprised that the hand had cost her 80,000 dollars!

(C) I decided to share the designs and software for my 3D robotic hand with others for free. Maybe someone can take what I have done and do something useful with it. No one person can change the world, but we can build a better world by working together.

19 자연스러운 글이 되도록 (A)~(C)를 바르게 나열한 것은?

① (A)–(C)–(B)　　② (B)–(A)–(C)
③ (B)–(C)–(A)　　④ (C)–(A)–(B)
⑤ (C)–(B)–(A)

20 주어진 단어를 활용하여 밑줄 친 ⓐ와 같은 의미의 문장을 쓰시오.

> (so / that)

➡ _____

21 How much did the girl pay for her robotic hand? Answer in English.

➡ _____

22 다음 중 위 글의 내용과 일치하는 것은?

① Easton gave the girl what he had made.

② Easton planned to meet the girl at a science fair.

③ The girl's robotic hand had so many functions.

④ Easton made a 3D printer with the robotic hand.

⑤ The designs and software for the 3D robotic hand are shared without cost.

[23~25] 다음 글을 읽고 물음에 답하시오.

Useless Corn Cobs as Useful Water Filters (Lalita Prasida)

As a young girl living in the countryside in India, I often found that the water around us was seriously polluted. (①) I wondered how I could solve this problem. Then I hit on the idea to use corn cobs. (②) Useless corn cobs were everywhere in my village. I thought that the small holes in the corn cobs could filter dirty matter out of the polluted water. (③) One day, I picked up some dried cobs along the road, washed them, and placed them in a bowl of dirty water. (④) After a while, I checked the water, and it looked much clearer. (⑤) My system removed 70 to 80 percent of the dirty matter from the water. I hope my filtering system can clean up all the lakes not only in my village but also in other areas.

23 (①)~(⑤) 중 주어진 문장이 들어가기에 가장 적절한 곳은?

> Then, using corn cobs that I had collected from farmers, I built a filtering system.

①   ②   ③   ④   ⑤

24 According to Lalita, what could filter dirty matter out of the polluted water? Answer in English with a full sentence.

➡ _____

_____

25 위 글을 읽고 답할 수 있는 것은?

① When did Lalita make the filtering system?

② Who wanted Lalita to build the filtering system?

③ What did Lalita use to make the filtering system?

④ What did people in India think about what Lalita had made?

⑤ How long did it take for Lalita to build the filtering system?

[26~27] 다음 글을 읽고 물음에 답하시오.

> To Genie,
>
> I have three wishes. I wonder ①if you can make my wishes ②come true. First, I wish I ③lived in Hawaii. Then, I could swim at a beautiful beach. Second, I wish every Wednesday ④were a holiday. Then, I could be more relaxed. Finally, I wish I were the president of Korea. Then, I would try hard to make my country a happier place ⑤to live. (A)나는 네가 나를 도와줄 수 있을지 모르겠지만, 네가 할 수 있길 바란다.
>
> Best Wishes,
> Sohee

26 밑줄 친 ①~⑤ 중 어법상 바르지 않은 것은?

①   ②   ③   ④   ⑤

27 주어진 단어를 활용하여 밑줄 친 우리말 (A)를 영어로 쓰시오.

> (know / can / help / hope)

➡ _____

_____

단원별 예상문제

01 다음과 같이 풀이되는 단어로 가장 적절한 것은?

> to stitch with thread

① manage   ② collect   ③ coin
④ realize   ⑤ sew

02 다음 중 밑줄 친 단어의 우리말 의미가 바르지 <u>않은</u> 것은?

① She was clearly <u>relaxed</u> and in a good mood. (편안한)
② The system can <u>filter</u> dirty matter. (여과하다)
③ We should <u>get together</u> to discuss the issue. (협조하다)
④ He got to the place <u>for himself</u>. (스스로)
⑤ Filters do not <u>remove</u> all bad things from water. (없애다)

03 주어진 단어를 적절히 활용하여 빈칸에 알맞은 말을 쓰시오.

(1) She tried her best, but it was _____. But she didn't give up. (use)
(2) Sue bought a _____ vacuum cleaner recently. It looks terrific. (robot)

04 주어진 단어를 활용하여 다음 우리말을 아홉 단어로 이루어진 한 문장의 영어로 쓰시오.

> 네가 이 퍼즐을 푸는 것이 가능하니? (possible / the puzzle)

➡ _____

05 자연스러운 대화가 되도록 (A)~(E)를 바르게 나열하시오.

W: Hi, Tom. What are you doing?
(A) No, I'm not very good right now, but I'm practicing hard.
(B) Cool! Are you good at it?
(C) As you know, I run a sandwich restaurant. Is it possible for you to deliver orders with your drone?
(D) No, it isn't. But I think it will be possible in one or two years.
(E) I'm flying my drone.
W: That will be great.

➡ _____

[06~08] 다음 대화를 읽고 물음에 답하시오.

W: Hi. I'm looking for a backpack for my son.
M: How old is your son?
W: He is five years old.
M: I want to recommend this one.
W: Oh, ①it's so cute.
M: Yes, isn't it? ②It has a cap that looks like a penguin, so kids love ③it.
W: Is ④it possible for me to take the cap off for washing?
M: Sure. You can easily take it off and put it back on.
W: That's wonderful. I'll take ⑤it.

06 Where is this conversation likely to take place?

① at a grocery store   ② at the library
③ at a mall   ④ in a house
⑤ at the bus stop

07 밑줄 친 ①~⑤ 중 가리키는 것이 나머지 넷과 <u>다른</u> 하나는?

①   ②   ③   ④   ⑤

08 Choose one that is NOT true.

① The woman has a five-year-old son.

② The woman buys the backpack that the man recommends to her.

③ It is impossible for her to wash the cap.

④ The backpack is popular among kids.

⑤ The backpack has a cap that looks like a penguin on it.

[09~10] 다음 대화를 읽고 물음에 답하시오.

Bora: What are you doing, Jessie?

Jessie: I'm drawing Dr. Rebecca, my favorite superhero.

Bora: Wow, that's great.

Jessie: Thanks. I wish I could read people's minds like her.

Bora: (A)<u>Is it possible for her to control them, too?</u>

Jessie: Yes. She can control your mind if she wants to.

Bora: That's very cool.

Jessie: What about you? Do you also have any favorite superheroes?

Bora: Sure. I love Sky X. (B)<u>I wish I could fly like him.</u>

Jessie: I like him, too. He can even breathe in space.

09 주어진 단어를 활용하여 밑줄 친 (B)와 같은 의미의 문장을 쓰시오.

(would like)

➡ _____

10 밑줄 친 (A)를 대신하여 쓸 수 있는 것은?

① Can you control them, too?

② Is it likely that she can control them, too?

③ Are you sure she can control them, too?

④ Do you think it is possible to control them, too?

⑤ Is it probable that you can control them, too?

11 다음 중 어법상 올바른 문장을 <u>모두</u> 고르면?

① The owner of the shop asked her whether she liked the rosemary flavor.

② All the children at the kindergarten want to know if it is fine next Monday.

③ The P.E. teacher couldn't tell if the girl was lying or telling the truth.

④ I wonder whether your sister will come to the library last weekend.

⑤ I'm not quite sure if or not there is a grocery store around my house.

12 다음 문장을 'I wish 가정법' 구문으로 알맞게 전환한 것은?

> I'm sorry that I can't pay the school fees for many poor girls in Africa.

① I wish I can't pay the school fees for many poor girls in Africa.

② I wish I can pay the school fees for many poor girls in Africa.

③ I wish I couldn't pay the school fees for many poor girls in Africa.

④ I wish I could pay the school fees for many poor girls in Africa.

⑤ I wish could I pay the school fees for many poor girls in Africa.

13 다음 주어진 문장을 가정법으로 바르게 고친 것은? *출제율 90%*

> As I am not smart enough, I won't be one of those who changed the world.

① If I am smart enough, I will be one of those who changed the world.
② If I'm not smart enough, I will be one of those who changed the world.
③ If I weren't smart enough, I would be one of those who changed the world.
④ If I were smart enough, I would be one of those who changed the world.
⑤ If I were smart enough, I wouldn't be one of those who changed the world.

14 다음 〈보기〉와 같이 if를 사용하여 주어진 문장을 완성하시오. *출제율 95%*

> ┤ 보기 ├
> Can I make a cheaper robotic hand?
> ➡ I'm not sure if I can make a cheaper robotic hand.

(1) Is he going to come back here?
→ I wonder _____.

(2) Did she have breakfast with the man?
→ I want to know _____
_____.

(3) Has anyone seen my teacher's book on the bench?
→ I don't know _____
_____.

(4) Can the professor and her students come on time for dinner?
→ I'm not sure _____
_____.

(5) Are there any clothes for us to give out to the poor villagers?
→ I want to know _____
_____.

(6) Will it be cloudy the day after tomorrow?
→ I have no idea _____
_____.

[15~16] 다음 각 가정법 과거 문장에서 어법상 옳은 것을 고르시오. *출제율 95%*

15 ① I wish their younger brother doesn't live far from New York.
② I wish I can see the concert of the idol band this coming Saturday.
③ I wish I knew a lot about the Great King Sejong.
④ I wish my daddy can speak English so well that he could be promoted.
⑤ I wish Sunny follows your advice when she is in trouble.

16 ① If we work together, we could build a better world. *출제율 100%*
② I wish the small holes in the corn cobs could filter dirty matter out of the polluted water.
③ If the farmers had helped me, I can make the filtering system using the corn cobs.
④ I wish they know the solution to the problem of the polluted water.
⑤ I wish my filtering system will remove all the dirty matter from the water.

17 다음 간접의문이 사용된 문장들 중 어법상 옳은 것을 고르시오.

① I don't know whether is the rumor true or not.
② Whether my daughter will join them or not depend on you.
③ It doesn't matter whether did Mr. Parker make a mistake or not.
④ I wonder if what you broke at the museum is an expensive item.
⑤ I have no idea that or not the boss will attend the meeting.

[18~20] 다음에 주어진 두 문장을 합쳐서 가정법의 한 문장으로 영작하되, 주어진 단어로 시작하시오.

18
- I'm sorry that I'm not as tall as Jordan.
- I want to be as tall as Jordan.

➡ I _____.

19
- Bob doesn't know Judy's SNS address.
- He wants to visit her SNS.

➡ If _____
_____.

20
- I was able to make a useful robotic hand for the price of only 300 dollars.
- That was due to 3D printing technology.

➡ Had _____
_____
_____.

21 다음 그림과 각 캐릭터의 생각이나 대화를 기록한 〈보기〉를 읽고, 내용에 맞게 빈칸에 들어갈 알맞은 말을 쓰시오. (단, whether는 쓸 수 없으며, 모든 캐릭터는 여성으로 간주할 것.)

─┤ 보기 ├─

Aunt Mary: Is it going to rain today?
Becky: Can I wash the parrot?
Parrot: Did she get a cleaner's license?
Snake: Will anyone come to see me?
Kitty: Is there anything left to eat?
Tree: Has Becky washed me before?

(1) Aunt Mary wonders _____
_____.
(2) Becky asks _____.
(3) Parrot doubts _____.
(4) Snake wants to know _____
_____.
(5) Kitty has no idea _____
_____.
(6) Tree doesn't know _____
_____.

22 다음 각 가정법 문장에서 어법상 어색한 단어를 한 개씩만 찾아 바르게 고치시오. (고친 부분은 두 단어라도 상관 없음.)

(1) I wish my wife is strong enough to move the rock.

_____ ➡ _____

단원별 예상문제 **213**

(2) If you are in her situation, you would understand how much the girls in Africa want to go to school.

_____ ➡ _____

(3) I wish I have a lot of robotic hands so that I can take care of my little sisters.

_____ ➡ _____

(4) I wish my girl friend is the president of the company.

_____ ➡ _____

(5) Tony wouldn't be late for the meeting yesterday if his bike had not been broken.

_____ ➡ _____

(6) I wish someone can take what I have done and do something useful with it.

_____ ➡ _____

출제율 90%

23 다음 각 문장을 읽고, 괄호 안에 주어진 동사와 if를 이용한 간접의문문을 사용하여 같은 내용이 되도록 만드시오.

(1) Peter's girl friend said to him, "Do you really love me?" (ask)

➡ _____

(2) Easton thought to himself, "Can I make her a better dress?" (be sure)

➡ _____
_____

(3) Mary said to her parents, "Will you buy me a sewing machine for my birthday?" (ask)

➡ _____
_____

[24~28] 다음 글을 읽고 물음에 답하시오.

Headbands for (A)_____ (Mary Grace Henry)

'Why can't many girls in Africa go to school as I can? I wish they could go to school, too.' I had this thought when I was twelve. I realized that their families couldn't ①afford it. I wondered if I could do something for those girls. Then I had an idea. For my birthday, I asked my parents to buy me a sewing machine. They bought me one, and I learned how to make headbands for myself. I created ten headbands and ②sold them at my school. Soon, I ③raised enough money to send one girl in Africa to school. I couldn't stop there. I started a business to help girls in Africa who couldn't go to school. Thanks to the ④success of my business, I can pay the school fees for many poor girls in countries like Kenya and Uganda to go to school. I also pay (B)_____ their textbooks, uniforms, and pencils.

Isn't (C)it amazing? My advice to you is to just do something. When you see a need, act. Start small, taking little steps. Your ⑤cold heart can change lives.

출제율 100%

24 빈칸 (A)에 들어갈 말로 가장 적절한 것은?

① My Fortune   ② Girls' Education
③ Girls' Clothes   ④ Enough Food
⑤ Poor Pets

출제율 95%

25 다음 중 빈칸 (B)에 들어갈 말과 같은 말이 들어가는 것은?

① It is rude _____ him to reject the offer.
② How kind _____ you to say so!
③ It was careless _____ me to behave like that.
④ We stepped aside _____ her to pass.
⑤ Isn't it generous _____ them to give this information?

26 밑줄 친 (C)의 의미로 가장 적절한 것은?

① making so many headbands
② helping friends with a sewing machine
③ helping many poor girls go to school
④ giving food to girls in Africa
⑤ helping poor girls in Africa stand on their own feet

27 Write the reason why Mary started a business. Answer in English.

➡ _____

_____

28 ①~⑤ 중 글의 흐름상 어색한 것을 찾아 바르게 고쳐 쓰시오.

➡ _____

[29~31] 다음 글을 읽고 물음에 답하시오.

Useless Corn Cobs as Useful Water Filters (Lalita Prasida)

As a young girl living in the countryside in India, I often found that the water around us was seriously polluted. I wondered how I could solve this problem. Then I hit on the idea to use corn cobs. Useless corn cobs were everywhere in my village. I thought that the small holes in the corn cobs could filter dirty matter into the polluted water.

One day, I picked up some dried cobs along the road, washed them, and placed them in a bowl of dirty water. After a while, I checked the water, and it looked much clearer. Then, using corn cobs (A)that I had collected from farmers, I built a filtering system. My system removed 70 to 80

percent of the dirty matter from the water. I hope my filtering system can clean up all the lakes not only in my village but also in other areas.

29 밑줄 친 (A)와 쓰임이 같은 것은?

① Did you say that I stole the money?
② The news that he came back spread.
③ Who is the man that she is looking at?
④ The problem was that I couldn't afford it.
⑤ We didn't know that he wasn't satisfied with our service.

30 What does Lalita hope? Answer in English with a full sentence.

➡ _____

_____

_____

31 위 글의 내용과 일치하는 것은?

① Lalita collected wet corn cobs to make the filtering system.
② Lalita didn't wash cobs before placing them in a bowl of dirty water.
③ Farmers didn't give corn cobs to Lalita for free.
④ The filtering system couldn't make entirely clear water.
⑤ Lalita wasn't interested in water around her.

[01~03] 다음 대화를 읽고 물음에 답하시오.

Bora: What are you doing, Jessie?

Jessie: I'm drawing Dr. Rebecca, my favorite superhero.

Bora: Wow, that's great.

Jessie: Thanks. (A)I wish I could read people's minds like her.

Bora: Is it possible for her to control them, too?

Jessie: Yes. She can control your mind if she wants to.

Bora: That's very cool.

Jessie: What about you? Do you also have any favorite superheroes?

Bora: Sure. I love Sky X. I wish I could fly like him.

Jessie: I like him, too. He can even breathe in space.

Bora: Yes. He can do anything in space.

01 다음은 밑줄 친 문장 (A)의 의미이다. 빈칸에 알맞은 말을 쓰시오.

Jessie can't _____, but Dr. Rebecca can.

02 Who is Jessie's favorite superhero? Answer in English.

➡ _____

03 According to the dialogue, what can Sky X do? Answer in English.

➡ _____

04 다음 주어진 〈보기〉와 같이 각 그림과 설명을 보고 해당하는 문장을 'I wish 가정법' 형태로 영작하시오.

┌─ 보기 ─┐

The math teacher likes me.

➡ I wish the math teacher liked me.

(1) I live in Hawaii.

(2) I am the president of Korea.

(3) I have a million dollars.

(4) Every Wednesday is a holiday.

(1) I wish _____.

(2) I wish _____.

(3) I wish _____.

(4) I wish _____.

05 다음 중에서 틀린 문장을 찾아 기호를 쓰고, 바르게 고쳐 문장을 다시 쓰시오.

① Andy wondered if he really enjoyed the job of guarding the entrance.

② Father asked me if I wanted to get a chance to go abroad.

③ Parker didn't know if watching stars and taking pictures could lead to a job.

④ I don't know if that the professor wrote is worth reading.

⑤ I wonder if I have courage to make decisions that will change my life.

➡ _____

_____

Useless Corn Cobs as Useful Water Filters (Lalita Prasida)

As a young girl living in the countryside in India, I often found that the water around us was seriously polluted. I wondered (A)_____. Then I hit on the idea to use corn cobs. Useless corn cobs were everywhere in my village. I thought that the small holes in the corn cobs could filter dirty matter out of the polluted water.

One day, I picked up some dried cobs along the road, washed them, and placed them in a bowl of dirty water. After a while, I checked the water, and it looked much clearer. Then, using corn cobs that I had collected from farmers, I built a filtering system. My system removed 70 to 80 percent of the dirty matter from the water. I hope my filtering system can clean up all the lakes not only in my village but also in other areas.

06 주어진 단어를 바르게 배열하여 빈칸 (A)에 들어갈 말을 완성하시오.

(this / solve / how / could / I / problem)

➡ _____

07 What was the idea that Lalita came up with to clear the polluted water? Answer in English with six words.

➡ _____

08 What was everywhere in Lalita's village? Answer in English with a full sentence.

➡ _____

09 다음은 위 글을 요약한 것이다. 위 글의 내용과 일치하지 않는 곳을 세 군데 찾아 바르게 고쳐 쓰시오.

Lalita wondered how she could clean the air. Using corn leaves, she made a filtering system. It moved 70 to 80 percent of the dirty matter from the water.

➡ _____

To Genie,

I have three wishes. I wonder (A)_____ you can make my wishes come true. First, (B)나는 하와이에 살았으면 좋겠다. Then, I could swim at a beautiful beach. Second, I wish every Wednesday were a holiday. Then, I could be more relaxed. Finally, I wish I were the president of Korea. Then, I would try hard to make my country a happier place to live in. I don't know (C)_____ you can help me, but I hope you can.

Best Wishes,
Sohee

10 빈칸 (A)와 (C)에 공통으로 들어갈 말을 쓰시오.

➡ _____

11 동사 wish를 활용하여 밑줄 친 우리말 (B)를 영어로 쓰시오. (6 words)

➡ _____

01 다음은 슈퍼 영웅 SKY X의 능력이다. 빈칸에 알맞은 말을 써서 대화를 완성하시오.

> • What he can do: fly to the moon
> • What he can't do: travel to the sun

A: I'm Sky X. I can fly.

B: Hi, Sky X. Nice to meet you.

C: I wish I could fly like you. Is it possible _____?

A: Sure.

D: Then is it possible _____?

A: No. That's impossible.

02 다음 〈보기〉와 같이 원하는 번호의 그림을 골라, 그림에 맞게 가정법 과거 시제의 조건문과 주절을 영작하시오.

보기

> ① If I knew his phone number, I would call him.

➡ _____

➡ _____

➡ _____

03 다음 소원과, 소원이 이루어진다면 하고 싶은 일을 참고하여 램프의 요정에게 쓰는 편지를 완성하시오.

> I have a million dollars. — I can help all the children who can't afford to go to school.
> I am a famous singer. — I will be on TV and my grandma will be happy.
> I am a bird. — I can fly all around the world.

> To Genie,
> I have three wishes. I wonder if you can make my wishes come true. First, I wish _____. Then, I could _____. Second, I wish _____. Then, _____. Finally, I wish _____. Then, _____. I don't know if you can help me, but I hope you can.
>
> Best Wishes,
> Sohee

단원별 모의고사

01 다음 중 빈칸에 들어갈 말이 <u>다른</u> 하나는?

① Did you pay _____ each item?
② Thank you _____ understanding me.
③ She has built a house _____ herself.
④ He hit _____ creative ideas to make the situation better.
⑤ She has used the machines _____ free since last year.

02 다음 대화의 밑줄 친 부분과 의미가 가장 가까운 것은?

> A: What are you doing here?
> B: I'm looking at the club poster. I'd like to play the drums.

① I want you to play the drums.
② I wish I could play the drums.
③ I'm sure I can play the drums.
④ It is possible for me to play the drums.
⑤ I think I have to learn how to play the drums.

03 짝지어진 두 단어의 관계가 같도록 빈칸에 알맞은 말을 쓰시오.

> fee – charge : contaminate – _____

04 주어진 단어를 활용하여 다음 우리말을 7단어로 이루어진 한 문장의 영어로 쓰시오.

> 그녀는 내일 너를 만나기를 고대하고 있어.
> (look / to)

➡ _____

05 다음 중 단어의 영영 풀이가 바르지 <u>않은</u> 것은?

① business: a work of producing, buying, and selling of goods and services
② coin: a round piece of metal used as money
③ headband: a narrow strip of material worn around the head, usually to keep your hair or sweat out of your eyes
④ come across: to pass by someone
⑤ software: the operating applications programs that are used in a computer system

06 자연스러운 대화가 되도록 (A)~(D)를 바르게 나열하시오.

> (A) Yes, but I'm not good at speaking yet.
> (B) I've been learning it for a month.
> (C) Is it possible for you to read Korean now?
> (D) How long have you been learning Korean?

➡ _____

[07~08] 다음 대화를 읽고 물음에 답하시오.

> W: Hi. I'm looking for a backpack for my son.
> M: How old is your son?
> W: He is five years old.
> M: I want to recommend this one.
> W: Oh, it's so cute.
> M: Yes, isn't it? It has a cap that looks like a penguin, so kids love it.
> W: (A)Is it possible for me to take the cap off for washing?
> M: Sure. You can easily take it off and put it back on.
> W: That's wonderful. I'll take it.

07 주어진 단어를 활용하여 밑줄 친 (A)와 같은 의미의 문장을 쓰시오.

> (can)

➡ _____

08 위 대화를 읽고 답할 수 없는 것은?

① What is the woman looking for?
② How old is the woman's son?
③ What does the man recommend?
④ What is the backpack made with?
⑤ Can the woman wash the cap?

09 다음 대화의 빈칸에 알맞은 말을 세 단어로 쓰시오.

> A: Can you swim well?
> B: No, I _____ , but I can't.

[10~12] 다음 대화를 읽고 물음에 답하시오.

> B: Wendy, you have been late for school a lot ①lately. ②What's wrong?
> G: (A)_____ , but I just can't.
> B: Doesn't your mom wake you up?
> G: She does, but I don't get up ③right away. ④ I wish I could have an AI robot.
> B: An AI robot?
> G: Yes. I mean one that could make sure I ⑤got up and gave me breakfast in the morning.
> B: That sounds great.

10 빈칸 (A)에 들어갈 말로 적절하지 않은 것을 모두 고르시오.

① I want to wake up early
② I'd like to wake up early
③ I wish I could wake up early
④ I can't wait to wake up early
⑤ I always wake up early

11 What does Wendy's mother do? Answer in English.

➡ _____

12 ①~⑤ 중 주어진 말로 바꾸어 쓸 수 없는 것은?

① recently
② What's the matter with you?
③ at once
④ It is possible for me to have an AI robot.
⑤ woke up

13 다음 빈칸 ⓐ, ⓑ, ⓒ에 공통으로 들어갈 말로 가장 적절한 것은?

> • Lalita wanted to know ⓐ_____ she could help her village with the filter she made using corn cobs.
> • You can make your dream come true ⓑ_____ you dream it specifically.
> • Fabien is asking the man ⓒ_____ there is an art museum near the building.

① when   ② that   ③ how
④ if   ⑤ whether

14 다음 중 어법상 어색한 것은?

① If Minsu got up earlier this morning, he wouldn't miss the bus.
② If Jay had put on his glasses, he would have noticed her.
③ If Mary missed the bus, she would not have been late for work.
④ If the organization could be awarded the prize, I would be proud of it.
⑤ If Bruce told the truth to his mom, she would be impressed with what he did for her.

15 다음 중 〈보기〉의 문장과 의미가 가장 가까운 것을 고르시오.

> ┤ 보기 ├
>
> If Yeon-kyoung were in good condition, she would make twice as many attacks of spikes as any other players.

① As Yeon-kyoung is not in good condition, she didn't make as many attacks of spikes as any other players.

② As Yeon-kyoung is not in good condition, she doesn't make as many attacks of spikes as any other players.

③ Though Yeon-kyoung were not in good condition, she made as many attacks of spikes as any other players.

④ As Yeon-kyoung was not in good condition, she didn't make as many attacks of spikes as any other players.

⑤ As Yeon-kyoung was in good condition, she made twice as many attacks of spikes as any other players.

[16~17] 다음 〈보기〉의 밑줄 친 부분과 쓰임이 다른 하나는?

16

> I wish I could please my mother.

① I wish the visitor could speak Korean.

② She could get freedom if you told the truth to the police.

③ I wish I could make as many foreign friends as possible.

④ Could you find me a job suitable for my age?

⑤ If he knew her number, he could make a phone call.

17

> I wonder if my filter will completely remove the dirty matter in the water.

① Sean asked his cousins if the game titles would look interesting.

② I'm not sure if the actress will come to my city tomorrow or not.

③ My teacher wondered if the war broke out in 1904 or in 1905.

④ The player wasn't sure if the girl in first row was seeing him or not.

⑤ David won't attend the meeting if his friend Tom appears this evening.

[18~21] 다음 글을 읽고 물음에 답하시오.

A Robotic Hand from a Helpful Mind (Easton LaChappelle)

One day, when I was fourteen, I came across a little girl at a science fair. (①) She had a robotic hand that could only open and close. I was surprised that the hand had cost her 80,000 dollars! (②) 'I wish she had a better robotic hand,' I thought to myself. (③) After many failures, finally, by using 3D printing technology, I was able to make a useful robotic hand for the price of only 300 dollars. (④) I decided to share the designs and software for my 3D robotic hand with others for free. (⑤) Maybe someone can take what I have done and do something useful with it. (A) No one person can change the world, but we can build a better world by working together.

18 (①)~(⑤) 중 주어진 문장이 들어가기에 가장 적절한 곳은?

> With that, I started to make a much cheaper and better robotic hand.

①　　②　　③　　④　　⑤

19 According to the passage, what did Easton decide to do after inventing the robotic hand with 3D printing technology? Answer in English.

➡ _____

_____

20 밑줄 친 (A)의 의미로 가장 적절한 것은?

① No one can change the world.
② None of us change the world.
③ Not all of us can change the world.
④ The world can be changed by one person.
⑤ The world can't be changed by a single person.

21 위 글을 읽고 답할 수 있는 것은?

① How old was the little girl who had a robotic hand?
② Who did Easton meet at a science fair?
③ How did Easton get the 3D printer?
④ How many times did Easton fail to invent the robotic hand?
⑤ What brought Easton to the science fair?

[22~25] 다음 글을 읽고 물음에 답하시오.

Headbands for Girls' Education (Mary Grace Henry)

'Why can't many girls in Africa go to school as I can? (A)나는 그들도 학교에 갈 수 있으면 좋을 텐데.' I had this thought when I was twelve. I realized ①that their families couldn't afford it. I wondered ②that I could do something for those girls. Then I had an idea. For my birthday, I asked my parents to buy me a sewing machine. They bought me one, and I learned how to make headbands ③for myself. I created ten headbands and sold them at my school. Soon, I raised enough money ④to send one girl in Africa to school. I couldn't stop there. I started a business to help girls in Africa who couldn't go to school. Thanks to the success of my business, I can pay the school fees for many poor girls in countries like Kenya and Uganda to go to school. I also pay for their textbooks, uniforms, and pencils.

Isn't it amazing? My advice to you ⑤is to just do something. When you see a need, act. Start small, taking little steps. Your warm heart can change lives.

22 주어진 단어를 활용하여 밑줄 친 우리말 (A)를 영어로 쓰시오.

(wish / go / too) (8 words)

➡ _____

23 밑줄 친 ①~⑤ 중 어법상 바르지 않은 것은?

① ② ③ ④ ⑤

24 What did Mary start to help girls in Africa who couldn't go to school? Answer in English with seven words.

➡ _____

25 위 글의 내용과 일치하지 않는 것은?

① Mary wanted the poor girls in Africa to go to school like her.
② Mary taught herself how to make headbands.
③ Mary's parents bought her a sewing machine as she asked them.
④ Mary also helps the poor girls in her neighborhood.
⑤ Mary thinks our warm heart can change lives of people.

Lesson

Special

The Necklace

교과서

Words & Expressions

Key Words

- **admire** [ədmáiər] 통 존경하다, 칭찬하다, 감탄하며 바라보다
- **ambassador** [æmbǽsədər] 명 대사
- **amount** [əmáunt] 명 양, 액수
- **ball** [bɔːl] 명 무도회
- **beauty** [bjúːtj] 명 아름다움, 미
- **borrow** [bɑ́rou] 통 빌리다
- **certainly** [sə́ːrtnli] 부 확실히, 틀림없이
- **couple** [kʌ́pl] 명 부부
- **cry** [krai] 통 울다
- **diamond** [dáiəmənd] 명 다이아몬드
- **fancy** [fǽnsi] 형 화려한
- **franc** [fræŋ] 명 프랑 (프랑스, 스위스 등의 화폐 단위)
- **huge** [hjuːdʒ] 형 거대한, 엄청난
- **invitation** [ìnvitéiʃən] 명 초대, 초대장
- **jeweler** [dʒúːələr] 명 보석 상인

- **jewelry** [dʒúːəlri] 명 보석류
- **lend** [lend] 통 빌려주다
- **lie** [lai] 명 거짓말
- **look** [luk] 명 보기, 눈길
- **nearly** [níərli] 부 거의
- **necklace** [néklis] 명 목걸이
- **piece** [piːs] 명 한 개, 한 부분, 조각
- **replace** [ripléis] 통 (다른 사람·사물을) 대신하다
- **second job** 부업
- **shocked** [ʃakt] 형 충격을 받은
- **similar** [símələr] 형 비슷한, 유사한
- **whatever** [hwʌtévər] 대 ～이든지, ～한 어떤 것이든
- **whisper** [hwíspər] 통 속삭이다, 귓속말을 하다
- **worth** [wəːrθ] 형 ～의 가치가 있는
- **worn** [wɔːrn] 형 지친

Key Expressions

- **at once** 즉시, 당장
- **call on** ～에게 청하다, 부탁하다
- **Do I know you**? 절 아시나요?
- **It takes**+목적어+시간+**to**부정사 (목적어)가 ～하는 데 (시간)이 걸리다

- **pay back** 갚다, 돌려주다
- **run into** ～을 우연히 만나다
- **spend**+시간+동명사 ～하는 데 (시간)을 소비하다

Word Power

※ 서로 비슷한 뜻을 가진 어휘

□ **admire** 존경하다 – **respect** 존경하다

□ **amount** 양, 액수 – **quantity** 양

□ **huge** 거대한, 엄청난 – **vast** 광대한, 거대한

□ **replace** ~을 대신하다 – **substitute** ~을 대신하다, 대리하다

□ **similar** 비슷한, 유사한 – **alike** 비슷한

□ **whisper** 속삭이다, 귓속말을 하다 – **murmur** 속삭이다

※ 서로 반대되는 뜻을 가진 어휘

□ **borrow** 빌리다 ↔ **lend** 빌려주다

□ **huge** 거대한, 엄청난 ↔ **tiny** 아주 작은

□ **similar** 비슷한, 유사한 ↔ **different** 다른, 상이한

□ **whisper** 속삭이다, 귓속말을 하다 ↔ **shout** 큰소리를 내다, 외치다, 소리[고함]치다

English Dictionary

□ **admire** 존경하다, 칭찬하다, 감탄하며 바라보다
→ to like and respect someone or something very much
누군가 또는 어떤 것을 매우 좋아하고 존경하다

□ **ambassador** 대사
→ a diplomat of the highest rank who is the official representative of his or her country in another country
다른 나라에서 자신의 나라의 공식적인 대표인 가장 높은 지위의 외교관

□ **amount** 양, 액수
→ a quantity of something 어떤 것의 양

□ **ball** 무도회
→ a large formal place where people dance
사람들이 춤추는 큰 정식의 장소

□ **certainly** 확실히, 틀림없이
→ surely; without doubt
확실히, 의심 없이

□ **couple** 부부
→ two people who are married
결혼한 두 사람

□ **cry** 울다
→ to let tears come from the eyes because of sadness, hurt, etc.
슬픔, 아픔 등 때문에 눈에서 눈물이 나오게 하다

□ **diamond** 다이아몬드
→ a hard, bright, precious stone which is clear and colorless
깨끗하고 무색인 단단하고 밝고 귀중한 돌

□ **invitation** 초대, 초대장
→ a request to come to an event or somewhere
행사나 어느 곳으로 오라는 요청

□ **jeweler** 보석 상인
→ a person who makes, sells, and repairs jewelry and watches
보석류나 시계를 만들고, 팔고, 수리하는 사람

□ **jewelry** 보석류
→ decorative objects worn on clothes or on the body, such as rings and necklaces
반지나 목걸이 같은 옷이나 몸에 걸치는 장식물

□ **lie** 거짓말
→ a statement which you know is not true
진실이 아닌 것을 알고 있는 진술

□ **nearly** 거의
→ almost but not quite
완전하게는 아니지만 거의

□ **replace** ~을 대신하다
→ to take a place of
~을 대신하다

□ **shocked** 충격을 받은
→ feeling very upset or surprised
매우 혼란하거나 놀란 느낌

□ **similar** 비슷한, 유사한
→ alike in many ways
여러 방식으로 비슷한

□ **whisper** 속삭이다, 귓속말을 하다
→ to speak or say something very softly and low
무언가를 매우 부드럽고 낮게 말하다

□ **worn** 지친
→ very tired
매우 피곤한

The Necklace
Scene 1

This is Mr. and Mrs. Loisel's home in Paris. **Although** the home is nice, Mrs. Loisel is not happy. She is young and pretty, and wants a fancier life.

Mrs. Loisel: (*to herself*) Same old house and same boring dinners. I hate living here!

Mr. Loisel: Matilda, I am home. Look what I have got for you!

Mrs. Loisel: What is that?

Mr. Loisel: An invitation to the Ambassador's Ball. I had to fight to get it. Everybody wanted it.

Mrs. Loisel: (*crying*) Why would I want it?

Mr. Loisel: Matilda. What is wrong?

Mrs. Loisel: I have nothing to wear to such a fancy party. I cannot go.

Mr. Loisel: Don't be sad. Here, I will give you 400 francs. Get yourself a beautiful new dress.

Scene 2

Mr. Loisel: (*looking at Matilda's new dress*) Amazing, Matilda. Beautiful!

Mrs. Loisel: Something is not right.

Mr. Loisel: What could be wrong?

Mrs. Loisel: (*crying*) Oh, no. What am I going to do?

Mr. Loisel: What is it, Matilda?

necklace: 목걸이
invitation: 초대장, 초청장
ambassador: 대사
ball: 무도회
franc: 프랑 (스위스 등의 화폐 단위)

확인문제

● 다음 문장이 본문의 내용과 일치하면 T, 일치하지 않으면 F를 쓰시오.

1   The Loisels live in Paris. ☐

2   What Mr. Loisel wants is a fancier life. ☐

3   Mrs. Loisel is not happy with the invitation because she doesn't have beautiful clothes to wear. ☐

4   Mrs. Loisel will buy a jewel with 400 francs. ☐

Mrs. Loisel: I have no jewelry to wear with my beautiful dress. I
will look so poor!

Mr. Loisel: Call on your friend, Mrs. Forestier. I am sure she will
lend you some of her jewelry.

Mrs. Loisel: That is a good idea! Let me go at once.

Scene 3

Mrs. Forestier: Matilda, it is so nice to see you! What brings you here?

Mrs. Loisel: We are invited to the Ambassador's Ball.

Mrs. Forestier: The Ambassador's Ball! That is wonderful! You must
be excited.

Mrs. Loisel: Yes… And no. I am sad to say I have no jewelry. May
I borrow something from you?

Mrs. Forestier: Sure! Here is my case.

Mrs. Loisel: Wow, you have so many wonderful pieces!

Mrs. Forestier: Choose whatever you like.

Mrs. Loisel: Would you lend me this diamond necklace? It is beautiful!

Mrs. Forestier: Certainly! Now go enjoy the ball.

Scene 4

Matilda has a perfect evening. Everybody at the ball admires her
beauty. It is very late when the Loisels leave the ball.

Mr. Loisel: It was such a long night. I am so tired.

Mrs. Loisel: But it was worth it. Do you know I danced with the
Ambassador?

jewelry: 보석 장식, 장신구
call on: ~에게 청하다, 부탁하다
piece: 한 개, 한 부분, 조각
whatever: ~한 어떤 것이든
diamond: 다이아몬드
certainly: 틀림없이, 분명히
admire: ~에 감탄하다, 칭찬하다
beauty: 아름다움, 미
worth: ~의 가치가 있는

확인문제

● 다음 문장이 본문의 내용과 일치하면 T, 일치하지 않으면 F를 쓰시오.

1   Mrs. Loisel is satisfied with her dress and wants nothing more. ☐

2   Mrs. Loisel sends her husband to borrow a necklace from her friend. ☐

3   Mrs. Forestier willingly lends her necklace to Matilda. ☐

Mr. Loisel: I am glad you <u>enjoyed yourself</u>, but I have to go to
enjoy oneself: 즐기다

work in the morning.

Mrs. Loisel: (*looking in the mirror*) Just one more look.

(*shocked*) The necklace… It is gone!

Mr. Loisel: What? Did you have it <u>when</u> we left the ball?
부사절을 이끄는 접속사(~할 때)

Mrs. Loisel: Yes, I surely <u>did</u>. Please go find it!
had it when we left the ball

Mr. Loisel searches the streets. He returns to the ball and then goes

to the police. When the necklace is not found, Mr. Loisel tells Matilda
tell+목적어+to부정사: 목적어에게 …하라고 말하다

<u>to lie</u> to her friend. Matilda tells Mrs. Forestier she broke the necklace

and would fix it before returning it. The couple needs time <u>to find</u> a
to부정사의 형용사적 용법(time 수식)

similar <u>one</u>.
necklace를 가리키는 부정대명사

Scene 5

Mr. Loisel: (*to the jeweler*) Excuse me? <u>May</u> we look at that
정중히 요청할 때

diamond necklace?

Mrs. Loisel: (*whispering*) It is nearly the same. We <u>must</u> have it!
필요성이나 중요성을 나타낼 때

Mr. Loisel: How much is it?

Jeweler: 40,000 francs.

Mrs. Loisel: How about 36,000?

Mr. Loisel: Please, we really need it.

Jeweler: Well, then… 36,000 it is.

They do not have 36,000 francs. It is a huge amount of money. So

they borrow <u>it</u>. After <u>buying</u> the necklace <u>for</u> Mrs. Forestier, the couple
a huge amount of money·지칭   4형식을 3형식으로 전환할 때 간접목적어에 전치사 for

<u>spends</u> ten years paying back the money.
spend+시간/돈+Ving: V하느라 시간이나 돈을 쓰다

look: 보기, 눈길
surely: 확실히, 분명히
couple: 남녀, 커플, 부부
similar: 비슷한, 유사한
jeweler: 보석상
whisper: 속삭이다
huge: 거대한, 엄청난
amount: 금액, 액수, 양
pay back: 갚다, 돌려주다

📎 **확인문제**

● 다음 문장이 본문의 내용과 일치하면 T, 일치하지 <u>않으면</u> F를 쓰시오.

1 Mr. Loisel has to go to work the next day of the party. ☐

2 Matilda is sure that she lost her necklace at the ball. ☐

3 The Loisels manage to find just the same necklace as Mrs. Forestier's. ☐

4 The Loisels borrow money from the jeweler. ☐

5 It took a decade for the couple to pay back the money. ☐

They move to a very small place. Mr. Loisel gets a second job. Matilda

washes clothes for others. Ten years of hard work makes Matilda old
                                                                 make+목적어+목적격보어(목적어를 ~하게 만들다)

and worn. After ten years, Matilda runs into Mrs. Forestier on the street.

worn: 몹시 지친, 수척한

second job: 부업

run into: ~를 우연히 만나다, 마주치다

replace: 대신하다

tell ~ the truth: ~에게 진실을 말하다

Scene 6

Mrs. Loisel: Mrs. Forestier, good morning.

Mrs. Forestier: Do I know you?

Mrs. Loisel: Yes, it is me, Matilda.

Mrs. Forestier: Oh, I cannot believe it! You have changed so much.

Mrs. Loisel: I have had some difficult times because of you.
             현재완료(계속 용법)   전치사(+명사)

Mrs. Forestier: Because of me? What do you mean?
                  ~ 때문에

Mrs. Loisel: Do you remember the diamond necklace you lent me?
                                    목적격 관계대명사 that 생략 (that) you lent me

Well, I lost it.

Mrs. Forestier: But you returned it to me.

Mrs. Loisel: No, I returned another one just like it. It took us ten
                                      = necklace

years to pay for it.
It takes 사람 시간 to V: 사람이 V하느라 ~만큼의 시간이 걸리다

Mrs. Forestier: You bought a diamond necklace to replace mine?
                                              to부정사의 부사적 용법 중 목적(~하기 위해서)

Mrs. Loisel: Yes.

Mrs. Forestier: Oh, my poor Matilda. Why didn't you come to me
                                         Why didn't you+동사원형 ~?: 왜 ~하지 않았니?

and tell me the truth? My diamond necklace was not real.

It was worth only 500 francs!

확인문제

● 다음 문장이 본문의 내용과 일치하면 T, 일치하지 <u>않으면</u> F를 쓰시오.

1 Matilda washes clothes for others to pay back the money. ☐

2 Matilda becomes old and worn because of the ten years of hard work. ☐

3 Mrs. Forestier recognizes Matilda as soon as she sees her. ☐

4 The necklace that Matilda returned to Mrs. Forestier wasn't what she had borrowed

from Mrs. Forestier. ☐

5 The necklace Matilda borrowed from Mrs. Forestier was real. ☐

6 Mrs. Forestier didn't know the truth that Matilda lost her necklace. ☐

● 우리말을 참고하여 빈칸에 알맞은 말을 쓰시오.

Scene 1

1 _____ _____ Mr. and Mrs. Loisel's home _____ _____.

2 _____ the home is _____, Mrs. Loisel is _____.

3 She is young and pretty, _____ _____ a _____ life.

4 Mrs. Loisel: (_____ _____) Same _____ _____ and same _____ dinners. I hate _____ here!

5 Mr. Loisel: Matilda, I _____ _____. Look _____ I _____ _____ for you!

6 Mrs. Loisel: What is _____?

7 Mr. Loisel: An _____ _____ the Ambassador's Ball. I _____ _____ _____ _____ _____ _____. Everybody wanted it.

8 Mrs. Loisel: (*crying*) _____ _____ I want it?

9 Mr. Loisel: Matilda. What _____ _____?

10 Mrs. Loisel: I have _____ _____ _____ to _____ _____ _____ _____. I cannot go.

11 Mr. Loisel: _____ _____ sad. Here, I will _____ _____ 400 francs. _____ a beautiful new dress.

Scene 2

12 Mr. Loisel: (_____ _____ *Matilda's new dress*) _____, Matilda. Beautiful!

13 Mrs. Loisel: Something is _____ _____.

14 Mr. Loisel: _____ _____?

15 Mrs. Loisel: (*crying*) Oh, no. What am I _____ _____ _____?

장면 1

1 이곳은 파리의 Loisel 부부의 집이다.

2 그들의 집은 멋지지만, Loisel 부인은 행복하지 않다.

3 그녀는 젊고 예뻐서 더 화려하고 고급스러운 삶을 원한다.

4 Mrs. Loisel: (혼잣말로) 똑같은 낡은 집과 매일 같이 똑같은 지겨운 저녁 식사. 여기서 사는 게 너무 싫어!

5 Mr. Loisel: Matilda, 나 집에 왔어요. 내가 당신을 위해 무엇을 가져왔는지 봐요!

6 Mrs. Loisel: 뭐예요?

7 Mr. Loisel: 대사님이 여는 무도회 초대장이에요. 이걸 얻기 위해 엄청난 노력을 했단 말이에요. 모두가 갖고 싶어 했거든요.

8 Mrs. Loisel: (울면서) 내가 그걸 왜 갖고 싶겠어요?

9 Mr. Loisel: Matilda. 무슨 문제 있어요?

10 Mrs. Loisel: 그런 고급스러운 파티에 입고 갈 옷이 하나도 없는걸요. 못가요.

11 Mr. Loisel: 슬퍼하지 말아요. 자, 여기 400프랑을 줄게요. 아름다운 새 드레스를 사요.

장면 2

12 Mr. Loisel: (Matilda의 새 드레스를 보며) 멋져요, Matilda. 아름답군요!

13 Mrs. Loisel: 뭔가 제대로 맞지 않아요.

14 Mr. Loisel: 뭐가 안 맞을 수 있죠?

15 Mrs. Loisel: (울면서) 오, 안 돼. 어쩌면 좋아요?

16 Mr. Loisel: _____ _____ _____, Matilda?

17 Mrs. Loisel: I have _____ _____ _____ _____ with my beautiful dress. I will look _____ _____!

18 Mr. Loisel: _____ _____ your friend, Mrs. Forestier. I am sure _____ _____ _____ _____ some of her jewelry.

19 Mrs. Loisel: That is a good idea! _____ _____ _____ at once.

Scene 3

20 Mrs. Forestier: Matilda, it is so nice _____ _____ you! _____ _____ _____ _____?

21 Mrs. Loisel: We are _____ _____ the Ambassador's Ball.

22 Mrs. Forestier: The Ambassador's Ball! That is _____! You must be _____.

23 Mrs. Loisel: Yes… And no. I am sad _____ _____ I have _____ _____. May I _____ _____ _____ _____?

24 Mrs. Forestier: Sure! _____ _____ my case.

25 Mrs. Loisel: Wow, you have _____ _____ _____!

26 Mrs. Forestier: Choose _____ _____ _____.

27 Mrs. Loisel: Would you _____ _____ _____? It is beautiful!

28 Mrs. Forestier: _____! Now _____ _____ the ball.

Scene 4

29 Matilda has _____ _____ _____. Everybody at the ball _____ _____ _____.

30 _____ _____ very late _____ _____ _____ _____ the ball.

31 Mr. Loisel: It was _____ _____ _____ _____ _____. I am so tired.

16 Mr. Loisel: 뭐예요, 부인?

17 Mrs. Loisel: 이 아름다운 드레스에 어울릴 보석이 하나도 없어요. 내가 너무 불쌍해 보일 거예요!

18 Mr. Loisel: 당신 친구 Forestier 부인에게 부탁해 봐요. 그녀는 자신이 가진 보석을 분명히 빌려줄 거예요.

19 Mrs. Loisel: 그거 좋은 생각이에요! 지금 당장 가봐야겠어요.

장면 3

20 Mrs. Forestier: Matilda, 이렇게 보게 되어서 정말 좋아요! 무슨 일로 왔어요?

21 Mrs. Loisel: 우리 부부가 대사의 무도회에 초대되었어요.

22 Mrs. Forestier: 대사의 무도회라! 멋지네요! 당신은 분명 신났겠군요.

23 Mrs. Loisel: 네… 그리고 아니기도 해요. 말하기 슬프지만 난 보석이 없어요. 부인에게서 좀 빌릴 수 있을까요?

24 Mrs. Forestier: 물론이죠! 여기 내 보석함이에요.

25 Mrs. Loisel: 와, 부인은 정말 멋진 보석들이 많네요!

26 Mrs. Forestier: 원하는 것 아무거나 골라요.

27 Mrs. Loisel: 이 다이아몬드 목걸이를 빌려줄 수 있나요? 이거 정말 아름다워요!

28 Mrs. Forestier: 당연하죠! 자, 이제 가서 무도회를 즐겨요.

장면 4

29 Matilda는 완벽한 저녁을 보낸다. 무도회장에 있는 모든 사람들이 아름다운 그녀를 감탄하며 바라본다.

30 Loisel 부부는 아주 늦은 시간이 되어서야 무도회를 떠났다.

31 Mr. Loisel: 정말 길고 긴 밤이었어요. 정말 피곤해요.

32 Mrs. Loisel: But _____ _____ _____ _____. Do you know I _____ _____ the Ambassador?

33 Mr. Loisel: I am glad _____ _____ _____, but I have to go to work in the morning.

34 Mrs. Loisel: (_____ _____ *the mirror*) Just one _____ _____. (*shocked*) The necklace… It is gone!

35 Mr. Loisel: What? Did you have it _____ _____ _____ _____ _____?

36 Mrs. Loisel: Yes, I surely _____. Please _____ _____ it!

37 Mr. Loisel _____ the streets.

38 He _____ _____ the ball and then _____ _____ the police.

39 When the necklace _____ _____ _____, Mr. Loisel tells Matilda _____ _____ _____ her friend.

40 Matilda tells Mrs. Forestier she _____ the necklace and would _____ before _____ _____.

41 The couple needs time _____ _____ _____ _____ _____.

Scene 5

42 Mr. Loisel: (*to the jeweler*) Excuse me? _____ _____ _____ _____ that diamond necklace?

43 Mrs. Loisel: (_____) It is _____ _____ _____. We must have it!

44 Mr. Loisel: _____ _____ is it?

45 Jeweler: 40,000 _____.

46 Mr. Loisel: _____ _____ 36,000?

47 Mrs. Loisel: Please, we _____ _____ _____.

48 Jeweler: Well, then… 36,000 _____ _____.

49 They _____ _____ _____ 36,000 francs. It is _____ _____ _____ money.

50 So they _____ _____.

32 Mrs. Loisel: 그렇지만 충분히 가치가 있었어요. 당신, 제가 대사님과 춤춘 것을 아나요?

33 Mr. Loisel: 당신이 즐거웠다니 기쁘지만 나 아침에 출근해야 해요.

34 Mrs. Loisel: (거울을 보며) 한 번만 더 볼게요. (충격을 받고) 목걸이… 목걸이가 없어졌어요!

35 Mr. Loisel: 뭐라고요? 무도회를 떠날 때 걸고 있었소?

36 Mrs. Loisel: 네, 분명히 하고 있었는데. 가서 찾아 줘요!

37 Loisel 씨는 길거리를 수색한다.

38 그는 무도회장으로 되돌아가 본 다음 경찰서에도 간다.

39 목걸이가 발견되지 않자, Loisel 씨는 Matilda에게 그녀의 친구에게 거짓말을 하라고 한다.

40 Matilda는 Forestier 부인에게 목걸이를 망가뜨려서 돌려주기 전에 고쳐 주겠다고 말한다.

41 부부는 비슷한 것을 찾을 시간이 필요하다.

장면 5

42 Mr. Loisel: (보석상에게) 실례합니다. 저 다이아몬드 목걸이 좀 볼 수 있을까요?

43 Mrs. Loisel: (속삭이며) 거의 똑같아요. 저걸 꼭 사야만 해요!

44 Mr. Loisel: 이거 얼마인가요?

45 Jewler: 40,000프랑이에요.

46 Mr. Loisel: 36,000에 안 될까요?

47 Mrs. Loisel: 부탁드려요. 우린 이게 정말 필요하거든요.

48 Jewler: 음. 그럼… 36,000프랑에 하시죠.

49 그들은 36,000프랑이 없다. 그건 큰돈이다.

50 그래서 그들은 돈을 빌린다.

51 After _____ the necklace _____ Mrs. Forestier, the couple _____ ten years _____ back the money.

52 They _____ _____ a very small place.

53 Mr. Loisel _____ _____ _____ _____. Matilda _____ clothes _____ others.

54 Ten years of hard work _____ Matilda _____ and _____.

55 After ten years, Matilda _____ _____ Mrs. Forestier _____ the street.

Scene 6

56 Mrs. Loisel: Mrs. Forestier, _____ _____.

57 Mrs. Forestier: _____ _____ _____ _____ ?

58 Mrs. Loisel: Yes, _____ _____ _____ , Matilda.

59 Mrs. Forestier: Oh, I cannot _____ _____ ! You _____ so much.

60 Mrs. Loisel: I _____ _____ some _____ because of you.

61 Mrs. Forestier: Because of me? _____ _____ _____ ?

62 Mrs. Loisel: Do you remember the diamond necklace _____ _____ _____ ? Well, I _____ _____ .

63 Mrs. Forestier: But you _____ _____ to me.

64 Mrs. Loisel: No, I returned _____ _____ just _____ _____ . _____ took us ten years _____ _____ _____ .

65 Mrs. Forestier: You _____ a diamond necklace _____ _____ mine?

66 Mrs. Loisel: Yes.

67 Mrs. Forestier: Oh, my poor Matilda. _____ _____ _____ to me and _____ _____ the truth? My diamond necklace _____ _____ _____ . It was _____ only 500 francs!

51 부부는 Forestier 부인에게 돌려줄 목걸이를 산 후 돈을 갚는 데 십 년이 걸린다.

52 그들은 아주 작은 곳으로 이사한다.

53 Loisel 씨는 부업을 구한다. Matilda는 다른 사람들을 위해 빨래를 해 준다.

54 10년 동안의 고된 일로 Matilda는 늙고 지쳤다.

55 십 년 후, Matilda는 Forestier 부인과 거리에서 마주친다.

장면 6

56 Mrs. Loisel: Forestier 부인, 좋은 아침이에요.

57 Mrs. Forestier: 제가 당신을 아나요?

58 Mrs. Loisel: 네, 저예요, Matilda.

59 Mrs. Forestier: 오, 믿을 수 없어요! 당신 너무 많이 변했어요.

60 Mrs. Loisel: 저는 당신 때문에 힘든 시간을 보냈거든요.

61 Mrs. Forestier: 나 때문에요? 무슨 말이에요?

62 Mrs. Loisel: 당신이 빌려준 목걸이 기억하죠? 음, 제가 그걸 잃어버렸어요.

63 Mrs. Forestier: 그런데 그거 나한테 돌려줬잖아요.

64 Mrs. Loisel: 아니요, 나는 당신 것과 똑같은 다른 목걸이를 돌려줬어요. 그 값을 치르느라 십 년이 걸렸어요.

65 Mrs. Forestier: 내 것을 대체하려고 다이아몬드 목걸이를 샀다고요?

66 Mrs. Loisel: 네, 맞아요.

67 Mrs. Forestier: 오, 가엾은 Matilda. 왜 내게 와서 사실을 말하지 않았어요? 제 다이아몬드 목걸이는 진품이 아니었어요. 그건 단돈 오백 프랑짜리였다고요!

● 우리말을 참고하여 본문을 영작하시오.

Scene 1

1 이곳은 파리의 Loisel 부부의 집이다.

➡ _____

2 그들의 집은 멋지지만, Loisel 부인은 행복하지 않다.

➡ _____

3 그녀는 젊고 예뻐서 더 화려하고 고급스러운 삶을 원한다.

➡ _____

4 Mrs. Loisel: (혼잣말로) 똑같은 낡은 집과 매일 같이 똑같은 지겨운 저녁 식사. 여기서 사는 게 너무 싫어!

➡ _____

5 Mr. Loisel: Matilda, 나 집에 왔어요. 내가 당신을 위해 무엇을 가져왔는지 봐요!

➡ _____

6 Mrs. Loisel: 뭐예요?.

➡ _____

7 Mr. Loisel: 대사님이 여는 무도회 초대장이에요. 이걸 얻기 위해 엄청난 노력을 했단 말이에요. 모두가 갖고 싶어 했거든요.

➡ _____

8 Mrs. Loisel: (울면서) 내가 그걸 왜 갖고 싶겠어요?

➡ _____

9 Mr. Loisel: Matilda. 무슨 문제 있어요?

➡ _____

10 Mrs. Loisel: 그런 고급스러운 파티에 입고 갈 옷이 하나도 없는걸요. 못가요.

➡ _____

11 Mr. Loisel: 슬퍼하지 말아요. 자, 여기 400프랑을 줄게요. 아름다운 새 드레스를 사요.

➡ _____

Scene 2

12 Mr. Loisel: (Matilda의 새 드레스를 보며) 멋져요, Matilda. 아름답군요!

➡ _____

13 Mrs. Loisel: 뭔가 제대로 맞지 않아요.

➡ _____

14 Mr. Loisel: 뭐가 안 맞을 수 있죠?

➡ _____

15 Mrs. Loisel: (울면서) 오, 안 돼. 어쩌면 좋아요?

➡ _____

16 Mr. Loisel: 뭐예요, 부인?

➡ _____

17 Mrs. Loisel: 이 아름다운 드레스에 어울릴 보석이 하나도 없어요. 내가 너무 불쌍해 보일 거예요!

➡ _____

18 Mr. Loisel: 당신 친구 Forestier 부인에게 부탁해 봐요. 그녀는 자신이 가진 보석을 분명히 빌려줄 거예요.

➡ _____

19 Mrs. Loisel: 그거 좋은 생각이에요! 지금 당장 가봐야겠어요.

➡ _____

Scene 3

20 Mrs. Forestier: Matilda, 이렇게 보게 되어서 정말 좋아요! 무슨 일로 왔어요?

➡ _____

21 Mrs. Loisel: 우리 부부가 대사의 무도회에 초대되었어요.

➡ _____

22 Mrs. Forestier: 대사의 무도회라! 멋지네요! 당신은 분명 신났겠군요.

➡ _____

23 Mrs. Loisel: 네… 그리고 아니기도 해요. 말하기 슬프지만 난 보석이 없어요. 부인에게서 좀 빌릴 수 있을까요?

➡ _____

24 Mrs. Forestier: 물론이죠! 여기 내 보석함이에요.

➡ _____

25 Mrs. Loisel: 와, 부인은 정말 멋진 보석들이 많네요!

➡ _____

26 Mrs. Forestier: 원하는 것 아무거나 골라요.

➡ _____

27 Mrs. Loisel: 이 다이아몬드 목걸이를 빌려줄 수 있나요? 이거 정말 아름다워요!

➡ _____

28 Mrs. Forestier: 당연하죠! 자, 이제 가서 무도회를 즐겨요.

➡ _____

Scene 4

29 Matilda는 완벽한 저녁을 보낸다. 무도회장에 있는 모든 사람들이 아름다운 그녀를 감탄하며 바라본다.

➡ _____

30 Loisel 부부는 아주 늦은 시간이 되어서야 무도회를 떠났다.

➡ _____

31 Mr. Loisel: 정말 길고 긴 밤이었어요. 정말 피곤해요.

➡ _____

32 Mrs. Loisel: 그렇지만 충분히 가치가 있었어요. 당신, 제가 대사님과 춤춘 것을 아나요?

➡ _____

33 Mr. Loisel: 당신이 즐거웠다니 기쁘지만 나 아침에 출근해야 해요.

➡ _____

34 Mrs. Loisel: (거울을 보며) 한 번만 더 볼게요. (충격을 받고) 목걸이… 목걸이가 없어졌어요!

➡ _____

35 Mr. Loisel: 뭐라고요? 무도회를 떠날 때 걸고 있었소?

➡ _____

36 Mrs. Loisel: 네, 분명히 하고 있었는데. 가서 찾아 줘요!

➡ _____

37 Loisel 씨는 길거리를 수색한다.

➡ _____

38 그는 무도회장으로 되돌아가 본 다음 경찰서에도 간다.

➡ _____

39 목걸이가 발견되지 않자, Loisel 씨는 Matilda에게 그녀의 친구에게 거짓말을 하라고 한다.

➡ _____

40 Matilda는 Forestier 부인에게 목걸이를 망가뜨려서 돌려주기 전에 고쳐 주겠다고 말한다.

➡ _____

41 부부는 비슷한 것을 찾을 시간이 필요하다.

➡ _____

Scene 5

42 Mr. Loisel: (보석상에게) 실례합니다. 저 다이아몬드 목걸이 좀 볼 수 있을까요?

➡ _____

43 Mrs. Loisel: (속삭이며) 거의 똑같아요. 저걸 꼭 사야만 해요!

➡ _____

44 Mr. Loisel: 이거 얼마인가요?

➡ _____

45 Jewler: 40,000프랑이에요.

➡ _____

46 Mr. Loisel: 36,000에 안 될까요?

➡ _____

47 Mrs. Loisel: 부탁드려요, 우린 이게 정말 필요하거든요.

➡ _____

48 Jewler: 음, 그럼… 36,000프랑에 하시죠.

➡ _____

49 그들은 36,000프랑이 없다. 그건 큰돈이다.

➡ _____

50 그래서 그들은 돈을 빌린다.

➡ _____

51 부부는 Forestier 부인에게 돌려줄 목걸이를 산 후 돈을 갚는 데 십 년이 걸린다.

➡ _____

52 그들은 아주 작은 곳으로 이사한다.

➡ _____

53 Loisel 씨는 부업을 구한다. Matilda는 다른 사람들을 위해 빨래를 해 준다.

➡ _____

54 10년 동안의 고된 일로 Matilda는 늙고 지쳤다.

➡ _____

55 십 년 후, Matilda는 Forestier 부인과 거리에서 마주친다.

➡ _____

Scene 6

56 Mrs. Loisel: Forestier 부인, 좋은 아침이에요.

➡ _____

57 Mrs. Forestier: 제가 당신을 아나요?

➡ _____

58 Mrs. Loisel: 네, 저예요, Matilda.

➡ _____

59 Mrs. Forestier: 오, 믿을 수 없어요! 당신 너무 많이 변했어요.

➡ _____

60 Mrs. Loisel: 저는 당신 때문에 힘든 시간을 보냈거든요.

➡ _____

61 Mrs. Forestier: 나 때문에요? 무슨 말이에요?

➡ _____

62 Mrs. Loisel: 당신이 빌려준 목걸이 기억하죠? 음, 제가 그걸 잃어버렸어요.

➡ _____

63 Mrs. Forestier: 그런데 그거 나한테 돌려줬잖아요.

➡ _____

64 Mrs. Loisel: 아니요, 나는 당신 것과 똑같은 다른 목걸이를 돌려줬어요. 그 값을 치르느라 십 년이 걸렸어요.

➡ _____

65 Mrs. Forestier: 내 것을 대체하려고 다이아몬드 목걸이를 샀다고요?

➡ _____

66 Mrs. Loisel: 네, 맞아요.

➡ _____

67 Mrs. Forestier: 오, 가엾은 Matilda. 왜 내게 와서 사실을 말하지 않았어요? 제 다이아몬드 목걸이는 진품이 아니었어요. 그건 단돈 오백 프랑짜리였다고요!

➡ _____

_____

01 다음 빈칸에 알맞은 단어를 〈보기〉에서 골라 쓰시오.

┤ 보기 ├

ball   invitation   admire   replace

(1) You have to _____ the way he handled the situation.

(2) He goes to the _____, wearing a mask.

(3) Machines have _____d human labour in many industries.

(4) I regret that I am unable to accept your kind _____.

02 다음 주어진 단어의 영영풀이가 <u>잘못된</u> 것을 고르시오.

① certainly: surely; without doubt

② amount: an essential and distinguishing attribute of something or someone

③ jewelry: decorative objects worn on clothes or on the body, such as rings and necklaces

④ cry: to let tears come from the eyes because of sadness, hurt, etc.

⑤ ambassador: a diplomat of the highest rank who is the official representative of his or her country in another country

03 밑줄 친 부분과 바꿔 쓸 수 있는 말을 고르시오.

The UN has <u>called on</u> both sides to start peace talks.

① respected   ② delayed

③ recommended   ④ invited

⑤ asked

04 다음 우리말에 맞도록 빈칸에 알맞은 말을 쓰시오. (철자가 주어진 것도 있음.)

(1) 이것이 우리에게 엄청난 문제가 될 것이다.
➡ This is going to be a h_____ problem for us.

(2) 변화에 대한 반대로 그 산업이 거의 파괴되었다.
➡ Resistance to change has n_____ destroyed the industry.

(3) 내가 한 번 봐도 될까?
➡ Do you mind if I have a _____?

05 빈칸 (A)와 (B)에 들어갈 알맞은 말이 바르게 짝지어진 것을 고르시오.

• It (A)_____ on Japan to withdraw the plan.

• I can't (B)_____ back the debt by next year.

(A)	(B)
① took	pay
② took	keep
③ called	take
④ called	pay
⑤ called	keep

06 다음 우리말에 맞게 주어진 어휘를 알맞게 배열하시오.

(1) 나는 대사님의 무도회 초대장을 얻기 위해 싸워야만 했다. (to get, had to, to, the Ambassador's Ball, the invitation, I, fight)

➡ _____

_____

(2) 나는 그런 화려한 파티에 입고 갈 것이 없다. (to wear, nothing, such, to, a fancy party, have, I)

➡ _____

(3) 나는 보석이 없다는 말을 하기가 슬프다. (to say, jewelry, am, no, I, I, sad, have)

➡ _____

(4) Matilda는 그녀의 친구에게 거짓말을 하게 되어 미안했다. (to lie, sorry, her friend, Matilda, to, was)

➡ _____

(5) 그 부부가 비슷한 목걸이를 찾을 시간이 필요하다. (to find, similar, the couple, time, a, needs, necklace)

➡ _____

(6) 우리가 그 목걸이 값을 치르느라 10년이 걸렸다. (to pay, ten years, took, for, us, the necklace, it)

➡ _____

07 중요 다음 문장에서 어법상 어색한 부분을 찾아 바르게 고치시오.

> After buying the necklace for Mrs. Forestier, the couple spends ten years to pay back the money.

➡ _____

08 다음 그림을 보고, 우리말에 맞게 괄호 안의 단어를 배열하여 빈칸을 채우시오.

> 그 목걸이는 겨우 5백 프랑짜리였어!
>
> ➡ _____ francs!
>
> (only, worth, 500, was, the necklace)

[09~11] 다음 글을 읽고 물음에 답하시오.

Scene 1

This is Mr. and Mrs. Loisel's home in Paris. Although the home is nice, Mrs. Loisel is not happy. She is young and pretty, and wants a fancier life.

Mrs. Loisel: (*to herself*) Same old house and same boring dinners. I hate living here!

Mr. Loisel: Matilda, I am home. Look what I have got for you!

Mrs. Loisel: What is that?

Mr. Loisel: An invitation to the Ambassador's Ball. I had to fight to get it. Everybody wanted it.

Mrs. Loisel: (*crying*) Why would I want it?

Mr. Loisel: Matilda. What is wrong?

Mrs. Loisel: I have nothing to wear to such a fancy party. I cannot go.

Mr. Loisel: Don't be sad. Here, I will give you 400 francs. Get yourself a beautiful new dress.

09 What has Mr. Loisel got for Matilda? Answer in English.

➡ _____

10 Write the reason why Mrs. Loisel says that she can't go to the Ambassador's Ball. Use the phrase 'It is because.'

➡ _____

➡ _____

11 How much money does Mr. Loisel give to his wife? Answer in English.

➡ _____

[12~13] 다음 글을 읽고 물음에 답하시오.

Scene 2

Mr. Loisel: (*looking at Matilda's new dress*) Amazing, Matilda. Beautiful!

Mrs. Loisel: Something is not right.

Mr. Loisel: What could be wrong?

Mrs. Loisel: (*crying*) Oh, no. What am I going to do?

Mr. Loisel: What is it, Matilda?

Mrs. Loisel: I have no jewelry to wear with my beautiful dress. I will look so poor!

Mr. Loisel: Call on your friend, Mrs. Forestier. (A)그녀가 틀림없이 보석을 빌려줄 거예요.

Mrs. Loisel: That is a good idea! Let me go at once.

12 주어진 단어를 활용하여 밑줄 친 우리말 (A)를 영어로 쓰시오.

(I / sure / she / some of)

➡ _____

13 위 글의 내용과 일치하도록 빈칸에 알맞은 말을 쓰시오.

Although Matilda has got _____, she still doesn't feel satisfied because she doesn't have _____ with it.

[14~16] 다음 글을 읽고 물음에 답하시오.

Scene 3

Mrs. Forestier: Matilda, it is so nice to see you! What brings you here?

Mrs. Loisel: We are invited to the Ambassador's Ball.

Mrs. Forestier: The Ambassador's Ball! That is wonderful! You must be excited.

Mrs. Loisel: Yes⋯ And no. I am sad to say I have no jewelry. May I borrow (A)something from you?

Mrs. Forestier: Sure! Here is my case.

Mrs. Loisel: Wow, you have so many wonderful pieces!

Mrs. Forestier: ⓐ _____

Mrs. Loisel: Would you lend me this diamond necklace? It is beautiful!

Mrs. Forestier: Certainly! Now go enjoy the ball.

14 주어진 단어를 바르게 배열하여 빈칸 ⓐ에 들어갈 말을 쓰시오.

(like / whatever / choose / you)

➡ _____

15 밑줄 친 (A)가 의미하는 것을 위 글에서 찾아 쓰시오.

➡ _____

16 Why is Mrs. Loisel visiting Mrs. Forestier now? Answer in English.

➡ _____

_____

[17~19] 다음 글을 읽고 물음에 답하시오.

Scene 4

Matilda has a perfect evening. Everybody at the ball admires her beauty. It is very late when the Loisels leave the ball.

Mr. Loisel: It was such a long night. I am so tired.

Mrs. Loisel: But it was worth it. Do you know I danced with the Ambassador?

Mr. Loisel: I am glad you enjoyed (A)you, but I have to go to work in the morning.

Mrs. Loisel: (*looking in the mirror*) Just one more look. (*shocked*) The necklace... It is gone!

Mr. Loisel: What? Did you have it when we left the ball?

Mrs. Loisel: Yes, I surely did. Please go find it!

Mr. Loisel searches the streets. He returns to the ball and then goes to the police. When the necklace is not found, Mr. Loisel tells Matilda to lie to her friend. Matilda tells Mrs. Forestier she broke the necklace and would fix it before returning it. The couple needs time to find a similar one.

17 밑줄 친 (A)you를 어법에 맞게 쓰시오.

➡ _____

18 What is admired at the ball? Answer in English.

➡ _____

19 What does Mr. Loisel tell Matilda to do when the necklace is not found? Answer in English.

➡ _____

[20~22] 다음 글을 읽고 물음에 답하시오.

Scene 5

Mr. Loisel: (*to the jeweler*) Excuse me? May we look at that diamond necklace?

Mrs. Loisel: (*whispering*) It is nearly the same. We must have it!

Mr. Loisel: How much is it?

Jeweler: 40,000 francs.

Mr. Loisel: How about 36,000?

Mrs. Loisel: Please, we really need it.

Jeweler: Well, then... 36,000 it is.

They do not have 36,000 francs. It is a huge amount of money. So they borrow it. After buying the necklace for Mrs. Forestier, the couple spends ten years paying back the money. They move to a very small place. Mr. Loisel gets a second job. Matilda washes clothes for others. Ten years of hard work makes Matilda old and worn. After ten years, Matilda runs into Mrs. Forestier on the street.

20 What do Mr. and Mrs. Loisel do to pay back the money? Answer in English.

➡ _____

_____

21 How does ten years of hard work make Matilda look? Answer in English.

➡ _____

_____

22 How much does they pay for the diamond necklace?

➡ _____

[01~02] 다음 빈칸에 공통으로 들어갈 말을 쓰시오.

01 출제율 90%

- Very few of his books are worth _____.
- I spend almost every day _____ a book in the library.

02 출제율 95%

- I ran _____ an old friend of mine.
- Dolphins can't fall _____ a deep sleep.

03 출제율 100%

다음 빈칸에 알맞은 단어를 〈보기〉에서 골라 쓰시오.

┌─ 보기 ─┐
shocked   worn   similar   once

(1) Can we sit down? I'm _____ out.
(2) It is a good plan to go at _____.
(3) Others have met _____ problems.
(4) I was _____ when I heard the news.

04 출제율 95%

다음 짝지어진 단어의 관계가 같도록 빈칸에 알맞은 말을 주어진 철자로 시작하여 쓰시오.

(1) borrow – lend : similar – d_____
(2) deep – shallow : tiny – h_____
(3) replace – substitute : respect – a_____

05 출제율 95%

다음 영영풀이를 보고 빈칸에 알맞은 단어를 주어진 철자로 시작하여 쓰시오.

to take a place of

Can anything r_____ a mother's love and care?

06 출제율 90%

다음 괄호 안의 어휘를 우리말에 맞게 배열하시오.

내가 거기까지 걸어갔다가 돌아오는 데 1시간이 걸린다. (it, an hour, me, and, there, takes, walk, back, to)

➡ _____

07 출제율 90%

다음 그림을 보고, 우리말에 맞게 괄호 안의 단어를 배열하여 빈칸을 채우시오.

10년 동안의 고된 일로 Matilda는 늙고 수척해진다.
➡ Ten _____
_____. (make, wear, hard, year, work, old, Matilda, of, and, 3 단어의 어형을 변화시킬 것.)

08 다음 중 〈보기〉의 밑줄 친 to부정사와 쓰임이 같은 것은?

┌─ 보기 ─┐

She complained that she had no jewelry to wear with her beautiful dress.

① Jane was disappointed to have lost the luxury bag.
② Mr. Loisel had to fight to get the invitation to the King's Ball.
③ The couple had to work hard to pay back the money for the new necklace.
④ The fake diamond necklace was too cheap to replace the real one.
⑤ Matilda has nothing to wear to such a fancy party.

09 다음 밑줄 친 부분 중 어법상 어색한 것을 고르시오.

① Ten years of hard work has made Matilda old and worn.
② I have had some difficult times because of you.
③ You and your husband have changed so much for the past 10 years.
④ Have you had the necklace when we left the ball?
⑤ Have you bought a diamond necklace to replace mine?

10 다음 중 〈보기〉의 밑줄 친 to부정사와 쓰임이 다른 것은?

┌─ 보기 ─┐

Matilda is sad to tell her friend that she has no jewelry.

① Have you come here to buy the diamond necklace?
② Mrs. Frostier feels sorry to hear her friend had difficulty paying back money.
③ He determined to pay for the ring he had lost.
④ Matilda went to her friend's office to return the ring she had borrowed.
⑤ The Loisels must be crazy to buy the real diamond necklace without checking.

11 다음 〈보기〉와 같이 빈칸에 알맞은 단어를 넣어 같은 의미의 문장을 완성하시오.

┌─ 보기 ─┐

Choose anything that you like.
→ Choose whatever you like.

(1) Anyone who comes to this village will be welcomed.
➡ _____ will be welcomed.

(2) I hate anyone that tries to make fool of good people.
➡ I hate _____
_____.

(3) The boy always throws any things that he has in his hands.
➡ The boy always throws _____
_____.

12 다음 중 밑줄 친 부분의 성격이 다른 하나를 고르시오.

① The prince left the girl crying over the torn dress.

② Matilda tells her friend that she would fix the necklace before returning it.

③ The couple spent ten years paying back the money.

④ They have had a difficult time doing so many kinds of works.

⑤ After buying the necklace for the lady, the man visited her.

13 다음 주어진 우리말에 맞게 괄호 안의 단어만을 사용하여, The couple을 포함한 총 10 단어로 영작하시오. (어법에 맞게 단어의 형태 변화 가능.)

> 그 부부는 비슷한 다이아몬드 목걸이를 찾을 시간이 필요하다.
>
> (find, similar, necklace, time, need, a, to, diamond)

➡ The couple _____

_____.

14 다음 각 문장의 밑줄 친 that 중 생략할 수 없는 것은?

① I am sure that she will lend you some of her jewelry.

② It is very late that the Loisels leave the ball.

③ Do you remember the diamond necklace that you lent me?

④ I have nothing that I would wear to such a fancy party.

⑤ I am sad to say that I have no jewelry to put on.

[15~18] 다음 글을 읽고 물음에 답하시오.

Scene 1

This is Mr. and Mrs. Loisel's home in Paris. Although the home is nice, Mrs. Loisel is not happy. She is young and pretty, and wants a fancier life.

Mrs. Loisel: (*to herself*) Same old house and same boring dinners. I hate living here!

Mr. Loisel: Matilda, I am home. Look (A)_____ I have got for you!

Mrs. Loisel: What is that?

Mr. Loisel: An invitation to the Ambassador's Ball. I had to fight to get it. Everybody wanted it.

Mrs. Loisel: (*crying*) Why would I want it?

Mr. Loisel: Matilda. What is wrong?

Mrs. Loisel: I have nothing (B)_____. I cannot go.

Mr. Loisel: Don't be sad. Here, I will give you 400 francs. Get yourself a beautiful new dress.

15 빈칸 (A)에 들어갈 말과 다른 말이 들어가는 것은?

① I don't understand _____ she is saying.

② I think _____ he wants doesn't matter to us.

③ Can you please tell me _____ you are doing now?

④ The reason is _____ I don't believe they are our friends.

⑤ Watching you enjoy your work is _____ I want most.

16 What did Mr. Loisel have to do to get the invitation? Answer in English.

➡ _____

17 위 글의 흐름상 빈칸 (B)에 들어갈 말로 가장 적절한 것은?

① to eat for the great life
② to see at the boring party
③ to wear to such a fancy party
④ to talk with such a fancy people
⑤ to buy for such a great place

18 위 글의 내용과 일치하는 것은?

① The Loisels' house is humble.
② Mrs. Loisel feels happy about her life.
③ Mrs. Loisel tells her husband she hates living in the house.
④ Matilda thinks her life is boring and is not enjoyable.
⑤ Mr. Loisel will give some money to his wife in order that she can get some jewelry.

[19~24] 다음 글을 읽고 물음에 답하시오.

Scene 4

Matilda has a perfect evening. Everybody at the ball ①admires her beauty. It is very late ②when the Loisels leave the ball.

Mr. Loisel: It was such a long night. I am so tired.

Mrs. Loisel: But it was worth ③it. Do you know I danced with the Ambassador?

Mr. Loisel: I am glad you enjoyed yourself, but I have to go to work in the morning.

Mrs. Loisel: (*looking in the mirror*) Just one ④more look. (*shocked*) The necklace... It is gone!

Mr. Loisel: What? Did you have it when we left the ball?

Mrs. Loisel: Yes, I surely ⑤was. Please go find it!

Mr. Loisel searches the streets. He returns to the ball and then goes to the police. When the necklace is not found, Mr. Loisel tells Matilda to lie to her friend. Matilda tells Mrs. Forestier she broke the necklace and would ⓐfix it before returning it. The couple needs time to find a similar one.

19 ①~⑤ 중 어법상 바르지 않은 것을 바르게 고쳐 쓰시오.

➡ _____

20 다음 중 밑줄 친 ⓐ와 같은 의미로 쓰인 것은?

① She'll fix a meeting.
② I always fix dinner for you.
③ You need to fix the picture on the wall.
④ Let's fix the date of the next meeting.
⑤ My car won't start. Can you fix it?

21 Choose one that is TRUE.

① Nobody cares about Matilda's presence.
② The Loisels leave the ball as early as possible.
③ Mrs. Loisel thinks it wasn't a good idea to go to the party.
④ Mr. Loisel feels great because his wife enjoyed herself.
⑤ Matilda goes out to find the necklace by herself.

✍️ 출제율 100%

22 위 장면에서 Matilda의 심경 변화로 가장 적절한 것은?

① excited → happy
② embarrassed → sad
③ pleased → anxious
④ bored → embarrassed
⑤ delighted → threatened

✍️ 출제율 95%

23 What does the couple need? Answer in English.

➡ _____

✍️ 출제율 95%

24 What does Matilda tell Mrs. Forestier? Answer in English.

➡ _____
_____

[25~28] 다음 글을 읽고 물음에 답하시오.

Scene 3
Mrs. Forestier: Matilda, it is so nice to see you! ⓐ무슨 일로 왔어요?
Mrs. Loisel: We are invited to the Ambassador's Ball.
Mrs. Forestier: The Ambassador's Ball! That is wonderful! You must be (A)_____.
Mrs. Loisel: Yes... And no. I am sad to say I have no jewelry. (B)_____
Mrs. Forestier: Sure! Here is my case.
Mrs. Loisel: Wow, you have so many wonderful pieces!
Mrs. Forestier: Choose whatever you like.
Mrs. Loisel: Would you lend me this diamond necklace? It is beautiful!
Mrs. Forestier: Certainly! Now go enjoy the ball.

✍️ 출제율 95%

25 빈칸 (A)에 동사 excite를 어법에 맞게 쓰시오.

➡ _____

✍️ 출제율 90%

26 빈칸 (B)에 들어갈 말로 가장 적절한 것은?

① May I look around here?
② Can I use your bathroom?
③ May I lend you jewelry?
④ Can you buy me a new one?
⑤ May I borrow something from you?

✍️ 출제율 95%

27 주어진 단어를 활용하여 밑줄 친 우리말 ⓐ를 영어로 쓰시오.

(bring) (4 words)

➡ _____

✍️ 출제율 100%

28 Choose one that is TRUE.

① Matilda is Mrs. Loisel's relative.
② Mrs. Forestier was invited to the Ambassador's Ball.
③ Unlike Mrs. Loisel, Mrs. Forestier has many pieces of jewelry.
④ Mrs. Forestier chose the diamond necklace for Mrs. Loisel.
⑤ The beautiful diamond necklace is given to Mrs. Loisel as a gift.

[29~31] 다음 글을 읽고 물음에 답하시오.

Scene 2
Mr. Loisel: (*looking at Matilda's new dress*) Amazing, Matilda. Beautiful!
Mrs. Loisel: Something is not right.
Mr. Loisel: What could be wrong?
Mrs. Loisel: (*crying*) Oh, no. What am I going to do?
Mr. Loisel: What is it, Matilda?

Mrs. Loisel: I have no jewelry to wear with my beautiful dress. I will look so poor!

Mr. Loisel: Call on your friend, Mrs. Forestier. I am sure she will lend you some of her jewelry.

Mrs. Loisel: That is a good idea! Let me (A)_____ at once.

✏ 출제율 90%

29 빈칸 (A)에 동사 go를 어법에 맞게 쓰시오.

➡ _____

✏ 출제율 95%

30 Write the reason why Matilda thinks she will look so poor despite of her new dress. Use the phrase 'It is because.'

➡ _____

_____

✏ 출제율 100%

31 다음 중 위 장면에 이어질 내용으로 가장 적절한 것은?

① making Mr. Loisel go to Mrs. Forestier to lend jewelry

② Mr. Loisel going to work to make money for buying beautiful jewelry

③ forcing Mrs. Forestier to give up her jewelry for Mrs. Loisel

④ Mrs. Loisel buying more dresses for herself

⑤ asking Mrs. Forestier to lend her jewelry to Matilda

[32~35] 다음 글을 읽고 물음에 답하시오.

Scene 5

Mr. Loisel: (*to the jeweler*) Excuse me? May we look at that diamond necklace?

Mrs. Loisel: (*whispering*) It is nearly the same. We must have it!

Mr. Loisel: How much is it?

Jeweler: 40,000 francs.

Mr. Loisel: How about 36,000?

Mrs. Loisel: Please, we really need it.

Jeweler: Well, then... 36,000 it is.

They do not have 36,000 francs. It is a huge amount of money. So they borrow it. After buying the necklace for Mrs. Forestier, the couple spends ten years paying back the money. They move to a very small place. Mr. Loisel gets a second job. Matilda washes clothes for others. Ten years of hard work makes Matilda old and worn. After ten years, Matilda runs into Mrs. Forestier on the street.

✏ 출제율 95%

32 Wirte the reason why Mr. and Mrs. Loisel move to a very small place. Use the phrase 'It is because.'

➡ _____

_____

✏ 출제율 100%

33 위 글을 읽고 답할 수 있는 것은?

① How many diamond necklaces does the jeweler have?

② Why did Matilda borrow a necklace from Mrs. Forestier?

③ How much is the necklace that Matilda borrowed?

④ Where did Matilda lose Mrs. Forestier's necklace?

⑤ What makes Matilda look old and worn?

✏ 출제율 95%

34 How long does it take for the couple to pay back the money? Answer in English with a full sentence.

➡ _____

_____

35 위 글의 내용과 일치하지 <u>않는</u> 곳을 한 군데 찾아 바르게 고쳐 쓰시오.

> The Loisels go to the jeweler to buy a necklace which looks like the one Matilda borrowed from Mrs. Forestier. After buying the necklace with borrowed money, they have to work hard to pay back the money. Ten years have passed and Matilda meets Mrs. Forestier on purpose.

➡ _____

[36~40] 다음 글을 읽고 물음에 답하시오.

Scene 6

Mrs. Loisel: Mrs. Forestier, good morning.

Mrs. Forestier: Do I know you?

Mrs. Loisel: Yes, it is me, Matilda.

Mrs. Forestier: Oh, I cannot believe it! (A)_____

Mrs. Loisel: I have had some difficult times because of you.

Mrs. Forestier: Because of me? What do you mean?

Mrs. Loisel: Do you remember the diamond necklace you lent me? Well, I lost ①it.

Mrs. Forestier: But you returned ②it to me.

Mrs. Loisel: No, I returned another one just like ③it. It took us ten years to pay for ④it.

Mrs. Forestier: You bought a diamond necklace (B)<u>to replace</u> mine?

Mrs. Loisel: Yes.

Mrs. Forestier: Oh, my poor Matilda. Why didn't you come to me and tell me (C)<u>the truth</u>? My diamond necklace was not real. ⑤It was worth only 500 francs!

36 대화의 흐름상 빈칸 (A)에 들어갈 말로 가장 적절한 것은?

① What makes you so happy?

② You have changed so much.

③ I don't remember who you are.

④ You finally made it!

⑤ How come you are here?

37 ①~⑤ 중 지칭하는 것이 <u>다른</u> 하나는?

①   ②   ③   ④   ⑤

38 다음 중 밑줄 친 (B)와 쓰임이 같은 것은?

① There is a chance <u>to talk</u> with her.

② It was nice <u>to feel</u> proud of myself.

③ <u>To make</u> him do his best matters.

④ He promised <u>to trust</u> us again.

⑤ She went out <u>to find</u> something to drink.

39 How much was Mrs. Forestier's necklace worth? Answer in English.

➡ _____

40 밑줄 친 (C)가 의미하는 것을 우리말로 쓰시오.

➡ _____

중간 + 기말 **plus**

영어 **기출문제집**

영어 중 **3**

시사 | 박준언

Best Collection

내용문의 중등영어발전소 적중100 편집부 TEL 070-7707-0457

INSIGHT
on the textbook

교과서 파헤치기

영어 기출 문제집

적중 100 plus
2학기 전과정

영어 중 **3**

시사 | 박준언

INSIGHT
on the textbook

교과서 파헤치기

※ 다음 영어를 우리말로 쓰시오.

01 success _____

02 match _____

03 abroad _____

04 achieve _____

05 symbol _____

06 experience _____

07 regularly _____

08 appreciate _____

09 clearly _____

10 trail _____

11 amaze _____

12 hot spring _____

13 landscape _____

14 throughout _____

15 main _____

16 confused _____

17 natural _____

18 plaid _____

19 culture _____

20 recommend _____

21 wildly _____

22 view _____

23 surely _____

24 rival _____

25 several _____

26 society _____

27 wedding _____

28 suggest _____

29 traditional _____

30 someday _____

31 village _____

32 waterfall _____

33 native _____

34 nickname _____

35 long before _____

36 be covered with _____

37 filled with _____

38 with the help of _____

39 be famous for _____

40 all year round _____

41 be known as _____

42 prepare for _____

43 come to one's mind _____

※ 다음 우리말을 영어로 쓰시오.

01	경쟁자
02	추천하다
03	(특정한 곳의) 토박이의
04	해외에(서), 해외로
05	언젠가, 언제든
06	달성하다, 성취하다
07	풍경
08	도처에
09	몇몇의
10	폭포
11	성공, 성과
12	경관, 전망
13	확실히, 분명히
14	가지고 가다
15	진가를 알아보다
16	격자무늬, 격자무늬 천
17	흔한
18	명확하게
19	경기, 시합
20	결혼(식)
21	자취, 오솔길

22	(대단히) 놀라게 하다
23	쌍둥이의; 쌍둥이
24	마을, 부락, 촌락
25	자연의, 천연의
26	겪다, 경험하다
27	별명
28	제안하다
29	상징, 상징물
30	온천
31	주요한, 주된
32	(사람이) 혼란스러워 하는
33	전통적인
34	정보
35	(옷을) 입어보다
36	~로 가득 찬
37	~로 유명하다
38	~을 준비하다
39	일 년 내내
40	~로 알려져 있다
41	~으로 덮이다
42	~의 도움을 받아서
43	생각이 나다, 생각이 떠오르다

※ 다음 영영풀이에 알맞은 단어를 <보기>에서 골라 쓴 후, 우리말 뜻을 쓰시오.

1 _____ : a New Zealand bird that cannot fly: _____

2 _____ : in or to a foreign country: _____

3 _____ : a place where hot water flows out of the ground: _____

4 _____ : a pattern of crossed lines and squares: _____

5 _____ : a contest between two or more players or teams: _____

6 _____ : a rough path across countryside or through a forest: _____

7 _____ : a ceremony at which two people are married to each other: _____

8 _____ : to successfully complete something or get a good result: _____

9 _____ : happening often and to many people or in many places: _____

10 _____ : someone who belongs to the race of people that first lived in New Zealand: _____

11 _____ : a person, company or thing that competes with another in sport, business, etc.: _____

12 _____ : a meal in which everyone who is invited brings something to eat: _____

13 _____ : an outdoor game played by two teams with an oval(= egg-shaped) ball: _____

14 _____ : everything you can see when you look across a large area of land, especially in the country: _____

15 _____ : an area of land that is higher than the land around it, but not as high as a mountain: _____

16 _____ : a picture or shape that has a particular meaning or represents a particular organization or idea: _____

보기			
rugby	abroad	common	wedding
Maori	match	landscape	plaid
hill	hot spring	rival	achieve
symbol	trail	potluck	kiwi

※ 다음 우리말과 일치하도록 빈칸에 알맞은 말을 쓰시오.

Listen & Speak 1 A

1. B: _____ _____ about _____ _____ from _____ countries.

   G: Hmm... Do you know _____ _____ _____ _____?

   B: No, I don't. What is it?

   G: It is _____ _____ from Scotland. It _____ _____ a _____ skirt and has a _____ _____.

   B: A skirt of knee length _____ a _____ _____?

   G: Yes. It is _____ _____ it is a skirt for men.

   B: That sounds _____. I want _____ _____ one _____.

2. G: Brian, _____ _____ _____ _____ we will _____ for the World Food Festival.

   B: I will make a meat pie. It is _____ in Australia. _____ _____ you, Sera?

   G: I want to make a _____ English _____, fish and chips.

   B: Fish and chips? _____ does it _____ _____?

   G: It's _____ fish _____ hot _____ _____.

   B: That sounds _____. _____ _____ them.

Listen & Speak 2 A

1. B: Wow, we _____ _____ _____ Hong Kong, Mom.

   W: I'm _____ _____ _____ our visit. What _____ we _____ today, Mike?

   B: I _____ we _____ Victoria Peak.

   W: Victoria Peak?

   B: It is _____ _____ _____ in Hong Kong and is _____ _____ _____ movies. We can enjoy the _____ _____.

   W: That _____ good. _____ go.

1. B: 다른 나라의 전통 의상에 대해 이야기해 보자.
   G: 흠… 너는 킬트가 뭔지 아니?
   B: 아니, 몰라. 그게 뭐야?
   G: 킬트는 스코틀랜드의 전통 의상이야. 그건 무릎길이의 치마같이 생겼고, 체크무늬가 있어.
   B: 무릎길이의 체크무늬 치마라고?
   G: 응. 킬트는 남자를 위한 치마이기 때문에 특이해.
   B: 흥미롭게 들린다. 나는 킬트를 입어보고 싶어.

2. G: Brian, 우리 세계 음식 축제에 무엇을 준비할 것인지 이야기해 보자.
   B: 나는 미트 파이를 만들 거야. 그건 호주에서 유명해. 너는 어때, 세라야?
   G: 나는 영국의 유명한 요리인 피시 앤 칩스를 만들고 싶어.
   B: 피시앤칩스? 그건 어떻게 생겼어?
   G: 그건 뜨거운 감자튀김이 곁들여진 튀긴 생선이야.
   B: 그거 흥미롭다. 우리 함께 그것들을 준비하자.

1. B: 와, 엄마, 우리가 마침내 홍콩에 도착했어요.
   W: 우리가 방문할 곳들이 기대된다. 오늘 우리는 무엇을 해야 하니, Mike?
   B: 저는 우리가 빅토리아 피크에 가는 것을 제안해요.
   W: 빅토리아 피크?
   B: 빅토리아 피크는 홍콩에서 가장 높은 산이고, 영화에도 많이 나왔어요. 우리는 환상적인 경관을 즐길 수 있어요.
   W: 그거 좋겠구나. 가 보자.

2. **G:** My American friend _____ me to a _____ dinner next Friday.

   B: You _____, you should take _____ _____ _____ at the dinner.

   G: What would you _____ _____ I take?

   B: I _____ you _____ some Korean food. _____ Gimbap, Suji?

   G: Yes. It's not _____ and it's _____ _____ _____.

   B: I think it'll be good _____ dinner.

2. G: 나의 미국인 친구가 다음 주 금요일에 있을 포틀럭 저녁 식사에 나를 초대했어.
   B: 네가 알다시피, 너는 저녁 식사에 함께 나눠 먹을 음식을 가지고 가야 해.
   G: 무엇을 가져갈지 추천해 줄래?
   B: 나는 네가 한국 음식을 가져가는 것을 추천해. 수지야, 김밥 어때?
   G: 그래. 김밥은 맵지도 않고, 들고 가기도 쉽겠다.
   B: 내 생각에는 김밥이 저녁 식사에 좋을 것 같아.

Real Life Talk

Seho: Good morning.

Jessie, Andy: Hi, Seho.

Seho: I will visit my uncle in Philadelphia this winter. _____ _____ _____ _____ _____ the city?

Jessie: Sure. I was there _____ _____ _____ _____. _____, _____ _____ about food.

Seho: Okay. _____ _____ is Philadelphia _____ _____?

Jessie: _____ _____ _____ food in Philadelphia is the cheese steak sandwich. It is a big sandwich _____ _____ beef and _____ cheese.

Seho: Good _____. I _____ _____ it. _____ _____ any places _____ _____ _____ _____ tourists?

Andy: I _____ you visit _____ Hall. It is very important in American _____.

Seho: Wonderful. Thank you for the _____.

Andy: My _____.

세호: 안녕.
Jessie, Andy: 안녕, 세호야.
세호: 나 이번 겨울에 필라델피아에 계신 삼촌을 뵈러 가. 너희들 나한테 그 도시에 대해 알려줄 수 있니?
Jessie: 물론이지. 난 몇 년 전에 거기에 갔었어. 먼저 음식에 대해 이야기해 보자.
세호: 좋아. 필라델피아는 어떤 음식이 유명해?
Jessie: 필라델피아에서 가장 유명한 음식은 치즈 스테이크 샌드위치야. 소고기와 녹인 치즈로 채워진 큰 샌드위치지.
세호: 멋진 제안이다. 먹어 볼게. 여행자들에게 인기 있는 장소가 있니?
Andy: 나는 네가 독립 기념관에 방문하는 것을 제안해. 그곳은 미국 역사에서 아주 중요해.
세호: 멋지겠다. 정보 고마워.
Andy: 천만에.

Wrap Up

M: _____ to Australia. The _____ of Australia is Canberra. People speak English. Meat pie is a _____ _____ in Australia. _____ _____, _____ _____ _____ _____ visit the Sydney Opera House and the _____ _____ in Melbourne.

M: 호주에 온 것을 환영한다. 호주의 수도는 캔버라다. 사람들은 영어로 말한다. 고기 파이는 호주에서 인기 있는 음식이다. 매년 많은 관광객들이 시드니 오페라 하우스와 멜버른의 아름다운 해변을 방문한다.

※ 다음 우리말에 맞도록 대화를 영어로 쓰시오.

Listen & Speak 1 A

1. B: _____
   G: _____
   B: _____
   G: _____

   B: _____
   G: _____
   B: _____

2. G: _____
   B: _____
   G: _____
   B: _____
   G: _____
   B: _____

Listen & Speak 2 A

1. B: _____
   W: _____
   B: _____
   W: _____
   B: _____

   W: _____

1. B: 다른 나라의 전통 의상에 대해 이야기해 보자.
   G: 흠… 너는 킬트가 뭔지 아니?
   B: 아니, 몰라. 그게 뭐야?
   G: 킬트는 스코틀랜드의 전통 의상이야. 그건 무릎길이의 치마같이 생겼고, 체크무늬가 있어.
   B: 무릎길이의 체크무늬 치마라고?
   G: 응. 킬트는 남자를 위한 치마이기 때문에 특이해.
   B: 흥미롭게 들린다. 나는 킬트를 입어 보고 싶어.

2. G: Brian, 우리 세계 음식 축제에 무엇을 준비할 것인지 이야기해 보자.
   B: 나는 미트 파이를 만들 거야. 그건 호주에서 유명해. 너는 어때, 세라야?
   G: 나는 영국의 유명한 요리인 피시 앤 칩스를 만들고 싶어.
   B: 피시앤칩스? 그건 어떻게 생겼어?
   G: 그건 뜨거운 감자튀김이 곁들여진 튀긴 생선이야.
   B: 그거 흥미롭다. 우리 함께 그것들을 준비하자.

1. B: 와, 엄마, 우리가 마침내 홍콩에 도착했어요.
   W: 우리가 방문할 곳들이 기대된다. 오늘 우리는 무엇을 해야 하니, Mike?
   B: 저는 우리가 빅토리아 피크에 가는 것을 제안해요.
   W: 빅토리아 피크?
   B: 빅토리아 피크는 홍콩에서 가장 높은 산이고, 영화에도 많이 나왔어요. 우리는 환상적인 경관을 즐길 수 있어요.
   W: 그거 좋겠구나. 가 보자.

2. G: _____

B: _____

G: _____

B: _____

G: _____

B: _____

2. G: 나의 미국인 친구가 다음 주 금요일에 있을 포틀럭 저녁 식사에 나를 초대했어.
B: 네가 알다시피, 너는 저녁 식사에 함께 나눠 먹을 음식을 가지고 가야 해.
G: 무엇을 가져갈지 추천해 줄래?
B: 나는 네가 한국 음식을 가져가는 것을 추천해. 수지야, 김밥 어때?
G: 그래. 김밥은 맵지도 않고, 들고 가기도 쉽겠다.
B: 내 생각에는 김밥이 저녁 식사에 좋을 것 같아.

Real Life Talk

Seho: _____

Jessie, Andy: _____

Seho: _____

_____

Jessie: _____

Seho: _____

Jessie: _____

_____

Seho: _____

_____

Andy: _____

_____

Seho: _____

Andy: _____

세호: 안녕.
Jessie, Andy: 안녕, 세호야.
세호: 나 이번 겨울에 필라델피아에 계신 삼촌을 뵈러 가. 너희들 나한테 그 도시에 대해 알려줄 수 있니?
Jessie: 물론이지. 난 몇 년 전에 거기에 갔었어. 먼저 음식에 대해 이야기해 보자.
세호: 좋아. 필라델피아는 어떤 음식이 유명해?
Jessie: 필라델피아에서 가장 유명한 음식은 치즈 스테이크 샌드위치야. 소고기와 녹인 치즈로 채워진 큰 샌드위치지.
세호: 멋진 제안이다. 먹어 볼게. 여행자들에게 인기 있는 장소가 있니?
Andy: 나는 네가 독립 기념관에 방문하는 것을 제안해. 그곳은 미국 역사에서 아주 중요해.
세호: 멋지겠다. 정보 고마워.
Andy: 천만에.

Wrap Up

M: _____

_____

_____

M: 호주에 온 것을 환영한다. 호주의 수도는 캔버라다. 사람들은 영어로 말한다. 고기 파이는 호주에서 인기 있는 음식이다. 매년 많은 관광객들이 시드니 오페라 하우스와 멜버른의 아름다운 해변을 방문한다.

※ 다음 우리말과 일치하도록 빈칸에 알맞은 것을 골라 쓰시오.

Hello! New Zealand

1 New Zealand is a _____ of _____ _____. It has many beautiful lakes and _____.
    A. waterfalls   B. natural   C. place   D. beauty

2 New Zealand _____ _____ _____ _____, the South Island and the North Island.
    A. main   B. two   C. islands   D. has

3 In the South Island, there are mountains that are _____ _____ snow _____ year _____.
    A. covered   B. round   C. all   D. with

4 You will _____ _____ _____ the fantastic _____.
    A. by   B. be   C. views   D. amazed

5 In the North Island, there are many _____ _____, lakes, and _____ _____ green grass.
    A. with   B. hot   C. areas   D. springs

6 _____ _____ its natural beauty, many famous movies have _____ _____ in New Zealand.
    A. been   B. of   C. made   D. because

7 If you visit New Zealand, you _____ _____ _____ its _____.
    A. nature   B. surely   C. will   D. appreciate

8 When you _____ the word kiwi, what _____ _____ your _____?
    A. mind   B. comes   C. hear   D. to

9 _____ a fruit, _____, in New Zealand the word kiwi has a _____ of _____.
    A. couple   B. maybe   C. meanings   D. but

10 First, kiwi is the _____ of a _____, green _____.
    A. delicious   B. name   C. fruit

11 A lot of kiwi fruit is _____ there, _____ New Zealand is _____ _____ the land of kiwi fruit.
    A. known   B. grown   C. as   D. so

12 Kiwi is _____ the name of _____ of New Zealand's _____ _____.
    A. native   B. one   C. also   D. birds

13 The kiwi is _____ to New Zealanders _____ it is the _____ of the _____.
    A. because   B. special   C. nation   D. symbol

14 _____, kiwi is a _____ _____ people _____ New Zealand.
    A. from   B. nickname   C. also   D. for

15 Today, New Zealanders _____ _____ _____ Kiwis _____ the world.
    A. called   B. throughout   C. sometimes   D. are

16 Now, you know _____ kiwi is the _____ of a _____, a bird, and _____ a people.
    A. fruit   B. that   C. also   D. name

안녕! 뉴질랜드

1 뉴질랜드는 자연의 아름다움이 가득한 곳이다. 뉴질랜드는 아름다운 호수와 폭포들이 많다.

2 뉴질랜드에는 남섬과 북섬, 두 개의 본섬이 있다.

3 남섬에는 일 년 내내 눈으로 덮인 산들이 있다.

4 당신은 굉장히 멋진 경관에 놀랄 것이다.

5 북섬에는 많은 온천과 호수, 초원 지역이 있다.

6 뉴질랜드 자연의 아름다움 때문에 많은 유명한 영화들이 뉴질랜드에서 촬영되었다.

7 뉴질랜드를 방문하면, 분명히 그 자연의 진가를 인정할 것이다.

8 키위라는 단어를 들을 때, 무엇이 떠오르는가?

9 아마도 과일이 떠오르겠지만, 뉴질랜드에서 키위는 몇 가지 뜻이 있다.

10 먼저, 키위는 맛있는 초록색 과일의 이름이다.

11 많은 키위가 그곳에서 자라기 때문에 뉴질랜드는 키위의 나라로 알려져 있다.

12 키위는 뉴질랜드 토종 새의 이름이기도 하다.

13 키위 새는 국가의 상징이기 때문에, 뉴질랜드 사람들에게 특별하다.

14 또한, 키위는 뉴질랜드 출신의 사람들을 부르는 별명이기도 하다.

15 오늘날 뉴질랜드인들은 전 세계적으로 키위라고 불리기도 한다.

16 이제, 당신은 키위가 과일과 새, 그리고 국민의 명칭이라는 것을 알았다.

17 Next time, don't become _____ when someone _____ the word kiwi, _____ has several _____.

A. uses　　　B. which　　　C. confused　　　D. meanings

18 Now, _____ _____ about the Maori. They are the _____ _____ of New Zealand.

A. native　　　B. talk　　　C. people　　　D. let's

19 They went to live _____ the islands _____ _____ Europeans _____.

A. arrived　　　B. long　　　C. on　　　D. before

20 The Maori culture is an _____ _____ of _____ New Zealand _____.

A. part　　　B. society　　　C. today's　　　D. important

21 The Maori language _____ _____ at some schools and _____ _____ Maori language radio and TV stations.

A. are　　　B. taught　　　C. there　　　D. is

22 There are Maori _____ in _____ _____ of the _____.

A. country　　　B. many　　　C. villages　　　D. parts

23 You can _____ Maori _____ and _____ Maori _____.

A. experience　　　B. visit　　　C. culture　　　D. villages

24 If you _____ "kia ora" to the villagers, they will be _____ to _____ it. It _____ "hi" in English.

A. means　　　B. say　　　C. hear　　　D. glad

25 _____ you _____ _____ the haka?

A. ever　　　B. have　　　C. watched

26 The haka may look _____ because haka dancers _____ and _____ their bodies _____.

A. wildly　　　B. move　　　C. shout　　　D. scary

27 The Maori people, _____ you've already _____ about, started _____ the haka _____ a war dance.

A. as　　　B. who　　　C. doing　　　D. heard

28 Today, _____, New Zealanders do the haka at sport _____, weddings, or _____ important _____.

A. matches　　　B. other　　　C. however　　　D. events

29 For _____, New Zealand's _____ rugby team members do the haka _____ every _____.

A. before　　　B. example　　　C. national　　　D. match

30 It is _____ _____ _____ the world.

A. all　　　B. famous　　　C. over

31 If you see the haka, you will probably _____ _____ the rival team _____ be _____.

A. scared　　　B. agree　　　C. that　　　D. must

32 _____ the kiwi bird, the haka is a _____ _____.

A. symbol　　　B. like　　　C. national

17 다음에는 누군가가 키위라는 단어를 사용할 때 혼동하지 마라. 그 단어는 여러 뜻을 가지고 있기 때문이다.

18 이제, 마오리족에 대해 이야기해 보자. 마오리족은 뉴질랜드의 원주민이다.

19 그들은 유럽인들이 도착하기 오래 전에 이 섬에 와서 살았다.

20 마오리족의 문화는 오늘날 뉴질랜드 사회의 중요한 부분이다.

21 몇몇 학교에서 마오리어를 가르치고 있으며, 마오리어의 라디오와 TV 방송국이 있다.

22 나라의 여러 곳에 마오리 마을이 있다.

23 당신은 마오리 마을을 방문해 마오리 문화를 경험할 수 있다.

24 당신이 마을 사람들에게 "kia ora"라고 말한다면 그들은 그것을 듣고 좋아할 것이다. 그것은 영어로 "안녕"이라는 뜻이다.

25 하카를 본 적이 있는가?

26 하카 춤을 추는 사람들이 소리 지르고, 그들의 몸을 사납게 움직이기 때문에 하카는 무서워 보일 수도 있다.

27 당신이 이미 그들에 대해 들은 적이 있겠지만, 마오리인들은 전쟁 춤으로 하카를 추기 시작했다.

28 하지만, 오늘날 뉴질랜드 사람들은 하카를 운동 경기, 결혼식 또는 다른 중요한 행사가 있을 때 한다.

29 예를 들어, 뉴질랜드의 럭비 국가 대표 팀 선수들은 모든 경기 전에 하카를 춘다.

30 그것은 전 세계적으로 유명하다.

31 당신이 하카를 본다면, 상대 팀이 틀림없이 겁을 먹을 것이라는 것에 아마 동의할 것이다.

32 키위와 마찬가지로 하카는 나라의 상징이다.

※ 다음 우리말과 일치하도록 빈칸에 알맞은 것을 골라 쓰시오.

Hello! New Zealand

1 New Zealand is ＿＿＿＿ ＿＿＿＿ ＿＿＿＿ ＿＿＿＿.
It has many beautiful ＿＿＿＿ and ＿＿＿＿.

2 New Zealand has ＿＿＿＿ ＿＿＿＿ ＿＿＿＿, the South Island
and the North Island.

3 In the South Island, there ＿＿＿＿ ＿＿＿＿ that ＿＿＿＿
＿＿＿＿ ＿＿＿＿ snow ＿＿＿＿ ＿＿＿＿ ＿＿＿＿.

4 You will ＿＿＿＿ ＿＿＿＿ ＿＿＿＿ the ＿＿＿＿ ＿＿＿＿.

5 In the North Island, there are ＿＿＿＿ ＿＿＿＿ ＿＿＿＿, lakes,
and areas ＿＿＿＿ green grass.

6 ＿＿＿＿ ＿＿＿＿ its ＿＿＿＿ ＿＿＿＿, many famous movies
＿＿＿＿ ＿＿＿＿ ＿＿＿＿ in New Zealand.

7 If you visit New Zealand, you ＿＿＿＿ ＿＿＿＿ ＿＿＿＿ its
nature.

8 When you ＿＿＿＿ the word kiwi, what ＿＿＿＿ ＿＿＿＿
＿＿＿＿ ＿＿＿＿?

9 Maybe a fruit, but, in New Zealand the word kiwi has ＿＿＿＿
＿＿＿＿ ＿＿＿＿ ＿＿＿＿.

10 First, kiwi is ＿＿＿＿ ＿＿＿＿ of a ＿＿＿＿, green fruit.

11 A lot of kiwi fruit ＿＿＿＿ ＿＿＿＿ there, ＿＿＿＿ New
Zealand ＿＿＿＿ ＿＿＿＿ ＿＿＿＿ the land of kiwi fruit.

12 Kiwi is also the name of ＿＿＿＿ of ＿＿＿＿ ＿＿＿＿
＿＿＿＿.

13 The kiwi is ＿＿＿＿ ＿＿＿＿ New Zealanders ＿＿＿＿ it is
the ＿＿＿＿ of the nation.

14 Also, kiwi is ＿＿＿＿ ＿＿＿＿ ＿＿＿＿ people ＿＿＿＿ New
Zealand.

15 Today, New Zealanders ＿＿＿＿ ＿＿＿＿ ＿＿＿＿ Kiwis
＿＿＿＿ ＿＿＿＿ ＿＿＿＿.

16 Now, you know ＿＿＿＿ kiwi is ＿＿＿＿ ＿＿＿＿ ＿＿＿＿ a
fruit, a bird, and also a people.

안녕! 뉴질랜드

1 뉴질랜드는 자연의 아름다움이 가득한 곳이다. 뉴질랜드는 아름다운 호수와 폭포들이 많다.

2 뉴질랜드에는 남섬과 북섬, 두 개의 본섬이 있다.

3 남섬에는 일 년 내내 눈으로 덮인 산들이 있다.

4 당신은 굉장히 멋진 경관에 놀랄 것이다.

5 북섬에는 많은 온천과 호수, 초원 지역이 있다.

6 뉴질랜드 자연의 아름다움 때문에 많은 유명한 영화들이 뉴질랜드에서 촬영되었다.

7 뉴질랜드를 방문하면, 분명히 그 자연의 진가를 인정할 것이다.

8 키위라는 단어를 들을 때, 무엇이 떠오르는가?

9 아마도 과일이 떠오르겠지만, 뉴질랜드에서 키위는 몇 가지 뜻이 있다.

10 먼저, 키위는 맛있는 초록색 과일의 이름이다.

11 많은 키위가 그곳에서 자라기 때문에 뉴질랜드는 키위의 나라로 알려져 있다.

12 키위는 뉴질랜드 토종 새의 이름이기도 하다.

13 키위 새는 국가의 상징이기 때문에, 뉴질랜드 사람들에게 특별하다.

14 또한, 키위는 뉴질랜드 출신의 사람들을 부르는 별명이기도 하다.

15 오늘날 뉴질랜드인들은 전 세계적으로 키위라고 불리기도 한다.

16 이제, 당신은 키위가 과일과 새, 그리고 국민의 명칭이라는 것을 알았다.

17 Next time, don't become _____ when someone _____ the word kiwi, _____ _____ _____ _____ .

18 Now, _____ _____ about the Maori. _____ are _____ _____ _____ of New Zealand.

19 They went to _____ _____ the islands _____ _____ _____ _____ .

20 The Maori culture is _____ _____ _____ of _____ New Zealand _____ .

21 The Maori language _____ _____ _____ at some schools and _____ _____ Maori language radio and TV stations.

22 _____ _____ Maori villages _____ _____ _____ _____ the country.

23 You can _____ Maori _____ and _____ Maori _____ .

24 If you _____ "kia ora" _____ the villagers, they _____ _____ _____ _____ _____ it. It _____ "hi" in English.

25 _____ you _____ _____ the haka?

26 The haka may _____ _____ _____ haka dancers _____ and _____ their bodies _____ .

27 The Maori people, _____ you've already _____ _____ , started _____ the haka _____ a war dance.

28 Today, _____ , New Zealanders _____ the haka _____ _____ _____ , weddings, or _____ _____ _____ .

29 _____ _____ , New Zealand's _____ _____ do the haka _____ _____ _____ _____ .

30 It is _____ _____ _____ the world.

31 If you see the haka, you _____ probably _____ the rival team _____ _____ .

32 _____ the kiwi bird, the haka is _____ _____ .

17 다음에는 누군가가 키위라는 단어를 사용할 때 혼동하지 마라. 그 단어는 여러 뜻을 가지고 있기 때문이다.

18 이제, 마오리족에 대해 이야기해 보자. 마오리족은 뉴질랜드의 원주민이다.

19 그들은 유럽인들이 도착하기 오래 전에 이 섬에 와서 살았다.

20 마오리족의 문화는 오늘날 뉴질랜드 사회의 중요한 부분이다.

21 몇몇 학교에서 마오리어를 가르치고 있으며, 마오리어의 라디오와 TV 방송국이 있다.

22 나라의 여러 곳에 마오리 마을이 있다.

23 당신은 마오리 마을을 방문해 마오리 문화를 경험할 수 있다.

24 당신이 마을 사람들에게 "kia ora"라고 말한다면 그들은 그것을 듣고 좋아할 것이다. 그것은 영어로 "안녕"이라는 뜻이다.

25 하카를 본 적이 있는가?

26 하카 춤을 추는 사람들이 소리 지르고, 그들의 몸을 사납게 움직이기 때문에 하카는 무서워 보일 수도 있다.

27 당신이 이미 그들에 대해 들은 적이 있겠지만, 마오리인들은 전쟁 춤으로 하카를 추기 시작했다.

28 하지만, 오늘날 뉴질랜드 사람들은 하카를 운동 경기, 결혼식 또는 다른 중요한 행사가 있을 때 한다.

29 예를 들어, 뉴질랜드의 럭비 국가 대표 팀 선수들은 모든 경기 전에 하카를 춘다.

30 그것은 전 세계적으로 유명하다.

31 당신이 하카를 본다면, 상대 팀이 틀림없이 겁을 먹을 것이라는 것에 아마 동의할 것이다.

32 키위와 마찬가지로 하카는 나라의 상징이다.

※ 다음 문장을 우리말로 쓰시오.

1 New Zealand is a place of natural beauty. It has many beautiful lakes and waterfalls.
➡ _____

2 New Zealand has two main islands, the South Island and the North Island.
➡ _____

3 In the South Island, there are mountains that are covered with snow all year round.
➡ _____

4 You will be amazed by the fantastic views.
➡ _____

5 In the North Island, there are many hot springs, lakes, and areas with green grass.
➡ _____

6 Because of its natural beauty, many famous movies have been made in New Zealand.
➡ _____

7 If you visit New Zealand, you will surely appreciate its nature.
➡ _____

8 When you hear the word kiwi, what comes to your mind?
➡ _____

9 Maybe a fruit, but, in New Zealand the word kiwi has a couple of meanings.
➡ _____

10 First, kiwi is the name of a delicious, green fruit.
➡ _____

11 A lot of kiwi fruit is grown there, so New Zealand is known as the land of kiwi fruit.
➡ _____

12 Kiwi is also the name of one of New Zealand's native birds.
➡ _____

13 The kiwi is special to New Zealanders because it is the symbol of the nation.
➡ _____

14 Also, kiwi is a nickname for people from New Zealand.
➡ _____

15 Today, New Zealanders are sometimes called Kiwis throughout the world.
➡ _____

16 Now, you know that kiwi is the name of a fruit, a bird, and also a people.
➡ _____

17 Next time, don't become confused when someone uses the word kiwi, which has several meanings.

➡ _____

18 Now, let's talk about the Maori. They are the native people of New Zealand.

➡ _____

19 They went to live on the islands long before Europeans arrived.

➡ _____

20 The Maori culture is an important part of today's New Zealand society.

➡ _____

21 The Maori language is taught at some schools and there are Maori language radio and TV stations.

➡ _____

22 There are Maori villages in many parts of the country.

➡ _____

23 You can visit Maori villages and experience Maori culture.

➡ _____

24 If you say "kia ora" to the villagers, they will be glad to hear it. It means "hi" in English.

➡ _____

25 Have you ever watched the haka?

➡ _____

26 The haka may look scary because haka dancers shout and move their bodies wildly.

➡ _____

27 The Maori people, who you've already heard about, started doing the haka as a war dance.

➡ _____

28 Today, however, New Zealanders do the haka at sport matches, weddings, or other important events.

➡ _____

29 For example, New Zealand's national rugby team members do the haka before every match.

➡ _____

30 It is famous all over the world.

➡ _____

31 If you see the haka, you will probably agree that the rival team must be scared.

➡ _____

32 Like the kiwi bird, the haka is a national symbol.

➡ _____

※ 다음 괄호 안의 단어들을 우리말에 맞도록 바르게 배열하시오.

Hello! New Zealand

1 (Zealand / New / a / is / place / natural / of / beauty. // has / it / beautiful / many / and / waterfalls. / lakes)
➡ _____

2 (Zealand / New / two / has / islands, / main / South / the / and / Island / North / the / Island.)
➡ _____

3 (the / in / Island, / South / are / there / that / mountains / are / with / covered / all / snow / round. / year)
➡ _____

4 (will / you / amazed / be / the / by / views. / fantastic)
➡ _____

5 (the / in / Island, / North / are / there / hot / many / lakes, / springs, / areas / and / with / grass. / green)
➡ _____

6 (of / because / its / beauty, / natural / famous / many / have / movies / been / in / made / Zealand. / New)
➡ _____

7 (you / if / New / visit / Zealand, / will / you / appreciate / surely / nature. / its)
➡ _____

8 (you / when / hear / word / the / kiwi, / comes / what / your / to / mind?)
➡ _____

9 (a / maybe / fruit, / in / but, / Zealand / New / word / the / has / kiwi / a / of / couple / meanings.)
➡ _____

10 (kiwi / first, / the / is / of / name / delicious, / a / fruit. / green)
➡ _____

11 (lot / a / kiwi / of / is / fruit / there, / grown / New / so / Zealand / known / is / as / land / the / kiwi / of / fruit.)
➡ _____

12 (is / kiwi / the / also / of / name / of / one / Zealand's / New / birds. / native)
➡ _____

13 (kiwi / the / special / is / New / to / because / Zealanders / is / it / the / symbol / the / of / nation.)
➡ _____

14 (kiwi / also, / is / a / nickname / people / for / New / from / Zealand.)
➡ _____

15 (New / today, / Zealanders / sometimes / are / called / throughout / Kiwis / world. / the)
➡ _____

16 (you / now, / that / know / is / kiwi / the / of / name / fruit, / a / bird, / a / also / and / people. / a)
➡ _____

안녕! 뉴질랜드

1 뉴질랜드는 자연의 아름다움이 가득한 곳이다. 뉴질랜드는 아름다운 호수와 폭포들이 많다.

2 뉴질랜드에는 남섬과 북섬, 두 개의 본섬이 있다.

3 남섬에는 일 년 내내 눈으로 덮인 산들이 있다.

4 당신은 굉장히 멋진 경관에 놀랄 것이다.

5 북섬에는 많은 온천과 호수, 초원 지역이 있다.

6 뉴질랜드 자연의 아름다움 때문에 많은 유명한 영화들이 뉴질랜드에서 촬영되었다.

7 뉴질랜드를 방문하면, 분명히 그 자연의 진가를 인정할 것이다.

8 키위라는 단어를 들을 때, 무엇이 떠오르는가?

9 아마도 과일이 떠오르겠지만, 뉴질랜드에서 키위는 몇 가지 뜻이 있다.

10 먼저, 키위는 맛있는 초록색 과일의 이름이다.

11 많은 키위가 그곳에서 자라기 때문에 뉴질랜드는 키위의 나라로 알려져 있다.

12 키위는 뉴질랜드 토종 새의 이름이기도 하다.

13 키위 새는 국가의 상징이기 때문에, 뉴질랜드 사람들에게 특별하다.

14 또한, 키위는 뉴질랜드 출신의 사람들을 부르는 별명이기도 하다.

15 오늘날 뉴질랜드인들은 전 세계적으로 키위라고 불리기도 한다.

16 이제, 당신은 키위가 과일과 새, 그리고 국민의 명칭이라는 것을 알았다.

17 (time, / next / become / don't / when / confused / uses / someone / word / the / kiwi, / has / which / meanings. / several)
➡ _____

18 (let's / now, / about / talk / Maori. / the // are / they / native / the / people / New / of / Zealand.)
➡ _____

19 (went / they / live / to / the / on / long / islands / before / arrived. / Europeans)
➡ _____

20 (Maori / the / culture / an / is / part / important / an / of / New / today's / society. / Zealand)
➡ _____

21 (Maori / the / language / taught / is / some / at / schools / there / and / Maori / are / radio / lauguage / TV / and / stations.)
➡ _____

22 (are / there / villages / Maori / many / in / of / parts / country. / the)
➡ _____

23 (can / you / Maori / visit / villages / and / Maori / experience / culture.)
➡ _____

24 (you / if / say / ora" / "kia / the / to / villagers, / will / they / glad / be / hear / to / it. // means / it / in / "hi" / English.)
➡ _____

25 (you / have / watched / ever / haka? / the)
➡ _____

26 (haka / the / look / may / because / scary / dancers / haka / and / shout / their / move / widely. / bodies)
➡ _____

27 (Maori / the / people, / you've / who / heard / already / about, / doing / started / haka / the / a / as / dance. / war)
➡ _____

28 (however, / today, / Zealanders / New / the / do / haka / sport / at / matches, / or / weddings, / important / other / events.)
➡ _____

29 (example, / for / Zealand's / New / rugby / national / memebers / team / the / do / before / haka / match. / every)
➡ _____

30 (is / it / all / famous / the / over / world.)
➡ _____

31 (you / if / the / see / haka, / will / you / agree / probably / the / that / team / rival / be / must / scared.)
➡ _____

32 (the / like / bird, / kiwi / haka / the / a / is / symbol. / national)
➡ _____

17 다음에는 누군가가 키위라는 단어를 사용할 때 혼동하지 마라. 그 단어는 여러 뜻을 가지고 있기 때문이다.

18 이제, 마오리족에 대해 이야기해 보자. 마오리족은 뉴질랜드의 원주민이다.

19 그들은 유럽인들이 도착하기 오래 전에 이 섬에 와서 살았다.

20 마오리족의 문화는 오늘날 뉴질랜드 사회의 중요한 부분이다.

21 몇몇 학교에서 마오리어를 가르치고 있으며, 마오리어의 라디오와 TV 방송국이 있다.

22 나라의 여러 곳에 마오리 마을이 있다.

23 당신은 마오리 마을을 방문해 마오리 문화를 경험할 수 있다.

24 당신이 마을 사람들에게 "kia ora"라고 말한다면 그들은 그것을 듣고 좋아할 것이다. 그것은 영어로 "안녕"이라는 뜻이다.

25 하카를 본 적이 있는가?

26 하카 춤을 추는 사람들이 소리 지르고, 그들의 몸을 사납게 움직이기 때문에 하카는 무서워 보일 수도 있다.

27 당신이 이미 그들에 대해 들은 적이 있겠지만, 마오리인들은 전쟁 춤으로 하카를 추기 시작했다.

28 하지만, 오늘날 뉴질랜드 사람들은 하카를 운동 경기, 결혼식 또는 다른 중요한 행사가 있을 때 한다.

29 예를 들어, 뉴질랜드의 럭비 국가 대표 팀 선수들은 모든 경기 전에 하카를 춘다.

30 그것은 전 세계적으로 유명하다.

31 당신이 하카를 본다면, 상대 팀이 틀림없이 겁을 먹을 것이라는 것에 아마 동의할 것이다.

32 키위와 마찬가지로 하카는 나라의 상징이다.

※ **다음 우리말을 영어로 쓰시오.**

1 뉴질랜드는 자연의 아름다움이 가득한 곳이다. 뉴질랜드는 아름다운 호수와 폭포들이 많다.

➡ _____

2 뉴질랜드에는 남섬과 북섬, 두 개의 본섬이 있다.

➡ _____

3 남섬에는 일 년 내내 눈으로 덮인 산들이 있다.

➡ _____

4 당신은 굉장히 멋진 경관에 놀랄 것이다.

➡ _____

5 북섬에는 많은 온천과 호수, 초원 지역이 있다.

➡ _____

6 뉴질랜드 자연의 아름다움 때문에 많은 유명한 영화들이 뉴질랜드에서 촬영되었다.

➡ _____

7 뉴질랜드를 방문하면, 분명히 그 자연의 진가를 인정할 것이다.

➡ _____

8 키위라는 단어를 들을 때, 무엇이 떠오르는가?

➡ _____

9 아마도 과일이 떠오르겠지만, 뉴질랜드에서 키위는 몇 가지 뜻이 있다.

➡ _____

10 먼저, 키위는 맛있는 초록색 과일의 이름이다.

➡ _____

11 많은 키위가 그곳에서 자라기 때문에 뉴질랜드는 키위의 나라로 알려져 있다.

➡ _____

12 키위는 뉴질랜드 토종 새의 이름이기도 하다.

➡ _____

13 키위 새는 국가의 상징이기 때문에, 뉴질랜드 사람들에게 특별하다.

➡ _____

14 또한, 키위는 뉴질랜드 출신의 사람들을 부르는 별명이기도 하다.

➡ _____

15 오늘날 뉴질랜드인들은 전 세계적으로 키위라고 불리기도 한다.

➡ _____

16 이제, 당신은 키위가 과일과 새, 그리고 국민의 명칭이라는 것을 알았다.

➡ _____

17 다음에는 누군가가 키위라는 단어를 사용할 때 혼동하지 마라. 그 단어는 여러 뜻을 가지고 있기 때문이다.

➡ _____

18 이제, 마오리족에 대해 이야기해 보자. 마오리족은 뉴질랜드의 원주민이다.

➡ _____

19 그들은 유럽인들이 도착하기 오래 전에 이 섬에 와서 살았다.

➡ _____

20 마오리족의 문화는 오늘날 뉴질랜드 사회의 중요한 부분이다.

➡ _____

21 몇몇 학교에서 마오리어를 가르치고 있으며, 마오리어의 라디오와 TV 방송국이 있다.

➡ _____

_____

22 나라의 여러 곳에 마오리 마을이 있다.

➡ _____

23 당신은 마오리 마을을 방문해 마오리 문화를 경험할 수 있다.

➡ _____

24 당신이 마을 사람들에게 "kia ora"라고 말한다면 그들은 그것을 듣고 좋아할 것이다. 그것은 영어로 "안녕"이라는 뜻이다.

➡ _____

25 하카를 본 적이 있는가?

➡ _____

26 하카 춤을 추는 사람들이 소리 지르고, 그들의 몸을 사납게 움직이기 때문에 하카는 무서워 보일 수도 있다.

➡ _____

27 당신이 이미 그들에 대해 들은 적 있겠지만, 마오리인들은 전쟁 춤으로 하카를 추기 시작했다.

➡ _____

28 하지만, 오늘날 뉴질랜드 사람들은 하카를 운동 경기, 결혼식 또는 다른 중요한 행사가 있을 때 한다.

➡ _____

29 예를 들어, 뉴질랜드의 럭비 국가 대표 팀 선수들은 모든 경기 전에 하카를 춘다.

➡ _____

30 그것은 전 세계적으로 유명하다.

➡ _____

31 당신이 하카를 본다면, 상대 팀이 틀림없이 겁을 먹을 것이라는 것에 아마 동의할 것이다.

➡ _____

32 키위와 마찬가지로 하카는 나라의 상징이다.

➡ _____

※ 다음 우리말과 일치하도록 빈칸에 알맞은 말을 쓰시오.

Before You Read

1. Rugby is _____ _____ _____ in New Zealand.

2. New Zealand is _____ _____ _____ _____ _____ the world.

3. The Maori people are _____ _____ _____ of New Zealand and _____ _____ _____ .

Enjoy Writing

1. We _____ You

2. _____ you _____ _____ New Zealand?

3. It has _____ _____ _____ and 600 _____ _____ .

4. _____ _____ is Wellington.

5. The kiwi, _____ is _____ _____ _____ to New Zealand, is _____ _____ _____ _____ of the country.

6. _____ you _____ _____ New Zealand, you _____ _____ a _____ _____ , shows _____ _____ _____ of New Zealand.

7. We _____ you _____ a _____ _____ of the Maori people.

8. They _____ _____ and _____ in the ground _____ _____ _____ . It is great.

9. Many people visit New Zealand _____ _____ _____ _____ _____ .

10. We are _____ _____ you to this _____ _____ .

Project Step 1

1. A: _____ _____ about which country we _____ _____ _____ _____ .

2. B: _____ _____ do you _____ , Australia _____ the UK?

3. C: I _____ we _____ information _____ the UK.

4. There is _____ _____ _____ information _____ _____ .

5. D: _____ .

1. 럭비는 뉴질랜드에서 인기 있는 운동이다.
2. 뉴질랜드는 남반구에 있다.
3. 마오리족은 뉴질랜드의 원주민들이고, 그들의 문화가 있다.

1. 우리는 당신을 초대합니다
2. 당신은 뉴질랜드에 대해 아는가?
3. 그곳은 두 개의 본섬과 600개의 작은 섬들로 되어 있다.
4. 그곳의 수도는 웰링턴이다.
5. 키위는 뉴질랜드 태생의 새인데, 그 나라의 상징 중 하나이다.
6. 뉴질랜드에 온다면 마오리 마을을 반드시 방문해야 하는데, 왜냐하면 그 마을이 뉴질랜드 원주민들의 문화를 보여 주기 때문이다.
7. 우리는 당신이 마오리족의 전통 요리를 먹어 보는 것을 제안한다.
8. 그들은 열을 가한 돌로 땅 속에서 고기와 채소를 요리한다. 그것은 훌륭하다.
9. 많은 사람들은 아름다운 자연을 즐기기 위해 뉴질랜드를 방문한다.
10. 우리는 당신을 이 아름다운 나라에 초대하게 되어 기쁘다.

1. A: 어느 나라를 조사할 것인지 이야기해 보자.
2. B: 호주와 영국 중에서 어느 나라를 선호하니?
3. C: 나는 영국에 관한 정보를 찾아볼 것을 제안해.
4. 우리가 작업해야 할 많은 정보들이 있잖아.
5. D: 그래

※ 다음 우리말을 영어로 쓰시오.

Before You Read

1. 럭비는 뉴질랜드에서 인기 있는 운동이다.
➡ _____

2. 뉴질랜드는 남반구에 있다.
➡ _____

3. 마오리족은 뉴질랜드의 원주민들이고, 그들의 문화가 있다.
➡ _____

Enjoy Writing

1. 우리는 당신을 초대합니다
➡ _____

2. 당신은 뉴질랜드에 대해 아는가?
➡ _____

3. 그곳은 두 개의 본섬과 600개의 작은 섬들로 되어 있다.
➡ _____

4. 그곳의 수도는 웰링턴이다.
➡ _____

5. 키위는 뉴질랜드 태생의 새인데, 그 나라의 상징 중 하나이다.
➡ _____

6. 뉴질랜드에 온다면 마오리 마을을 반드시 방문해야 하는데, 왜냐하면 그 마을이 뉴질랜드 원주민들의 문화를 보여 주기 때문이다.
➡ _____
_____

7. 우리는 당신이 마오리족의 전통 요리를 먹어 보는 것을 제안한다.
➡ _____

8. 그들은 열을 가한 돌로 땅 속에서 고기와 채소를 요리한다. 그것은 훌륭하다.
➡ _____

9. 많은 사람들은 아름다운 자연을 즐기기 위해 뉴질랜드를 방문한다.
➡ _____

10. 우리는 당신을 이 아름다운 나라에 초대하게 되어 기쁘다.
➡ _____

Project Step 1

1. A: 어느 나라를 조사할 것인지 이야기해 보자.
➡ _____

2. B: 호주와 영국 중에서 어느 나라를 선호하니?
➡ _____

3. C: 나는 영국에 관한 정보를 찾아볼 것을 제안해.
➡ _____

4. 우리가 작업해야 할 많은 정보들이 있잖아.
➡ _____

5. D: 그래.
➡ _____

※ 다음 영어를 우리말로 쓰시오.

01 sincerely _____

02 accidentally _____

03 relationship _____

04 delete _____

05 emotional _____

06 prepare _____

07 especially _____

08 responsibility _____

09 proper _____

10 generous _____

11 humorous _____

12 include _____

13 break _____

14 case _____

15 serious _____

16 casual _____

17 suggestion _____

18 thoughtful _____

19 necessary _____

20 mind _____

21 regret _____

22 apology _____

23 relaxed _____

24 sincere _____

25 wound _____

26 apologize _____

27 brave _____

28 ignore _____

29 appreciate _____

30 borrow _____

31 nervous _____

32 loud _____

33 intend _____

34 tray _____

35 trip over _____

36 care about _____

37 bump into _____

38 at once _____

39 with all one's heart _____

40 turn down _____

41 laugh off _____

42 take responsibility for _____

43 think nothing of _____

※ 다음 우리말을 영어로 쓰시오.

01 삭제하다 _____

02 의견, 제안 _____

03 사려 깊은, 생각에 잠긴 _____

04 우연히, 뜻하지 않게 _____

05 꺼리다, 싫어하다 _____

06 고마워하다, 감사하다 _____

07 대충하는, 건성의 _____

08 특히, 유난히 _____

09 너그러운 _____

10 사례, 경우 _____

11 책임 _____

12 ~을 준비하다 _____

13 (관계를) 끝내다, 끊다 _____

14 의도하다 _____

15 심각한, 진지한 _____

16 진정한, 진심 어린 _____

17 적절한, 제대로 된 _____

18 후회하다 _____

19 무시하다 _____

20 포함하다 _____

21 느긋한, 여유 있는 _____

22 사과하다 _____

23 감정적인 _____

24 재미있는, 유머러스한 _____

25 용감한 _____

26 실수, 잘못 _____

27 사과 _____

28 관계 _____

29 진심으로 _____

30 상처, 부상 _____

31 소리가 큰, 시끄러운 _____

32 처리하다, 대우하다 _____

33 빌리다 _____

34 필요한 _____

35 ~에 부딪히다 _____

36 ~을 웃어넘기려 하다 _____

37 지나가다 _____

38 ~에 걸려 넘어지다 _____

39 (소리를) 줄이다 _____

40 ~에 책임을 지다 _____

41 선택하다, 고르다 _____

42 진심으로 _____

43 ~와 잘 지내다 _____

※ 다음 영영풀이에 알맞은 단어를 <보기>에서 골라 쓴 후, 우리말 뜻을 쓰시오.

1 _____ : to be grateful for something: _____

2 _____ : a wrong action, statement, or judgment: _____

3 _____ : to intentionally not listen or give attention to: _____

4 _____ : the way in which two things are connected: _____

5 _____ : something that it is your job or duty to deal with: _____

6 _____ : in a way that was not planned or intended: _____

7 _____ : showing no fear of dangerous or difficult things: _____

8 _____ : done without much thought, effort, or concern: _____

9 _____ : to remove part or all of a written or electronic text: _____

10 _____ : an act of saying that you are sorry for something wrong you have done:

_____

11 _____ : honest and true, and based on what you really feel and believe: _____

12 _____ : an idea, plan, or action that is suggested or the act of suggesting it:

_____

13 _____ : always thinking of the things you can do to make people happy or

comfortable: _____

14 _____ : to make or get something or someone ready for something that will

happen in the future: _____

15 _____ : to feel sorry about something you have done or about something that you

have not been able to do: _____

16 _____ : willing to give money, help, kindness, etc., especially more than is usual

or expected: _____

sincere	accidentally	generous	brave
thoughtful	ignore	suggestion	mistake
apology	responsibility	prepare	relationship
regret	casual	delete	appreciate

※ 다음 우리말과 일치하도록 빈칸에 알맞은 말을 쓰시오.

Listen & Speak 1 A-1

B: Judy, do you _____ _____ _____ the volume?

G: _____, _____ _____. Is it too _____?

B: Yes, it is. I can _____ it in my room.

G: I'm sorry. I'll _____ _____ _____.

B: _____ a _____.

B: Judy, 볼륨을 좀 낮춰 줄래?
G: 그래. 소리가 너무 크니?
B: 응, 소리가 커. 내 방에서도 들려
G: 미안해. 내가 볼륨을 낮출게.
B: 정말 고마워.

Listen & Speak 1 A-2

G: I _____ _____ my mom's _____ _____.

B: _____ _____ _____, Mina.

G: _____ _____ _____ _____ me _____ _____ _____ _____ _____ her?

B: No, _____ _____ _____. You should _____ _____.

G: I see. I'll talk to her _____ _____ _____ _____.

G: 내가 실수로 엄마가 제일 좋아하는 접시를 깼어.
B: 그것 참 안됐구나, 미나야.
G: 엄마한테 미안하다고 어떻게 말해야 하는지 말해 줄래?
B: 응, 물론이지. 너는 진심으로 사과해야 해.
G: 알겠어. 엄마에게 진심으로 이야기해야겠어.

Listen & Speak 1 A-3

B: Karen, do you _____ _____ to my house tomorrow at 7 a.m.?

G: That's very _____.

B: I know, but I need the book _____ you _____ _____ _____.

G: I see. Then _____ meet at seven.

B: See you _____.

B: Karen, 내일 오전 7시에 우리 집에 와 줄래?
G 그건 너무 이른데.
B: 그건 알지만, 수업 시작하기 전에 네가 빌려간 책이 필요하거든.
G: 알겠어. 그럼 7시에 보자.
B: 그때 보자.

Listen & Speak 1 B

A: Hellen, do you _____ _____ _____?

B: No, I don't. / Sorry _____ I _____.

A: Hellen, do you _____ _____ _____ _____?

B: No, I don't. / Sorry but I _____.

A: Hellen, 조용히 좀 해 줄래?
B: 알았어. / 미안하지만 그럴 수 없어.

A: Hellen, 쓰레기 좀 주워 줄래?
B: 알았어. / 미안하지만 그럴 수 없어.

Listen & Speak 2 A-1

G: You _____ _____ _____ _____, Minsu. Can I come in?

B: Sure. I'm _____ _____ the dance _____, but it's not easy.

G: I can help you. I was in the _____ _____ _____.

B: Really? That would be _____, Amy.

G: You _____ _____ _____ _____ into the _____. But one thing you _____ _____ do is to be more _____. You are too _____.

B: Your _____ is very _____. I really _____ your _____.

G: It's my _____.

Listen & Speak 2 A-2

B: Irene, what are you doing?

G: Well, I've _____ my favorite cap. I can't find it.

B: _____ _____ _____ you. _____ does it look _____?

G: It's red. My name _____ _____ in black on the side.

B: Oh, is this _____? It was _____ the table.

G: Yes, it is. Thank you, Jim. I _____ your _____.

B: _____ _____.

Listen & Speak 2 B

A: _____ me _____ you the way.

B: I _____ your time.

A: _____ _____ _____ your _____.

B: I _____ _____.

Real Life Talk

Jessie: Hi, Andy. _____ _____?

Andy: Hi, Jessie. I'm going to buy a _____ for Amy. You'_____ _____ friends with her _____ a long time, _____ you?

Jessie: Yes, _____ first grade in _____ school.

Andy: Well, I know you're really _____ _____, but _____ _____ _____ me? I am sure you could _____ _____ _____ _____ _____ _____.

G: 민수야, 너 바빠 보인다. 나 들어가도 되니?

B: 물론. 나 춤 경연대회를 준비하고 있는데 쉽지 않아.

G: 내가 도와줄게. 나 작년에 대회에 참가했었거든.

B: 정말? Amy, 그거 정말 좋을 거 같아.

G: 너는 리듬을 타는 건 잘하는 편이야. 하지만 네가 해야 할 한 가지는 긴장을 더 푸는 것이야. 너는 너무 긴장을 해.

B: 네 조언이 정말 도움이 된다. 너의 조언 정말 고마워.

G: 도움이 됐다니 기뻐.

B: Irene, 너 뭐 하고 있어?

G: 음, 내가 제일 좋아하는 모자를 잃어버렸어. 그 모자를 못 찾겠어.

B: 내가 도와줄게. 그것은 어떻게 생겼어?

G: 그건 빨간색이야. 모자 옆 부분에 내 이름이 검은색으로 쓰여 있어.

B: 오, 이거 네 것이니? 이거 탁자 아래에 있었어.

G: 응, 맞아. 고마워, Jim. 도와줘서 고마워.

B: 천만에.

A: 제가 길을 알려 줄게요.

B: 시간 내 줘서 감사합니다.

A: 내가 너의 가방을 들어 줄게.

B: 도와 줘서 고마워.

Jessie: 안녕, Andy. 무슨 일이니?

Andy: 안녕, Jessie. 나는 Amy한테 줄 선물을 사려고 해. 너는 그 애와 오랫동안 친구로 지냈지, 그렇지 않니?

Jessie: 응, 초등학교 1학년 때부터.

Andy: 음, 네가 공부하느라 바쁘다는 것을 알지만, 나를 좀 도와줄 수 있니? 괜찮은 것을 고르도록 네가 도와줄 수 있을 것이라고 확신해.

Jessie: No _____. What's the _____ _____? It's not her birthday.

Andy: Well, two months ago, when my leg _____ _____, she _____ my backpack to school.

Jessie: That was nice _____ _____.

Andy: Yes, it was. What should I get for her?

Jessie: Well, _____ _____ a case for her smartphone? She _____ her case _____.

Andy: Really? _____ _____ for your _____.

Wrap Up 1

G: I _____ _____ _____ _____ to Jejudo.

B: That's _____, Suhee. I _____ _____ _____ there.

G: _____ _____ _____ _____ me _____ _____ _____ in Jejudo?

B: _____ _____ _____. Jejudo has many beautiful _____. You _____ _____ them.

G: Good. I will go _____. What _____ can I do?

B: Why _____ _____ hike Halla Mountain? You can see the mountain from _____ on the island.

G: Great. _____ _____ food?

B: If you like fish, on Jejudo _____ _____ is _____ and _____.

G: I'll try everything. I _____ your _____.

Wrap Up 2

W: Mike does not feel very _____. He _____ _____ _____ a cold. He _____ _____ see a doctor, but he has a meeting with Jane _____ _____ _____ _____. He wants _____ _____ her tomorrow _____. What _____ he _____ to her?

Jessie: 좋아. 무엇을 위한 선물이니? 그 애의 생일은 아닌데.
Andy: 음, 두 달 전에 내 다리가 부러졌을 때, 그 애가 학교까지 내 가방을 들어줬어.
Jessie: 그 애는 정말 친절했구나.
Andy: 응, 그랬어. 그 애를 위해 무엇을 사야 할까?
Jessie: 음, 스마트폰 케이스는 어떠니? 그 애는 최근에 케이스를 깨뜨렸어.
Andy: 정말? 제안해 줘서 고마워.

G: 나는 제주도에 갈 계획이야.
B: 그거 멋지다, 수희야. 나 예전에 제주도에 살았어.
G: 내가 제주도에서 뭘 해야 하는지 말해 줄래?
B: 물론. 제주도에는 아름다운 해변들이 많아. 그 해변들을 꼭 가봐야 해.
G: 좋아. 나는 수영하러 갈 거야. 그 밖에 내가 할 수 있는 것은 무엇이니?
B: 한라산을 등반해 보는 건 어때? 섬의 모든 곳에서 그 산을 볼 수 있어.
G: 좋아. 음식은 어때?
B: 네가 생선을 좋아한다면, 제주도에서는 회가 신선하고 맛있어.
G: 나는 모든 걸 다 해 볼 거야. 조언해 줘서 고마워.

W: Mike는 몸이 별로 좋지 않아. 그는 감기에 걸렸을지도 몰라. 그는 병원에 가야 하지만, 한 시간 후에 Jane과 회의가 있어. 그는 대신 내일 그녀를 만나기를 원해. 그는 그녀에게 뭐라고 말해야 할까?

Step2

※ 다음 우리말에 맞도록 대화를 영어로 쓰시오.

해석

Listen & Speak 1 A-1

B: _____

G: _____

B: _____

G: _____

B: _____

B: Judy, 볼륨을 좀 낮춰 줄래?
G: 그래. 소리가 너무 크니?
B: 응, 소리가 커. 내 방에서도 들려
G: 미안해. 내가 볼륨을 낮출게.
B: 정말 고마워.

Listen & Speak 1 A-2

G: _____

B: _____

G: _____

B: _____

G: _____

G: 내가 실수로 엄마가 제일 좋아하는 접시를 깼어.
B: 그것 참 안됐구나, 미나야.
G: 엄마한테 미안하다고 어떻게 말해야 하는지 말해 줄래?
B: 응, 물론이지. 너는 진심으로 사과해야 해.
G: 알겠어. 엄마에게 진심으로 이야기해야겠어.

Listen & Speak 1 A-3

B: _____

G: _____

B: _____

G: _____

B: _____

B: Karen, 내일 오전 7시에 우리 집에 와 줄래?
G 그건 너무 이른데.
B: 그건 알지만, 수업 시작하기 전에 네가 빌려간 책이 필요하거든.
G: 알겠어. 그럼 7시에 보자.
B: 그때 보자.

Listen & Speak 1 B

A: _____

B: _____

A: _____

B: _____

A: Hellen, 조용히 좀 해 줄래?
B: 알았어. / 미안하지만 그럴 수 없어.

A: Hellen, 쓰레기 좀 주워 줄래?
B: 알았어. / 미안하지만 그럴 수 없어.

G: _____

B: _____

G: _____

B: _____

G: _____

_____

B: _____

G: _____

G: 민수야, 너 바빠 보인다. 나 들어가도 되니?
B: 물론. 나 춤 경연대회를 준비하고 있는데 쉽지 않아.
G: 내가 도와줄게. 나 작년에 대회에 참가했었거든.
B: 정말? Amy, 그거 정말 좋을 거 같아.
G: 너는 리듬을 타는 건 잘하는 편이야. 하지만 네가 해야 할 한 가지는 긴장을 더 푸는 것이야. 너는 너무 긴장을 해.
B: 네 조언이 정말 도움이 된다. 너의 조언 정말 고마워.
G: 도움이 됐다니 기뻐.

B: _____

G: _____

B: _____

G: _____

B: _____

G: _____

B: _____

B: Irene, 너 뭐 하고 있어?
G: 음, 내가 제일 좋아하는 모자를 잃어버렸어. 그 모자를 못 찾겠어.
B: 내가 도와줄게. 그것은 어떻게 생겼어?
G: 그건 빨간색이야. 모자 옆 부분에 내 이름이 검은색으로 쓰여 있어.
B: 오, 이거 네 것이니? 이거 탁자 아래에 있었어.
G: 응, 맞아. 고마워, Jim. 도와줘서 고마워.
B: 천만에.

A: _____

B: _____

A: _____

B: _____

A: 제가 길을 알려 줄게요.
B: 시간 내 줘서 감사합니다.

A: 내가 너의 가방을 들어 줄게.
B: 도와 줘서 고마워.

Jessie: _____

Andy: _____

_____

Jessie: _____

Andy: _____

_____

Jessie: 안녕, Andy. 무슨 일이니?
Andy: 안녕, Jessie. 나는 Amy한테 줄 선물을 사려고 해. 너는 그 애와 오랫동안 친구로 지냈지, 그렇지 않니?
Jessie: 응, 초등학교 1학년 때부터.
Andy: 음, 네가 공부하느라 바쁘다는 것을 알지만, 나를 좀 도와줄 수 있니? 괜찮은 것을 고르도록 네가 도와줄 수 있을 것이라고 확신해.

Jessie: _____

Andy: _____

_____

Jessie: _____

Andy: _____

Jessie: _____

Andy: _____

Jessie: 좋아. 무엇을 위한 선물이니? 그 애의 생일은 아닌데.
Andy: 음, 두 달 전에 내 다리가 부러졌을 때, 그 애가 학교까지 내 가방을 들어줬어.
Jessie: 그 애는 정말 친절했구나.
Andy: 응, 그랬어. 그 애를 위해 무엇을 사야 할까?
Jessie: 음, 스마트폰 케이스는 어떠니? 그 애는 최근에 케이스를 깨뜨렸어.
Andy: 정말? 제안해 줘서 고마워.

Wrap Up 1

G: _____

B: _____

G: _____

B: _____

G: _____

B: _____

G: _____

B: _____

G: _____

G: 나는 제주도에 갈 계획이야.
B: 그거 멋지다, 수희야. 나 예전에 제주도에 살았어.
G: 내가 제주도에서 뭘 해야 하는지 말해 줄래?
B: 물론. 제주도에는 아름다운 해변들이 많아. 그 해변들을 꼭 가봐야 해.
G: 좋아. 나는 수영하러 갈 거야. 그 밖에 내가 할 수 있는 것은 무엇이니?
B: 한라산을 등반해 보는 건 어때? 섬의 모든 곳에서 그 산을 볼 수 있어.
G: 좋아. 음식은 어때?
B: 네가 생선을 좋아한다면, 제주도에서는 회가 신선하고 맛있어.
G: 나는 모든 걸 다 해 볼 거야. 조언해 줘서 고마워.

Wrap Up 2

W: _____

_____

_____

W: Mike는 몸이 별로 좋지 않아. 그는 감기에 걸렸을지도 몰라. 그는 병원에 가야 하지만, 한 시간 후에 Jane과 회의가 있어. 그는 대신 내일 그녀를 만나기를 원해. 그는 그녀에게 뭐라고 말해야 할까?

※ 다음 우리말과 일치하도록 빈칸에 알맞은 것을 골라 쓰시오.

1 _____ we are _____, we all make _____. It is not easy to get _____ with everyone all the time.

  A. mistakes   B. along   C. human   D. because

2 Sometimes we hurt people's feelings _____ _____ to. Sometimes, we do something _____ and _____ it later.

  A. wrong   B. without   C. regret   D. intending

3 When _____ _____, what should we do? We _____ _____.

  A. happens   B. apologize   C. that   D. should

4 Read the _____ _____ studies and learn three things about a _____ _____.

  A. proper   B. case   C. apology   D. following

5 When June _____ _____ a backpack and fell, Mike found it funny and _____. He took a picture and _____ it on an SNS.

  A. uploaded   B. tripped   C. laughed   D. over

6 June saw the picture and _____ _____. Mike said, _____ a laugh, "Sorry, June!" and _____ it.

  A. angry   B. deleted   C. became   D. with

7 After that, June felt _____ more _____ of Mike's _____ apology.

  A. because   B. even   C. casual   D. hurt

8 June didn't like how Mike had _____. Mike _____ to think it was _____ _____.

  A. seemed   B. nothing   C. acted   D. serious

9 What did you learn from this _____? Yes. You _____ right. You should be _____ when you _____.

  A. guessed   B. apologize   C. case   D. sincere

10 _____ is necessary to _____ good friendships. _____ you're sorry is more than just _____.

  A. saying   B. build   C. apologizing   D. words

11 You need to show that you _____ the other person and _____ his or her _____.

  A. about   B. feelings   C. care   D. respect

12 If you truly want to _____ _____ _____, be _____ in your apology.

  A. sincere   B. things   C. make   D. right

13 The _____ sincere your _____ is, the _____ it will be _____.

  A. better   B. more   C. received   D. apology

14 Here is _____ case. While Kate was hurrying across the cafeteria, she _____ _____ _____ Hojun.

  A. bumped   B. another   C. into   D. accidently

15 Some food on Hojun's _____ _____ on his jacket. Kate didn't _____. Hojun felt _____.

  A. fell   B. apologize   C. bad   D. tray

1 우리는 인간이기 때문에 모두가 실수한다. 모든 사람과 항상 잘 지내기는 쉽지 않다.

2 때때로 우리는 의도하지 않게 다른 사람의 감정을 상하게 한다. 때때로 우리는 나쁜 일을 하고 나중에 그것을 후회한다.

3 이런 일이 생기면, 우리는 무엇을 해야 할까? 우리는 사과해야 한다.

4 다음 사례 연구들을 읽고 올바른 사과를 위한 세 가지를 알아보자.

5 June이 가방에 걸려 넘어졌을 때, Mike는 그것이 재미있다고 생각하고 웃었다. 그는 사진을 찍어서 SNS에 올렸다.

6 June은 그 사진을 보고 화가 났다. Mike는 웃으면서 "미안해, June!"이라고 말하고 사진을 삭제했다.

7 그 후, June은 Mike의 가벼운 사과에 한층 더 화가 났다.

8 June은 Mike의 행동 방식이 마음에 들지 않았다. Mike는 이 일이 심각한 일이 아니라고 생각하는 것처럼 보였다.

9 이 사례로부터 무엇을 배웠는가? 맞다. 당신은 바르게 추측했다. 당신은 사과할 때에 진실해야 한다.

10 사과하는 것은 좋은 교우 관계를 만들기 위해 필요하다. 미안하다고 말하는 것은 단지 말 이상이다.

11 당신이 타인을 존중하고, 타인의 감정에 관심을 갖고 있음을 보여주어야 한다.

12 당신이 진실로 일을 바로잡기를 원한다면, 당신의 사과는 진실해야 한다.

13 당신의 사과가 진실할수록, 그것은 더 잘 받아들여질 것이다.

14 또 다른 사례가 있다. Kate가 급식실을 가로질러 급하게 뛰어갈 때, 호준이와 실수로 부딪쳤다.

15 호준이의 급식판에 있던 음식이 그의 재킷에 떨어졌다. Kate는 사과하지 않았다. 호준이는 기분이 나빴다.

16 He thought, 'Why _____ she _____ something? It would be nothing _____ she apologized _____ now.'
A. right   B. say   C. doesn't   D. if

17 This case shows _____ when an apology is _____, you should _____ at _____.
A. necessary   B. once   C. that   D. apologize

18 A quick apology _____ that you are _____ and take _____ for your _____.
A. action   B. shows   C. responsibility   D. thoughtful

19 All you need to do is to say, "I'm sorry." Then, the hurt friend will _____ _____ of it and _____ it _____.
A. laugh   B. nothing   C. off   D. think

20 _____, apologies are necessary _____ family members and _____ ones, _____.
A. among   B. finally   C. loved   D. too

21 One day, Sunmin _____ her sister's _____ book. _____, she _____ it.
A. favorite   B. borrowed   C. lost   D. later

22 Sunmin didn't _____ because she _____ it was not _____. She thought, 'We're sisters, _____ all.'
A. important   B. apologize   C. after   D. thought

23 Sunmin's sister _____ _____ Sunmin had _____ her. How could her own sister _____ her feelings?
A. treated   B. disliked   C. ignore   D. how

24 This was not the first time Sunmin _____ _____ to her _____ _____.
A. sister   B. little   C. hadn't   D. apologized

25 People need to _____ when they do _____ _____. This includes family members and the people who are _____ to you.
A. close   B. apologize   C. wrong   D. something

26 People _____ _____ more _____ when the hurt _____ from a family member or a friend.
A. comes   B. hurt   C. easily   D. get

27 We may think that they will _____ it _____ _____ they are _____ to us.
A. close   B. let   C. because   D. go

28 Remember, however, that small _____ and no apology _____ _____ to big _____ wounds.
A. add   B. mistakes   C. up   D. emotional

29 This is _____ true _____ family members and _____ _____.
A. among   B. especially   C. ones   D. loved

30 Have you ever _____ of the _____, "No _____ apologies, no more _____"?
A. chances   B. heard   C. more   D. saying

31 People make _____, but don't _____ one mistake _____ a beautiful _____.
A. break   B. mistakes   C. relationship   D. let

32 Do you want to _____ to someone? _____ to do it now. A quick and _____ "I'm sorry" can _____ many problems.
A. try   B. sincere   C. apologize   D. solve

16 그는 '왜 그녀는 아무 말도 하지 않지? 그녀가 즉시 사과한다면 아무 일도 아닐 텐데.' 라고 생각했다.

17 이 사례는 사과가 필요할 때는 사과를 즉시 해야 한다는 것을 보여준다.

18 신속한 사과는 당신이 사려 깊고, 당신의 행동에 책임을 진다는 것을 보여준다.

19 당신이 해야 할 행동은 "미안해."라고 말하는 것뿐이다. 그러면 상처받은 친구는 당신의 잘못을 아무렇지 않게 생각하고, 웃어넘길 것이다.

20 마지막으로 사과는 가족이나 사랑하는 사람들 사이에서도 필요하다.

21 어느 날, 선민이는 여동생이 가장 좋아하는 책을 빌렸다. 나중에 그녀는 그것을 잃어버렸다.

22 선민이는 그것이 중요하지 않고 생각하여 사과하지 않았다. 그녀는 '우리는 어쨌든 자매니까.'라고 생각했다.

23 선민이의 여동생은 언니가 본인을 대했던 방식이 마음에 들지 않았다. 어떻게 자신의 언니가 그녀의 기분을 무시할 수 있는가?

24 선민이가 여동생에게 사과하지 않았던 것은 이번이 처음이 아니었다.

25 사람들은 잘못했을 때, 사과해야 한다. 이것은 가족이나 당신에게 가까운 사람도 포함한다.

26 사람들은 마음의 상처가 가족이나 친구에게서 올 때 더 쉽게 상처 받는다.

27 우리는 아마 그들이 가깝기 때문에 그냥 넘어갈 것이라고 생각할지 모른다.

28 하지만 작은 실수를 하고 사과하지 않는 것은 큰 감정적인 상처가 된다는 것을 기억하라.

29 이것은 가족과 사랑하는 사람들에게 특히 더 그러하다.

30 당신은 "더 이상 사과하지 않는다면 더 이상 기회가 없다."는 말을 들어본 적이 있는가?

31 사람들은 실수하지만, 그 실수가 아름다운 관계를 깨뜨리게 해서는 안 된다.

32 누군가에게 사과하고 싶은가? 지금 하려고 노력해라. 빠르고 진정한 "미안해."라는 말이 많은 문제를 해결해 줄 것이다.

※ 다음 우리말과 일치하도록 빈칸에 알맞은 것을 골라 쓰시오.

1 _____ we are human, we all make mistakes. _____ _____ not easy _____ _____ _____ _____ everyone _____ _____ _____.

2 Sometimes we _____ people's feelings _____ _____ _____. Sometimes, we do _____ _____ and _____ it later.

3 When _____ happens, what should we do? We _____ _____.

4 Read the _____ _____ studies and learn three things about _____ _____ _____.

5 When June _____ _____ a backpack and fell, Mike found _____ _____ and _____. He _____ a picture and _____ it _____ an SNS.

6 June _____ the picture and _____ _____. Mike said, _____ a _____, "Sorry, June!" and _____ _____.

7 After that, June felt _____ more hurt _____ _____ Mike's _____ _____.

8 June didn't like _____ _____ _____ _____. Mike _____ _____ _____ it was _____ _____.

9 What did you learn from this case? Yes. You guessed right. You _____ _____ _____ when you _____.

10 _____ is necessary _____ build good _____. _____ you're sorry is _____ _____ just words.

11 You need to show _____ you _____ the _____ person and _____ _____ his or her _____.

12 If you truly want to _____ _____ _____, be _____ in your apology.

13 _____ _____ _____ your apology is, _____ _____ it will be _____.

14 Here is _____ case. While Kate was _____ _____ the cafeteria, she _____ _____ _____ Hojun.

15 Some food _____ Hojun's tray _____ _____ his jacket. Kate didn't _____. Hojun _____ _____.

---

1 우리는 인간이기 때문에 모두가 실수한다. 모든 사람과 항상 잘 지내기는 쉽지 않다.

2 때때로 우리는 의도하지 않게 다른 사람의 감정을 상하게 한다. 때때로 우리는 나쁜 일을 하고 나중에 그것을 후회한다.

3 이런 일이 생기면, 우리는 무엇을 해야 할까? 우리는 사과해야 한다.

4 다음 사례 연구들을 읽고 올바른 사과를 위한 세 가지를 알아보자.

5 June이 가방에 걸려 넘어졌을 때, Mike는 그것이 재미있다고 생각하고 웃었다. 그는 사진을 찍어서 SNS에 올렸다.

6 June은 그 사진을 보고 화가 났다. Mike는 웃으면서 "미안해, June!"이라고 말하고 사진을 삭제했다.

7 그 후, June은 Mike의 가벼운 사과에 한층 더 화가 났다.

8 June은 Mike의 행동 방식이 마음에 들지 않았다. Mike는 이 일이 심각한 일이 아니라고 생각하는 것처럼 보였다.

9 이 사례로부터 무엇을 배웠는가? 맞다. 당신은 바르게 추측했다. 당신은 사과할 때에 진실해야 한다.

10 사과하는 것은 좋은 교우 관계를 만들기 위해 필요하다. 미안하다고 말하는 것은 단지 말 이상이다.

11 당신이 타인을 존중하고, 타인의 감정에 관심을 갖고 있음을 보여주어야 한다.

12 당신이 진실로 일을 바로잡기를 원한다면, 당신의 사과는 진실해야 한다.

13 당신의 사과가 진실할수록, 그것은 더 잘 받아들여질 것이다.

14 또 다른 사례가 있다. Kate가 급식실을 가로질러 급하게 뛰어갈 때, 호준이와 실수로 부딪쳤다.

15 호준이의 급식판에 있던 음식이 그의 재킷에 떨어졌다. Kate는 사과하지 않았다. 호준이는 기분이 나빴다.

16 He thought, '_____ _____ she _____ something? It would be nothing _____ she _____ _____ _____.'

17 This case shows _____ when an apology _____ _____, you should _____ _____ _____.

18 A quick apology _____ _____ you are _____ and _____ _____ your action.

19 _____ you need _____ _____ is to say, "I'm sorry." Then, the hurt friend will _____ _____ of it and _____ _____ _____.

20 Finally, apologies _____ necessary _____ family _____ and _____ _____, too.

21 One day, Sunmin _____ her sister's _____ book. _____, she _____ it.

22 Sunmin didn't _____ because she thought it was _____ _____. She thought, 'We're sisters, _____ _____.'

23 Sunmin's sister disliked how Sunmin _____ _____ her. How could her own sister _____ her feelings?

24 This was not the first time Sunmin _____ _____ _____ her _____ _____.

25 People need _____ _____ when they do _____ _____. This _____ family members and the people _____ _____ to you.

26 People _____ _____ _____ _____ when the hurt _____ _____ a family member or a friend.

27 We may think that they will _____ _____ _____ because they _____ _____ to us.

28 Remember, however, that _____ _____ and _____ _____ _____ _____ big _____ _____.

29 This is especially true _____ family members and _____ _____.

30 Have you ever _____ _____ the saying, "_____ _____ apologies, _____ _____ _____"?

31 People _____ mistakes, but don't _____ one mistake _____ a _____ _____.

32 Do you want to _____ _____ someone? _____ _____ it now. A _____ and _____ "I'm sorry" _____ _____ many problems.

---

16 그는 '왜 그녀는 아무 말도 하지 않지? 그녀가 즉시 사과한다면 아무 일도 아닐 텐데.' 라고 생각했다.

17 이 사례는 사과가 필요할 때는 사과를 즉시 해야 한다는 것을 보여준다.

18 신속한 사과는 당신이 사려 깊고, 당신의 행동에 책임을 진다는 것을 보여준다.

19 당신이 해야 할 행동은 "미안해."라고 말하는 것뿐이다. 그러면 상처받은 친구는 당신의 잘못을 아무렇지 않게 생각하고, 웃어넘길 것이다.

20 마지막으로 사과는 가족이나 사랑하는 사람들 사이에서도 필요하다.

21 어느 날, 선민이는 여동생이 가장 좋아하는 책을 빌렸다. 나중에 그녀는 그것을 잃어버렸다.

22 선민이는 그것이 중요하지 않다고 생각하여 사과하지 않았다. 그녀는 '우리는 어쨌든 자매니까.'라고 생각했다.

23 선민이의 여동생은 언니가 본인을 대했던 방식이 마음에 들지 않았다. 어떻게 자신의 언니가 그녀의 기분을 무시할 수 있는가?

24 선민이가 여동생에게 사과하지 않았던 것은 이번이 처음이 아니었다.

25 사람들은 잘못했을 때, 사과해야 한다. 이것은 가족이나 당신에게 가까운 사람도 포함한다.

26 사람들은 마음의 상처가 가족이나 친구에게서 올 때 더 쉽게 상처 받는다.

27 우리는 아마 그들이 가깝기 때문에 그냥 넘어갈 것이라고 생각할지 모른다.

28 하지만 작은 실수를 하고 사과하지 않는 것은 큰 감정적인 상처가 된다는 것을 기억하라.

29 이것은 가족과 사랑하는 사람들에게 특히 더 그러하다.

30 당신은 "더 이상 사과하지 않는다면 더 이상 기회가 없다."는 말을 들어본 적이 있는가?

31 사람들은 실수하지만, 그 실수가 아름다운 관계를 깨뜨리게 해서는 안 된다.

32 누군가에게 사과하고 싶은가? 지금 하려고 노력해라. 빠르고 진정한 "미안해."라는 말이 많은 문제를 해결해 줄 것이다.

※ 다음 문장을 우리말로 쓰시오.

1 ▸ Because we are human, we all make mistakes. It is not easy to get along with everyone all the time.
➡ _____

2 ▸ Sometimes we hurt people's feelings without intending to. Sometimes, we do something wrong and regret it later.
➡ _____

3 ▸ When that happens, what should we do? We should apologize.
➡ _____

4 ▸ Read the following case studies and learn three things about a proper apology.
➡ _____

5 ▸ When June tripped over a backpack and fell, Mike found it funny and laughed. He took a picture and uploaded it on an SNS.
➡ _____

6 ▸ June saw the picture and became angry. Mike said, with a laugh, "Sorry, June!" and deleted it.
➡ _____

7 ▸ After that, June felt even more hurt because of Mike's casual apology.
➡ _____

8 ▸ June didn't like how Mike had acted. Mike seemed to think it was nothing serious.
➡ _____

9 ▸ What did you learn from this case? Yes. You guessed right. You should be sincere when you apologize.
➡ _____

10 ▸ Apologizing is necessary to build good friendships. Saying you're sorry is more than just words.
➡ _____

11 ▸ You need to show that you respect the other person and care about his or her feelings.
➡ _____

12 ▸ If you truly want to make things right, be sincere in your apology.
➡ _____

13 ▸ The more sincere your apology is, the better it will be received.
➡ _____

14 ▸ Here is another case. While Kate was hurrying across the cafeteria, she accidentally bumped into Hojun.
➡ _____

15 ▸ Some food on Hojun's tray fell on his jacket. Kate didn't apologize. Hojun felt bad.
➡ _____

16 He thought, 'Why doesn't she say something? It would be nothing if she apologized right now.'

➡ _____

17 This case shows that when an apology is necessary, you should apologize at once.

➡ _____

18 A quick apology shows that you are thoughtful and take responsibility for your action.

➡ _____

19 All you need to do is to say, "I'm sorry." Then, the hurt friend will think nothing of it and laugh it off.

➡ _____

20 Finally, apologies are necessary among family members and loved ones, too.

➡ _____

21 One day, Sunmin borrowed her sister's favorite book. Later, she lost it.

➡ _____

22 Sunmin didn't apologize because she thought it was not important. She thought, 'We're sisters, after all.'

➡ _____

23 Sunmin's sister disliked how Sunmin had treated her. How could her own sister ignore her feelings?

➡ _____

24 This was not the first time Sunmin hadn't apologized to her little sister.

➡ _____

25 People need to apologize when they do something wrong. This includes family members and the people who are close to you.

➡ _____

26 People get hurt more easily when the hurt comes from a family member or a friend.

➡ _____

27 We may think that they will let it go because they are close to us.

➡ _____

28 Remember, however, that small mistakes and no apology add up to big emotional wounds.

➡ _____

29 This is especially true among family members and loved ones.

➡ _____

30 Have you ever heard of the saying, "No more apologies, no more chances"?

➡ _____

31 People make mistakes, but don't let one mistake break a beautiful relationship.

➡ _____

32 Do you want to apologize to someone? Try to do it now. A quick and sincere "I'm sorry" can solve many problems.

➡ _____

※ 다음 괄호 안의 단어들을 우리말에 맞도록 바르게 배열하시오.

1 (we / because / human, / are / all / we / mistakes. / make // is / it / easy / not / get / to / along / everyone / with / the / all / time.)
➡ _____

2 (we / sometimes / people's / hurt / without / feelings / to. / intending // we / sometimes, / something / do / and / wrong / it / regret / later.)
➡ _____

3 (that / when / happens, / should / what / do? / we // should / we / apologize.)
➡ _____

4 (the / read / case / following / studies / learn / and / things / three / about / proper / a / apology.)
➡ _____

5 (June / when / over / tripped / backpack / a / fell, / and / found / Mike / funny / it / laughed. / and // took / he / picture / a / and / it / uploaded / on / SNS. / an)
➡ _____

6 (saw / June / picture / the / and / angry. / became // said, / Mike / a / with / laugh, / June!" / "sorry, / and / it. / deleted)
➡ _____

7 (that, / after / felt / June / more / even / hurt / of / because / Mike's / apology. / causal)
➡ _____

8 (didn't / June / how / like / had / Mike / acted. // seemed / Mike / think / to / was / it / serious. / nothing)
➡ _____

9 (did / what / learn / you / this / from / case? // yes. // guessed / you / right. // should / you / sincere / be / you / when / apologize.)
➡ _____

10 (is / apologizing / to / necessary / good / build / friendships. // you're / saying / is / sorry / than / more / words. / just)
➡ _____

11 (need / you / show / to / you / that / the / respect / other / and / person / about / care / her / or / feelings. / her)
➡ _____

12 (you / if / want / truly / to / things / make / right, / sincere / be / your / in / apology.)
➡ _____

13 (more / the / your / sincere / is, / apology / better / the / will / it / received. / be)
➡ _____

14 (is / here / case. / another // Kate / while / hurrying / was / the / across / cafeteria, / accidentally / she / into / bumped / Hojun.)
➡ _____

15 (food / some / Hojun's / on / fell / tray / his / on / jacket. // didn't / Kate / apologize. // felt / bad. / Hojun)
➡ _____

---

1 우리는 인간이기 때문에 모두가 실수한다. 모든 사람과 항상 잘 지내기는 쉽지 않다.

2 때때로 우리는 의도하지 않게 다른 사람의 감정을 상하게 한다. 때때로 우리는 나쁜 일을 하고 나중에 그것을 후회한다.

3 이런 일이 생기면, 우리는 무엇을 해야 할까? 우리는 사과해야 한다.

4 다음 사례 연구들을 읽고 올바른 사과를 위한 세 가지를 알아보자.

5 June이 가방에 걸려 넘어졌을 때, Mike는 그것이 재미있다고 생각하고 웃었다. 그는 사진을 찍어서 SNS에 올렸다.

6 June은 그 사진을 보고 화가 났다. Mike는 웃으면서 "미안해, June!"이라고 말하고 사진을 삭제했다.

7 그 후, June은 Mike의 가벼운 사과에 한층 더 화가 났다.

8 June은 Mike의 행동 방식이 마음에 들지 않았다. Mike는 이 일이 심각한 일이 아니라고 생각하는 것처럼 보였다.

9 이 사례로부터 무엇을 배웠는가? 맞다. 당신은 바르게 추측했다. 당신은 사과할 때에 진실해야 한다.

10 사과하는 것은 좋은 교우 관계를 만들기 위해 필요하다. 미안하다고 말하는 것은 단지 말 이상이다.

11 당신이 타인을 존중하고, 타인의 감정에 관심을 갖고 있음을 보여주어야 한다.

12 당신이 진실로 일을 바로잡기를 원한다면, 당신의 사과는 진실해야 한다.

13 당신의 사과가 진실할수록, 그것은 더 잘 받아들여질 것이다.

14 또 다른 사례가 있다. Kate가 급식실을 가로질러 급하게 뛰어갈 때, 호준이와 실수로 부딪쳤다.

15 호준이의 급식판에 있던 음식이 그의 재킷에 떨어졌다. Kate는 사과하지 않았다. 호준이는 기분이 나빴다.

16 (thought, / he / doesn't / 'why / she / something? / say // would / it / nothing / be / she / if / right / apologized / now.')

➡ _____

17 (case / this / that / shows / an / when / is / apology / necessary, / should / you / at / apologize / once.)

➡ _____

18 (quick / a / shows / apology / you / that / thoughtful / are / responsibility / and / take / your / for / action.)

➡ _____

19 (you / all / to / need / is / do / say, / to / sorry." / "I'm // the / then, / friend / hurt / think / will / of / nothing / it / laugh / and / off. / it)

➡ _____

20 (apologies / finally, / necessary / are / family / among / and / members / ones, / loved / too.)

➡ _____

21 (day, / one / borrowed / Sunmin / sister's / her / book. / favorite // she / later, / it. / lost)

➡ _____

22 (didn't / Sunmin / because / apologize / she / it / thought / not / was / important. // thought, / she / sisters, / 'we're / all.' / after)

➡ _____

23 (sister / Sunmin's / how / disliked / had / Sunmin / her. / treated // could / how / own / her / ignore / sister / feelings? / her)

➡ _____

24 (was / this / the / not / time / first / hadn't / Sunmin / to / apologized / her / sister. / little)

➡ _____

25 (need / people / apologize / to / they / when / something / do / wrong. // includes / this / members / family / the / and / who / people / close / are / you. / to)

➡ _____

26 (get / people / more / hurt / when / easily / hurt / the / from / comes / family / a / or / member / friend. / a)

➡ _____

27 (may / think / we / that / will / they / it / let / because / go / are / they / to / close / us.)

➡ _____

28 (however, / remember, / small / that / and / mistakes / no / add / apology / up / big / to / wounds. / emotional)

➡ _____

29 (is / this / true / especially / family / among / and / members / ones. / loved)

30 (you / have / heard / ever / the / of / saying, / more / "no / apologies, / more / no / chances?")

➡ _____

31 (make / people / mistakes, / don't / but / one / let / break / mistake / beautiful / a / relationship.)

➡ _____

32 (you / do / to / want / to / apologize / someone? // to / try / it / do / now. // quick / a / sincere / and / sorry" / "I'm / solve / can / problems. / many)

➡ _____

※ 다음 우리말을 영어로 쓰시오.

1 우리는 인간이기 때문에 모두가 실수한다. 모든 사람과 항상 잘 지내기는 쉽지 않다.

➡ _____

2 때때로 우리는 의도하지 않게 다른 사람의 감정을 상하게 한다. 때때로 우리는 나쁜 일을 하고 나중에 그것을 후회한다.

➡ _____

_____

3 이런 일이 생기면, 우리는 무엇을 해야 할까? 우리는 사과해야 한다.

➡ _____

4 다음 사례 연구들을 읽고 올바른 사과를 위한 세 가지를 알아보자.

➡ _____

5 June이 가방에 걸려 넘어졌을 때, Mike는 그것이 재미있다고 생각하고 웃었다. 그는 사진을 찍어서 SNS에 올렸다.

➡ _____

_____

6 June은 그 사진을 보고 화가 났다. Mike는 웃으면서 "미안해, June!"이라고 말하고 사진을 삭제했다.

➡ _____

7 그 후, June은 Mike의 가벼운 사과에 한층 더 화가 났다.

➡ _____

8 June은 Mike의 행동 방식이 마음에 들지 않았다. Mike는 이 일이 심각한 일이 아니라고 생각하는 것처럼 보였다.

➡ _____

9 이 사례로부터 무엇을 배웠는가? 맞다. 당신은 바르게 추측했다. 당신은 사과할 때에 진실해야 한다.

➡ _____

10 사과하는 것은 좋은 교우 관계를 만들기 위해 필요하다. 미안하다고 말하는 것은 단지 말 이상이다.

➡ _____

11 당신이 타인을 존중하고, 타인의 감정에 관심을 갖고 있음을 보여 주어야 한다.

➡ _____

12 당신이 진실로 일을 바로잡기를 원한다면, 당신의 사과는 진실해야 한다.

➡ _____

13 당신의 사과가 진실할수록, 그것은 더 잘 받아들여질 것이다.

➡ _____

14 또 다른 사례가 있다. Kate가 급식실을 가로질러 급하게 뛰어갈 때, 호준이와 실수로 부딪쳤다.

➡ _____

_____

15 호준이의 급식판에 있던 음식이 그의 재킷에 떨어졌다. Kate는 사과하지 않았다. 호준이는 기분이 나빴다.

➡ _____

16 그는 '왜 그녀는 아무 말도 하지 않지? 그녀가 즉시 사과한다면 아무 일도 아닐 텐데.'라고 생각했다.

➡ _____

17 이 사례는 사과가 필요할 때는 사과를 즉시 해야 한다는 것을 보여준다.

➡ _____

18 신속한 사과는 당신이 사려 깊고, 당신의 행동에 책임을 진다는 것을 보여준다.

➡ _____

19 당신이 해야 할 행동은 "미안해."라고 말하는 것뿐이다. 그러면 상처받은 친구는 당신의 잘못을 아무렇지 않게 생각하고, 웃어넘길 것이다.

➡ _____

20 마지막으로 사과는 가족이나 사랑하는 사람들 사이에서도 필요하다.

➡ _____

21 어느 날, 선민이는 여동생이 가장 좋아하는 책을 빌렸다. 나중에 그녀는 그것을 잃어버렸다.

➡ _____

22 선민이는 그것이 중요하지 않다고 생각하여 사과하지 않았다. 그녀는 '우리는 어쨌든 자매니까.'라고 생각했다.

➡ _____

23 선민이의 여동생은 언니가 본인을 대했던 방식이 마음에 들지 않았다. 어떻게 자신의 언니가 그녀의 기분을 무시할 수 있는가?

➡ _____

24 선민이가 여동생에게 사과하지 않았던 것은 이번이 처음이 아니었다.

➡ _____

25 사람들은 잘못했을 때, 사과해야 한다. 이것은 가족이나 당신에게 가까운 사람도 포함한다.

➡ _____

26 사람들은 마음의 상처가 가족이나 친구에게서 올 때 더 쉽게 상처 받는다.

➡ _____

27 우리는 아마 그들이 가깝기 때문에 그냥 넘어갈 것이라고 생각할지 모른다.

➡ _____

28 하지만 작은 실수를 하고 사과하지 않는 것은 큰 감정적인 상처가 된다는 것을 기억하라.

➡ _____

29 이것은 가족과 사랑하는 사람들에게 특히 더 그러하다.

➡ _____

30 당신은 "더 이상 사과하지 않는다면 더 이상 기회가 없다."는 말을 들어본 적이 있는가?

➡ _____

31 사람들은 실수하지만, 그 실수가 아름다운 관계를 깨뜨리게 해서는 안 된다.

➡ _____

32 누군가에게 사과하고 싶은가? 지금 하려고 노력해라. 빠르고 진정한 "미안해."라는 말이 많은 문제를 해결해 줄 것이다.

➡ _____

_____

※ 다음 우리말과 일치하도록 빈칸에 알맞은 말을 쓰시오.

After You Read C

1. Inho went to a _____ _____ _____ _____.

2. He _____ _____ _____ a woman's bag accidentally _____ _____ _____ _____.

3. The woman said, "Sorry," and she _____ _____ _____.

4. Inho was angry _____ the woman did not make a _____ and _____ _____.

5. He thought _____ the woman should _____ _____ _____ _____.

1. 인호는 신발을 사려고 가게에 갔다.
2. 어떤 여자가 지나갈 때 그는 우연히 그 여자의 가방에 부딪혔다.
3. 그 여자는 "미안해."라고 말하고는 빠르게 걸어갔다.
4. 인호는 그녀가 진실되고 올바른 사과를 하지 않았다고 생각했기 때문에 화가 났다.
5. 그는 그 여자가 그의 감정에 신경 써야 한다고 생각했다.

Enjoy Writing C

1. My _____ _____, Jinsu

2. I'd _____ _____ _____ my friend, Jinsu.

3. I _____ _____ him _____ elementary school.

4. He is always _____, _____, and _____.

5. This is _____ _____ _____ me.

6. Last Friday I was _____ and _____ _____ _____.

7. Jinsu _____ _____ _____ _____ _____ _____.

8. I am _____ _____ _____ _____ him _____ my friend.

9. _____ _____ I know him, _____ _____ our friendship becomes.

1. 나의 훌륭한 친구, 진수
2. 나는 나의 친구 진수를 소개하고 싶어.
3. 나는 그를 초등학교 때부터 알았어.
4. 그는 항상 재미있고, 용감하고, 발랄해.
5. 이게 그가 나를 도와주었던 방법이야.
6. 지난 금요일 나는 아파서 수학 수업을 못 들었어.
7. 진수가 내게 자신의 수업 노트를 보여줬어.
8. 나는 그를 친구로 두어서 행운이야.
9. 내가 그를 많이 알수록 우리의 우정은 더 깊어져.

Project Step 1

1. A: Do you know _____ _____ _____ _____ _____ _____ _____?

2. B: Yes. First, write about _____ _____ _____.

3. C: Then write _____ _____ _____ _____ _____ _____ it.

4. D: _____ _____ _____ _____ _____ for our actions.

5. A: Thank you _____ _____ _____. I _____ _____ it.

1. A: 너는 우리가 어떻게 사과 편지를 쓰는지 아니?
2. B: 응. 먼저, 우리가 뭘 했는지 써야 해.
3. C: 그리고 나서 그것에 대해 미안하다고 써야 해.
4. D: 우리 행동에 대해 변명은 하면 안 돼.
5. A: 조언해 줘서 고마워. 정말 고마워.

※ **다음 우리말을 영어로 쓰시오.**

After You Read C

1. 인호는 신발을 사려고 가게에 갔다.
➡ _____

2. 어떤 여자가 지나갈 때 그는 우연히 그 여자의 가방에 부딪혔다.
➡ _____

3. 그 여자는 "미안해."라고 말하고는 빠르게 걸어갔다.
➡ _____

4. 인호는 그녀가 진실되고 올바른 사과를 하지 않았다고 생각했기 때문에 화가 났다.
➡ _____

5. 그는 그 여자가 그의 감정에 신경 써야 한다고 생각했다.
➡ _____

Enjoy Writing C

1. 나의 훌륭한 친구, 진수
➡ _____

2. 나는 나의 친구 진수를 소개하고 싶어.
➡ _____

3. 나는 그를 초등학교 때부터 알았어.
➡ _____

4. 그는 항상 재미있고, 용감하고, 발랄해.
➡ _____

5. 이게 그가 나를 도와주었던 방법이야.
➡ _____

6. 지난 금요일 나는 아파서 수학 수업을 못 들었어.
➡ _____

7. 진수가 내게 자신의 수업 노트를 보여 줬어.
➡ _____

8. 나는 그를 친구로 두어서 행운이야.
➡ _____

9. 내가 그를 많이 알수록 우리의 우정은 더 깊어져.
➡ _____

Project Step 1

1. A: 너는 우리가 어떻게 사과 편지를 쓰는지 아니?
➡ _____

2. B: 응. 먼저, 우리가 뭘 했는지 써야 해.
➡ _____

3. C: 그러고 나서 그것에 대해 미안하다고 써야 해.
➡ _____

4. D: 우리 행동에 대해 변명은 하면 안 돼.
➡ _____

5. A: 조언해 줘서 고마워. 정말 고마워.
➡ _____

※ 다음 영어를 우리말로 쓰시오.

01 goods _____

02 probably _____

03 subject _____

04 huge _____

05 popular _____

06 include _____

07 ability _____

08 traditional _____

09 plain _____

10 lively _____

11 cone _____

12 main character _____

13 exhibition _____

14 plate _____

15 outdoor _____

16 fever _____

17 advertising _____

18 performance _____

19 common _____

20 creativity _____

21 familiar _____

22 art work _____

23 special effects _____

24 creative _____

25 lesson _____

26 artistic _____

27 copy _____

28 run _____

29 colorful _____

30 classical _____

31 refreshing _____

32 sculpture _____

33 decoration _____

34 worth _____

35 be made up of _____

36 set up _____

37 the other day _____

38 be regarded as _____

39 in other words _____

40 instead of _____

41 pay attention to _____

42 break down _____

43 turn one's eyes to _____

※ 다음 우리말을 영어로 쓰시오.

01 대중적인, 인기 있는

02 예술적인

03 지루한, 지겨운

04 접시

05 광고

06 전시회

07 화려한

08 친숙한

09 조각품

10 연기, 공연

11 창의적인

12 활기 넘치는, 생생한

13 열, 발열

14 창의력

15 진심으로, 정말로

16 ~의 가치가 있는

17 흔한, 평범한, 공통의

18 변기, 화장실

19 상품, 제품

20 능력

21 예술 작품

22 거대한, 큰

23 포함하다, 넣다

24 아마

25 신선한, 참신한

26 교훈

27 주인공

28 전통적인

29 실외의

30 장식

31 보통의, 평범한

32 운영하다

33 원뿔, 원뿔형 물체

34 특수효과

35 ~로 만들어지다

36 다시 말해서, 즉

37 ~을 부수다

38 ~로 여겨지다

39 ~에 주의를 기울이다

40 A를 B로 바꾸다

41 ~의 줄임말이다

42 ~로 구성되다

43 요전 날, 며칠 전

※ 다음 영영풀이에 알맞은 단어를 <보기>에서 골라 쓴 후, 우리말 뜻을 쓰시오.

1 _____ : not interesting or exciting: _____

2 _____ : not decorated in any way; with nothing added: _____

3 _____ : liked, enjoyed, or supported by many people: _____

4 _____ : the way an actor performs a part in a play, movie, etc.: _____

5 _____ : the physical or mental power or skill needed to do something: _____

6 _____ : the ability to produce or use original and unusual ideas: _____

7 _____ : a thing that makes something look more attractive on special occasions: _____

8 _____ : to do or play something regularly or repeatedly in order to become skilled at it: _____

9 _____ : easy to recognize because of being seen, met, heard, etc. before: _____

10 _____ : a shape with a flat, round or oval base and a top that becomes narrower until it forms a point: _____

11 _____ : an opinion that someone offers you about what you should do or how you should act in a particular situation: _____

12 _____ : traditional in style or form, or based on methods developed over a long period of time, and considered to be of lasting value: _____

13 _____ : to contain something as a part of something else, or to make something part of something else: _____

14 _____ : a work of art that is a solid figure or object made by carving or shaping wood, stone, clay, metal, etc.: _____

15 _____ : following or belonging to the customs or ways of behaving that have continued in a group of people or society for a long time without changing: _____

16 _____ : an event at which objects such as paintings are shown to the public, a situation in which someone shows a particular skill or quality to the public, or the act of showing these things: _____

보기			
traditional	creativity	exhibition	ability
cone	boring	classical	popular
include	practice	sculpture	decoration
advice	performance	familiar	plain

※ 다음 우리말과 일치하도록 빈칸에 알맞은 말을 쓰시오.

Listen & Speak 1 A

1. B: Sandy, you can _____ _____ many _____ of music in this _____ _____.

   G: That's _____, Bob. Can I _____ _____ _____ music?

   B: _____. Do you like _____ _____?

   G: Yes, Beethoven is _____ _____ _____ _____. How _____ you?

   B: I like pop music _____ _____ _____ _____.

   G: I see. _____ _____ _____ _____ most about pop music?

   B: I'm really _____ _____ its _____ rhythms.

2. G: Jim, did you _____ your _____ _____?

   B: Yes. I _____ the face of my role model on a _____.

   G: _____ _____. Who is your role model?

   B: My dad. He always gives me good _____. Who _____ you _____, Amy?

   G: Well, I drew _____ _____ in the sea.

   B: Wonderful! I'm _____ _____ _____ _____.

   G: Thank you.

1. B: Sandy, 너는 이 음악 도서관에서 많은 종류의 음악을 들을 수 있어.
   G: 그거 멋지다, Bob. 클래식 음악도 들을 수 있어?
   B: 물론이지. 너 클래식 음악 좋아하니?
   G: 응. 베토벤이 내가 가장 좋아하는 음악가 중의 하나야. 너는 어때?
   B: 나는 클래식보다는 대중음악이 더 좋아.
   G: 그렇구나. 너는 대중음악의 어떤 점이 가장 마음에 들어?
   B: 나는 대중음악의 신나는 리듬이 정말 좋아.

2. G: Jim, 미술 숙제 다 끝냈어?
   B: 응. 나는 접시에 나의 롤 모델을 그렸어.
   G: 그거 흥미롭구나. 너의 롤 모델은 누구야?
   B: 우리 아빠야. 아빠는 나에게 항상 좋은 조언을 해 주셔. 너는 누구를 그렸어, Amy?
   G: 음, 나는 내가 바다에서 서핑하는 것을 그렸어.
   B: 멋지다! 나는 네 그림에 푹 빠졌어.
   G: 고마워.

Listen & Speak 2 A

1. B: _____ _____ _____ I watched a _____, *A Love Story in the War*.

   G: Oh, _____ _____ _____ _____ the play?

   B: I liked the _____ _____. The _____ _____ were _____.

   G: Was the story good _____ _____?

   B: No. It was _____ _____ _____, but the music was _____ _____.

   G: So, do you think I _____ _____ it?

   B: _____ _____ you have _____ _____ _____ time and money.

1. B: 며칠 전에 '전쟁 속의 사랑 이야기'라는 연극을 봤어.
   G: 오, 그 연극 어땠어?
   B: 주인공들이 좋았어. 배우들의 연기가 끝내줬거든.
   G: 이야기도 좋았어?
   B: 아니. 이야기는 조금 지루했는데, 음악은 꽤 괜찮았어.
   G: 그럼, 너는 내가 그 연극을 보러 가야 한다고 생각하니?
   B: 네가 돈과 시간이 많을 경우에만.

2. **B:** Caire, _____ _____ _____ _____ your art class?

   G: It's great. I learn _____ _____ in the _____.

   B: _____ _____ _____ _____ about it?

   G: I enjoy _____ _____ _____ _____. _____ about you, Allen?

   B: I also like the class. I learn good _____ _____. I love painting _____ many colors.

   G: Oh, I saw your _____ _____ _____. I _____ it was very _____.

   B: Thanks. I _____ _____ _____.

Real Life Talk

Bora: Andy, you went to the art museum, _____ _____?

Andy: Yes. They had a _____ Chagall exhibition.

Bora: _____ _____ _____ _____ it?

Andy: It was _____! I _____ _____ _____ the colors in his _____ and his _____.

Bora: _____ _____. He was _____ _____ _____ _____ _____ ever. _____ _____ did you see in the museum?

Andy: I went to _____ _____ _____ and saw things like umbrellas, cups, and backpacks. _____ _____ of art _____ _____ on them.

Bora: Did you buy _____?

Andy: Yes. I bought this T-shirt. _____ _____ _____ _____ it?

Bora: It _____ _____ _____ you.

Andy: Thank you.

Wrap Up 1

B: Cindy, you went to the music _____, _____ you?

G: Yes. _____ _____ famous musicians _____ there.

B: _____ _____ _____ _____ the festival?

G: It was fantastic! I really liked the _____ _____. Do you know the band _____ _the Brothers_?

B: Oh, I've _____ about them. The singer is _____.

G: Yes. His _____ was great.

B: _____ _____.

2. **B:** Claire, 미술 수업 어때?
  G: 훌륭해. 나는 그 수업에서 많은 것을 배워.
  B: 배우는 것 중에 어떤 것이 가장 좋아?
  G: 다양한 그림 기술 배우는 것이 재미있어. 너는 어때, Allen?
  B: 나도 미술 수업이 좋아. 괜찮은 색칠하기 기술들을 배우잖아. 나는 다양한 색깔을 사용해서 그림 그리는 것이 정말 좋아.
  G: 오, 지난번에 네 작품을 봤어. 나는 그게 굉장히 창의적이라고 생각했어.
  B: 고마워. 연습을 많이 했거든.

보라: Andy야, 너 미술관에 갔었지, 그렇지 않니?
Andy: 응. 샤갈 특별 전시회가 있었어.
보라: 그거 어땠니?
Andy: 멋졌어! 나는 그의 그림에 쓰인 색깔과 그의 창의성에 매료됐어.
보라: 당연해. 그는 가장 위대한 화가 중 한 명이었잖아. 너는 미술관에서 또 무엇을 봤니?
Andy: 기념품점에 갔었는데 우산, 컵, 가방 같은 것들을 봤어. 유명 예술 작품들이 그것들에 그려져 있었어.
보라: 구입한 게 있니?
Andy: 응. 나 이 티셔츠 샀어. 어때?
보라: 네게 잘 어울린다.
Andy: 고마워.

B: Cindy, 너 음악 축제에 갔었지, 그렇지 않니?
G: 응. 많은 유명 가수들이 거기서 공연을 했어.
B: 그 축제는 어땠어?
G: 아주 환상적이었어. 나는 특별 손님이 정말 좋았어. 너 '더 브라더스'라고 불리는 밴드를 아니?
B: 오, 들어본 적이 있어. 가수가 유명하잖아.
G: 맞아. 그의 공연은 굉장했어.
B: 놀랄 일도 아니지.

※ 다음 우리말에 맞도록 대화를 영어로 쓰시오.

Listen & Speak 1 A

1. B: _____

   G: _____

   B: _____

   G: _____

   B: _____

   G: _____

   B: _____

2. G: _____

   B: _____

   G: _____

   B: _____

   G: _____

   B: _____

   G: _____

Listen & Speak 2 A

1. B: _____

   G: _____

   B: _____

   G: _____

   B: _____

   G: _____

   B: _____

해석

1. B: Sandy, 너는 이 음악 도서관에서 많은 종류의 음악을 들을 수 있어.
   G: 그거 멋지다, Bob. 클래식 음악도 들을 수 있어?
   B: 물론이지. 너 클래식 음악 좋아하니?
   G: 응. 베토벤이 내가 가장 좋아하는 음악가 중의 하나야. 너는 어때?
   B: 나는 클래식보다는 대중음악이 더 좋아.
   G: 그렇구나. 너는 대중음악의 어떤 점이 가장 마음에 들어?
   B: 나는 대중음악의 신나는 리듬이 정말 좋아.

2. G: Jim, 미술 숙제 다 끝냈어?
   B: 응. 나는 접시에 나의 롤 모델을 그렸어.
   G: 그거 흥미롭구나. 너의 롤 모델은 누구야?
   B: 우리 아빠야. 아빠는 나에게 항상 좋은 조언을 해 주셔. 너는 누구를 그렸어, Amy?
   G: 음, 나는 내가 바다에서 서핑하는 것을 그렸어.
   B: 멋지다! 나는 네 그림에 푹 빠졌어.
   G: 고마워.

1. B: 며칠 전에 '전쟁 속의 사랑 이야기'라는 연극을 봤어.
   G: 오, 그 연극 어땠어?
   B: 주인공들이 좋았어. 배우들의 연기가 끝내줬거든.
   G: 이야기도 좋았어?
   B: 아니. 이야기는 조금 지루했는데, 음악은 꽤 괜찮았어.
   G: 그럼, 너는 내가 그 연극을 보러 가야 한다고 생각하니?
   B: 네가 돈과 시간이 많을 경우에만.

2. B: _____

G: _____

B: _____

G: _____

B: _____

_____

G: _____

B: _____

Real Life Talk

Bora: _____

Andy: _____

Bora: _____

Andy: _____

Bora: _____

_____

Andy: _____

_____

Bora: _____

Andy: _____

Bora: _____

Andy: _____

Wrap Up 1

B: _____

G: _____

B: _____

G: _____

_____

B: _____

G: _____

B: _____

2. B: Claire, 미술 수업 어때?
G: 훌륭해. 나는 그 수업에서 많은 것을 배워.
B: 배우는 것 중에 어떤 것이 가장 좋아?
G: 다양한 그림 기술 배우는 것이 재미있어. 너는 어때, Allen?
B: 나도 미술 수업이 좋아. 괜찮은 색칠하기 기술들을 배우잖아. 나는 다양한 색깔을 사용해서 그림 그리는 것이 정말 좋아.
G: 오, 지난번에 네 작품을 봤어. 나는 그게 굉장히 창의적이라고 생각했어.
B: 고마워. 연습을 많이 했거든.

보라: Andy야, 너 미술관에 갔었지, 그렇지 않니?
Andy: 응. 샤갈 특별 전시회가 있었어.
보라: 그거 어땠니?
Andy: 멋졌어! 나는 그의 그림에 쓰인 색깔과 그의 창의성에 매료됐어.
보라: 당연해. 그는 가장 위대한 화가 중한 명이었잖아. 너는 미술관에서 또 무엇을 봤니?
Andy: 기념품점에 갔었는데 우산, 컵, 가방 같은 것들을 봤어. 유명 예술 작품들이 그것들에 그려져 있었어.
보라: 구입한 게 있니?
Andy: 응. 나 이 티셔츠 샀어. 어때?
보라: 네게 잘 어울린다.
Andy: 고마워.

B: Cindy, 너 음악 축제에 갔었지, 그렇지 않니?
G: 응. 많은 유명 가수들이 거기서 공연을 했어.
B: 그 축제는 어땠어?
G: 아주 환상적이었어. 나는 특별 손님이 정말 좋았어. 너 '더 브라더스'라고 불리는 밴드를 아니?
B: 오, 들어본 적이 있어. 가수가 유명하잖아.
G: 맞아. 그의 공연은 굉장했어.
B: 놀랄 일도 아니지.

※ 다음 우리말과 일치하도록 빈칸에 알맞은 것을 골라 쓰시오.

Pop Art: Art for Everyone

1 _____ to the Pop Art _____! What do you see? _____ of soup cans? Big _____?

    A. cartoons   B. Welcome   C. paintings   D. Exhibition

2 Do they look like art works? _____ not, but _____ again. They are all _____ _____ of pop art.

    A. works   B. probably   C. think   D. famous

3 Pop is _____ for popular. _____ pop art means _____ _____, or art for people.

    A. art   B. short   C. popular   D. so

4 It _____ in the 1950s in America. Pop artists at that time wanted to _____ _____ fun and _____.

    A. create   B. began   C. easy   D. something

5 _____ of difficult _____ art _____, they _____ their eyes to popular culture.

    A. traditional   B. turned   C. instead   D. works

6 They _____ images _____ TV, comic books, _____, and _____.

    A. from   B. magazines   C. used   D. advertising

7 When people saw _____ _____ in art _____, they found them _____.

    A. images   B. refreshing   C. exhibitions   D. familiar

8 _____ then, pop art has _____ _____ _____.

    A. become   B. since   C. popular   D. truly

9 People thought _____ art was _____ difficult _____ _____.

    A. too   B. understand   C. that   D. to

10 By _____ daily images and _____ colors, pop artists _____ that _____.

    A. changed   B. using   C. thought   D. bright

11 Using _____ images, pop art looks _____. In other _____, it doesn't look _____.

    A. words   B. common   C. artistic   D. plain

12 But it is still _____ _____ _____ to. Although it looks plain, it is _____ with meaning.

    A. attention   B. filled   C. paying   D. worth

13 _____ _____ about some _____ pop _____.

    A. famous   B. let's   C. artists   D. learn

14 They became _____ for their special artistic _____. They were able to _____ common _____ into amazing art.

    A. ability   B. objects   C. famous   D. change

15 Andy Warhol is _____ the King of Pop Art. He _____ his _____ _____ magazines and stores.

    A. found   B. called   C. in   D. subjects

1 팝 아트 전시회에 온 것을 환영한다! 무엇이 보이는가? 수프 통조림들을 모아 놓은 그림? 커다란 만화 그림?

2 그것들이 예술 작품처럼 보이는가? 아마 그렇게 보이지 않겠지만, 다시 생각해 봐라. 그것들은 모두 유명한 팝 아트 작품들이다.

3 'pop'은 'popular(대중적인)'의 줄임말이다. 그래서 팝 아트는 대중 예술 또는 사람들을 위한 예술이라는 뜻이다.

4 팝 아트는 1950년대 미국에서 시작됐다. 그 당시 팝 아트 작가들은 재미있고 쉬운 것을 만들고 싶어 했다.

5 어려운 전통 예술 작품 대신 그들은 대중문화로 눈을 돌렸다.

6 그들은 텔레비전, 만화책, 잡지 및 광고에 나오는 이미지들을 사용했다.

7 미술 전시회에서 친숙한 이미지들을 봤을 때 사람들은 그것들이 신선하다는 걸 알게 되었다.

8 그때부터 팝 아트는 정말 유명해졌다.

9 사람들은 예술이 너무 어려워서 이해할 수 없는 것으로 생각했었다.

10 일상적인 이미지와 밝은 색을 씀으로써, 팝 아트 작가들은 그러한 관점을 바꿨다.

11 흔한 이미지를 사용하기 때문에 팝 아트는 평범해 보인다. 즉, 팝 아트는 예술적으로 보이지 않는다.

12 하지만 여전히 주목할 만한 가치가 있다. 평범해 보일지라도 그것은 의미로 가득 차 있다.

13 몇 명의 유명한 팝 아트 작가들에 대해 알아보자.

14 그들은 특별한 예술적인 능력으로 유명해졌다. 그들은 흔한 대상을 놀라운 예술로 바꿀 수 있었다.

15 Andy Warhol은 팝 아트의 왕이라 불린다. 그는 잡지와 상점에서 주제를 찾았다.

16 One of his _____ works is _____ _____ of pictures of Marilyn Monroe, the American _____.

A. made   B. actor   C. famous   D. up

17 _____ work shows cans of soup. He _____ many _____ of these _____.

A. works   B. another   C. made   D. copies

18 Why did he make _____ of his _____? He wanted to _____ that art is _____ you see every day.

A. works   B. show   C. copies   D. something

19 Claes Oldenburg is _____ pop artist _____ _____ art _____.

A. made   B. another   C. fun   D. who

20 He made _____ of _____, such as a hamburger, cookies, and a _____.

A. brush   B. sculptures   C. items   D. everyday

21 In the _____, he _____ soft sculptures. They were _____ of plastic, paper, and other soft _____.

A. made   B. beginning   C. materials   D. created

22 For example, he used _____ to make toilets. Later, he made _____ _____ of daily items, such _____ an ice cream cone.

A. sculptures   B. cloth   C. as   D. huge

23 _____ everyone to enjoy his art, he _____ _____ his works in _____ places.

A. set   B. outdoor   C. wanting   D. up

24 He also _____ a store _____ his studio to _____ his works. For him, artistic works were funs _____ for people.

A. inside   B. ran   C. goods   D. sell

25 Roy Lichtenstein _____ cartoons in his _____. They were large and _____ in _____ colors.

A. works   B. lively   C. used   D. painted

26 He even _____ speech balloons in his paintings. Back then, cartoons _____ not _____ _____ an art form.

A. regarded   B. included   C. were   D. as

27 _____, Roy Lichtenstein thought _____. He asked _____, '_____ are they not?'

A. differently   B. however   C. himself   D. why

28 Then Roy Lichtenstein _____ the wall _____ high art and popular culture by _____ cartoons to art.

A. down   B. between   C. broke   D. adding

29 Pop artists _____ art _____ be easy. _____ can _____ and enjoy art.

A. create   B. believed   C. anyone   D. should

30 How about _____ a _____ of _____ _____ today?

A. work   B. creating   C. art   D. pop

31 By _____ daily images in a _____ way, you can make a work of art for everyone. This is the most _____ _____ from pop art.

A. lesson   B. creative   C. important   D. using

16 그의 유명 작품들 중 하나는 미국 배우인 Marilyn Monroe의 사진으로 구성되어 있다.

17 또 다른 작품은 수프 통조림들을 보여준다. 그는 이 작품들의 사본을 많이 만들었다.

18 그는 왜 작품의 복사본을 만들었나? 그는 예술은 여러분이 매일 보는 것임을 보여 주고 싶어 했다.

19 Claes Oldenburg는 예술을 재미있게 만들었던 또 다른 팝 아트 작가이다.

20 그는 햄버거와 쿠키, 붓 같은 일상적인 물품들의 조각품을 만들었다.

21 초기에 그는 부드러운 조각품을 만들었다. 그것들은 플라스틱, 종이, 그리고 다른 부드러운 재료들로 만들어졌다.

22 예를 들어서 그는 변기를 만들기 위해 천을 사용했다. 나중에 그는 아이스크림콘 같은 일상 물품의 거대한 조각품을 만들었다.

23 그는 모든 사람이 그의 작품을 보고 즐기기를 원했기 때문에 그의 작품들을 실외에 설치했다.

24 그는 작품 판매를 위해 그의 작업실 안에 상점을 운영하기도 했다. 그에게 예술적인 작품들은 사람들을 위한 재미있는 제품이었다.

25 Roy Lichtenstein은 그의 작품에 만화를 사용했다. 그것들은 크고 생기 넘치는 색들로 그려졌다.

26 그는 심지어 그의 작품에 말풍선을 넣었다. 그 당시에 만화는 예술 형식으로 여겨지지 않았다.

27 하지만 Roy Lichtenstein은 다르게 생각했다. 그는 스스로에게 '왜 만화는 예술로 간주되지 않을까?'라고 물었다.

28 만화를 예술에 첨가함으로써 Roy Lichtenstein은 순수 예술과 대중문화 사이의 벽을 허물었다.

29 팝 아트 작가들은 예술은 쉬워야 한다고 믿었다. 누구나 예술을 만들 수 있고, 즐길 수 있다.

30 오늘 팝 아트 작품 하나를 만들어 보는 것은 어떤가?

31 일상적인 이미지를 창의적인 방식으로 사용함으로써, 모든 사람을 위한 예술 작품을 만들 수 있다. 이것이 팝 아트의 가장 중요한 교훈이다.

Step2

※ 다음 우리말과 일치하도록 빈칸에 알맞은 것을 골라 쓰시오.

Pop Art: Art for Everyone

1 _____ _____ the Pop Art _____! _____ do you see? Paintings of soup cans? Big _____?

2 Do they _____ _____ art works? _____ not, but _____ again. They _____ all _____ _____ of pop art.

3 Pop _____ _____ _____ _____. So pop art means _____ _____, or art for people.

4 _____ _____ _____ the 1950s in America. Pop artists at that time _____ _____ _____ create _____ _____ and easy.

5 _____ _____ difficult _____ art works, they _____ their eyes _____ _____ _____.

6 They _____ images _____ TV, comic books, magazines, and _____.

7 When people saw _____ _____ in _____ _____, they found _____ _____.

8 _____ then, pop art has _____ _____ _____.

9 People thought _____ art was _____ difficult _____ _____.

10 _____ _____ daily images and _____ _____, pop artists _____ _____ _____.

11 _____ common images, pop art _____ _____. _____ _____ _____, it doesn't look _____.

12 But it is still _____ _____ _____ _____. Although it _____ _____, it _____ _____ _____ _____ meaning.

13 _____ learn about some _____ _____ _____.

14 They became _____ _____ their special artistic _____. They were _____ _____ _____ _____ _____ _____ _____ art.

15 Andy Warhol _____ _____ the King of Pop Art. He _____ his _____ _____ magazines and stores.

1 팝 아트 전시회에 온 것을 환영한다! 무엇이 보이는가? 수프 통조림들을 모아 놓은 그림? 커다란 만화 그림?

2 그것들이 예술 작품처럼 보이는가? 아마 그렇게 보이지 않겠지만, 다시 생각해 봐라. 그것들은 모두 유명한 팝 아트 작품들이다.

3 'pop'은 'popular(대중적인)'의 줄임말이다. 그래서 팝 아트는 대중 예술 또는 사람들을 위한 예술이라는 뜻이다.

4 팝 아트는 1950년대 미국에서 시작됐다. 그 당시 팝 아트 작가들은 재미있고 쉬운 것을 만들고 싶어 했다.

5 어려운 전통 예술 작품 대신 그들은 대중문화로 눈을 돌렸다.

6 그들은 텔레비전, 만화책, 잡지 및 광고에 나오는 이미지들을 사용했다.

7 미술 전시회에서 친숙한 이미지들을 봤을 때 사람들은 그것들이 신선하다는 걸 알게 되었다.

8 그때부터 팝 아트는 정말 유명해졌다.

9 사람들은 예술이 너무 어려워서 이해할 수 없는 것으로 생각했었다.

10 일상적인 이미지와 밝은 색을 씀으로써, 팝 아트 작가들은 그러한 관점을 바꿨다.

11 흔한 이미지를 사용하기 때문에 팝 아트는 평범해 보인다. 즉, 팝 아트는 예술적으로 보이지 않는다.

12 하지만 여전히 주목할 만한 가치가 있다. 평범해 보일지라도 그것은 의미로 가득 차 있다.

13 몇 명의 유명한 팝 아트 작가들에 대해 알아보자.

14 그들은 특별한 예술적인 능력으로 유명해졌다. 그들은 흔한 대상을 놀라운 예술로 바꿀 수 있었다.

15 Andy Warhol은 팝 아트의 왕이라 불린다. 그는 잡지와 상점에서 주제를 찾았다.

16 One of his famous works _____ _____ _____ of pictures of Marilyn Monroe, the American actor.

17 _____ _____ _____ cans of soup. He _____ many _____ of these _____.

18 Why did he make _____ _____ _____ _____? He wanted _____ _____ _____ art is something _____ _____ every day.

19 Claes Oldenburg is _____ pop artist _____ _____ art _____.

20 He made _____, _____ _____ a hamburger, cookies, and a _____.

21 _____ _____ _____, he _____ _____ _____ _____. They were _____ _____ plastic, paper, and other _____ _____.

22 _____ _____, he used _____ _____ _____ toilets. Later, he made _____ _____ of _____ _____, _____ _____ an ice cream cone.

23 _____ everyone _____ _____ his art, he _____ _____ his works in _____ places.

24 He also _____ a store _____ his studio _____ _____ his works. For him, artistic works _____ _____ for people.

25 Roy Lichtenstein _____ cartoons _____ _____ _____. They _____ large and _____ in _____ _____.

26 He even _____ speech balloons in his paintings. _____ _____, cartoons _____ not _____ _____ an art form.

27 _____, Roy Lichtenstein thought _____. He asked _____, '_____ are _____ _____?'

28 Then Roy Lichtenstein _____ _____ the wall _____ high art _____ popular culture _____ _____ cartoons to art.

29 Pop artists _____ art _____ _____ easy. _____ can _____ and _____ art.

30 How about _____ a work of _____ _____ today?

31 _____ _____ daily images _____ a _____ _____, you can _____ a work of art _____ everyone. This is _____ _____ _____ _____ from pop art.

16 그의 유명 작품들 중 하나는 미국 배우인 Marilyn Monroe의 사진으로 구성되어 있다.

17 또 다른 작품은 수프 통조림들을 보여준다. 그는 이 작품들의 사본을 많이 만들었다.

18 그는 왜 작품의 복사본을 만들었나? 그는 예술은 여러분이 매일 보는 것임을 보여 주고 싶어 했다.

19 Claes Oldenburg는 예술을 재미있게 만들었던 또 다른 팝 아트 작가이다.

20 그는 햄버거와 쿠키, 붓 같은 일상적인 물품들의 조각품을 만들었다.

21 초기에 그는 부드러운 조각품을 만들었다. 그것들은 플라스틱, 종이, 그리고 다른 부드러운 재료들로 만들어졌다.

22 예를 들어서 그는 변기를 만들기 위해 천을 사용했다. 나중에 그는 아이스크림콘 같은 일상 물품의 거대한 조각품을 만들었다.

23 그는 모든 사람이 그의 작품을 보고 즐기기를 원했기 때문에 그의 작품들을 실외에 설치했다.

24 그는 작품 판매를 위해 그의 작업실 안에 상점을 운영하기도 했다. 그에게 예술적인 작품들은 사람들을 위한 재미있는 제품이었다.

25 Roy Lichtenstein은 그의 작품에 만화를 사용했다. 그것들은 크고 생기 넘치는 색들로 그려졌다.

26 그는 심지어 그의 작품에 말풍선을 넣었다. 그 당시에 만화는 예술 형식으로 여겨지지 않았다.

27 하지만 Roy Lichtenstein은 다르게 생각했다. 그는 스스로에게 '왜 만화는 예술로 간주되지 않을까?'라고 물었다.

28 만화를 예술에 첨가함으로써 Roy Lichtenstein은 순수 예술과 대중문화 사이의 벽을 허물었다.

29 팝 아트 작가들은 예술은 쉬워야 한다고 믿었다. 누구나 예술을 만들 수 있고, 즐길 수 있다.

30 오늘 팝 아트 작품 하나를 만들어 보는 것은 어떤가?

31 일상적인 이미지를 창의적인 방식으로 사용함으로써, 모든 사람을 위한 예술 작품을 만들 수 있다. 이것이 팝 아트의 가장 중요한 교훈이다.

※ 다음 문장을 우리말로 쓰시오.

Pop Art: Art for Everyone

1 Welcome to the Pop Art Exhibition! What do you see? Paintings of soup cans? Big cartoons?

➡ _____

2 Do they look like art works? Probably not, but think again. They are all famous works of pop art.

➡ _____

3 Pop is short for popular. So pop art means popular art, or art for people.

➡ _____

4 It began in the 1950s in America. Pop artists at that time wanted to create something fun and easy.

➡ _____

5 Instead of difficult traditional art works, they turned their eyes to popular culture.

➡ _____

6 They used images from TV, comic books, magazines, and advertising.

➡ _____

7 When people saw familiar images in art exhibitions, they found them refreshing.

➡ _____

8 Since then, pop art has become truly popular.

➡ _____

9 People thought that art was too difficult to understand.

➡ _____

10 By using daily images and bright colors, pop artists changed that thought.

➡ _____

11 Using common images, pop art looks plain. In other words, it doesn't look artistic.

➡ _____

12 But it is still worth paying attention to. Although it looks plain, it is filled with meaning.

➡ _____

13 Let's learn about some famous pop artists.

➡ _____

14 They became famous for their special artistic ability. They were able to change common objects into amazing art.

➡ _____

15 Andy Warhol is called the King of Pop Art. He found his subjects in magazines and stores.

➡ _____

16 One of his famous works is made up of pictures of Marilyn Monroe, the American actor.

➡ _____

17 Another work shows cans of soup. He made many copies of these works.

➡ _____

18 Why did he make copies of his works? He wanted to show that art is something you see every day.

➡ _____

19 Claes Oldenburg is another pop artist who made art fun.

➡ _____

20 He made sculptures of everyday items, such as a hamburger, cookies, and a brush.

➡ _____

21 In the beginning, he created soft sculptures. They were made of plastic, paper, and other soft materials.

➡ _____

22 For example, he used cloth to make toilets. Later, he made huge sculptures of daily items, such as an ice cream cone.

➡ _____

23 Wanting everyone to enjoy his art, he set up his works in outdoor places.

➡ _____

24 He also ran a store inside his studio to sell his works. For him, artistic works were fun goods for people.

➡ _____

25 Roy Lichtenstein used cartoons in his works. They were large and painted in lively colors.

➡ _____

26 He even included speech balloons in his paintings. Back then, cartoons were not regarded as an art form.

➡ _____

27 However, Roy Lichtenstein thought differently. He asked himself, 'Why are they not?'

➡ _____

28 Then Roy Lichtenstein broke down the wall between high art and popular culture by adding cartoons to art.

➡ _____

29 Pop artists believed art should be easy. Anyone can create and enjoy art.

➡ _____

30 How about creating a work of pop art today?

➡ _____

31 By using daily images in a creative way, you can make a work of art for everyone. This is the most important lesson from pop art.

➡ _____

_____

※ 다음 괄호 안의 단어들을 우리말에 맞도록 바르게 배열하시오.

1
Pop Art: Art for Everyone
(to / Welcome / the / Art / Pop / Exhibition! // do / what / see? / you // of / paintings / cans? / soup // cartoons? / big)
➡ _____

2
(they / do / like / look / works? / art // not, / probably / think / but / again. // are / they / famous / all / of / works / art. / pop)
➡ _____

3
(is / pop / for / short / popular. // pop / so / means / art / art, / popular / art / or / people. / for)
➡ _____

4
(began / it / the / in / 1950s / America. // in // artists / pop / that / at / wanted / time / to / something / create / easy. / and / fun)
➡ _____

5
(of / instead / traditional / difficult / works, / art / turned / they / eyes / their / popular / to / culture.)
➡ _____

6
(used / they / from / images / TV, / books, / comic / advertising. / and / magazines,)
➡ _____

7
(people / when / familiar / saw / in / images / art / they / exhibitions, / found / refreshing. / them)
➡ _____

8
(then, / since / art / pop / become / has / popular. / truly)
➡ _____

9
(thought / people / art / that / too / was / to / understand. / difficult)
➡ _____

10
(using / by / images / daily / and / colors, / bright / artists / pop / changed / thought. / that)
➡ _____

11
(common / using / pop / images, / looks / art / plain. // other / in / words, / doesn't / it / artistic. / look)
➡ _____

12
(it / but / is / worth / is / still / attention / paying / to. // it / although / plain, / looks / is / it / with / filled / meaning.)
➡ _____

13
(learn / let's / some / about / pop / famous / artists.)
➡ _____

14
(became / they / for / famous / special / their / ability. / artistic // were / they / to / able / common / change / into / objects / art. / amazing)
➡ _____

15
(Warhol / Andy / called / is / King / the / Pop / of / Art. // found / he / subjects / his / magazines / in / stores. / and)
➡ _____

1 팝 아트 전시회에 온 것을 환영한다! 무엇이 보이는가? 수프 통조림들을 모아 놓은 그림? 커다란 만화 그림?

2 그것들이 예술 작품처럼 보이는가? 아마 그렇게 보이지 않겠지만, 다시 생각해 봐라. 그것들은 모두 유명한 팝 아트 작품들이다.

3 'pop'은 'popular(대중적인)'의 줄임말이다. 그래서 팝 아트는 대중 예술 또는 사람들을 위한 예술이라는 뜻이다.

4 팝 아트는 1950년대 미국에서 시작됐다. 그 당시 팝 아트 작가들은 재미있고 쉬운 것을 만들고 싶어 했다.

5 어려운 전통 예술 작품 대신 그들은 대중문화로 눈을 돌렸다.

6 그들은 텔레비전, 만화책, 잡지 및 광고에 나오는 이미지들을 사용했다.

7 미술 전시회에서 친숙한 이미지들을 봤을 때 사람들은 그것들이 신선하다는 걸 알게 되었다.

8 그때부터 팝 아트는 정말 유명해졌다.

9 사람들은 예술이 너무 어려워서 이해할 수 없는 것으로 생각했었다.

10 일상적인 이미지와 밝은 색을 씀으로써, 팝 아트 작가들은 그러한 관점을 바꿨다.

11 흔한 이미지를 사용하기 때문에 팝 아트는 평범해 보인다. 즉, 팝 아트는 예술적으로 보이지 않는다.

12 하지만 여전히 주목할 만한 가치가 있다. 평범해 보일지라도 그것은 의미로 가득 차 있다.

13 몇 명의 유명한 팝 아트 작가들에 대해 알아보자.

14 그들은 특별한 예술적인 능력으로 유명해졌다. 그들은 흔한 대상을 놀라운 예술로 바꿀 수 있었다.

15 Andy Warhol은 팝 아트의 왕이라 불린다. 그는 잡지와 상점에서 주제를 찾았다.

16 (of / one / famous / his / is / works / up / made / of / pictures / Marilyn / of / Monroe, / the / actor. / American)
➡ _____

17 (work / another / cans / shows / soup. / of // he / many / made / copies / these / of / works.)
➡ _____

18 (did / why / make / he / of / copies / works? / his // wanted / he / show / that / to / art / something / is / see / you / day. / every)
➡ _____

19 (Oldenburg / Claes / is / pop / another / who / artist / art / made / fun.)
➡ _____

20 (made / he / of / sculptures / everyday / such / items, / as / hamburger, / a / cookies, / and / brush. / a)
➡ _____

21 (the / in / beginning, / created / he / sculptures. / soft // were / they / of / made / plastic, / and / paper, / soft / other / materials.)
➡ _____

22 (example, / for / used / he / to / cloth / toilets. / make // he / later, / huge / made / of / sculptures / items, / daily / as / such / ice / an / cone. / cream)
➡ _____

23 (everyone / wanting / enjoy / to / art, / his / set / he / up / works / his / outdoor / in / places.)
➡ _____

24 (also / he / a / ran / inside / store / studio / his / sell / to / works. / his // him, / for / works / artistic / were / goods / fun / people. / for)
➡ _____

25 (Lichtenstein / Roy / cartoons / used / his / in / works. // were / they / and / large / in / painted / colors. / lively)
➡ _____

26 (even / he / speech / included / balloons / his / in / paintings. // then, / back / were / cartoons / regarded / not / an / as / form. / art)
➡ _____

27 (however, / Lichtenstein / Roy / differently. / thought // asked / he / himself, / are / 'why / not?' / they)
➡ _____

28 (Roy / then / broke / Lichtenstein / down / the / between / wall / art / high / and / culture / popular / by / cartoons / adding / art. / to)
➡ _____

29 (artists / pop / art / believed / be / should / easy. // can / anyone / enjoy / and / create / art.)
➡ _____

30 (about / how / a / creating / of / work / art / pop / today?)
➡ _____

31 (using / by / images / daily / a / in / way, / creative / can / you / a / make / work / art / of / everyone. / for // is / this / the / important / most / from / lesson / art. / pop)
➡ _____
_____

16 그의 유명 작품들 중 하나는 미국 배우인 Marilyn Monroe의 사진으로 구성되어 있다.

17 또 다른 작품은 수프 통조림들을 보여준다. 그는 이 작품들의 사본을 많이 만들었다.

18 그는 왜 작품의 복사본을 만들었나? 그는 예술은 여러분이 매일 보는 것임을 보여 주고 싶어 했다.

19 Claes Oldenburg는 예술을 재미있게 만들었던 또 다른 팝 아트 작가이다.

20 그는 햄버거와 쿠키, 붓 같은 일상적인 물품들의 조각품을 만들었다.

21 초기에 그는 부드러운 조각품을 만들었다. 그것들은 플라스틱, 종이, 그리고 다른 부드러운 재료들로 만들어졌다.

22 예를 들어서 그는 변기를 만들기 위해 천을 사용했다. 나중에 그는 아이스크림콘 같은 일상 물품의 거대한 조각품을 만들었다.

23 그는 모든 사람이 그의 작품을 보고 즐기기를 원했기 때문에 그의 작품들을 실외에 설치했다.

24 그는 작품 판매를 위해 그의 작업실 안에 상점을 운영하기도 했다. 그에게 예술적인 작품들은 사람들을 위한 재미있는 제품이었다.

25 Roy Lichtenstein은 그의 작품에 만화를 사용했다. 그것들은 크고 생기 넘치는 색들로 그려졌다.

26 그는 심지어 그의 작품에 말풍선을 넣었다. 그 당시에 만화는 예술 형식으로 여겨지지 않았다.

27 하지만 Roy Lichtenstein은 다르게 생각했다. 그는 스스로에게 '왜 만화는 예술로 간주되지 않을까?'라고 물었다.

28 만화를 예술에 첨가함으로써 Roy Lichtenstein은 순수 예술과 대중문화 사이의 벽을 허물었다.

29 팝 아트 작가들은 예술은 쉬워야 한다고 믿었다. 누구나 예술을 만들 수 있고, 즐길 수 있다.

30 오늘 팝 아트 작품 하나를 만들어 보는 것은 어떤가?

31 일상적인 이미지를 창의적인 방식으로 사용함으로써, 모든 사람을 위한 예술 작품을 만들 수 있다. 이것이 팝 아트의 가장 중요한 교훈이다.

※ 다음 우리말을 영어로 쓰시오.

Pop Art: Art for Everyone

1 팝 아트 전시회에 온 것을 환영한다! 무엇이 보이는가? 수프 통조림들을 모아 놓은 그림? 커다란 만화 그림?

➡ _____

2 그것들이 예술 작품처럼 보이는가? 아마 그렇게 보이지 않겠지만, 다시 생각해 봐라. 그것들은 모두 유명한 팝 아트 작품들이다.

➡ _____

3 'pop'은 'popular(대중적인)'의 줄임말이다. 그래서 팝 아트는 대중 예술 또는 사람들을 위한 예술이라는 뜻이다.

➡ _____

4 팝 아트는 1950년대 미국에서 시작됐다. 그 당시 팝 아트 작가들은 재미있고 쉬운 것을 만들고 싶어 했다.

➡ _____

5 어려운 전통 예술 작품 대신 그들은 대중문화로 눈을 돌렸다.

➡ _____

6 그들은 텔레비전, 만화책, 잡지 및 광고에 나오는 이미지들을 사용했다.

➡ _____

7 미술 전시회에서 친숙한 이미지들을 봤을 때 사람들은 그것들이 신선하다는 걸 알게 되었다.

➡ _____

8 그때부터 팝 아트는 정말 유명해졌다.

➡ _____

9 사람들은 예술이 너무 어려워서 이해할 수 없는 것으로 생각했었다.

➡ _____

10 일상적인 이미지와 밝은 색을 씀으로써, 팝 아트 작가들은 그러한 관점을 바꿨다.

➡ _____

11 흔한 이미지를 사용하기 때문에 팝 아트는 평범해 보인다. 즉, 팝 아트는 예술적으로 보이지 않는다.

➡ _____

12 하지만 여전히 주목할 만한 가치가 있다. 평범해 보일지라도 그것은 의미로 가득 차 있다.

➡ _____

13 몇 명의 유명한 팝 아트 작가들에 대해 알아보자.

➡ _____

14 그들은 특별한 예술적인 능력으로 유명해졌다. 그들은 흔한 대상을 놀라운 예술로 바꿀 수 있었다.

➡ _____

15 Andy Warhol은 팝 아트의 왕이라 불린다. 그는 잡지와 상점에서 주제를 찾았다.

➡ _____

16 그의 유명 작품들 중 하나는 미국 배우인 Marilyn Monroe의 사진으로 구성되어 있다.

➡ _____

17 또 다른 작품은 수프 통조림들을 보여준다. 그는 이 작품들의 사본을 많이 만들었다.

➡ _____

18 그는 왜 작품의 복사본을 만들었나? 그는 예술은 여러분이 매일 보는 것임을 보여 주고 싶어 했다.

➡ _____

19 Claes Oldenburg는 예술을 재미있게 만들었던 또 다른 팝 아트 작가이다.

➡ _____

20 그는 햄버거와 쿠키, 붓 같은 일상적인 물품들의 조각품을 만들었다.

➡ _____

21 초기에 그는 부드러운 조각품을 만들었다. 그것들은 플라스틱, 종이, 그리고 다른 부드러운 재료들로 만들어졌다.

➡ _____

22 예를 들어서 그는 변기를 만들기 위해 천을 사용했다. 나중에 그는 아이스크림콘 같은 일상 물품의 거대한 조각품을 만들었다.

➡ _____
_____

23 그는 모든 사람이 그의 작품을 보고 즐기기를 원했기 때문에 그의 작품들을 실외에 설치했다.

➡ _____

24 그는 작품 판매를 위해 그의 작업실 안에 상점을 운영하기도 했다. 그에게 예술적인 작품들은 사람들을 위한 재미있는 제품이었다.

➡ _____
_____

25 Roy Lichtenstein은 그의 작품에 만화를 사용했다. 그것들은 크고 생기 넘치는 색들로 그려졌다.

➡ _____

26 그는 심지어 그의 작품에 말풍선을 넣었다. 그 당시에 만화는 예술 형식으로 여겨지지 않았다.

➡ _____

27 하지만 Roy Lichtenstein은 다르게 생각했다. 그는 스스로에게 '왜 만화는 예술로 간주되지 않을까?'라고 물었다.

➡ _____

28 만화를 예술에 첨가함으로써 Roy Lichtenstein은 순수 예술과 대중문화 사이의 벽을 허물었다.

➡ _____

29 팝 아트 작가들은 예술은 쉬워야 한다고 믿었다. 누구나 예술을 만들 수 있고, 즐길 수 있다.

➡ _____

30 오늘 팝 아트 작품 하나를 만들어 보는 것은 어떤가?

➡ _____

31 일상적인 이미지를 창의적인 방식으로 사용함으로써, 모든 사람을 위한 예술 작품을 만들 수 있다. 이것이 팝 아트의 가장 중요한 교훈이다.

➡ _____
_____

※ 다음 우리말과 일치하도록 빈칸에 알맞은 말을 쓰시오.

Project Step 1

1. A: What do you _____ _____ _____ _____ these paper cups?
2. B: _____ _____ _____ make a tower?
3. C: Wonderful! _____ _____ a tower _____ the Leaning Tower of Pisa.
4. D: _____ _____ _____ something on the cups?
5. B: Sounds great. First, _____ _____ everyone _____ _____ _____.

Enjoy Writing B

1. _____ _____ _____ of _____ _____.
2. _____ _____ I went to the concert hall _____ _____ _____ _____.
3. _____ _____ _____ _____ _____ was *You and Me*.
4. I watched it _____ my favorite actor was _____ _____.
5. I liked the _____ and _____ _____ _____ _____.
6. The story was about _____ _____ _____ _____ _____ _____ to her birthday party.
7. They _____ _____ _____ _____ _____.
8. The _____ _____ was Sophie. She sang _____ _____ _____. It was fantastic.
9. _____ _____ _____ the songs _____ _____ _____, I was _____.
10. The musical was really _____ _____.

Enjoy Writing B

1. A _____ _____ _____ Me
2. Last Saturday I _____ _____ my friend's house _____ _____ _____.
3. _____ _____ _____ _____ _____ _____ was *My Son*. I watched it _____ _____ _____ it.
4. I liked the _____ _____ _____ _____ _____. The story was about _____ _____ _____ _____ _____ _____ his lost son.
5. _____ _____ _____ was John. He _____ _____ the actor Roy Jones, _____ was fantastic.
6. It was touching. Watching the _____ _____, I was _____.
7. The movie _____ _____ _____ _____ _____.

※ 다음 우리말을 영어로 쓰시오.

Project Step 1

1. A: 이 종이컵들로 무엇을 만들고 싶어?
   ➡ _____

2. B: 우리 탑을 만드는 게 어때?
   ➡ _____

3. C: 훌륭해! 피사의 사탑과 같은 탑을 만들어 보자.
   ➡ _____

4. D: 종이컵에 뭔가를 그리는 게 어때?
   ➡ _____

5. B: 좋은 생각이야. 먼저 모두에게 종이컵을 몇 개 나누어 주자.
   ➡ _____

Enjoy Writing B

1. 내 생애 최고의 뮤지컬
   ➡ _____

2. 지난 토요일 나는 뮤지컬을 보러 콘서트홀에 갔다.
   ➡ _____

3. 뮤지컬 제목은 '너와 나'였다.
   ➡ _____

4. 내가 가장 좋아하는 배우가 그 뮤지컬에 나왔기 때문에 그것을 보았다.
   ➡ _____

5. 나는 공연의 노래와 춤이 좋았다.
   ➡ _____

6. 뮤지컬의 내용은 가장 친한 친구들을 자신의 생일 파티에 초대했던 여자 아이에 관한 것이었다.
   ➡ _____

7. 그들은 자신들의 우정에 대해 이야기했다.
   ➡ _____

8. 주인공은 Sophie였다. 그녀는 많은 아름다운 노래들을 불렀다. 그것은 환상적이었다.
   ➡ _____

9. 공연 중에 노래를 따라 부르며 매우 신났었다.
   ➡ _____

10. 그 뮤지컬은 정말 볼 가치가 있었다.
   ➡ _____

Enjoy Writing B

1. 나에게 감동을 준 영화
   ➡ _____

2. 지난 토요일 나는 영화를 보러 친구 집에 갔다.
   ➡ _____

3. 영화의 제목은 '나의 아들'이었다. 나는 내 친구가 그 영화를 추천해서 봤다.
   ➡ _____

4. 나는 그 영화의 이야기가 마음에 들었다. 그것은 잃어버린 아들을 찾으려 했던 용감한 남자에 관한 이야기였다.
   ➡ _____

5. 주인공은 John이었다. 그 역은 배우 Roy Jones가 연기했는데 아주 멋졌다.
   ➡ _____

6. 그 영화는 감동적이었다. 나는 감동적인 장면들을 보며 감동받았다.
   ➡ _____

7. 그 영화는 정말 볼 가치가 있었다.
   ➡ _____

※ 다음 영어를 우리말로 쓰시오.

01	afford	
02	business	
03	corn cob	
04	filter	
05	collect	
06	invention	
07	useful	
08	relaxed	
09	sew	
10	control	
11	sewing machine	
12	useless	
13	system	
14	match	
15	cost	
16	countryside	
17	pollute	
18	entrance fee	
19	triangle	
20	stay	
21	failure	

22	fair	
23	raise	
24	fee	
25	remove	
26	success	
27	president	
28	whether	
29	step	
30	recommend	
31	pollution	
32	realize	
33	teenager	
34	headband	
35	hit on	
36	come across	
37	thanks to	
38	for oneself	
39	change A into B	
40	for free	
41	pay for	
42	think to oneself	
43	not only A but also B	

※ 다음 우리말을 영어로 쓰시오.

01 오염		22 꿰매다, 바느질하다	
02 ~할 여유가 되다		23 오염시키다	
03 깨닫다, 인식하다		24 (자금을) 모으다	
04 머무르다		25 통제하다, 조절하다, 조정하다	
05 사업		26 십 대	
06 수집하다		27 추천하다	
07 성공		28 삼각형	
08 제거하다		29 유용한	
09 값이 들다		30 발명(품)	
10 편안한, 여유 있는		31 대통령, 회장	
11 박람회		32 체계, 장치	
12 재봉틀		33 발명가	
13 요금		34 단계	
14 시골		35 지불하다	
15 입장료		36 ~ 덕분에	
16 여과장치; 여과하다		37 스스로	
17 옥수수 속대		38 마음속으로 생각하다	
18 쓸모없는, 소용없는		39 A를 B로 바꾸다	
19 실패		40 우연히 마주치다	
20 ~인지 (아닌지)		41 무료로	
21 성냥		42 만나다	
		43 A 뿐만 아니라 B도	

※ 다음 영영풀이에 알맞은 단어를 <보기>에서 골라 쓴 후, 우리말 뜻을 쓰시오.

1 _____ : relating to or like a robot: _____

2 _____ : to stitch with thread: _____

3 _____ : to be able to do something: _____

4 _____ : to be obtained at the price of: _____

5 _____ : the achievement of an aim or purpose: _____

6 _____ : without having to pay: _____

7 _____ : a round piece of metal used as money: _____

8 _____ : to meet or find by chance: _____

9 _____ : to think of a plan, a solution, etc. suddenly or by chance: _____

10 _____ : a work of producing, buying, and selling of goods and services: _____

11 _____ : to damage the water, air, land, etc. by using harmful chemicals: _____

12 _____ : the operating applications programs that are used in a computer system: _____

13 _____ : a large public event where goods are bought and sold, usually from tables that have been specially arranged for the event: _____

14 _____ : a narrow strip of material worn around the head, usually to keep your hair or sweat out of your eyes: _____

15 _____ : to make an organization, person, or system do what you want or have in the way you want: _____

16 _____ : a short, thin piece of wood or thick paper with a special tip that produces fire when it is scratched against something else: _____

fair	success	headband	coin
hit on	cost	pollute	robotic
match	come across	control	for free
software	sew	business	afford

대화문 Test

※ 다음 우리말과 일치하도록 빈칸에 알맞은 말을 쓰시오.

Listen & Speak 1 A-1

G: _____ _____ _____ this _____ the paper?

B: Sure. _____ the middle point, I draw _____ _____. Then I _____ the _____, _____ _____.

G: Good. Now, is it _____ _____ _____ to draw it _____ _____ your pencil _____ the paper?

B: I'll try. Hmm... No, _____ _____ _____ _____ _____?

G: Well, start _____ one of the _____ _____ _____.

B: Do you mean _____ _____ _____ _____ _____ _____ _____?

G: Yes. Draw the circle _____ and then _____ _____ _____ _____ _____. Or you can draw the _____ _____, like this.

B: Oh, now _____ _____ _____.

Listen & Speak 1 A-2

W: Hi. I'm _____ _____ a backpack _____ my son.

M: _____ _____ is your son?

W: He is _____ _____ _____.

M: I want _____ _____ this one.

W: Oh, it's _____ _____.

M: Yes, _____ _____? It has a cap _____ _____ _____ a penguin, _____ kids _____ _____.

W: Is it possible _____ _____ _____ _____ _____ the cap _____ for _____?

M: Sure. You can easily _____ _____ _____ and _____ _____ _____ on.

W: That's _____. I'll _____ _____.

Listen & Speak 2 A-1

B: Wendy, _____ _____ _____ _____ _____ _____ school a lot _____. What's _____?

G: I want to _____ _____ _____, but I just _____.

B: Doesn't your mom _____ _____ _____?

G: She _____, but I don't get up _____ _____. _____ I _____ have an AI robot.

B: _____ _____ _____?

G: Yes. I mean one _____ _____ _____ _____ _____ I _____ and _____ _____ _____ _____ in the morning.

B: That sounds _____.

해석

G: 너 이걸 종이에 그릴 수 있겠니?

B: 물론이지. 가운데 지점으로부터 두 개의 삼각형을 그리면 돼. 그러고 나서 이렇게 원을 그리면 되지.

G: 좋아. 그럼 종이에서 연필을 떼지 않고 그것을 그리는 것이 가능하니?

B: 시도해 볼게. 흠… 아니, 그게 어떻게 가능하니?

G: 음, 네 개의 빨간 점 중 한 곳에서 시작하면 돼.

B: 빨간 점 중에 아무 점이나 말하는 거야?

G: 응. 원을 먼저 그리고, 그 다음에 삼각형 두 개를 이렇게 그려. 아니면 이렇게 삼각형을 먼저 그릴 수도 있어.

B: 오, 이제 알겠어.

W: 안녕하세요. 아들을 위한 배낭을 찾고 있어요.

M: 아들이 몇 살인가요?

W: 아들은 다섯 살이에요.

M: 이것을 추천하고 싶네요.

W: 오, 이거 정말 귀엽네요.

M: 네, 그렇지 않나요? 펭귄과 같이 생긴 모자가 있어서 아이들이 좋아하죠.

W: 제가 세탁을 위해 모자를 분리하는 것도 가능한가요?

M: 물론이죠. 모자를 쉽게 분리했다가 다시 붙일 수도 있어요.

W: 훌륭해요. 이걸 살게요.

B: Wendy, 너 요즘 계속 지각하네. 무슨 일 있어?

G: 일찍 일어나고 싶은데, 그게 안 돼.

B: 네 엄마가 널 깨워 주시지 않니?

G: 엄마가 깨워주시긴 하는데, 바로 일어나지 않아. 인공지능 로봇이 있으면 좋겠어.

B: 인공지능 로봇?

G: 응. 내가 아침에 꼭 일어나도록 확인해 주고, 아침밥을 가져다주는 그런 로봇 말이야.

B: 그거 좋은 생각이야.

Listen & Speak 2 A-2

B: I'm _____ _____ _____ my uncle in Mexico.

G: What are you _____ _____ _____ _____, Mike?

B: I'll _____ _____ _____ _____ _____ at his house _____ he has a big _____ _____.

G: That's great. _____ you _____ _____?

B: No, _____ _____ _____ _____, but I can't. _____ I'll _____ _____ _____ a water walking ball _____.

G: A water walking ball? _____ _____ _____?

B: _____ a large ball. We _____ _____ it and _____ _____ the water.

G: That _____ _____ fun.

Real Life Talk

Bora: What _____ you _____, Jessie?

Jessie: I'm _____ Dr. Rebecca, _____ _____ _____.

Bora: Wow, that's _____.

Jessie: Thanks. I wish I _____ _____ _____ _____ like her.

Bora: Is it possible _____ _____ _____ _____ them, too?

Jessie: Yes. She can _____ your mind _____ _____ _____ _____.

Bora: That's very _____.

Jessie: What about you? Do you also _____ _____ _____ _____?

Bora: Sure. I love Sky X. I wish I _____ _____ _____ _____.

Jessie: I like him, too. He can _____ _____ _____ _____.

Bora: Yes. He _____ _____ _____ in space.

Wrap Up 1

W: Hi, Tom. _____ _____ _____ _____?

B: I'm _____ my drone.

W: Cool! _____ you _____ _____ it?

B: No, I'm not very good _____, but I'm _____ _____.

W: _____ _____ _____, I _____ a sandwich restaurant. Is it _____ _____ _____ _____ _____ _____ with your drone?

B: No, it _____. But I think _____ _____ _____ _____ one or two years.

W: _____ will _____ _____.

B: 나는 멕시코에 있는 삼촌을 방문할 계획이야.

G: 거기서 뭐 할 거야, Mike?

B: 삼촌이 큰 수영장을 가지고 계셔서 난 대부분의 시간을 삼촌 집에서 보낼 거야.

G: 멋지다. 너 수영 잘하니?

B: 아니, 잘했으면 좋겠는데, 못해. 그래서 대신 나는 물 위를 걷는 공을 가지고 놀 거야.

G: 물 위를 걷는 공? 그게 뭐야?

B: 그건 큰 공이야. 그 안에 들어가서 물 위를 걸으면 돼.

G: 그거 분명 재밌겠다.

Bora: Jessie야, 뭐 하고 있어?

Jessie: 내가 제일 좋아하는 슈퍼 영웅인 닥터 레베카를 그리고 있어.

Bora: 와, 훌륭해.

Jessie: 고마워. 나는 그녀처럼 사람들의 마음을 읽을 수 있으면 좋겠어.

Bora: 그녀가 사람들의 마음을 통제하는 것도 가능하니?

Jessie: 응. 그녀가 원하면 네 마음을 통제할 수 있어.

Bora: 그거 정말 멋지다.

Jessie: 너는 어때? 너도 좋아하는 슈퍼 영웅이 있니?

Bora: 물론. 나는 스카이 X를 좋아해. 스카이 X처럼 하늘을 날 수 있으면 좋겠어.

Jessie: 나도 그가 좋아. 그는 우주에서 숨을 쉴 수도 있잖아.

Bora: 응. 그는 우주에서 뭐든 할 수 있어.

W: 안녕, Tom. 무엇을 하는 중이니?

B: 지금 드론을 날리고 있어요.

W: 멋지구나! 드론 조종을 잘하니?

B: 아니요, 전 지금은 별로 잘하지 못하지만 열심히 연습하고 있어요.

W: 네가 알다시피, 내가 샌드위치 가게를 운영하고 있잖아. 너는 네 드론으로 주문한 음식을 배달하는 것이 가능하니?

B: 아니요, 불가능해요. 하지만 1~2년 후에는 가능할 거라 생각해요.

W: 그러면 좋겠구나.

※ 다음 우리말에 맞도록 대화를 영어로 쓰시오.

Listen & Speak 1 A-1

G: _____

B: _____

G: _____

_____

B: _____

G: _____

B: _____

G: _____

_____

B: _____

G: 너 이걸 종이에 그릴 수 있겠니?
B: 물론이지. 가운데 지점으로부터 두 개의 삼각형을 그리면 돼. 그러고 나서 이렇게 원을 그리면 되지.
G: 좋아. 그럼 종이에서 연필을 떼지 않고 그것을 그리는 것이 가능하니?
B: 시도해 볼게. 흠… 아니, 그게 어떻게 가능하니?
G: 음, 네 개의 빨간 점 중 한 곳에서 시작하면 돼.
B: 빨간 점 중에 아무 점이나 말하는 거야?
G: 응. 원을 먼저 그리고, 그 다음에 삼각형 두 개를 이렇게 그려. 아니면 이렇게 삼각형을 먼저 그릴 수도 있어.
B: 오, 이제 알겠어.

Listen & Speak 1 A-2

W: _____

M: _____

W: _____

M: _____

W: _____

M: _____

W: _____

M: _____

W: _____

W: 안녕하세요. 아들을 위한 배낭을 찾고 있어요.
M: 아들이 몇 살인가요?
W: 아들은 다섯 살이에요.
M: 이것을 추천하고 싶네요.
W: 오, 이거 정말 귀엽네요.
M: 네, 그렇지 않나요? 펭귄과 같이 생긴 모자가 있어서 아이들이 좋아하죠.
W: 제가 세탁을 위해 모자를 분리하는 것도 가능한가요?
M: 물론이죠. 모자를 쉽게 분리했다가 다시 붙일 수도 있어요.
W: 훌륭해요. 이걸 살게요.

Listen & Speak 2 A-1

B: _____

G: _____

B: _____

G: _____

B: _____

G: _____

B: _____

B: Wendy, 너 요즘 계속 지각하네. 무슨 일 있어?
G: 일찍 일어나고 싶은데, 그게 안 돼.
B: 네 엄마가 널 깨워 주시지 않니?
G: 엄마가 깨워주시긴 하는데, 바로 일어나지 않아. 인공지능 로봇이 있으면 좋겠어.
B: 인공지능 로봇?
G: 응. 내가 아침에 꼭 일어나도록 확인해 주고, 아침밥을 가져다주는 그런 로봇 말이야.
B: 그거 좋은 생각이야.

Listen & Speak 2 A-2

B: _____

G: _____

B: _____

G: _____

B: _____

G: _____

B: _____

G: _____

B: 나는 멕시코에 있는 삼촌을 방문할 계획이야.

G: 거기서 뭐 할 거야, Mike?

B: 삼촌이 큰 수영장을 가지고 계셔서 난 대부분의 시간을 삼촌 집에서 보낼 거야.

G: 멋지다. 너 수영 잘하니?

B: 아니, 잘했으면 좋겠는데, 못해. 그래서 대신 나는 물 위를 걷는 공을 가지고 놀 거야.

G: 물 위를 걷는 공? 그게 뭐야?

B: 그건 큰 공이야. 그 안에 들어가서 물 위를 걸으면 돼.

G: 그거 분명 재밌겠다.

Real Life Talk

Bora: _____

Jessie: _____

Bora: _____

Jessie: _____

Bora: _____

Jessie: _____

Bora: _____

Jessie: _____

Bora: _____

Jessie: _____

Bora: _____

Bora: Jessie야, 뭐 하고 있어?

Jessie: 내가 제일 좋아하는 슈퍼 영웅인 닥터 레베카를 그리고 있어.

Bora: 와, 훌륭해.

Jessie: 고마워. 나는 그녀처럼 사람들의 마음을 읽을 수 있으면 좋겠어.

Bora: 그녀가 사람들의 마음을 통제하는 것도 가능하니?

Jessie: 응. 그녀가 원하면 네 마음을 통제할 수 있어.

Bora: 그거 정말 멋지다.

Jessie: 너는 어때? 너도 좋아하는 슈퍼 영웅이 있니?

Bora: 물론. 나는 스카이 X를 좋아해. 스카이 X처럼 하늘을 날 수 있으면 좋겠어.

Jessie: 나도 그가 좋아. 그는 우주에서 숨을 쉴 수도 있잖아.

Bora: 응. 그는 우주에서 뭐든 할 수 있어.

Wrap Up 1

W: _____

B: _____

W: _____

B: _____

W: _____

B: _____

W: _____

W: 안녕, Tom. 무엇을 하는 중이니?

B: 지금 드론을 날리고 있어요.

W: 멋지구나! 드론 조종을 잘하니?

B: 아니요, 전 지금은 별로 잘하지 못하지만 열심히 연습하고 있어요.

W: 네가 알다시피, 내가 샌드위치 가게를 운영하고 있잖아. 너는 네 드론으로 주문한 음식을 배달하는 것이 가능하니?

B: 아니요, 불가능해요. 하지만 1~2년 후에는 가능할 거라 생각해요.

W: 그러면 좋겠구나.

※ 다음 우리말과 일치하도록 빈칸에 알맞은 것을 골라 쓰시오.

1 Who are the people who _____ the world? Do you think you are _____ young _____ be _____ of these people?

    A. too   B. change   C. to   D. one

2 In the _____ stories you will meet three teenagers who _____ their ideas to _____ the world a better _____.

    A. following   B. place   C. used   D. make

A Robotic Hand from a Helpful Mind (Easton LaChappelle)

3 One day, _____ I was fourteen, I _____ _____ a little girl at a science _____.

    A. across   B. fair   C. came   D. when

4 She had a _____ hand _____ could only _____ and _____.

    A. open   B. robotic   C. close   D. that

5 I was _____ the hand _____ her 80,000 dollars!

    A. cost   B. that   C. had   D. surprised

6 'I _____ she _____ a _____ robotic hand,' I thought to _____.

    A. myself   B. wish   C. better   D. had

7 _____ that, I started to make a _____ and _____ robotic hand.

    A. cheaper   B. with   C. much   D. better

8 After many _____, finally, by _____ 3D printing technology, I was _____ to make a useful robotic hand for the _____ of only 300 dollars.

    A. able   B. failures   C. price   D. using

9 I decided to _____ the designs and software for my 3D robotic hand _____ _____ for _____.

    A. others   B. share   C. free   D. with

10 Maybe someone can take _____ I have _____ and do _____ _____ with it.

    A. useful   B. what   C. something   D. done

11 No _____ person can _____ the world, but we can _____ a better world by _____ together.

    A. working   B. change   C. one   D. build

Headbands for Girls' Education (Mary Grace Henry)

12 'Why _____ many girls in Africa _____ to school _____ I can? I wish they _____ go to school, too.'

    A. as   B. can't   C. could   D. go

13 I _____ this _____ when I was twelve. I _____ that their families couldn't _____ it.

    A. realized   B. thought   C. afford   D. had

14 I wondered _____ I _____ do _____ for those girls. Then I _____ an idea.

    A. something   B. had   C. could   D. if

15 For my birthday, I _____ my parents to _____ me a _____ _____.

    A. sewing   B. asked   C. buy   D. machine

---

1 세상을 바꾸는 사람들은 누구인가요? 여러분은 너무 어려서 이런 사람들 중 하나가 될 수 없다고 생각하나요?

2 다음 이야기에서 여러분은 세상을 더 나은 곳으로 만들기 위해 자신들의 아이디어를 사용한 세 명의 십 대들을 만날 겁니다.

돕는 마음으로부터 탄생한 로봇 손 (Easton LaChappelle)

3 내가 열네 살이었을 때, 어느 날 한 과학 박람회에서 어린 소녀를 우연히 만났다.

4 그녀는 겨우 접었다 펴지기만 하는 로봇 손을 가지고 있었다.

5 나는 그녀가 그 손에 8만 달러를 지불했다는 데 놀랐다!

6 '나는 그녀가 더 나은 로봇 손을 가질 수 있으면 좋겠어.'라고 마음속으로 생각했다.

7 나는 이런 생각을 가지고 더 싸고 좋은 로봇 손을 만들기 시작했다.

8 많은 실패 뒤 마침내 3D 프린트 기술을 사용해서 나는 단 300달러짜리의 유용한 로봇 손을 만들 수 있었다.

9 나는 내 3D 로봇 손의 디자인과 소프트웨어를 다른 사람들과 무료로 공유하기로 결심했다.

10 아마도 누군가는 내가 만든 것을 이용해 다른 유용한 것을 할 수 있을 것이다.

11 혼자 세상을 바꿀 수는 없지만, 함께 일 하면서 더 나은 세상을 만들 수 있다.

여학생 교육을 위한 머리띠 (Mary Grace Henry)

12 '아프리카의 많은 소녀들은 왜 나처럼 학교에 갈 수 없지? 나는 그들도 학교에 갈 수 있으면 좋을 텐데.'

13 내가 12살 때, 이런 생각을 했었다. 나는 그들의 가족이 그럴 금전적 여유가 없다는 것을 깨달았다.

14 나는 내가 그 소녀들을 위해서 어떤 것을 할 수 있을까 생각했다. 그때 아이디어가 떠올랐다.

15 나는 내 생일에 부모님께 재봉틀을 사 달라고 부탁드렸다.

16 They _____ me one, and I learned _____ to _____ headbands for _____.
    A. make   B. bought   C. myself   D. how

17 I _____ ten _____ and _____ them _____ my school.
    A. headbands   B. sold   C. created   D. at

18 Soon, I _____ money to _____ one girl in Africa to school. I couldn't _____ there.
    A. stop   B. send   C. enough   D. raised

19 I started a _____ to _____ girls in Africa _____ couldn't _____ to school.
    A. who   B. business   C. go   D. help

20 Thanks to the _____ of my business, I can _____ the school _____ for many poor girls in countries _____ Kenya and Uganda to go to school.
    A. fees   B. success   C. pay   D. like

21 I also _____ for their _____, _____, and pencils. Isn't it _____?
    A. amazing   B. pay   C. uniforms   D. textbooks

22 My _____ to you is to just do _____. When you see a _____, _____.
    A. need   B. advice   C. act   D. something

23 Start small, _____ little _____. Your warm _____ can change _____.
    A. steps   B. lives   C. taking   D. heart

Useless Corn Cobs as Useful Water Filters (Lalita Prasida)

24 As a young girl _____ in the countryside in India, I often _____ that the water around us was _____ _____.
    A. polluted   B. found   C. living   D. seriously

25 I wondered _____ I could _____ this problem. Then I _____ the idea to use corn cobs.
    A. on   B. hit   C. solve   D. how

26 _____ corn cobs _____ everywhere _____ my _____.
    A. village   B. useless   C. in   D. were

27 I thought that the small _____ in the corn cobs could filter _____ out of the _____ water.
    A. dirty   B. holes   C. polluted   D. matter

28 One day, I _____ up some dried cobs along the road, _____ them, and _____ them in a _____ of dirty water.
    A. placed   B. picked   C. bowl   D. washed

29 _____ a _____, I checked the water, and it looked _____.
    A. clearer   B. while   C. much   D. after

30 Then, _____ corn cobs that I had _____ _____ farmers, I built a _____ system.
    A. filtering   B. using   C. from   D. collected

31 My system _____ 70 to 80 percent of the _____ _____ the water.
    A. matter   B. removed   C. dirty   D. from

32 I hope my filtering system can _____ _____ all the lakes not _____ in my village but _____ in other areas.
    A. only   B. up   C. clean   D. also

16 그들은 재봉틀을 사 주셨고 나는 머리띠 만드는 법을 혼자 배웠다.

17 10개의 머리띠를 만들어 학교에서 팔았다.

18 나는 곧 아프리카에 있는 한 명의 소녀를 학교에 보낼 수 있는 충분한 자금을 모았다. 나는 거기서 멈출 수 없었다.

19 나는 학교에 갈 수 없는 아프리카의 소녀들을 돕기 위해 사업을 시작했다.

20 내 사업의 성공 덕분에 나는 케냐와 우간다 같은 나라에 있는 많은 가난한 소녀들이 학교에 갈 수 있게 수업료를 지불할 수 있다.

21 나는 또한 그들의 교과서와 교복, 연필을 위한 비용도 지불한다. 놀랍지 않은가?

22 나의 조언은 그냥 무엇이든 하라는 것이다. 필요성이 보인다면 행동하라.

23 작은 단계를 밟아가면서 작은 것부터 시작하라. 너의 따뜻한 마음이 삶을 바꿀 수 있다.

유용한 물 여과 장치로 쓰인 쓸모없는 옥수수 속대 (Lalita Prasida)

24 인도의 시골에 살고 있었던 어린 소녀인 나는 종종 내 주변에 있는 물이 심각하게 오염되어 있는 것을 발견했다.

25 나는 이 문제를 어떻게 해결할 수 있을지 궁금했다. 그때 나는 옥수수 속대를 이용해야겠다는 생각이 불현듯 떠올랐다.

26 내가 사는 마을에는 쓸모없는 옥수수 속대가 곳곳에 널려 있다.

27 나는 옥수수 속대의 작은 구멍들이 더러운 물질을 오염된 물 밖으로 걸러 낼 수 있을 거라고 생각했다.

28 어느 날 나는 길을 따라 마른 옥수수 속대를 주운 뒤, 그것들을 씻어서 더러운 물이 담긴 그릇에 넣었다.

29 잠시 뒤 물을 확인했는데 훨씬 더 맑게 보였다.

30 그러고 나서 나는 농부들로부터 모은 옥수수 속대를 이용하여 여과 장치를 만들었다.

31 내 장치는 물에서 70~80%의 더러운 물질을 제거했다.

32 나는 내 여과 장치가 내 마을뿐만 아니라 다른 지역에 있는 모든 호수를 깨끗하게 해 줄 수 있기를 희망한다.

※ 다음 우리말과 일치하도록 빈칸에 알맞은 것을 골라 쓰시오.

1 Who are the people _____ _____ the world? Do you think you are _____ _____ _____ _____ one of these people?

2 In the following stories you _____ _____ three teenagers who used their ideas _____ _____ the world a better place.

A Robotic Hand from a Helpful Mind (Easton LaChappelle)

3 One day, _____ I was fourteen, I _____ _____ a little girl _____ a _____ _____ .

4 She had a _____ hand _____ could only _____ and _____ .

5 I was _____ _____ the hand _____ _____ _____ 80,000 dollars!

6 'I _____ she _____ a better robotic hand,' I _____ _____ _____ .

7 _____ that, I started to make _____ _____ _____ and _____ robotic hand.

8 After many _____, finally, _____ _____ 3D printing technology, I _____ _____ _____ make a useful robotic hand _____ the _____ _____ only 300 dollars.

9 I decided _____ _____ the designs and software _____ my 3D robotic hand _____ _____ _____ _____ .

10 _____ someone can _____ _____ _____ _____ and do _____ _____ it.

11 _____ _____ person can _____ the world, but we can _____ a better world _____ _____ _____ .

Headbands for Girls' Education (Mary Grace Henry)

12 'Why _____ many girls in Africa _____ _____ _____ as I can? I wish they _____ _____ to school, too.'

13 I _____ _____ _____ when I was twelve. I _____ _____ their families _____ _____ it.

14 I wondered _____ _____ _____ _____ _____ _____ for those girls. Then I _____ an idea.

1 세상을 바꾸는 사람들은 누구인 가? 여러분은 너무 어려서 이런 사람들 중 하나가 될 수 없다고 생각하나요?

2 다음 이야기에서 여러분은 세상을 더 나은 곳으로 만들기 위해 자신들의 아이디어를 사용한 세 명의 십 대들을 만날 겁니다.

돕는 마음으로부터 탄생한 로봇 손 (Easton LaChappelle)

3 내가 열네 살이었을 때, 어느 날 한 과학 박람회에서 어린 소녀를 우연히 만났다.

4 그녀는 겨우 접었다 펴지기만 하는 로봇 손을 가지고 있었다.

5 나는 그녀가 그 손에 8만 달러를 지불했다는 데 놀랐다!

6 '나는 그녀가 더 나은 로봇 손을 가질 수 있으면 좋겠어.'라고 마음 속으로 생각했다.

7 나는 이런 생각을 가지고 더 싸고 좋은 로봇 손을 만들기 시작했다.

8 많은 실패 뒤 마침내 3D 프린트 기술을 사용해서 나는 단 300달 러짜리의 유용한 로봇 손을 만들 수 있었다.

9 나는 내 3D 로봇 손의 디자인과 소프트웨어를 다른 사람들과 무료로 공유하기로 결심했다.

10 아마도 누군가는 내가 만든 것을 이용해 다른 유용한 것을 할 수 있을 것이다.

11 혼자 세상을 바꿀 수는 없지만, 함께 일 하면서 더 나은 세상을 만들 수 있다.

여학생 교육을 위한 머리띠 (Mary Grace Henry)

12 '아프리카의 많은 소녀들은 왜 나처럼 학교에 갈 수 없지? 나는 그들도 학교에 갈 수 있으면 좋을 텐데.'

13 내가 12살 때, 이런 생각을 했었다. 나는 그들의 가족이 그럴 금전적 여유가 없다는 것을 깨달았다.

14 나는 내가 그 소녀들을 위해서 어떤 것을 할 수 있을까 생각했다. 그때 아이디어가 떠올랐다.

15 For my birthday, I _____ my parents _____ _____ _____ _____ _____ _____ .

16 They _____ _____ _____ , and I learned _____ _____ _____ headbands _____ _____ .

17 I created _____ _____ and sold _____ at my school.

18 Soon, I _____ _____ _____ to send one girl in Africa to school. I couldn't _____ there.

19 I started _____ _____ _____ _____ girls in Africa _____ couldn't _____ to school.

20 Thanks _____ _____ of my business, I can pay the school _____ _____ many poor girls in countries _____ Kenya and Uganda _____ _____ _____ _____ .

21 I also _____ _____ their _____ , _____ , and pencils. _____ it _____ ?

22 My _____ to you _____ to just _____ _____ . When you see _____ _____ , _____ .

23 Start _____ , _____ little steps. Your _____ _____ can change _____ .

Useless Corn Cobs as Useful Water Filters (Lalita Prasida)

24 _____ a young girl _____ in the countryside in India, I _____ _____ _____ the water _____ us was _____ _____ .

25 I wondered _____ _____ _____ _____ this problem. Then I _____ _____ the idea _____ _____ corn cobs.

26 _____ corn cobs _____ everywhere _____ my village.

27 I thought that _____ _____ _____ in the corn cobs _____ _____ _____ out of the _____ water.

28 One day, I _____ _____ _____ some dried cobs along the road, _____ , and _____ them _____ _____ _____ dirty water.

29 _____ _____ _____ , I checked the water, and _____ looked _____ _____ .

30 Then, _____ corn cobs _____ I had _____ _____ _____ farmers, I _____ a _____ system.

31 My system _____ 70 to 80 percent of _____ _____ from the water.

32 I hope my _____ _____ can _____ _____ all the lakes _____ in my village _____ _____ in _____ _____ .

---

15 나는 내 생일에 부모님께 재봉틀을 사 달라고 부탁드렸다.

16 그들은 재봉틀을 사 주셨고 나는 머리띠 만드는 법을 혼자 배웠다.

17 10개의 머리띠를 만들어 학교에서 팔았다.

18 나는 곧 아프리카에 있는 한 명의 소녀를 학교에 보낼 수 있는 충분한 자금을 모았다. 나는 거기서 멈출 수 없었다.

19 나는 학교에 갈 수 없는 아프리카의 소녀들을 돕기 위해 사업을 시작했다.

20 내 사업의 성공 덕분에 나는 케냐와 우간다 같은 나라에 있는 많은 가난한 소녀들이 학교에 갈 수 있게 수업료를 지불할 수 있다.

21 나는 또한 그들의 교과서와 교복, 연필을 위한 비용도 지불한다. 놀랍지 않은가?

22 나의 조언은 그냥 무엇이든 하라는 것이다. 필요성이 보인다면 행동하라.

23 작은 단계를 밟아가면서 작은 것부터 시작하라. 너의 따뜻한 마음이 삶을 바꿀 수 있다.

유용한 물 여과 장치로 쓰인 쓸모없는 옥수수 속대 (Lalita Prasida)

24 인도의 시골에 살고 있었던 어린 소녀인 나는 종종 내 주변에 있는 물이 심각하게 오염되어 있는 것을 발견했다.

25 나는 이 문제를 어떻게 해결할 수 있을지 궁금했다. 그때 나는 옥수수 속대를 이용해야겠다는 생각이 불현듯 떠올랐다.

26 내가 사는 마을에는 쓸모없는 옥수수 속대가 곳곳에 널려 있다.

27 나는 옥수수 속대의 작은 구멍들이 더러운 물질을 오염된 물 밖으로 걸러 낼 수 있을 거라고 생각했다.

28 어느 날 나는 길을 따라 마른 옥수수 속대를 주운 뒤, 그것들을 씻어서 더러운 물이 담긴 그릇에 넣었다.

29 잠시 뒤 물을 확인했는데 훨씬 더 맑게 보였다.

30 그리고 나서 나는 농부들로부터 모은 옥수수 속대를 이용하여 여과 장치를 만들었다.

31 내 장치는 물에서 70~80%의 더러운 물질을 제거했다.

32 나는 내 여과 장치가 내 마을뿐만 아니라 다른 지역에 있는 모든 호수를 깨끗하게 해 줄 수 있기를 희망한다.

※ 다음 문장을 우리말로 쓰시오.

1 Who are the people who change the world? Do you think you are too young to be one of these people?

➡ _____

2 In the following stories you will meet three teenagers who used their ideas to make the world a better place.

➡ _____
_____

A Robotic Hand from a Helpful Mind (Easton LaChappelle)

3 One day, when I was fourteen, I came across a little girl at a science fair.

➡ _____

4 She had a robotic hand that could only open and close.

➡ _____

5 I was surprised that the hand had cost her 80,000 dollars!

➡ _____

6 'I wish she had a better robotic hand,' I thought to myself.

➡ _____

7 With that, I started to make a much cheaper and better robotic hand.

➡ _____

8 After many failures, finally, by using 3D printing technology, I was able to make a useful robotic hand for the price of only 300 dollars.

➡ _____

9 I decided to share the designs and software for my 3D robotic hand with others for free.

➡ _____

10 Maybe someone can take what I have done and do something useful with it.

➡ _____

11 No one person can change the world, but we can build a better world by working together.

➡ _____

Headbands for Girls' Education (Mary Grace Henry)

12 'Why can't many girls in Africa go to school as I can? I wish they could go to school, too.'

➡ _____

13 I had this thought when I was twelve. I realized that their families couldn't afford it.

➡ _____

14 I wondered if I could do something for those girls. Then I had an idea.

➡ _____

15 For my birthday, I asked my parents to buy me a sewing machine.

➡ _____

16 They bought me one, and I learned how to make headbands for myself.
➡ _____

17 I created ten headbands and sold them at my school.
➡ _____

18 Soon, I raised enough money to send one girl in Africa to school. I couldn't stop there.
➡ _____

19 I started a business to help girls in Africa who couldn't go to school.
➡ _____

20 Thanks to the success of my business, I can pay the school fees for many poor girls in countries like Kenya and Uganda to go to school.
➡ _____
_____

21 I also pay for their textbooks, uniforms, and pencils. Isn't it amazing?
➡ _____

22 My advice to you is to just do something. When you see a need, act.
➡ _____

23 Start small, taking little steps. Your warm heart can change lives.
➡ _____

Useless Corn Cobs as Useful Water Filters (Lalita Prasida)

24 As a young girl living in the countryside in India, I often found that the water around us was seriously polluted.
➡ _____

25 I wondered how I could solve this problem. Then I hit on the idea to use corn cobs.
➡ _____

26 Useless corn cobs were everywhere in my village.
➡ _____

27 I thought that the small holes in the corn cobs could filter dirty matter out of the polluted water.
➡ _____

28 One day, I picked up some dried cobs along the road, washed them, and placed them in a bowl of dirty water.
➡ _____

29 After a while, I checked the water, and it looked much clearer.
➡ _____

30 Then, using corn cobs that I had collected from farmers, I built a filtering system.
➡ _____

31 My system removed 70 to 80 percent of the dirty matter from the water.
➡ _____

32 I hope my filtering system can clean up all the lakes not only in my village but also in other areas.
➡ _____

※ 다음 괄호 안의 단어들을 우리말에 맞도록 바르게 배열하시오.

1 (are / who / people / the / change / who / world? / the // you / do / think / are / you / young / too / be / to / of / one / people? / these)
➡ _____

2 (the / in / stories / following / you / meet / will / teenagers / three / used / who / ideas / their / make / to / world / the / better / a / place.)
➡ _____

A Robotic Hand from a Helpful Mind (Easton LaChappelle)

3 (day, / one / I / when / fourteen, / was / came / I / across / little / a / girl / a / at / fair. / science)
➡ _____

4 (had / she / robotic / a / that / hand / could / open / only / close. / and)
➡ _____

5 (was / I / that / surprised / the / had / hand / cost / 80,000 / her / dollars!)
➡ _____

6 (wish / 'I / had / she / better / a / hand,' / robotic / thought / I / myself. / to)
➡ _____

7 (that, / with / started / I / make / to / much / a / and / cheaper / robotic / better / hand.)
➡ _____

8 (many / after / finally, / failures, / using / by / printing / 3D / technology, / was / I / to / able / a / make / robotic / useful / for / hand / price / the / only / of / dollars. / 300)
➡ _____

9 (decided / I / share / to / designs / the / software / and / my / for / robotic / 3D / with / hand / others / free. / for)
➡ _____

10 (someone / maybe / take / can / I / what / done / have / and / something / do / with / useful / it.)
➡ _____

11 (one / no / can / person / the / change / world, / we / but / build / can / world / better / a / by / together. / working)
➡ _____

Headbands for Girls' Education (Mary Grace Henry)

12 (can't / 'why / girls / many / Africa / in / to / go / as / school / can? / I // wish / I / could / they / to / go / too.' / school,)
➡ _____

13 (had / I / thought / this / I / when / twelve. / was // realized / I / their / that / couldn't / families / it. / afford)
➡ _____

14 (wondered / I / I / if / do / could / for / something / girls. / those // I / then / an / had / idea.)
➡ _____

15 (my / for / birthday, / asked / I / parents / my / buy / to / a / me / machine. / sewing)
➡ _____

16 (bought / they / one, / me / I / and / how / learned / make / to / myself. / headbands / for)
➡ _____

1 세상을 바꾸는 사람들은 누구인가? 여러분은 너무 어려서 이런 사람들 중 하나가 될 수 없다고 생각하나요?

2 다음 이야기에서 여러분은 세상을 더 나은 곳으로 만들기 위해 자신들의 아이디어를 사용한 세 명의 십 대들을 만날 겁니다.

돕는 마음으로부터 탄생한 로봇 손 (Easton LaChappelle)

3 내가 열네 살이었을 때, 어느 날 한 과학 박람회에서 어린 소녀를 우연히 만났다.

4 그녀는 겨우 접었다 펴지기만 하는 로봇 손을 가지고 있었다.

5 나는 그녀가 그 손에 8만 달러를 지불했다는 데 놀랐다!

6 '나는 그녀가 더 나은 로봇 손을 가질 수 있으면 좋겠어.'라고 마음속으로 생각했다.

7 나는 이런 생각을 가지고 더 싸고 좋은 로봇 손을 만들기 시작했다.

8 많은 실패 뒤 마침내 3D 프린트 기술을 사용해서 나는 단 300달러짜리의 유용한 로봇 손을 만들 수 있었다.

9 나는 내 3D 로봇 손의 디자인과 소프트웨어를 다른 사람들과 무료로 공유하기로 결심했다.

10 아마도 누군가는 내가 만든 것을 이용해 다른 유용한 것을 할 수 있을 것이다.

11 혼자 세상을 바꿀 수는 없지만, 함께 일 하면서 더 나은 세상을 만들 수 있다.

여학생 교육을 위한 머리띠 (Mary Grace Henry)

12 '아프리카의 많은 소녀들은 왜 나처럼 학교에 갈 수 없지? 나는 그들도 학교에 갈 수 있으면 좋을 텐데.'

13 내가 12살 때, 이런 생각을 했었다. 나는 그들의 가족이 그럴 금전적 여유가 없다는 것을 깨달았다.

14 나는 내가 그 소녀들을 위해서 어떤 것을 할 수 있을까 생각했다. 그때 아이디어가 떠올랐다.

15 나는 내 생일에 부모님께 재봉틀을 사 달라고 부탁드렸다.

16 그들은 재봉틀을 사 주셨고 나는 머리띠 만드는 법을 혼자 배웠다.

17 (created / I / headbands / ten / sold / and / at / them / school. / my)

➡ _____

18 (I / soon, / enough / raised / to / money / one / send / girl / Africa / in / school. / to // couldn't / I / there. / stop)

➡ _____

19 (started / I / business / a / help / to / in / girls / who / Africa / couldn't / to / school. / go)

➡ _____

20 (to / thanks / success / the / my / of / business, / can / I / the / pay / fees / school / many / for / girls / poor / countries / in / Kenya / like / Uganda / and / go / to / school. / to)

➡ _____

21 (also / I / for / pay / textbooks, / their / and / uniforms, / pencils. // it / amazing? / isn't)

➡ _____

22 (advice / my / you / to / is / just / to / something. / do // you / when / a / see / act. / need,)

➡ _____

23 (small, / start / little / taking / steps. // warm / your / can / heart / lives / change)

➡ _____

Useless Corn Cobs as Useful Water Filters (Lalita Prasida)

24 (a / as / girl / young / living / the / in / countryside / India, / in / often / I / that / found / water / the / us / around / seriously / was / polluted.)

➡ _____

25 (wondered / I / I / how / solve / could / problem. / this // I / then / on / hit / idea / the / use / to / cobs. / corn)

➡ _____

26 (corn / useless / were / cobs / in / everywhere / village. / my)

➡ _____

27 (thought / I / the / that / small / in / holes / the / cobs / corn / filter / could / matter / dirt / of / out / polluted / the / water.)

➡ _____

28 (day, / one / picked / I / some / up / cobs / dried / along / road, / the / them, / washed / and / them / placed / a / in / of / bowl / water. / dirty)

➡ _____

29 (a / after / while, / checked / I / water, / the / it / and / much / looked / clearer.)

➡ _____

30 (using / then, / cobs / corn / I / that / collected / had / farmers, / from / built / I / a / system. / filtering)

➡ _____

31 (system / my / 70 / removed / to / percent / 80 / of / dirty / the / from / matter / water. / the)

➡ _____

32 (hope / I / filtering / my / can / system / clean / all / up / the / not / lakes / only / in / village / my / also / but / in / areas. / other)

➡ _____

17 10개의 머리띠를 만들어 학교에서 팔았다.

18 나는 곧 아프리카에 있는 한 명의 소녀를 학교에 보낼 수 있는 충분한 자금을 모았다. 나는 거기서 멈출 수 없었다.

19 나는 학교에 갈 수 없는 아프리카의 소녀들을 돕기 위해 사업을 시작했다.

20 내 사업의 성공 덕분에 나는 케냐와 우간다 같은 나라에 있는 많은 가난한 소녀들이 학교에 갈 수 있게 수업료를 지불할 수 있다.

21 나는 또한 그들의 교과서와 교복, 연필을 위한 비용도 지불한다. 놀랍지 않은가?

22 나의 조언은 그냥 무엇이든 하라는 것이다. 필요성이 보인다면 행동하라.

23 작은 단계를 밟아가면서 작은 것부터 시작하라. 너의 따뜻한 마음이 삶을 바꿀 수 있다.

유용한 물 여과 장치로 쓰인 쓸모없는 옥수수 속대 (Lalita Prasida)

24 인도의 시골에 살고 있었던 어린 소녀인 나는 종종 내 주변에 있는 물이 심각하게 오염되어 있는 것을 발견했다.

25 나는 이 문제를 어떻게 해결할 수 있을지 궁금했다. 그때 나는 옥수수 속대를 이용해야겠다는 생각이 불현듯 떠올랐다.

26 내가 사는 마을에는 쓸모없는 옥수수 속대가 곳곳에 널려 있다.

27 나는 옥수수 속대의 작은 구멍들이 더러운 물질을 오염된 물 밖으로 걸러 낼 수 있을 거라고 생각했다.

28 어느 날 나는 길을 따라 마른 옥수수 속대를 주운 뒤, 그것들을 씻어서 더러운 물이 담긴 그릇에 넣었다.

29 잠시 뒤 물을 확인했는데 훨씬 더 맑게 보였다.

30 그리고 나서 나는 농부들로부터 모은 옥수수 속대를 이용하여 여과 장치를 만들었다.

31 내 장치는 물에서 70~80%의 더러운 물질을 제거했다.

32 나는 내 여과 장치가 내 마을뿐만 아니라 다른 지역에 있는 모든 호수를 깨끗하게 해 줄 수 있기를 희망한다.

※ 다음 우리말을 영어로 쓰시오.

1 세상을 바꾸는 사람들은 누구인가? 여러분은 너무 어려서 이런 사람들 중 하나가 될 수 없다고 생각하나요?
➡ _____
_____

2 다음 이야기에서 여러분은 세상을 더 나은 곳으로 만들기 위해 자신들의 아이디어를 사용한 세 명의 십 대들을 만날 겁니다.
➡ _____
_____

A Robotic Hand from a Helpful Mind (Easton LaChappelle)

3 내가 열네 살이었을 때, 어느 날 한 과학 박람회에서 어린 소녀를 우연히 만났다.
➡ _____

4 그녀는 겨우 접었다 펴지기만 하는 로봇 손을 가지고 있었다.
➡ _____

5 나는 그녀가 그 손에 8만 달러를 지불했다는 데 놀랐다!
➡ _____

6 '나는 그녀가 더 나은 로봇 손을 가질 수 있으면 좋겠어.'라고 마음속으로 생각했다.
➡ _____

7 나는 이런 생각을 가지고 더 싸고 좋은 로봇 손을 만들기 시작했다.
➡ _____

8 많은 실패 뒤 마침내 3D 프린트 기술을 사용해서 나는 단 300달러짜리의 유용한 로봇 손을 만들 수 있었다.
➡ _____
_____

9 나는 내 3D 로봇 손의 디자인과 소프트웨어를 다른 사람들과 무료로 공유하기로 결심했다.
➡ _____

10 아마도 누군가는 내가 만든 것을 이용해 다른 유용한 것을 할 수 있을 것이다.
➡ _____

11 혼자 세상을 바꿀 수는 없지만, 함께 일 하면서 더 나은 세상을 만들 수 있다.
➡ _____

Headbands for Girls' Education (Mary Grace Henry)

12 '아프리카의 많은 소녀들은 왜 나처럼 학교에 갈 수 없지? 나는 그들도 학교에 갈 수 있으면 좋을 텐데.'
➡ _____

13 내가 12살 때, 이런 생각을 했었다. 나는 그들의 가족이 그럴 금전적 여유가 없다는 것을 깨달았다.
➡ _____

14 나는 내가 그 소녀들을 위해서 어떤 것을 할 수 있을까 생각했다. 그때 아이디어가 떠올랐다.
➡ _____

15 나는 내 생일에 부모님께 재봉틀을 사 달라고 부탁드렸다.
➡ _____

16 그들은 재봉틀을 사 주셨고 나는 머리띠 만드는 법을 혼자 배웠다.
➡ _____

17 10개의 머리띠를 만들어 학교에서 팔았다.
➡ _____

18 나는 곧 아프리카에 있는 한 명의 소녀를 학교에 보낼 수 있는 충분한 자금을 모았다. 나는 거기서 멈출 수 없었다.
➡ _____

19 나는 학교에 갈 수 없는 아프리카의 소녀들을 돕기 위해 사업을 시작했다.
➡ _____

20 내 사업의 성공 덕분에 나는 케냐와 우간다 같은 나라에 있는 많은 가난한 소녀들이 학교에 갈 수 있게 수업료를 지불할 수 있다.
➡ _____
_____

21 나는 또한 그들의 교과서와 교복, 연필을 위한 비용도 지불한다. 놀랍지 않은가?
➡ _____

22 나의 조언은 그냥 무엇이든 하라는 것이다. 필요성이 보인다면 행동하라.
➡ _____

23 작은 단계를 밟아가면서 작은 것부터 시작하라. 너의 따뜻한 마음이 삶을 바꿀 수 있다.
➡

Useless Corn Cobs as Useful Water Filters (Lalita Prasida)
24 인도의 시골에 살고 있었던 어린 소녀인 나는 종종 내 주변에 있는 물이 심각하게 오염되어 있는 것을 발견했다.
➡ _____
_____

25 나는 이 문제를 어떻게 해결할 수 있을지 궁금했다. 그때 나는 옥수수 속대를 이용해야겠다는 생각이 불현 듯 떠올랐다.
➡ _____

26 내가 사는 마을에는 쓸모없는 옥수수 속대가 곳곳에 널려 있다.
➡ _____

27 나는 옥수수 속대의 작은 구멍들이 더러운 물질을 오염된 물 밖으로 걸러 낼 수 있을 거라고 생각했다.
➡ _____

28 어느 날 나는 길을 따라 마른 옥수수 속대를 주운 뒤, 그것들을 씻어서 더러운 물이 담긴 그릇에 넣었다.
➡ _____
_____

29 잠시 뒤 물을 확인했는데 훨씬 더 맑게 보였다.
➡ _____

30 그러고 나서 나는 농부들로부터 모은 옥수수 속대를 이용하여 여과 장치를 만들었다.
➡ _____

31 내 장치는 물에서 70~80%의 더러운 물질을 제거했다.
➡ _____

32 나는 내 여과 장치가 내 마을뿐만 아니라 다른 지역에 있는 모든 호수를 깨끗하게 해 줄 수 있기를 희망한다.
➡ _____

※ 다음 우리말과 일치하도록 빈칸에 알맞은 말을 쓰시오.

Communication Task

1. A: I'm Sky X. I _____ _____.
2. B: Hi, Sky X. Nice _____ _____ _____.
3. C: I _____ I _____ _____ _____ you. _____ _____ _____ _____ _____ to fly to the moon?
4. A: _____.
5. D: Then _____ _____ _____ _____ _____ _____ _____ to the sun?
6. A: No. That's _____.

1. A: 나는 스카이 X야. 나는 하늘을 날 수 있어.
2. B: 안녕, 스카이 X. 만나서 반가워.
3. C: 나는 너처럼 하늘을 날 수 있으면 좋겠어. 너는 달까지 날아가는 것이 가능하니?
4. A: 물론이지.
5. D: 그럼 너는 태양으로 여행하는 것이 가능하니?
6. A: 아니. 그건 불가능해.

Enjoy Writing

1. _____ Genie,
2. I have three wishes. _____ _____ _____ you can _____ _____ _____ _____.
3. First, I _____ I _____ in Hawaii. Then I _____ _____ _____ _____ _____.
4. Second, I _____ every Wednesday _____ a holiday. Then, I _____ _____ _____ _____.
5. _____, _____ _____ _____ _____ _____ the president of Korea.
6. Then I would try hard to _____ _____ _____ _____ _____ _____ _____ _____.
7. I don't know _____ _____ _____ _____ _____ _____, but _____ _____ you _____.
8. _____ _____, Sohee

1. Genie에게
2. 나는 세 가지 소원이 있다. 네가 나의 소원들을 모두 이루어 줄 수 있을지 궁금하다.
3. 첫 번째로, 나는 하와이에 살았으면 좋겠다. 그럼 하와이의 아름다운 해변에서 수영할 수 있을 것이다.
4. 두 번째로, 나는 모든 수요일이 휴일이었으면 좋겠다. 그럼 나는 더 편히 쉴 수 있을 것이다.
5. 마지막으로, 나는 한국의 대통령이었으면 좋겠다.
6. 그럼 나는 이 나라를 살기에 더 행복한 곳으로 만들기 위해 열심히 노력할 것이다.
7. 나는 네가 나를 도와줄 수 있을지 모르겠지만, 네가 할 수 있길 바란다.
8. 행운을 빌며, 소희가

After Your Read

1. _____ _____!
2. Easton _____ _____ _____ a girl's expensive robotic hand and wanted _____ _____ _____ _____ _____ _____ one.
3. Finally he made one _____ _____ _____ _____ _____ and _____ _____ _____ his designs and software _____ _____.
4. Mary _____ she _____ _____ girls in Africa to school.
5. She _____ and _____ _____.
6. Now she _____ the school _____, textbooks, uniforms, and pencils of _____ _____ _____ _____ _____ _____ _____ _____.
7. Lalita wondered _____ _____ _____ _____ _____ _____ _____.
8. _____ _____ _____ _____, she made _____ _____ _____ _____.
9. It _____ 70 to 80 percent of _____ _____ _____ _____ _____ _____.

1. 창의적인 십 대들!
2. Easton은 어떤 소녀의 비싼 로봇 손을 보고 놀라서, 더 싸고 좋은 로봇 손을 만들고 싶었다.
3. 마침내 그는 단 300달러짜리 로봇 손을 만들었고 그의 디자인과 소프트웨어를 무료로 나누기로 결심했다.
4. Mary는 아프리카 소녀들을 학교에 보낼 수 있기를 바랐다.
5. 그녀는 머리띠를 만들어 팔았다.
6. 이제 그녀는 아프리카의 많은 가난한 소녀들의 학비와 교과서, 교복 그리고 연필의 비용을 지불한다.
7. Lalita는 어떻게 물을 깨끗하게 할 수 있을지 궁금했다.
8. 그녀는 옥수수 속대를 이용해서 정수 장치를 만들었다.
9. 그 정수 장치는 오염된 물에서 70~80 퍼센트의 더러운 물질을 제거했다.

※ 다음 우리말을 영어로 쓰시오.

Communication Task

1. A: 나는 스카에 X야. 나는 하늘을 날 수 있어.
➡ _____

2. B: 안녕, 스카이 X. 만나서 반가워.
➡ _____

3. C: 나는 너처럼 하늘을 날 수 있으면 좋겠어. 너는 달까지 날아가는 것이 가능하니?
➡ _____

4. A: 물론이지.
➡ _____

5. D: 그럼 너는 태양으로 여행하는 것이 가능하니?
➡ _____

6. A: 아니. 그건 불가능해.
➡ _____

Enjoy Writing

1. Genie에게
➡ _____

2. 나는 세 가지 소원이 있다. 네가 나의 소원들을 모두 이루어 줄 수 있을지 궁금하다.
➡ _____

3. 첫 번째로, 나는 하와이에 살았으면 좋겠다. 그럼 하와이의 아름다운 해변에서 수영할 수 있을 것이다.
➡ _____

4. 두 번째로, 나는 모든 수요일이 휴일이었으면 좋겠다. 그럼 나는 더 편히 쉴 수 있을 것이다.
➡ _____

5. 마지막으로, 나는 한국의 대통령이었으면 좋겠다.
➡ _____

6. 그럼 나는 이 나라를 살기에 더 행복한 곳으로 만들기 위해 열심히 노력할 것이다.
➡ _____

7. 나는 네가 나를 도와줄 수 있을지 모르겠지만, 네가 할 수 있길 바란다.
➡ _____

8. 행운을 빌며, 소희가
➡ _____

After Your Read

1. 창의적인 십 대들!
➡ _____

2. Easton은 어떤 소녀의 비싼 로봇 손을 보고 놀라서, 더 싸고 좋은 로봇 손을 만들고 싶었다.

3. 마침내 그는 단 300달러짜리 로봇 손을 만들었고 그의 디자인과 소프트웨어를 무료로 나누기로 결심했다.
➡ _____

4. Mary는 아프리카 소녀들을 학교에 보낼 수 있기를 바랐다.

5. 그녀는 머리띠를 만들어 팔았다.
➡ _____

6. 이제 그녀는 아프리카의 많은 가난한 소녀들의 학비와 교과서, 교복 그리고 연필의 비용을 지불한다.
➡ _____

7. Lalita는 어떻게 물을 깨끗하게 할 수 있을지 궁금했다.
➡ _____

8. 그녀는 옥수수 속대를 이용해서 정수 장치를 만들었다.
➡ _____

9. 그 정수 장치는 오염된 물에서 70~80퍼센트의 더러운 물질을 제거했다.
➡ _____

※ 다음 영어를 우리말로 쓰시오.

01 necklace _____

02 piece _____

03 amount _____

04 beauty _____

05 whisper _____

06 couple _____

07 diamond _____

08 shocked _____

09 ball _____

10 worn _____

11 similar _____

12 whatever _____

13 fancy _____

14 admire _____

15 cry _____

16 lend _____

17 franc _____

18 huge _____

19 worth _____

20 invitation _____

21 ambassador _____

22 jeweler _____

23 replace _____

24 nearly _____

25 second job _____

26 jewelry _____

27 lie _____

28 borrow _____

29 certainly _____

30 look _____

31 run into _____

32 pay back _____

33 at once _____

34 call on _____

35 Do I know you? _____

36 spend+시간+동명사 _____

37 It takes+목적어+
    시간+to부정사 _____

※ 다음 우리말을 영어로 쓰시오.

01 속삭이다, 귓속말을 하다 _____

02 프랑 (프랑스, 스위스 등의 화폐 단위) _____

03 거대한, 엄청난 _____

04 양, 액수 _____

05 무도회 _____

06 ~이든지, ~한 어떤 것이든 _____

07 확실히, 틀림없이 _____

08 존경하다, 칭찬하다 _____

09 목걸이 _____

10 한 개, 한 부분, 조각 _____

11 대사 _____

12 다이아몬드 _____

13 울다 _____

14 화려한 _____

15 충격을 받은 _____

16 거의 _____

17 ~의 가치가 있는 _____

18 초대, 초대장 _____

19 보석 상인 _____

20 아름다움, 미 _____

21 비슷한, 유사한 _____

22 빌리다 _____

23 보석류 _____

24 부부 _____

25 빌려주다 _____

26 (다른 사람·사물을) 대신하다 _____

27 부업 _____

28 거짓말 _____

29 지친 _____

30 보기, 눈길 _____

31 ~을 우연히 만나다 _____

32 절 아시나요? _____

33 즉시, 당장 _____

34 ~에게 청하다, 부탁하다 _____

35 갚다, 돌려주다 _____

※ 다음 영영풀이에 알맞은 단어를 <보기>에서 골라 쓴 후, 우리말 뜻을 쓰시오.

1 _____ : very tired: _____

2 _____ : two people who are married: _____

3 _____ : a quantity of something: _____

4 _____ : alike in many ways: _____

5 _____ : almost but not quite: _____

6 _____ : to take a place of: _____

7 _____ : surely, without doubt: _____

8 _____ : feeling very upset or surprised: _____

9 _____ : a large formal place where people dance: _____

10 _____ : a statement which you know is not true: _____

11 _____ : to let tears come from the eyes because of sadness, hurt, etc.: _____

12 _____ : hard, bright, precious stone which is clear and colorless: _____

13 _____ : a request to come to an event or somewhere: _____

14 _____ : to like and respect someone or something very much:

_____

15 _____ : to speak or say something very softly and low: _____

16 _____ : a diplomat of the highest rank who is the official representative of his or her country in another country: _____

보기			
whisper	amount	ambassador	similar
invitation	shocked	lie	replace
admire	worn	diamond	couple
ball	certainly	cry	nearly

※ 다음 우리말과 일치하도록 빈칸에 알맞은 것을 골라 쓰시오.

Scene 1

1 _____ _____ Mr. and Mrs. Loisel's home _____ _____.

A. in   B. is   C. Paris   D. this

2 _____ the home is _____, Mrs. Loisel is _____.

A. nice   B. although   C. happy   D. not

3 She is young and _____, and _____ a _____ _____.

A. fancier   B. pretty   C. wants   D. life

4 Mrs. Loisel: (to _____) Same old house and _____ _____ dinners. I hate _____ here!

A. boring   B. living   C. herself   D. same

5 Mr. Loisel: Matilda, I am _____. Look _____ I _____ for you!

A. what   B. got   C. have   D. home

6 Mrs. Loisel: _____ is _____?

A. that   B. what

7 Mr. Loisel: An _____ to the Ambassador's Ball. I _____ to _____ to _____ it. Everybody wanted it.

A. fight   B. invitation   C. get   D. had

8 Mrs. Loisel: (crying) _____ _____ I _____ it?

A. would   B. why   C. want

9 Mr. Loisel: Matilda. _____ is _____?

A. wrong   B. what

10 Mrs. Loisel: I have _____ to _____ to _____ a _____ party. I cannot go.

A. fancy   B. nothing   C. such   D. wear

11 Mr. Loisel: _____ _____ sad. Here, I will give you 400 francs. _____ _____ a beautiful new dress.

A. yourself   B. be   C. get   D. don't

Scene 2

12 Mr. Loisel: (_____ _____ *Matilda's new dress*) _____, Matilda. Beautiful!

A. amazing   B. at   C. looking

13 Mrs. Loisel: _____ is _____ _____.

A. right   B. something   C. not

14 Mr. Loisel: What _____ _____ _____?

A. wrong   B. be   C. could

15 Mrs. Loisel: (crying) Oh, no. What am I _____ _____ _____?

A. to   B. going   C. do

장면 1

1 이곳은 파리의 Loisel 부부의 집이다.

2 그들의 집은 멋지지만, Loisel 부인은 행복하지 않다.

3 그녀는 젊고 예뻐서 더 화려하고 고급스러운 삶을 원한다.

4 Mrs. Loisel: (혼잣말로) 똑같은 낡은 집과 매일 같이 똑같은 지겨운 저녁 식사. 여기서 사는 게 너무 싫어!

5 Mr. Loisel: Matilda, 나 집에 왔어요. 내가 당신을 위해 무엇을 가져왔는지 봐요!

6 Mrs. Loisel: 뭐예요?

7 Mr. Loisel: 대사님이 여는 무도회 초대장이에요. 이걸 얻기 위해 엄청난 노력을 했단 말이에요. 모두가 갖고 싶어 했거든요.

8 Mrs. Loisel: (울면서) 내가 그걸 왜 갖고 싶겠어요?

9 Mr. Loisel: Matilda. 무슨 문제 있어요?

10 Mrs. Loisel: 그런 고급스러운 파티에 입고 갈 옷이 하나도 없는걸요. 못가요.

11 Mr. Loisel: 슬퍼하지 말아요. 자, 여기 400프랑을 줄게요. 아름다운 새 드레스를 사요.

장면 2

12 Mr. Loisel: (Matilda의 새 드레스를 보며) 멋져요, Matilda. 아름답군요!

13 Mrs. Loisel: 뭔가 제대로 맞지 않아요.

14 Mr. Loisel: 뭐가 안 맞을 수 있죠?

15 Mrs. Loisel: (울면서) 오, 안 돼. 어쩌면 좋아요?

16 Mr. Loisel: _____ _____ _____, Matilda?

    A. is   B. what   C. it

17 Mrs. Loisel: I have no _____ to _____ with my beautiful dress. I will look _____ _____!

    A. poor   B. jewelry   C. wear   D. so

18 Mr. Loisel: _____ _____ your friend, Mrs. Forestier. I am _____ she will _____ you some of her jewelry.

    A. lend   B. call   C. sure   D. on

19 Mrs. Loisel: That is a good idea! _____ me _____ _____ _____.

    A. once   B. let   C. at   D. go

Scene 3

20 Mrs. Forestier: Matilda, it is _____ nice _____ see you! What _____ you _____?

    A. brings   B. so   C. here   D. to

21 Mrs. Loisel: We _____ _____ _____ the Ambassador's Ball.

    A. invited   B. are   C. to

22 Mrs. Forestier: The Ambassador's Ball! That is _____! You _____ _____ _____ _____.

    A. wonderful   B. excited   C. be   D. must

23 Mrs. Loisel: Yes… And no. I am sad to _____ I have no _____. May I _____ something _____ you?

    A. jewelry   B. from   C. say   D. borrow

24 Mrs. Forestier: Sure! _____ is _____ _____.

    A. case   B. here   C. my

25 Mrs. Loisel: Wow, you have _____ _____ _____ _____!

    A. wonderful   B. so   C. pieces   D. many

26 Mrs. Forestier: _____ _____ you _____.

    A. whatever   B. like   C. choose

27 Mrs. Loisel: Would you _____ _____ this _____ _____? It is beautiful!

    A. necklace   B. lend   C. diamond   D. me

28 Mrs. Forestier: _____! Now _____ _____ the ball.

    A. go   B. certainly   C. enjoy

Scene 4

29 Matilda has a _____ _____. Everybody at the ball _____ her _____.

    A. admires   B. perfect   C. beauty   D. evening

30 _____ _____ very late _____ the Loisels _____ the ball.

    A. leave   B. it   C. when   D. is

31 Mr. Loisel: It was _____ a _____ _____. I am _____ tired.

    A. night   B. such   C. long   D. so

---

16 Mr. Loisel: 뭐예요, 부인?

17 Mrs. Loisel: 이 아름다운 드레스에 어울릴 보석이 하나도 없어요. 내가 너무 불쌍해 보일 거예요!

18 Mr. Loisel: 당신 친구 Forestier 부인에게 부탁해 봐요. 그녀는 자신이 가진 보석을 분명히 빌려줄 거예요.

19 Mrs. Loisel: 그거 좋은 생각이에요! 지금 당장 가봐야겠어요.

장면 3

20 Mrs. Forestier: Matilda, 이렇게 보게 되어서 정말 좋아요! 무슨 일로 왔어요?

21 Mrs. Loisel: 우리 부부가 대사의 무도회에 초대되었어요.

22 Mrs. Forestier: 대사의 무도회라! 멋지네요! 당신은 분명 신났겠군요.

23 Mrs. Loisel: 네… 그리고 아니기도 해요. 말하기 슬프지만 난 보석이 없어요. 부인에게서 좀 빌릴 수 있을까요?

24 Mrs. Forestier: 물론이죠! 여기 내 보석함이에요.

25 Mrs. Loisel: 와, 부인은 정말 멋진 보석들이 많네요!

26 Mrs. Forestier: 원하는 것 아무거나 골라요.

27 Mrs. Loisel: 이 다이아몬드 목걸이를 빌려줄 수 있나요? 이거 정말 아름다워요!

28 Mrs. Forestier: 당연하죠! 자, 이제 가서 무도회를 즐겨요.

장면 4

29 Matilda는 완벽한 저녁을 보낸다. 무도회장에 있는 모든 사람들이 아름다운 그녀를 감탄하며 바라본다.

30 Loisel 부부는 아주 늦은 시간이 되어서야 무도회를 떠났다.

31 Mr. Loisel: 정말 길고 긴 밤이었어요. 정말 피곤해요.

---

32 Mrs. Loisel: But it was _____ _____. Do you know I _____ _____ the Ambassador?
A. worth   B. with   C. it   D. danced

33 Mr. Loisel: I am glad you _____ _____, but I _____ to go to _____ in the morning.
A. yourself   B. have   C. enjoyed   D. work

34 Mrs. Loisel: (_____ _in the mirror_) Just one _____ _____. (_shocked_) The necklace… It is _____!
A. look   B. looking   C. gone   D. more

35 Mr. Loisel: What? Did you have it _____ _____ _____ the _____?
A. when   B. left   C. we   D. ball

36 Mrs. Loisel: Yes, I _____ _____. Please _____ it!
A. go   B. did   C. find   D. surely

37 Mr. Loisel _____ the _____.
A. streets   B. searches

38 He _____ _____ the ball and _____ _____ to the police.
A. goes   B. to   C. then   D. returns

39 When the _____ is not _____, Mr. Loisel tells Matilda _____ to her friend.
A. lie   B. necklace   C. found   D. to

40 Matilda tells Mrs. Forestier she _____ the _____ and would _____ it before _____ it.
A. returning   B. broke   C. fix   D. necklace

41 The _____ needs time to _____ a _____ _____.
A. similar   B. couple   C. one   D. find

Scene 5

42 Mr. Loisel: (_to the jeweler_) Excuse me? _____ _____ _____ _____ that diamond necklace?
A. at   B. may   C. look   D. we

43 Mrs. Loisel: (_____) It is _____ the _____. We _____ have it!
A. must   B. nearly   C. same   D. whispering

44 Mr. Loisel: _____ _____ is it?
A. much   B. how

45 Jeweler: _____ _____.
A. francs   B. 40,000

46 Mr. Loisel: _____ _____ 36,000?
A. about   B. how

47 Mrs. Loisel: Please, we _____ _____ _____.
A. need   B. really   C. it

48 Jeweler: Well, _____ … 36,000 _____ _____.
A. it   B. then   C. is

49 They do not _____ 36,000 francs. It is a _____ _____ money.
A. amount   B. have   C. huge   D. of

50 _____ they _____ it.
A. borrow   B. so

32 Mrs. Loisel: 그렇지만 충분히 가치가 있었어요. 당신, 제가 대사님과 춤춘 것을 아나요?

33 Mr. Loisel: 당신이 즐거웠다니 기쁘지만 나 아침에 출근해야 해요.

34 Mrs. Loisel: (거울을 보며) 한 번만 더 볼게요. (충격을 받고) 목걸이… 목걸이가 없어졌어요!

35 Mr. Loisel: 뭐라고요? 무도회를 떠날 때 걸고 있었소?

36 Mrs. Loisel: 네, 분명히 하고 있었는데. 가서 찾아 줘요!

37 Loisel 씨는 길거리를 수색한다.

38 그는 무도회장으로 되돌아가 본 다음 경찰서에도 간다.

39 목걸이가 발견되지 않자, Loisel 씨는 Matilda에게 그녀의 친구에게 거짓말을 하라고 한다.

40 Matilda는 Forestier 부인에게 목걸이를 망가뜨려서 돌려주기 전에 고쳐 주겠다고 말한다.

41 부부는 비슷한 것을 찾을 시간이 필요하다.

장면 5

42 Mr. Loisel: (보석상에게) 실례합니다. 저 다이아몬드 목걸이 좀 볼 수 있을까요?

43 Mrs. Loisel: (속삭이며) 거의 똑같아요. 저걸 꼭 사야만 해요!

44 Mr. Loisel: 이거 얼마인가요?

45 Jewler: 40,000프랑이에요.

46 Mr. Loisel: 36,000에 안 될까요?

47 Mrs. Loisel: 부탁드려요. 우린 이게 정말 필요하거든요.

48 Jewler: 음, 그럼… 36,000프랑에 하시죠.

49 그들은 36,000프랑이 없다. 그건 큰돈이다.

50 그래서 그들은 돈을 빌린다.

51 After _____ the necklace _____ Mrs. Forestier, the couple _____ ten years _____ back the money.

    A. spends   B. for   C. paying   D. buying

52 They _____ _____ a very small _____.

    A. to   B. move   C. place

53 Mr. Loisel gets a _____ _____. Matilda _____ clothes for _____.

    A. washes   B. second   C. others   D. job

54 Ten years of _____ work _____ Matilda _____ and _____.

    A. makes   B. hard   C. worn   D. old

55 After ten _____, Matilda _____ _____ Mrs. Forestier _____ the street.

    A. into   B. on   C. years   D. runs

Scene 6

56 Mrs. Loisel: Mrs. Forestier, _____ _____.

    A. morning   B. good

57 Mrs. Forestier: _____ _____ _____ you?

    A. know   B. do   C. I

58 Mrs. Loisel: Yes, _____ _____ _____, Matilda.

    A. is   B. it   C. me

59 Mrs. Forestier: Oh, I _____ _____ it! You _____ _____ so much.

    A. changed   B. believe   C. have   D. cannot

60 Mrs. Loisel: I _____ _____ some _____ _____ because of you.

    A. times   B. had   C. difficult   D. have

61 Mrs. Forestier: _____ _____ me? _____ do you _____?

    A. mean   B. because   C. what   D. of

62 Mrs. Loisel: Do you _____ the diamond necklace you _____ _____? Well, I _____ it.

    A. lent   B. remember   C. lost   D. me

63 Mrs. Forestier: But you _____ _____ _____ me.

    A. to   B. it   C. returned

64 Mrs. Loisel: No, I returned _____ one just _____ it. It took us ten years to _____ _____ it.

    A. pay   B. another   C. like   D. for

65 Mrs. Forestier: You _____ a diamond necklace _____ _____ _____?

    A. to   B. bought   C. mine   D. replace

66 Mrs. Loisel: Yes.

67 Mrs. Forestier: Oh, my poor Matilda. Why _____ you come to me and tell me the _____? My diamond necklace was not _____. It was _____ only 500 francs!

    A. worth   B. truth   C. real   D. didn't

51 부부는 Forestier 부인에게 돌려줄 목걸이를 산 후 돈을 갚는 데 십 년이 걸린다.

52 그들은 아주 작은 곳으로 이사한다.

53 Loisel 씨는 부업을 구한다. Matilda는 다른 사람들을 위해 빨래를 해 준다.

54 10년 동안의 고된 일로 Matilda는 늙고 지쳤다.

55 십 년 후, Matilda는 Forestier 부인과 거리에서 마주친다.

장면 6

56 Mrs. Loisel: Forestier 부인, 좋은 아침이에요.

57 Mrs. Forestier: 제가 당신을 아나요?

58 Mrs. Loisel: 네, 저예요, Matilda.

59 Mrs. Forestier: 오, 믿을 수 없어요! 당신 너무 많이 변했어요.

60 Mrs. Loisel: 저는 당신 때문에 힘든 시간을 보냈거든요.

61 Mrs. Forestier: 나 때문에요? 무슨 말이에요?

62 Mrs. Loisel: 당신이 빌려준 목걸이 기억하죠? 음, 제가 그걸 잃어버렸어요.

63 Mrs. Forestier: 그런데 그거 나한테 돌려줬잖아요.

64 Mrs. Loisel: 아니요, 나는 당신 것과 똑같은 다른 목걸이를 돌려줬어요. 그 값을 치르느라 십 년이 걸렸어요.

65 Mrs. Forestier: 내 것을 대체하려고 다이아몬드 목걸이를 샀다고요?

66 Mrs. Loisel: 네, 맞아요.

67 Mrs. Forestier: 오, 가엾은 Matilda. 왜 내게 와서 사실을 말하지 않았어요? 제 다이아몬드 목걸이는 진품이 아니었어요. 그건 단돈 오백 프랑짜리였다고요!

※ 다음 우리말과 일치하도록 빈칸에 알맞은 것을 골라 쓰시오.

Scene 1

1 _____ _____ Mr. and Mrs. Loisel's home _____ _____.

2 _____ the home is _____, Mrs. Loisel is _____ _____.

3 She is young and pretty, _____ _____ a _____ _____.

4 Mrs. Loisel: (_____ _____) Same _____ _____ and same _____ dinners. I _____ _____ here!

5 Mr. Loisel: Matilda, I _____ _____. Look _____ I _____ _____ for you!

6 Mrs. Loisel: What is _____?

7 Mr. Loisel: An _____ _____ the Ambassador's Ball. I _____ _____ _____ _____ _____ _____. Everybody wanted it.

8 Mrs. Loisel: (*crying*) _____ _____ I want it?

9 Mr. Loisel: Matilda. What _____ _____?

10 Mrs. Loisel: I have _____ _____ _____ to _____ _____ _____ _____. I cannot go.

11 Mr. Loisel: _____ _____ sad. Here, I will _____ 400 francs. _____ _____ a _____ _____ _____.

Scene 2

12 Mr. Loisel: (_____ _____ *Matilda's new dress*) _____, Matilda. Beautiful!

13 Mrs. Loisel: Something is _____ _____.

14 Mr. Loisel: _____ _____ _____ _____ _____?

15 Mrs. Loisel: (*crying*) Oh, no. What am I _____ _____ _____?

1 이곳은 파리의 Loisel 부부의 집이다.

2 그들의 집은 멋지지만, Loisel 부인은 행복하지 않다.

3 그녀는 젊고 예뻐서 더 화려하고 고급스러운 삶을 원한다.

4 Mrs. Loisel: (혼잣말로) 똑같은 낡은 집과 매일 같이 똑같은 지겨운 저녁 식사. 여기서 사는 게 너무 싫어!

5 Mr. Loisel: Matilda, 나 집에 왔어요. 내가 당신을 위해 무엇을 가져왔는지 봐요!

6 Mrs. Loisel: 뭐예요?

7 Mr. Loisel: 대사님이 여는 무도회 초대장이에요. 이걸 얻기 위해 엄청난 노력을 했단 말이에요. 모두가 갖고 싶어 했거든요.

8 Mrs. Loisel: (울면서) 내가 그걸 왜 갖고 싶겠어요?

9 Mr. Loisel: Matilda. 무슨 문제 있어요?

10 Mrs. Loisel: 그런 고급스러운 파티에 입고 갈 옷이 하나도 없는걸요. 못가요.

11 Mr. Loisel: 슬퍼하지 말아요. 자, 여기 400프랑을 줄게요. 아름다운 새 드레스를 사요.

12 Mr. Loisel: (Matilda의 새 드레스를 보며) 멋져요, Matilda. 아름답군요!

13 Mrs. Loisel: 뭔가 제대로 맞지 않아요.

14 Mr. Loisel: 뭐가 안 맞을 수 있죠?

15 Mrs. Loisel: (울면서) 오, 안 돼. 어쩌면 좋아요?

16 Mr. Loisel: _____ _____ _____, Matilda?

17 Mrs. Loisel: I have _____ _____ _____ _____ with my _____ _____. I will look _____ _____!

18 Mr. Loisel: _____ _____ your friend, Mrs. Forestier. I am sure _____ _____ _____ _____ _____ some of her _____.

19 Mrs. Loisel: That is a good idea! _____ _____ _____ _____ _____.

Scene 3

20 Mrs. Forestier: Matilda, it is so nice _____ _____ you! _____ _____ _____ _____ _____?

21 Mrs. Loisel: We are _____ _____ the Ambassador's Ball.

22 Mrs. Forestier: The Ambassador's Ball! That is _____! You _____ _____ _____ _____.

23 Mrs. Loisel: Yes… And no. I am sad _____ _____ I have _____ _____ _____. May I _____ _____ _____ _____ _____?

24 Mrs. Forestier: Sure! _____ _____ my _____.

25 Mrs. Loisel: Wow, you have _____ _____ _____ _____!

26 Mrs. Forestier: Choose _____ _____ _____.

27 Mrs. Loisel: Would you _____ _____ _____ _____? It is beautiful!

28 Mrs. Forestier: _____! Now _____ _____ _____ the ball.

Scene 4

29 Matilda has _____ _____ _____. Everybody at the ball _____ _____ _____.

30 _____ _____ very late _____ _____ _____ _____ the ball.

31 Mr. Loisel: It was _____ _____ _____ _____ _____. I am so _____.

장면 옆 번역란:

16 Mr. Loisel: 뭐예요, 부인?

17 Mrs. Loisel: 이 아름다운 드레스에 어울릴 보석이 하나도 없어요. 내가 너무 불쌍해 보일 거예요!

18 Mr. Loisel: 당신 친구 Forestier 부인에게 부탁해 봐요. 그녀는 자신이 가진 보석을 분명히 빌려줄 거예요.

19 Mrs. Loisel: 그거 좋은 생각이에요! 지금 당장 가봐야겠어요.

장면 3

20 Mrs. Forestier: Matilda, 이렇게 보게 되어서 정말 좋아요! 무슨 일로 왔어요?

21 Mrs. Loisel: 우리 부부가 대사의 무도회에 초대되었어요.

22 Mrs. Forestier: 대사의 무도회라! 멋지네요! 당신은 분명 신났겠군요.

23 Mrs. Loisel: 네… 그리고 아니기도 해요. 말하기 슬프지만 난 보석이 없어요. 부인에게서 좀 빌릴 수 있을까요?

24 Mrs. Forestier: 물론이죠! 여기 내 보석함이에요.

25 Mrs. Loisel: 와, 부인은 정말 멋진 보석들이 많네요!

26 Mrs. Forestier: 원하는 것 아무거나 골라요.

27 Mrs. Loisel: 이 다이아몬드 목걸이를 빌려줄 수 있나요? 이거 정말 아름다워요!

28 Mrs. Forestier: 당연하죠! 자, 이제 가서 무도회를 즐겨요.

장면 4

29 Matilda는 완벽한 저녁을 보낸다. 무도회장에 있는 모든 사람들이 아름다운 그녀를 감탄하며 바라본다.

30 Loisel 부부는 아주 늦은 시간이 되어서야 무도회를 떠났다.

31 Mr. Loisel: 정말 길고 긴 밤이었어요. 정말 피곤해요.

32 Mrs. Loisel: But _____ _____ _____ _____. Do you know I _____ _____ the Ambassador?

33 Mr. Loisel: I am glad _____ _____ _____, but I have to _____ _____ _____ in the morning.

34 Mrs. Loisel: (_____ _____ *the mirror*) Just one _____ _____. (*shocked*) The necklace… It is gone!

35 Mr. Loisel: What? Did you have it _____ _____ _____ _____ _____?

36 Mrs. Loisel: Yes, I surely _____. Please _____ _____ it!

37 Mr. Loisel _____ the streets.

38 He _____ _____ the ball and then _____ _____ the police.

39 When the necklace _____ _____ _____, Mr. Loisel tells Matilda _____ _____ _____ her friend.

40 Matilda tells Mrs. Forestier she _____ the _____ and would _____ _____ before _____ _____.

41 The couple needs time _____ _____ _____ _____ _____.

Scene 5

42 Mr. Loisel: (*to the jeweler*) Excuse me? _____ _____ _____ _____ that diamond necklace?

43 Mrs. Loisel: (_____) It is _____ _____ _____. We _____ _____ it!

44 Mr. Loisel: _____ _____ is it?

45 Jeweler: 40,000 _____.

46 Mr. Loisel: _____ _____ 36,000?

47 Mrs. Loisel: Please, we _____ _____ _____.

48 Jeweler: Well, then… 36,000 _____ _____.

49 They _____ _____ _____ 36,000 francs. It is _____ _____ _____ _____ money.

50 So they _____ _____.

32 Mrs. Loisel: 그렇지만 충분히 가치가 있었어요. 당신, 제가 대사님과 춤춘 것을 아나요?

33 Mr. Loisel: 당신이 즐거웠다니 기쁘지만 나 아침에 출근해야 해요.

34 Mrs. Loisel: (거울을 보며) 한 번만 더 볼게요. (충격을 받고) 목걸이… 목걸이가 없어졌어요!

35 Mr. Loisel: 뭐라고요? 무도회를 떠날 때 걸고 있었소?

36 Mrs. Loisel: 네, 분명히 하고 있었는데. 가서 찾아 줘요!

37 Loisel 씨는 길거리를 수색한다.

38 그는 무도회장으로 되돌아가 본 다음 경찰서에도 간다.

39 목걸이가 발견되지 않자, Loisel 씨는 Matilda에게 그녀의 친구에게 거짓말을 하라고 한다.

40 Matilda는 Forestier 부인에게 목걸이를 망가뜨려서 돌려주기 전에 고쳐 주겠다고 말한다.

41 부부는 비슷한 것을 찾을 시간이 필요하다.

장면 5

42 Mr. Loisel: (보석상에게) 실례합니다. 저 다이아몬드 목걸이가 좀 볼 수 있을까요?

43 Mrs. Loisel: (속삭이며) 거의 똑같아요. 저걸 꼭 사야만 해요!

44 Mr. Loisel: 이거 얼마인가요?

45 Jweler: 40,000프랑이에요.

46 Mr. Loisel: 36,000에 안 될까요?

47 Mrs. Loisel: 부탁드려요, 우린 이게 정말 필요하거든요.

48 Jeweler: 음, 그럼… 36,000프랑에 하시죠.

49 그들은 36,000프랑이 없다. 그건 큰돈이다.

50 그래서 그들은 돈을 빌린다.

51 After _____ the necklace _____ Mrs. Forestier, the couple _____ ten years _____ _____ the money.

52 They _____ _____ a very _____ _____.

53 Mr. Loisel _____ _____ _____ _____. Matilda _____ clothes _____ _____.

54 Ten years of hard work _____ Matilda _____ and _____.

55 After ten years, Matilda _____ _____ Mrs. Forestier _____ the street.

Scene 6

56 Mrs. Loisel: Mrs. Forestier, _____ _____.

57 Mrs. Forestier: _____ _____ _____ _____ _____?

58 Mrs. Loisel: Yes, _____ _____ _____, Matilda.

59 Mrs. Forestier: Oh, I cannot _____ _____! You _____ _____ so much.

60 Mrs. Loisel: I _____ _____ some _____ _____ _____ _____ you.

61 Mrs. Forestier: Because of me? _____ _____ _____?

62 Mrs. Loisel: Do you remember the diamond necklace _____ _____ _____? Well, I _____ _____.

63 Mrs. Forestier: But you _____ _____ to me.

64 Mrs. Loisel: No, I returned _____ _____ just _____. _____ _____ us ten years _____ _____.

65 Mrs. Forestier: You _____ a diamond necklace _____ _____ _____?

66 Mrs. Loisel: Yes.

67 Mrs. Forestier: Oh, my poor Matilda. _____ _____ _____ to me and _____ _____ the truth? My diamond necklace _____ _____ _____. It was _____ only 500 francs!

51 부부는 Forestier 부인에게 돌려 줄 목걸이를 산 후 돈을 갚는 데 십 년이 걸린다.

52 그들은 아주 작은 곳으로 이사한다.

53 Loisel 씨는 부업을 구한다. Matilda는 다른 사람들을 위해 빨래를 해 준다.

54 10년 동안의 고된 일로 Matilda는 늙고 지쳤다.

55 십 년 후, Matilda는 Forestier 부인과 거리에서 마주친다.

장면 6

56 Mrs. Loisel: Forestier 부인, 좋은 아침이에요.

57 Mrs. Forestier: 제가 당신을 아나요?

58 Mrs. Loisel: 네, 저예요, Matilda.

59 Mrs. Forestier: 오, 믿을 수 없어요! 당신 너무 많이 변했어요.

60 Mrs. Loisel: 저는 당신 때문에 힘든 시간을 보냈거든요.

61 Mrs. Forestier: 나 때문에요? 무슨 말이에요?

62 Mrs. Loisel: 당신이 빌려준 목걸이 기억하죠? 음, 제가 그걸 잃어버렸어요.

63 Mrs. Forestier: 그런데 그거 나한테 돌려줬잖아요.

64 Mrs. Loisel: 아니요, 나는 당신 것과 똑같은 다른 목걸이를 돌려줬어요. 그 값을 치르느라 십 년이 걸렸어요.

65 Mrs. Forestier: 내 것을 대체하려고 다이아몬드 목걸이를 샀다고요?

66 Mrs. Loisel: 네, 맞아요.

67 Mrs. Forestier: 오, 가엾은 Matilda. 왜 내게 와서 사실을 말하지 않았어요? 제 다이아몬드 목걸이는 진품이 아니었어요. 그건 단돈 오백 프랑짜리였다고요!

※ 다음 문장을 우리말로 쓰시오.

Scene 1

1 This is Mr. and Mrs. Loisel's home in Paris.

➡ _____

2 Although the home is nice, Mrs. Loisel is not happy.

➡ _____

3 She is young and pretty, and wants a fancier life.

➡ _____

4 Mrs. Loisel: (*to herself*) Same old house and same boring dinners. I hate living here!

➡ _____

5 Mr. Loisel: Matilda, I am home. Look what I have got for you!

➡ _____

6 Mrs. Loisel: What is that?

➡ _____

7 Mr. Loisel: An invitation to the Ambassador's Ball. I had to fight to get it. Everybody wanted it.

➡ _____

8 Mrs. Loisel: (*crying*) Why would I want it?

➡ _____

9 Mrs. Loisel: Matilda. What is wrong?

➡ _____

10 Mrs. Loisel: I have nothing to wear to such a fancy party. I cannot go.

➡ _____

11 Mr. Loisel: Don't be sad. Here, I will give you 400 francs. Get yourself a beautiful new dress.

➡ _____

Scene 2

12 Mr. Loisel: (*looking at Matilda's new dress*) Amazing, Matilda. Beautiful!

➡ _____

13 Mrs. Loisel: Something is not right.

➡ _____

14 Mr. Loisel: What could be wrong?

➡ _____

15 Mrs. Loisel: (*crying*) Oh, no. What am I going to do?

➡ _____

16 Mr. Loisel: What is it, Matilda?

➡ _____

17 Mrs. Loisel: I have no jewelry to wear with my beautiful dress. I will look so poor!

➡ _____

18 Mr. Loisel: Call on your friend, Mrs. Forestier. I am sure she will lend you some of her jewelry.

➡ _____

19 Mrs. Loisel: That is a good idea! Let me go at once.

➡ _____

Scene 3

20 Mrs. Forestier: Matilda, it is so nice to see you! What brings you here?

➡ _____

21 Mrs. Loisel: We are invited to the Ambassador's Ball.

➡ _____

22 Mrs. Forestier: The Ambassador's Ball! That is wonderful! You must be excited.

➡ _____

23 Mrs. Loisel: Yes… And no. I am sad to say I have no jewelry. May I borrow something from you?

➡ _____

24 Mrs. Forestier: Sure! Here is my case.

➡ _____

25 Mrs. Loisel: Wow, you have so many wonderful pieces!

➡ _____

26 Mrs. Forestier: Choose whatever you like.

➡ _____

27 Mrs. Loisel: Would you lend me this diamond necklace? It is beautiful!

➡ _____

28 Mrs. Forestier: Certainly! Now go enjoy the ball.

➡ _____

Scene 4

29 Matilda has a perfect evening. Everybody at the ball admires her beauty.

➡ _____

30 It is very late when the Loisels leave the ball.

➡ _____

31 Mr. Loisel: It was such a long night. I am so tired.

➡ _____

32 Mrs. Loisel: But it was worth it. Do you know I danced with the Ambassador?
➡ _____

33 Mr. Loisel: I am glad you enjoyed yourself, but I have to go to work in the morning.
➡ _____

34 Mrs. Loisel: (*looking in the mirror*) Just one more look. (*shocked*) The necklace... It is gone!
➡ _____

35 Mr. Loisel: What? Did you have it when we left the ball?
➡ _____

36 Mrs. Loisel: Yes, I surely did. Please go find it!
➡ _____

37 Mr. Loisel searches the streets.
➡ _____

38 He returns to the ball and then goes to the police.
➡ _____

39 When the necklace is not found, Mr. Loisel tells Matilda to lie to her friend.
➡ _____

40 Matilda tells Mrs. Forestier she broke the necklace and would fix it before returning it.
➡ _____

41 The couple needs time to find a similar one.
➡ _____

Scene 5

42 Mr. Loisel: (*to the jeweler*) Excuse me? May we look at that diamond necklace?
➡ _____

43 Mrs. Loisel: (*whispering*) It is nearly the same. We must have it!
➡ _____

44 Mr. Loisel: How much is it?
➡ _____

45 Jeweler: 40,000 francs.
➡ _____

46 Mr. Loisel: How about 36,000?
➡ _____

47 Mrs. Loisel: Please, we really need it.
➡ _____

48 Jeweler: Well, then... 36,000 it is.
➡ _____

49 They do not have 36,000 francs. It is a huge amount of money.
➡ _____

50 So they borrow it.
➡ _____

51 After buying the necklace for Mrs. Forestier, the couple spends ten years paying back the money.

➡ _____

52 They move to a very small place.

➡ _____

53 Mr. Loisel gets a second job. Matilda washes clothes for others.

➡ _____

54 Ten years of hard work makes Matilda old and worn.

➡ _____

55 After ten years, Matilda runs into Mrs. Forestier on the street.

➡ _____

Scene 6

56 Mrs. Loisel: Mrs. Forestier, good morning.

➡ _____

57 Mrs. Forestier: Do I know you?

➡ _____

58 Mrs. Loisel: Yes, it is me, Matilda.

➡ _____

59 Mrs. Forestier: Oh, I cannot believe it! You have changed so much.

➡ _____

60 Mrs. Loisel: I have had some difficult times because of you.

➡ _____

61 Mrs. Forestier: Because of me? What do you mean?

➡ _____

62 Mrs. Loisel: Do you remember the diamond necklace you lent me? Well, I lost it.

➡ _____

63 Mrs. Forestier: But you returned it to me.

➡ _____

64 Mrs. Loisel: No, I returned another one just like it. It took us ten years to pay for it.

➡ _____

65 Mrs. Forestier: You bought a diamond necklace to replace mine?

➡ _____

66 Mrs. Loisel: Yes.

➡ _____

67 Mrs. Forestier: Oh, my poor Matilda. Why didn't you come to me and tell me the truth? My diamond necklace was not real. It was worth only 500 francs!

➡ _____

_____

※ 다음 괄호 안의 단어들을 우리말에 맞도록 바르게 배열하시오.

Scene 1

1 (is / this / Mrs. / and / Mr. / home / Loisel's / Paris. / in)
➡ _____

2 (the / although / is / home / nice, / Loisel / Mrs. / not / is / happy.)
➡ _____

3 (is / she / young / pretty, / and / wants / and / a / life. / fancier)
➡ _____

4 (Mrs. Loisel: / *herself*) (*to* // old / same / and / house / boring / same / dinners. // hate / I / here! / living)
➡ _____
_____

5 (Mr. Loisel: / Matilda, / am / I / home. // what / look / have / I / for / got / you!)
➡ _____

6 (Mrs. Loisel: / is / that? / what)
➡ _____

7 (Mr. Loisel: / invitation / an / the / to / Ball. / Ambassador's // had / I / fight / to / get / it. / to // wanted / everybody / it.)
➡ _____
_____

8 (Mrs. Loisel: / (*crying*) / would / why / want / I / it?)
➡ _____

9 (Mr. Loisel: / Matilda. / is / what / wrong?)
➡ _____

10 (Mrs. Loisel: / have / I / to / nothing / wear / such / to / a / party. / fancy // cannot / I / go.)
➡ _____

11 (Mr. Loisel: / be / don't / sad. // I / here, / give / will / 400 / you / francs. // yourself / get / beautiful / a / dress. / new)
➡ _____
_____

Scene 2

12 (Mr. Loisel: / (*looking / Matilda's / at / dress*) / *new* // Matilda, / Amazing, / Beautiful!)
➡ _____

13 (Mrs. Loisel: / is / something / right. / not)
➡ _____

14 (Mr. Loisel: / could / what / wrong? / be)
➡ _____

15 (Mrs. Loisel: / (*crying*) / no. / oh, // am / what / going / I / do? / to)
➡ _____

장면 1

1 이곳은 파리의 Loisel 부부의 집이다.

2 그들의 집은 멋지지만, Loisel 부인은 행복하지 않다.

3 그녀는 젊고 예뻐서 더 화려하고 고급스러운 삶을 원한다.

4 Mrs. Loisel: (혼잣말로) 똑같은 낡은 집과 매일 같이 똑같은 지겨운 저녁 식사. 여기서 사는 게 너무 싫어!

5 Mr. Loisel: Matilda, 나 집에 왔어요. 내가 당신을 위해 무엇을 가져왔는지 봐요!

6 Mrs. Loisel: 뭐예요?

7 Mr. Loisel: 대사님이 여는 무도회 초대장이에요. 이걸 얻기 위해 엄청난 노력을 했단 말이에요. 모두가 갖고 싶어 했거든요.

8 Mrs. Loisel: (울면서) 내가 그걸 왜 갖고 싶겠어요?

9 Mr. Loisel: Matilda. 무슨 문제 있어요?

10 Mrs. Loisel: 그런 고급스러운 파티에 입고 갈 옷이 하나도 없는걸요. 못가요.

11 Mr. Loisel: 슬퍼하지 말아요. 자, 여기 400프랑을 줄게요. 아름다운 새 드레스를 사요.

장면 2

12 Mr. Loisel: (Matilda의 새 드레스를 보며) 멋져요, Matilda. 아름답군요!

13 Mrs. Loisel: 뭔가 제대로 맞지 않아요.

14 Mr. Loisel: 뭐가 안 맞을 수 있죠?

15 Mrs. Loisel: (울면서) 오, 안 돼. 어쩌면 좋아요?

16 (Mr. Loisel: / is / what / it, / Matilda?)
➡ _____

17 (Mrs. Loisel: / have / I / jewelry / no / wear / to / my / with / dress. / beautiful // will / I / so / look / poor!)
➡ _____
_____

18 (Mr. Loisel: / on / call / friend, / your, / Forestier. / Mrs. // am / I / she / sure / will / you / lend / of / some / jewelry. / her)
➡ _____
_____

19 (Mrs. Loisel: / is / that's / a / idea! / good // me / let / at / go / once.)
➡ _____

Scene 3

20 (Mrs. Forestier: / Matilda, / is / it / nice / so / see / you! / to // brings / what / here? / you)
➡ _____

21 (Mrs. Loisel: / are / we / to / invited / the / Ball. / Ambassador's)
➡ _____

22 (Mrs. Forestier: / Ambassador's / The / Ball! // is / that / wonderful! // must / you / excited. / be)
➡ _____

23 (Mrs. Loisel: / Yes... / no. / and // am / I / to / sad / say / have / I / jewelry. / no // I / may / something / borrow / you? / from)
➡ _____

24 (Mrs. Forestier: / sure! // is / here / case. / my)
➡ _____

25 (Mrs. Loisel: / you / wow, / so / have / wonderful / many / pieces!)
➡ _____

26 (Mrs. Forestier: / whatever / chose / like. / you)
➡ _____

27 (Mrs. Loisel: / you / would / me / lend / this / necklace? // diamond // is / it / beautiful!)
➡ _____

28 (Mrs. Forestier: / certainly! // go / now / the / enjoy / ball.)
➡ _____

Scene 4

29 (has / Matilda / a / evening. / perfect // at / everybody / ball / the / her / admires / beauty.)
➡ _____

30 (is / it / late / very / the / when / Loisels / the / leave / ball.)
➡ _____

31 (Mr. Loisel: / was / it / a / such / night. / long // am / I / tired. / so)
➡ _____

16 Mr. Loisel: 뭐예요, 부인?

17 Mrs. Loisel: 이 아름다운 드레스에 어울릴 보석이 하나도 없어요. 내가 너무 불쌍해 보일 거예요!

18 Mr. Loisel: 당신 친구 Forestier 부인에게 부탁해 봐요. 그녀는 자신이 가진 보석을 분명히 빌려줄 거예요.

19 Mrs. Loisel: 그거 좋은 생각이에요! 지금 당장 가봐야겠어요.

장면 3

20 Mrs. Forestier: Matilda, 이렇게 보게 되어서 정말 좋아요! 무슨 일로 왔어요?

21 Mrs. Loisel: 우리 부부가 대사의 무도회에 초대되었어요.

22 Mrs. Forestier: 대사의 무도회라! 멋지네요! 당신은 분명 신났겠군요.

23 Mrs. Loisel: 네… 그리고 아니기도 해요. 말하기 슬프지만 난 보석이 없어요. 부인에게서 좀 빌릴 수 있을까요?

24 Mrs. Forestier: 물론이죠! 여기 내 보석함이에요.

25 Mrs. Loisel: 와, 부인은 정말 멋진 보석들이 많네요!

26 Mrs. Forestier: 원하는 것 아무거나 골라요.

27 Mrs. Loisel: 이 다이아몬드 목걸이를 빌려줄 수 있나요? 이거 정말 아름다워요!

28 Mrs. Forestier: 당연하죠! 자, 이제 가서 무도회를 즐겨요.

장면 4

29 Matilda는 완벽한 저녁을 보낸다. 무도회장에 있는 모든 사람들이 아름다운 그녀를 감탄하며 바라본다.

30 Loisel 부부는 아주 늦은 시간이 되어서야 무도회를 떠났다.

31 Mr. Loisel: 정말 길고 긴 밤이었어요. 정말 피곤해요.

32 (Mrs. Loisel: / it / but / worth / was / it. // you / know / do / danced / I / the / with / Ambassador?)
➡ _____

33 (Mr. Loisel: / am / I / you / glad / yourself, / enjoyed / I / but / go / to / have / to / in / work / morning. / the)
➡ _____

34 (Mrs. Loisel: / in / (*looking / mirror*) / *the* // one / just / look. / more // (*shocked*) // necklace... / the // is it / gone!)
➡ _____

35 (Mr. Loisel: / what? / you / did / it / have / we / when / the / left / ball?)
➡ _____

36 (Mrs. Loisel: / I / yes, / did. / surely // go / please / it! / find)
➡ _____

37 (Loisel / Mr. / the / searches / streets.)
➡ _____

38 (returns / he / the / to / ball / and / goes / then / the / to / police.)
➡ _____

39 (the / when / is / necklace / found, / not / Loisel / Mr. / Matilda / tells / to / lie / friend. / her / to)
➡ _____

40 (Matilda / Mrs. / tells / Forestier / broke / she / necklace / the / and / fix / would / before / it / it. / returning)
➡ _____

41 (couple /the / time / needs / find / to / a / one. / similar)
➡ _____

Scene 5

42 (Mr. Loisel: / *the / jeweler*) / (*to* // me? / excuse // we / may / at / look / diamond / that / necklace?)
➡ _____

43 (Mrs. Loisel: / (*whispering*) / is / it / the / nearly / same. // must / we / it! / have)
➡ _____

44 (Mr. Loisel: / much / how / it? / is)
➡ _____

45 (Jeweler: / francs. / 40,000)
➡ _____

46 (Mr. Loisel: / about / how / 36,000?)
➡ _____

47 (Mrs. Loisel: / we / please, / need / really / it.)
➡ _____

48 (Jeweler: / then... / well, / it / 36,000 / is.)
➡ _____

49 (do / they / have / not / francs. / 36,000 // is / it / a / amount / huge / money. / of)
➡ _____

50 (they / so / it. / borrow)
➡ _____

32 Mrs. Loisel: 그렇지만 충분히 가치가 있었어요. 당신, 제가 대사님과 춤춘 것을 아나요?

33 Mr. Loisel: 당신이 즐거웠다니 기쁘지만 나 아침에 출근해야 해요.

34 Mrs. Loisel: (거울을 보며) 한 번만 더 볼게요. (충격을 받고) 목걸이… 목걸이가 없어졌어요!

35 Mr. Loisel: 뭐라고요? 무도회를 떠날 때 걸고 있었소?

36 Mrs. Loisel: 네, 분명히 하고 있었는데. 가서 찾아 줘요!

37 Loisel 씨는 길거리를 수색한다.

38 그는 무도회장으로 되돌아가 본 다음 경찰서에도 간다.

39 목걸이가 발견되지 않자, Loisel 씨는 Matilda에게 그녀의 친구에게 거짓말을 하라고 한다.

40 Matilda는 Forestier 부인에게 목걸이를 망가뜨려서 돌려주기 전에 고쳐 주겠다고 말한다.

41 부부는 비슷한 것을 찾을 시간이 필요하다.

장면 5

42 Mr. Loisel: (보석상에게) 실례합니다. 저 다이아몬드 목걸이 좀 볼 수 있을까요?

43 Mrs. Loisel: (속삭이며) 거의 똑같아요. 저걸 꼭 사야만 해요!

44 Mr. Loisel: 이거 얼마인가요?

45 Jewler: 40,000프랑이에요.

46 Mr. Loisel: 36,000에 안 될까요?

47 Mrs. Loisel: 부탁드려요, 우린 이게 정말 필요하거든요.

48 Jewler: 음, 그럼… 36,000프랑에 하시죠.

49 그들은 36,000프랑이 없다. 그건 큰돈이다.

50 그래서 그들은 돈을 빌린다.

51 (buying / after / necklace / the / Mrs. / for / Forestier, / couple / the / ten / spends / paying / years / the / back / money.)
➡ _____

52 (move / they / to / very / a / place. / small)
➡ _____

53 (Loisel / Mr. / a / gets / job. / second // washes / Matilda / for / clothes / others.)
➡ _____

54 (years / ten / hard / of / makes / work / old / Matilda / worn. / and)
➡ _____

55 (ten / after / years, / runs / Matilda / into / Forestier / Mrs. / the / on / street.)
➡ _____

Scene 6

56 (Mrs. Loisel: / Forestier, / Mrs. / morning. / good)
➡ _____

57 (Mrs. Forestier: / I / do / you? / know)
➡ _____

58 (Mrs. Loisel: / it / yes, / me, / is / Matilda.)
➡ _____

59 (Mrs. Forestier: / I / oh, / believe / cannot / it! // have / you / so / changed / much.)
➡ _____

60 (Mrs. Loisel: / have / I / some / had / times / difficult / of / because / you.)
➡ _____

61 (Mrs. Forestier: / of / because / me? // do / what / mean? / you)
➡ _____

62 (Mrs. Loisel: / you / do / the / remember / diamond / you / necklace / me? / lent // I / well, / it. / lost)
➡ _____

63 (Mrs. Forestier: / you / but / it / returned / to / me.)
➡ _____

64 (Mrs. Loisel: / I / no, / another / returned / just / one / it. / like // took / it / ten / us / to / years / for / pay / it.)
➡ _____

65 (Mrs. Forestier: / bought / you / diamond / a / necklace / replace / to / mine?)
➡ _____

66 (Mrs. Loisel: / yes.)
➡ _____

67 (Mrs. Forestier: / my / oh, / Matilda. / poor // didn't / why / come / you / me / to / and / me / tell / truth? / the // diamond / my / was / necklace / real. / not // was / it / only / worth / francs! / 500)
➡ _____
_____

51 부부는 Forestier 부인에게 돌려줄 목걸이를 산 후 돈을 갚는 데 십 년이 걸린다.

52 그들은 아주 작은 곳으로 이사한다.

53 Loisel 씨는 부업을 구한다. Matilda는 다른 사람들을 위해 빨래를 해 준다.

54 10년 동안의 고된 일로 Matilda는 늙고 지쳤다.

55 십 년 후, Matilda는 Forestier 부인과 거리에서 마주친다.

장면 6

56 Mrs. Loisel: Forestier 부인, 좋은 아침이에요.

57 Mrs. Forestier: 제가 당신을 아나요?

58 Mrs. Loisel: 네, 저예요, Matilda.

59 Mrs. Forestier: 오, 믿을 수 없어요! 당신 너무 많이 변했어요.

60 Mrs. Loisel: 저는 당신 때문에 힘든 시간을 보냈거든요.

61 Mrs. Forestier: 나 때문에요? 무슨 말이에요?

62 Mrs. Loisel: 당신이 빌려준 목걸이 기억하죠? 음, 제가 그걸 잃어버렸어요.

63 Mrs. Forestier: 그런데 그거 나한테 돌려줬잖아요.

64 Mrs. Loisel: 아니요, 나는 당신 것과 똑같은 다른 목걸이를 돌려줬어요. 그 값을 치르느라 십 년이 걸렸어요.

65 Mrs. Forestier: 내 것을 대체하려고 다이아몬드 목걸이를 샀다고요?

66 Mrs. Loisel: 네, 맞아요.

67 Mrs. Forestier: 오, 가엾은 Matilda. 왜 내게 와서 사실을 말하지 않았어요? 제 다이아몬드 목걸이는 진품이 아니었어요. 그건 단돈 오백 프랑짜리였다고요!

※ 다음 우리말을 영어로 쓰시오.

Scene 1

1 이곳은 파리의 Loisel 부부의 집이다.

➡ _____

2 그들의 집은 멋지지만, Loisel 부인은 행복하지 않다.

➡ _____

3 그녀는 젊고 예뻐서 더 화려하고 고급스러운 삶을 원한다.

➡ _____

4 Mrs. Loisel: (혼잣말로) 똑같은 낡은 집과 매일 같이 똑같은 지겨운 저녁 식사. 여기서 사는 게 너무 싫어!

➡ _____

5 Mr. Loisel: Matilda, 나 집에 왔어요. 내가 당신을 위해 무엇을 가져왔는지 봐요!

➡ _____

6 Mrs. Loisel: 뭐예요?.

➡ _____

7 Mr. Loisel: 대사님이 여는 무도회 초대장이에요. 이걸 얻기 위해 엄청난 노력을 했단 말이에요. 모두가 갖고 싶어 했거든요.

➡ _____

8 Mrs. Loisel: (울면서) 내가 그걸 왜 갖고 싶겠어요?

➡ _____

9 Mr. Loisel: Matilda. 무슨 문제 있어요?

➡ _____

10 Mrs. Loisel: 그런 고급스러운 파티에 입고 갈 옷이 하나도 없는걸요. 못가요.

➡ _____

11 Mr. Loisel: 슬퍼하지 말아요. 자, 여기 400프랑을 줄게요. 아름다운 새 드레스를 사요.

➡ _____

Scene 2

12 Mr. Loisel: (Matilda의 새 드레스를 보며) 멋져요, Matilda. 아름답군요!

➡ _____

13 Mrs. Loisel: 뭔가 제대로 맞지 않아요.

➡ _____

14 Mr. Loisel: 뭐가 안 맞을 수 있죠?

➡ _____

15 Mrs. Loisel: (울면서) 오, 안 돼. 어쩌면 좋아요?

➡ _____

16 Mr. Loisel: 뭐예요, 부인?

➡ _____

17 Mrs. Loisel: 이 아름다운 드레스에 어울릴 보석이 하나도 없어요. 내가 너무 불쌍해 보일 거예요!

➡ _____

18 Mr. Loisel: 당신 친구 Forestier 부인에게 부탁해 봐요. 그녀는 자신이 가진 보석을 분명히 빌려줄 거예요.

➡ _____

19 Mrs. Loisel: 그거 좋은 생각이에요! 지금 당장 가봐야겠어요.

➡ _____

Scene 3

20 Mrs. Forestier: Matilda, 이렇게 보게 되어서 정말 좋아요! 무슨 일로 왔어요?

➡ _____

21 Mrs. Loisel: 우리 부부가 대사의 무도회에 초대되었어요.

➡ _____

22 Mrs. Forestier: 대사의 무도회라! 멋지네요! 당신은 분명 신났겠군요.

➡ _____

23 Mrs. Loisel: 네… 그리고 아니기도 해요. 말하기 슬프지만 난 보석이 없어요. 부인에게서 좀 빌릴 수 있을까요?

➡ _____

24 Mrs. Forestier: 물론이죠! 여기 내 보석함이에요.

➡ _____

25 Mrs. Loisel: 와, 부인은 정말 멋진 보석들이 많네요!

➡ _____

26 Mrs. Forestier: 원하는 것 아무거나 골라요.

➡ _____

27 Mrs. Loisel: 이 다이아몬드 목걸이를 빌려줄 수 있나요? 이거 정말 아름다워요!

➡ _____

28 Mrs. Forestier: 당연하죠! 자, 이제 가서 무도회를 즐겨요.

➡ _____

Scene 4

29 Matilda는 완벽한 저녁을 보낸다. 무도회장에 있는 모든 사람들이 아름다운 그녀를 감탄하며 바라본다.

➡ _____

30 Loisel 부부는 아주 늦은 시간이 되어서야 무도회를 떠났다.

➡ _____

31 Mr. Loisel: 정말 길고 긴 밤이었어요. 정말 피곤해요.

➡ _____

32 ▶ Mrs. Loisel: 그렇지만 충분히 가치가 있었어요. 당신, 제가 대사님과 춤춘 것을 아나요?

➡ _____

33 ▶ Mr. Loisel: 당신이 즐거웠다니 기쁘지만 나 아침에 출근해야 해요.

➡ _____

34 ▶ Mrs. Loisel: (거울을 보며) 한 번만 더 볼게요. (충격을 받고) 목걸이… 목걸이가 없어졌어요!

➡ _____

35 ▶ Mr. Loisel: 뭐라고요? 무도회를 떠날 때 걸고 있었소?

➡ _____

36 ▶ Mrs. Loisel: 네, 분명히 하고 있었는데. 가서 찾아 줘요!

➡ _____

37 ▶ Loisel 씨는 길거리를 수색한다.

➡ _____

38 ▶ 그는 무도회장으로 되돌아가 본 다음 경찰서에도 간다.

➡ _____

39 ▶ 목걸이가 발견되지 않자, Loisel 씨는 Matilda에게 그녀의 친구에게 거짓말을 하라고 한다.

➡ _____

40 ▶ Matilda는 Forestier 부인에게 목걸이를 망가뜨려서 돌려주기 전에 고쳐 주겠다고 말한다.

➡ _____

41 ▶ 부부는 비슷한 것을 찾을 시간이 필요하다.

➡ _____

Scene 5

42 ▶ Mr. Loisel: (보석상에게) 실례합니다. 저 다이아몬드 목걸이 좀 볼 수 있을까요?

➡ _____

43 ▶ Mrs. Loisel: (속삭이며) 거의 똑같아요. 저걸 꼭 사야만 해요!

➡ _____

44 ▶ Mr. Loisel: 이거 얼마인가요?

➡ _____

45 ▶ Jewler: 40,000프랑이에요.

➡ _____

46 ▶ Mr. Loisel: 36,000에 안 될까요?

➡ _____

47 ▶ Mrs. Loisel: 부탁드려요, 우린 이게 정말 필요하거든요.

➡ _____

48 ▶ Jewler: 음, 그럼… 36,000프랑에 하시죠.

➡ _____

49 ▶ 그들은 36,000프랑이 없다. 그건 큰돈이다.

➡ _____

50 ▶ 그래서 그들은 돈을 빌린다.

➡ _____

51 부부는 Forestier 부인에게 돌려줄 목걸이를 산 후 돈을 갚는 데 십 년이 걸린다.

➡ _____

52 그들은 아주 작은 곳으로 이사한다.

➡ _____

53 Loisel 씨는 부업을 구한다. Matilda는 다른 사람들을 위해 빨래를 해 준다.

➡ _____

54 10년 동안의 고된 일로 Matilda는 늙고 지쳤다.

➡ _____

55 십 년 후, Matilda는 Forestier 부인과 거리에서 마주친다.

➡ _____

Scene 6

56 Mrs. Loisel: Forestier 부인, 좋은 아침이에요.

➡ _____

57 Mrs. Forestier: 제가 당신을 아나요?

➡ _____

58 Mrs. Loisel: 네, 저예요, Matilda.

➡ _____

59 Mrs. Forestier: 오, 믿을 수 없어요! 당신 너무 많이 변했어요.

➡ _____

60 Mrs. Loisel: 저는 당신 때문에 힘든 시간을 보냈거든요.

➡ _____

61 Mrs. Forestier: 나 때문에요? 무슨 말이에요?

➡ _____

62 Mrs. Loisel: 당신이 빌려준 목걸이 기억하죠? 음, 제가 그걸 잃어버렸어요.

➡ _____

63 Mrs. Forestier: 그런데 그거 나한테 돌려줬잖아요.

➡ _____

64 Mrs. Loisel: 아니요, 나는 당신 것과 똑같은 다른 목걸이를 돌려줬어요. 그 값을 치르느라 십 년이 걸렸어요.

➡ _____

65 Mrs. Forestier: 내 것을 대체하려고 다이아몬드 목걸이를 샀다고요?

➡ _____

66 Mrs. Loisel: 네, 맞아요.

➡ _____

67 Mrs. Forestier: 오, 가엾은 Matilda. 왜 내게 와서 사실을 말하지 않았어요? 제 다이아몬드 목걸이는 진품이 아니었어요. 그건 단돈 오백 프랑짜리였다고요!

➡ _____

_____

MEMO

MEMO

2학기 전과정 적중100 plus

영어 기출 문제집

영어 기출 문제집

적중100 plus
2학기 전과정

2학기

정답 및 해설

시사 | 박준언

중 3

적중100

영어 기출 문제집

적중'100

2학기

정답 및 해설

시사 | 박준언

중 3

Lesson 6

Meet the World

시험대비 실력평가
p.08

01 ③   02 knee   03 ④   04 ②
05 be covered with   06 ①
07 suggest   08 ⑤

01 • 이 옷감은 천연(natural) 섬유로 만들어졌다. • 북악산은 방문객들에게 경탄할 만한 자연의(natural) 아름다움과 문화적 자산으로 깊은 인상을 남긴다.

02 헬멧과 무릎 보호대를 포함한 안전 장비를 착용하는 것 또한 권고된다. <영영풀이> '다리가 구부러지는 관절'의 의미로 'knee(무릎)'가 적절하다.

03 '외국에 있거나 외국으로 가는'의 의미로 'abroad(해외에, 해외로)'가 적절하다. 'aboard'는 '(배·항공기·열차·버스 등을) 타고'의 의미이다.

04 '자주 그리고 많은 사람에게 또는 많은 장소에서 일어나는'의 의미로 'common(흔한)'이 적절하다.

05 be covered with: ~로 덮여 있다

06 (A) 그녀는 네 명의 심사위원들을 놀라게 했고, 그들 모두로부터 '합격'을 얻었습니다. (B) 그들은 요한 바흐, 게오르그 헨델, 그리고 안토니오 비발디가 작곡한 음악을 추천합니다.

07 유의어 관계다. 풍경 : 제안하다

08 너한테서 멋진 생일 선물 받기를 기대하고 있을게! / '~을 기대하다'는 'look forward to+동명사'를 쓴다.

서술형 시험대비
p.09

01 (1) filled (2) suggests (3) appreciate
   (4) landscape
02 waterfall
03 (1) throughout (2) confused (3) wildly
   (4) hot spring
04 (1) length, 길이 (2) north, 북쪽 (3) rival, 경쟁자
   (4) wedding, 결혼식
05 tradition(s), traditional

01 (1) 그는 세상을 건강한 사람들로 가득 찬 더 나은 곳으로 만들길 희망합니다. (2) 아처 교수는 여러분의 삶에서 좋고 긍정적인 것을 보라고 제안합니다. (3) 이 행사는 어린이들로 하여금 모든 형태의 예술의 진가를 알아보는 것을 가르칩니다. (4) 뉴질랜드는 숨이 멎을 듯한 아름다운 경치와 풍부한 야생동물로 유명한 나라

이다.

02 나이아가라 폭포는 북아메리카에서 가장 인기 있는 폭포입니다.

03 (1) throughout: 도처에 (2) confused: 혼란스러워 하는 (3) wildly: 거칠게 (4) hot spring: 온천

04 (1) 한쪽 끝에서 반대편 끝까지 어떤 것을 측정하는 것 (2) 일출을 바라볼 때 당신의 왼쪽에 있는 방향 (3) 다른 사람과 같은 목적이나 목표를 위해 경쟁하는 사람 (4) 결혼식과 그에 따르는 식사나 파티와 같은 축하 행사

05 • 한국은 훌륭한 문화와 독특한 전통(tradition)을 가진 아름다운 나라입니다. • 그것은 "이열치열"이라는 전통적인(traditional) 방법이야. 명사 'way'를 수식하는 형용사가 적절하다.

교과서
Conversation

핵심 Check
p.10~11

1 let's talk about what we will prepare for the World Food Festival
2 visit

교과서 대화문 익히기

Check(√) True or False
p.12

1 T 2 F 3 T 4 T

교과서 확인학습
p.14~15

Listen & Speak 1 A

1. Let's talk, other / what a kilt is / traditional clothing, looks like, knee-length, plaid pattern / with / unique because / interesting, to try, on

2. about, prepare / famous / popular, dish / What, look like / fried, with / interesting. Let's prepare

Listen & Speak 2 A

1. arrived in / looking forward to / suggest, visit / the highest, in a lot of / fantastic view / sounds

2. invited, potluck / know, share / recommend that /

suggest, take, How / spicy, to carry / for

Can you tell me about / a few years ago. First, let's / What food, famous for / The most famous, filled with, melted / suggestion, that are popular / suggest, Independence, history / information / pleasure

Welcome, capital, popular dish, lots of, beaches

시험대비 기본평가　　　　　　　　　　p.16

01 suggest, visit　　　02 ④　　　03 ②
04 ⑤

01 상대방에게 무언가를 제안하거나 권유할 때 쓰는 표현으로 'I suggest (that)+주어+(should)+동사원형'을 사용한다.
02 B의 대답으로 보아 여행에 관한 주제로 이야기를 한다는 것을 알 수 있다. 'Let's talk about ~.(~에 대하여 이야기해 봅시다.)'라는 주제를 소개하는 표현이 적절하다.
03 '인도를 방문하면 무엇을 할 수 있을까?'라는 물음에 '나는 우리가 그곳을 방문할 것을 제안해.'라고 말하는 것은 어색하다.
04 'Let's talk about ~.(~에 대하여 이야기해 봅시다.)'는 주제를 소개하는 표현이다.

시험대비 실력평가　　　　　　　　　p.17~18

01 ⑤　　　02 ④　　　03 ③　　　04 ②
05 it is a skirt for men　　　06 ②
07 the highest mountain in Hong Kong and is in a lot of movies
08 visit Victoria Peak, enjoy the fantastic view　09 ④

01 Jessie가 몇 년 전에 거기에 갔었다는 말을 한 다음 '먼저 음식에 대해 이야기해 보자.'라고 말하는 것으로 보아 빈칸에는 그 도시에 관한 정보를 알려달라는 표현이 적절하다.
02 독립 기념관이 Andy가 가장 좋아하는 장소라는 내용은 대화에 언급되어 있지 않다.
03 포틀럭 저녁 모임에 나를 초대했다는 말에 이어서 → (C) 'the dinner'가 'a potluck dinner'를 받는 명사로 이어지고→ (B) 가져갈 음식을 추천해 달라고 부탁하고 → (A) 김밥을 추천한다. 마지막으로 (D) 긍정의 대답이 오는 것이 자연스럽다.
04 학생들은 다섯 살에 학교에 간다는 B의 대답으로 보아 영국의 학교생활에 관해 이야기해 보자는 ②가 자연스럽다.
05 남자를 위한 치마이기 때문에 킬트가 독특하다.

---

06 단수 주어인 It 다음에 looks와 병렬 관계인 단수 동사 has가 되어야 한다.
07 'the 최상급+단수 명사' 형태로 정관사 'the'를 추가하고, 'high'는 'highest'로 변형시킨다.
08 Mike와 그의 어머니는 빅토리아 피크를 방문하고 홍콩의 환상적인 경관을 즐길 것이다.
09 ④번은 '어느 나라를 조사할 것인지 이야기해 보자.'라는 말에 '그러고 싶지만, 그곳을 방문하는 것이 기대 돼.'라고 말하는 것은 어색하다.

서술형 시험대비　　　　　　　　　　p.19

01 It is Independence Hall.
02 I suggest you visit Independence Hall, which is very important in American history.
03 I suggest you take some Korean food.
04 'Let's talk about traditional clothing from other countries.

01 질문: 필라델피아에서 관광객들에게 인기 있는 장소는 어디인가?
02 '명사, who/which ~'에서 'who/which ~'는 앞에 오는 명사의 추가적인 설명을 하고 '접속사+대명사'로 바꾸어 쓸 수 있다.
03 동사 'suggest(제안하다)' 다음에는 명사절을 이끄는 접속사 'that'이 생략되고 'that'절에서는 조동사 'should'를 쓰는데, 이를 생략하고 동사원형을 사용하여 'I suggest (that)+주어+(should)+동사원형 ~.'의 구문으로 나타낸다.
04 'Let's talk about ~(~에 대하여 이야기해 보자.)'를 이용하여 영작한다.

교과서

Grammar

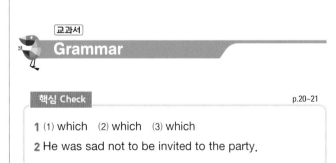

핵심 Check　　　　　　　　　　　p.20~21

1 (1) which　(2) which　(3) which
2 He was sad not to be invited to the party.

시험대비 기본평가　　　　　　　　　　p.22

01 ③　　　02 ⑤　　　03 ④　　　04 ⑤

01 '접속사+대명사'는 관계대명사로 바꿀 수 있고, 앞에 콤마가 있으면 '계속적 용법'의 관계대명사가 된다. 선행사가 사물이므로

3

계속적 용법의 관계대명사 which가 적절하다.

02 ① 부사적 용법(목적) ② 부사적 용법(목적) ③ 부사적 용법(감정의 원인) ④ 부사적 용법(판단의 근거) 조동사 must는 '~임에 틀림없다'는 의미로 판단에 쓰인다. ⑤ 명사적 용법(목적어)

03 who는 계속적 용법의 관계대명사로서, 선행사는 사람인 the boy이다. 콤마 뒤에 접속사 and와 주어로 대명사 he로 바꿔 쓸 수 있다.

04 <보기>는 부사적 용법(감정의 원인)이다. ①, ② 부사적 용법(목적) ③ 명사적 용법(목적어) ④ 부사적 용법(판단의 근거) 조동사 can't는 '~일 리 없다'라는 의미로 '판단'에 쓰인다. ⑤ 부사적 용법(감정의 원인)

시험대비 실력평가   p.23~25

01 ⓑ that → which, ⓒ which → who, ⓓ speak → speaks 또는 spoke, ⓔ which → that 또는 생략 또는 in which, ⓕ where → which 또는 lived in → lived

02 ③   **03** who you have already heard about

04 ⑤   **05** ④   **06** ⑤   **07** ④

08 ①   **09** ④

10 She goes there to feed the cats.   **11** ④

12 ④   **13** ④   **14** ①   **15** ②

---

01 ⓑ 선행사는 the lecture of the professor Potter인데 계속적 용법이므로 that은 쓸 수 없다. ⓒ 선행사가 사람이므로 who ⓓ 선행사 a parrot이 단수이므로 관계대명사 뒤의 동사도 일치시킨다. ⓔ the way+that[in which] ⓕ 전치사 in이 있으므로, where를 which로 고치거나 in을 생략한다.

02 ③은 to부정사의 명사적 용법으로 사용되었다. 나머지는 모두 부사적 용법이다.

03 관계대명사의 계속적 용법으로 선행사 The Maori people을 받아 who로 시작하여 about으로 마무리하는 것이 적절하다.

04 빈칸은 모두 계속적 용법의 관계대명사가 들어가는 자리이다. 문장의 선행사는 각각 (A) 앞 문장 전체, (B) Wellington, (C) someone이다.

05 ①, ②, ③번은 계속적 용법의 관계대명사 which가 적절하다. ⑤번은 동사의 수의 일치가 부적절, ① that → which, ② who → which, ③ of which → which, ⑤ come → comes

06 to부정사의 부정은 to부정사 바로 앞에 not을 쓴다. not to see는 in order not to see 또는 so as not to see로도 표현 가능하다.

07 be동사 뒤에 감정을 나타내는 형용사와 to부정사가 결합하면, '감정의 원인이나 이유'가 되는데, be동사 앞에 조동사 will이 오면, '~한다면'의 뜻이 되어, '조건'의 용법으로 쓰인다. ②의 경우, 'be heard to say' 형태는 '마을 사람들이 말하는 것이 들리다'는 내용

이 되므로 옳지 않다.

08 ① 내가 삼촌에게 수리를 맡겼고, '삼촌이 차를 수리한 것'이 선행사이므로, 관계대명사 which가 적절하다.

09 ④ 내용상 '코로나 전염병이 발발한' 2019년을 선행사로 받는 관계대명사이므로, 관계대명사 앞에 in이 있어야 한다. basketball court와는 무관하다. which를 in which 또는 관계부사 when으로 바꾸는 것이 적절하다.

10 엄마가 미주에게 미나가 공원에 매일 가는 이유를 물었고, 고양이들에게 '먹이를 주기 위해' 가는 것이므로, to부정사의 부사적 용법을 활용한다. 3인칭 단수 현재시제이므로 go를 goes로 하는 것에 유의한다.

11 주어진 문장의 to threaten과 ④번은 to부정사의 부사적 용법의 '목적'으로 쓰였다. ① 명사적 용법 ② 부사적 용법의 '결과' ③ 부사적 용법의 '감정의 원인' ⑤ 가주어 It과 함께 쓰인 진주어로 명사적 용법 *threaten: 위협하다

12 주어진 문장의 to watch와 ④번은 부사적 용법의 '판단의 근거'로 쓰였다. '적은 마오리 전사들의 하카 동작들을 보고 두려웠음에 틀림없다' ① 부사적 용법의 '목적' ② 부사적 용법의 '결과' ③ 부사적 용법의 '감정의 이유, 원인' ⑤ 형용사적 용법의 '명사 수식'(아기 고양이들을 덮어 줄 어떤 것)

13 주어진 문장의 to learn은 to부정사의 부사적 용법의 '목적'으로 쓰였다. ④만 부사적 용법 중 '감정의 원인, 이유'이다.

14 주어진 문장의 to scare는 to부정사의 부사적 용법의 '목적'으로 쓰였다. ①만 형용사적 용법(명사 수식)으로 사용되었다.

15 옳은 문장은 ⓐ, ⓔ 2개이다. ⓑ who → which, ⓒ and who → who, 또는 and who → and she ⓓ who → which

---

서술형 시험대비   p.26~27

01 (1) The Maori people dance to scare the enemy.

(2) Dolphins come up to the surface to breathe.

(3) She must be unwise to believe the word.

(4) The native people of New Zealand will be glad to hear the word.

(5) Jiho's room is not easy to clean.

(6) Simcheong was pleased to see her father again.

02 (1) George Washington is widely known for the episode of his honesty, which was not true.

(2) Sumin fell in love with Brian, who met her only twice.

(3) The Maori people were so good at haka dancing, which made the visitors also dance with excitement.

(4) I added some more hot sauce into the food, which made my mom upset.

---

03 (1) Jack walked to school to save some money.
   (2) Caroline exercises hard every day to lose weight.
   (3) Potter was surprised to watch the news.
   (4) Angela woke up to find herself alone in the dark.
   (5) Sam must be happy to meet her old friend.

04 Jisoo's parents volunteered to serve the meal during lunchtime, which made her feel proud.

05 (1) My grandma exercises every day to keep healthy.
   (2) She was pleased to receive thank-you notes from her neighbors.
   (3) Sandra went to the river to catch some fish.
   (4) The stone was too heavy for me to lift.
   (5) You need ice and sugar to make Bingsu.
   (6) The problem was impossible for Peter to solve in an hour.
   (7) A lot of firefighters ran into the woods to rescue the koalas.

06 (1) that → which
   (2) who → which
   (3) who → which

07 we learned the word kiwi, which has several meanings

01 (1) to부정사의 부사적 용법 중 '목적'이다. (2) to부정사의 부사적 용법 중 '목적'이다. '~로 올라오다'는 come up to로 표현한다. (3) to부정사의 부사적 용법 중 '판단의 근거'이다. 조동사 must는 '~임에 틀림없다'로 사용한다. (4) to부정사의 부사적 용법 중 '조건'이다. (5) to부정사의 부사적 용법 중 '형용사 수식'이다. '형용사+to부정사'는 '~하기에 ⋯한'으로 해석한다. (6) to부정사의 부사적 용법 중 '감정의 원인'이다.

02 각 문장의 관계대명사의 선행사는 (1)은 the episode, (2)는 Brian, (3), (4)는 앞 문장 전체이다.

03 각 문장의 to부정사는 부사적 용법 중 (1) 목적, (2) 목적, (3) 감정의 원인 (4) 결과 (5) 판단의 근거 등으로 사용되었다. (5)에 조동사 must를 반드시 사용해야 하기 때문에 Sam must be happy로 문장을 만드는 것에 유의한다.

04 앞 문장 전체 내용을 선행사로, '계속적' 용법의 관계대명사 which를 사용한다. volunteer가 동사로 사용되는 것에 유의한다.

05 to부정사의 부사적 용법을 사용하는 것이므로, 해석과 어법에 맞게 고친다. (1) 내 할머니는 건강을 유지하기 위해 매일 운동하신다. (2) 그녀는 이웃들로부터 감사 쪽지들을 받아서 기뻤다. (3) Sandra는 물고기를 잡으러 강에 갔다. (4) 그 돌은 내가 들기에는 너무 무거웠다. (5) 네가 빙수를 만들기 위해서는 얼음과

설탕이 필요하다. (6) 그 문제는 Peter가 한 시간 안에 풀기에 불가능했다. (7) 수많은 소방관들이 코알라들을 구출하기 위해서 숲으로 뛰어들었다.

06 모든 문장이 앞 문장 전체가 선행사이므로, 계속적 용법의 which가 적절하다.

07 우리말을 영작하면 Yesterday, we learned the word kiwi, and it has several meanings.가 된다. 이 문장에서 and it을 계속적 용법의 관계대명사 which로 바꿔 영작하는 것이 적절하다.

교과서 Reading

확인문제 p.28

1 T 2 F 3 F 4 T

확인문제 p.29

1 T 2 F 3 T 4 T 5 T 6 F

교과서 확인학습 A p.30~31

01 a place of natural beauty, lakes, waterfalls
02 two main islands
03 are mountains, are covered with
04 be amazed by
05 many hot springs, with
06 Because of, have been made
07 will surely appreciate
08 hear, comes to
09 a couple of meanings
10 the name, delicious
11 is grown, is known as
12 one, New Zealand's native birds
13 special to, because, symbol
14 a nickname for, from
15 are sometimes called
16 that, the name of
17 confused, uses, which has
18 let's talk, They, the native people
19 live on, long before, arrived
20 an important part, today's
21 is taught, there are
22 in many parts of

23 visit, villages, experience, culture

24 say, to, will be glad to hear, means

25 Have, watched

26 look scary because, shout, move, wildly

27 who, heard about, doing, as

28 however, do, at sport matches

29 For example, national rugby team members, before

30 famous all over

31 will, agree that, must be scared

32 Like, a national symbol

교과서 확인학습 B
p.32~33

1 New Zealand is a place of natural beauty. It has many beautiful lakes and waterfalls.

2 New Zealand has two main islands, the South Island and the North Island.

3 In the South Island, there are mountains that are covered with snow all year round.

4 You will be amazed by the fantastic views.

5 In the North Island, there are many hot springs, lakes, and areas with green grass.

6 Because of its natural beauty, many famous movies have been made in New Zealand.

7 If you visit New Zealand, you will surely appreciate its nature.

8 When you hear the word kiwi, what comes to your mind?

9 Maybe a fruit, but, in New Zealand the word kiwi has a couple of meanings.

10 First, kiwi is the name of a delicious, green fruit.

11 A lot of kiwi fruit is grown there, so New Zealand is known as the land of kiwi fruit.

12 Kiwi is also the name of one of New Zealand's native birds.

13 The kiwi is special to New Zealanders because it is the symbol of the nation.

14 Also, kiwi is a nickname for people from New Zealand.

15 Today, New Zealanders are sometimes called Kiwis throughout the world.

16 Now, you know that kiwi is the name of a fruit, a bird, and also a people.

17 Next time, don't become confused when someone uses the word kiwi, which has several meanings.

18 Now, let's talk about the Maori. They are the native people of New Zealand.

19 They went to live on the islands long before Europeans arrived.

20 The Maori culture is an important part of today's New Zealand society.

21 The Maori language is taught at some schools and there are Maori language radio and TV stations.

22 There are Maori villages in many parts of the country.

23 You can visit Maori villages and experience Maori culture.

24 If you say "kia ora" to the villagers, they will be glad to hear it. It means "hi" in English.

25 Have you ever watched the haka?

26 The haka may look scary because haka dancers shout and move their bodies wildly.

27 The Maori people, who you've already heard about, started doing the haka as a war dance.

28 Today, however, New Zealanders do the haka at sport matches, weddings, or other important events.

29 For example, New Zealand's national rugby team members do the haka before every match.

30 It is famous all over the world.

31 If you see the haka, you will probably agree that the rival team must be scared.

32 Like the kiwi bird, the haka is a national symbol.

시험대비 실력평가
p.34~37

01 ④   02 ③

03 New Zealand is made up with two main islands, the South Island and the North Island.

04 It's because it is the symbol of the nation.

05 ④   06 ②   07 ④   08 ③

09 ⑤

10 They do the haka before every match.

11 the rival team must be scared

12 ③   13 ⑤

14 They do the haka at sport matches, weddings, or other important events.

15 ④   16 ②   17 ④

18 It's because a lot of kiwi fruit is grown there.

19 ⑤   20 We can experience Maori culture.

21 ④   22 appreciate 23 ③   24 ③

01 이어지는 내용은 뉴질랜드 자연의 아름다움에 관하여 이야기하고 있으므로 ④번이 가장 적절하다.

02 ⓑ는 '일 년 내내'라는 의미이다. ①, ④ 가끔, ② 갑자기, ③ 일 년 내내, ⑤ 여기저기에

03 뉴질랜드는 두 개의 주요한 섬인 남섬과 북섬으로 이루어져 있다.

04 키위새가 뉴질랜드 사람들에게 특별한 이유는 그 새가 국가의 상징이기 때문이다.

05 키위는 뉴질랜드 출신 사람에 대한 별명이라고 하였다.

06 위 글은 뉴질랜드에서 키위라는 단어가 갖는 여러 가지 의미에 관한 글이다. 따라서 ②번이 가장 적절하다.

07 마오리어를 몇몇 학교에서 가르친다고 하였다.

08 마오리족은 전쟁 춤으로 하카를 추었지만 오늘날 뉴질랜드 사람들은 하카를 운동 경기, 결혼식, 또는 다른 중요한 행사가 있을 때 한다는 연결이 자연스럽다. 따라서 however가 적절하다.

09 마오리족은 하카 춤을 줄 때 소리 지르고 몸을 사납게 움직인다고 하였다.

10 뉴질랜드의 럭비 국가 대표 팀 선수들은 모든 경기 전에 하카를 춘다고 하였다.

11 must는 강한 추측을 나타내는 의미로 쓰일 수 있다.

12 하카는 무섭게 보이고 전쟁 춤으로 추었다고 하였으므로 문맥상 ③번이 가장 적절하다.

13 당신이 하카를 본다면, 상대 팀이 겁을 먹을 것이라는 것에 동의할 것이라고 하였으므로 ⑤번이 글의 내용과 일치한다.

14 오늘날 사람들은 운동 경기나 결혼식, 다른 중요한 행사에서 하카를 춘다고 하였다.

15 every 뒤에는 단수 명사가 온다. 따라서 match라고 써야 한다.

16 키위는 여러 뜻을 가지고 있기 때문에 그 단어를 사용할 때 혼동하지 말라는 말이 문맥상 가장 적절하다.

17 키위가 뉴질랜드 출신의 사람들을 부르는 별명이라고 말하고 난 후 오늘날 뉴질랜드인들이 전 세계적으로 키위라고 불린다는 설명이 이어지는 것이 적절하다.

18 뉴질랜드가 키위의 나라로 알려진 이유는 많은 키위가 그곳에서 자라기 때문이다.

19 마오리족에 대해 이야기해 보자고 말하며 (C) 마오리족이 누구인지 설명, 그들이 오늘날 뉴질랜드 사회의 중요한 부분이라고 말함. - (B) 그것에 대한 뒷받침 문장을 진술. - (A) (B)에서 언급한 마오리 마을에 방문하여 그들의 문화를 경험할 수 있다고 말함.

20 마오리 마을을 방문하면 마오리 문화를 경험할 수 있다.

21 밑줄 친 ⓐ는 감정의 원인을 나타내는 to부정사의 부사적 용법으로 쓰였다. ① 부사적 용법 중 판단의 이유 ② 진주어 ③ 형용사

적 용법(paper 수식) ④ 부사적 용법 중 감정의 원인 ⑤ 부사적 용법 중 목적(~하기 위해서)

22 무언가의 좋은 질을 알아봤기 때문에 그것을 좋아하게 되는 것은 '진가를 알아보다, 인정하다(appreciate)'이다.

23 사물을 선행사로 취하는 관계대명사이므로 which가 적절하다.

24 굉장히 멋진 경관에 놀랄 것이라고 하였으므로 ③번이 글의 내용과 일치한다.

🦉 서술형 시험대비   p.38~39

01 In the South Island, there are mountains that are covered with snow all year around.

02 We should go to the North Island.

03 If you visit New Zealand, you will surely appreciate its nature.

04 It is famous for its natural beauty.

05 a fruit, a bird, and also a people

06 which

07 A lot of kiwi fruit is grown in New Zealand.

08 several meanings of kiwi

09 The Maori went to live on New Zealand long before Europeans arrived.

10 We can find Maori villages in many parts of the country.

11 We should say "kia ora."

12 Canada → New Zealand
their food → their culture

13 Have you ever watched the haka?

14 It's because haka dancers shout and move their bodies wildly.

15 We are likely to see them do the haka before their match.

16 The haka, the kiwi bird

01 뉴질랜드의 남섬에는 일 년 내내 눈으로 덮인 산들이 있다고 하였다.

02 북섬에는 많은 온천이 있다고 하였으므로, 온천을 즐기고 싶다면 북섬으로 가야한다.

03 시간이나 조건의 부사절에서 현재시제로 미래를 표현한다. 따라서 will visit이 아닌 visit이라고 쓰는 것이 적절하다.

04 뉴질랜드는 자연의 아름다움으로 유명한 곳임을 알 수 있다.

05 위 글에 언급된 키위의 다양한 의미로는 과일, 새, 그리고 국민의 명칭이 있다.

06 불완전한 절을 이끌며 콤마 뒤에서 쓰이는 것은 관계대명사 which이다.

07 많은 키위들이 뉴질랜드에서 자란다고 하였다.

7

08 해석: 키위의 몇 가지 의미를 이해하지 않으면, 당신은 혼란을 느낄 것이다.

09 마오리족은 유럽인들이 도착하기 오래 전에 뉴질랜드에 와서 살았다고 하였다.

10 나라의 여러 곳에 마오리 마을이 있다고 하였다.

11 "kia ora"는 영어로 "안녕"이라는 의미의 마오리어라고 하였다.

12 마오리족은 뉴질랜드의 원주민이며 그들의 문화는 오늘날 뉴질랜드 사회의 중요한 부분이라고 하였다.

13 하카를 본 적이 있는지 경험을 묻고 있으므로 현재완료 시제를 사용하여 답하는 것이 적절하다.

14 하카 춤을 추는 사람들이 소리 지르고, 그들의 몸을 사납게 움직이기 때문에 하카는 무서워 보일 수도 있다고 하였다.

15 위 글의 내용에 따르면, 우리는 뉴질랜드 럭비 선수들이 경기 전에 하카를 추는 것을 볼 수 있다.

16 키위뿐만 아니라 하카는 나라의 상징이다.

영역별 핵심문제   p.41~45

01 (a)chieve   02 ④   03 ⑤   04 ①
05 With the help of   06 ③   07 ④
08 I suggest we watch a soccer game.   09 ④
10 It is a big sandwich filled with beef and melted cheese.
11 ③   12 ③, ⑤   13 ④   14 ④
15 ⑤
16 The public library introduced a new system, which would help the people to easily borrow the audio books that had always been difficult to borrow.   17 ②
18 ①
19 do the haka to scare their opponents
20 There are many hot springs, lakes, and areas with green grass in the North Island of New Zealand.   21 ②   22 ⑤   23 ③
24 scare   25 ⑤   26 (C)–(B)–(A)
27 We should visit a Maori village.
28 Many people visit New Zealand to enjoy the beautiful nature.   29 ④

01 유의어 관계다. 해외에 – 성취하다, 달성하다

02 (A) 중국인들은 판다를 용기의 상징으로 여깁니다. (B) 마오리족 사람들은 뉴질랜드의 원주민입니다.

03 십자 모양의 선과 사각형으로 된 무늬

04 '초대받은 사람들이 먹을 것을 가지고 오는 식사'의 의미로 'potluck(각자 준비한 음식을 나눠먹는 식사)'이 적절하다.

05 with the help of: ~의 도움을 받아서

06 ③ recommend: 추천하다

07 '그룹 1의 사진이 매우 좋다고 생각한다.'라는 B의 답으로 보아 그룹 1의 사진에 대한 주제로 이야기를 하고 있다는 것을 알 수 있다.

08 제안하는 표현은 'I suggest (that)+주어+(should)+동사원형'을 이용한다.

09 주어진 문장이 '멋진 제안이야. 먹어볼게.'라는 뜻이므로 샌드위치에 관한 이야기 다음인 ④가 적절하다.

10 cheese steak sandwich는 '소고기와 녹인 치즈로 채워진 큰 샌드위치'라고 하고 있다.

11 '미국의 독립 기념관은 무엇을 위한 것인가?'에 대한 답은 대화에 언급되어 있지 않다.

12 ① 선행사가 lecture이고, 계속적 용법이다. that → which ② 계속적 용법의 관계대명사 which는 맞게 쓰였으나 선행사가 a traditional market이므로, 동사는 단수 형태를 써야 한다. sell → sells ④ 내용상 선행사가 사람이 아닌 the works이다. 관계대명사 뒤의 be동사도 are이다. who → which

13 '모든 문장이 '회사에 늦지 않기 위해서'라는 목적을 나타내는데, ④만 '일찍 일어나지만 늦지 않는다'라는 이상한 내용이 되고 있다.

14 주어진 문장의 to find는 부사적 용법의 '목적'으로 사용되었으며, ④를 제외한 모든 문장은 쓰임이 같다. ④의 to make는 동사 like의 '목적어'로서, 명사적 용법으로 사용되었다.

15 주어진 문장의 to film은 부사적 용법의 '목적'으로 사용되었다. ⑤의 to smoke는 동사 promised의 '목적어'로서, 명사적 용법으로 사용되었다. 나머지는 각각 ①, ④ 부사적 용법의 '목적' ② 부사적 용법의 '원인' ③ 부사적 용법의 '결과'이다.

16 본문에 나온 표현만으로 계속적 관계대명사와 제한적 관계대명사를 모두 사용해야 하기 때문에, 보충 설명이 필요한 두 번째 문장을 계속적 용법의 'which'로 연결하는 것이 적절하다.

17 관계대명사 뒤의 동사는 선행사의 수에 일치시켜야 한다. 선행사가 class이므로, which are → which is로 하는 것이 적절하다.

18 '접속사와 대명사 and it은 관계대명사 which로 쓸 수 있고, 'the one that(선행사+관계대명사)'는 what과 같다. ①은 선행사 뒤에 what이 있어 부적절하다.

19 to부정사의 부사적 용법을 활용하여 알맞게 영작한다.

20 뉴질랜드의 북섬에는 많은 온천과 호수, 초원 지역이 있다고 하였다.

21 빈칸 (A)에는 전치사 with가 들어간다. ① be anxious about: 조바심을 내다 ② be crowded with: ~으로 붐비다 ③ devote oneself to: ~에 전념하다, 몰두하다 ④ apply for: ~에 지원하다 ⑤ be accustomed to: ~에 익숙하다

22 Because는 접속사이므로 주어와 동사가 포함된 절을 이끌어야

한다. 따라서 Because of라고 쓰는 것이 적절하다.

23 마오리인들이 전쟁 춤으로 하카를 추기 시작했다는 문장에 이어지는 예시문은 뉴질랜드 럭비 국가 대표 팀이 경기 전에 하카를 하는 것에 관한 내용이므로, 오늘날 뉴질랜드 사람이 운동 경기에서 하카를 한다는 말이 ③번에 들어가는 것이 적절하다.

24 '당신이 하카를 본다면, 상대 팀이 겁을 먹을 것이라는 것에 아마 동의할 것이다'라고 하였으므로 뉴질랜드 럭비 국가 대표 팀 선수들이 경기 전에 하카를 추는 이유는 상대 팀 선수들을 겁주기 위해서임을 알 수 있다.

25 하카 춤을 추는 사람들이 소리 지르고, 그들의 몸을 사납게 움직이기 때문에 하카는 무서워 보일 수 있다고 하였다.

26 (C) 뉴질랜드에 대해 아는지 물으며 간단한 소개 (B) 뉴질랜드에 온다면 마오리 마을을 방문하여 마오리족의 전통 요리를 먹어 보는 것을 제안함 (A) 그들의 요리 방법에 관한 이야기로 이어지는 것이 가장 자연스럽다.

27 뉴질랜드 원주민 문화를 보고 싶다면 마오리 마을을 방문해야 한다.

28 많은 사람들은 아름다운 자연을 즐기기 위해 뉴질랜드를 방문한다고 하였다.

29 뉴질랜드는 두 개의 본섬과 600개의 작은 섬들로 되어 있다고 하였다.

단원별 예상문제 p.46~49

01 natural 02 ③
03 I'm looking forward to our visit. 04 ③
05 ④ 06 traditional 07 ③
08 ⑤
09 are spoken → speak, visits → visit
10 ①
11 (1) ⓐ (2) ⓒ (3) ⓕ (4) ⓓ (5) ⓓ (6) ⓔ (7) ⓖ (8) ⓑ
   (9) ⓕ (10) ⓒ (11) ⓔ (12) ⓖ (13) ⓐ
12 ③ 13 ② 14 ④ 15 ⑤
16 ③ 17 Because of its natural beauty.
18 hills → mountains / tall trees → green grass
19 ③ 20 ③

01 반의어 관계다. 혼란스러워 하는-침착한 : 인위적인-자연의, 천연의

02 시골을 가로지르거나 숲을 지나가는 거친 길

03 '~을 기대하다'라는 표현으로 'I'm looking forward to+명사/동명사'를 사용한다.

04 Victoria Peak은 홍콩에서 가장 높은 산이다.

05 남자를 위한 치마라고 했기 때문에 'common'을 'unique'로 바꾸어야 한다.

06 '오랜 시간 동안 한 무리의 사람들에게 계속되어 온 관습이나 행

동 방식을 따르는'의 의미로 'traditional(전통적인)'이 적절하다.

07 빈칸 다음에 '그건 뜨거운 감자튀김이 곁들여진 튀긴 생선이야.'라고 G가 말하는 것으로 보아 'fish and chips'가 어떻게 생겼는지 묻는 말이 적절하다.

08 미트 파이가 어떻게 생겼는지는 대화에서 언급되어 있지 않다.

09 사람들이 영어를 사용하는 능동의 의미이므로 수동태 'are spoken'을 'speak'로 고치고, 복수 주어 'lots of tourists' 뒤에 복수 동사 'visit'이 적절하다.

10 관계대명사 '계속적' 용법의 문장들이다. ①번의 that을 which로 고쳐야 한다.

11 (3) only to V는 '~했으나 결국 ~하다'라는 뜻이다. (6) must have p.p.는 '~했음에 틀림없다'는 뜻이므로 '판단'을 표현한다. (13) '진주어'로 쓰인 '명사적 용법'

12 ③번은 선행사가 sea water가 아니라 '앞 문장 전체'이다.

13 ⓐ, ⓒ, ⓓ, ⓔ는 to부정사의 부사적 용법 중 '목적'이다. 나머지는 각각 명사적 용법으로 ⓑ, ⓕ는 목적어로, ⓖ는 진주어로 쓰였다.

14 주어진 문장의 to부정사는 부사적 용법 중 '감정의 원인'으로 쓰였다. 일반적으로 '감정의 형용사+to부정사'의 결합에서 앞에 조동사 will이 오면, 부사적 용법 중 '조건'이 되는데, 지금 주어진 문장의 경우에는 조건의 If절이 있으므로, '감정의 원인'으로 보는 것이 적절하다. ④만 부사적 용법 중 '감정의 원인, 이유'이다. ① 부사적 용법 중 '결과' ② 명사적 용법(진주어) ③ 부사적 용법 중 '목적' ⑤ 명사적 용법(목적어)

15 이어지는 내용으로 보아 마오리족의 문화는 오늘날 뉴질랜드 사회의 중요한 부분이라고 말하는 것이 가장 적절하다.

16 나라의 여러 곳에 마오리 마을이 있다고 하였으므로 한 장소에 집중되어 있다는 ③번은 글의 내용과 일치하지 않는다.

17 뉴질랜드 자연의 아름다움 때문에 많은 유명한 영화들이 뉴질랜드에서 촬영되었다.

18 남섬에는 일 년 내내 눈으로 덮인 산들이 있으며, 북섬에는 높은 나무가 아닌 초원 지역이 있다고 하였다.

19 주격 관계대명사 which의 선행사는 a Maori village이므로 단수 취급하는 것이 적절하다.

20 뉴질랜드의 상징이 몇 개가 있는지는 위 글을 읽고 알 수 없다.

서술형 실전문제 p.50~51

01 She will prepare fish and chips for the festival.
02 Why don't we visit Victoria Peak?
03 (1) New Zealand is known as the land of kiwi fruit, where a lot of kiwi fruit is grown.
   (2) I won't get confused when somebody uses the word kiwi, which has several meanings.

(3) Janet received a letter of invitation from her friend, which she didn't read.

(4) All the employees in the company stop working at noon, when they go out for lunch.

(5) The boss praised Sean, who didn't mean to do well this time.

04 to take pictures of the beautiful night scenery

05 you will probably agree that the rival team must be scared

06 sing → shout / happy → scary

07 The Maori people started doing the haka as a war dance.

08 which is a bird native to New Zealand

09 600 smaller islands

01 세라는 음식 축제를 위해 무엇을 준비할 것인가?

02 제안이나 권유를 나타내는 표현으로 'Why don't we ~?(~하는 것이 어때?)'를 사용할 수 있다.

03 선행사에 따라 who, which, when, where 등에 유의하여 영작한다.

04 to부정사의 부사적 용법 중 '목적'을 이용한다.

05 상대팀이 겁을 먹는 것은 감정을 느끼는 것이므로 과거분사 scared를 쓰는 것에 유의한다.

06 하카 춤 추는 사람들은 소리 지르고 그들의 몸을 사납게 움직이기 때문에 하카는 무서워 보일 수도 있다고 하였다.

07 마오리인들은 전쟁 춤으로 하카를 추기 시작했다고 하였다. 는 뉴질랜드 태생의 새라는 부연 설명을 제시하는 절이다.

09 뉴질랜드는 두 개의 본섬과 600개의 작은 섬들로 되어 있다고 하였다.

창의사고력 서술형 문제   p.52

|모범답안|

01 (1) A: Let's talk about school life in Canada.
   B: Students start a new school year in September.

(2) A: Let's talk about school life in the UK.
   B: Students go to school at the age of five.

(3) A: Let's talk about school life in New Zealand.
   B: Students learn the Maori language.

02 (1) which means she likes foreign cultures (2) which can offer her opportunities to study foreign cultures more (3) where she can study foreign languages deeply 등 어법과 내용에 맞으면 정답

03 the third largest island in Europe, Dublin, which stands for the green land, the Cliffs of Moher,

which show the beautiful nature of Ireland, traditional dish, bread boiled in milk with some sugar, get refreshed

단원별 모의고사   p.53~57

| 01 ⑤ | 02 activity | 03 ③ | 04 ④ |
| 05 ⑤ | 06 ③ | 07 ⑤ | |

08 What would you recommend that I take?

09 I suggest we look to the right before

10 ③

11 (1) People are afraid of the corona virus, which causes the critical disease.

(2) People hope the cure will come out soon not to worry any longer.

12 ③   13 ③

14 (1) Ladders are linked with a strange belief, and it is that passing under them brings bad luck.

(2) Ladders are linked with a strange belief, which is that passing under them brings bad luck.

15 ②   16 ③

17 which would bring me good luck   18 ③

19 (B) a fruit   (C) a bird   (D) a people

20 We can call them kiwi.   21 ③

22 ①   23 ④

24 It means "hi" in English.   25 ②

01 ⑤번은 'collaborator(협력자)'에 관한 설명이다. 'rival(경쟁자)'에 대한 영어 설명은 'a person who is competing for the same object or goal as another'이다.

02 '동사-명사'의 관계이다. 성취하다-업적 : 행동하다-활동

03 '갑자기 어떤 생각을 하다'라는 의미로 'come to one's mind(생각이 떠오르다)'가 적절하다.

04 '키위라는 단어를 들으면 무엇이 떠오르니?'라는 A의 물음에 '사과보다 키위를 더 좋아해.'라고 말하는 것은 어색하다.

05 ⑤번은 요청을 하는 표현이다.

06 ③번의 'filled'는 명사 'sandwich'를 수식하는 과거분사로 올바르게 사용되었다.

07 미국 역사에서 중요하기 때문에 독립 기념관을 방문해 보라고 제안한다.

09 'look to the right'를 이용하여 '길을 건너기 전에 오른쪽을 보는 것을 제안해'라고 말하는 것이 적절하다.

10 나머지는 제안이나 권유를 나타내는 표현이고, ③은 이야기하고 싶은 주제를 소개할 때 사용하는 표현이다.

11 내용을 정확히 이해하고, 조건에 맞게 질문에 답하도록 한다. (1) 관계대명사 which를 활용한다. (2) to부정사의 '부사적' 용법을 사용해야 하므로 to worry를 쓰되, not은 to 앞에 쓰는 것에 유의한다.

12 ③의 to call은 동사 like의 목적어로 쓰인 명사적 용법이고, 다른 문장들은 모두 부사적 용법으로 쓰였다. 내용상으로도, Kiwi라고 부르는 것이 아니라, 다른 나라 사람들에 의해 불리는 것이므로 to be called라고 하는 것이 적절하다.

13 ③의 to learn은 부사적 용법 중 '감정의 원인'으로 쓰였다. ①, ④, ⑤는 명사적 용법, ②는 형용사적 용법이다.

14 선행사는 a strange belief이고, 'and it is that'은 'which is that'으로 명사절 접속사 that을 쓰는 것에 유의한다.

15 밑줄 친 which는 '계속적' 용법의 관계대명사이다. ①, ④는 의문대명사, ③, ⑤번은 전치사의 목적어 역할로 쓰인 관계대명사의 제한적 용법이다.

16 to be는 '늦지 않기 위해서'라는 부사적 용법 중 '목적'으로 쓰였다. ③만 부사적 용법 중 '목적'이다. ① likes의 목적어로 쓰인 명사적 용법 ② 진주어로 쓰인 명사적 용법 ④ forget의 목적어로 쓰인 명사적 용법 ⑤ 주어로 쓰인 명사적 용법이다.

17 글자 수를 맞추려면 계속적 용법의 관계대명사 which를 사용해야 한다. 7 단어로 영작한다면 which 대신 and it을 쓰는 것이 적절하다.

18 (A) be known as ~: ~로 알려지다 ① introduce A to B: A를 B에게 소개하다 ② be worried about: ~에 대해 걱정하다 ③ think of A as B: A를 B로 여기다 ④ look into: ~을 조사하다 ⑤ deal with: ~를 상대하다, 다루다

19 키위는 과일, 새, 그리고 국민의 명칭이라고 하였다.

20 뉴질랜드 출신 사람들을 부르는 별명이 키위라고 하였다. 따라서 우리는 그들을 키위라고 부를 수 있다.

21 뉴질랜드에서 많은 키위가 자란다고 했을 뿐, 키위가 뉴질랜드 사람들이 가장 좋아하는 과일이라는 말은 나와 있지 않다.

22 뉴질랜드에는 두 개의 본섬이 있다는 문장이 제시된 후 남섬과 북섬에 대한 소개가 이어지는 것이 적절하다.

23 뉴질랜드에서 몇 편의 영화가 촬영되었는지는 위 글을 읽고 답할 수 없다.

24 "kia ora"는 영어로 "안녕하세요."를 의미한다.

25 밑줄 친 (A)에 이어지는 문장에서 제시된 바와 같이, 몇몇 학교에서 마오리어를 가르치고 있고, 마오리어의 라디오와 TV 방송국이 있고, 그 나라의 여러 곳에 마오리 마을이 있으므로 ②번이 가장 적절하다.

How to Get Along with People

01 ③   02 thoughtful   03 ⑤
04 ②   05 get along, with   06 ④
07 ⑤

01 • 저것들은 인터뷰를 위한 적절한 옷이 아니다. • 그들의 목표는 한국인들 사이에서 적절한 한국어 사용을 촉진하는 것이다.

02 그 고등학교 교장은 그러한 사려 깊은 표현에 감동을 받았다. <영영풀이> '사람들을 행복하게 하거나 편안하게 하기 위해 할 수 있는 일들을 항상 생각하는'의 의미로 'thoughtful(사려 깊은)'이 적절하다.

03 '정직하고 진실하며, 당신이 정말로 느끼고 믿는 것에 근거하는'이라는 의미로 'sincere(진심어린)'가 적절하다.

04 '어떤 일이나 사람이 미래에 일어날 일에 준비가 되도록 하다'의 의미로 'prepare(준비하다)'가 적절하다.

05 get along with: ~와 어울리다, 잘 지내다

06 (A) 당신이 인터넷에 게시하는 정보는 삭제할지라도 영원히 인터넷에 남아 있다는 것을 기억하라. (B) 여러분이 이 프로그램에 관심이 있다면, 단지 100명의 운이 좋은 학생들만이 이 학교에 다닐 수 있기 때문에 서둘러야 합니다.

07 나머지는 '형용사-명사'의 관계이지만, ⑤는 '동사-명사'의 관계이다.

01 (1) suggestions (2) emotional (3) relaxed
(4) appreciate
02 (n)ervous
03 (1) ignore (2) regret (3) accidentally (4) mind
04 (1) responsibility, 책임 (2) apology, 사과
(3) relationship, 관계 (4) generous, 너그러운

01 (1) 교육과 여러분의 학교를 나아지게 하기 위한 제안이나 의견이 있으세요? (2) 어떤 사람들은 애완동물들이 감정적인 지원으로 환자들이 더 빨리 회복되도록 도울 수도 있다고 믿습니다. (3) 스트레칭은 건강하고 느긋한 마음을 갖기 위한 좋은 방법이다. (4) 누군가 우리말을 경청해 주면 그건 그 사람의 관심을 나타내는 것이므로 그것을 고마워한다.

02 • 만약 당신이 긴장한다면, 당신의 어깨를 뒤로 한 채 똑바로 서려

고 노력하라. • 비록 초조하다 할지라도 자신 있게 행동하려고 해라. • 차분하게 있을 거라고 생각했지만 TV 카메라와 마주했을 때나는 매우 긴장했다.

03 (1) ignore: 무시하다 (2) regret: 후회하다 (3) accidentally: 우연히 (4) mind: 꺼리다

04 (1) 당신이 처리해야 할 일이나 의무인 것 (2) 당신이 저지른 잘못된 일에 미안하다고 말하는 행위 (3) 두 가지가 연결되는 방식 (4) 평소 또는 예상 했던 것 보다 더 많이 돈, 도움, 친절을 기꺼이 주는

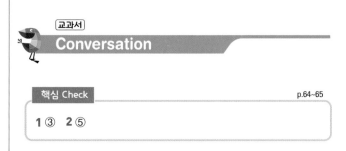

Conversation 〔교과서〕

1 ③   2 ⑤

교과서 대화문 익히기

1 F   2 T   3 F   4 T

5 F   6 T   7 F   8 T

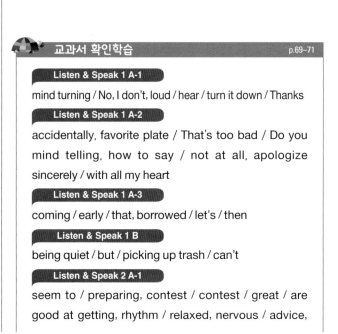

교과서 확인학습   p.69~71

Listen & Speak 1 A-1
mind turning / No, I don't, loud / hear / turn it down / Thanks

Listen & Speak 1 A-2
accidentally, favorite plate / That's too bad / Do you mind telling, how to say / not at all, apologize sincerely / with all my heart

Listen & Speak 1 A-3
coming / early / that, borrowed / let's / then

Listen & Speak 1 B
being quiet / but / picking up trash / can't

Listen & Speak 2 A-1
seem to / preparing, contest / contest / great / are good at getting, rhythm / relaxed, nervous / advice,

helpful, appreciate / pleasure

lost / Let me help, What, like / is written / yours / appreciate / No problem

Listen & Speak 2 B

Let, show / appreciate / Let me carry / appreciate your help

Real Life Talk

What's up / (You')ve, been, haven't / since, elementary / busy studying, do you mind helping, help me pick out / problem. for / was broken / of her / how about, recently / suggestion

Wrap Up 1

am planning to go / cool, used to live / Do you mind telling, what to do / Not at all, beaches / swimming, else / don't you, everywhere / How about / raw fish, fresh, delicious / appreciate, tips

Wrap Up 2

well, might have caught, needs to, to meet, instead

시험대비 기본평가   p.72

01 mind helping   02 ①, ④, ⑤   03 ②
04 ⑤

01 'Do you mind ~ing?'는 '당신은 ~하는 것이 괜찮으신가요?' 라는 뜻으로 상대방에게 무엇인가를 조심스럽고 정중하게 요청 할 때 사용하는 표현이다.

02 상대방의 도움에 대해 감사하는 표현이 적절하다.

03 빈칸 다음의 대답으로 보아, 상대방의 요청에 승낙한다는 것을 알 수 있다. 요청을 승낙할 때 mind는' 꺼리다'라는 뜻이므로 부 정어(not)를 써서 승낙을 표현한다. Of course not. / Not at all. / Surely not. / Certainly not. / No, I don't (mind). 등으로 표현한다.

04 I appreciate ~.'는 감사하는 표현이다.

시험대비 실력평가   p.73~74

01 ④   02 ①   03 ④   04 ②
05 He is good at getting into the rhythm.
06 ④   07 ③
08 I need the book that[which] you borrowed before class.
09 has to return, borrowed
10 Do you mind putting off the meeting until tomorrow?

01 빈칸 다음의 Andy가 한 말로 보아 도움을 요청하는 표현이 적 절하다.

02 Amy와 Jessie가 초등학교 1학년 때부터 친구로 지내고 있다.

03 무엇을 하고 있는지 묻는 말에 → (C) 모자를 잃어버려서 찾을 수 없다는 내용이 오고 → (D) 도와준다는 말과 함께 모자가 어 떻게 생겼는지 묻고 → (A) 모자의 색깔과 모자에 이름이 적혔 다는 것을 말해주고 → (B) 식탁 아래에 모자가 있었다고 모자 를 찾아주는 내용이 자연스럽다.

04 B의 대답이 'Of course not.'인 것으로 보아 요청하는 말은 'Do you mind ~?'로 표현하는 것이 적절하다.

05 질문: Amy의 말에 의하면 민수는 무엇을 잘하는가?

06 단수 주어인 'one thing' 다음에 단수 동사 is가 와야 한다.

07 ③ 'Do you mind ~?'로 요청하는 말에 'Of course.'로 답하는 것은 거절을 할 때 사용하는 표현으로 'Go ahead.(그렇게 하세 요.)'와 어울리지 않는다.

08 선행사 'the book'을 수식하는 목적격 관계대명사절을 이용하고 목적격 관계대명사 'that' 또는 'which'를 추가한다.

09 '~해야 한다'라는 의미로 'have to'는 3인칭 단수 주어 뒤에서 'has to'로 바꾸어 쓰고, 수식받는 명사 'book'이 '빌려진' 수동의 의미로 주어진 동사 'borrow'를 과거분사로 변형하여 쓴다

10 'Do you mind+동명사 ~?' 형태로 상대방에게 요청하는 표현을 사용한다.

서술형 시험대비   p.75

01 Because his leg was broken.
02 You've been friends with her for a long time, haven't you?
03 Do you mind telling me what to do in Jejudo?
04 What does it look like?

01 질문: 두 달 전에 왜 Amy는 Andy의 가방을 들어 주었는가?

02 (a)의 'since first grade in elementary school'로 보아 과 거부터 현재까지 친구로 지내고 있음을 알 수 있다. 현재완료를 사용하고, 부가의문문도 조동사 have의 부정문인 haven't로 바 꾸어 주어야 한다.

03 'Do you mind+-ing?' 형태를 사용하고, '무엇을 ~할지'는 'what to do'를 사용한다.

04 대화의 흐름상 모자의 모습을 묻는 표현이 적절하다. 'What ~ look like?'를 사용한다.

핵심 Check p.76~77

1 (1) how (2) why
2 The more homework they have, the more tired the students feel.

시험대비 기본평가 p.78

01 ③
02 (1) in which / how (2) in which / where
03 ②
04 (1) The hotter, more (2) higher, to climb
  (3) older, less flexible

01 often의 비교급은 more 또는 less를 앞에 쓰는 것이 좋고 (oftener를 쓸 수도 있음), 의미상 less often이 적절하다.

02 '전치사+관계대명사'는 관계부사로 표현한다. 선행사가 the way일 때, 관계부사는 how이지만, 둘을 동시에 쓰지 않는다. 선행사가 장소일 때 where를 쓴다.

03 관계부사가 오면 뒤의 문장은 완전한 절의 형태여야 한다. 선행사 the way와 관계부사 how는 함께 쓸 수 없다.

04 'The+비교급 ~, the+비교급 …' 구문이다. 형용사 또는 부사의 비교급에 대해 꼼꼼하게 공부해야 하며, hot, high 등은 er을 뒤에 쓰지만, flexible은 more 또는 less를 쓰고, much나 many는 more처럼 다른 단어가 비교급이 된다. (2)번 문장은 내용상 가주어-진주어 구문이므로 동사 climb을 to부정사로 변형하는 것이 적절하다.

시험대비 실력평가 p.79~81

01 ④	**02** ④	**03** ③	**04** ④
05 ⑤	**06** ④	**07** ②	**08** ④
09 ③	**10** ⑤	**11** ③	**12** how

13 when
14 The more you watch the news, the better you know
15 The more expensive some products are, the more people want to buy them.
16 ③ **17** ④

01 ④ 선행사 the way와 관계부사 how는 함께 쓸 수 없다. 둘 중 하나를 삭제하면 옳은 문장이 된다.

02 'The+비교급 ~, the+비교급 …' 구문이다. '당신이 더 열심히

일할수록 더 많은 돈을 벌 수 있다.'

03 'The+비교급 ~, the+비교급 …' 구문이다. '한국의 역사에 대해 방문객들이 더 알게 될수록, 그들은 아마도 더 많이 흥미를 느끼게 될 것이다.'

04 선행사가 the reason일 때, '전치사+관계대명사'는 for which를, '관계부사'는 why를 쓰는 것이 적절하며, the reason과 why 둘 중 하나만 쓰는 것도 가능하다. ① 선행사 the reason 필요 ② which 앞에 for 필요 ③ 마지막에 for 불필요 ⑤ on → for

05 선행사가 the place이므로 '관계부사' where 또는 '전치사+관계대명사'로 at which 또는 in which 등으로 연결해서 표현 가능하며, 일반적 장소인 the place를 생략해도 괜찮다. ① where 뒤의 어순은 '주어+동사'가 되어야 한다. ② know 동사가 있을 때 의문사를 문두로 보낼 수 없다. ③ 관계부사 where 앞에 전치사 불필요 ④ 마지막에 in이 있으므로 on 불필요

06 '친한 친구가 자신의 실수에 대해 진심으로 사과하지 않을수록, 사람들은 더 쉽게 상처 받는다.'라는 내용이다.

07 '당신의 사과가 더욱 진실할수록, 그것들은 더 잘 받아들여진다'는 내용이다. ① 더 많이 필요해진다 ③ 더 가볍게 여겨진다 ④ 더욱 건성으로 받아들여진다 ⑤ 더 많이 무시된다

08 선행사가 the way일 때, 관계부사 how는 같이 쓰지 않으며, 관계부사 앞에 전치사 in을 쓰지도 않는다.

09 선행사가 the time일 때, 관계부사는 when을 쓰며, that으로도 바꿔 쓸 수 있다. 일반적으로 관계대명사 which를 쓸 때는 전치사 at, on, in 등이 쓰이지만, 선행사가 the first time일 경우 in과 함께 for which도 가능하다. of는 시간을 나타내는 선행사 뒤에 쓰지 않는다.

10 선행사가 the reason일 때, 관계부사는 why를 쓰며, that으로도 바꿔 쓸 수 있다. the reason 또는 why 둘 중 하나를 생략해도 무방하며, 관계대명사를 쓸 때는 for가 함께 온다. ⑤는 관계부사 뒤의 어순이 잘못되었다.

11 <보기>는 '더 빠른 사과가 당신이 더 사려 깊고 책임감 있음을 보여줄 것이다'라는 뜻이다. 'The+비교급 ~, the+비교급 …' 구문을 사용해서 정확하게 표현한 문장은 ③이다. '당신의 사과가 더 빠를수록, 당신은 더 사려 깊고 책임감 있게 보인다.' 나머지는 모두 어법상 옳지 않은 문장들이다.

12 두 문장을 연결해 주는 빈칸 뒤에 완전한 문장이 오고, 선행사가 the way일 때는 관계부사 how를 쓰는데, 둘 중 하나만 써야 한다. 두 단어를 쓰는 것이 조건이라면 the way를 쓴다.

13 두 문장을 연결해 주는 빈칸 뒤에 완전한 문장이 오고, 선행사가 시간일 때는 관계부사 when을 쓰는 것이 적절하다. 두 단어를 쓰는 것이 조건이라면 선행사 the day가 있으므로 on which가 좋다.

14 'The+비교급 ~, the+비교급 …' 구문을 사용한 문장이다. '뉴스를 많이 보는 것'을 'the more'로, '더 잘 알게 되는 것'을 'the better'로 쓰는 것에 유의한다.

15 'The+비교급 ~, the+비교급 …' 구문을 사용한 문장이다. '더 많은 사람들'을 'the more people'로 쓰는 것에 유의한다.

16 (A) the way가 있으므로 how는 불가능하고, that 또는 in which를 써야 한다. (B) 관계대명사 주격이 필요하므로 which[that]가 적절하다. (C) 선행사가 the day이며 뒤에 완전한 문장이므로 when 또는 on which가 적절하다.

17 (A)는 관계부사 why, how, when 모두 가능하다. (B) the reason 뒤에 관계부사 why 또는 for which가 적절하다. (C) 장소의 선행사 cafe 뒤에 where 또는 at[in] which가 적절하다.

서술형 시험대비
p.82~83

01 (1) The sooner you apologize for the mistake, the less hurt people get.
   (2) The more we have, the more we want.
   (3) The more options you have, the more difficult it is to decide.
   (4) The more I know the friend, the stronger my trust in her becomes.
   (5) The more we give, the more we will get in return.
   (6) The harder he works, the brighter his future will be.

02 (1) like the way her son made excuses
   (2) how the turtle has managed his health
   (3) where people line up every morning to eat Bulgogi

03 (1) The older, the more
   (2) The more, the more intelligent
   (3) The louder, the better
   (4) The farther, the healthier

04 (1) the way how → the way 또는 how 삭제
   (2) the more happier → more 삭제

05 (1) The researchers found the special planet where life can live.
   (2) The director taught us how he made his films.
   (3) Her favorite season is winter when she can enjoy white snow and skiing.
   (4) Please let me know the reason why my professor was mad at me.
   (5) This is the hotel where the President of Brazil stayed.
   (6) I would never forget the day when my daughter walked for herself.

01 'The+비교급 ~, the+비교급 …' 구문을 사용한 문장이다.
   *trust in A: A에 대한 신뢰

02 (1) 'Ms. Kim은 그녀의 아들이 그 문제에 대해 변명하는 방식이 마음에 들지 않았다.' (2) '동물들은 거북이가 어떻게 그의 건강을 유지해왔는지 궁금하다.' (3) 저기가 사람들이 불고기를 먹으러 매일 아침 줄을 서는 그 유명한 식당이다.

03 (1) 그 학생이 나이를 먹을수록, 그의 할아버지를 더 닮아 보인다. (2) 당신의 자녀들이 더 많은 책들을 읽을수록, 그들은 더욱 똑똑해질 것이다. (3) 당신이 더 큰 소리로 연습할수록, 당신은 외국어를 더 잘 말할 수 있다. (4) 그 환자가 매일 더 멀리 걸을수록, 그녀는 더욱 건강해질 것이다.

04 (1) 선행사가 the way일 때, 관계부사 how는 함께 쓸 수 없다. 둘 중 하나만 써도 어법상 문제 없다. (2) happy의 비교급은 happier이다. more는 불필요하다.

05 (1) 그 연구자들이 생명체가 살 수 있는 특별한 행성을 발견했다. (2) 그 감독이 우리에게 자신이 영화를 만드는 방법을 가르쳐 줬다. (3) 그녀가 가장 좋아하는 계절은 흰 눈과 스키를 즐길 수 있는 겨울이다. (4) 제발 교수님이 나에게 화가 난 이유를 나에게 알려주세요. (5) 이곳이 브라질의 대통령이 머물렀던 호텔이다. (6) 나는 나의 딸이 스스로 걸었던 날을 결코 잊을 수 없다.

교과서 Reading

확인문제
p.84

1 T 2 F 3 T

확인문제
p.85

1 T 2 F 3 T

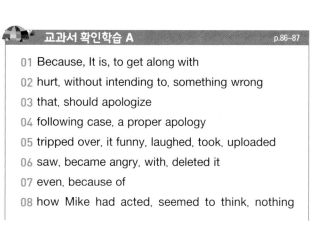

교과서 확인학습 A
p.86~87

01 Because, It is, to get along with
02 hurt, without intending to, something wrong
03 that, should apologize
04 following case, a proper apology
05 tripped over, it funny, laughed, took, uploaded
06 saw, became angry, with, deleted it
07 even, because of
08 how Mike had acted, seemed to think, nothing

serious

09 should be sincere

10 Apologizin, to, Saying, more than

11 that, respect, care about, feelings

12 make things right, sincere

13 The more, the better, received

14 another, accidentally bumped into

15 on, fell on, apologize, felt bad

16 Why doesn't, say, if, right now

17 that, is necessary, apologize at once

18 shows that, thoughtful, responsibility

19 All, to do, think nothing, laugh it off

20 are, among, members, loved ones

21 borrowed, favorite, lost

22 apologize, not important

23 ignore

24 hadn't apologized to

25 to apologize, something wrong, includes, who are close

26 get hurt more easily, comes from

27 let it go, are close

28 small mistakes, no apology add up to

29 among, loved ones

30 heard of, No more, no more chances

31 make, let, break

32 apologize to, Try to do, can solve

교과서 확인학습 B
p.88~89

1 Because we are human, we all make mistakes. It is not easy to get along with everyone all the time.

2 Sometimes we hurt people's feelings without intending to. Sometimes, we do something wrong and regret it later.

3 When that happens, what should we do? We should apologize.

4 Read the following case studies and learn three things about a proper apology.

5 When June tripped over a backpack and fell, Mike found it funny and laughed. He took a picture and uploaded it on an SNS.

6 June saw the picture and became angry. Mike said, with a laugh, "Sorry, June!" and deleted it.

7 After that, June felt even more hurt because of Mike's casual apology.

8 June didn't like how Mike had acted. Mike seemed to think it was nothing serious.

9 What did you learn from this case? Yes. You guessed right. You should be sincere when you apologize.

10 Apologizing is necessary to build good friendships. Saying you're sorry is more than just words.

11 You need to show that you respect the other person and care about his or her feelings.

12 If you truly want to make things right, be sincere in your apology.

13 The more sincere your apology is, the better it will be received.

14 Here is another case. While Kate was hurrying across the cafeteria, she accidentally bumped into Hojun.

15 Some food on Hojun's tray fell on his jacket. Kate didn't apologize. Hojun felt bad.

16 He thought, 'Why doesn't she say something? It would be nothing if she apologized right now.'

17 This case shows that when an apology is necessary, you should apologize at once.

18 A quick apology shows that you are thoughtful and take responsibility for your action.

19 All you need to do is to say, "I'm sorry." Then, the hurt friend will think nothing of it and laugh it off.

20 Finally, apologies are necessary among family members and loved ones, too.

21 One day, Sunmin borrowed her sister's favorite book. Later, she lost it.

22 Sunmin didn't apologize because she thought it was not important. She thought, 'We're sisters, after all.'

23 Sunmin's sister disliked how Sunmin had treated her. How could her own sister ignore her feelings?

24 This was not the first time Sunmin hadn't apologized to her little sister.

25 People need to apologize when they do something wrong. This includes family members and the people who are close to you.

26 People get hurt more easily when the hurt comes from a family member or a friend.

27 We may think that they will let it go because they are close to us.

28 Remember, however, that small mistakes and no apology add up to big emotional wounds.

29 This is especially true among family members and loved ones.

30 Have you ever heard of the saying, "No more

apologies, no more chances"?

31 People make mistakes, but don't let one mistake break a beautiful relationship.

32 Do you want to apologize to someone? Try to do it now. A quick and sincere "I'm sorry" can solve many problems..

시험대비 실력평가
p.90~93

01 ⑤　　　　02 proper　　　03 ②　　　　04 ③
05 ④　　　　06 ④
07 We should be sincere.　　08 ③
09 some food on his tray　　10 ⑤　　　　11 ②
12 ④　　　　13 ②
14 People need to apologize when they do something wrong.
15 (C)–(A)–(D)–(B)　　　16 ②　　　　17 ④
18 ②　　　　19 ⑤
20 We should apologize at once when an apology is necessary
21 She lost it later.　　　22 ③
23 when they do something wrong　　　24 ④
25 ⑤번 → now

01 나쁜 일을 하고 그것을 후회하는 일이 생기면 무엇을 해야 하는지를 묻고 이에 대한 답으로 주어진 문장이 제시되는 것이 가장 자연스럽다.

02 '옳거나 가장 적합한'이라는 의미는 '적절한, 제대로 된 (proper)'이다.

03 사례 연구들을 읽고 올바른 사과를 위한 세 가지를 알아보자고 하였으므로 '적절히 사과하는 법'이 가장 적절하다.

04 빈칸 (A)에는 비교급을 강조하는 부사가 들어가야 한다. very는 원급의 형용사나 부사를 강조하는 말이다.

05 이어지는 조언에서 사과는 진실해야 함을 강조하고 있다. 따라서 Mike의 사과가 가벼웠기 때문에 June이 더 화가 난 것이다.

06 June은 Mike의 행동 방식이 마음에 들지 않았다.

07 사과할 때는 진실해야 한다고 하였다.

08 '즉시'라는 의미의 ③번이 가장 적절하다. for once: 이번 한 번만, from time to time: 이따금씩

09 Kate가 호준이와 부딪쳤을 때, 그는 급식판에 음식을 들고 있었다. 그 부딪힘은 음식이 그의 재킷에 떨어지게 했다.

10 호준이는 Kate가 사과하지 않아서 기분이 나빴다고 하였으므로 ⑤번이 글의 내용과 일치한다.

11 여동생이 가장 좋아하는 책을 빌리고 이것을 잃어버린 것을 가

리키는 말이다.

12 모두 선민이를 가리키지만 ④번은 선민이의 여동생을 가리키는 말이다.

13 가깝기 때문에 사과하지 않고 그냥 넘어갈 수도 있지만 이것이 쌓이면 큰 감정적 상처가 된다는 연결이 자연스럽다.

14 잘못했을 때 사과해야 한다고 하였다.

15 (C) June이 가방에 걸려 넘어짐 (A) Mike는 사진을 찍어서 SNS에 올리고 June은 사진을 보고 화가 남 (D) Mike가 가볍게 사과함 (B) June은 그의 행동 방식에 더 화가 남

16 receive는 '받다'라는 의미이다. 사과가 더 잘 받아들여질 것이라는 의미이므로 ②번이 적절하다.

17 사과하는 것은 좋은 교우 관계를 만들기 위해 필요하다고 하였다. be related to: ~와 관계가 있다

18 이어지는 조언은 사과를 즉시 해야 한다는 것이므로 ②번이 적절하다.

19 빈칸 (B)에는 off가 들어간다. ① work out: 운동하다 ② come across: 우연히 만나다 ③ consist of: ~으로 구성되다 ④ keep ~ from Ving: ~가 V하지 못하게 막다 ⑤ give off: 발산하다

20 사과가 필요할 때는 즉시 해야 한다.

21 선민이는 여동생이 가장 좋아하는 책을 빌렸다가 나중에 그것을 잃어버렸다.

22 글의 내용으로 미루어보아 선민이의 여동생은 선민이가 그녀의 기분을 무시하고 사과하지 않는 방식이 마음에 들지 않는 것임을 알 수 있다

23 -thing으로 끝나는 대명사는 형용사의 수식을 뒤에서 받는 것에 유의한다.

24 위 글은 사과하는 것의 중요성에 관한 글이다.

25 이어지는 문장에서 빠르고 진정한 사과가 많은 문제를 해결해 줄 것이라고 하였으므로 '지금 하려고 노력해라'고 말하는 것이 적절하다.

서술형 시험대비
p.94~95

01 to hurt people's feelings
02 It is not easy to get along with everyone all the time.
03 apology
04 The more sincere your apology is, the better it will be received.
05 He uploaded it on an SNS.
06 It's because Mike apologized to him casually.
07 you respect the other person and care about his or her feelings
08 Because Kate bumped into him.

01 다른 사람의 감정을 상하게 할 의도 없이 그들의 감정을 상하게
한다는 의미이다.

02 모든 사람과 항상 잘 지내기는 쉽지 않다고 하였다.

03 누군가에게 상처주거나 그들에게 물의를 일으켜 미안하다고 말
하기 위해 말하거나 쓰는 어떤 것은 '사과(apology)'이다.

04 사과가 받아들여지는 것이므로 receive를 과거분사 형태로 써
서 수동태를 만드는 것에 유의한다.

05 Mike는 June의 사진을 찍어서 SNS에 올렸다.

06 Mike가 June에게 가볍게 사과했기 때문에 June은 더 화가 났
다.

07 당신의 사과를 진실하게 만드는 것은 당신이 타인을 존중하고
타인의 감정에 관심을 갖고 있음을 보여주는 것이다.

08 음식이 호준이의 재킷에 떨어진 이유는 Kate가 그와 부딪쳤기
때문이다.

09 호준이는 Kate로부터 어떠한 사과도 받지 못했고, 그래서 그는
기분이 나빴다.

10 해석: 당신의 행동에 책임을 진다는 것을 보여주고 싶다면, 가능
한 빨리 사과해라.

11 선민이의 여동생은 언니가 그녀의 기분을 무시한다고 생각해서
화가 난 것이다.

12 앞 문장을 가리키는 말이다.

13 사람들은 마음의 상처가 가족이나 친구에게서 올 때 더 쉽게 상
처 받는다고 하였다.

14 아무리 당신과 가까운 사람이라 할지라도, 당신이 무언가를 잘
못한다면 그들에게 사과해야 한다.

영역별 핵심문제 p.97~101

01 solve   02 ④   03 ⑤   04 ①

05 with all my heart

06 Do you mind changing seats with me?

07 Do you mind telling me how to say sorry to her?

08 ②

09 She suggests that he buy a case for her
smartphone.

10 ④   11 ①   12 ③   13 ②

14 ①   15 ①   16 ③   17 ③

---

01 '동사-명사'의 관계이다. 포함하다-포함 : 해결하다-해결

02 (A) 너는 친구들과 부딪힌다. 그러면 너와 친구들은 다치게 될
거야. (B) 학생들은 아침에 그들의 옷을 고르기 위한 충분한 시
간이 없다.

03 계획되거나 의도되지 않은 방식으로

04 서면이나 전자 텍스트의 일부 또는 전부를 제거하다

05 with all my heart: 진심으로

06 요청하는 표현으로 'Do you mind+-ing?'를 사용한다.

07 도움을 요청하는 표현으로 'Do you mind+-ing?' 형태를 사용
한다.

08 주어진 문장이 '괜찮은 것을 고르도록 네가 도와줄 수 있을 것이
라고 확신해.'라는 뜻이므로 요청하는 말 다음에 오는 것이 적절
하다.

09 질문: Jessie는 Andy가 Amy를 위해 무엇을 사라고 제안하는
가? / 동사 'suggest'의 목적절인 'that'절의 해석이 '~해야 한다'
는 '당위성'을 나타낼 때는 '주어+should+동사원형' 형태를 사
용하고 이때 'should'는 생략 가능하다.

10 두 달 전에 Andy가 다리를 다친 이유는 대화에 언급되어 있지
않다.

11 '날씨가 더 추워질수록 사람들이 전보다 더 감기에 많이 걸리는
경향이 있다.'라는 문장은 '날씨가 더 추워질수록 더 많은 사람들
이 감기에 걸린다.'와 가장 유사하며, 'The 비교급, the 비교급'
구문을 통해 표현하는 것이 적절하다.

12 선행사가 the way일 때는 관계부사 how를 쓰는데, 둘 중 하나
만 써야 한다. the way 뒤에 how 대신 that을 쓸 수 있다. 관
계대명사로 표현할 때는 the way in which를 쓴다.

13 ② '어항은 물고기나 수중 생물들을 집어넣는 유리 용기이다.'라
는 문장에서 마지막에 전치사 in이 있으므로 선행사 container
뒤에는 관계대명사 which만 있으면 된다. in을 모두 지우고, 관
계부사 where로 쓰는 것도 적절하다.

14 ① '더 높이 올라갈수록, 우리가 숨 쉬는 것이 더 어려워졌다.'
는 문장이다. the more it was difficult가 아니라, the more
difficult it was의 어순이 적절하다.

15 나는 Paul이 그 어려운 문제를 푼 방법을 알아내고 싶다.'라는

문장이다. 일반적으로 선행사 the way는 관계부사 how와 짝이고, 둘은 나란히 쓸 수 없어서 둘 중 하나만 쓰면 된다. 그러나, how 대신에 that을 썼을 경우 the way를 생략하면 that이 더 이상 관계부사가 아니라 접속사가 되어 의미가 달라지고, 어법상으로도 옳지 않게 된다.

16 ① in which → which ② which → to which 또는 where ④ where → which ⑤ where → which

17 ① do → are 또는 will be ② More → The more, more → the more ④ the more earlier → the earlier ⑤ the more you will be careful → the more careful you will be
*destination: 목적지

18 ① 선행사 the way와 관계부사 how는 함께 쓸 수 없다. the way how → the way 또는 how ② why → which ③ when → which ④ at when → at which 또는 at 삭제

19 글의 내용으로 미루어 보아 Mike는 심각한 일이 아니라고 생각하는 것처럼 보였다고 말하는 것이 자연스럽다. 따라서 serious라고 쓰는 것이 적절하다.

20 (A)는 to부정사의 부사적 용법으로 쓰였다. ① 형용사적 용법 ② 진주어 ③ 부사적 용법 ④, ⑤ 동사의 목적어

21 글의 내용은 사과를 진실하게 해야 한다는 것이다.

22 Mike가 사진을 올리기 위해서 어떤 SNS를 사용했는지는 알 수 없다.

23 주어진 문장의 This가 가리키는 것은 사람들은 잘못했을 때 사과해야 한다는 문장이다. 따라서 ②번이 가장 적절하다.

24 result in을 대신하여 add up to를 써서 답해도 좋다.

25 선민이의 여동생은 선민이가 자신의 기분을 무시한다고 생각했다. 따라서 ③번이 글의 내용과 일치한다.

26 위 글은 글쓴이를 도와준 친구를 소개하는 글이다. 따라서 ②번이 가장 적절하다.

27 지난 금요일에 글쓴이는 아파서 수학 수업을 못 들었다고 하였다.

28 진수는 항상 재미있고, 용감하고, 발랄하다고 하였다.

단원별 예상문제 p.102~105

01 thoughtful 02 ⑤ 03 ① 04 ④
05 one thing you need to do is to be more relaxed
06 appreciate 07 ① 08 ⑤
09 might catch → might have caught
10 ① 11 ④ 12 ⑤ 13 ⑤
14 ② 15 ⑤ 16 ② 17 ⑤
18 ② 19 ⑤번 → how Mike had acted
20 ③
21 We need to show that we respect the other person and care about his or her feelings.

01 유의어 관계이다. 무시하다 : 사려 깊은

02 위험하거나 어려운 일에 대해 어떠한 두려움도 보이지 않는

03 과거의 상태를 나타내어 '~했었다'는 'used to+동사원형'을 사용한다.

04 Minjun이가 'Why don't you hike Halla Mountain?' (한라산을 등반해 보는 건 어때?)이라고 제안하고 있다.

05 우리말에서 '네가 해야 할'이 명사를 수식한다는 것을 알 수 있다. 주어부는 one thing 뒤에 관계대명사절인 'you need to do'를 쓰고, 동사 is를 쓴다. 마지막으로 부정사 to be를 사용하면 된다.

06 '무언가에 고마워하다'라는 의미로 'appreciate'가 적절하다.

07 빈칸 앞에서 Irene이 '도와줘서 고마워.'라고 말하고 있으므로 '천만에.'라고 답하는 말이 적절하다.

08 Irene이 왜 모자를 잃어버렸는지를 알 수 없다.

09 Mike가 몸이 좋지 않다는 말 다음에 그가 감기에 걸렸을지 모른다는 과거의 추측을 나타내는 말이 오는 것이 자연스럽다. 'might catch'는 'may catch'보다 가능성이 약한 현재의 추측으로, 과거의 추측은 'might have+과거분사'를 사용해야 한다.

10 평서문의 동사가 'have+과거분사'인 현재완료이므로, 부가의문문은 조동사 have를 부정해야 한다. 'weren't'를 'haven't'로 바꾸어야 한다.

11 방법을 나타내는 관계부사 how와 용법이 다른 것을 찾는 문제이다. ④는 의문사로 사용되었다. '나는 그 곰들이 성숙한 상태가 되면 얼마나 강해질지 궁금해.'라는 문장이다.

12 관계부사가 아닌 것을 찾는 문제이다. ⑤는 접속사로서 부사절을 이끄는 역할을 한다. *the Mediterranean Sea: 지중해

13 'The+비교급 ~, the+비교급 ⋯' 구문과 특수한 경우를 제외하고는 비교급 앞에 the를 쓰지 않는다. 접속사 when과 as가 있는 ①, ②번 문장과 ④번에서 the+비교급은 적절하지 않고, ③은 worse 앞에 more가 있어 부적절하다.

14 'The+비교급 ~, the+비교급 ⋯' 구문이다. 형용사 hot은 ①과 ④처럼 more hotter 또는 more hot으로 비교급을 쓰지 않는다. ③은 시제가 부적절하며, ⑤는 내용상 better보다는 more를 쓰는 것이 적절하다.

15 (A)는 to부정사의 명사적 용법으로 진주어로 쓰였다. ① 형용사적 용법 ②, ③ 부사적 용법 중 목적 ④ 부사적 용법 중 결과 ⑤ 진주어

16 나쁜 일을 하고 그것을 후회한다는 의미이므로 ②번이 가장 적절하다.

17 잘못을 하면 가까운 사람에게도 반드시 사과해야 하며, 그들이 나와 가깝기 때문에 그냥 넘어갈 것이라고 생각해서는 안 된다는 내용이므로 ⑤번이 가장 적절하다.

18 실수에 대해 즉시 사과하지 않으면, 그것은 아름다운 관계를 깨뜨

19 간접의문문이므로 '의문사+주어+동사'의 어순이 옳다.

20 사과는 좋은 교우 관계를 만들기 위해 필요하다고 하였다.

21 사과할 때 타인을 존중하고 타인의 감정에 관심을 갖고 있음을 보여 주어야 한다.

서술형 실전문제
p.106~107

01 (A) studying (B) helping (C) (to) pick
(D) was broken

02 I appreciate

03 You seem to be busy, Minsu.

04 (1) how (2) where (3) why

05 (1) harder, more (2) clearer, longer
(3) fewer, happier (4) older, smarter
(5) sooner, better

06 (1) Tell me how Mary persuaded her parents to give her the car.
(2) No one knows the day when Minju will marry the handsome guy of the idol group.
(3) Bucheon is the city where International Fantastic Film Festival will take place.

07 작은 실수를 하고 사과하지 않는 것이 큰 감정적인 상처가 되는 것.

08 necessary, oved, hurt, close

09 It's because she thought it was not important.

01 (A) be busy –ing: ~하느라 바쁘다, (B) mind는 목적어로 동명사를 취한다, (C) help는 목적보어 자리에 '동사원형' 또는 'to부정사'를 취한다. (D) 다리가 부러졌다는 수동의 의미이므로 'was broken'이 적절하다.

02 감사하는 표현으로 'Thank you for ~'나 'I appreciate ~'를 사용할 수 있다.

03 'It seems that+주어+동사 ~'는 '주어+seem to+부정사'로 바꾸어 쓸 수 있다.

04 각각의 선행사가 (1) 방법, (2) 장소, (3) 이유 등이다. 관계부사 how는 선행사 the way와 함께 쓰지 않는다.

05 (1) 더 열심히 일할수록, 너는 더 많은 돈을 번다. (2) 동영상의 화질이 더 선명할수록, 그것을 내려 받는 데 더 오랜 시간이 걸린다. (3) 더운 여름 날 수업이 더 적을수록, 학생들은 더 행복하게 느낀다. (4) 그 소녀가 나이를 먹을수록, 그녀는 더 똑똑해졌다. (5) 당신이 그 프로젝트를 일찍 끝낼수록, 협상에서 더 유리한 위치를 차지할 수 있다.

06 각각의 선행사에 맞게 관계부사를 쓰되, the way는 how와 같이 쓸 수 없으므로, (1)에서 선행사 없이 관계부사 이끄는 절만 쓰는 것에 유의한다.

07 앞 문장의 내용을 가리키는 말이다.

08 사과는 가족이나 사랑하는 사람들 사이에서도 필요하며, 사람들은 마음의 상처가 가족이나 친구에게서 올 때 더 쉽게 상처받는다고 하였다.

09 선민이가 그녀의 여동생에게 사과하지 않은 이유는 책을 잃어버린 것이 중요하지 않다고 생각했기 때문이다.

창의사고력 서술형 문제
p.108

|모범답안|

01 (1) I'll let you know how you can find the way.
(2) This is how I help you walk freely.
(3) I know how you set the table.
(4) I wonder how you read the directions.

02 for ten years / funny, generous, and cheerful / she helped me / Two weeks ago / I forgot to take my lunch to school / shared her lunch with me

01 보기의 단어들을 적절히 조합하여 그림과 어법에 맞게 영작한 답이면 된다.

단원별 모의고사
p.109~113

01 ⑤   02 (s)tingy   03 ③   04 ④
05 ⑤   06 ②

07 I know you're really busy studying, but do you mind helping me?

08 Andy asks her[Jessie] to help him pick out something nice for Amy.

09 ④   10 ③   11 ①   12 ④
13 ④

14 (1) for which (2) in which (3) in which
(4) on which

15 (1) The more it rained, the more depressed she felt.
(2) The more sincere her apology is, the better he will accept it.

16 ②   17 ⑤   18 ④   19 ③

20 Mike seemed to think it was nothing serious.

21 ③   22 sincere

01 ⑤번은 'lend(빌려주다)'에 관한 설명이다. 'borrow(빌리다)'의 영어 설명은 'to get or receive something from someone with the intention of giving it back after a period of time(일정 기간 후에 돌려줄 의도를 가지고 어떤 사람에게서 무언가를 얻거나 받다)'이다.

02 반의어 관계다. 바른-틀린 : 후한-인색한

03 '걷거나 달리고 있을 때 무언가에 발을 부딪친 후 균형을 잃거나, 누군가에게 이렇게 하도록 하다'는 의미로 'trip over(~에 걸려 넘어지다)'가 적절하다.

04 ④번은 'Do you mind ~?'로 요청하는 표현이므로 직역을 하면 '당신은 ~을 싫어하나요?'가 된다. B의 대답 'Yes, I do.'는 '네, 싫어합니다.'라는 거절의 표현인데, '볼륨을 줄일게.'라고 말하는 것은 어색하다.

05 ⑤번은 'Do you mind ~?'로 묻는 요청의 말에 대한 거절의 표현이다.

06 ②번의 'mind'의 목적어 자리에는 동명사만 사용 가능하기 때문에 부정사 'to tell'로 바꾸어 쓸 수 없다.

07 'be busy+-ing' 구문을 이용하여 '~하느라 바쁘다'를 표현하고, 'do you mind+-ing' 구문을 이용하여 '~해 주겠니?'라는 요청의 표현을 쓴다.

08 Andy는 Jessie에게 Amy에게 줄 선물로 괜찮은 것을 고르는 것을 도와달라고 부탁하고 있다.

09 Minsu가 여유를 가지기 위해 무엇을 할지는 대화에서 언급되어 있지 않다.

10 Mina는 엄마에게 미안하다고 어떻게 말해야 할지 조언을 구하고 있고, 상대방이 진심으로 사과해야 한다고 충고하고 있으므로 ③번이 가장 적절하다.

11 '산 위로 더 높이 올라갈수록, 날씨가 더 추워진다.'라는 문장이다. as로 시작하는 부사절로 바꿀 수 있다. ① '당신이 산을 더 높이 올라감에 따라 날씨가 더 추워진다.'의 뜻이다.

12 '우리가 나이를 먹을수록, 우리의 근육과 뼈는 유연성이 덜해진다.'는 내용이다. 'The+비교급 ~, the+비교급 …' 구문이 정확하게 사용된 문장이 답이다.

13 선행사가 the way일 때 how는 같이 사용하지 않는다.

14 일반적으로 선행사가 the way일 때, '전치사+관계대명사'는 in which를, 선행사가 the reason일 때 for which를 쓰며, 장소나 시간의 명사가 선행사로 쓰일 경우, 각 단어에 알맞게 at/on/in 등과 관계대명사 which를 활용하는 것이 적절하다. (2)의 경우 in 외에도 at이 가능하다.

15 (1) 비가 내린다는 표현은 비인칭주어 it을 활용한다. 과거 시제임에 유의하여 영작한다. (2) well의 비교급이 better임에 유의한다.

16 빈칸 (A)에는 동사 take가 쓰인다. 모두 take가 사용되지만 ②번에는 동사 make가 쓰여 '결심하다'라는 의미의 make up one's mind라는 의미를 완성한다.

17 신속한 사과는 당신이 사려 깊고, 당신의 행동에 책임을 진다는 것을 보여준다는 의미가 자연스러우므로 thoughtful이라고 쓰는 것이 적절하다.

18 주어진 문장은 '누군가에게 사과하고 싶은가?'에 대한 답이며, it이 가리키는 것 역시 to apologize to someone이다. 따라서 ④번에 들어가는 것이 가장 적절하다.

19 가족과 사랑하는 사람들에게 작은 실수를 하고 사과하지 않는 것은 큰 감정적인 상처가 된다고 하였고, 가깝다는 이유로 사과하지 않고 그냥 넘어가는 것은 옳지 않으므로 ③번은 글의 내용과 일치하지 않는다.

20 Mike는 그 일이 심각한 일이 아니라고 생각하는 것처럼 보였다.

21 (A) Mike의 가벼운 사과에 더 상처를 받았다는 의미이고, (B) 사과할 때 타인을 존중하고 타인의 감정에 관심을 갖고 있음을 보여 주어야 하며, (C) 사과가 진실할수록 그것이 더 잘 받아들여진다는 의미가 자연스럽다. reject: 거절하다

22 Mike의 사과는 진실하지 않았고, 그 결과 June은 더 화가 난 것이다.

Have Fun with Art!

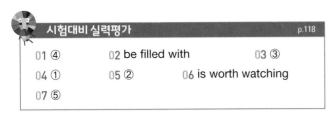

시험대비 실력평가 p.118

01 ④　　　02 be filled with　　　03 ③
04 ①　　　05 ②　　　06 is worth watching
07 ⑤

01 • '대학은 우리가 특정한 과목에 대한 지식을 배우는 곳이다.' • '학생들은 주어진 주제로 찬반 토론을 벌였습니다.' '과목, 주제'라는 의미를 가지는 단어는 'subject'가 맞다.

02 '흥미롭게도, 이 도서관은 종이로 된 책 대신에 전자책으로 가득 찰 것입니다.' <영영풀이> '비어 있는 공간에 어떤 물질을 넣다'의 의미로 'be filled with'가 적절하다.

03 (A) '아테네가 민주주의의 발생지라는 것은 당연하다.'라는 의미로 'no wonder'가 '~은 (별로) 놀랄 일이 아니다'의 의미로 적절하다. 'as well'은 '또한'의 의미이다. (B) '불가리아'라는 이름은 유럽에서 가장 오래된 나라 이름으로 여겨진다. '~로 여겨지다'는 'be regarded as'가 적절하다.

04 '오랜 시간 동안 변화 없이 한 무리의 사람들 또는 사회에서 지속되어 온 관습이나 행동 방식을 따르거나 속해 있는'의 의미로 'traditional(전통적인)'이 적절하다.

05 '어떤 식으로든 장식되지 않은; 아무것도 추가하지 않은'의 의미로 'plain(평범한)'이 적절하다.

06 'be worth+동명사' 형태로 '~할 만한 가치가 있다'는 뜻이다. 'watch'를 동명사 'watching'으로 바꾸어야 한다.

07 ⑤의 '포함하다-제외하다'는 반의어 관계이고, 나머지는 유의어 관계이다. ①은 '만들다, 창조하다', ②는 '생생한, 활기찬', ③은 '흔한, 평범한', ④는 '운영하다'라는 의미이다.

서술형 시험대비 p.119

01 (1) goods　(2) meaning　(3) amazing　(4) creative
02 plain, Plain, plain
03 (1) performances　(2) Back then
　　(3) pay attention to　(4) break down
04 (1) boring, 지루한　(2) practice, 연습하다
　　(3) cone, 원뿔

01 (1) 가격은 상품에 표시되어 있다. (2) 태극기에는 수많은 역사와 의미가 담겨 있다. / '의미'라는 명사로 사용되기 때문에 'meaning'이 적절하다. (3) 말은 놀라운 동물입니다. 그들은 아

름답고, 강하며, 영리합니다. / 동사 'amaze'를 'animals'를 수식하는 형용사로 '놀라운'의 의미를 가진 'amazing'으로 바꾸어 준다. (4) 창의적인 사람은 흥미로운 아이디어를 생각하는 능력을 가지고 있습니다. / 명사 'person'을 수식해야 하므로 동사 'create'의 형용사 'creative'가 적절하다.

02 • 우리 집은 갈색이고 장식이 없습니다. • 평원과 사막이 수목이 울창한 해안지대의 산맥과 태평양 연안에까지 뻗쳐 있었다. • 그들은 평범한 얼굴보다는 아름다운 얼굴을 보기를 좋아합니다. / 'plain'은 명사로 '평원, 평야', 형용사로 '보통의, 평범한, 수수한'의 의미를 가지고 있다.

03 (1) performance: 공연 (2) back then: 그 당시에 (3) pay attention to: ~에 주의를 기울이다 (4) break down: 부수다, 분해하다

04 (1) 재미있거나 흥미롭지 않은 (2) 어떤 것에 숙련되기 위해 그것을 규칙적으로 또는 반복적으로 하거나 연주하다 (3) 평평한, 둥근 또는 타원형의 기초와 점이 형성될 때까지 좁아지는 꼭대기를 가진 형태

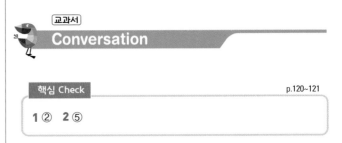

교과서
Conversation

핵심 Check p.120~121

1 ②　　2 ⑤

교과서 대화문 익히기

Check(√) True or False p.122

1 T　2 F　3 F　4 T

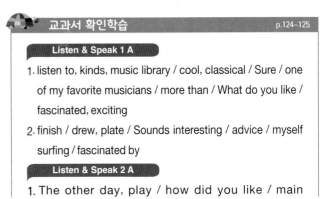

교과서 확인학습 p.124~125

Listen & Speak 1 A

1. listen to, kinds, music library / cool, classical / Sure / one of my favorite musicians / more than / What do you like / fascinated, exciting

2. finish / drew, plate / Sounds interesting / advice / myself surfing / fascinated by

Listen & Speak 2 A

1. The other day, play / how did you like / main

characters, performance, fantastic / as well / a little boring / should see / Only if, a lot of

2. how do you like / a lot / What do you like most / learning different drawing skills, What / painting skills, with / work, creative / practice a lot

Real Life Talk

didn't you / special / How did you like / fantastic / was fascinated by / creativity / No wonder, one of the greatest painters, What else / a gift shop, were printed / anything / How do you like / looks great on

Wrap Up 1

festival, didn't / performed / How did you like / special guest, called / heard / performance / No wonder

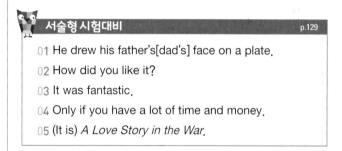

시험대비 기본평가   p.126

01 How do you like   02 ④   03 ③
04 ②

01 'How do you like ~?'는 '~은 어때?'라는 뜻으로 어떤 것에 대해 만족하는지 아니면 불만족하는지 묻는 표현이다.

02 '~에 매료되다, ~에 관심이 있다'는 표현이 적절하다. ④번은 '~에 만족하다'라는 의미가 되려면 'be satisfied with'를 사용해야 한다.

03 빈칸 다음의 대답으로 보아, 빈칸에는 축제가 어땠는지 묻는 말이 적절하다.

04 'How do you like ~?'는 어떤 것에 대해 만족하는지 아니면 불만족하는지 묻는 표현이다.

시험대비 실력평가   p.127~128

01 ②, ④   02 ①   03 ④   04 ②
05 She likes classical music.
06 ②   07 ④
08 how do you like your art class?
09 She thought it was very creative.
10 were fascinated by

01 빈칸 다음의 Andy가 한 말로 보아 만족이나 불만족을 묻는 표현이 적절하다.

02 Bora는 미술관에 가지 않았다.

03 며칠 전에 연극을 봤다는 말에 → (C) 그 연극이 어땠는지 묻고 → (D) 주인공들이 좋았고, 그들의 연기가 훌륭했다는 말을 하고 → (A) 이야기도 또한 좋았는지 묻는 말에 → (B) 그것은 약간 지루했다는 말을 하는 것이 자연스럽다.

04 '오페라의 유령'이라는 노래에 관한 대화 내용이므로 ②가 가장 적절하다.

05 질문: Sandy는 어떤 종류의 음악을 좋아하는가?

06 'one of+복수 명사'이므로 'musicians'가 되어야 한다.

07 ④번은 '축제는 어땠니?'라는 물음에, B가 '그것에 관해 들어봤어. 가수가 유명해.'라고 말하는 것은 자연스럽지 못하다.

08 어떤 것에 대해 만족하는지 아니면 불만족하는지 묻는 표현인 'How do you like ~?'를 이용한다.

09 질문: Claire는 Allen의 작품에 관해 어떻게 생각했는가?

10 '~에 매료되다'라는 의미로 동사 'fascinate'를 과거분사 'fascinated'로 바꾸어 준다.

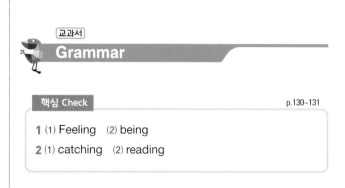

서술형 시험대비   p.129

01 He drew his father's[dad's] face on a plate.
02 How did you like it?
03 It was fantastic.
04 Only if you have a lot of time and money.
05 (It is) *A Love Story in the War.*

01 질문: Jim은 미술 과제로 무엇을 그렸는가? / Jim의 롤 모델은 그의 아버지이므로 my role model을 his father 또는 his dad로 바꾼다.

02 Andy의 대답 'It was fantastic!'으로 보아 빈칸에는 샤갈 전시회에 대해 어떤지 묻는 말이 오는 것이 자연스럽다.

03 질문: Andy는 Chagall 전시회를 어떻게 생각했는가?

04 '~해야만'의 의미로 'Only if+주어+동사 -'를 사용한다.

05 질문: 소년이 본 연극의 제목은 무엇인가?

교과서
Grammar

핵심 Check   p.130~131

1 (1) Feeling   (2) being
2 (1) catching   (2) reading

시험대비 기본평가   p.132

01 ⑤   02 ④   03 ②
04 (1) working   (2) paying attention to
    (3) crying

01 부사절을 분사구문으로 바꿀 때, 주어가 같으면 주어를 생략하고 분사를 쓴다.

02 'be worth V-ing'를 활용한다. worth에서 파생된 같은 의미의 다양한 표현도 익혀두는 것이 좋다.

03 두 문장을 하나로 만들어 보면 'As[While] Billy watched the emotional scenes, she was moved.'가 된다. ②가 분사구문으로 적절한 답이다. ① 과거분사 부적절 ③ 수동태형 부적절 ④ '접속사+주어'가 있을 때는 분사구문 불가능 ⑤ 의미상 '양보'의 접속사 Though 부적절

04 동명사의 관용적 표현들과 관련된 문제들이다. 'be worth V-ing'에서 동명사를 수동형으로 쓰지 않는 것에 유의한다.

시험대비 실력평가   p.133~135

01 ⑤	02 ①	03 ②	04 ④
05 ②	06 Changed → Changing		07 ③
08 ③	09 ③	10 ②	

11 Cartoons not being regarded as an art form at that time

12 Wanting everyone to enjoy his art   13 ①

14 ④	15 ③	16 ⑤

01 'be worth'는 V-ing(동명사)를 받는다. 'be worthy of V-ing[being p.p.]'로도 표현 가능하며, 'It is worth paying attention to ~' 형태로도 쓸 수 있다.

02 동명사의 관용적 표현에 관련된 문제이다. 'can't help'는 V-ing(동명사)를 받는다. 'can't but V(동사원형)', 'can't help but V(동사원형)'로도 표현 가능하며, 'have no choice but to V' 형태로도 쓸 수 있다.

03 부사절을 써서 영작하면, 'When people saw familiar images in art exhibitions, they found them refreshing.'이 된다. ②가 부사절을 분사구문으로 적절히 전환했다.

04 부사절을 써서 영작하면, 'Although pop art looks plain, it is filled with meaning.'이 된다. ④는 looks를 looking으로 적절하게 표현한 분사구문 앞에 접속사 Although를 덧붙였다.

05 각 문장을 해석하면, (1) '세계 역사와 문화 발전에 관한 책들은 읽을 가치가 있다.', (2) '그 집은 최소 50만 달러의 가치가 있음에 틀림없다.'이다, 명사나 동명사를 목적어로 받으며, '가치'의 의미를 가진 것은 worth이다.

06 '흔한 물건들을 놀라운 예술로 변모시키면서'(능동의 분사 구문)이므로 Changing으로 고치는 것이 적절하다.

07 ③의 knowing은 '현재분사'로 쓰였다. 'Brian은 그의 친구들이

참여하지 않을 것을 알고 그 계획을 포기했다.' 나머지는 모두 동명사이다. ① '그 작가의 책들은 알 가치가 없다.' ② '미래의 우리의 삶이 어떻게 될지 알 수 없다.' ④ '주변에 한국인들이 거의 살지 않기 때문에, 우리는 그녀를 알 수밖에 없다.' ⑤ '그녀의 문제가 불안감에서 왔다는 것을 알아도 소용없었다.'

08 내용상 Though의 역접 관계가 아닌, As 또는 Because 등과 같은 이유를 나타내는 접속사가 적절하다.

09 'be worth'는 V-ing(동명사)를 받는다. 'be worthy of V-ing[being p.p.]'로도 표현 가능하며, 'It is worth seeing and collecting the works ~' 형태도 가능하다.

10 <보기>는 '약간 평범하고 흔해보일지라도, 팝 아트는 수많은 의미로 가득 차 있다.'는 뜻으로, ② '11년간 마드리드에서 살아왔지만, Angella는 여전히 스페인어를 잘 못한다.'는 문장과 함께 '양보'의 의미인 '역접'으로 사용되었다. ① '조건' ③ '이유' ④ '이유' 또는 '시간' ⑤ '이유'

11 주어진 우리말의 부사절을 표현하면, 'Though cartoons were not regarded as an art form at that time,'이고, 종속절과 주절의 주어가 달라, 독립분사구문으로 Cartoons를 문두에 쓰고, 분사구문 앞에 부정어 not을 쓰면 'Cartoons not being regarded as ~' 형태가 된다.

12 주어진 우리말의 부사절을 표현하면, 'As he wanted everyone to enjoy his art,'이고, 접속사와 주어를 생략하고 Wanting으로 표현하면, 적절한 답이 된다.

13 모든 문장이 'be worth V-ing'이다. 일반적으로 '주어가 V할 가치가 있다'는 뜻인데, 주어는 V-ing의 대상이다. ①은 '팝 아트는 주목할 만한 가치가 있다.'라는 문장인데, pay attention은 전치사 to가 동반되어야 대상을 취할 수 있다. 그러므로 문미에 to를 추가하는 것이 적절하다.

14 동명사의 관용적 표현들이 사용된 문장들이다. ④는 '엎질러진 우유를 보며 우는 것은 소용없다.'라는 문장으로 'It is no use V-ing'일 때, crying이 맞는 표현이고, 'of no use'가 쓰였을 때는 'to V'를 쓰는 것이 적절하다.

15 'be worth'는 V-ing(동명사)를 취한다. 'be worthy of V-ing(being p.p.)'와 뜻이 같고, 'It is worth V-ing', 또는 'It is worth while V-ing(또는 to V)' 형태로도 표현 가능하다.

16 '내가 가장 좋아하는 시인이 쓰는 글은 세 번 읽을 가치가 있다.'라는 문장이다. ⑤는 '시인이 쓰는 글' 또는 '시인에 의해 쓰여진 글'이 아닌, '내가 가장 좋아하는 시'이므로 주어의 성격이 다르고, be worth 뒤의 동명사도 수동형으로 썼기 때문에 어법상 틀린 문장이다.

01 (1) visiting　(2) checking　(3) seeing　(4) buying
　(5) laughing　(6) laugh　(7) laugh　(8) to laugh
　(9) advertising　(10) knowing　(11) to know
　(12) carrying　(13) prepare　(14) preparing

02 (1) Being able to turn common objects into amazing art
　(2) Believing that art should be easy, pop artists broke
　(3) There not being any friends left around here
　(4) Finding his subjects in magazines and stores

03 (1) Gloria's mom couldn't help drinking the sour beverage to save her.
　(2) The expensive TV set was worth paying for.
　(3) It was no use fixing the ceiling unless the water problem is resolved.
　(4) Those men were busy preparing for the awards ceremony.
　(5) Pop art is worth paying attention to.

04 (1) As Andy Warhol wanted to show that art is something you see every day, he made many copies of his works.
　(2) Using daily images in a creative way, you can make a work of art for everyone.
　(3) When seeing familiar images in art exhibitions, people found them refreshing.
　(4) Using common images and everyday items, pop art looks plain.
　(5) Though[Although] looking plain, pop art is filled with meaning that art should be easy to understand. 또는 Looking plain, pop art is filled with meaning that art should be easy to understand.
　(6) Wanting everyone to enjoy his art, a pop artist set[sets] up his works in outdoor places.
　(7) Though cartoons were not regarded as an art form at that time, Roy Lichtenstein used them in making his works.

01 동명사의 관용적 표현에 관련된 문제이다. 다양한 동명사의 관용적 표현들을 알아두어야 한다. 'be worth V-ing = be worthy of V-ing[being p.p.] = It be worth V-ing'이며, 'can't help V-ing = can't but V(동사원형) = can't help but V(동사원형) = have no choice but to V'이다. 'It is no use V-ing = It is useless[of no use] to V', 'There is no V-ing = It is impossible to V'이다.

02 분사구문으로 시작하는 문장들이다. 각 분사구문의 원래의 부사절을 쓰면, (1) 'As they were able to turn common objects into amazing art', (2) 'Since[As] they believed that art should be easy', (3) 'As[Since, Because] there were not any friends left around here', (4) 'While he was finding his subjects in magazines and stores'이다. (3)은 주절과 종속절의 주어가 다르므로 유도부사 there를 문두에 쓴 독립분사구문이다.

03 'be worth V-ing'를 포함한 다양한 동명사의 관용적 표현들과 같은 의미의 다른 표현들을 많이 숙지하는 것이 좋다. 문제의 조건에서 가장 짧은 형태의 문장을 영작하는 것이 조건이므로, (3)의 경우 of no use를 useless로 바꾸면 단어들의 수가 더 줄어들겠지만 동명사를 받을 수 없음에 유의한다.

04 어법상 어색한 것을 '한 단어'로 고치거나 이동하라고 언급한 문제의 조건에 유의한다. (1) 접속사 As가 있으므로, wanting을 wanted로 고친다. 동사가 과거 시제임에 유의. 주절과 종속절의 주어가 같으므로 As만을 생략하는 것은 불가능하다. (2) Use → Using (3) seen → seeing (4) Used → Using (5) 구조는 접속사가 있는 분사구문 형태이나, 의미상 Because가 어색하다. 역접의 접속사 Though 또는 Although로 바꾸든가, 생략하는 것이 적절하다. (6) 분사구문이 양쪽에 나온 형태이다. 주절에 setting을 동사 set로 바꾸는 것이 적절하다. (현재시제로 보고 sets라고 해도 무방하다.) (7) 부사절과 종속절의 주어가 다른데, 독립분사구문 형태를 쓰려면 접속사가 없어야 한다. 그러나 Though를 생략해도, being not의 순서가 좋지 않아서, 차라리 being을 동사 were로 고쳐 부사절을 만든다.

교과서
Reading

확인문제　　　　　　　　p.138

1 T　2 T　3 F　4 F

확인문제　　　　　　　　p.139

1 T　2 F　3 T　4 F

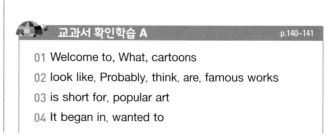

교과서 확인학습 A　　　　　　　p.140~141

01 Welcome to, What, cartoons
02 look like, Probably, think, are, famous works
03 is short for, popular art
04 It began in, wanted to

05 Instead of, traditional, turned, to

06 used, from, advertising

07 familiar images, them refreshing

08 become truly popular

09 that, too, to understand

10 By using, changed that thought

11 Using, looks plain. In other words, artistic

12 worth paying attention to, is filled with

13 famous pop artists

14 famous for, ability, able to change, into amazing

15 is called, found, subjects in

16 is made up

17 Another work shows, made, copies

18 copies of his works, to show that, you see

19 another, who made, fun

20 sculptures of everyday items

21 In the beginning, created, made of, soft materials

22 For example, cloth to make, huge sculptures, such as

23 Wanting, to enjoy, set up, outdoor

24 ran, inside, to sell, were fun goods

25 used, in his works, were, painted, lively colors

26 included, were, regarded as

27 However, differently, himself, Why, they not

28 broke down, between, and, by adding

29 believed, should be, Anyone, create, enjoy

30 creating, pop art

31 By using, in, make, for, the most important lesson

교과서 확인학습 B

p.142~143

1 Welcome to the Pop Art Exhibition! What do you see? Paintings of soup cans? Big cartoons?

2 Do they look like art works? Probably not, but think again. They are all famous works of pop art.

3 Pop is short for popular. So pop art means popular art, or art for people.

4 It began in the 1950s in America. Pop artists at that time wanted to create something fun and easy.

5 Instead of difficult traditional art works, they turned their eyes to popular culture.

6 They used images from TV, comic books, magazines, and advertising.

7 When people saw familiar images in art exhibitions, they found them refreshing.

8 Since then, pop art has become truly popular.

9 People thought that art was too difficult to understand.

10 By using daily images and bright colors, pop artists changed that thought.

11 Using common images, pop art looks plain. In other words, it doesn't look artistic.

12 But it is still worth paying attention to. Although it looks plain, it is filled with meaning.

13 Let's learn about some famous pop artists.

14 They became famous for their special artistic ability. They were able to change common objects into amazing art.

15 Andy Warhol is called the King of Pop Art. He found his subjects in magazines and stores.

16 One of his famous works is made up of pictures of Marilyn Monroe, the American actor.

17 Another work shows cans of soup. He made many copies of these works.

18 Why did he make copies of his works? He wanted to show that art is something you see every day.

19 Claes Oldenburg is another pop artist who made art fun.

20 He made sculptures of everyday items, such as a hamburger, cookies, and a brush.

21 In the beginning, he created soft sculptures. They were made of plastic, paper, and other soft materials.

22 For example, he used cloth to make toilets. Later, he made huge sculptures of daily items, such as an ice cream cone.

23 Wanting everyone to enjoy his art, he set up his works in outdoor places.

24 He also ran a store inside his studio to sell his works. For him, artistic works were fun goods for people.

25 Roy Lichtenstein used cartoons in his works. They were large and painted in lively colors.

26 He even included speech balloons in his paintings. Back then, cartoons were not regarded as an art form.

27 However, Roy Lichtenstein thought differently. He asked himself, 'Why are they not?'

28 Then Roy Lichtenstein broke down the wall between high art and popular culture by adding cartoons to art.

29 Pop artists believed art should be easy. Anyone can create and enjoy art.

30 How about creating a work of pop art today?

31 By using daily images in a creative way, you can make a work of art for everyone. This is the most important lesson from pop art.

 시험대비 실력평가 p.144~147

01 cartoon

02 They used images from TV, comic books, magazines, and advertising.

03 ③ 04 ④

05 He is called the King of Pop Art. 06 ④

07 ②

08 He wanted everyone to enjoy his art.

09 ③ 10 [C]–[B]–[A] 11 ③

12 ②

13 Pop artists believed art should be easy.

14 ④ 15 ⑤ 16 It began in 1950s.

17 ②, ④ 18 ④ 19 ④

20 He found his subjects in magazines and stores.

21 ③

22 He created soft sculptures in the beginning.

23 ④ 24 ⑤ 25 cartoons

26 He added cartoons to art. 27 ⑤

01 신문이나 잡지에 나오는 익살스러운 그림 혹은 연속적인 그림은 '만화(cartoon)'이다.

02 팝 아트 작가들은 텔레비전, 만화책, 잡지 및 광고에 나오는 이미지들을 사용했다.

03 사람들은 예술이 너무 어려워서 이해할 수 없는 것으로 생각했었다.

04 Andy Warhol이 자신의 작품들의 사본을 많이 만들었다고 말한 후 사본을 많이 만든 이유를 묻는 말이 들어가는 것이 자연스럽다.

05 그는 팝 아트의 왕이라 불린다.

06 글쓴이는 팝 아트는 여전히 주목할 만한 가치가 있다고 하였다.

07 Claes Oldenburg는 부드러운 조각품을 만들었다고 말하며 재료를 언급하고, 변기를 만들기 위해 천을 사용했다고 좀 더 자세히 말하고 있으므로 예시를 이끄는 For example이 가장 적절하다.

08 Claes Oldenburg는 모든 사람이 그의 작품을 보고 즐기기를 원했다.

09 Claes Oldenburg는 일상적인 물품들의 조각을 만든 예술가로, 초기에 플라스틱이나 종이, 그리고 다른 부드러운 재료들로 조각품을 만들었고, 나중에는 일상 물품의 거대한 조각품을 만들었다

고 하였으므로 ③번이 그의 작품에 해당한다고 볼 수 있다.

10 Roy Lichtenstein은 작품에 만화를 사용했는데 [C] 당시에 만화는 예술 형식으로 여겨지지 않음 [B] 하지만 Roy Lichtenstein은 다르게 생각하고 만화가 왜 예술로 간주되지 않는지 의문을 품음 [A] 만화를 예술에 첨가함으로써 Roy Lichtenstein은 순수 예술과 대중문화 사이의 벽을 허물음

11 be regarded as: ~라고 여겨지다

12 글의 내용은 누구나 예술 작품을 만들고 즐길 수 있다는 의미이다. 따라서 ②번이 가장 적절하다.

13 팝 아티스트들은 예술이 쉬워야 한다고 믿었다.

14 (A)는 '작품'이라는 의미로 쓰이고 있다. ① 일하다 ② 작동하다 ③ 일, 직장 ④ 작품 ⑤ 효과가 있다

15 팝 아티스트들은 일상적인 이미지를 사용하였다.

16 팝 아트는 1950년대에 시작됐다.

17 팝 아트는 일상적인 이미지와 밝은 색을 사용하여 만들어지며, 팝 아트의 의미는 사람들을 위한 예술이라고 하였으므로 ②, ④번이 가장 적절하다.

18 Andy Warhol의 작품들로 미루어 보아 흔한 대상을 놀라운 예술로 바꾸었다고 말하는 것이 자연스럽다. 따라서 ④번을 common이라고 쓰는 것이 적절하다.

19 수프 통조림으로 팝 아트 작품을 만든 예시가 나와 있다.

20 Andy Warhol은 잡지와 상점에서 주제를 찾았다.

21 예시로 이어지고 있는 것은 일상적인 물품들이다.

22 Claes Oldenburg는 초기에 부드러운 조각품을 만들었다고 하였다.

23 Claes Oldenburg는 변기를 만들기 위해서 천을 사용했다.

24 밑줄 친 (A)는 목적어로 사용된 재귀대명사이다. ⑤번은 강조 용법으로 사용되었다.

25 만화를 가리키는 말이다.

26 Roy Lichtenstein은 만화를 예술에 첨가하였다.

27 ⑤ Roy Lichtenstein은 순수 예술과 대중문화 사이의 벽을 허물었다. built → broke down

 서술형 시험대비 p.148~149

01 It means popular art or art for people.

02 popular culture, difficult traditional art works

03 미술 전시회에서 친숙한 이미지를 보고 사람들이 그것들이 신선하다는 걸 알게 되었을 때

04 By using daily images and bright colors, pop artists changed people's thought toward art.

05 It's because it uses common images.

06 They were able to change common objects into amazing art.

07 pictures, the American actor[actress], common objects

08 another pop artist who made art fun

09 Because[As] he wanted to everyone to enjoy his art

10 He used plastic, paper, and other soft materials.

11 They were painted in lively colors.

12 Why are cartoons not an art form?

13 일상적인 이미지를 창의적인 방식으로 사용함으로써 모든 사람을 위한 예술 작품을 만들 수 있는 것

01 팝 아트란 대중 예술 또는 사람들을 위한 예술이라는 뜻이다.

02 1950년대에, 미국의 팝 아티스트들은 전통 예술 작품보다는 대중문화에 흥미가 있었다.

03 앞 문장의 상황을 가리키는 말이다.

04 팝 아티스트들은 일상적인 이미지와 밝은 색을 씀으로써 예술을 향한 사람들의 생각을 바꾸었다.

05 팝 아트가 평범해 보이는 이유는 흔한 이미지를 사용하기 때문이다.

06 몇 명의 유명한 팝 아트 작가들은 흔한 대상을 놀라운 예술로 바꿀 수 있었다.

07 Andy Warhol의 유명한 작품 중 하나는 미국 배우인 Marilyn Monroe의 사진으로 구성되어 있다. 그 작품 외에도, 그는 쉽게 구할 수 있는 흔한 대상을 사용하여 예술작품을 만들었다.

08 '예술'이 '재미있는' 것이므로 목적격보어로 형용사 fun을 쓰는 것에 유의한다. 여기에서 쓰인 동사 make는 5형식 동사이다. '또 다른 하나'를 말할 때는 'another'를 사용하며, '예술을 재미있게 만들었던'이 '작가'를 수식하므로 관계대명사를 활용하여 문장을 완성한다.

09 원인을 나타내는 분사구문이므로 Because 혹은 As를 써서 같은 의미의 절을 완성할 수 있다.

10 부드러운 조각품을 만들기 위해서 Claes Oldenburg는 플라스틱, 종이, 그리고 다른 부드러운 재료들을 사용하였다.

11 Roy Lichtenstein의 그림은 생기 넘치는 색들로 그려졌다고 하였다.

12 '왜 만화는 예술로 간주되지 않을까?'라는 의미이다.

13 앞 문장을 가리키는 말이다.

영역별 핵심문제
p.151~155

01 unfamiliar　02 ④　　　03 ②　　　04 ⑤
05 be made up of　　　06 ④　　　07 ③
08 How do you like your food?
09 ③　　　10 ④　　　11 ④
12 I have an interest in your drawing.　　　13 ③

14 ④

15 (1) works were[are] worth seeing
　　(2) was so busy watching the show that

16 ⑤　　　17 ③　　　18 ④

19 Pop is short for popular. 20 ③

21 People thought that art was too difficult to understand.　　　22 ④　　　23 ⑤

24 He included speech balloons in his paintings.

25 ③

26 The writer liked the story of the movie.

27 ⑤

01 반의어 관계이다. 활기 없는-활기 넘치는 : 친숙한-낯선

02 (A) 나는 텐트를 설치할 괜찮은 장소를 알고 있어. (B) 그들은 나에게 떠나라고 했다. 다시 말해서, 나는 해고되었다.

03 독창적이고 특이한 아이디어를 생산하거나 사용하는 능력

04 전통적 스타일이나 형식, 또는 오랜 기간에 걸쳐 개발된 방법에 기초하고, 지속적인 가치가 있는 것으로 여겨지는

05 be made up of: ~로 구성되다

06 ④번은 '나는 에릭 칼 특별전이라는 전시회에 갔습니다.'라는 말로 'exhibition'은 '전시회'라는 의미이다.

07 '대중음악의 신나는 리듬이 정말 좋아.'라는 대답으로 보아 ③번이 가장 적절하다.

08 어떤 것에 대해 만족하는지 아니면 불만족하는지 묻는 표현인 'How do you like ~?'를 사용한다.

09 주어진 문장이 '너는 미술관에서 또 무엇을 봤니?'라는 뜻이므로 ③번에 들어가는 것이 자연스럽다.

10 Andy가 왜 티셔츠를 구입했는지는 대화에서 언급되어 있지 않다.

11 이것은 내가 가장 소중히 여기는 거라는 말에 → (D) '그건 머그컵이지 않니?'라고 묻고 → (B) '응'이라고 답을 하며 7년 동안 사용해 왔다는 말에 → (A) 놀라움을 표현하고 → (C) 머그컵이 어떤지 물어보고 → (E) 좋아 보인다는 말을 하는 것이 자연스럽다.

12 관심을 표현하는 말로 'be fascinated by', 'have an interest in', 'be interested in', 'be into' 등을 사용하여 표현할 수 있다.

13 ③의 meeting은 현재분사이다. 나머지는 모두 동명사로 사용되었다.

14 There가 있는 '독립분사구문'이다. 해석을 해보면 '비록 만화가 예술에 속할 수 없다는 오해가 있었지만, 몇몇 팝 아티스트들은 만화를 사용함으로써 훌륭한 예술작품들을 만들었다.'라는 내용이다. 부사구와 주절이 역접 관계이므로, '조건'이나 '이유'가 아닌, '양보'임을 알 수 있다. '양보'의 접속사 Though가 쓰인 ④

가 적절하다.

15 동명사의 관용적 용법을 활용하는 문제이다. (1) '세계적으로 유명한 팝 아티스트 Florentijn Hofman의 작품들은 볼 만한 가치가 있었다.'는 문장이다. works가 복수이므로 'was → were'로 고쳐 넣고, 동명사 visiting을 활용한다. were 대신 are를 써도 좋다. (2) '민준이는 쇼를 보느라 너무 바빠서 전화를 받을 수 없었다.'는 문장이다. be busy V-ing를 활용 'watch → watching'으로 고쳐 단어를 배열한다.

16 분사구문의 부정은 not을 분사 앞에 쓴다. 접속사를 쓸 경우, 접속사 뒤에 주어가 오면 분사구문은 쓸 수 없으므로 ①은 안 된다. ②, ④는 내용이 반대가 되고, ③은 not의 위치가 틀렸다.

17 '작년에 뉴욕에서 열린 Andy Warhol의 작품전은 방문할만한 가치가 있었다.'라는 문장이다. '주어+be worth V-ing'에서 주어가 V-ing의 의미상 목적어가 될 때, V-ing 뒤에 추가로 목적어를 쓰지 않는다.

18 모두 팝 아티스트들을 지칭하지만 ④번은 일반 사람들을 가리키는 말이다.

19 'pop'은 'popular(대중적인)'의 줄임말이라고 하였다.

20 팝 아트 작가들은 재미있고 쉬운 것을 만들고 싶어 했다고 하였으므로 ③번이 글의 내용과 일치한다.

21 사람들은 예술이 너무 어려워서 이해할 수 없는 것으로 생각했었다.

22 그 당시에 만화는 예술 형식으로 여겨지지 않았지만 Roy Lichtenstein은 다르게 생각하였다고 말하고 그의 남다른 생각이 이어지는 것이 자연스럽다.

23 일상적인 이미지를 창의적인 방식으로 사용함으로써 모든 사람을 위한 예술 작품을 만들 수 있고 이것이 바로 팝 아트의 가장 중요한 교훈이라고 하였다.

24 Roy Lichtenstein은 자신의 작품에 말풍선을 넣었다.

25 관계대명사 that은 계속적 용법으로 쓰일 수 없다. 따라서 who 라고 쓰는 것이 적절하다.

26 글쓴이는 영화의 이야기가 마음에 들었다고 하였다.

27 영화를 보는 데 얼마만큼의 시간을 소요했는지는 위 글을 읽고 답할 수 없다.

단원별 예상문제   p.156~159

01 popularity   02 ④   03 ①   04 ②
05 Was the story good as well?   06 boring
07 ⑤
08 I prefer pop music to classical music.
09 ④   10 ④   11 ①   12 ②
13 ②, ④   14 ①, ④   15 ③
16 They are famous for their special artistic ability.
17 ⑤   18 ⑤

19 He set up his works in outdoor places.
20 ③
21 magazines and stores, sculptor, cartoons

01 '형용사-명사' 관계다. 창의적인-창의성 : 인기 있는-인기

02 어떤 사람이 특정한 상황에서 당신이 무엇을 해야 하는지 또는 어떻게 행동해야 하는지에 대해 당신에게 제안하는 의견

03 만족이나 불만족에 대해 묻는 표현으로 'How do you like ~?'를 사용한다. 'What'을 'How'로 바꾸어야 한다.

04 Bora가 'Andy 야, 너 미술관에 갔었지, 그렇지 않니?'라고 묻는 것으로 보아 미술관에서 이야기하고 있지 않다는 것을 알 수 있다.

05 'as well'은 문장 끝에서 '또한'의 의미로 사용된다.

06 '재미있거나 흥미롭지 않은'의 의미로 'boring'이 적절하다.

07 음악 도서관에서 얼마나 많은 종류의 음악을 들을 수 있는지는 언급되어 있지 않다.

08 'like A more than B'는 'B보다 A를 더 좋아한다'라는 의미로 'prefer A to B'로 바꾸어 쓸 수 있다.

09 주어와 목적어가 동일할 때는 재귀대명사를 사용한다. 'me'를 'myself'로 고친다.

10 종속절이 주절보다 앞선 시제이므로, 완료분사구문이 필요하며 준동사의 부정은 not을 앞에 쓰는 것이므로, Not having been invited로 시작하는 ④가 적절하다.

11 동명사의 관용적 용법 중 'be worth V-ing'에서 동명사는 능동형으로 써야 한다. 단, be worthy of V-ing는 수동형 동명사 being p.p.가 좋다.

12 동명사의 관용적 용법 중 'can't help V-ing = can't but V(동사원형) = can't help but V(동사원형) = have no choice but to V'와 관련된 문제이다. ② crying → cry

13 'be worth V-ing = be worthy of V-ing[being p.p.] =It be worth V-ing' ② to buy → buying ④ 'worth of being visited'에서 worth → worthy 또는 of being visited → visiting

14 앞선 문장과 같은 맥락의 문장을 연결하는 것이므로 '다시 말해서' 혹은 '즉'이라는 의미의 연결어가 들어가는 것이 적절하다.

15 밑줄 친 (B)는 '주제'라는 의미로 쓰였다. ① 과목 ② 피실험자 ③ 주제 ④ ~될 수 있는 ⑤ 주어

16 그들은 특별한 예술적인 능력으로 유명해졌다고 하였다.

17 Andy Warhol의 또 다른 작품으로 수프 통조림들을 보여준다고 하였으므로 ⑤번이 옳다.

18 Claes Oldenburg는 일상적인 물품들을 주제로 삼았다. 따라서 ⑤번은 적절하지 않다.

19 Claes Oldenburg는 자신의 작품을 실외에 설치했다.

29

20 답변은 팝 아트에 관한 설명이 주를 이루고 있으므로 ③번이 가장 적절하다.

21 Andy Warhol은 잡지와 상점에서 주제를 찾는 것을 좋아했고, Claes Oldenburg는 훌륭한 조각가였으며, Roy Lichtenstein은 그의 그림에 만화를 사용한 것으로 유명했다.

서술형 실전문제   p.160~161

01 (A) fascinated   (B) painters   (C) were

02 (2) I was fascinated by its design.

03 (1) Though other people laughing at cartoons,

   (2) Using common everyday objects and images,

04 the island in the East Sea, is worth protecting

05 There is no knowing how long the

06 (1) It having rained heavily the day before,

   (2) Strictly speaking,

   (3) Exhausted from a series of overtime work,

   (4) Finding the kitty the old lady had lost,

07 Pop art began in America in 1950s.

08 Pop artists at that time wanted to create something fun and easy.

09 familiar images

10 (A) touching   (B) Watching   (C) moved

11 He went to his friend's house to watch a movie.

01 (A): '~에 매료되다'라는 의미로 'be fascinated by'를 사용한다. (B) 'one of the 최상급+복수 명사'로 단수인 'painter'를 복수명사로 바꾸어 준다. (C) 주어가 복수 명사인 'Famous works'이므로 복수 동사 'were'가 적절하다.

02 밝은 색깔이 아니라 디자인에 매료되었다고 소개하고 있다.

03 분사구문을 배열하는 문제이다. 각각 (1) '양보', (2) '이유'의 부사절을 분사구문으로 만든 것이다.

04 동명사의 관용적 용법 'be worth V-ing'를 활용한 문장이다.

05 동명사의 관용적 용법 'there is no V-ing'를 활용한 문장이다. 'V하는 것은 불가능하다.'라는 뜻이다.

06 (1) 원래의 부사절에서 비인칭 주어 it이 있으므로, 'It having rained'와 같이 독립분사구문 형태로 표현하는 것이 적절하다. (2) 비인칭 독립분사구문이므로, 문 두에 People을 쓸 필요가 없다. (3) 수동이므로 Exhausting을 Exhausted로 고쳐야 한다. (4) 능동이므로 Found → Finding이 적절하다.

07 팝 아트는 1950년대에 미국에서 시작되었다.

08 -thing으로 끝나는 부정대명사는 형용사가 뒤에서 수식하는 것에 유의하여 답한다.

09 사람들이 전시회에서 본 친숙한 이미지들을 가리키는 말이다.

10 감정을 유발할 때에는 현재분사를, 감정을 느낄 때에는 과거분사

를 쓰며, (B)는 주절의 주어가 분사구문의 주어와 같으므로 생략되었다. 따라서 내가 감동적인 장면을 본 것이므로 현재분사를 쓰는 것이 적절하다. (A)에 moving, (C)에 touched라고 써도 좋다.

11 글쓴이는 영화를 보러 친구 집에 갔다고 하였다.

창의사고력 서술형 문제   p.162

|모범답안|

01 ① Playing the guitar, she composed a song.

   ② Holding something in her mouth, she is lying on the bed.

   ③ Walking in the bird park, he talked to the parrot.

   ④ Watching TV, he didn't hear the phone ringing.

02 Last Saturday / the concert hall / a musical / *You and Me* / my favorite actor was in it / the songs and dances / about a girl who invited her best friends to her birthday party / about their friendship / The main character was / sang many beautiful songs / fantastic / Singing along to the songs during the performance, excited

01 단어들을 적절히 조합하여 내용과 어법에 맞게 영작한 답이면 된다.

단원별 모의고사   p.163~167

01 ⑤   02 familiar   03 ③   04 ④

05 ③   06 ④   07 ④

08 I drew myself surfing in the sea.   09 ②

10 I couldn't take my eyes off it.   11 ②

12 ③   13 ③   14 ④

15 (1) used everyday items

   (2) If they watch the pop artist making

   (3) she got interested in the film

   (4) Though she was unhealthy

16 ②   17 (C)-(B)-(A)

18 But it is still worth paying attention to.   19 ④

20 ③

21 It's because he wanted to show that art is something you see every day.

22 other → another   23 ④   24 ⑤

25 He ran a store inside his studio to sell his works.

01 ⑤번은 'original(원본)'에 관한 설명이다. 'copy(복사본)'의 영어 설명은 'something that has been made to be

exactly like something else(다른 것과 똑같도록 만들어진 것)'이다.

02 유의어 관계이다. 조언, 충고 : 친숙한

03 '누군가 또는 어떤 것 대신에'의 의미로 'instead of'가 적절하다.

04 ④번은 책을 읽었다는 말에 대해 B가 그것을 혼자 시청했다고 답하는 것은 어색하다.

05 앞의 말에 동의할 때 사용하는 말로 '놀랄 일이 아니다.'라는 'No wonder.'가 적절하다.

06 (d)의 'them'은 'things like umbrellas, cups, and backpacks'를 가리킨다.

07 미술 과제에 관한 대화이므로 ④번이 가장 적절하다.

08 주어와 목적어가 동일할 때 재귀대명사를 목적어 자리에 사용한다.

09 대화의 흐름상 연극이 어땠는지 묻는 말이 적절하다.

10 'can't take A off B': 'B에서 A를 떼지 못하다'

11 ①, ④는 주절과 종속절의 주어가 다르므로, 분사구문의 주어를 쓴다. 날씨를 나타내는 '독립분사구문'은 주어 It을 쓴다. ③, ⑤는 반대로 주절과 종속절의 주어가 같으므로, 주어를 분사구문 앞에 쓸 필요가 없다. ① Drawing → My sister drawing ③ The structures observed → Observed ④ Not snowing → It not snowing ⑤ Maggy memorizing → Memorizing

12 동명사의 관용적 용법 'be worth V-ing'와 관련된 문제이다. 'be worthy of V-ing[being p.p.] = It be worth V-ing' 모두 같은 의미이며, ③과 같이 be worth가 있을 때는 능동형으로 visiting을 쓴다. be worthy of가 있을 때는 being visited 가능하다.

13 동명사의 관용적 용법 중 'can't help V-ing'와 관련된 문제이다. 'can't but V(동사원형) = can't help but V(동사원형) = have no choice but to V' 모두 같은 의미를 나타낸다. ③ crying → cry

14 ④ 부사절로 고치면, 'As there were no coins left'이다. 주어가 다르므로, 유도부사 there는 생략할 수 없다. 'Being no coins left → There being no coins left'가 적절하다.

15 각 문장의 분사구문은, (1) '양태'(그가 일상의 물건들을 사용하듯이) (2) '조건'(그 팝 아티스트가 그림을 제작하는 것을 본다면) (3) '이유'(그 영화에 흥미를 느껴서) (4) '양보'(건강하지 않은데도 불구하고) 등이다. 각각에 맞는 접속사와 대명사를 활용하는 것에 유의한다.

16 위 글은 팝 아트의 의미와 팝 아트가 어떻게 발전하게 되었는지

에 관한 글이다. 따라서 ②번이 가장 적절하다.

17 (C)의 그 당시는 1950년대를 의미한다. 전통 예술 작품 대신 대중문화로 눈을 돌렸다고 하였으므로 (B)에서 대중문화에 해당하는 텔레비전, 만화책 등이 제시가 되고, 사람들의 반응이 나온 후 (A)에서 그때부터 팝 아트는 정말 유명해졌다고 말하는 순서가 가장 자연스럽다.

18 be worth Ving: V할 가치가 있다, pay attention to: ~에 주목하다

19 팝 아트는 평범해 보일지라도 의미로 가득 차 있다고 하였다.

20 위 글은 Andy Warhol의 작품에 관한 설명이므로 Marilyn Monroe가 그 당시에 미국에서 가장 사랑받았던 배우이며 이른 나이에 죽었다는 문장은 글의 흐름상 어색하다.

21 Andy Warhol은 예술은 매일 보는 것임을 보여 주고 싶었기 때문에 자신의 작품 사본을 많이 만들었다.

22 other+복수명사, another+단수명사

23 빈칸 뒤에 other soft materials의 예가 오므로 ④ '예를 들면'이 적절하다.

24 (A)는 to부정사의 부사적 용법 중 목적(~하기 위해서)으로 쓰였다. ①, ③ 형용사적 용법 ② 진주어 ④ 동사의 목적어 ⑤ 부사적 용법 중 목적

25 Claes Oldenburg는 작품 판매를 위해 작업실 안에 상점을 운영하였다.

Lesson 9

You Can Do It, Too

시험대비 실력평가
p.172

01 ③	02 afford	03 ②	04 ③
05 ⑤	06 ⑤		

01 주어진 단어는 반의어 관계에 있다. 따라서 ③번이 적절하다. ①, ④ 매우 귀중한, ② 귀중한, ⑤ 돈이 많이 드는, 비싼

02 '어떤 것을 할 수 있다'는 '~할 여유가 되다(afford)'이다.

03 ① 그 연설자는 논의를 위한 몇 가지 진지한 주제를 제안함으로써 끝냈다. by Ving: V함으로써 ② 그는 사람들의 삶을 더 편안하게 만들어 줄 새로운 방법을 생각해 냈다. hit on: ~을 생각해 내다 ③ 당신의 노력 덕분에, 우리는 이 프로젝트를 가까스로 끝낼 수 있었습니다. ④ 매주 그들은 노래를 만들고 함께 연주하기 위해서 만난다. ⑤ 당신은 그녀가 그것을 공짜로 해주리라고 기대할 순 없어요.

04 ① 우리가 이 물건들을 집안에 두는 것은 쓸모가 없어. useless: 쓸모없는 ② 정부는 이민을 통제하려고 시도한다. control: 조종하다, 통제하다 ③ 사람들은 쓰레기로 환경을 오염시킨다. pollute: 오염시키다 ④ 필터가 물속의 모든 오염물질들을 제거하는 것은 아니다. remove: 제거하다, 없애다 ⑤ 우리는 그가 살아 있는지 죽었는지 모른다. whether: ~인지 아닌지

05 thanks to: ~ 덕분에, look forward to ~ing: ~하기를 고대하다

06 모두 '동사-명사'의 관계이지만 attempt는 동사와 명사의 형태가 같으며 attemption이라는 단어는 존재하지 않는다.

서술형 시험대비
p.173

01 (1) coin (2) control (3) business (4) cost
   (5) for free

02 fair

03 (1) pollution (2) limitation (3) beautiful

04 (1) We can collect things like shoes and clothes that people no longer need.
   (2) The entrance fee is $10 for adults.
   (3) Sam rides a bike not to pollute the air.

05 (A) to   (B) by   (C) for

06 success

01 (1) 나는 중국 동전 하나를 가지고 있어. (2) 너는 너의 소비를 통

제하는 방법을 배울 필요가 있어. (3) 그녀는 언젠가 자신의 사업체를 가지길 원해요. (4) 나는 그것이 전부 5달러만 들었다는 것을 믿을 수 없어요. (5) 사람들이 무료로 일을 해 주길 기대할 수는 없다.

02 fair는 '박람회'라는 의미 외에도 형용사로 '공정한, 타당한'이라는 의미를 갖는다.

03 (1), (2) 동사에 어미 '-tion'을 붙여서 명사가 된 것이다. pollute의 명사형은 pollution으로 만들 수 있다. (3) 명사에 어미 '-ful'을 붙여서 형용사가 된 것으로, beauty의 형용사형은 beautiful이다.

04 각각 (1) '모으다' (2) '요금' (3) '오염시키다'라는 말이 빠져 있으므로 collect, fee, pollute를 써서 문장을 완성한다.

05 (A) look forward to Ving: ~을 고대하다, think to oneself: 마음속으로 생각하다 (B) by Ving: V함으로써, by oneself: 혼자서, 혼자 힘으로 (C) pay for: ~을 지불하다, blame A for B: A를 B라는 이유로 비난하다

06 '목적 또는 목표의 성취'는 '성공'이다.

교과서
Conversation

핵심 Check
p.174~175

1 Is it possible for her to control them, too?
2 she can drive the truck
3 I wish I lived in a big city.

교과서 대화문 익히기

Check(√) True or False
p.176

1 F   2 T   3 F   4 F

교과서 확인학습
p.178~179

Listen & Speak 1 A-1

Can you draw / From, two triangles / like this / possible for you, without taking, off / how is that / at, four red points / any of the red points / first, the two triangles like this, triangles first / I get it

Listen & Speak 1 A-2

looking for, for / How old / five years old / to recommend / so / isn't it, that looks like, love it / for me to take, off / ake it off, put it back / wonderful, take it

Listen & Speak 2 A-1

you have been late for, wrong / wake up early, can't / wake you up / does, right away. I wish, could / An AI robot / that could make sure, gave me breakfast / great

Listen & Talk 2 A-2

planning to visit / going to do there / spend most of my time, because, swimming pool / Can, swim well / I wish I could, have fun with, instead / What is that / It's, go inside, walk on / must be

Real Life Talk

are, doing / drawing, my favorite superhero / great / could read people's minds / for her to control / if she wants to / cool / have any favorite superheroes / could fly like him / even breathe in / can do anything

Wrap Up 1

What are you doing / flying / Are, good at / right now, practicing hard / As you know, run / for you to deliver orders / isn't, it will be possible in / That, be great

시험대비 기본평가   p.180

01 (A) Is it possible for you   (B) Is it possible for you

02 ③   03 ③

04 I could have an AI robot.

01 달이나 태양까지 날아가는 것이 가능한지 묻는 말이므로 가주어 it과 의미상의 주어 'for+목적격'을 적절히 이용하여 문장을 완성할 수 있다.

02 가능을 묻는 표현인 'Is it possible for ~ to V?'는 'Is it likely that 주어 can V ~?'로 바꾸어 쓸 수 있다.

03 Wendy는 계속해서 지각을 하고 있으므로, 일찍 일어나고 싶지만 그렇게 안 된다는 의미가 자연스럽다.

04 이어지는 대화 내용으로 보아 Wendy는 인공지능 로봇이 있으면 좋겠다는 바람의 말을 했음을 알 수 있다.

시험대비 실력평가   p.181~182

01 ③   02 ④   03 (D)-(A)-(C)-(E)-(B)

04 ②

05 It is because she can't wake up early.

06 I wish I could invent a time machine.   07 ⑤

08 ②   09 ③   10 ③   11 ④

12 Can you deliver orders with your drone?

01 가능성을 묻는 말에 긍정으로 답하고 있으므로 ③번이 적절하다.

02 종이에서 연필을 떼지 않고 그림을 그릴 때 빨간 점 중에서 아무 점에서 시작해도 된다고 하였다.

03 일찍 일어나고 싶지만 그럴 수 없다는 말에 (D) 엄마가 깨워주시지 않느냐고 묻고 (A) 엄마가 깨워주시지만 자신이 바로 일어나지 않는다며, 인공지능 로봇이 있으면 좋겠다는 소망을 말함 (C) 인공지능 로봇이냐고 되묻자 (E) 그것을 원하는 이유를 설명하고 (B) 이 말에 좋은 생각이라고 답하는 순서가 자연스럽다.

04 ⓐ는 '최근에'라는 말이다. 따라서 ②번이 적절하다.

05 Wendy는 일찍 일어날 수 없어서 지각한 것이다.

06 이어지는 말로 보아 A는 타임머신을 발명하고 싶다는 소망을 나타냈음을 알 수 있다.

07 스마트폰을 가지고 있다면 친구들에게 메시지를 보낼 것이라는 내용이 가장 적절하다.

08 밑줄 친 부분은 가능성을 묻는 말이다. 따라서 ②번이 적절하다.

09 모자를 더 큰 것으로 교환할 수 있냐고 묻는 말에 긍정으로 대답하고 그럴 수 있을 것 같지 않다는 말이 이어지고 있으므로 어색한 대화이다.

10 hardly는 '거의 ~하지 않는'이라는 의미의 부사이다. hard는 형용사와 부사의 형태가 같으므로 'I'm practicing hard'라고 쓰는 것이 적절하다.

11 여자는 Tom이 드론으로 샌드위치 배달을 할 수 있는지 묻고 있으므로 ④번이 글의 내용과 일치한다.

12 가능을 묻는 말이므로 'Can you ~?'로 표현할 수 있다.

서술형 시험대비   p.183

01 Is it possible for you to draw this on the paper?

02 to draw it without taking your pencil off the paper

03 (1) 원을 먼저 그리고 그 다음에 삼각형 두 개를 그린다.
   (2) 삼각형 두 개를 먼저 그리고 원을 그린다.

04 I wish I could keep calm and pass the time.
   I wish I could create a shelter.
   I wish I could wait for help.
   I wish I could find food.

05 It is possible for Dr. Rebecca to read people's

minds and control them.

06 Bora's favorite superhero is Sky X.

01 가능성을 묻는 표현이므로 'Is it possible ~?'로 물을 수 있으며 to부정사의 의미상 주체로 'for+목적격'을 이용할 수 있다.

02 연필을 떼지 않고 그것을 그리는 것을 의미하는 말이다.

03 원을 먼저 그린 후 삼각형 두 개를 그리거나, 삼각형 두 개를 먼저 그린 후 원을 그리는 두 가지 방법이 제시되어 있다.

04 바람이나 소원을 말할 때 'I wish'를 써서 나타낼 수 있다. 해석: 내가 차분함을 유지하며 시간을 보낼 수 있으면 좋겠어. 내가 피신처를 만들 수 있다면 좋겠어. 내가 도움을 기다릴 수 있으면 좋겠어. 내가 음식을 찾을 수 있으면 좋겠어.

05 닥터 레베카는 사람들의 마음을 읽고 조종하는 것이 가능하다.

06 보라가 가장 좋아하는 슈퍼 영웅은 스카이 X이다.

교과서
Grammar

핵심 Check   p.184~185

1 (1) lived   (2) were[was]   (3) could

2 (1) if   (2) whether

시험대비 기본평가   p.186

01 (1) can → could   (2) has → had
   (3) work → worked   (4) may might

02 ④   03 ④   04 ③

01 모든 문장이 가정법이라는 조건이 주어졌고, 구조는 '가정법 과거' 형태이므로, 조건절의 동사를 과거시제로, 주절의 조동사도 과거형이 적절하다.

02 세 문장 모두 '~인지 아닌지' 여부를 나타내는 명사절로서 접속사가 들어가는 자리이다. 문두 또는 바로 다음에 or not이 오는 경우 if는 불가능하므로, whether가 적절하다.

03 I wish 가정법 문장이다. 주절에 '동사의 과거형' 또는 '조동사 과거+동사원형'의 구조가 오는 답을 선택하는 것이 적절하다.

04 명사절 접속사 if를 찾는 문제이다. ①, ②, ④, ⑤는 모두 조건의 부사절 접속사로 쓰였다.

01 ④   02 ⑤   03 ③

04 I don't know if you can help me.

05 I wish I were the President of the United States.

06 David asked me whether there was a bathroom

07 If I were the girl, I would give up.   08 ④

09 ②   10 ③   11 ②   12 ⑤

13 ②   14 ④   15 ⑤   16 ④

01 'I wish 가정법 과거' 문장에서 주절에는 '동사의 과거형' 또는 '조동사의 과거+동사원형'이 온다. will make → would make 또는 made가 적절하다.

02 ⑤ 가정법 문장이라면 can을 could로, 직설법 문장이라면 pushed를 push로 쓰는 것이 적절하다.

03 간접의문문을 이끄는 명사절 접속사 if는 whether와 달리 'or not'을 바로 붙여서 쓸 수 없다.

04 의문사가 없을 때 간접의문문은 if로 시작한다. 주절의 I don't know에 맞는 if 이하를 적절히 배열한다.

05 'I wish 가정법' 문장에서 '~라면 좋을 텐데'라는 뜻을 나타낼 때, 주절에는 'were'가 온다.

06 의문사가 없을 때 간접의문문은 whether로 시작한다. 주절의 어순은 'whether+주어+동사'인데, 유도부사 there가 오는 문장은 'there+동사+주어'가 바른 어순이 된다.

07 가정법 과거 시제의 문장이다. If절에 과거동사 were를 쓰고, 주절에 조동사의 과거형 would를 쓴다.

08 ④만 조건의 부사절 접속사이며, 나머지는 모두 간접의문문을 이끄는 명사절 접속사이다.

09 ②를 제외한 나머지는 모두 가정법의 주절에서 쓰이는 조동사이다. ②의 could는 can의 과거시제이다.

10 ③만 조건의 부사절을 이끄는 접속사이다. 나머지는 모두 간접의문문의 명사절을 이끈다.

11 '~가 없다면'이라는 가정법 표현은 'If there were no ~'로 나타내며, without 또는 'If it were not for ~'로 대체할 수 있고, 이 경우 if를 생략해서 'were it not for ~'로 표현 가능하다. ② is → were

12 'I wish 가정법 과거'는 직설법 현재 시제의 반대 의미이므로, 직설법의 couldn't make를 can't make로 고치는 것이 적절하다.

13 ① 직설법으로는, 'Vanessa의 동생이 휴대폰이 없어서 한 대 갖고 싶어 한다.'는 내용인데, 가정법으로는 '갖고자 한다면 얻을 수 있다'가 되어 의미가 다르다. ③ 직설법과 같은 뜻이 되려면, 가정법 과거완료 시제가 필요하다. ④ 가정법과 직설법에 모두

not이 있어서 뜻이 반대된다. ⑤ 직설법으로 '비가 억수같이 와서 가족 모두가 집에 있었다.'는 내용인데, 가정법은 '비가 억수같이 온다면, 모든 가족이 집에 머무르지 않을 텐데.'가 되어 어색하다.

14 의문사가 없는 의문문의 간접의문문을 이끄는 명사절 접속사 if/whether를 적절히 사용하여, 동사 ask의 목적어 자리에 쓰고, 내용상 can의 과거시제 could를 활용한 ④가 정답이다. ① '소녀가 로봇 손을 만들어 달라고 부탁했다.'가 되어, 우리말과 일치하지 않는다. ②, ③ 접속사 that을 쓰는 경우는 '~인지'라는 의사를 묻기보다 '~이라는 것'이라는 사실과 관계될 때 쓴다. ⑤ 접속사 whether는 올바르지만, could make는 '만들 수 있는지'라는 뜻이고, made는 '만들었는지'가 되어 뜻이 같지 않다.

15 ① can → could ② can → could ③ will → would ④ is → could be

16 (A)와 (C)는 'I wish 가정법' 형태이다. 주절에 동사 또는 조동사의 과거형을 쓴다. (B)는 가정법 과거 문장이고, 주절에 조동사의 과거형 would가 적절하다.

서술형 시험대비 p.190~191

01 (1) I wish I could pay the school fees for many poor girls to
(2) I wish the small holes in the corn cobs could filter
(3) I wish the girl I met at a science fair had
(4) the villagers helped me, I could build

02 (1) I asked myself that night if[whether] I could solve the problem of the polluted water.
(2) Tony wasn't sure if[whether] he could make it but he decided to try.
(3) Whether Jane will follow her heart or not is important in her life.
(4) Even her closest friends doubted whether she could do something for the girls in Africa.
(5) Most people in my town are wondering if it will rain next week.
(6) Sean couldn't decide whether to reject the job offer or not.
(7) The researchers want to know if[whether] my filtering system can clean up all the lakes not only in my village but also in other areas.

03 (1) But for (2) If it were not for
(3) Were it not for
(4) As there is her invention, the town does

04 (1) Matilda wondered if she could borrow something from Mrs. Forestier.
(2) Matilda asked Mrs. Forestier if she would lend her that diamond necklace.

05 wish the poor girls in Africa could go

06 wish I sang well like

07 Ask Mike if Susan speaks Korean.

08 Gloria was not sure if her baby was hungry or sad.

01 'I wish 가정법', 'If절의 가정법 과거' 등에 유의하여, 주어진 단어들을 적절히 배열한다.

03 '그녀의 발명이 없다면, 마을은 수질 오염 문제로 고통을 겪을 텐데.'라는 내용으로 직설법으로 표현하면, '그녀의 발명이 있어서, 마을은 수질 오염 문제로 고통을 겪지 않는다.'가 된다. 가정법 과거를 전제로, 'Without = But for = If it were not for = Were it not for'를 기억해 두는 것이 좋다.

04 간접의문문을 이끄는 명사절 접속사 if를 사용하여, 대화의 내용 (1) 'Matilda는 Mrs. Forestier로부터 뭔가를 빌릴 수 있을지 궁금해 했다.'와, (2) 'Matilda는 Mrs. Forestier에게 그 다이아몬드 목걸이를 빌려줄 것인지 물어봤다.'에 알맞게 바른 어순으로 배열한다.

05 '아프리카의 가난한 소녀들이 학교에 갈 수 없기 때문에, 나는 안타깝게 느껴졌다.'라는 직설법 문장을 가정법으로 표현하면, '아프리카의 가난한 소녀들이 학교에 갈 수 있으면 좋을 텐데.'가 된다. 'I wish 가정법'을 활용하되, can't가 could로 바뀌는 것에 유의하여 영작한다.

06 '가수인 나의 할아버지처럼 노래를 잘하면 좋을 텐데.'라는 의미가 되도록 I wish 가정법에 동사 과거형 sang을 활용한다.

07 Susan이 3인칭 단수임에 유의하여, 적절하게 영작한다. 간접의문문의 어순은 'if+주어+동사'임에 유의한다.

08 '확신할 수 없었다'는 내용으로 보아, 과거시제와 not이 쓰였음을 알 수 있다. 시제에 유의하여, 적절히 영작한다.

교과서
Reading

확인문제 p.192

1 T 2 T 3 F

확인문제 p.193

1 F 2 T 3 F

01 who change, too young to be

02 will meet, to make

03 when, came across, at, fair

04 robotic, that, open, close

05 surprised that, had cost her

06 wish, had, to myself

07 a much cheaper, better

08 failures, by using, was able to, for, of

09 to share, for, with others for free

10 take what I have done, something useful

11 No one, change, build, by working

12 can't, go to school, could go

13 had this thought, realized that, afford

14 if I could do something, had

15 asked, buy me a sewing machine

16 bought me one, how to make

17 ten headbands, them

18 raised enough money, stop

19 a business, who, go

20 to the success, fees for, like, to go to school

21 pay for, textbooks, uniforms, amazing

22 advice, is, do something, a need, act

23 small, taking, lives

24 As, living, often found that, seriously polluted

25 how I could solve, hit on, to use

26 Useless, were, in

27 the small holes, could filter dirty matter, polluted

28 picked, washed them, placed, in a bowl of

29 After a while, it, much clearer

30 using, that, collected from, filtering

31 removed, the dirty matter

32 filtering system, clean up, not only, but also

교과서 확인학습 B   p.196~197

1 Who are the people who change the world? Do you think you are too young to be one of these people?

2 In the following stories you will meet three teenagers who used their ideas to make the world a better place.

3 One day, when I was fourteen, I came across a little girl at a science fair.

4 She had a robotic hand that could only open and close.

5 I was surprised that the hand had cost her 80,000 dollars!

6 'I wish she had a better robotic hand,' I thought to myself.

7 With that, I started to make a much cheaper and better robotic hand.

8 After many failures, finally, by using 3D printing technology, I was able to make a useful robotic hand for the price of only 300 dollars.

9 I decided to share the designs and software for my 3D robotic hand with others for free.

10 Maybe someone can take what I have done and do something useful with it.

11 No one person can change the world, but we can build a better world by working together.

12 'Why can't many girls in Africa go to school as I can? I wish they could go to school, too.'

13 I had this thought when I was twelve. I realized that their families couldn't afford it.

14 I wondered if I could do something for those girls. Then I had an idea.

15 For my birthday, I asked my parents to buy me a sewing machine.

16 They bought me one, and I learned how to make headbands for myself.

17 I created ten headbands and sold them at my school.

18 Soon, I raised enough money to send one girl in Africa to school. I couldn't stop there.

19 I started a business to help girls in Africa who couldn't go to school.

20 Thanks to the success of my business, I can pay the school fees for many poor girls in countries like Kenya and Uganda to go to school.

21 I also pay for their textbooks, uniforms, and pencils. Isn't it amazing?

22 My advice to you is to just do something. When you see a need, act.

23 Start small, taking little steps. Your warm heart can change lives.

24 As a young girl living in the countryside in India, I often found that the water around us was seriously polluted.

25 I wondered how I could solve this problem. Then I hit on the idea to use corn cobs.

26 Useless corn cobs were everywhere in my village.

27 I thought that the small holes in the corn cobs could filter dirty matter out of the polluted water.

28 One day, I picked up some dried cobs along the

road, washed them, and placed them in a bowl of dirty water.

29 After a while, I checked the water, and it looked much clearer.

30 Then, using corn cobs that I had collected from farmers, I built a filtering system.

31 My system removed 70 to 80 percent of the dirty matter from the water.

32 I hope my filtering system can clean up all the lakes not only in my village but also in other areas.

시험대비 실력평가
p.198~201

01 the people who change the world   02 ②
03 ④   04 ⑤
05 He used 3D printing technology.   06 ③
07 Because their families couldn't afford it.
08 afford   09 ⑤
10 Useless Corn Cobs as Useful Water Filters
11 ④   12 ④   13 ⑤   14 ②
15 It's because the girl's robotic hand had cost her 80,000 dollars.   16 ④   17 to go
18 ②   19 (D)—(B)—(A)—(C)   20 ⑤
21 ④
22 The small holes in the corn cobs could filter dirty matter out of the polluted water.
23 ③
24 주변에 있는 물이 심각하게 오염되어 있는 것
25 ③

01 세상을 바꾸는 사람들을 의미하는 말이다.

02 세상을 더 나은 곳으로 만들기 위해 자신들의 아이디어를 사용한 세 명의 십대들을 만날 것이라고 하였으므로 ②번이 가장 적절하다.

03 글쓴이는 자신이 발명한 로봇 손 디자인을 다른 사람들과 무료로 공유했다고 하였다. 따라서 혼자 세상을 바꿀 수는 없지만 함께 일하면서 더 나은 세상을 만들 수 있다고 말하는 것이 자연스럽다.

04 많은 실패 뒤에 마침내 300달러짜리의 유용한 로봇 손을 만들었고 이 로봇 손의 디자인과 소프트웨어를 다른 사람들과 무료로 공유하기로 결심했다는 것이 적절하다.

05 글쓴이는 3D 프린트 기술을 이용하여 로봇 손을 만들었다.

06 ③번 뒤에 나오는 대명사 They와 one이 가리키는 것은 주어진 문장의 my parents와 a sewing machine이다.

07 아프리카의 많은 소녀들이 학교를 갈 수 없는 이유는 그들의 가족

들에게 금전적 여유가 없기 때문이었다.

08 무언가에 돈을 지불할 만큼 충분한 돈을 가지고 있는 것은 '~할 여유가 되다(afford)'이다.

09 글쓴이는 머리띠를 10개 만들어 학교에서 팔았다고 하였다.

10 위 글은 쓸모없는 옥수수 속대로 유용한 물 여과 장치를 만든 이야기이다.

11 과거동사의 병렬이므로 placed라고 쓰는 것이 적절하다.

12 Lalita는 농부들로부터 옥수수 속대를 모았다.

13 빈칸에는 비교급을 강조하는 부사(구) much, still, even, far, a lot이 들어갈 수 있다. very는 원급을 강조한다.

14 글쓴이가 만든 3D 로봇 손의 디자인과 소프트웨어를 의미한다.

15 소녀가 로봇 손에 8만 달러를 지불했다는 말에 글쓴이는 놀랐다고 하였다.

16 Easton은 겨우 접었다 펴지기만 하는 로봇 손에 8만 달러를 지불한 소녀를 돕고 싶은 마음에 로봇 손을 만들기 시작했다.

17 for many poor girls in countries like Kenya and Uganda라는 의미상의 주어가 존재하므로 to부정사형으로 쓰는 것이 적절하다.

18 이어지는 내용과 글 전체의 내용은 행동을 하라는 것이다. 따라서 act가 가장 적절하다.

19 (D) 아프리카 소녀들이 학교에 갈 수 없는 이유가 궁금함 (B) 가족들에게 금전적인 여유가 없기 때문임을 알게 되고, 소녀들을 돕기 위한 아이디어를 떠올려 부모님에게 재봉틀을 사달라고 말함 (A) 재봉틀로 머리띠를 만들어 한 명의 소녀를 도움 (C) 여러 소녀들을 돕기 위해 사업을 시작함

20 Mary는 아프리카의 가난한 소녀들을 돕기 위해 머리띠를 만들어 파는 아이디어를 떠올렸다.

21 주어진 문장의 the water는 글쓴이가 옥수수 속대를 넣은 더러운 물을 지칭한다. 따라서 ④번에 들어가는 것이 가장 적절하다.

22 옥수수 속대의 작은 구멍들이 더러운 물질을 오염된 물 밖으로 걸러 낼 수 있었다.

23 (A)는 '~로(서)'라는 의미로 쓰인 전치사이다. ① ~이기 때문에 ② ~처럼, ~같이 ③ ~로(서) ④ ~하는 대로 ⑤ ~하다시피

24 Lalita가 살고 있는 주변의 물이 심각하게 오염된 문제를 의미한다.

25 옥수수 속대에는 좁은 하나의 구멍이 아니라 작은 구멍들이 있다.

서술형 시험대비
p.202~203

01 He met her at a science fair.
02 소녀가 더 나은 로봇 손을 가질 수 있으면 좋겠다는 생각
03 He was able to make a useful robotic hand for the price of only 300 dollars.

37

04 We can build a better world by working together.

05 cheap → expensive, foot → hand, sell → share

06 She asked her parents to buy her a sewing machine.

07 the school fees, their textbooks, uniforms, and pencils, to go to school

08 My advice to you is to just do something.

09 clearer

10 She lived in the countryside in India.

11 She decided to use corn cobs to filter water.

12 Her system removed 70 to 80 percent of the dirty matter from the water.

01 Easton은 한 과학 박람회에서 어린 소녀를 만났다고 하였다.

02 앞 문장에서 Easton이 마음속으로 생각했던 것을 가리키는 말이다.

03 Easton은 3D 프린트 기술을 사용해서 단 300달러짜리의 유용한 로봇 손을 만들 수 있었다.

04 혼자 세상을 바꿀 수는 없지만, 함께 일하면서 더 나은 세상을 만들 수 있다고 하였다.

05 소녀는 비싼 로봇 손을 가지고 있었고 Easton은 자신의 디자인과 소프트웨어를 무료로 공유하기로 결심하였다.

06 Mary는 부모님께 자신의 생일에 재봉틀을 사 달라고 부탁드렸다.

07 사업의 성공 덕분에 Mary는 케냐와 우간다 같은 나라에 있는 많은 가난한 소녀들이 학교에 갈 수 있게 수업료를 지불할 뿐만 아니라 교과서와 교복, 연필을 위한 비용도 지불할 수 있다.

08 조언은 셀 수 없으므로 단수 취급하며, '무엇이든 하라는 것'이므로 to just do something이라고 쓰는 것이 적절하다.

09 물이 더 깨끗해져 있었다고 말하는 것이 자연스러우며, 비교급 강조 부사 much가 있으므로 clearer라고 쓰는 것이 가장 적절하다.

10 그녀는 인도의 시골에 살고 있었다.

11 물을 걸러내기 위해 Lalita는 옥수수 속대를 사용하기로 결정하였다.

12 Lalita의 여과장치는 물에서 70~80%의 더러운 물질을 제거하였다.

영역별 핵심문제 p.205~209

01 ⑤　　02 ④　　03 ②　　04 ④
05 ④　　06 ⑤
07 Is it possible for you to swim well?
08 Because his uncle has a big swimming pool.
09 ③　　10 ④　　11 ③　　12 ④

13 (1) If I were an inventor, I could make cheaper and more convenient robotic arms.
(2) If Jake weren't wearing the skirt, he would not look like a school girl.
(3) If there were a pen, I could write or draw a thing right now.
(4) If Henry had the violin, it would be easy for him to perform the songs.

14 whether to study in England or Canada　15 ①

16 ②　　　17 ⑤　　　18 ④　　　19 ②

20 Do you think you are so young that you can't be one of these people?

21 She paid 80,000 dollars for it.　　22 ⑤

23 ⑤

24 The small holes in the corn cobs could filter dirty matter out of the polluted water.

25 ③　　　26 ⑤

27 I don't know if you can help me, but I hope you can.

01 모두 '동사-명사'의 관계이지만, ⑤번은 ment라는 단어는 존재하지 않는다. ① 참가하다 - 참가 ② 느끼다 - 느낌 ③ 빛나다 - 빛 ④ (정보를) 알아내다, 알리다 - 정보 ⑤ mention: 언급

02 '~할 여유가 있다'는 의미로 쓰이는 단어는 afford이다.

03 hit on: ~을 생각해 내다, come across: 우연히 마주치다, By Ving: V함으로써

04 <보기>에서 쓰인 fair는 '박람회'라는 의미이다. ①, ③ 공정한 ② 상당한, 제법 큰 ④ 박람회 ⑤ (날씨가) 맑은

05 대답에서 '너는 원하는 무엇이든 될 수 있다'고 답하는 것으로 보아, 말하는 이의 가능성에 관해 묻는 말이 들어가는 것이 적절하다.

06 사막에서 살 수 있으면 좋겠다는 말에 동감을 표현하면서 아주 위험해 보인다고 말하고 있으므로 어색하다.

07 가능성을 묻는 말이므로 'Is it possible ~?'을 이용할 수 있으며 to부정사의 의미상의 주체로 'for+목적격'을 명시해야 한다.

08 Mike의 삼촌이 큰 수영장을 가지고 계셔서 Mike는 대부분의 시간을 삼촌 집에서 보낼 것이라고 하였다.

09 수영을 잘 못하기 때문에 물 위를 걷는 공을 가지고 놀 것이라고 말하는 것이 자연스럽다.

10 Mike가 삼촌의 집에서 얼마나 머무를지는 대화에 나와 있지 않다.

11 동사 asked의 목적어가 되는 명사절로서, 뒤의 or not과 호응하는 것은 whether뿐이다. if를 사용해야 할 경우에는 or not을 문미로 보내면 가능하다. ① if or not 불가능 ② however는 명사절을 이끌 수 없다. ④ could I는 어순 부적절 ⑤

succeeded → could succeed

12 주어 역할의 명사절을 이끄는 접속사가 필요하다. Though, As 등은 부사절을 이끌기 때문에 부적절하고, 내용상 '학생이 A를 받을지 여부는 중요하지 않다'는 것이므로, whether가 맞다. if 는 문두에서 명사절을 이끌 수 없다.

13 직설법 현재 문장을 가정법으로 바꿀 때, 종속절에는 동사의 과거형을, 주절에는 '조동사의 과거형+동사원형'을 쓰는 것에 유의하여, 문장을 전환한다. (4)에서 'it is not easy'는 가정법으로 바꿀 때, 조동사 would를 활용하고, 내용이 반대가 되므로 'it would be easy'로 바뀌는 것에 유의한다.

14 윤호는 영국에서 공부할지 캐나다에서 공부할지 결정할 수 없었다.

15 ①은 조건문의 부사절을 만드는 접속사로 쓰였다. 나머지는 모두 의문사가 없는 간접의문문을 이끄는 명사절 접속사이다.

16 우리말은 'I wish 가정법'에 해당한다. 조동사의 과거형 could 를 활용하되, 어순과 내용에 유의한다.

17 우리말은 '가정법 과거시제'를 의미한다. 가정법 과거에 맞게 동사의 과거형을 쓰되, 이 예문의 경우 비인칭 주어 it과 동사의 과거형 rained를 사용하는 것에 유의한다.

18 <보기>의 if는 가정법 과거 시제의 부사절을 이끄는 종속접속사로 쓰였다. ④를 제외하면, 모두 간접의문문의 명사절을 이끄는 접속사로서 '~인지'라는 뜻이다.

19 (B) 과학 박람회에서 로봇 손을 가진 소녀를 만남 (A) 소녀가 더 나은 로봇 손을 가지길 바라며 로봇 손을 만들기 시작하고, 3D 프린트 기술을 사용하여 만듦 (C) 자신이 만든 로봇 손의 디자인과 소프트웨어를 다른 사람들과 무료로 공유하기로 결심함

20 '너무 ~해서 …할 수 없는'이라는 의미로 쓰이는 'too ~ to V'는 'so ~ that S can't V'와 같다.

21 소녀는 로봇 손에 8만 달러를 지불했다고 하였다.

22 Easton은 3D 로봇 손의 디자인과 소프트웨어를 다른 사람들과 무료로 공유하기로 결심하였다. 따라서 ⑤번이 글의 내용과 일치한다.

23 ⑤번에 이어지는 글쓴이의 여과장치는 주어진 문장의 a filtering system을 의미한다.

24 Lalita는 옥수수 속대의 작은 구멍들이 더러운 물질을 오염된 물 밖으로 걸러낼 수 있을 것이라고 생각했다.

25 Lalita는 여과 장치를 만들기 위해 옥수수 속대를 사용하였다.

26 'live in a happier place'이므로 'to live in'으로 쓰는 것이 적절하다.

27 know의 목적어로 '~인지 아닌지'로 해석되는 명사절 접속사 if 혹은 whether를 쓰는 것에 유의한다.

단원별 예상문제 p.210~215

01 ⑤ **02** ③ **03** (1) useless (2) robotic
04 Is it possible for you to solve the puzzle?
05 (E)-(B)-(A)-(C)-(D) **06** ③ **07** ④
08 ③ **09** I would like to fly like him.
10 ② **11** ①, ③ **12** ④ **13** ④
14 (1) if he is going to come back here
   (2) if she had breakfast with the man
   (3) if anyone has seen my teacher's book on the bench
   (4) if the professor and her students can come on time for dinner
   (5) if there are any clothes for us to give out to the poor villagers
   (6) if it will be cloudy the day after tomorrow
15 ③ **16** ② **17** ④
18 wish I were[was] as tall as Jordan
19 Bob knew Judy's SNS address, he would visit her SNS
20 it not been for 3D printing technology, I wouldn't have been able to make a useful robotic hand for the price of only 300 dollars
21 (1) if it is going to rain today
   (2) if she can wash the parrot
   (3) if she got a cleaner's license
   (4) if anyone will come to see her
   (5) if there is anything left to eat
   (6) if Becky has washed her before
22 (1) is → were[was] (2) are → were
   (3) have → had (4) is → were[was]
   (5) be → have been (6) can → could
23 (1) Peter's girl friend asked him if he really loved her.
   (2) Easton was not sure if he could make her a better dress.
   (3) Mary asked her parents if they would buy her a sewing machine for her birthday.
24 ② **25** ④ **26** ③
27 She started a business to help girls in Africa who couldn't go to school.
28 ⑤번 → warm **29** ③
30 She hopes her filtering system can clean up all the lakes not only in her village but also in other areas.
31 ④

---

01 '실로 꿰매다'는 '바느질하다(sew)'이다.

02 get together는 '만나다, 모이다'라는 의미이다.

03 (1) 그녀는 최선을 다했지만, 소용없었다. 하지만 그녀는 포기하지 않았다. (2) Sue는 최근에 로봇 진공청소기를 샀어. 그것은 멋져 보여.

04 가능을 묻는 표현은 'Is it possible to V ~?'이며, to부정사의 의미상 주어로 'for+목적격'을 써서 나타낼 수 있다.

05 무엇을 하고 있느냐는 물음에 (E) 드론을 날리고 있다고 말함 (B) 드론 조종을 잘하는지 묻자 (A) 지금은 별로 잘하지 못하지만 열심히 연습하고 있다고 함 (C) 드론으로 샌드위치 배달을 할 수 있느냐는 물음에 (D) 불가능하다고 답하며 1~2년 후에는 가능할 것이라고 말함

06 아들을 위한 배낭을 구매하고 있으므로 대화가 벌어지는 장소는 쇼핑몰이 가장 적절하다.

07 모두 배낭을 지칭하는 말이지만 ④번은 가주어 it이다.

08 배낭에 붙어 있는 모자는 세탁을 위해 분리하는 것이 가능하다고 하였다.

09 소망을 표현하는 말은 'would like to V'이다.

10 가능을 묻는 말이므로 ②번이 적절하다. 의미상의 주어가 'for her'로 제시되고 있으므로 that절에서 주어를 she로 쓰는 것에 유의한다.

11 ② next Monday가 있으므로, 미래시제이다. 간접의문문의 명사절에서 미래시제는 will을 써야 한다. ④ 부사 last weekend는 과거시제이다. will come → came ⑤ 'if or not'은 쓰지 않는다. or not을 삭제 또는 문장 끝에 두거나 if 대신에 whether를 쓰는 것이 적절하다.

12 I wish 가정법 문장에서 조동사는 과거형으로 쓴다.

13 '직설법 현재'를 가정법으로 고치면 '가정법 과거'가 된다. If절에 '과거동사(be동사일 경우 were 또는 was)'를, 주절에 '조동사 과거+동사원형'을 쓰되, 직설법과 반대되도록 쓰는 것에 유의한다.

14 의문사 없는 간접의문문의 명사절을 이끄는 접속사 if를 활용하는 문제이다. 수와 시제, 어순 등에 유의한다.

15 ① doesn't → didn't ② can see → could see ④ can → could ⑤ follows → followed

16 ① work → worked ③ had helped → helped, can → could ④ know → knew ⑤ will → would

17 ① is the rumor → the rumor is ② depend → depends ③ did Mr. Parker make → Mr. Parker made ⑤ that → whether

18 직설법에서 'Jordan만큼 키가 크고 싶다'고 했으므로, 가정법으로는 'Jordan처럼 키가 크면 좋을 텐데'를 표현하는 'I wish 가정법'이 적절하다.

19 직설법 문장을 해석해 보면, 'Bob이 Judy의 SNS 주소를 모르고 있고, 그녀의 SNS를 방문하고 싶어한다.'이므로, 가정법 과거시제 'Bob이 Judy의 SNS 주소를 안다면 그녀의 SNS를 방문할 텐데.'라고 표현하는 것이 적절하다.

20 직설법에서 '300달러 가격에 유용한 로봇 손을 만들 수 있었고, 그것은 3D 프린팅 기술 때문이었다.'라고 했으므로, 가정법 과거완료시제 '3D 프린팅 기술이 없었더라면, 로봇 손을 만들 수 없었을 것이다.'라고 표현하는 것이 적절하다. 원래는 'If it had not been for'와 같이 해야 하나, Had가 문두에 있으므로, If가 생략된 형태인 'Had it not been for'로 종속절을 만들고, 주절에는 '조동사 과거+have+p.p.' 형태를 쓰는 것에 유의한다.

21 그림에 등장하는 모든 생각은 의문사가 없는 의문문이다. 간접의문문으로 전환할 때, if 또는 whether를 사용하되, 문제의 조건에서 whether는 쓸 수 없다고 했으므로 if를 이용하여, 수와 시제에 맞추되, (3)과 같은 경우 과거시제에 맞게 if절에 과거 동사 got을 쓰는 것 등에 유의한다.

22 문제에서 각 문장이 가정법이라고 했으므로, (1), (2), (3), (4)에 나온 'if절' 또는 'I wish' 뒤의 동사를 과거형으로 쓴다. be동사는 were로 고친다. 주어가 3인칭 단수이거나 I인칭일 경우 was를 쓸 수도 있다. (5) 내용상 과거시제이므로 '가정법 과거완료'로 표현한다. 가정법 과거완료의 주절에는 '조동사+have+p.p.'를 쓴다. (6) and를 기준으로 동사원형 병렬 구조이므로, 조동사만 고친다. can → could

23 기본적으로 간접의문문으로 전환할 때, 시제와 대명사, 수 일치, 부사구 등에 유의하도록 한다.

24 글의 내용은 아프리카 소녀들이 교육을 받을 수 있도록 돕고자 한 글쓴이의 노력이다. 따라서 ②번이 가장 적절하다.

25 빈칸 (B)에는 전치사 for가 들어간다. 사람의 성질을 나타내는 형용사 뒤에는 'of+목적격'으로 to부정사의 의미상 주어를 나타낸다.

26 글쓴이는 아프리카 소녀들이 학교에 갈 수 있도록 머리띠를 만들어 팔았고, 이로 인하여 많은 소녀들을 학교에 보낼 수 있게 되었다고 하였다. 따라서 ③번이 가장 적절하다.

27 Mary가 사업을 시작한 이유는 학교에 갈 수 없는 아프리카 소녀들을 돕기 위해서였다.

28 타인을 돕는 행동에 관해 말하고 있으므로 '따뜻한 마음이 삶을 바꿀 수 있다'고 말하는 것이 자연스럽다.

29 밑줄 친 (A)는 불완전한 절을 이끄는 목적격 관계대명사이다. 모두 명사절 접속사로 쓰였지만 ③번은 전치사 at의 목적어가 빠져 있으므로 관계대명사 that이다.

30 Lalita는 자신의 여과 장치가 자신의 마을뿐만 아니라 다른 지역에 있는 모든 호수를 깨끗하게 해 줄 수 있기를 희망한다.

31 Lalita가 만든 여과 장치는 물에서 70~80%의 더러운 물질을 제거했다고 하였다. 따라서 완전히 깨끗한 물을 만들 수는 없었다.

01 read people's minds
02 Dr. Rebecca is Jessie's favorite superhero.
03 Sky X can fly and do anything in space.
04 (1) I lived in Hawaii
   (2) I were[was] the president of Korea
   (3) I had a million dollars
   (4) every Wednesday were[was] a holiday
05 ④, ④ I don't know if what the professor wrote is worth reading.
06 how I could solve this problem
07 It was to use corn cobs.
08 Useless corn cobs were everywhere in Lalita's village.
09 air → water, leaves → cobs, moved → removed
10 if (또는 whether)
11 I wish I lived in Hawaii.

01 'I wish+주어+과거동사'는 소망을 나타내는 표현으로, 주로 현재의 사실과 반대되는 상황을 나타낼 때 쓴다. 따라서 Jessie는 닥터 레베카와 달리 사람들의 마음을 읽을 수 없다는 의미이다.

02 Jessie가 가장 좋아하는 슈퍼 영웅은 닥터 레베카이다.

03 Sky X는 하늘을 날 수 있고 우주에서 무엇이든 할 수 있다고 하였다.

04 'I wish 가정법' 문장에서, 주절에 '동사의 과거형' 또는 '조동사 과거+동사원형'의 구조가 오도록 영작한다.

05 의문사가 없는 간접의문문을 이끄는 접속사 if 뒤에 that절이 왔는데, 불완전할 경우 what을 생각할 필요가 있다. if 뒤에 쓰인 'what the professor wrote'가 명사절 주어이다. 해석해 보면 '나는 교수님이 쓴 것이 읽을 가치가 있는지 모른다.'가 된다. 그러므로 that → what이 적절하다.

06 간접의문문의 어순은 '의문사+주어+동사'임에 유의하여 답한다.

07 오염된 물을 깨끗하게 만들기 위해 Lalita가 생각해 낸 아이디어는 옥수수 속대를 사용하는 것이었다.

08 Lalita의 마을에는 쓸모없는 옥수수 속대가 어디에나 있었다.

09 Lalita는 심각하게 오염된 물을 깨끗하게 만들기 위해 옥수수 속대를 이용하여 오염 물질의 70~80%를 제거하였다.

10 '~인지 아닌지'라는 의미로 불확실한 명사절을 이끌 때 쓰는 접속사 if 또는 whether가 적절하다.

11 'I wish ~'는 '~하면 좋을 텐데'라는 의미로 현재 사실과 반대되거나 이룰 수 없는 일에 대한 아쉬움을 나타낼 때 쓰인다.

|모범답안|
01 for you to fly to the moon /
   for you to travel to the sun

02 ② If I had a puppy, I would walk it every day.
   ③ If it weren't raining, I could go backpacking.
   ④ If Sam stayed longer, I would make some pizza for him.
03 I had a million dollars / help all the children who can't afford to go to school / I were a famous singer / I would be on TV and my grandma would be happy / I were a bird / I could fly all around the world

02 가정법 과거시제의 조건절과 함께 주절에 조동사 과거형을 적절히 이용하여 어법에 맞게 쓰면 정답.

01 ④   02 ②   03 pollute
04 She looks forward to meeting you tomorrow.
05 ④   06 (D)-(B)-(C)-(A)
07 Can I take the cap off for washing?
08 ④   09 wish I could   10 ④, ⑤
11 She wakes Wendy up.   12 ④   13 ④
14 ③   15 ②   16 ④   17 ⑤
18 ③
19 He decided to share the designs and software for his 3D robotic hand with others for free.
20 ⑤   21 ②
22 I wish they could go to school, too.   23 ②
24 She started a business to help them.   25 ④

01 ① pay for: ~을 지불하다 ② thank A for B: A에게 B라는 이유로 고마워하다 ③ for oneself: 스스로 ④ hit on: (생각을) 떠올리다 ⑤ for free: 공짜로

02 소망을 표현하는 말이므로 ②번이 가장 적절하다.

03 유의어 관계에 있는 단어이다. 따라서 '오염시키다'라는 의미로 쓰이는 pollute를 쓸 수 있다.

04 look forward to Ving: V하기를 고대하다

05 come across는 '우연히 만나다'라는 의미로 'to meet or find by chance'로 풀이될 수 있다.

06 (D) 한국어를 배운지 얼마나 되었는지 물음 (B) 한 달 동안 배워왔다고 답함 (C) 한국어를 읽는 것이 가능한지 물음 (A) 읽을 수는 있지만 말하는 것은 아직 미숙하다고 답함

07 세탁을 위해 모자를 분리하는 것이 가능한지를 묻는 표현이다. 따라서 'Can 주어 V ~?'로 표현할 수 있다.

08 ④ 가방이 무엇으로 만들어졌는지는 위 대화를 읽고 알 수 없다.

09 수영을 잘하냐고 묻는 말에 '아니'라고 답하며 '그렇지만 할 수

41

없다'는 말이 이어지고 있으므로 '아니, 잘했으면 좋겠는데, 못해.'라고 말하는 것이 자연스럽다.

10 모두 일찍 일어나고 싶다는 소망을 나타내는 말이지만, ④번은 일찍 일어나길 몹시 기다린다는 표현이며 ⑤번은 항상 일찍 일어나는 습관을 나타내는 말이다.

11 Wendy의 어머니는 그녀를 깨워준다고 하였다.

12 소망을 나타내는 표현과 가능성을 나타내는 표현은 같지 않다. ④번은 'I want to have ~' 혹은 'I'd like to have ~' 등으로 표현할 수 있다.

13 when은 ⓐ와 ⓑ에 넣으면 무리가 없으나, ⓒ에는 내용상 부적절하다. whether는 ⓑ에 적절하지 않다. 따라서, 세 개의 빈칸에 공통으로 가능한 것은 if 뿐이다.

14 ③ 'Mary가 버스를 놓친다면, 지각하지 않았을 것이다.'라는 문장은 어법과 의미에서 모두 어색하다. 가정법을 적절히 적용하여 고치면, 'If Mary missed the bus, she would be late for work.'가 된다.

15 주어진 문장은 '연경이 컨디션이 좋으면, 다른 선수들보다 두 배의 스파이크 공격을 해낼 텐데.'라는 가정법 과거 문장이다. 직설법으로는 반대의 현재시제이므로, As가 이끄는 종속절과 주절에 모두 현재시제가 있는 ②가 정답이다. '연경이 컨디션이 좋지 않아서, 두 배의 공격을 해내지 않는다.'

16 보기에 주어진 could는 가정법의 주절에 사용된 can의 과거시제형이다. ④는 공손한 질문을 위한 조동사이다.

17 보기에 주어진 if는 간접의문문의 명사절을 이끄는 접속사이다. ⑤번을 제외한 나머지 모두 같은 역할이다. ⑤번은 조건의 부사절을 만드는 if가 쓰였다.

18 주어진 문장의 that이 의미하는 것은 소녀가 더 나은 로봇 손을 가지기를 바라는 Easton의 생각이다. 따라서 ③번이 가장 적절하다.

19 Easton은 자신이 만든 3D 로봇 손 디자인과 소프트웨어를 다른 사람들과 무료로 공유하기로 결심했다.

20 혼자서 세상을 바꿀 수는 없다는 의미이므로 '세상이 한 사람에 의해 바뀔 수는 없다'는 ⑤번이 가장 적절하다.

21 Easton은 과학 박람회에서 우연히 한 소녀를 만났다.

22 현실과 반대되는 상황을 가정하는 가정법이므로 'I wish'가 이끄는 절은 과거시제임에 유의하자.

23 자신이 소녀들을 위해서 어떤 것을 할 수 있을까 생각했다는 의미이다. 불확실한 절을 이끄는 접속사는 if이다.

24 Mary는 학교에 갈 수 없는 아프리카 소녀들을 돕기 위해 사업을 시작하였다.

25 Mary는 자신의 이웃이 아닌 아프리카에 있는 소녀들을 돕고 있다.

The Necklace

교과서
Reading

📎 **확인문제**   p.226

1 T 2 F 3 T 4 F

📎 **확인문제**   p.227

1 F 2 F 3 T

📎 **확인문제**   p.228

1 T 2 F 3 F 4 F 5 T

📎 **확인문제**   p.229

1 T 2 T 3 F 4 T 5 F 6 T

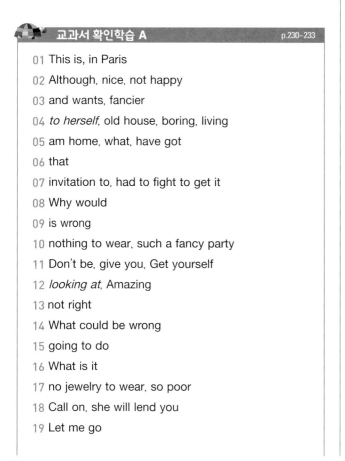

교과서 확인학습 A   p.230~233

01 This is, in Paris

02 Although, nice, not happy

03 and wants, fancier

04 *to herself*, old house, boring, living

05 am home, what, have got

06 that

07 invitation to, had to fight to get it

08 Why would

09 is wrong

10 nothing to wear, such a fancy party

11 Don't be, give you, Get yourself

12 *looking at*, Amazing

13 not right

14 What could be wrong

15 going to do

16 What is it

17 no jewelry to wear, so poor

18 Call on, she will lend you

19 Let me go

20 to see, What brings you here

21 invited to

22 wonderful, excited

23 to say, no jewelry, borrow something from you

24 Here is

25 so many wonderful pieces

26 whatever you like

27 lend me this diamond necklace

28 Certainly, go enjoy

29 a perfect evening, admires her beauty

30 It is, when the Loisels leave

31 such a long night

32 it was worth it, danced with

33 you enjoyed yourself

34 *looking in*, more look.

35 when we left the ball

36 did, go find

37 searches

38 returns to, goes to

39 is not found, to lie to

40 broke, fix it, returning it

41 to find a similar one

42 May we look at

43 *whispering*, nearly the same

44 How much

45 francs

46 How about

47 really need it

48 it is

49 do not have, a huge amount of

50 borrow it

51 buying, for, spends, paying

52 move to

53 gets a second job, washes, for

54 makes, old, worn

55 runs into, on

56 good morning

57 Do I know you

58 it is me

59 believe it, have changed

60 have had, difficult times

61 What do you mean

62 you lent me, lost it

63 returned it

64 another one, like it, It, to pay for it

65 bought, to replace

66 Why didn't you come, tell me, was not real, worth

43

1 This is Mr. and Mrs. Loisel's home in Paris.

2 Although the home is nice, Mrs. Loisel is not happy.

3 She is young and pretty, and wants a fancier life.

4 Mrs. Loisel: (*to herself*) Same old house and same boring dinners. I hate living here!

5 Mr. Loisel: Matilda, I am home. Look what I have got for you!

6 Mrs. Loisel: What is that?

7 Mr. Loisel: An invitation to the Ambassador's Ball. I had to fight to get it. Everybody wanted it.

8 Mrs. Loisel: (*crying*) Why would I want it?

9 Mr. Loisel: Matilda. What is wrong?

10 Mrs. Loisel: I have nothing to wear to such a fancy party. I cannot go.

11 Mr. Loisel: Don't be sad. Here, I will give you 400 francs. Get yourself a beautiful new dress.

12 Mr. Loisel: (*looking at Matilda's new dress*) Amazing, Matilda. Beautiful!

13 Mrs. Loisel: Something is not right.

14 Mr. Loisel: What could be wrong?

15 Mrs. Loisel: (*crying*) Oh, no. What am I going to do?

16 Mr. Loisel: What is it, Matilda?

17 Mrs. Loisel: I have no jewelry to wear with my beautiful dress. I will look so poor!

18 Mr. Loisel: Call on your friend, Mrs. Forestier. I am sure she will lend you some of her jewelry.

19 Mrs. Loisel: That is a good idea! Let me go at once.

20 Mrs. Forestier: Matilda, it is so nice to see you! What brings you here?

21 Mrs. Loisel: We are invited to the Ambassador's Ball.

22 Mrs. Forestier: The Ambassador's Ball! That is wonderful! You must be excited.

23 Mrs. Loisel: Yes… And no. I am sad to say I have no jewelry. May I borrow something from you?

24 Mrs. Forestier: Sure! Here is my case.

25 Mrs. Loisel: Wow, you have so many wonderful pieces!

26 Mrs. Forestier: Choose whatever you like.

27 Mrs. Loisel: Would you lend me this diamond necklace? It is beautiful!

28 Mrs. Forestier: Certainly! Now go enjoy the ball.

29 Matilda has a perfect evening. Everybody at the ball admires her beauty.

30 It is very late when the Loisels leave the ball.

31 Mr. Loisel: It was such a long night. I am so tired.

32 Mrs. Loisel: But it was worth it. Do you know I danced with the Ambassador?

33 Mr. Loisel: I am glad you enjoyed yourself, but I have to go to work in the morning.

34 Mrs. Loisel: (*looking in the mirror*) Just one more look. (*shocked*) The necklace… It is gone!

35 Mr. Loisel: What? Did you have it when we left the ball?

36 Mrs. Loisel: Yes, I surely did. Please go find it!

37 Mr. Loisel searches the streets.

38 He returns to the ball and then goes to the police.

39 When the necklace is not found, Mr. Loisel tells Matilda to lie to her friend.

40 Matilda tells Mrs. Forestier she broke the necklace and would fix it before returning it.

41 The couple needs time to find a similar one.

42 Mr. Loisel: (*to the jeweler*) Excuse me? May we look at that diamond necklace?

43 Mrs. Loisel: (*whispering*) It is nearly the same. We must have it!

44 Mr. Loisel: How much is it?

45 Jeweler: 40,000 francs.

46 Mr. Loisel: How about 36,000?

47 Mrs. Loisel: Please, we really need it.

48 Jeweler: Well, then… 36,000 it is.I

49 They do not have 36,000 francs. It is a huge amount of money.

50 So they borrow it.

51 After buying the necklace for Mrs. Forestier, the couple spends ten years paying back the money.

52 They move to a very small place.

53 Mr. Loisel gets a second job. Matilda washes clothes for others.

54 Ten years of hard work makes Matilda old and worn.

55 After ten years, Matilda runs into Mrs. Forestier on the street.

56 Mrs. Loisel: Mrs. Forestier, good morning.

57 Mrs. Forestier: Do I know you?

58 Mrs. Loisel: Yes, it is me, Matilda.

59 Mrs. Forestier: Oh, I cannot believe it! You have changed so much.

60 Mrs. Loisel: I have had some difficult times because of you.

61 Mrs. Forestier: Because of me? What do you mean?

62 Mrs. Loisel: Do you remember the diamond necklace you lent me? Well, I lost it.

63 Mrs. Forestier: But you returned it to me.

64 Mrs. Loisel: No, I returned another one just like it. It took us ten years to pay for it.

65 Mrs. Loisel: You bought a diamond necklace to replace mine?

66 Mrs. Loisel: Yes.

67 Mrs. Forestier: Oh, my poor Matilda. Why didn't you come to me and tell me the truth? My diamond necklace was not real. It was worth only 500 francs!

서술형 실전문제
p.238~241

01 (1) admire (2) ball (3) replace (4) invitation

02 ②   03 ⑤

04 (1) (h)uge (2) (n)early (3) look

05 ④

06 (1) I had to fight to get the invitation to the Ambassador's Ball.

(2) I have nothing to wear to such a fancy party.

(3) I am sad to say I have no jewelry.

(4) Matilda was sorry to lie to her friend.

(5) The couple needs time to find a similar necklace.

(6) It took us ten years to pay for the necklace.

07 to pay → paying

08 The necklace was worth only 500

09 He has got an invitation to the Ambassador's Ball.

10 It is because she has nothing to wear to such a fancy party.

11 He gives her 400 francs.

12 I am sure she will lend you some of her jewelry.

13 a new dress, jewelry to wear

14 Choose whatever you like.

15 jewelry

16 She is visiting Mrs. Forestier because she wants to borrow her jewelry.

17 yourself

18 Matilda's beauty is admired at the ball.

19 He tells her to lie to her friend.

20 They move to a very small place. Mr. Loisel gets a second job and Matilda washes clothes for others.

21 Ten years of hard work makes Matilda look old and worn.

22 They pay 36,000 francs to pay for it.

01 (1) admire: 존경하다, 칭찬하다. 당신은 그가 그 상황에 대처한 방식을 존경해야 해요. (2) ball: 무도회. 그는 가면을 쓰고 무도회에 간다. (3) replace: ~을 대신하다. 많은 산업에서 기계가 인간 노동을 대신하게 되었다. (4) invitation: 초대, 초대장. 제가 안타깝게도 당신의 친절한 초대를 받아들일 수가 없답니다.

02 ②의 영영풀이는 quality의 영영풀이이다. ① certainly: 확실히, 틀림없이, 그럼요. 확실히, 의심 없이. ② amount: 양, 액수. 어떤 것의 양. ③ jewelry: 보석류. 반지나 목걸이 같은 옷이나 몸에 걸치는 장식물. ④ cry: 울다ㆍ슬픔, 아픔 등 때문에 눈에서 눈물이 나오게 하다. ⑤ ambassador: 대사. 다른 나라에서 자신의 나라의 공식적인 대표인 가장 높은 지위의 외교관

03 call on: 요청하다, ① respect: 존경하다 ② delay: 연기하다 ③ recommend: 추천하다 ④ invite: 초대하다

04 (1) huge: 거대한, 엄청난 (2) nearly: 거의 (3) look: 보기, 눈길

05 (A) call on: 요청하다. 그것은 일본에게 계획을 취소할 것을 요청했다. take on: 떠맡다, 고용하다 (B) pay back: 갚다, 돌려주다. 나는 내년까지 빚을 못 갚을 것 같아. take back: 취소[철회]하다

06 'to부정사'가 들어가는 다양한 문장들이다. 각각 (1) to부정사의 '부사적' 용법 중 '목적(~하기 위해서)'이다. (2) to부정사의 '형용사적' 용법으로, '앞의 명사를 수식'하고 있다. (3), (4) to부정사의 '부사적' 용법 중 '감정의 원인, 이유'이다. (5) to부정사의 '형용사적' 용법으로 쓰였다. (6) to부정사의 '명사적' 용법으로 사용되었고, 가주어-진주어 구문이다. '주어'로 쓰였다.

07 「spend+시간[돈]+동명사」는 '~하느라 시간, 돈 등을 소비하다'라는 뜻을 가지고 있다. '그 돈을 갚느라 10년을 보낸다.'는 문장이므로, to pay를 paying으로 고치는 것이 적절하다.

09 Loisel 씨는 아내 Matilda를 위해 대사님이 여는 무도회 초대장을 가지고 왔다.

10 Loisel 부인이 무도회에 갈 수 없다고 말한 이유는 그런 고급스러운 파티에 입고 갈 옷이 하나도 없기 때문이다.

12 be sure (that) ~: ~을 확신하다

13 해석: Matilda는 새 드레스를 가졌지만, 그녀는 그것에 어울릴 보석이 없기 때문에 여전히 만족하지 못한다.

14 whatever는 복합관계대명사로 불완전한 절을 이끌며 주절 내에서 명사 역할을 한다. 이 문장의 경우 choose의 목적어를 이끌고 있다.

15 보석을 의미하는 말이다.

16 Loisel 부인이 Forestier 부인을 방문 중인 이유는 목걸이를 빌리고 싶어서이다.

17 주어와 목적어가 같을 때, 목적어로 재귀대명사를 쓴다. 이를 재귀대명사의 재귀적 용법이라고 부른다.

18 무도회에서 모든 사람들이 아름다운 Matilda를 감탄하며 바라본

19 Loisel 씨는 목걸이가 발견되지 않자 Matilda에게 그녀의 친구에게 거짓말을 하라고 한다.

20 두 사람은 아주 작은 곳으로 이사 가서 Loisel 씨는 부업을 구하고 Matilda는 다른 사람들을 위해 빨래를 해준다.

21 10년 동안의 고된 일은 Matilda를 늙고 지쳐 보이게 만든다.

22 두 사람은 다이아몬드 목걸이에 36,000프랑을 지불한다.

단원별 예상문제
p.242~248

01 reading 02 into
03 (1) worn (2) once (3) similar (4) shocked
04 (1) (d)ifferent (2) (h)uge (3) (a)dmire
05 (r)eplace
06 It takes me an hour to walk there and back.
07 years of hard work makes Matilda old and worn
08 ⑤ 09 ④ 10 ③
11 (1) Whoever comes to this village
   (2) whoever tries to make fool of good people
   (3) whatever he has in his hands 12 ①
13 needs time to find a similar diamond necklace
14 ② 15 ④
16 He had to fight to get it. 17 ③ 18 ④
19 ⑤번 → did 20 ⑤ 21 ④ 22 ③
23 The couple needs time to find a similar necklace.
24 Matilda tells Mrs. Forestier she broke the necklace and would fix it before returning it.
25 excited 26 ⑤
27 What brings you here? 28 ③ 29 go
30 It is because she has no jewelry to wear with her beautiful dress.
31 ⑤
32 It is because they have to pay back the money they borrowed. 33 ⑤
34 It takes ten years for the couple to pay back the money.
35 on purpose → accidentally 36 ②
37 ④ 38 ⑤
39 It was worth only 500 francs.
40 Matilda가 Forestier 부인의 목걸이를 잃어버렸다는 것

01 • worth: ~의 가치가 있는(형용사이지만 전치사처럼 쓰여, 뒤에 명사, 대명사, 동명사 등이 옴). 그의 책들 중 극히 소수만이 읽을 가치가 있다. • spend 돈·시간 ~ing: 돈·시간 등을 ~하는 데 보내다. 나는 거의 매일 도서관에서 책을 읽으면서 보낸다.

02 • run into: ~을 우연히 만나다. 나는 우연히 옛 친구를 만났다. • fall into: ~에 빠지다. 돌고래는 깊이 잠들 수가 없다.

03 (1) worn: 지친. 우리 좀 앉을까? 난 너무 지쳤어. (2) at once: 당장. 당장 가는 것이 상책이다. (3) similar: 비슷한, 유사한. 다른 사람들도 비슷한 문제를 겪어 왔다. (4) shocked: 충격을 받은. 그 소식을 들었을 때 충격을 받았어요.

04 (1) 반의어 관계이다. borrow: 빌리다, lend: 빌려주다, similar: 비슷한, 유사한, different: 다른, 상이한 (2) 반의어 관계이다. deep: 깊은, shallow: 얕은, tiny 아주 작은, huge 거대한, 엄청난 (3) 동의어 관계이다. replace: ~을 대신하다, substitute: ~을 대신하다, 대리하다, respect 존경하다, admire 존경하다

05 replace: ~을 대신하다. 어떤 것이 엄마의 사랑과 관심을 대신할 수 있을까?

06 it takes+목적어+시간+to부정사: (목적어)가 ~하는 데 (시간)이 걸리다

07 '10년'은 'ten years'이다. 또한, 주어가 '10년'이라는 '단위'를 말하고, 현재시제이므로 make를 makes로 고치는 것이 적절하고, '늙고 수척해진'이라는 표현은 'old and worn'이므로 wear를 worn으로 고쳐서 알맞게 배열한다.

08 보기의 'to 부정사'는 '형용사'적 용법으로 쓰여서 '앞의 명사를 수식'한다. ⑤번의 'to부정사'도 같은 역할이다. ① '부사적' 용법 '감정의 원인' ②, ③ '부사적' 용법 '목적' ④ '부사적' 용법 '형용사 수식' 09 소망을 표현하는 말은 'would like to V'이다.

10 보기의 'to 부정사'는 '부사적' 용법으로 쓰여서 '감정의 원인'을 나타낸다. ③번의 'to 부정사'는 명사적 용법이다. ①, ④ '부사적' 용법-'목적'(~하기 위해서) ② '부사적' 용법 '감정의 원인' ⑤ '부사적' 용법-'판단의 근거'

12 ①은 '현재분사'이다. 해석하면, 그 왕자는 찢어진 드레스에 울고 있는 소녀를 두고 떠났다.라는 뜻이다. 나머지는 모두 '동명사'로 사용되었다. 특히 ②, ⑤는 전치사의 목적어로 쓰였고, ③, ④는 동명사의 관용적 용법으로 'spend+시간+V-ing', 'have a difficult time V-ing' 등으로, 꼭 암기하는 것이 좋다.

13 '필요하다'라는 우리말로 보아 '현재시제'임을 알 수 있다. 동사 need를 needs로 형태 변화하는 것에 유의하여, 'to부정사'가 명사 뒤에서 '수식'하는 형태로 영작한다.

14 일반적으로 that이 관계대명사 목적격으로 사용되었을 경우와, 명사절로서 목적어를 이끄는 접속사로 사용되었을 경우 생략 가능하다. ②는 It ~ that 강조구문으로 사용되었고, 문맥상 when으로 바꿀 수는 있으나, 생략은 불가능하다. ①과 ⑤는 명사절 목적어를 이끄는 접속사이며, ③, ④는 관계대명사의 목적격이다.

15 관계대명사 what은 불완전한 절을 이끌며 주절에서 명사 역할을 한다. ④번의 문장은 완전한 절을 이끌고 있으므로 명사절 접속사 that이 들어가는 것이 적절하다.

16 Loisel 씨는 초대장을 얻어 내기 위해 싸워야 했다고 하였다.

17 이어지는 대화에서 Loisel 씨가 아내에게 옷을 살 돈을 주겠다고 말하고 있으므로 ③번이 가장 적절하다.

18 Matilda는 자신의 삶이 지루하고 즐길만한 것이 아니라고 생각한다. Matilda는 이곳에서 살기 싫다는 말을 남편에게 한 것이 아니라 혼잣말로 한다.

19 'I surely had it when we left the ball.'을 받아주는 문장이므로 'I surely did.'라고 쓰는 것이 적절하다. 일반동사의 대동사는 do(es), did를 쓴다.

20 밑줄 친 ⓐ는 '수리하다, 고치다'라는 의미로 쓰였다. ① 준비[주선]하다 ② (음식을) 준비하다, 마련하다 ③ (움직이지 않게) 고정시키다 ④ (날짜, 시간, 양 등을) 정하다 ⑤ 수리하다, 고치다

21 Loisel 씨는 아내가 즐거웠다고 말하자 기쁘다고 말했다.

22 Matilda는 대사와 춤을 추며 즐거운 시간을 보냈지만 목걸이가 사라진 것을 알고 초조해하고 있다. 따라서 ③번이 가장 적절하다.

23 부부는 비슷한 것을 찾을 시간이 필요하다고 하였다.

24 Matilda는 Forestier 부인에게 목걸이를 망가뜨려서 돌려주기 전에 고쳐 주겠다고 말한다.

25 감정을 느낄 때는 과거분사를 쓰는 것이 적절하다.

26 마땅한 보석이 없으므로 빌려달라고 요청하는 말이 가장 자연스럽다. lend: ~을 빌려주다, borrow: ~을 빌리다

27 무슨 일로 왔느냐는 물음을 사물을 주어로 하여 표현할 수 있다.

28 Loisel 부인과는 달리 Forestier 부인에게는 많은 보석이 있다.

29 사역동사의 목적격 보어로 동사원형이 쓰인다.

30 Matilda는 아름다운 드레스에 어울릴 보석이 하나도 없어서 자신이 불쌍해 보일 것이라고 한다.

31 드레스에 어울릴 보석이 하나도 없다는 이유로 슬퍼하는 부인에게 Loisel 씨는 친구 Forestier 부인에게 가서 보석을 빌려달라는 부탁을 해 보라고 제안하고, 이에 부인은 지금 당장 가봐야겠다고 말하고 있으므로 ⑤번이 가장 적절하다.

32 빌린 돈을 갚아야 했기 때문에 두 사람은 아주 작은 곳으로 이사한다고 하였다.

33 Matilda를 늙고 지쳐 보이게 만든 것은 10년 동안의 고된 일이다.

34 커플이 Forestier 부인에게 돌려줄 목걸이를 산 후 돈을 갚는 데 십 년이 걸린다.

35 Matilda는 Forestier 부인을 우연히 만난다고 하였다. '우연히'는 accidentally, by accident, by chance로 표현할 수 있다.

36 이어지는 대화의 내용으로 미루어 보아 Matilda가 10년 동안 힘든 시간을 보내어 외모에 많은 변화가 있었기 때문에 Mrs. Forestier가 그녀를 알아볼 수 없음을 알 수 있다.

37 모두 Matilda가 Forestier 부인에게서 빌린 목걸이를 가리키는 말이지만, ④번은 Matilda가 부인에게 사준 목걸이를 가리키는 말이다.

38 밑줄 친 (B)는 to부정사의 부사적 용법 중 목적으로 쓰였다. ① 형용사적 용법 ② 명사적 용법 중 진주어 ③ 명사적 용법 중 주어 ④ 명사적 용법 중 목적어 ⑤ 부사적 용법 중 목적 (~하기 위해서

39 Forestier 부인의 목걸이는 500프랑이었다.

40 Matilda가 Forestier 부인의 목걸이를 잃어버렸다는 것을 뜻한다.

교과서 파헤치기

Lesson **6**

01 성공, 성과	02 경기, 시합	03 해외에(서), 해외로
04 달성하다, 성취하다		05 상징, 상징물
06 흔한	07 겪다, 경험하다	
08 진가를 알아보다, 인정하다		09 명확하게
10 자취, 오솔길	11 (대단히) 놀라게 하다	
12 온천	13 풍경	14 도처에
15 주요한, 주된	16 (사람이) 혼란스러워 하는	
17 자연의, 천연의	18 격자무늬, 격자무늬 천	
19 문화	20 추천하다	
21 걷잡을 수 없이, 극도로		22 경관, 전망
23 확실히, 분명히	24 경쟁자, 경쟁 상대	
25 몇몇의	26 사회	27 결혼(식)
28 제안하다	29 전통적인	
30 언젠가, 언제든, 훗날		31 마을, 부락, 촌락
32 폭포	33 (특정한 곳의) 토박이의	
34 별명	35 훨씬 이전에	36 ~으로 덮이다
37 ~로 가득 찬	38 ~의 도움을 받아서	
39 ~로 유명하다	40 일 년 내내	41 ~로 알려져 있다
42 ~을 준비하다	43 생각이 나다, 생각이 떠오르다	

01 rival	02 recommend	03 native
04 abroad	05 someday	06 achieve
07 landscape	08 throughout	09 several
10 waterfall	11 success	12 view
13 surely	14 carry	15 appreciate
16 plaid	17 common	18 clearly
19 match	20 wedding	21 trail
22 amaze	23 twin	24 village
25 natural	26 experience	27 nickname
28 suggest	29 symbol	30 hot spring
31 main	32 confused	33 traditional
34 information	35 try on	36 filled with
37 be famous for	38 prepare for	39 all year round
40 be known as	41 be covered with	
42 with the help of	43 come to one's mind	

1 kiwi, 키위새   2 abroad, 해외에(서), 해외로

3 hot spring, 온천   4 plaid, 격자무늬   5 match, 경기, 시합

6 trail, 오솔길   7 wedding, 결혼식

8 achieve, 달성하다, 성취하다   9 common, 흔한

10 Maori, 마오리인   11 rival, 경쟁자, 경쟁 상대

12 potluck, 각자 준비한 음식을 나눠먹는 식사

13 rugby, 럭비   14 landscape, 풍경   15 hill, 언덕

16 symbol, 상징, 상징물

Listen & Speak 1 A

1. Let's talk, traditional clothing, other / what a kilt is / traditional clothing, looks like, knee-length, plaid pattern / with, plaid pattern / unique because / interesting, to try, on

2. let's talk about what, prepare / famous, How about / popular, dish / What, look like / fried, with, potato chips / interesting. Let's prepare

Listen & Speak 2 A

1. finally arrived in / looking forward to, should, do / suggest, visit / the highest mountain, in a lot of / fantastic view / sounds, Let's

2. invited, potluck / know, food to share / recommend that / suggest, take, How about / spicy, easy to carry / for

Real Life Talk

Can you tell me about / a few years ago. First, let's talk / What food, famous for / The most famous, filled with, melted / suggestion, will try, Are there, that are popular with / suggest, Independence, history / information / pleasure

Wrap Up

Welcome, capital, popular dish, Every year, lots of tourists, beautiful beaches

Listen & Speak 1 A

1. B: Let's talk about traditional clothing from other countries.

   G: Hmm... Do you know what a kilt is?

   B: No, I don't. What is it?

   G: It is traditional clothing from Scotland. It looks like a knee-length skirt and has a plaid pattern.

B: A skirt of knee length with a plaid pattern?

G: Yes. It is unique because it is a skirt for men.

B: That sounds interesting. I want to try one on.

2. G: Brian, let's talk about what we will prepare for the World Food Festival.

B: I will make a meat pie. It is famous in Australia. How about you, Sera?

G: I want to make a popular English dish, fish and chips.

B: Fish and chips? What does it look like?

G: It's fried fish with hot potato chips.

B: That sounds interesting. Let's prepare them.

Listen & Speak 2 A

1. B: Wow, we finally arrived in Hong Kong, Mom.

W: I'm looking forward to our visit. What should we do today, Mike?

B: I suggest we visit Victoria Peak.

W: Victoria Peak?

B: It is the highest mountain in Hong Kong and is in a lot of movies. We can enjoy the fantastic view.

W: That sounds good. Let's go.

2. G: My American friend invited me to a potluck dinner next Friday.

B: You know, you should take food to share at the dinner.

G: What would you recommend that I take?

B: I suggest you take some Korean food. How about Gimbap, Suji?

G: Yes. It's not spicy and it's easy to carry.

B: I think it'll be good for dinner.

Real Life Talk

Seho: Good morning.

Jessie, Andy: Hi, Seho.

Seho: I will visit my uncle in Philadelphia this winter. Can you tell me about the city?

Jessie: Sure. I was there a few years ago. First, let's talk about food.

Seho: Okay. What food is Philadelphia famous for?

Jessie: The most famous food in Philadelphia is the cheese steak sandwich. It is a big sandwich filled with beef and melted cheese.

Seho: Good suggestion. I will try it. Are there any places that are popular with tourists?

Andy: I suggest you visit Independence Hall. It is bery important in American histoy.

Seho: Wonderful. Thank you for the information.

Andy: My pleasure.

Wrap Up

M: Welcome to Australia. The capital of Australia is Canberra. People speak English. Meat pie is a popular dish in Australia. Every year, lots of tourists visit the Sydney Opera House and the beautiful beaches in Melbourne.

본문 TEST Step 1 — p.09~10

01 place, natural beauty, waterfalls

02 has two main islands

03 covered with, all, round

04 be amazed by, views

05 hot springs, areas with

06 Because of, been made

07 will surely appreciate, nature

08 hear, comes to, mind

09 Maybe, but, couple, meanings

10 name, delicious, fruit

11 grown, so, known as

12 also, one, native birds

13 special, because, symbol, nation

14 Also, nickname for, from

15 are sometimes called, throughout

16 that, name, fruit, also

17 confused, uses, which, meanings

18 let's talk, native people

19 on, long before, arrived

20 important part, today's, society

21 is taught, there are

22 villages, many parts, country

23 visit, villages, experience, culture

24 say, glad, hear, means

25 Have, ever watched

26 scary, shout, move, wildly

27 who, heard, doing, as

28 however, matches, other, events

29 example, national, before, match

30 famous all over

31 agree that, must, scared

32 Like, national symbol

본문 TEST Step 2 — p.11~12

01 a place of natural beauty, lakes, waterfalls

02 two main islands

03 are mountains, are covered with, all year round

04 be amazed by, fantastic views

05 many hot springs, with

06 Because of, natural beauty, have been made

07 will surely appreciate

08 hear, comes to your mind

09 a couple of meanings

10 the name, delicious

11 is grown, so, is known as

12 one, New Zealand's native birds

13 special to, because, symbol

14 a nickname for, from

15 are sometimes called, throughout the world

16 that, the name of

17 confused, uses, which has several meanings

18 let's talk, They, the native people

19 live on, long before Europeans arrived

20 an important part, today's, society

21 is taught, there are

22 There are, in many parts of

23 visit, villages, experience, culture

24 say, to, will be glad to hear, means

25 Have, ever watched

26 look scary because, shout, move, wildly

27 who, heard about, doing, as

28 however, do, at sport matches, other important events

29 For example, national rugby team members, before every match

30 famous all over

31 will, agree that, must be scared

32 Like, a national symbol

본문 TEST Step 3   p.13~14

1 뉴질랜드는 자연의 아름다움이 가득한 곳이다. 뉴질랜드는 아름다운 호수와 폭포들이 많다.

2 뉴질랜드에는 남섬과 북섬, 두 개의 본섬이 있다.

3 남섬에는 일 년 내내 눈으로 덮인 산들이 있다.

4 당신은 굉장히 멋진 경관에 놀랄 것이다.

5 북섬에는 많은 온천과 호수, 초원 지역이 있다.

6 뉴질랜드 자연의 아름다움 때문에 많은 유명한 영화들이 뉴질랜드에서 촬영되었다.

7 뉴질랜드를 방문하면, 분명히 그 자연의 진가를 인정할 것이다.

8 키위라는 단어를 들을 때, 무엇이 떠오르는가?

9 아마도 과일이 떠오르겠지만, 뉴질랜드에서 키위는 몇 가지 뜻이 있다.

10 먼저, 키위는 맛있는 초록색 과일의 이름이다.

11 많은 키위가 그곳에서 자라기 때문에 뉴질랜드는 키위의 나라로 알려져 있다.

12 키위는 뉴질랜드 토종 새의 이름이기도 하다.

13 키위 새는 국가의 상징이기 때문에, 뉴질랜드 사람들에게 특별하다.

14 또한, 키위는 뉴질랜드 출신의 사람들을 부르는 별명이기도 하다.

15 오늘날 뉴질랜드인들은 전 세계적으로 키위라고 불리기도 한다.

16 이제, 당신은 키위가 과일과 새, 그리고 국민의 명칭이라는 것을 알았다.

17 다음에는 누군가가 키위라는 단어를 사용할 때 혼동하지 마라. 그 단어는 여러 뜻을 가지고 있기 때문이다.

18 이제, 마오리족에 대해 이야기해 보자. 마오리족은 뉴질랜드의 원주민이다.

19 그들은 유럽인들이 도착하기 오래 전에 이 섬에 와서 살았다.

20 마오리족의 문화는 오늘날 뉴질랜드 사회의 중요한 부분이다.

21 몇몇 학교에서 마오리어를 가르치고 있으며, 마오리어의 라디오와 TV 방송국이 있다.

22 나라의 여러 곳에 마오리 마을이 있다.

23 당신은 마오리 마을을 방문해 마오리 문화를 경험할 수 있다.

24 당신이 마을 사람들에게 "kia ora"라고 말한다면 그들은 그것을 듣고 좋아할 것이다. 그것은 영어로 "안녕"이라는 뜻이다.

25 하카를 본 적이 있는가?

26 하카 춤을 추는 사람들이 소리 지르고, 그들의 몸을 사납게 움직이기 때문에 하카는 무서워 보일 수도 있다.

27 당신이 이미 그들에 대해 들은 적이 있겠지만, 마오리인들은 전쟁 춤으로 하카를 추기 시작했다.

28 하지만, 오늘날 뉴질랜드 사람들은 하카를 운동 경기, 결혼식 또는 다른 중요한 행사가 있을 때 한다.

29 예를 들어, 뉴질랜드의 럭비 국가 대표 팀 선수들은 모든 경기 전에 하카를 춘다.

30 그것은 전 세계적으로 유명하다.

31 당신이 하카를 본다면, 상대 팀이 틀림없이 겁을 먹을 것이라는 것에 아마 동의할 것이다.

32 키위와 마찬가지로 하카는 나라의 상징이다.

본문 TEST Step 4· Step 5   p.15~18

1 New Zealand is a place of natural beauty. It has many beautiful lakes and waterfalls.

2 New Zealand has two main islands, the South Island and the North Island.

3 In the South Island, there are mountains that are covered with snow all year round.

4 You will be amazed by the fantastic views.

5 In the North Island, there are many hot springs, lakes, and areas with green grass.

6 Because of its natural beauty, many famous movies have been made in New Zealand.

7 If you visit New Zealand, you will surely appreciate its nature.

8 When you hear the word kiwi, what comes to your mind?

9 Maybe a fruit, but, in New Zealand the word kiwi has a couple of meanings.

10 First, kiwi is the name of a delicious, green fruit.

11 A lot of kiwi fruit is grown there, so New Zealand is known as the land of kiwi fruit.

12 Kiwi is also the name of one of New Zealand's native birds.

13 The kiwi is special to New Zealanders because it is the symbol of the nation.

14 Also, kiwi is a nickname for people from New Zealand.

15 Today, New Zealanders are sometimes called Kiwis throughout the world.

16 Now, you know that kiwi is the name of a fruit, a bird, and also a people.

17 Next time, don't become confused when someone uses the word kiwi, which has several meanings.

18 Now, let's talk about the Maori. They are the native people of New Zealand.

19 They went to live on the islands long before Europeans arrived.

20 The Maori culture is an important part of today's New Zealand society.

21 The Maori language is taught at some schools and there are Maori language radio and TV stations.

22 There are Maori villages in many parts of the country.

23 You can visit Maori villages and experience Maori culture.

24 If you say "kia ora" to the villagers, they will be glad to hear it. It means "hi" in English.

25 Have you ever watched the haka?

26 The haka may look scary because haka dancers shout and move their bodies wildly.

27 The Maori people, who you've already heard about, started doing the haka as a war dance.

28 Today, however, New Zealanders do the haka at sport matches, weddings, or other important events.

29 For example, New Zealand's national rugby team members do the haka before every match.

30 It is famous all over the world.

31 If you see the haka, you will probably agree that the rival team must be scared.

32 Like the kiwi bird, the haka is a national symbol.

구석구석지문 TEST Step 1   p.19

Before You Read

1. a popular sport
2. in the southern part of
3. the native people, have their culture

Enjoy Writing

1. Invite
2. Do, know about
3. two main islands, smaller islands
4. Its capital
5. which, a bird native, one of the symbols
6. If, come to, should visit, Maori village, which, the native culture
7. suggest, try, traditional dish
8. cook meat, vegetables, with heated rocks
9. to enjoy the beautiful nature
10. happy to invite, beautiful country

Project Step 1

1. Let's talk, are going to look into
2. Which country, prefer, or
3. suggest, search for, on
4. a lot of, to work with
5. Okay

구석구석지문 TEST Step 2   p.20

Before You Read

1. Rugby is a popular sport in New Zealand.
2. New Zealand is in the southern part of the world.
3. The Maori people are the native people of New Zealand and have their culture.

Enjoy Writing

1. We Invite You
2. Do you know about New Zealand?
3. It has two main islands and 600 smaller islands.
4. Its capital is Wellington.

5. The kiwi, which is a bird native to New Zealand, is one of the symbols of the country.

6. If you come to New Zealand, you should visit a Maori village, which shows the native culture of New Zealand.

7. We suggest you try a traditional dish of the Maori people.

8. They cook meat and vegetables in the ground with heated rocks. It is great.

9. Many people visit New Zealand to enjoy the beautiful nature.

10. We are happy to invite you to this beautiful country.

Project Step 1

1. A: Let's talk about which country we are going to look into.
2. B: Which country do you prefer, Australia or the UK?
3. C: I suggest we search for information on the UK.
4. There is a lot of information to work with.
5. D: Okay.

Lesson 7

단어 TEST Step 1 p.21

01 진심으로	02 우연히, 뜻하지 않게	
03 관계	04 삭제하다	05 감정적인
06 ~을 준비하다	07 특히, 유난히	08 책임
09 적절한, 제대로 된	10 너그러운	
11 재미있는, 유머러스한		12 포함하다
13 (관계를) 끝내다, 끊다		14 사례, 경우
15 심각한, 진지한	16 대충하는, 건성의	17 의견, 제안
18 사려 깊은, 생각에 잠긴		19 필요한
20 꺼리다, 싫어하다	21 후회하다	22 사과
23 느긋한, 여유 있는	24 진정한, 진심 어린	25 상처, 부상
26 사과하다	27 용감한	28 무시하다
29 고마워하다, 감사하다		30 빌리다
31 긴장하는, 초조해 하는		
32 소리가 큰, 시끄러운		33 의도하다
34 식판, 쟁반	35 ~에 걸려 넘어지다	
36 ~에 마음을 쓰다, ~에 관심을 가지다		37 ~에 부딪히다
38 즉시	39 진심으로	40 (소리를) 줄이다
41 ~을 웃어넘기려 하다		42 ~에 책임을 지다
43 ~를 아무렇지 않게 여기다		

단어 TEST Step 2 p.22

01 delete	02 suggestion	03 thoughtful
04 accidentally	05 mind	06 appreciate
07 casual	08 especially	09 generous
10 case	11 responsibility	12 prepare
13 break	14 intend	15 serious
16 sincere	17 proper	18 regret
19 ignore	20 include	21 relaxed
22 apologize	23 emotional	24 humorous
25 brave	26 mistake	27 apology
28 relationship	29 sincerely	30 wound
31 loud	32 treat	33 borrow
34 necessary	35 bump into	36 laugh off
37 pass by	38 trip over	39 turn down
40 take responsibility for		41 pick out
42 with all one's heart		43 get along with

단어 TEST Step 3 p.23

1 appreciate, 감사하다 2 mistake, 실수
3 ignore, 무시하다 4 relationship, 관계

5 responsibility, 책임   6 accidentally, 우연히

7 brave, 용감한   8 casual, 대충하는, 건성의

9 delete, 삭제하다   10 apology, 사과

11 sincere, 진정한, 진심어린   12 suggestion, 제안

13 thoughtful, 사려 깊은   14 prepare, 준비하다

15 regret, 후회하다   16 generous, 관대한, 너그러운

대화문 TEST Step 1
p.24~26

Listen & Speak 1 A-1

mind turning down / No, I don't, loud / hear / turn it down / Thanks, lot

Listen & Speak 1 A-2

accidentally broke, favorite plate / That's too bad / Do you mind telling, how to say sorry to / not at all, apologize sincerely / with all my heart

Listen & Speak 1 A-3

mind coming / early / that, borrowed before class / let's / then

Listen & Speak 1 B

mind being quiet / but, can't / mind picking up trash / can't

Listen & Speak 2 A-1

seem to be busy / preparing for, contest / contest last year / great / are good at getting, rhythm / need to, relaxed, nervous / advice, helpful, appreciate, advice / pleasure

Listen & Speak 2 A-2

lost / Let me help, What, like / is written / yours, under / appreciate, help / No problem

Listen & Speak 2 B

Let, show / appreciate / Let me carry, backpack / appreciate your help

Real Life Talk

What's up / present, (You')ve, been, for, haven't / since, elementary / busy studying, do you mind helping, help me pick out something nice / problem, present for / was broken, carried / of her / how about, broke, recently / Thank you, suggestion

Wrap Up 1

am planning to go / cool, used to live / Do you mind telling, what to do / Not at all, beaches, should visit / swimming, else / don't you, everywhere / How about / raw fish, fresh, delicious / appreciate, tips

Wrap Up 2

well, might have caught, needs to, in an hour, to meet, instead, should, say

대화문 TEST Step 2
p.27~29

Listen & Speak 1 A-1

B: Judy, do you mind turning down the volume?

G: No, I don't. Is it too loud?

B: Yes, it is. I can hear it in my room.

G: I'm sorry. I'll turn it down.

B: Thanks a lot.

Listen & Speak 1 A-2

G: I accidentally broke my mom's favorite plate.

B: That's too bad, Mina.

G: Do you mind telling me how to say sorry to her?

B: No, not at all. You should apologize sincerely.

G: I see. I'll talk to her with all my heart.

Listen & Speak 1 A-3

B: Karen, do you mind coming to my house tomorrow at 7 a.m.?

G: That's very early.

B: I know, but I need the book that you borrowed before class.

G: I see. Then let's meet at seven.

B: See you then.

Listen & Speak 1 B

A: Hellen, do you mind being quiet?

B: No, I don't. / Sorry but I can't.

A: Hellen, do you mind picking up trash?

B: No, I don't. / Sorry but I can't.

Listen & Speak 2 A-1

G: You seem to be busy, Minsu. Can I come in?

B: Sure. I'm preparing for the dance contest, but it's not easy.

G: I can help you. I was in the contest last year.

B: Really? That would be great, Amy.

G: You are good at getting into the rhythm. But one thing you need to do is to be more relaxed. You are too nervous.

B: Your advice is very helpful. I really appreciate your advice.

G: It's my pleasure.

Listen & Speak 2 A-2

B: Irene, what are you doing?

G: Well, I've lost my favorite cap. I can't find it.

B: Let me help you. What does it look like?

G: It's red. My name is written in black on the side.

B: Oh, is this yours? It was under the table.

G: Yes, it is. Thank you, Jim. I appreciate your help.

B: No problem.

Listen & Speak 2 B

A: Let me show you the way.

B: I appreciate your time.

A: Let me carry your backpack.

B: I appreciate your help.

Jessie: Hi, Andy. What's up?

Andy: Hi, Jessie. I'm going to buy a present for Amy. You've been friends with her for a long time, haven't you?

Jessie: Yes, since first grade in elementary school.

Andy: Well, I know you're really busy studying, but do you mind helping me? I am sure you could help me pick out something nice.

Jessie: No problem. What's the present for? It's not her birthday.

Andy: Well, two months ago, when my leg was broken, she carried my backpack to school.

Jessie: That was nice of her.

Andy: Yes, it was. What should I get for her?

Jessie: Well, how about a case for her smartphone? She broke her case recently.

Andy: Really? Thank you for your suggestion.

G: I am planning to go to Jejudo.

B: That's cool, Suhee. I used to live there.

G: Do you mind telling me what to do in Jejudo?

B: Not at all. Jejudo has many beautiful beaches. You should visit them.

G: Good. I will go swimming. What else can I do?

B: Why don't you hike Halla Mountain? You can see the mountain from everywhere on the island.

G: Great.

B: If you like fish, on Jejudo raw fish is fresh and delicious.

G: I'll try everything. I appreciate your tips.

W: Mike does not feel very well. He might have caught a cold. He needs to see a doctor, but he has a meeting with Jane in an hour. He wants to meet her tomorrow instead. What should he say to her?

01 Because, human, mistakes, along

02 without intending, wrong, regret

03 that happens, should apologize

04 following case, proper apology

05 tripped over, laughed, uploaded

06 became angry, with, deleted

07 even, hurt because, casual

08 acted, seemed, nothing serious

09 case, guessed, sincere, apologize

10 Apologizing, build, Saying, words

11 respect, care about, feelings

12 make things right, sincere

13 more, apology, better, received

14 another, accidentally bumped into

15 tray fell, apologize, bad

16 doesn't, say, if, right

17 that, necessary, apologize, once

18 shows, thoughtful, responsibility, action

19 think nothing, laugh, off

20 Finally, among, loved, too

21 borrowed, favorite, Later, lost

22 apologize, thought, important, after

23 disliked how, treated, ignore

24 hadn't apologized, little sister

25 apologize, something wrong, close

26 get hurt, easily, comes

27 let, go because, close

28 mistakes, add up, emotional

29 especially, among, loved ones

30 heard, saying, more, chances

31 mistakes, let, break, relationship

32 apologize, Try, sincere, solve

01 Because, It is, to get along with, all the time

02 hurt, without intending to, something wrong, regret

03 that, should apologize

04 following case, a proper apology

05 tripped over, it funny, laughed, took, uploaded, on

06 saw, became angry, with, laugh, deleted it

07 even, because of, casual apology

08 how Mike had acted, seemed to think, nothing serious

09 should be sincere, apologize

10 Apologizing, to, friendships, Saying, more than

11 that, respect, other, care about, feelings

12 make things right, sincere

13 The more sincere, the better, received

14 another, hurrying across, accidentally bumped into

15 on, fell on, apologize, felt bad

16 Why doesn't, say, if, apologized right now

17 that, is necessary, apologize at once

18 shows that, thoughtful, take responsibility for

19 All, to do, think nothing, laugh it off

20 are, among, members, loved ones

21 borrowed, favorite, Later, lost

22 apologize, not important, after all

23 had treated, ignore

24 hadn't apologized to, little sister

25 to apologize, something wrong, includes, who are close

26 get hurt more easily, comes from

27 let it go, are close

28 small mistakes, no apology add up to, emotional wounds

29 among, loved ones

30 heard of, No more, no more chances

31 make, let, break, beautiful relationship

32 apologize to, Try to do, quick, sincere, can solve

1 우리는 인간이기 때문에 모두가 실수한다. 모든 사람과 항상 잘 지내기는 쉽지 않다.

2 때때로 우리는 의도하지 않게 다른 사람의 감정을 상하게 한다. 때때로 우리는 나쁜 일을 하고 나중에 그것을 후회한다.

3 이런 일이 생기면, 우리는 무엇을 해야 할까? 우리는 사과해야 한다.

4 다음 사례 연구들을 읽고 올바른 사과를 위한 세 가지를 알아보자.

5 June이 가방에 걸려 넘어졌을 때, Mike는 그것이 재미있다고 생각하고 웃었다. 그는 사진을 찍어서 SNS에 올렸다.

6 June은 그 사진을 보고 화가 났다. Mike는 웃으면서 "미안해, June!"이라고 말하고 사진을 삭제했다.

7 그 후, June은 Mike의 가벼운 사과에 한층 더 화가 났다.

8 June은 Mike의 행동 방식이 마음에 들지 않았다. Mike는 이 일이 심각한 일이 아니라고 생각하는 것처럼 보였다.

9 이 사례로부터 무엇을 배웠는가? 맞다. 당신은 바르게 추측했다. 당신은 사과할 때에 진실해야 한다.

10 사과하는 것은 좋은 교우 관계를 만들기 위해 필요하다. 미안하다고 말하는 것은 단지 말 이상이다.

11 당신이 타인을 존중하고, 타인의 감정에 관심을 갖고 있음을 보여 주어야 한다.

12 당신이 진실로 일을 바로잡기를 원한다면, 당신의 사과는 진실해야 한다.

13 당신의 사과가 진실할수록, 그것은 더 잘 받아들여질 것이다.

14 또 다른 사례가 있다. Kate가 급식실을 가로질러 급하게 뛰어갈 때, 호준이와 실수로 부딪쳤다.

15 호준이의 급식판에 있던 음식이 그의 재킷에 떨어졌다. Kate는 사과하지 않았다. 호준이는 기분이 나빴다.

16 그는 '왜 그녀는 아무 말도 하지 않지? 그녀가 즉시 사과한다면 아무 일도 아닐 텐데.' 라고 생각했다.

17 이 사례는 사과가 필요할 때는 사과를 즉시 해야 한다는 것을 보여준다.

18 신속한 사과는 당신이 사려 깊고, 당신의 행동에 책임을 진다는 것을 보여준다.

19 당신이 해야 할 행동은 "미안해."라고 말하는 것뿐이다. 그러면 상처받은 친구는 당신의 잘못을 아무렇지 않게 생각하고, 웃어넘길 것이다.

20 마지막으로 사과는 가족이나 사랑하는 사람들 사이에서도 필요하다.

21 어느 날, 선민이는 여동생이 가장 좋아하는 책을 빌렸다. 나중에 그녀는 그것을 잃어버렸다.

22 선민이는 그것이 중요하지 않다고 생각하여 사과하지 않았다. 그녀는 '우리는 어쨌든 자매니까.'라고 생각했다.

23 선민이의 여동생은 언니가 본인을 대했던 방식이 마음에 들지 않았다. 어떻게 자신의 언니가 그녀의 기분을 무시할 수 있는가?

24 선민이가 여동생에게 사과하지 않았던 것은 이번이 처음이 아니었다.

25 사람들은 잘못했을 때, 사과해야 한다. 이것은 가족이나 당신에게 가까운 사람도 포함한다.

26 사람들은 마음의 상처가 가족이나 친구에게서 올 때 더 쉽게 상처 받는다.

27 우리는 아마 그들이 가깝기 때문에 그냥 넘어갈 것이라고 생각할지 모른다.

28 하지만 작은 실수를 하고 사과하지 않는 것은 큰 감정적인 상처가 된다는 것을 기억하라.

29 이것은 가족과 사랑하는 사람들에게 특히 더 그러하다.

30 당신은 "더 이상 사과하지 않는다면 더 이상 기회가 없다."는 말을 들어본 적이 있는가?

31 사람들은 실수하지만, 그 실수가 아름다운 관계를 깨뜨리게 해서는 안 된다.

32 누군가에게 사과하고 싶은가? 지금 하려고 노력해라. 빠르고 진정한 "미안해."라는 말이 많은 문제를 해결해 줄 것이다.

1 Because we are human, we all make mistakes. It is not easy to get along with everyone all the time.

2 Sometimes we hurt people's feelings without intending to. Sometimes, we do something wrong and regret it later.

3 When that happens, what should we do? We should apologize.

4 Read the following case studies and learn three things about a proper apology.

5 When June tripped over a backpack and fell, Mike found it funny and laughed. He took a picture and uploaded it on an SNS.

6 June saw the picture and became angry. Mike said, with a laugh, "Sorry, June!" and deleted it.

7 After that, June felt even more hurt because of Mike's casual apology.

8 June didn't like how Mike had acted. Mike seemed to think it was nothing serious.

9 What did you learn from this case? Yes. You guessed right. You should be sincere when you apologize.

10 Apologizing is necessary to build good friendships. Saying you're sorry is more than just words.

11 You need to show that you respect the other person and care about his or her feelings.

12 If you truly want to make things right, be sincere in your apology.

13 The more sincere your apology is, the better it will be received.

14 Here is another case. While Kate was hurrying across the cafeteria, she accidentally bumped into Hojun.

15 Some food on Hojun's tray fell on his jacket. Kate didn't apologize. Hojun felt bad.

16 He thought, 'Why doesn't she say something? It would be nothing if she apologized right now.'

17 This case shows that when an apology is necessary, you should apologize at once.

18 A quick apology shows that you are thoughtful and take responsibility for your action.

19 All you need to do is to say, "I'm sorry." Then, the hurt friend will think nothing of it and laugh it off.

20 Finally, apologies are necessary among family members and loved ones, too.

21 One day, Sunmin borrowed her sister's favorite book. Later, she lost it.

22 Sunmin didn't apologize because she thought it was not important. She thought, 'We're sisters, after all.'

23 Sunmin's sister disliked how Sunmin had treated her. How could her own sister ignore her feelings?

24 This was not the first time Sunmin hadn't apologized to her little sister.

25 People need to apologize when they do something wrong. This includes family members and the people who are close to you.

26 People get hurt more easily when the hurt comes from a family member or a friend.

27 We may think that they will let it go because they are close to us.

28 Remember, however, that small mistakes and no apology add up to big emotional wounds.

29 This is especially true among family members and loved ones.

30 Have you ever heard of the saying, "No more apologies, no more chances"?

31 People make mistakes, but don't let one mistake break a beautiful relationship.

32 Do you want to apologize to someone? Try to do it now. A quick and sincere "I'm sorry" can solve many problems..

After You Read C

1. a store buy shoes
2. was hit by, as she passed by
3. walked away quickly
4. because, sincere, proper apology
5. that, care about his feelings

Enjoy Writing C

1. Wonderful Friend
2. like to introduce
3. have known, since
4. humorous, brave, cheerful
5. how he helped
6. sick, missed a math class
7. showed me his class notes
8. lucky to have, as
9. The more, the deeper

Project Step 1

1. how we write a note of apology
2. what we did

3. that we are sorry for

4. Do not make excuses

5. for the tips, really appreciate

구석구석지문 TEST Step 2   p.41

After You Read C

1. Inho went to a a store buy shoes.

2. He was hit by a woman's bag accidentally as she passed by.

3. The woman said, "Sorry," and she walked away quickly.

4. Inho was angry because the woman did not make a sincere and proper apology.

5. He thought that the woman should care about his feelings.

Enjoy Writing C

1. My Wonderful Friend, Jinsu

2. I'd like to introduce my friend, Jinsu.

3. I have known him since elementary school.

4. He is always humorous, brave, and cheerful.

5. This is how he helped me.

6. Last Friday I was sick and missed a math class.

7. Jinsu showed me his class notes.

8. I am lucky to have him as my friend.

9. The more I know him, the deeper our friendship becomes.

Project Step 1

1. A: Do you know how we write a note of apology?

2. B: Yes. First, write about what we did.

3. C: Then write that we are sorry for it.

4. D: Do not make excuses for our actions.

5. A: Thank you for the tips. I really appreciate it.

단어 TEST Step 1   p.42

01 상품, 제품	02 아마
03 주제, 과목, 실험대상자	04 거대한, 큰
05 대중적인, 인기 있는	06 포함하다, 넣다
07 능력 08 전통적인	09 보통의, 평범한
10 활기 넘치는, 생생한	11 원뿔, 원뿔형 물체
12 주인공 13 전시회	14 접시
15 실외의 16 열, 발열	17 광고
18 연기, 공연 19 흔한, 평범한, 공통의	
20 창의력 21 친숙한	22 예술 작품
23 특수효과 24 창의적인	25 교훈
26 예술적인 27 복사본	28 운영하다
29 화려한 30 클래식의, 고전적인	31 신선한, 참신한
32 조각품 33 장식	34 ~의 가치가 있는
35 ~로 구성되다 36 설치하다	37 요전 날, 며칠 전
38 ~로 여겨지다 39 다시 말해서, 즉	40 ~ 대신에
41 ~에 주의를 기울이다	42 ~을 부수다
43 ~로 눈길을 돌리다	

단어 TEST Step 2   p.43

01 popular	02 artistic	03 boring
04 plate	05 advertising	06 exhibition
07 colorful	08 familiar	09 sculpture
10 performance	11 creative	12 lively
13 fever	14 creativity	15 truly
16 worth	17 common	18 toilet
19 goods	20 ability	21 art work
22 huge	23 include	24 probably
25 refreshing	26 lesson	27 main character
28 traditional	29 outdoor	30 decoration
31 plain	32 run	33 cone
34 special effects	35 be made of	36 in other words
37 break down	38 be regarded as	
39 pay attention to	40 change A into B	
41 be short for	42 be made up of	43 the other day

단어 TEST Step 3   p.44

1 boring, 지루한   2 plain, 평범한

3 popular, 대중적인, 인기 있는   4 performance, 연기

5 ability, 능력 6 creativity, 창의력 7 decoration, 장식

8 practice, 연습하다   9 familiar, 친숙한   10 cone, 원뿔

11 advice, 충고　12 classical, 클래식의, 고전적인

13 include, 포함하다　14 sculpture, 조각품

15 traditional, 전통적인　16 exhibition, 전시회

대화문 TEST Step 1　p.45~46

Listen & Speak 1 A

1. listen to, kinds, music library / cool, listen to classical / Sure, classical music / one of my favorite musicians, about / more than classical music / What do you like / fascinated by, exciting

2. finish, art homework / drew, plate / Sounds interesting / advice, did, draw / myself surfing / fascinated by your drawing

Listen & Speak 2 A

1. The other day, play / how did you like / main characters, actors', performance, fantastic / as well / a little boring, pretty good / should see / Only if, a lot of

2. how do you like / a lot, class / What do you like most / learning different drawing skills, What / painting skills, with / work last time, thought, creative / practice a lot

Real Life Talk

didn't you / special / How did you like / fantastic, was fascinated by, paintings, creativity / No wonder, one of the greatest painters, What else / a gift shop, Famous works, were printed / anything / How do you like / looks great on

Wrap Up 1

festival, didn't / A lot of, performed / How did you like / special guest, called / heard, famous / performance / No wonder

대화문 TEST Step 2　p.47~48

Listen & Speak 1 A

1. B: Sandy, you can listen to many kinds of music in this music library.

   G: That's cool, Bob. Can I listen to classical music?

   B: Sure. Do you like classical music?

   G: Yes, Beethoven is one of my favorite musicians. How about you?

   B: I like pop music more than classical music.

   G: I see. What do you like most about pop music?

B: I'm really fascinated by its exciting rhythms.

2. G: Jim, did you finish your art homework?

   B: Yes. I drew the face of my role model on a plate.

   G: Sounds interesting. Who is your role model?

   B: My dad. He always gives me good advice. Who did you draw, Amy?

   G: Well, I drew myself surfing in the sea.

   B: Wonderful! I'm fascinated by your drawing.

   G: Thank you.

Listen & Speak 2 A

1. B: The other day I watched a play, *A Love Story in the War*.

   G: Oh, how did you like the play?

   B: I liked the main characters. The actors' performances were fantastic.

   G: Was the story good as well?

   B: No. It was a little boring, but the music was pretty good.

   G: So, do you think I should see it?

   B: Only if you have a lot of time and money.

2. B: Caire, how do you like your art class?

   G: It's great. I learn a lot in the class.

   B: What do you like most about it?

   G: I enjoy learning different drawing skills. What about you, Allen?

   B: I also like the class. I learn good painting skills. I love painting with many colors.

   G: Oh, I saw your work last time. I thought it was very creative.

   B: Thanks. I practice a lot.

Real Life Talk

Bora: Andy, you went to the art museum, didn't you?

Andy: Yes. They had a special Chagall exhibition.

Bora: How did you like it?

Andy: It was fantastic! I was fascinated by the colors in his paintings and his creativity.

Bora: No wonder. He was one of the greatest painters ever. What else did you see in the museum?

Andy: I went to a gift shop and saw things like umbrellas, cups, and backpacks. Famous works of art were printed on them.

Bora: Did you buy anything?

Andy: Yes. I bought this T-shirt. How do you like it?

Bora: It looks great on you.

Andy: Thank you.

Wrap Up 1

B: Cindy, you went to the music festival, didn't you?

G: Yes. A lot of famous musicians performed there.

B: How did you like the festival?

G: It was fantastic! I really liked the special guest. Do you know the band called *the Brothers*?

B: Oh, I've heard about them. The singer is famous.

G: Yes. His performance was great.

B: No wonder.

본문 **TEST** Step 1   p.49~50

01 Welcome, Exhibition, Paintings, cartoons

02 Probably, think, famous works

03 short, so, popular art

04 began, create something, easy

05 Instead, traditional, works, turned

06 used, from, magazines, advertising

07 familiar images, exhibitions, refreshing

08 Since, become truly popular

09 that, too, to understand

10 using, bright, changed, thought

11 common, plain, words, artistic

12 worth paying attention, filled

13 Let's learn, famous, artists

14 famous, ability, change, objects

15 called, found, subjects in

16 famous, made up, actor

17 Another, made, copies, works

18 copies, works, show, something

19 another, who made, fun

20 sculptures, everyday items, brush

21 beginning, created, made, materials

22 cloth, huge sculptures, as

23 Wanting, set up, outdoor

24 ran, inside, sell, goods

25 used, works, painted, lively

26 included, were, regarded as

27 However, differently, himself, Why

28 broke down, between, adding

29 believed, should, Anyone, create

30 creating, work, pop art

31 using, creative, important lesson

본문 **TEST** Step 2   p.51~52

01 Welcome to, Exhibition, What, cartoons

02 look like, Probably, think, are, famous works

03 is short for popular, popular art

---

04 It began in, wanted to, something fun

05 Instead of, traditional, turned, to popular culture

06 used, from, advertising

07 familiar images, art exhibitions, them refreshing

08 Since, become truly popular

09 that, too, to understand

10 By using, bright colors, changed that thought

11 Using, looks plain. In other words, artistic

12 worth paying attention to, looks plain, is filled with

13 Let's, famous pop artists

14 famous for, ability, able to change common objects into amazing

15 is called, found, subjects in

16 is made up

17 Another work shows, made, copies, works

18 copies of his works, to show that, you see

19 another, who made, fun

20 sculptures of everyday items, such as, brush

21 In the beginning, created soft sculptures, made of, soft materials

22 For example, cloth to make, huge sculptures, daily items, such as

23 Wanting, to enjoy, set up, outdoor

24 ran, inside, to sell, were fun goods

25 used, in his works, were, painted, lively colors

26 included, Back then, were, regarded as

27 However, differently, himself, Why, they not

28 broke down, between, and, by adding

29 believed, should be, Anyone, create, enjoy

30 creating, pop art

31 By using, in, creative way, make, for, the most important lesson

---

본문 **TEST** Step 3   p.53~54

1 팝 아트 전시회에 온 것을 환영한다! 무엇이 보이는가? 수프 통조림들을 모아 놓은 그림? 커다란 만화 그림?

2 그것들이 예술 작품처럼 보이는가? 아마 그렇게 보이지 않겠지만, 다시 생각해 봐라. 그것들은 모두 유명한 팝 아트 작품들이다.

3 'pop'은 'popular(대중적인)'의 줄임말이다. 그래서 팝 아트는 대중 예술 또는 사람들을 위한 예술이라는 뜻이다.

4 팝 아트는 1950년대 미국에서 시작됐다. 그 당시 팝 아트 작가들은 재미있고 쉬운 것을 만들고 싶어 했다.

5 어려운 전통 예술 작품 대신 그들은 대중문화로 눈을 돌렸다.

6 그들은 텔레비전, 만화책, 잡지 및 광고에 나오는 이미지들을

사용했다.

7 미술 전시회에서 친숙한 이미지들을 봤을 때 사람들은 그것들이 신선하다는 걸 알게 되었다.

8 그때부터 팝 아트는 정말 유명해졌다.

9 사람들은 예술이 너무 어려워서 이해할 수 없는 것으로 생각했다.

10 일상적인 이미지와 밝은 색을 씀으로써, 팝 아트 작가들은 그러한 관점을 바꿨다.

11 흔한 이미지를 사용하기 때문에 팝 아트는 평범해 보인다. 즉, 팝 아트는 예술적으로 보이지 않는다.

12 하지만 여전히 주목할 만한 가치가 있다. 평범해 보일지라도 그것은 의미로 가득 차 있다.

13 몇 명의 유명한 팝 아트 작가들에 대해 알아보자.

14 그들은 특별한 예술적인 능력으로 유명해졌다. 그들은 흔한 대상을 놀라운 예술로 바꿀 수 있었다.

15 Andy Warhol은 팝 아트의 왕이라 불린다. 그는 잡지와 상점에서 주제를 찾았다.

16 그의 유명 작품들 중 하나는 미국 배우인 Marilyn Monroe의 사진으로 구성되어 있다.

17 또 다른 작품은 수프 통조림들을 보여준다. 그는 이 작품들의 사본을 많이 만들었다.

18 그는 왜 작품의 복사본을 만들었나? 그는 예술은 여러분이 매일 보는 것임을 보여 주고 싶어 했다.

19 Claes Oldenburg는 예술을 재미있게 만들었던 또 다른 팝 아트 작가이다.

20 그는 햄버거와 쿠키, 붓 같은 일상적인 물품들의 조각품을 만들었다.

21 초기에 그는 부드러운 조각품을 만들었다. 그것들은 플라스틱, 종이, 그리고 다른 부드러운 재료들로 만들어졌다.

22 예를 들어서 그는 변기를 만들기 위해 천을 사용했다. 나중에 그는 아이스크림콘 같은 일상 물품의 거대한 조각품을 만들었다.

23 그는 모든 사람이 그의 작품을 보고 즐기기를 원했기 때문에 그의 작품들을 실외에 설치했다.

24 그는 작품 판매를 위해 그의 작업실 안에 상점을 운영하기도 했다. 그에게 예술적인 작품들은 사람들을 위한 재미있는 제품이었다.

25 Roy Lichtenstein은 그의 작품에 만화를 사용했다. 그것들은 크고 생기 넘치는 색들로 그려졌다.

26 그는 심지어 그의 작품에 말풍선을 넣었다. 그 당시에 만화는 예술 형식으로 여겨지지 않았다.

27 하지만 Roy Lichtenstein은 다르게 생각했다. 그는 스스로에게 '왜 만화는 예술로 간주되지 않을까?'라고 물었다.

28 만화를 예술에 첨가함으로써 Roy Lichtenstein은 순수 예술과 대중문화 사이의 벽을 허물었다.

29 팝 아트 작가들은 예술은 쉬워야 한다고 믿었다. 누구나 예술을 만들 수 있고, 즐길 수 있다.

30 오늘 팝 아트 작품 하나를 만들어 보는 것은 어떤가?

31 일상적인 이미지를 창의적인 방식으로 사용함으로써, 모든 사람을 위한 예술 작품을 만들 수 있다. 이것이 팝 아트의 가장 중요한 교훈이다.

본문 TEST Step 4-Step 5 p.55~58

1 Welcome to the Pop Art Exhibition! What do you see? Paintings of soup cans? Big cartoons?

2 Do they look like art works? Probably not, but think again. They are all famous works of pop art.

3 Pop is short for popular. So pop art means popular art, or art for people.

4 It began in the 1950s in America. Pop artists at that time wanted to create something fun and easy.

5 Instead of difficult traditional art works, they turned their eyes to popular culture.

6 They used images from TV, comic books, magazines, and advertising.

7 When people saw familiar images in art exhibitions, they found them refreshing.

8 Since then, pop art has become truly popular.

9 People thought that art was too difficult to understand.

10 By using daily images and bright colors, pop artists changed that thought.

11 Using common images, pop art looks plain. In other words, it doesn't look artistic.

12 But it is still worth paying attention to. Although it looks plain, it is filled with meaning.

13 Let's learn about some famous pop artists.

14 They became famous for their special artistic ability. They were able to change common objects into amazing art.

15 Andy Warhol is called the King of Pop Art. He found his subjects in magazines and stores.

16 One of his famous works is made up of pictures of Marilyn Monroe, the American actor.

17 Another work shows cans of soup. He made many copies of these works.

18 Why did he make copies of his works? He wanted to show that art is something you see every day.

19 Claes Oldenburg is another pop artist who made art fun.

20 He made sculptures of everyday items, such as a hamburger, cookies, and a brush.

21 In the beginning, he created soft sculptures. They

were made of plastic, paper, and other soft materials.

22 For example, he used cloth to make toilets. Later, he made huge sculptures of daily items, such as an ice cream cone.

23 Wanting everyone to enjoy his art, he set up his works in outdoor places.

24 He also ran a store inside his studio to sell his works. For him, artistic works were fun goods for people.

25 Roy Lichtenstein used cartoons in his works. They were large and painted in lively colors.

26 He even included speech balloons in his paintings. Back then, cartoons were not regarded as an art form.

27 However, Roy Lichtenstein thought differently. He asked himself, 'Why are they not?'

28 Then Roy Lichtenstein broke down the wall between high art and popular culture by adding cartoons to art.

29 Pop artists believed art should be easy. Anyone can create and enjoy art.

30 How about creating a work of pop art today?

31 By using daily images in a creative way, you can make a work of art for everyone. This is the most important lesson from pop art.

구석구석지문 TEST Step 1 p.59

Project Step 1

1. want to make with
2. Why don't we
3. Let's build, like
4. How about drawing
5. let's give, some paper cups

Enjoy Writing B

1. The Best Musical, My Life
2. Last Saturday, to watch a musical
3. The title of the musical
4. because, in it
5. songs, dances of the musical
6. a girl who invited her best friends
7. talked about their friendship
8. main character, many beautiful songs
9. Singing along to, during the performance, excited
10. worth watching

Enjoy Writing B

1. Movie That Moved
2. went to, to watch a movie
3. The title of the movie, because my friend recommended
4. story of the movie, a brave man who tried to find
5. The main character, was played by, who
6. emotional scenes, moved
7. was really worth watching

구석구석지문 TEST Step 2 p.60

Project Step 1

1. A: What do you want to make with these paper cups?
2. B: Why don't we make a tower?
3. C: Wonderful! Let's build a tower like the Leaning Tower of Pisa.
4. D: How about drawing something on the cups?
5. B: Sounds great. First, let's give everyone some paper cups.

Enjoy Writing B

1. The Best Musical of My Life
2. Last Saturday I went to the concert hall to watch a musical.
3. The title of the musical was *You and Me*.
4. I watched it because my favorite actor was in it.
5. I liked the songs and dances of the musical.
6. The story was about a girl who invited her best friends to her birthday party.
7. They talked about their friendship.
8. The main character was Sophie. She sang many beautiful songs. It was fantastic.
9. Singing along to the songs during the performance, I was excited.
10. The musical was really worth watching.

Enjoy Writing B

1. A Movie That Moved Me
2. Last Saturday I went to my friend's house to watch a movie.
3. The title of the movie was *My Son*. I watched it because my friend recommended it.
4. I liked the story of the movie. The story was about a brave man who tried to find his lost son.
5. The main character was John. He was played by the actor Roy Jones, who was fantastic.
6. It was touching. Watching the emotional scenes, I was moved.
7. The movie was really worth watching.

단어 TEST Step 1

p.61

01 ~할 여유가 되다 02 사업 03 옥수수 속대
04 여과장치, 필터; 여과하다, 거르다 05 수집하다
06 발명(품) 07 유용한 08 편안한, 여유 있는
09 꿰매다, 바느질하다
10 통제하다, 조절하다, 조정하다 11 재봉틀
12 쓸모없는, 소용없는 13 체계, 장치
14 성냥 15 값이 들다 16 시골
17 오염시키다 18 입장료 19 삼각형
20 머무르다 21 실패 22 박람회
23 (자금을) 모으다 24 요금 25 제거하다
26 성공 27 대통령, 회장, 총재 28 ~인지 (아닌지)
29 단계 30 추천하다 31 오염
32 깨닫다, 인식하다 33 십 대(= teen) 34 머리띠
35 ~을 생각해 내다 36 우연히 마주치다 37 ~ 덕분에
38 스스로 39 A를 B로 바꾸다 40 무료로
41 지불하다 42 마음속으로 생각하다
43 A 뿐만 아니라 B도

단어 TEST Step 2

p.62

01 pollution 02 afford 03 realize
04 stay 05 business 06 collect
07 success 08 remove 09 cost
10 relaxed 11 fair
12 sewing machine 13 fee
14 countryside 15 entrance fee 16 filter
17 corn cob 18 useless 19 failure
20 whether 21 match 22 sew
23 pollute 24 raise 25 control
26 teenager 27 recommend 28 triangle
29 useful 30 invention 31 president
32 system 33 inventor 34 step
35 pay for 36 thanks to 37 for oneself
38 think to oneself
39 change A into B 40 come across
41 for free 42 get together
43 not only A but also B

단어 TEST Step 3

p.63

1 robotic, 로봇식의 2 sew, 꿰매다, 바느질하다
3 afford, ~할 여유가 되다 4 cost, 값이 들다

5 success, 성공 6 for free, 무료로 7 coin, 동전
8 come across, 우연히 마주치다
9 hit on, ~을 생각해 내다 10 business, 사업
11 pollute, 오염시키다 12 software, 소프트웨어
13 fair, 박람회 14 headband, 머리띠
15 control, 통제하다, 조정하다 16 match, 성냥

대화문 TEST Step 1

p.64~65

Listen & Speak 1 A-1

Can you draw, on / From, two triangles, draw, circle, like this / possible for you, without taking, off / how is that possible / at, four red points / any of the red points / first, the two triangles like this, triangles first / I get it

Listen & Speak 1 A-2

looking for, for / How old / five years old / to recommend / so cute / isn't it, that looks like, so, love it / for me to take, off, washing / take it off, put it back / wonderful, take it

Listen & Speak 2 A-1

you have been late for, lately, wrong / wake up early, can't / wake you up / does, right away, I wish, could / An AI robot / that could make sure, got up, gave me breakfast / great

Listen & Talk 2 A-2

planning to visit / going to do there / spend most of my time, because, swimming pool / Can, swim well / I wish I could, So, have fun with, instead / What is that / It's, go inside, walk on / must be

Real Life Talk

are, doing / drawing, my favorite superhero / great / could read people's minds / for her to control / control, if she wants to / cool / have any favorite superheroes / could fly like him / even breathe in space / can do anything

Wrap Up 1

What are you doing / flying / Are, good at / right now, practicing hard / As you know, run, possible for you to deliver orders / isn't, it will be possible in / That, be great

대화문 TEST Step 2

p.66~67

Listen & Speak 1 A-1

G: Can you draw this on the paper?
B: Sure. From the middle point, I draw two triangles.

Then I draw the circle, like this.

G: Good. Now, is it possible for you to draw it without taking your pencil off the paper?

B: I'll try. Hmm... No, how is that possible?

G: Well, start at one of the four red points.

B: Do you mean any of the red points?

G: Yes. Draw the circle first and then the two triangles like this. Or you can draw the triangles first, like this.

B: Oh, now I get it.

Listen & Speak 1 A-2

W: Hi. I'm looking for a backpack for my son.

M: How old is your son?

W: He is five years old.

M: I want to recommend this one.

W: Oh, it's so cute.

M: Yes, isn't it? It has a cap that looks like a penguin, so kids love it.

W: Is it possible for me to take the cap off for washing?

M: Sure. You can easily take it off and put it back on.

W: That's wonderful. I'll take it.

Listen & Speak 2 A-1

B: Wendy, you have been late for school a lot lately. What's wrong?

G: I want to wake up early, but I just can't.

B: Doesn't your mom wake you up?

G: She does, but I don't get up right away. I wish I could have an AI robot.

B: An AI robot?

G: Yes. I mean one that could make sure I got up and give me breakfast in the morning.

B: That sounds great.

Listen & Speak 2 A-2

B: I'm planning to visit my uncle in Mexico.

G: What are you going to do there, Mike?

B: I'll spend most of my time at his house because he has a big swimming pool.

G: That's great. Can you swim well?

B: No, I wish I could, but I can't. So I'll have fun with a water walking ball instead.

G: A water walking ball? What is that?

B: It's a large ball. We go inside it and walk on the water.

G: That must be fun.

Real Life Talk

Bora: What are you doing, Jessie?

Jessie: I'm drawing Dr. Rebecca, my favorite superhero.

Bora: Wow, that's great.

Jessie: Thanks. I wish I could read people's minds like her.

Bora: Is it possible for her to control them, too?

Jessie: Yes. She can control your mind if she wants to.

Bora: That's very cool.

Jessie: What about you? Do you also have any favorite superheroes?

Bora: Sure. I love Sky X. I wish I could fly like him.

Jessie: I like him, too. He can even breathe in space.

Bora: Yes. He can do anything in space.

Wrap Up 1

W: Hi, Tom. What are you doing?

B: I'm flying my drone.

W: Cool! Are you good at it?

B: No, I'm not very good right now, but I'm practicing hard.

W: As you know, I run a sandwich restaurant. Is it possible for you to deliver orders with your drone?

B: No, it isn't. But I think it will be possible in one or two years.

W: That will be great.

본문 TEST Step 1 p.68~69

01 change, too, to, one
02 following, used, make, place
03 when, came across, fair
04 robotic, that, open, close
05 surprised that, had cost
06 wish, had, better, myself
07 With, much cheaper, better
08 failures, using, able, price
09 share, with others, free
10 what, done, something useful
11 one, change, build, working
12 can't, go, as, could
13 had, thought, realized, afford
14 if, could, something, had
15 asked, buy, sewing machine
16 bought, how, make, myself
17 created, headbands, sold, at
18 raised enough, send, stop
19 business, help, who, go
20 success, pay, fees, like,
21 pay, textbooks, uniforms, amazing

22 advice, something, need, act

23 taking, steps, heart, lives

24 living, found, seriously polluted

25 how, solve, hit on

26 Useless, were, in, village

27 holes, dirty matter, polluted

28 picked, washed, placed, bowl

29 After, while, much clearer

30 using, collected from, filtering

31 removed, dirty matter from

32 clean up, only, also

01 who change, too young to be

02 will meet, to make

03 when, came across, at, science fair

04 robotic, that, open, close

05 surprised that, had cost her

06 wish, had, thought to myself

07 With, a much cheaper, better

08 failures, by using, was able to, for, price of

09 to share, for, with others for free

10 Maybe, take what I have done, something useful with

11 No one, change, build, by working together

12 can't, go to school, could go

13 had this thought, realized that, couldn't afford

14 if I could do something, had

15 asked, to buy me a sewing machine

16 bought me one, how to make, for myself

17 ten headbands, them

18 raised enough money, stop

19 a business to help, who, go

20 to the success, fees for, like, to go to school

21 pay for, textbooks, uniforms, Isn't, amazing

22 advice, is, do something, a need, act

23 small, taking, warm heart, lives

24 As, living, often found that, around, seriously polluted

25 how I could solve, hit on, to use

26 Useless, were, in

27 the small holes, could filter dirty matter, polluted

28 picked up, washed them, placed, in a bowl of

29 After a while, it, much clearer

30 using, that, collected from, built, filtering

31 removed, the dirty matter

32 filtering system, clean up, not only, but also, other areas

1 세상을 바꾸는 사람들은 누구인가? 여러분은 너무 어려서 이런 사람들 중 하나가 될 수 없다고 생각하나요?

2 다음 이야기에서 여러분은 세상을 더 나은 곳으로 만들기 위해 자신들의 아이디어를 사용한 세 명의 십 대들을 만날 겁니다.

3 내가 열네 살이었을 때, 어느 날 한 과학 박람회에서 어린 소녀를 우연히 만났다.

4 그녀는 겨우 접었다 펴지기만 하는 로봇 손을 가지고 있었다.

5 나는 그녀가 그 손에 8만 달러를 지불했다는 데 놀랐다!

6 '나는 그녀가 더 나은 로봇 손을 가질 수 있으면 좋겠어.'라고 마음속으로 생각했다.

7 나는 이런 생각을 가지고 더 싸고 좋은 로봇 손을 만들기 시작했다.

8 많은 실패 뒤 마침내 3D 프린트 기술을 사용해서 나는 단 300달러짜리의 유용한 로봇 손을 만들 수 있었다.

9 나는 내 3D 로봇 손의 디자인과 소프트웨어를 다른 사람들과 무료로 공유하기로 결심했다.

10 아마도 누군가는 내가 만든 것을 이용해 다른 유용한 것을 할 수 있을 것이다.

11 혼자 세상을 바꿀 수는 없지만, 함께 일 하면서 더 나은 세상을 만들 수 있다.

12 '아프리카의 많은 소녀들은 왜 나처럼 학교에 갈 수 없지? 나는 그들도 학교에 갈 수 있으면 좋을 텐데.'

13 내가 12살 때, 이런 생각을 했었다. 나는 그들의 가족이 그럴 금전적 여유가 없다는 것을 깨달았다.

14 나는 내가 그 소녀들을 위해서 어떤 것을 할 수 있을까 생각했다. 그때 아이디어가 떠올랐다.

15 나는 내 생일에 부모님께 재봉틀을 사 달라고 부탁드렸다.

16 그들은 재봉틀을 사 주셨고 나는 머리띠 만드는 법을 혼자 배웠다.

17 10개의 머리띠를 만들어 학교에서 팔았다.

18 나는 곧 아프리카에 있는 한 명의 소녀를 학교에 보낼 수 있는 충분한 자금을 모았다. 나는 거기서 멈출 수 없었다.

19 나는 학교에 갈 수 없는 아프리카의 소녀들을 돕기 위해 사업을 시작했다.

20 내 사업의 성공 덕분에 나는 케냐와 우간다 같은 나라에 있는 많은 가난한 소녀들이 학교에 갈 수 있게 수업료를 지불할 수 있다.

21 나는 또한 그들의 교과서와 교복, 연필을 위한 비용도 지불한다. 놀랍지 않은가?

22 나의 조언은 그냥 무엇이든 하라는 것이다. 필요성이 보인다면 행동하라.

23 작은 단계를 밟아가면서 작은 것부터 시작하라. 너의 따뜻한

마음이 삶을 바꿀 수 있다.

24 인도의 시골에 살고 있었던 어린 소녀인 나는 종종 내 주변에 있는 물이 심각하게 오염되어 있는 것을 발견했다.

25 나는 이 문제를 어떻게 해결할 수 있을지 궁금했다. 그때 나는 옥수수 속대를 이용해야겠다는 생각이 불현듯 떠올랐다.

26 내가 사는 마을에는 쓸모없는 옥수수 속대가 곳곳에 널려 있다.

27 나는 옥수수 속대의 작은 구멍들이 더러운 물질을 오염된 물 밖으로 걸러 낼 수 있을 거라고 생각했다.

28 어느 날 나는 길을 따라 마른 옥수수 속대를 주운 뒤, 그것들을 씻어서 더러운 물이 담긴 그릇에 넣었다.

29 잠시 뒤 물을 확인했는데 훨씬 더 맑게 보였다.

30 그러고 나서 나는 농부들로부터 모은 옥수수 속대를 이용하여 여과 장치를 만들었다.

31 내 장치는 물에서 70~80%의 더러운 물질을 제거했다.

32 나는 내 여과 장치가 내 마을뿐만 아니라 다른 지역에 있는 모든 호수를 깨끗하게 해 줄 수 있기를 희망한다.

1 Who are the people who change the world? Do you think you are too young to be one of these people?

2 In the following stories you will meet three teenagers who used their ideas to make the world a better place.

3 One day, when I was fourteen, I came across a little girl at a science fair.

4 She had a robotic hand that could only open and close.

5 I was surprised that the hand had cost her 80,000 dollars!

6 'I wish she had a better robotic hand,' I thought to myself.

7 With that, I started to make a much cheaper and better robotic hand.

8 After many failures, finally, by using 3D printing technology, I was able to make a useful robotic hand for the price of only 300 dollars.

9 I decided to share the designs and software for my 3D robotic hand with others for free.

10 Maybe someone can take what I have done and do something useful with it.

11 No one person can change the world, but we can build a better world by working together.

12 'Why can't many girls in Africa go to school as I can? I wish they could go to school, too.'

13 I had this thought when I was twelve. I realized that their families couldn't afford it.

14 I wondered if I could do something for those girls. Then I had an idea.

15 For my birthday, I asked my parents to buy me a sewing machine.

16 They bought me one, and I learned how to make headbands for myself.

17 I created ten headbands and sold them at my school.

18 Soon, I raised enough money to send one girl in Africa to school. I couldn't stop there.

19 I started a business to help girls in Africa who couldn't go to school.

20 Thanks to the success of my business, I can pay the school fees for many poor girls in countries like Kenya and Uganda to go to school.

21 I also pay for their textbooks, uniforms, and pencils. Isn't it amazing?

22 My advice to you is to just do something. When you see a need, act.

23 Start small, taking little steps. Your warm heart can change lives.

24 As a young girl living in the countryside in India, I often found that the water around us was seriously polluted.

25 I wondered how I could solve this problem. Then I hit on the idea to use corn cobs.

26 Useless corn cobs were everywhere in my village.

27 I thought that the small holes in the corn cobs could filter dirty matter out of the polluted water.

28 One day, I picked up some dried cobs along the road, washed them, and placed them in a bowl of dirty water.

29 After a while, I checked the water, and it looked much clearer.

30 Then, using corn cobs that I had collected from farmers, I built a filtering system.

31 My system removed 70 to 80 percent of the dirty matter from the water.

32 I hope my filtering system can clean up all the lakes not only in my village but also in other areas.

Communication Task

1. can fly
2. to meet you
3. wish, could fly like, Is it possible for you
4. Sure
5. is it possible for you to travel
6. impossible

Enjoy Writing

1. To
2. I wonder if, make my wishes come true
3. wish, lived, could swim at a beautiful beach
4. wish, were, could he more relaxed
5. Finally, I wish I were
6. make my country a happier place to live in
7. if you can help me, I hope, can
8. Best Let's

After Your Read

1. Creative Teens
2. was surprised at, to make a cheaper and better
3. fo only 300 dollars, decided to share, for free
4. wished, could send
5. made, sold headbands
6. pays for, fees, many poor school girls in Africa
7. how she could clean the water
8. Using corn cobs, a filtering system
9. removed, the dirty matter from the water

6. Then I would try hard to make my country a happier place to live in.
7. I don't know if you can help me, but I hope you can.
8. Best Let's, Sohee

After Your Read

1. Creative Teens!
2. Easton was surprised at a girl's expensive robotic hand and wanted to make a cheaper and better one.
3. Finally he made one fo only 300 dollars and decided to share his designs and software for free.
4. Mary wished she could send girls in Africa to school.
5. She made and sold headbands.
6. Now she pays for the school fees, textbooks, uniforms, and pencils of many poor school girls in Africa.
7. Lalita wondered how she could clean the water.
8. Using corn cobs, she made a filtering system.
9. It removed 70 to 80 percent of the dirty matter from the water.

Communication Task

1. A: I'm Sky X. I can fly.
2. B: Hi, Sky X. Nice to meet you.
3. C: I wish I could fly like you. Is it possible for you to fly to the moon?
4. A: Sure.
5. D: Then is it possible for you to travel to the sun?
6. A: No. That's impossible.

Enjoy Writing

1. To Genie,
2. I have three wishes. I wonder if you can make my wishes come true.
3. First, I wish I lived in Hawaii. Then I could swim at a beautiful beach.
4. Second, I wish every Wednesday were a holiday. Then, I could he more relaxed.
5. Finally, I wish I were the president of Korea.

15 whisper, 속삭이다, 귓속말을 하다

16 ambassador, 대사

단어 TEST Step 1   p.80

01 목걸이   02 한 개, 한 부분, 조각

03 양, 액수   04 아름다움, 미

05 속삭이다, 귓속말을 하다   06 부부

07 다이아몬드   08 충격을 받은   09 무도회

10 지친   11 비슷한, 유사한

12 ~이든지, ~한 어떤 것이든   13 화려한

14 존경하다, 칭찬하다, 감탄하며 바라보다   15 울다

16 빌려주다   17 (프랑스, 스위스 등의 화폐 단위) 프랑

18 거대한, 엄청난   19 ~의 가치가 있는   20 초대, 초대장

21 대사   22 보석 상인

23 (다른 사람·사물을) 대신하다   24 거의

25 부업   26 보석류   27 거짓말

28 빌리다   29 확실히, 틀림없이   30 보기, 눈길

31 ~을 우연히 만나다   32 갚다, 돌려주다

33 즉시, 당장   34 ~에게 청하다, 부탁하다

35 절 아시나요?   36 ~하는 데 (시간)이 걸리다

37 (목적어)가 ~하는 데 (시간)을 소비하다

단어 TEST Step 2   p.81

01 whisper   02 franc   03 huge

04 amount   05 ball   06 whatever

07 certainly   08 admire   09 necklace

10 piece   11 ambassador   12 diamond

13 cry   14 fancy   15 shocked

16 nearly   17 worth   18 invitation

19 jeweler   20 beauty   21 similar

22 borrow   23 jewelry   24 couple

25 lend   26 replace   27 second job

28 lie   29 worn   30 look

31 run into   32 Do I know you?

33 at once   34 call on   35 pay back

단어 TEST Step 3   p.82

1 worn, 지친   2 couple, 부부   3 amount, 양, 액수

4 similar, 비슷한, 유사한   5 nearly, 거의

6 replace, ~을 대신하다   7 certainly, 확실히, 틀림없이

8 shocked, 충격을 받은   9 ball, 무도회   10 lie, 거짓말

11 cry, 울다   12 diamond, 다이아몬드

13 invitation, 초대, 초대장

14 admire, 존경하다, 칭찬하다, 감탄하며 바라보다

본문 TEST Step 1   p.83~86

01 This is, in Paris

02 Although, nice, not happy

03 pretty, wants, fancier life

04 *herself*, same boring, living

05 home, what, have got

06 What, that

07 invitation, had, fight, get

08 Why would, want

09 What, wrong

10 nothing, wear, such, fancy

11 Don't be, Get yourself

12 *looking at*, Amazing

13 Something, not right

14 could be wrong

15 going to do

16 What is it

17 jewelry, wear, so poor

18 Call on, sure, lend

19 Let, go at once

20 so, to, brings, here

21 are invited to

22 wonderful, must be excited

23 say, jewelry, borrow, from

24 Here, my case

25 so many wonderful pieces

26 Choose whatever, like

27 lend me, diamond necklace

28 Certainly, go enjoy

29 perfect evening, admires, beauty

30 It is, when, leave

31 such, long night, so

32 worth it, danced with

33 enjoyed yourself, have, work

34 *looking*, more look, gone

35 when we left, ball

36 surely did, go find

37 searches, streets

38 returns to, then goes

39 necklace, found, to lie

40 broke, necklace, fix, returning

41 couple, find, similar one

42 May we look at

43 *whispering*, nearly, same, must

44 How much

45 40,000 francs

46 How about

47 really need it

48 then, it is

49 have, huge amount of

50 So, borrow

51 buying, for, spends, paying

52 move to, place

53 second job, washes, others

54 hard, makes, old, worn

55 years, runs into, on

56 good morning

57 Do I know

58 it is me

59 cannot believe, have changed

60 have had, difficult times

61 Because of, What, mean

62 remember, lent me, lost

63 returned it to

64 another, like, pay for

65 bought, to replace mine

67 didn't, truth, real, worth

본문 TEST Step 2   p.87~90

01 This is, in Paris

02 Although, nice, not happy

03 and wants, fancier life

04 *to herself*, old house, boring, hate living

05 am home, what, have got

06 that

07 invitation to, had to fight to get it

08 Why would

09 is wrong

10 nothing to wear, such a fancy party

11 Don't be, give you, Get yourself, beautiful new dress

12 *looking at*, Amazing

13 not right

14 What could be wrong

15 going to do

16 What is it

17 no jewelry to wear, beautiful dress, so poor

18 Call on, she will lend you, jewelry

19 Let me go at once

20 to see, What brings you here

21 invited to

22 wonderful, must be excited

23 to say, no jewelry, borrow something from you

24 Here is, case

25 so many wonderful pieces

26 whatever you like

27 lend me this diamond necklace

28 Certainly, go enjoy

29 a perfect evening, admires her beauty

30 It is, when the Loisels leave

31 such a long night, tired

32 it was worth it, danced with

33 you enjoyed yourself, go to work

34 *looking in*, more look.

35 when we left the ball

36 did, go find

37 searches

38 returns to, goes to

39 is not found, to lie to

40 broke, necklace, fix it, returning it

41 to find a similar one

42 May we look at

43 *whispering*, nearly the same, must have

44 How much

45 francs

46 How about

47 really need it

48 it is

49 do not have, a huge amount of

50 borrow it

51 buying, for, spends, paying back

52 move to, small place

53 gets a second job, washes, for others

54 makes, old, worn

55 runs into, on

56 good morning

57 Do I know you

58 it is me

59 believe it, have changed

60 have had, difficult times because of

61 What do you mean

62 you lent me, lost it

63 returned it

64 another one, like it, It took, to pay for it

65 bought, to replace mine

67 Why didn't you come, tell me, was not real, worth

1 이곳은 파리의 Loisel 부부의 집이다.

2 그들의 집은 멋지지만, Loisel 부인은 행복하지 않다.

3 그녀는 젊고 예뻐서 더 화려하고 고급스러운 삶을 원한다.

4 Mrs. Loisel: (혼잣말로) 똑같은 낡은 집과 매일 같이 똑같은 지겨운 저녁 식사. 여기서 사는 게 너무 싫어!

5 Mr. Loisel: Matilda, 나 집에 왔어요, 내가 당신을 위해 무엇을 가져왔는지 봐요!

6 Mrs. Loisel: 뭐예요?

7 Mr. Loisel: 대사님이 여는 무도회 초대장이에요. 이걸 얻기 위해 엄청난 노력을 했단 말이에요. 모두가 갖고 싶어 했거든요.

8 Mrs. Loisel: (울면서) 내가 그걸 왜 갖고 싶겠어요?

9 Mr. Loisel: Matilda. 무슨 문제 있어요?

10 Mrs. Loisel: 그런 고급스러운 파티에 입고 갈 옷이 하나도 없는걸요. 못가요.

11 Mr. Loisel: 슬퍼하지 말아요. 자, 여기 400프랑을 줄게요. 아름다운 새 드레스를 사요.

12 Mr. Loisel: (Matilda의 새 드레스를 보며) 멋져요, Matilda. 아름답군요!

13 Mrs. Loisel: 뭔가 제대로 맞지 않아요.

14 Mr. Loisel: 뭐가 안 맞을 수 있죠?

15 Mrs. Loisel: (울면서) 오, 안 돼. 어쩌면 좋아요?

16 Mr. Loisel: 뭐예요, 부인?

17 Mrs. Loisel: 이 아름다운 드레스에 어울릴 보석이 하나도 없어요. 내가 너무 불쌍해 보일 거예요!

18 Mr. Loisel: 당신 친구 Forestier 부인에게 부탁해 봐요. 그녀는 자신이 가진 보석을 분명히 빌려줄 거예요.

19 Mrs. Loisel: 그거 좋은 생각이에요! 지금 당장 가봐야겠어요.

20 Mrs. Forestier: Matilda, 이렇게 보게 되어서 정말 좋아요! 무슨 일로 왔어요?

21 Mrs. Loisel: 우리 부부가 대사의 무도회에 초대되었어요.

22 Mrs. Forestier: 대사의 무도회라! 멋지네요! 당신은 분명 신났겠군요.

23 Mrs. Loisel: 네… 그리고 아니기도 해요. 말하기 슬프지만 난 보석이 없어요. 부인에게서 좀 빌릴 수 있을까요?

24 Mrs. Forestier: 물론이죠! 여기 내 보석함이에요.

25 Mrs. Loisel: 와, 부인은 정말 멋진 보석들이 많네요!

26 Mrs. Forestier: 원하는 것 아무거나 골라요.

27 Mrs. Loisel: 이 다이아몬드 목걸이를 빌려줄 수 있나요? 이거 정말 아름다워요!

28 Mrs. Forestier: 당연하죠! 자, 이제 가서 무도회를 즐겨요.

29 Matilda는 완벽한 저녁을 보낸다. 무도회장에 있는 모든 사람들이 아름다운 그녀를 감탄하며 바라본다.

30 Loisel 부부는 아주 늦은 시간이 되어서야 무도회를 떠났다.

31 Mr. Loisel: 정말 길고 긴 밤이었어요. 정말 피곤해요.

32 Mrs. Loisel: 그렇지만 충분히 가치가 있었어요. 당신, 제가 대사님과 춤춘 것을 아나요?

33 Mr. Loisel: 당신이 즐거웠다니 기쁘지만 나 아침에 출근해야

34 Mrs. Loisel: (거울을 보며) 한 번만 더 볼게요. (충격을 받고) 목걸이… 목걸이가 없어졌어요!

35 Mr. Loisel: 뭐라고요? 무도회를 떠날 때 걸고 있었소?

36 Mrs. Loisel: 네, 분명히 하고 있었는데. 가서 찾아 줘요!

37 Loisel 씨는 길거리를 수색한다.

38 그는 무도회장으로 되돌아가 본 다음 경찰서에도 간다.

39 목걸이가 발견되지 않자, Loisel 씨는 Matilda에게 그녀의 친구에게 거짓말을 하라고 한다.

40 Matilda는 Forestier 부인에게 목걸이를 망가뜨려서 돌려주기 전에 고쳐 주겠다고 말한다.

41 부부는 비슷한 것을 찾을 시간이 필요하다.

42 Mr. Loisel: (보석상에게) 실례합니다. 저 다이아몬드 목걸이 좀 볼 수 있을까요?

43 Mrs. Loisel: (속삭이며) 거의 똑같아요. 저걸 꼭 사야만 해요!

44 Mr. Loisel: 이거 얼마인가요?

45 Jewler: 40,000프랑이에요.

46 Mr. Loisel: 36,000에 안 될까요?

47 Mrs. Loisel: 부탁드려요, 우린 이게 정말 필요하거든요.

48 Jewler: 음, 그럼… 36,000프랑에 하시죠.

49 그들은 36,000프랑이 없다. 그건 큰돈이다.

50 그래서 그들은 돈을 빌린다.

51 부부는 Forestier 부인에게 돌려줄 목걸이를 산 후 돈을 갚는 데 십 년이 걸린다.

52 그들은 아주 작은 곳으로 이사한다.

53 Loisel 씨는 부업을 구한다. Matilda는 다른 사람들을 위해 빨래를 해 준다.

54 10년 동안의 고된 일로 Matilda는 늙고 지쳤다.

55 십 년 후, Matilda는 Forestier 부인과 거리에서 마주친다.

56 Mrs. Loisel: Forestier 부인, 좋은 아침이에요.

57 Mrs. Forestier: 제가 당신을 아나요?

58 Mrs. Loisel: 네, 저예요, Matilda.

59 Mrs. Forestier: 오, 믿을 수 없어요! 당신 너무 많이 변했어요.

60 Mrs. Loisel: 저는 당신 때문에 힘든 시간을 보냈거든요.

61 Mrs. Forestier: 나 때문에요? 무슨 말이에요?

62 Mrs. Loisel: 당신이 빌려준 목걸이 기억하죠? 음, 제가 그걸 잃어버렸어요.

63 Mrs. Forestier: 그런데 그거 나한테 돌려줬잖아요.

64 Mrs. Loisel: 아니요, 나는 당신 것과 똑같은 다른 목걸이를 돌려줬어요. 그 값을 치르느라 십 년이 걸렸어요.

65 Mrs. Forestier: 내 것을 대체하려고 다이아몬드 목걸이를 샀다고요?

66 Mrs. Loisel: 네, 맞아요.

67 Mrs. Forestier: 오, 가엾은 Matilda. 왜 내게 와서 사실을 말하지 않았어요? 제 다이아몬드 목걸이는 진품이 아니었어요. 그건 단돈 오백 프랑짜리였다고요!

1 This is Mr. and Mrs. Loisel's home in Paris.

2 Although the home is nice, Mrs. Loisel is not happy.

3 She is young and pretty, and wants a fancier life.

4 Mrs. Loisel: (*to herself*) Same old house and same boring dinners. I hate living here!

5 Mr. Loisel: Matilda, I am home. Look what I have got for you!

6 Mrs. Loisel: What is that?

7 Mr. Loisel: An invitation to the Ambassador's Ball. I had to fight to get it. Everybody wanted it.

8 Mrs. Loisel: (*crying*) Why would I want it?

9 Mr. Loisel: Matilda. What is wrong?

10 Mrs. Loisel: I have nothing to wear to such a fancy party. I cannot go.

11 Mr. Loisel: Don't be sad. Here, I will give you 400 francs. Get yourself a beautiful new dress.

12 Mr. Loisel: (*looking at Matilda's new dress*) Amazing, Matilda. Beautiful!

13 Mrs. Loisel: Something is not right.

14 Mr. Loisel: What could be wrong?

15 Mrs. Loisel: (*crying*) Oh, no. What am I going to do?

16 Mr. Loisel: What is it, Matilda?

17 Mrs. Loisel: I have no jewelry to wear with my beautiful dress. I will look so poor!

18 Mr. Loisel: Call on your friend, Mrs. Forestier. I am sure she will lend you some of her jewelry.

19 Mrs. Loisel: That is a good idea! Let me go at once.

20 Mrs. Forestier: Matilda, it is so nice to see you! What brings you here?

21 Mrs. Loisel: We are invited to the Ambassador's Ball.

22 Mrs. Forestier: The Ambassador's Ball! That is wonderful! You must be excited.

23 Mrs. Loisel: Yes… And no. I am sad to say I have no jewelry. May I borrow something from you?

24 Mrs. Forestier: Sure! Here is my case.

25 Mrs. Loisel: Wow, you have so many wonderful pieces!

26 Mrs. Forestier: Choose whatever you like.

27 Mrs. Loisel: Would you lend me this diamond necklace? It is beautiful!

28 Mrs. Forestier: Certainly! Now go enjoy the ball.

29 Matilda has a perfect evening. Everybody at the ball admires her beauty.

30 It is very late when the Loisels leave the ball.

31 Mr. Loisel: It was such a long night. I am so tired.

32 Mrs. Loisel: But it was worth it. Do you know I danced with the Ambassador?

33 Mr. Loisel: I am glad you enjoyed yourself, but I have to go to work in the morning.

34 Mrs. Loisel: (*looking in the mirror*) Just one more look. (*shocked*) The necklace… It is gone!

35 Mr. Loisel: What? Did you have it when we left the ball?

36 Mrs. Loisel: Yes, I surely did. Please go find it!

37 Mr. Loisel searches the streets.

38 He returns to the ball and then goes to the police.

39 When the necklace is not found, Mr. Loisel tells Matilda to lie to her friend.

40 Matilda tells Mrs. Forestier she broke the necklace and would fix it before returning it.

41 The couple needs time to find a similar one.

42 Mr. Loisel: (*to the jeweler*) Excuse me? May we look at that diamond necklace?

43 Mrs. Loisel: (*whispering*) It is nearly the same. We must have it!

44 Mr. Loisel: How much is it?

45 Jeweler: 40,000 francs.

46 Mr. Loisel: How about 36,000?

47 Mrs. Loisel: Please, we really need it.

48 Jeweler: Well, then… 36,000 it is.I

49 They do not have 36,000 francs. It is a huge amount of money.

50 So they borrow it.

51 After buying the necklace for Mrs. Forestier, the couple spends ten years paying back the money.

52 They move to a very small place.

53 Mr. Loisel gets a second job. Matilda washes clothes for others.

54 Ten years of hard work makes Matilda old and worn.

55 After ten years, Matilda runs into Mrs. Forestier on the street.

56 Mrs. Loisel: Mrs. Forestier, good morning.

57 Mrs. Forestier: Do I know you?

58 Mrs. Loisel: Yes, it is me, Matilda.

59 Mrs. Forestier: Oh, I cannot believe it! You have changed so much.

60 Mrs. Loisel: I have had some difficult times because of you.

61 Mrs. Forestier: Because of me? What do you mean?

62 Mrs. Loisel: Do you remember the diamond necklace you lent me? Well, I lost it.

63 Mrs. Forestier: But you returned it to me.

64 Mrs. Loisel: No, I returned another one just like it. It took us ten years to pay for it.

65 Mrs. Forestier: You bought a diamond necklace to replace mine?

66 Mrs. Loisel: Yes.

67 Mrs. Forestier: Oh, my poor Matilda. Why didn't you come to me and tell me the truth? My diamond necklace was not real. It was worth only 500 francs!

MEMO

2학기 전과정

적중100 plus

영어 기출 문제집

정답 및 해설

시사 | 박준언

적중 1○○ + 특별부록

Plan B

우리학교
최신기출

시사 · 박준언 교과서를 배우는

학교 시험문제 분석 · 모음 · 해설집

전국단위 학교 시험문제 수집 및 분석

출제 빈도가 높은 문제 위주로 선별

문제 풀이에 필요한 상세한 해설

중3-2
영어

시사 · 박준언

적중 100 + 특별부록

Plan B

우리학교 최신기출

중3-2
영어

시사 · 박준언

3학년 영어 2학기 중간고사(5과) 1회

문항수 : 선택형(28문항)　서술형(2문항)　　20 ． ． ．

◎ 선택형 문항의 답안은 컴퓨터용 수정 싸인펜을 사용하여 OMR 답안지에 바르게 표기하시오.

◎ 서술형 문제는 답을 답안지에 반드시 검정 볼펜으로 쓰시오.

◎ 총 30문항 100점 만점입니다. 문항별 배점은 각 문항에 표시되어 있습니다.

01 다음 빈칸에 가장 알맞은 표현은?　　　　(3점)　[부산 ○○중]

> Do you _____ any clubs? If not, you can join our basketball club.

① move
② fight
③ spend
④ spread
⑤ belong to

02 다음 우리말을 영작한 것 중 <u>어색한</u> 것은?　　(3점)　[충북 ○○중]

① 영국 사람들은 차를 많이 마신다.
　→ People in UK drink a lot of tea.
② 캐나다의 수도는 오타와이다.
　→ The capital of Canada is Ottawa.
③ 캐나다에서는 영어만 사용된다.
　→ Only English is used in Canada.
④ 뉴질랜드는 호주보다 더 작다.
　→ New Zealand is smaller than Australia.
⑤ 호주와 뉴질랜드는 같은 국기를 사용한다.
　→ Australia and New Zealand use the same nation flag.

03 다음 빈칸에 공통으로 들어갈 것은?　　　(3점)　[부산 ○○중]

> • Yun Bonggil was willing to _____ his life for his country.
> • Father Lee Taeseok spent his life working for poor people in Sudan. They will remember his _____.

① duty
② mission
③ respect
④ sacrifice
⑤ independence

04 다음 중 어법상 <u>어색한</u> 것은?　　　　(4점)　[충북 ○○중]

① I exercise so that I can stay healthy.
② I waved at my sister so that she could find me.
③ David went to China so that he can learn Chinese.
④ Jinsu got up early so that he could catch the first train to Barcelona.
⑤ Yi Sunsin made the Turtle Ship so that he could protect the people.

05 다음 중 어법상 옳지 <u>않은</u> 문장은?　　(4점)　[경기 ○○중]

① I have never traveled abroad before I was 20 years old.
② David asked me what present I had given to Jane.
③ They had left the restaurant before I got there.
④ I had a stomachache after my mom had gone out.
⑤ When my dad came home, I had just finished my homework.

06 〈보기〉의 두 문장을 시간의 차이가 나도록 한 문장으로 연결할 때, 가장 적절한 것을 고르면? (4점)

> 보기
>
> She started living there in 1990.
> + I met her there in 2010.

① She has lived there for twenty years when I meet her.

② She had lived there for twenty years when I met her.

③ She has lived there for twenty years when I met her.

④ She had lived there for twenty years when I was meeting her.

⑤ She had been lived there for twenty years when I met her.

07 두 문장을 조건에 맞게 한 문장으로 바꿔 쓰시오. (4점)

> • Jinsu got up early.
> • He caught the first train to Seoul.
> → Jinsu got up early _____.

> 조건
>
> • 「so that+주어+동사 ~」 구문을 이용할 것.
> • 적절한 조동사를 반드시 추가하여 쓸 것.

→ _____

08 다음 대화의 빈칸에 들어갈 말로 알맞은 것은? (3점)

> A: You know about Yun Dongju, don't you?
> B: _____ He wrote many beautiful poems when Korea was under Japanese rule.

① Not at all.

② I have no idea.

③ Yes, I'd love to.

④ I've heard his name.

⑤ I haven't got a clue.

09 다음 중 짝지어진 대화가 자연스러운 것은? (2점)

① A: The museum must be interesting.

  B: Yes. I'm looking forward to visiting it!

② A: Look at Suwon Hwaseong. It's huge.

  B: That sounds interesting. I want to try one on.

③ A: What would you recommend that I take?

  B: I suggest we visit Victoria Peak.

④ A: What kind of volunteer work did you do there?

  B: I went to Hyeonchungwon to do volunteer work.

⑤ A: I'm planning to go there again next Wednesday. Will you join me?

  B: I felt great respect for the people who died for the country.

10 다음 대화의 빈칸에 들어갈 말로 가장 <u>어색한</u> 것은? (3점)

> A: I really appreciate your advice on my singing contest.
> B: _____

① It's nothing.

② My pleasure.

③ You're welcome.

④ Don't mention it.

⑤ I can't thank you enough.

11 다음 〈보기〉 중에서 필요한 단어를 골라 문장을 완성하시오. (단, 필요한 경우 형태를 변형할 것.) (4점)

> 보기
> be / to / invite / disappointing /
> is / disappointed / invent / for / not

> 내 여동생은 파티에 초대받지 못해서 실망했다.
> → My sister was _____
> to the party.

→ _____

[12~13] 다음 대화를 읽고 물음에 답하시오.

> B: Look at Suwon Hwaseong. It's huge.
> G: It also looks strong.
> B: Because it (A)_____ to protect the people during wars.
> G: Wow. Do you know who built it?
> B: Yes. King Jeongjo ordered Jeong Yakyong to direct the building process. You know about Jeong Yakyong, don't you?
> G: Yes, I've heard of him. He was a great scientist in Joseon.

12 위 대화의 흐름상 빈칸 (A)에 들어갈 말로 어법상 알맞은 것은? (2점)

① was built

② was build

③ was building

④ is build

⑤ is building

13 위 대화의 중심 내용으로 가장 적절한 것은? (4점)

① King Jeongjo didn't try to protect the lives of people in Suwon.

② Suwon Hwaseong was built under Jeong Yakyong's direction to save people from wars.

③ Jeong Yakyong, a great scientist in Joseon, built many great buildings.

④ King Jeongjo was ordered to build Suwon Hwaseong.

⑤ Jeong Yakyong wanted to know how to keep the people safe from the war.

14 다음 밑줄 친 to부정사 중 쓰임이 <u>다른</u> 것은?   (3점)

① I must go home now <u>to do</u> my homework.

② She was happy <u>to be invited</u> to the party.

③ I was pleased <u>to hear</u> the news.

④ He was glad <u>to meet</u> his old friends.

⑤ We were sad <u>to say</u> goodbye to Jake.

15 다음 짝지어진 대화가 <u>어색한</u> 것은?   (2점)

① A: You know about Jeong Yakyong, don't you?

　B: Yes, I've heard of him.

② A: You know Taegeukgi, don't you?

　B: Sure. It's the national flag of Korea, isn't it?

③ A: The art museum must be interesting.

　B: Yes. I'm not interested in art.

④ A: What is the Gansong Museum?

　B: It's a museum built by Gansong Jeon Hyeongpil.

⑤ A: I'm planning to go there again next Wednesday. Will you join me?

　B: Sure. I'm looking forward to it.

[16~17] 다음 대화를 읽고 물음에 답하시오.

Andy: Bora, what are you reading?

Bora: I'm reading *Sky, Wind, Star, and Poetry* by Yun Dongju. You know about Yun Dongju, don't you?

Andy: I've heard his name, but I don't know much about him.

Bora: He wrote many beautiful poems when Korea was under Japanese rule. (A)<u>His love for the country and his desire for independence can be felt in his poems.</u>

Andy: Really? I didn't know that. (B)<u>I want to read his poems and learn more about him.</u>

Bora: Great. In fact, I'm planning to visit the Yun Dongju Museum soon. (C)<u>She led the March 1st Movement in Cheonan.</u> Do you want to come with me?

Andy: Yes, when are you going?

Bora: Next Saturday. It's near Gyeongbok Palace. (D)<u>Can you meet me at the palace at 2 p.m.?</u>

Andy: Sure. Let's meet there.

Bora: Great. (E)<u>I'm really looking forward to the visit.</u>

16 위 대화의 (A)~(E) 중 흐름상 적절하지 <u>않은</u> 것은?   (3점)

① (A)　　　② (B)　　　③ (C)

④ (D)　　　⑤ (E)

17 위 대화의 내용과 일치하는 것은? (3점)

① Andy is reading Yun Dongju's poems.

② Andy knows quite well about Yun Dongju.

③ Yun Dongju wrote poems during the Korean War.

④ Andy will visit the Yun Dongju Museum next Saturday.

⑤ Andy and Bora will meet at Gyeongbok Palace Station.

[18~21] 다음 글을 읽고 물음에 답하시오.

Last week my history club went to Hyochang Park. We visited the Kim Koo Museum inside the park. At the entrance of the museum, we saw a white statue of Kim Koo.

Kim Koo is a great ⓐnational hero who spent most of his life fighting for the ⓑdependence of Korea from Japanese rule. In the 1900s, he helped ⓒeducate young people by building schools. In 1919, when the indepencence movement had spread throughout the country, he moved to Shanghai, China. There he ⓓjoined the Government of the Republic of Korea and later became its ⓔpresident.

The exhibition hall in the museum shows a lot of things about Kim Koo's life. While looking around the hall, we stopped at a photo of the Korean Patriotic Organization's members. Kim Koo formed the secret organization in 1931 to fight against Japan. Lee Bongchang and Yun Bonggil belonged to the group.

18 위 글의 밑줄 친 ⓐ~ⓔ 중 글의 흐름상 어울리지 <u>않는</u> 것은? (3점)

① ⓐ   ② ⓑ   ③ ⓒ

④ ⓓ   ⑤ ⓔ

19 위 글의 내용과 일치하지 <u>않는</u> 것은? (4점)

① 나의 역사 동아리는 효창 공원 안에 있는 김구 박물관을 방문했다.

② 우리는 박물관 입구에서 김구의 흰색 동상을 보았다.

③ 박물관 내의 전시관은 김구의 생애에 대해 많은 것을 보여 준다.

④ 전시관을 둘러보던 중 우리는 한인 애국단 멤버의 사진 앞에서 멈췄다.

⑤ 이봉창과 윤봉길은 비밀 조직인 한인 애국단을 만들었다.

20 위 글에 나타난 김구에 관한 내용과 일치하는 것은? (3점)

① He is a great international hero.

② He fought against China for the independence of Korea.

③ He built stadiums and tried to educate young people.

④ He went to Shanghai when the independence movement had disappeared in Korea.

⑤ He became the president of the Government of the Republic of Korea.

21 위 글을 읽고 '김구의 일생'을 연대기 순으로 요약 정리해 보았다. 〈보기〉의 ⓐ~ⓓ를 빈칸 (A)~(D)에 넣을 때, 들어갈 말이 순서대로 알맞게 짝지어진 것은? (4점)

Kim Koo (1876~1949)

The great (A)_____ who fought for (B)_____ from Japanese rule.

· 1900s: Helped (C)_____ by building schools.

· 1919: Joined the Government of the Republic of Korea in Shanghai and (D)_____

보기

ⓐ national hero

ⓑ educate young people

ⓒ became its president

ⓓ the independence of Korea

① ⓐ - ⓓ - ⓑ - ⓒ

② ⓐ - ⓓ - ⓒ - ⓑ

③ ⓒ - ⓓ - ⓐ - ⓑ

④ ⓓ - ⓐ - ⓑ - ⓒ

⑤ ⓓ - ⓒ - ⓑ - ⓐ

[22~25] 다음 글을 읽고 물음에 답하시오.

When Yun left for the mission, he told Kim, "Sir, you are ⓐworn a very old watch. (가)Mine is new, but I won't need it anymore. Please take my watch, and let me ⓑhave yours." Kim Koo always carried Yun's watch in his jacket ⓒnot to forget Yun's sacrifice.

ⓓAfter completing the tour of the museum, we moved to the tombs of the three heroes, Lee Bongchang, Yun Bonggil, and Baek Jeonggi. Their bodies ⓔhave been in Japan, but after Korea's independence Kim Koo brought them to Hyochang Park. By doing so, he showed his deep love and respect for the sacrifice of the three heroes.

As I left Hyochang Park, I thought about Kim Koo's words in My Wish that I had read in the exhibition hall. It was written in *Baekbeomilji*.

22 위 글의 ⓐ~ⓔ 중 문법적으로 옳은 것의 개수는? (4점)

① 1개　　　　② 2개　　　　③ 3개

④ 4개　　　　⑤ 5개

23 위 글의 밑줄 친 (가)에 담긴 의미로 알맞은 것은? (3점)

① I'm ready to die.

② I'm sure I'll come back.

③ The mission is impossible.

④ I can live without a watch.

⑤ This watch is very valuable to me.

24 위 글을 통해 알 수 <u>없는</u> 것은? (4점)

① 3명의 묘지에는 누가 묻혀 있나요?

② 김구의 My Wish는 어디에 적혀 있나요?

③ 왜 김구는 3명의 시신을 효창 공원에 가져왔나요?

④ 왜 김구는 항상 윤봉길의 시계를 가지고 다녔나요?

⑤ 김구는 중국 상하이로 간 후에 무엇을 했나요?

25 위 글의 내용과 일치하는 것은? (4점)

① 윤봉길의 시계는 김구의 것보다 낡았다.

② 김구는 윤봉길의 시계를 박물관에 보관했다.

③ 글쓴이는 박물관 관람을 마친 후 삼의사의 묘소를 둘러보았다.

④ 삼의사의 유해는 일본에 있다가 독립 직전에 효창 공원으로 모셔졌다.

⑤ 삼의사의 희생을 기리기 위해 유해를 모셔 온 사람은 알려지지 않았다.

[26~30] 다음 글을 읽고 물음에 답하시오.

The exhibition hall in the museum shows a lot of things about Kim Koo's life. While ⓐ<u>looking</u> around the hall, we stopped at a photo of the Korean Patriotic Organization's members. Kim Koo formed the secret organization in 1931 to fight ⓑ<u>for</u> Japan.

In 1932, Kim Koo made a plan ⓒ<u>to kill</u> Japanese generals in a park in Shanghai. ⓓ<u>As</u> the leader of the Korean Patriotic Organization, he directed Yun ⓔ<u>to carry out</u> the mission.

(A) When Yun left for the mission, he told Kim, "Sir, you are wearing (가)<u>a very old watch</u>. (나)<u>Mine</u> is new, but I won't need (다)<u>it</u> anymore. Please take (라)<u>my watch</u>, and let me have (마)<u>yours</u>." (B) Kim Koo always carried Yun's watch in his jacket. (C)

After completing the tour of the museum, we moved to the tombs of the three heroes, Lee Bongchang, Yun Bonggil, and Baek Jeonggi. (D) Their bodies had been in Japan, but after Korea's independence Kim Koo brought them to Hyochang Park. (E)

26 위 글의 밑줄 친 ⓐ~ⓔ 중 내용상 옳지 <u>않은</u> 것은? (3점)

① ⓐ   ② ⓑ   ③ ⓒ

④ ⓓ   ⑤ ⓔ

27 위 글의 흐름으로 보아, 주어진 문장이 들어가기에 가장 적절한 곳은? (4점)

> By doing so, he showed his deep love and respect for the sacrifice of the three heroes.

① (A)　　　② (B)　　　③ (C)
④ (D)　　　⑤ (E)

28 위 글의 (가)~(마) 중 Kim Koo의 시계와 Yun의 시계를 알맞게 짝지은 것은? (3점)

Kim Koo의 시계	Yun의 시계
① (가)	(나), (다), (라), (마)
② (가), (마)	(나), (다), (라)
③ (가), (나), (마)	(다), (라)
④ (가), (나), (다)	(라), (마)
⑤ (가), (나), (다), (라)	(마)

29 위 글을 읽고, 김구에 대한 설명 중 옳지 <u>않은</u> 것을 고르면? (3점)

① 김구가 한인 애국단 사진을 찍었다.
② 김구는 1931년에 한인 애국단을 만들었다.
③ 1932년에 김구는 일본 장군들을 죽일 계획을 세웠다.
④ 김구는 윤에게 암살 임무를 수행하도록 지시했다.
⑤ 김구는 윤의 시계를 항상 가지고 다녔다.

30 다음 글을 쓴 화자의 심경으로 가장 적절한 것은? (4점)

> If God asks me what my wish is, I would say clearly, "It is Korea's Independence." If he asks me what my second wish is, I would say, "It is the independence of my country." If he asks me what my third wish is, I would say loudly, "It is the complete independence of my country." That is my answer.

① interested
② scared
③ excited
④ surprised
⑤ determined

◎ 선택형 문항의 답안은 컴퓨터용 수정 싸인펜을 사용하여 OMR 답안지에 바르게 표기하시오.

◎ 서술형 문제는 답을 답안지에 반드시 검정 볼펜으로 쓰시오.

◎ 총 30문항 100점 만점입니다. 문항별 배점은 각 문항에 표시되어 있습니다.

[대전 ○○중]

01 다음 영영 풀이에 해당하는 단어로 알맞은 것은? (3점)

a person or an animal that originally lived in a particular area

① native
② object
③ rival
④ symbol
⑤ subject

[부산 ○○중]

02 다음 문장의 빈칸에 들어갈 단어로 알맞게 짝지어진 것은?

(4점)

• I heard some countries are warm all year (A)_____.
• After achieving big success abroad, Mia returned to her (B)_____ country.
• James is the best swimmer and has no (C)_____ in his country.

	(A)	(B)	(C)
①	rival	native	round
②	rival	round	native
③	round	native	rival
④	round	rival	native
⑤	native	round	rival

[대전 ○○중]

03 다음 빈칸에 들어갈 말이 순서대로 바르게 짝지어진 것은?

(3점)

• When you saw the artwork in the museum, what came _____ your mind?
• Shakespeare is known _____ a great writer.

① as - to
② to - as
③ to - with
④ as - with
⑤ without - as

[서울 강남구 ○○중]

04 다음 대화의 빈칸에 들어갈 말로 적절하지 <u>않은</u> 것은? (4점)

A: Let's talk about your problem. What are the things that make you worried?
B: I'm worried about my future. I don't know what to do and what I can do.
A: _____ They will help you to know about yourself.

① How about visiting career centers?
② Why don't you visit career centers?
③ I recommend you visit career centers.
④ Would you like to visit career centers?
⑤ I don't think you should visit career centers.

05 다음 빈칸에 들어갈 말이 순서대로 바르게 연결된 것은? (3점)

> • Mike is a teacher, _____ has a clear way of speaking.
> • He wanted to buy the same watch _____ I was wearing.

① who – who
② that – that
③ who – that
④ that – which
⑤ which – that

06 다음 중 밑줄 친 부분이 어법상 어색한 것은? (3점)

① He broke his leg, <u>who</u> depressed me.
② He has two cars, <u>which</u> are expensive.
③ Tom met Jane, <u>who</u> is good at playing the piano.
④ I have two sons, <u>who</u> are interested in music.
⑤ We had dinner in a restaurant, <u>which</u> we liked.

07 다음 밑줄 친 우리말과 의미가 같도록 문장을 완성하시오. (4점)

> June: What can we do if we visit India?
> Sue: <u>나는 우리가 요가를 배우는 것을 제안해.</u>
> June: That's a good idea!

→ _____ _____ _____ _____ yoga.

08 다음 중 밑줄 친 형용사의 쓰임이 나머지 넷과 <u>다른</u> 것은?(4점)

① She is not <u>easy</u> to persuade.
② I'm so <u>proud</u> to win the race.
③ Jane was <u>pleased</u> to meet her friends.
④ She felt <u>disappointed</u> to fail her project.
⑤ He is <u>sad</u> not to be invited to the party.

09 다음 밑줄 친 부분 중 지칭하는 범위가 <u>다른</u> 것은? (4점)

① We had dinner in a restaurant, <u>which</u> is located in the town.
② I love these movies, <u>which</u> were made in New Zealand.
③ Tom sold his books, <u>which</u> are of great value.
④ Link has a boat, <u>which</u> is expensive.
⑤ He broke his leg, <u>which</u> made me sad.

10 다음 대화의 빈칸에 들어갈 말로 가장 알맞은 것은? (3점)

> A: _____ travel experiences.
> B: Last year, I visited the national museum in France and it was so great.

① I forgot
② Let's share
③ She must ignore
④ Let me introduce
⑤ You can complain about

---

11 다음 대화의 밑줄 친 ⓐ~ⓔ 중 어법상 어색한 것은 모두 몇 문장인가? (4점)

> Mike: ⓐLet's talk about traditional clothing from other countries.
> Elle: ⓑDo you know what a kilt is?
> Mike: No, I don't. What is it?
> Elle: It is traditional clothing from Scotland. ⓒIt looks like a knee-length skirt and have a plaid pattern.
> Mike: A skirt of knee length with a plaid pattern?
> Elle: ⓓYes. It is unique because of it is a skirt for men.
> Mike: That sounds interesting. ⓔI want to try one on.

① 0문장   ② 1문장   ③ 2문장
④ 3문장   ⑤ 4문장

[12~13] 다음 대화를 읽고 물음에 답하시오.

> G: My American friend invited me to a potluck dinner next Friday.
> (A) 내가 무엇을 가져가야 할지 추천해 주겠니?
> (B) I suggest you take some Korean food. How about Gimbap, Suji?
> (C) You know, you should take food to share at the dinner.
> G: Yes. It's not spicy and it's easy to carry.
> B: I think it will be good for dinner.

12 위 대화의 (A)~(C)를 대화의 흐름에 맞게 배열한 것은? (2점)

① (A)-(C)-(B)
② (B)-(A)-(C)
③ (B)-(C)-(A)
④ (C)-(A)-(B)
⑤ (C)-(B)-(A)

13 위 대화의 밑줄 친 (A)의 우리말을 주어진 조건에 맞게 영어로 작성하시오. (5점)

> take, that, what, recommend

조건
> 1. 의문문 형태일 것.
> 2. 위에 주어진 단어를 모두 사용할 것.
> 3. 필요한 단어를 추가하여 7단어로 된 문장으로 쓸 것.

→ _____?

14 다음 대화의 내용과 일치하는 것은? (3점)

Sera: Brian, what will you prepare for the World Food Festival?

Brian: I will make a meat pie. It is famous in Australia. How about you, Sera?

Sera: I want to make a popular English dish, fish and chips.

Brian: Fish and chips? What does it look like?

Sera: It's fried fish with hot potato chips.

Brian: That sounds interesting.

① 호주의 유명 음식은 두 가지로 구성되어 있다.

② Sera는 Brian이 준비할 음식을 도와줄 예정이다.

③ Brian은 Sera가 준비하고 싶어 하는 음식에 흥미를 보였다.

④ Brian은 fish and chips가 어떻게 생겼는지 소개해 주었다.

⑤ Sera는 향토 음식 축제에 감자가 들어간 음식을 준비하고 싶어 한다.

15 다음 대화의 빈칸에 들어갈 말로 가장 적절한 것은? (4점)

A: We finally arrived in Hong Kong, Mom.

B: Wow, it's wonderful. (A)_____ What should we do today, Mike?

A: (B)_____

B: Victoria Peak?

A: It is the highest mountain in Hong Kong and is in a lot of movies. We can enjoy the fantastic view.

① (A) I'm looking for a place to visit.
   (B) How about taking a rest?

② (A) I want you to go on a trip with me someday.
   (B) I think we should visit Victoria Peak.

③ (A) I'm glad to be here with you.
   (B) I don't know much about Victoria Peak.

④ (A) I'm planning to visit Victoria Peak.
   (B) What would you do if you were at Victoria Peak?

⑤ (A) I'm looking forward to our visit.
   (B) I suggest we visit Victoria Peak.

[16~17] 다음 대화를 읽고 물음에 답하시오.

Seho: Good morning.

Jessie, Andy: Hi, Seho.

Seho: I will visit my uncle in Philadelphia this winter. Can you tell me about the city?

Jessie: Sure. I was there a few years ago. First, let's talk about food.

Seho: Okay. What food is Philadelphia famous for?

Jessie: The most famous food in Philadelphia is the cheese steak sandwich. It is a big sandwich filled with beef and melted cheese.

Seho: Good suggestion. I will try it. Are there any places that are popular with tourists?

Andy: (가)I suggest you visit Independence Hall. It is very important in American history.

Seho: Wonderful. Thank you for the information.

Andy: My pleasure.

16 위 대화의 밑줄 친 (가)와 바꾸어 쓸 수 있는 것은?　(3점)

① Why don't we visit Independence Hall?

② How about visiting Independence Hall?

③ Let's visit Independence Hall.

④ I think we should visit Independence Hall.

⑤ What can we do if we visit Independence Hall?

17 위 대화를 읽고 질문에 답할 수 없는 것은?　(4점)

① Who will Seho visit?

② What will Seho do this winter?

③ What is a cheese steak sandwich like?

④ How long has Andy lived in Philadelphia?

⑤ What place is popular with tourists in Philadelphia?

[18~19] 다음 글을 읽고 물음에 답하시오.

When you hear the word kiwi, what comes to your mind? Maybe a fruit, but, in New Zealand the word kiwi has a couple of meanings. First, kiwi is the name of a delicious, green fruit. A lot of kiwi fruit is grown throughout the country, so New Zealand is known as the land of kiwi fruit.

Kiwi is also the name of the one of New Zealand's native birds. (A)Because it is the symbol of the nation, the kiwi is special to New Zealanders. Also, kiwi is a nickname for people from New Zealand. Today, New Zealanders are sometimes called Kiwis throughout the world. Now, you know that kiwi is the name of a fruit, a bird, and also a people. Next time, (B)don't become confused when someone uses the word kiwi, that has several meanings.

18 위 글의 밑줄 친 (A)를 분사구문으로 바꿔 쓰시오. (3점)

(A)Because it is the symbol of the nation

→ _____

19 위 글의 밑줄 친 (B)의 <u>어색한</u> 부분을 고쳐 올바른 문장으로 다시 쓰시오. (3점)

(B)don't become confused when someone uses the word kiwi, that has several meanings

→ _____

20 위 글의 (A)~(E) 중 주어진 문장이 들어갈 가장 올바른 위치는? (3점)

You can visit Maori villages and experience Maori culture.

① (A)   ② (B)   ③ (C)
④ (D)   ⑤ (E)

21 위 글의 빈칸 ⓐ~ⓒ 안에 들어갈 말이 바르게 짝지어진 것은? (4점)

	ⓐ	ⓑ	ⓒ
①	in	by	to
②	on	from	at
③	in	to	at
④	on	at	in
⑤	in	at	with

[20~23] 다음 글을 읽고 물음에 답하시오.

(A) The Maori are the native people of New Zealand. They went to live ⓐ_____ the islands long before Europeans arrived. (B) The Maori culture is an important part of today's New Zealand society. (C) The Maori language is taught ⓑ_____ some schools and there are Maori language radio and TV stations. (D) There are Maori villages in many parts of the country. (E) If you say "kia ora" to the villagers, they will be glad to hear it. It means "hi" ⓒ_____ English.

22 위 글을 읽고 대답할 수 <u>없는</u> 질문은? (3점)

① Who are the Maori people?
② What does "kia ora" mean in English?
③ Where can you experience Maori culture?
④ Is it possible to learn the Maori language in schools?
⑤ How do visitors feel when they say "kia ora" to the Maori?

23 위 글의 내용과 가장 일치하지 <u>않는</u> 것은? (3점)

① 마오리 마을은 여러 지역에 있다.

② 마오리 문화는 최근에도 남아 있다.

③ 마오리족은 뉴질랜드의 두 번째 이주민이다.

④ 마오리 주민들은 'kia ora'가 무슨 뜻인지 알고 있다.

⑤ 마오리 마을은 주민 외에 다른 사람들도 방문이 가능하다.

24 위 글의 밑줄 친 ⓐ~ⓔ 중 어법상 <u>어색한</u> 것은? (2점)

① ⓐ   ② ⓑ   ③ ⓒ

④ ⓓ   ⑤ ⓔ

25 위 글의 밑줄 친 (A)matches와 같은 뜻으로 쓰인 것은? (4점)

① We went to the stadium to watch the rival team <u>match</u>.

② He has an old box of <u>matches</u> his grandfather used.

③ Bobby and Julia are a good <u>match</u> for each other.

④ The ID and password does not <u>match</u>.

⑤ These shoes <u>matched</u> the jacket well.

[24~27] 다음 글을 읽고 물음에 답하시오.

Have you ever watched the haka? The haka may look scary ⓐbecause haka dancers shout and move their bodies ⓑwild. The Maori people, who you've already ⓒheard about, started ⓓdoing the haka as a war dance. Today, however, New Zealanders do the haka at sport (A)matches, weddings, or other important events. (가)_____, New Zealand's national rugby team members do the haka before every match. It is famous all over the world. If you see the haka, you will probably agree that the rival team must be ⓔscared. Like the kiwi bird, the haka is a national symbol.

26 위 글의 빈칸 (가)에 문맥상 들어가기에 가장 적절한 것은? (3점)

① Finally

② At last

③ Moreover

④ Therefore

⑤ For example

27 위 글의 haka에 관한 내용과 일치하지 <u>않는</u> 것은? (3점)

① haka는 댄서들이 소리치고 거칠게 몸을 움직이기 때문에 무서워 보일 수 있다.

② 마오리족이 스포츠 경기 춤으로 haka를 시작했다.

③ 오늘날 결혼식이나 중요한 이벤트 등에서 haka를 추곤 한다.

④ 뉴질랜드의 럭비 국가 대표팀은 매 경기 전에 haka를 춘다.

⑤ haka는 뉴질랜드 국가의 상징이다.

28 위 글의 빈칸 (A)와 (B)에 들어갈 말이 바르게 짝지어진 것은? (3점)

	(A)	(B)
①	by	from
②	with	by
③	by	with
④	without	with
⑤	with	to

29 위 글의 빈칸 (가)에 대한 설명으로 <u>어색한</u> 것을 <u>모두</u> 고르시오. (3점)

① 주격 관계대명사 자리이다.

② 관계대명사 that이 올 수 있다.

③ 관계대명사 who가 올 수 있다.

④ 관계대명사 which가 올 수 있다.

⑤ 「접속사+대명사」가 올 수 있다.

[28~30] 다음 글을 읽고 물음에 답하시오.

New Zealand is a place of natural beauty. It has many beautiful lakes and waterfalls. New Zealand has two main islands, the South Island and the North Island. In the South Island, there are mountains (가)_____ are covered with snow all year round. You will be amazed (A)_____ the fantastic views.

In the North Island, there are many hot springs, lakes, and areas (B)_____ green grass. Because of its natural beauty, many famous movies have been made in New Zealand. If you visit New Zealand, you will surely appreciate its nature.

30 위 글의 내용과 일치하지 <u>않는</u> 것은? (3점)

① 뉴질랜드에는 많은 호수와 폭포가 있다.

② 뉴질랜드에는 동섬과 서섬이라는 두 주요 섬이 있다.

③ 뉴질랜드에는 일 년 내내 눈으로 덮인 산들이 있다.

④ 뉴질랜드에는 온천과 초원이 있다.

⑤ 뉴질랜드에서 많은 유명한 영화가 제작되었다.

3학년 영어 2학기 중간고사(6과) 2회

반		점수
이름		

문항수 : 선택형(28문항) 서술형(2문항) | 20 . . .

◎ 선택형 문항의 답안은 컴퓨터용 수정 싸인펜을 사용하여 OMR 답안지에 바르게 표기하시오.
◎ 서술형 문제는 답을 답안지에 반드시 검정 볼펜으로 쓰시오.
◎ 총 30문항 100점 만점입니다. 문항별 배점은 각 문항에 표시되어 있습니다.

[경기 ○○중]
[대전 ○○중]

01 다음 영영 풀이에 해당하는 단어로 알맞은 것은? (3점)

> • to be grateful for
> • to understand the importance of something

① amaze ② cover
③ appreciate ④ suggest
⑤ confuse

[경기 ○○중]

02 다음 영영 풀이에 해당하는 단어로 가장 적절한 것은? (3점)

> an action, object, event, etc., that expresses or represents a particular idea or quality

① rival ② society
③ culture ④ symbol
⑤ beauty

[대전 ○○중]

03 다음 영영 풀이에 해당하는 단어로 알맞은 것은? (2점)

> a person who you are competing or fighting against in the same area or for the same thing

① rival ② role model
③ ability ④ creator
⑤ survivor

[서울 강남구 ○○중]

04 다음 〈보기〉의 우리말 의미를 참고하여 문맥에 맞도록 문장을 완성하시오. (교과서 내 표현으로 작성할 것.) (6점)

> **보기**
> ~가 다 떨어지다, 바닥나다, 바닥나다 / ~에 투자할 가치가 있다 / 진심으로 / 격자무늬

(1) The kilt looks like a knee-length skirt and has a ＿＿＿＿ ＿＿＿＿.
(2) I'll talk to her with ＿＿＿＿ ＿＿＿＿ ＿＿＿＿.
(3) We've ＿＿＿＿ ＿＿＿＿ ＿＿＿＿ patience with him.
(4) The company ＿＿＿＿ ＿＿＿＿ ＿＿＿＿ our money into.

[경기 ○○중]

05 다음 중 어법상 옳은 문장은? (4점)

① We know how is the machine operated.
② I don't like the way how he treats me.
③ The more you struggle, the more deep you'll sink.
④ June 24th is the day when I went to the hospital on.
⑤ This is the place in which I met her for the first time.

06 다음 밑줄 친 부분 중 지칭하는 범위가 <u>다른</u> 것은? (4점)

① He hurt his arm, <u>which</u> made me sad.

② He has two cars, <u>which</u> are expensive.

③ Jane sold her book, <u>which</u> was 100 dollars.

④ They use the word kiwi, <u>which</u> has several meanings.

⑤ I like the movie, <u>which</u> was made in New Zealand.

08 다음 대화의 흐름상 빈칸에 들어갈 가장 알맞은 말은? (3점)

G: Brian, let's talk about what we will prepare for the World Food Festival.

B: I will make a meat pie. It is famous in Australia. How about you, Sera?

G: I want to make a popular English dish, fish and chips.

B: Fish and chips? _____

G: It is fried fish with hot potato chips.

B: That sounds interesting. Let's prepare them.

① What does it look like?

② Where can you buy it?

③ How long does it take to cook?

④ Why do English people eat it?

⑤ How often do you make it?

07 다음 〈보기〉의 문장을 영작한 것 중 어법상 옳은 것은? (3점)

> 보기
> Brian은 형이 한 명 있는데, 그는 런던에 산다.

① Brain has an older brother who live in London.

② Brain has an older brother which lives in London.

③ Brain has an older brother, that lives in London.

④ Brain has an older brother, which lives in London.

⑤ Brain has an older brother, who lives in London.

09 다음 빈칸에 공통으로 들어갈 말로 가장 적절한 것은? (2점)

> • I have a brother, and he lives in China.
> →I have a brother, _____ lives in China.
> • I have a sister, and she is an English teacher.
> →I have a sister, _____ is an English teacher.

① who   ② that

③ which   ④ what

⑤ when

10 다음 글의 빈칸 (A)~(C)에 들어가기에 가장 적절한 관계대명사는? (4점)

> We Invite You!
>
> Do you know about New Zealand? It has two main islands and 600 smaller islands. Its capital is Wellington. The kiwi, (A)_____ is a bird native to New Zealand, is one of the symbols of the country. If you come to New Zealand, you should visit a Maori village, (B)_____ shows the native culture of New Zealand. These days, many people (C)_____ want to enjoy the beautiful nature visit New Zealand.

	(A)	(B)	(C)
①	which	that	what
②	that	what	that
③	which	which	who
④	which	which	what
⑤	that	who	who

11 다음 대화의 밑줄 친 단어에 대한 설명으로 가장 적절한 것은? (3점)

> G: My American friend invited me to a <u>potluck party</u> next Friday.
> B: You know, you should take food to share at the dinner.
> G: What would you recommend that I take?
> B: I suggest you take some Korean food. How about Gimbap, Suji?
> G: Yes. It's not spicy and it's easy to carry.
> B: I think it'll be good for dinner.

① a party for a woman who is expecting a baby

② a party for a woman who is about to get married

③ a party where everyone who is invited brings food to share

④ an annual celebration for people who attended a college or university

⑤ a formal dance party for high school students usually at the end of the school year

[12~13] 다음 대화를 읽고 물음에 답하시오.

Seho: Good morning.

Jessie, Andy: Hi, Seho.

Seho: I will visit my uncle in Philadelphia this winter. Can you tell me about the city?

Jessie: Sure. ⓐI was there few years ago. First, let's talk about food.

Seho: Okay. What food is Philadelphia famous for?

Jessie: ⓑMost famous food in Philadelphia is the cheese steak sandwich. ⓒIt is a big sandwich which filled with beef and melted cheese.

Seho: Good suggestion. I will try it. ⓓAre there any places that are popular with tourists?

Andy: ⓔI suggest you visited Independence Hall. It is very important in American history.

Seho: Wonderful. Thank you for the information.

Andy: My pleasure.

13 위 대화의 내용과 일치하지 <u>않는</u> 것은? (3점)

① Seho has been to the Independence Hall before.

② Jessie knows what a cheese steak sandwich is like.

③ It is Philadelphia that Seho is going to visit this winter.

④ Seho wants to get some information about Philadelphia.

⑤ The place Andy recommends is very important in American history.

14 다음 짝지어진 대화의 내용이 가장 <u>어색한</u> 것은? (2점)

① A: Do you know what a kilt is?
   B: No, I don't. Tell me what it is.

② A: I want to eat fish and chips.
   B: It's my favorite. What does it look like?

③ A: Do you mind turning down the volume?
   B: No, not at all. Is it too loud?

④ A: I drew her surfing in the sea.
   B: I'm fascinated by your drawing.

⑤ A: Blaire, you don't have to be nervous on your English exam.
   B: Thanks, Hailey. I feel much better. I appreciate your advice.

12 위 대화의 밑줄 친 ⓐ~ⓔ 중 어법상 옳은 것은? (4점)

① ⓐ   ② ⓑ   ③ ⓒ

④ ⓓ   ⑤ ⓔ

B: ⓐLet's talk about traditional clothing from other countries.
G: Hmm... Do you know what a kilt is?
B: No, I don't. What is it?
G: It is traditional clothing from Scotland. It looks like a ⓑ무릎까지 오는 skirt and has a plaid pattern.
B: A skirt of ⓑ무릎까지 오는 with a plaid pattern?
G: Yes. It is unique because it is a skirt for men.
B: That sounds interesting. I want to try one on.

[충북 ○○중]

15 위 대화의 밑줄 친 ⓐ의 대화 의도와 <u>다른</u> 표현은? (3점)

① I'd like to say something about ~.
② I want to talk about ~.
③ Why don't we talk about ~?
④ Shall we talk about ~?
⑤ Can I get your advice on ~?

[경기 ○○중]

17 다음 글을 읽고 요약할 때, 글의 내용과 일치하지 <u>않는</u> 것은? (5점)

Do you know about Ireland? It is the third largest island in Europe. Its capital is Dublin. The color green, which stands for the green land, is one of the symbols of the country. If you come to Ireland, you should visit the Cliffs of Moher, which show the beautiful nature of Ireland. We suggest you try a traditional dish in Ireland. They boil bread in milk and then add some sugar on it. It is great. Many people visit Ireland to get refreshed. We are happy to invite you to this beautiful country.

ⓐ land : the third biggest island in Europe
ⓑ symbol of the country : the color green
  - It represents the green land
ⓒ place to visit : the Cliffs of Moher
  - People can appreciate the beautiful nature of Ireland
ⓓ traditional dish : bread boiled in milk with some sugar
ⓔ how to visit Ireland : to get refreshed

① ⓐ   ② ⓑ   ③ ⓒ
④ ⓓ   ⑤ ⓔ

[충북 ○○중]

16 위 대화의 밑줄 친 ⓑ를 바르게 옮긴 것은? (2점)

① knee length
② knee depth
③ knee height
④ knee width
⑤ knee distance

[18~19] 다음 글을 읽고 물음에 답하시오.

Have you ever watched the haka? (A) The haka may look ⓐ_____ because haka dancers shout and move their bodies wildly. (B) The Maori people, who you've already heard about, started doing the haka as a war dance. It was done to ⓑ_____ their rivals. (C) Today, however, New Zealanders do the haka at sport matches, weddings, or other important events. (D) It is famous all over the world. If you see the haka, you will probably agree that the rival team must be ⓒ_____. (E) Like the kiwi bird, the haka is a national symbol.

[20~22] 다음 글을 읽고 물음에 답하시오.

Now, let's talk about ⓐthe Maori. ⓑThey are ⓒthe native people of New Zealand. ⓓThey went to live on the islands long before Europeans arrived. The Maori culture is an important part of today's New Zealand society. The Maori language is taught at some schools and there are Maori language radio and TV stations. There are Maori villages in many parts of the country. You can visit Maori villages and experience Maori culture. If you say "kia ora" to the villagers, they will be glad (A)to hear it. ⓔIt means "hi" in English.

[충북 ○○중]

20 위 글의 밑줄 친 ⓐ~ⓔ 중 가리키는 대상이 다른 하나는? (2점)

① ⓐ   ② ⓑ   ③ ⓒ

④ ⓓ   ⑤ ⓔ

[경기 ○○중]

18 위 글의 흐름상 다음 문장이 들어가기에 가장 적절한 곳은? (3점)

> For example, New Zealand's national rugby team members do the haka before every match.

① (A)   ② (B)   ③ (C)

④ (D)   ⑤ (E)

[충북 ○○중]

21 위 글의 내용과 일치하지 <u>않는</u> 것은? (3점)

① 마오리족은 뉴질랜드의 원주민이다.

② 마오리족은 유럽인들이 도착한 이후에 뉴질랜드의 섬에 와서 살았다.

③ 마오리 문화는 오늘날 뉴질랜드 사회의 중요한 일부분이다.

④ 몇몇 학교에서 마오리어를 가르치고, 마오리어로 하는 라디오와 TV 방송국들이 있다.

⑤ "kia ora"는 영어로 "안녕하세요"를 의미한다.

[경기 ○○중]

19 위 글의 빈칸 ⓐ, ⓑ, ⓒ에 들어갈 말로 가장 적절한 것은? (4점)

	ⓐ	ⓑ	ⓒ
①	scary	scare	scared
②	scared	scared	scare
③	scare	scare	scared
④	scary	scared	scared
⑤	scare	scary	scared

22 위 글의 밑줄 친 (A)와 같은 용법으로 쓰이지 <u>않은</u> 것은? (3점)

① Jason was sad <u>to break</u> up with Anne.

② Jack was proud <u>to win</u> the dance contest.

③ My brother was pleased <u>to be invited</u> to the party.

④ Ken was disappointed <u>to hear</u> that the trip had been canceled.

⑤ Tom was the first student <u>to answer</u> the English question.

24 위 글의 밑줄 친 (나)which에 대한 설명 중 옳은 것을 <u>모두</u> 고르면? (정답 2개) (3점)

① 선행사는 앞 문장 전체이다.

② who로 바꿔 쓸 수 있다.

③ that과 바꿔 쓸 수 있다.

④ 선행사는 the word kiwi이다.

⑤ 관계대명사의 계속적 용법이다.

[23~27] 다음 글을 읽고 물음에 답하시오.

When you hear (가)<u>the word kiwi</u>, what comes (A)_____ your mind? Maybe a fruit, but, in New Zealand the word kiwi has a couple (B)_____ meanings. First, kiwi is the name of a delicious, green fruit. A lot of kiwi fruit is grown throughout the country, so New Zealand is known (C)_____ the land of kiwi fruit.

Kiwi is also the name of one of New Zealand's native birds. The kiwi is special to New Zealanders because it is the symbol of the nation. Also, kiwi is a nickname for people from New Zealand. Today, New Zealanders are sometimes called Kiwis throughout the world. Now, you know that kiwi is the name of a fruit, a bird, and also a people. Next time, don't become confused when someone uses the word kiwi, (나)<u>which</u> has several meanings.

25 위 글의 빈칸 (A), (B), (C)에 들어갈 말로 가장 적절한 것은? (4점)

	(A)	(B)	(C)
①	to	of	as
②	up	in	for
③	to	in	as
④	into	of	to
⑤	up	of	for

26 다음 중 위 글의 제목으로 가장 알맞은 것은? (3점)

① The Taste of Kiwi Fruit

② The Three Symbols of New Zealand

③ What Is the Nickname for New Zealanders?

④ A Native Kiwi Bird, the Symbol of New Zealand

⑤ What Does the Word Kiwi Mean in New Zealand?

23 위 글의 밑줄 친 (가)the word kiwi의 의미에 해당하는 것을 모두 고르면? (정답 3개) (4점)

① a fruit   ② a bird

③ a people   ④ a tree

⑤ a land

27 위 글의 내용과 일치하지 <u>않는</u> 것은? (4점)

① One of the meanings of kiwi is a green fruit.

② New Zealanders grow a lot of kiwi fruit across the country.

③ Most people may think of fruit when they hear the word kiwi.

④ There are several meanings in the word kiwi in New Zealand.

⑤ The kiwi bird was brought to New Zealand from somewhere else.

28 위 글의 밑줄 친 ⓐ~ⓔ 중 어법상 <u>어색한</u> 것은? (3점)

① ⓐ   ② ⓑ   ③ ⓒ

④ ⓓ   ⑤ ⓔ

29 위 글을 통해 알 수 있는 뉴질랜드의 남섬과 북섬의 구체적인 특징을 우리말로 쓰시오. (5점)

(1) 남섬의 특징: _____

(2) 북섬의 특징: _____

[28~30] 다음 글을 읽고 물음에 답하시오.

New Zealand is a place of natural beauty. It has many beautiful lakes and waterfalls. New Zealand has two main islands, the South Island and the North Island. In the South Island, there are mountains ⓐ<u>which are covered</u> with snow all year round. You will ⓑ<u>be amazed</u> by the fantastic views. In the North Island, there are many hot springs, lakes, and ⓒ<u>areas</u> with green grass. Because of its natural beauty, many famous movies ⓓ<u>have made</u> in New Zealand. If you ⓔ<u>visit</u> New Zealand, you will surely appreciate its nature.

30 위 글의 제목으로 가장 적절한 것은? (3점)

① The Best Thing to Do in the North Island

② New Zealand's Fantastic Natural Environment

③ Places to Experience Ice in New Zealand

④ How to Protect Beautiful Nature in New Zealand

⑤ Serious Environmental Problems in New Zealand

◎ 선택형 문항의 답안은 컴퓨터용 수정 싸인펜을 사용하여 OMR 답안지에 바르게 표기하시오.
◎ 서술형 문제는 답을 답안지에 반드시 검정 볼펜으로 쓰시오.
◎ 총 30문항 100점 만점입니다. 문항별 배점은 각 문항에 표시되어 있습니다.

[충북 ○○중]

01 다음 중 두 단어의 관계가 〈보기〉와 같은 것은?　(3점)

> 보기
>
> hurt : wound

① borrow : lend
② accept : reject
③ national : natural
④ thoughtful : considerate
⑤ accidentally : intentionally

[서울 강남구 ○○중]

02 다음 ⓐ~ⓔ 중 짝지어진 단어와 영영 풀이가 올바른 것의 개수는?　(4점)

> ⓐ regret: to take no notice of
> ⓑ casual: extremely interested
> ⓒ wound: a physical hurt or injury
> ⓓ accidentally: well known because you experienced it before
> ⓔ advertising: the activity of persuading people to buy products or services

① 1개　　②2개　　③3개
④4개　　⑤5개

[부산 ○○중]

03 다음 중 밑줄 친 표현이 어색한 것은?　(3점)

① Kate accidentally bumped into Minho.
② Hallyu spread very fast throughout the world.
③ There are a couple of people ahead of you. Just hold on.
④ I am always proper when I see Amy with her twin sister.
⑤ James is the best swimmer and has no rival in his country.

[대전 ○○중]

04 다음 중 어법상 옳은 문장은?　(4점)

① This is the place where he was born.
② This is the company where my dad works for.
③ This is the way which she could get the map.
④ I want to know the reason which she always comes late.
⑤ December 25th is the day where Santa gives presents to children.

[부산 ○○중]

05 다음 우리말에 맞게 주어진 단어로 영작했을 때 앞에서 5번째 단어는?　(3점)

> 당신의 사과가 진실할수록, 그것은 더 잘 받아들여질 것이다.
> (sincere, received, your, apology, the, it, is, will, the, more, better, be)

① is　　　②the　　　③your
④ apology　　⑤ sincere

06 다음 중 어법상 옳은 문장은? (4점)

① Kevin shows how he plants a tree in.

② The restaurant where we visited at was nice.

③ Seoul is the city in where the festival is held.

④ Please tell me the reason what you quit smoking.

⑤ The bed in which I slept last Saturday was comfortable.

08 다음 우리말을 영어로 쓰시오. (단, 관계부사 how를 사용하여 현재시제로 쓸 것) (4점)

- Jason은 그가 그의 자동차를 어떻게 수리하는지 보여 준다.

→ _____

07 다음 두 문장을 우리말의 의미에 맞게 한 문장으로 바르게 바꾼 것은? (3점)

The way was still unknown.
+ The accident happened in the way.
그 사고가 어떻게 일어났는지는 아직 알려지지 않았다.

① How was still unknown the accident happened.

② The accident happened how was still unknown.

③ How the accident happened was still unknown.

④ The way was still unknown how the accident happened.

⑤ The accident happened in the way how was still unknown.

09 다음 중 어법상 옳은 문장의 개수는? (5점)

ⓐ I show you how I do CPR.

ⓑ She felt disappointed failing her project.

ⓒ I'm looking forward to playing the janggu.

ⓓ This is the house where I bought last year.

ⓔ The city is known for its beautiful view.

ⓕ I visited the town where the artist was born in.

ⓖ He'll visit the National Museum, that is near the city hall.

ⓗ The famous you get, the more polite you have to be.

ⓘ I had dinner in a restaurant, which I liked it very much.

ⓙ The more photos he takes, the better you will have photos.

① 2개　　② 3개　　③ 4개
④ 5개　　⑤ 6개

10 다음 설명을 읽고 빈칸 (A), (B)에 들어갈 말을 차례대로 쓰시오. (4점)

> That is how I solved the difficult problem.

> 관계부사는 시간, 장소, 방법, 이유와 관련된 선행사와 다른 절(주어+동사 ~)을 연결합니다. 위 문장에서 관계부사 how는 선행사가 (A)_____을 나타낼 때 쓰며, 주어진 문장을 우리말로 해석하면 (B)'_____' 입니다.

조건
• 빈칸 (A)에는 우리말로 적을 것.

(A) _____

(B) _____

11 다음 대화 중 어색한 것은? (2점)

① A: Judy, do you mind turning down the volume?

　 B: No, I don't. Is it too loud?

② A: I accidentally broke my mom's favorite plate.

　 B: You can see a doctor.

③ A: Karen, do you mind coming to my house tomorrow at 7 a.m.?

　 B: That's very early.

④ A: Let me open the door for you.

　 B: Oh, I appreciate your help.

⑤ A: How long have you known him?

　 B: I have known him for ten years.

[12~13] 다음 대화를 읽고 물음에 답하시오.

> Jessie: Hi, Andy. What's up?
> Andy: Hi, Jessie. I'm going to buy a present for Amy. You've been friends with her for a long time, (A)[have you / haven't you]?
> Jessie: Yes, since first grade in elementary school.
> Andy: Well, I know that you're really busy (B)[studying / to study] these days, but do you mind helping me? I am sure you could help me pick out something nice.
> Jessie: No problem. What's the present for? It's not her birthday.
> Andy: Well, two months ago, when my leg was broken, she carried my backpack to school.
> Jessie: That was nice (C)[for her / of her].
> Andy: Yes, it was. What should I get for her?
> Jessie: Well, how about a case for her smartphone? She broke her case recently.
> Andy: Really? Thank you for your suggestion.

12 위 대화의 괄호 (A), (B), (C) 안에 들어갈 표현으로 가장 적절한 것은? (4점)

	(A)	(B)	(C)
①	have you	studying	for her
②	have you	to study	of her
③	haven't you	to study	for her
④	haven't you	studying	of her
⑤	haven't you	studying	for her

13 위 대화를 읽고 답할 수 있는 질문만을 〈보기〉에서 있는 대로 고른 것은? (4점)

> **보기**
>
> ⓐ Does Jessie mind helping Andy?
> ⓑ How long have Andy and Jessie been friends?
> ⓒ What is Andy going to buy for Amy's birthday present?
> ⓓ Why does Jessie recommend a smartphone case as a present?
> ⓔ Two months ago, why did Amy carry Andy's backpack to school?

① ⓐ, ⓑ

② ⓐ, ⓒ

③ ⓐ, ⓓ, ⓔ

④ ⓑ, ⓒ, ⓔ

⑤ ⓑ, ⓒ, ⓓ, ⓔ

[15~16] 다음 대화를 읽고 물음에 답하시오.

> Suhee: ⓐI'm planning to go to Jejudo.
> Dustin: That's cool, Suhee. ⓑI was used to live there.
> Suhee: ⓒDo you mind tell me what to do in Jejudo?
> Dustin: Not at all. Jejudo has many beautiful beaches. You should visit them.
> Suhee: Good. I will go swimming. What else can I do, Dustin?
> Dustin: Why don't you hike Halla Mountain? You can see the mountain from everywhere on the island.
> Suhee: Great. How about food?
> Dustin: ⓓIf you like fish, raw fish is fresh and delicious on Jejudo.
> Suhee: ⓔI'll try everything. Thank you for your tips.

15 위 대화의 밑줄 친 ⓐ~ⓔ 중 어법상 어색한 것의 개수는? (4점)

① 1개 　　② 2개 　　③ 3개

④ 4개 　　⑤ 5개

---

14 다음 대화의 빈칸에 들어갈 말로 가장 적절한 것은? (3점)

> A: Judy, do you mind lowering the volume?
> B: No, I don't. Is it too loud?
> A: Yes, it is. I can hear it in my room.
> B: I'm sorry. I'll _____.
> A: Thanks a lot.

① pick it up

② take it off

③ turn it down

④ hand it in

⑤ laugh it off

---

16 위 대화의 내용과 가장 일치하지 <u>않는</u> 것은? (3점)

① 수희는 Dustin이 한 제안들을 수락했다.

② 수희는 한라산 어느 곳도 오를 수 있다.

③ 수희는 제주도에서 수영과 하이킹을 할 것이다.

④ Dustin은 제주도에서 할 것들을 추천해 주었다.

⑤ Dustin은 제주도의 회가 신선하고 맛있다고 말한다.

<Three Things about a Proper Apology>
Because we are human, we all make mistakes. (A)It is not easy to get along with everyone all the time. ⓐ때때로 우리는 의도하지 않게 다른 사람의 감정을 상하게 한다. Sometimes, we do something wrong and regret it later. When that happens, what should we do? We should apologize. Read the following case studies and learn three things about a proper apology.

17 위 글의 밑줄 친 (A)와 같은 용법으로 쓰인 것은? (3점)

① It is filled with mystery.
② It was very cold outside.
③ The hunters caught the bear and killed it.
④ It is difficult to get up early in the morning.
⑤ It was a dry summer and many people were dying of thirst.

18 위 글의 밑줄 친 ⓐ를 바르게 영작한 것은? (3점)

① We sometimes hurt people's feelings with intended.
② Sometimes we hurt people's feelings without intended.
③ Sometimes we hurt people's feelings with intending to.
④ We sometimes hurt people's feelings without be intended.
⑤ Sometimes we hurt people's feelings without intending to.

19 위 글 다음에 이어질 내용으로 가장 알맞은 것은? (3점)

① Human's mistakes
② Doing something wrong
③ How to write different studies
④ Three things about a proper apology
⑤ Hurting people's feelings without intention

One day, Sunmin (A)[borrowed / bought] her sister's favorite book. Later, she lost it. Sunmin didn't apologize because she thought it was not important. She thought, 'We're sisters, after all.' Sunmin's sister disliked how Sunmin had treated her. How could her own sister (B)[ignore / respect] her feelings? This was not the first time Sunmin hadn't apologized to her little sister. People need to apologize when they do something wrong. This includes family members and the people who are (C)[close / unfriendly] to you. People get hurt more easily when the hurt comes from a family member or a friend.

20 위 글에 드러난 Sunmin의 행동을 보고, 글쓴이가 Sunmin에게 해줄 조언으로 가장 적절한 것은? (4점)

① No one has ever become poor by giving.

② When eating fruit, think of the person who planted the tree.

③ A real friend is one who walks in when the rest of the world walks out.

④ The man who moves a mountain begins by carrying away small stones.

⑤ In some families, "please" is regarded as the magic word. In our house, however, it was "sorry".

[22~25] 다음 글을 읽고 물음에 답하시오.

People need to apologize when they do something wrong. This includes family members and the people who ⓐare close to you. People get hurt more easily when the (A)hurt comes from a family member or a friend. We may think that they will ⓑlet go it because they are close to us. Remember, however, that small mistakes and no apology add up to big emotional wounds. This is especially true among family members and ⓒloved ones.

Have you ever ⓓheard of the saying, "No more apologies, no more chances"? People make mistakes, but don't let one mistake break a beautiful relationship. Do you want to apologize to someone? (가)_____ A quick and sincere "I'm sorry" can ⓔsolve many problems.

21 위 글의 괄호 (A), (B), (C) 안에 들어갈 단어로 가장 적절한 것은? (3점)

	(A)	(B)	(C)
①	borrowed	ignore	close
②	borrowed	respect	unfriendly
③	borrowed	ignore	unfriendly
④	bought	respect	unfriendly
⑤	bought	ignore	close

22 위 글의 밑줄 친 ⓐ~ⓔ 중 어법상 어색한 것은? (3점)

① ⓐ   ② ⓑ   ③ ⓒ

④ ⓓ   ⑤ ⓔ

23 위 글의 밑줄 친 (A)와 쓰임이 같은 것은?　　　(2점)

① I <u>hurt</u> my arm.

② Did you <u>hurt</u> yourself?

③ The tight shoes <u>hurt</u> him.

④ My knee <u>hurts</u> when I bend it.

⑤ There was <u>hurt</u> and real anger in her voie.

24 위 글의 내용과 일치하지 <u>않는</u> 것은?　　　(3점)

① 사람들은 마음의 상처가 가족이나 친구에게서 올 때 더 쉽게 상처를 받는다.

② 작은 실수를 하고 사과하지 않는 것은 결국 큰 감정의 상처가 된다는 것을 기억해야 한다.

③ 사과를 할 수 있는 기회는 다시 온다.

④ 사람들은 실수를 하지만 하나의 실수가 아름다운 관계를 깨트리게 해서는 안 된다.

⑤ 빠르고 진정한 "미안해"라는 말이 많은 문제를 해결할 수 있다.

25 위 글의 빈칸 (가)에 들어갈 말로 가장 적절한 것은?　　　(3점)

① Try to do it right now.

② Just forgive his mistakes.

③ Let others apologize before you do.

④ Don't be afraid of breaking a relationship.

⑤ Remember that slow and steady wins the race.

[26~30] 다음 글을 읽고 물음에 답하시오.

When June tripped over a backpack and fell, Mike found it funny and laughed. He took a picture and uploaded it on an SNS. June saw the picture and became angry. Mike said, with a laugh, "Sorry, June!" and deleted it. After that, June felt even more hurt because of Mike's (A)_____ apology. June didn't like how Mike had acted. Mike seemed to think it was nothing serious.

What did you learn from this case? Yes. You guessed right. You should be sincere when you apologize. Apologizing is necessary to build good friendships. (가)당신이 미안하다고 말하는 것은 단지 말 그 이상이다. You need to show that you respect the other person and ⓐ<u>care about</u> his or her feelings. If you truly want to make things right, ⓑ<u>be sincere</u> in your apology. The more sincere your apology is, the better it will be received.

Here is another case. While Kate was hurrying across the cafeteria, she accidentally ⓒ<u>bumped up</u> Hojun. Some food on Hojun's tray fell on his jacket. Kate didn't apologize. Hojun felt bad. He thought, 'Why doesn't she say something? It would be nothing if she apologized right now.'

This case shows that when an apology is necessary, you should apologize at once. A quick apology shows that you are thoughtful and ⓓ<u>take responsibility for</u> your action. All you need to do is to say, "I'm sorry." Then, the hurt friend will think nothing of it and ⓔ<u>laugh it off</u>.

26 위 글의 밑줄 친 ⓐ~ⓔ 중 <u>어색한</u> 것은?　　　(2점)

① ⓐ　　　② ⓑ　　　③ ⓒ

④ ⓓ　　　⑤ ⓔ

27 위 글의 빈칸 (A)에 들어갈 말로 가장 적절한 것은?   (3점)

① casual

② serious

③ long

④ sincere

⑤ genuine

29 위 글의 밑줄 친 (가)의 우리말을 바르게 영작한 것은?   (3점)

> 당신이 미안하다고 말하는 것은 단지 말 그 이상이다.

① Say you're sorry is more than just words.

② Saying you're sorry is more than just words.

③ To say you're sorry are more than just words.

④ Saying you're sorry are more than just words.

⑤ Say you're sorry are more than just words.

28 위 글의 주제로 가장 알맞은 것은?   (4점)

① Choose the right time when you apologize.

② Upload funny pictures on an SNS.

③ Have a smile when you apologize.

④ Apologize at once when you are wrong.

⑤ Say you are sorry to show that you respect the other person.

30 위 글을 읽고 답할 수 없는 것은?   (4점)

① What did Mike do after taking a picture?

② What is necessary to build good friendships?

③ Did Kate apologize to Hojun?

④ What did Hojun think about Kate?

⑤ What do you need to do after saying "I'm sorry"?

◎ 선택형 문항의 답안은 컴퓨터용 수정 싸인펜을 사용하여 OMR 답안지에 바르게 표기하시오.
◎ 서술형 문제는 답을 답안지에 반드시 검정 볼펜으로 쓰시오.
◎ 총 30문항 100점 만점입니다. 문항별 배점은 각 문항에 표시되어 있습니다.

[서울 관악구 ○○중]
[대전 ○○중]

01 다음 영영 풀이에 해당하는 단어로 알맞은 것은? (3점)

> to feel sorry about something you have done or you have not been able to do

① ignore
② regret
③ delete
④ intend
⑤ receive

[경기 ○○중]

02 다음 빈칸 (A), (B)에 들어갈 말로 가장 적절한 것은? (3점)

> • If you (A)_____ something that you have done, you wish that you had not done it.
> • When you are traveling, (B)_____ clothes will make you feel comfortable.

	(A)	(B)
①	regret	casual
②	regret	sincere
③	regret	emotional
④	intend	casual
⑤	intend	sincere

[충북 ○○중]

03 다음 글의 빈칸 (A)~(D)에 들어갈 단어가 순서대로 알맞게 짝지어진 것은? (3점)

> Inho went to a store to buy shoes. He was hit by a woman's bag (A)_____ as she passed by. The woman said, "Sorry," and she walked away quickly. Inho was angry because the woman did not make a (B)_____ and proper (C)_____. He thought that the woman should (D)_____ his feelings.

> ⓐ apology   ⓑ care about
> ⓒ sincere   ⓓ accidentally

	(A)	(B)	(C)	(D)
①	ⓐ	ⓑ	ⓓ	ⓒ
②	ⓑ	ⓒ	ⓐ	ⓓ
③	ⓒ	ⓑ	ⓓ	ⓐ
④	ⓒ	ⓓ	ⓑ	ⓐ
⑤	ⓓ	ⓒ	ⓐ	ⓑ

[대전 ○○중]

04 다음 중 어법상 옳은 문장은? (4점)

① The more famous you get, the more kind you should be.
② More you read books, the smarter you will become.
③ The sooner you arrive, the good seat you will get.
④ The hard you study, the better your future will be.
⑤ The cheaper the jewelry is, the more people will buy it.

05 다음 밑줄 친 부분 중 어법상 옳은 것은? (정답 2개)　(3점)

① Jason shows us <u>how he makes pizza</u>.

② This is <u>the way how I solve</u> the problem.

③ <u>How happened the accident</u> was still unknown.

④ I wonder <u>how she could make</u> the baby sleep.

⑤ He doesn't know <u>how did his uncle fix</u> his laptop.

07 다음 중 어법상 올바른 것은?　(3점)

① This is the house how he lives.

② This is the house which he lives.

③ This is the house where he lives.

④ This is the house in that he lives.

⑤ This is the house where he lives in.

06 다음 대화의 밑줄 친 (A)를 〈보기〉의 주어진 어휘를 반드시 포함하여 영작하시오. (필요할 경우 어형을 변형할 것.)　(4점)

Mina: I accidentally broke my mom's favorite plate.

Tony: That's too bad, Mina.

Mina: (A)네가 나에게 말해 주겠니 how to say sorry to her?

Tony: No, not at all. You should apologize sincerely.

Mina: I see. I'll talk to her with all my heart.

<제시어>
do / mind / tell

→ ＿＿＿＿ ＿＿＿＿ ＿＿＿＿ ＿＿＿＿

＿＿＿＿ how to say sorry to her?

08 다음 〈보기〉에서 문법상 옳은 것만을 고른 것은?　(4점)

보기

ⓐ The harder you try, the better your future will be.

ⓑ The darker it gets, lower the temperature will be.

ⓒ The more famous you get, the more polite you have to be.

ⓓ The cheaper the product is, the most people will buy it.

ⓔ The farther we are away from the city, the more fresher the air will be.

① ⓐ, ⓑ

② ⓐ, ⓒ

③ ⓑ, ⓒ

④ ⓒ, ⓓ

⑤ ⓒ, ⓔ

09 다음 중 어법상 올바른 문장은? (3점)

① We should understand how live people their lives.

② He wants to find out how the machine works.

③ She told us how had she earned so much money.

④ I wonder she how could make the baby stop crying.

⑤ We have to decide how will we get to our destination.

10 다음 중 어법상 옳은 문장을 고른 것은? (5점)

ⓐ This is the house which he lives in.

ⓑ I know the date when he will go abroad.

ⓒ Do you know the reason for why he was late?

ⓓ How happened the accident was still unknown.

ⓔ He wants to find out which the machine works.

ⓕ The faster you finish your work, the earlier you can go home.

ⓖ The more expensive you buy a computer, the more you can use programs.

① ⓐ, ⓑ, ⓕ

② ⓐ, ⓓ, ⓖ

③ ⓑ, ⓒ, ⓕ

④ ⓑ, ⓓ, ⓔ, ⓖ

⑤ ⓒ, ⓓ, ⓔ, ⓕ

11 다음 대화의 빈칸 (A)에 들어갈 말로 가장 적절한 것은? (3점)

Mina: I accidentally broke my mom's favorite plate.

Kevin: That's too bad, Mina.

Mina: Do you (A)_____ telling me how to say sorry to her?

Kevin: No, not at all. You should apologize sincerely.

Mina: I see. I'll talk to her with all my heart.

① like   ② love   ③ mind

④ enjoy   ⑤ finish

12 〈보기〉에 주어진 우리말을 바르게 영작한 것을 고르시오. (3점)

> 보기
> 당신이 일을 더 빨리 끝낼수록, 당신은 더 일찍 집에 갈 수 있습니다.

① The more fast you finish your work, the more early you can go home.

② The more fast you are finishing your work, the more early you can go home.

③ The faster you finished your work, the earlier you could go home.

④ The faster you finish your work, the earlier you can go home.

⑤ The faster you are finishing your work, the earlier you will go home.

[13~14] 다음 대화를 읽고 물음에 답하시오.

Amy: You seem to be busy, Minsu. Can I come in?

Minsu: Sure. I'm preparing for the dance contest, but it's not easy.

Amy: I can help you. I was in the contest last year.

Minsu: Really? That would be great, Amy.

Amy: You are good at getting into the rhythm. But one thing you need to do is to be more relaxed. You are too nervous.

Minsu: Your advice is very helpful. I really (A)_____ your advice.

Amy: It's really my pleasure.

14 위 대화의 빈칸 (A)와 다음 문장의 빈칸에 공통으로 들어갈 가장 알맞은 것은? (2점)

I (A)_____ what you've done.

① ignore

② pass

③ intend

④ apologize

⑤ appreciate

13 위 대화의 내용과 가장 일치하는 것은? (3점)

① Amy는 춤을 출 때 너무 긴장한다.

② 민수는 리듬을 잘 타는 것이 필요하다.

③ Amy는 민수의 춤에 대해서 충고를 해 주었다.

④ 민수는 작년에 댄스 경연 대회에 나갔던 경험이 있다.

⑤ Amy는 민수의 충고에 감사해 했다.

15 다음 중 대화의 흐름이 서로 어색한 것은? (3점)

① A: Let me show you the way.

B: I appreciate your kindness.

② A: Do you mind opening the window?

B: No, I don't. I feel cold. It's too windy outside.

③ A: What kind of person is your father?

B: He is humorous, brave and cheerful.

④ A: What does your favorite cap look like?

B: It's red. My name is written in black on the side.

⑤ A: I accidentally broke my mom's favorite plate.

B: That's too bad, Mina.

16 다음 대화에서 Suhee가 추천받지 <u>않은</u> 것을 <u>모두</u> 고른 것은? (4점)

> G: I am planning to go to Jejudo.
>
> B: That's cool, Suhee. I used to live there.
>
> G: Do you mind telling me what to do in Jejudo?
>
> B: Not at all. Jejudo has many beautiful beaches. You should visit them.
>
> G: Good. I will go swimming. What else can I do?
>
> B: Why don't you hike Halla Mountain? You can see the mountain from everywhere on the island.
>
> G: Great. How about food?
>
> B: If you like fish, on Jejudo, raw fish is fresh and delicious.
>
> G: I'll try everything. I appreciate your tips.

> ⓐ 해변 방문하기   ⓑ 등산하기
> ⓒ 생선회 먹기   ⓓ 요트 타기
> ⓔ 수영하기

① ⓐ, ⓑ

② ⓑ

③ ⓑ, ⓒ

④ ⓒ

⑤ ⓓ, ⓔ

17 다음 중 짝지어진 대화가 <u>어색한</u> 것은? (3점)

① A: Do you mind turning down the volume?

   B: No, I don't. Is it too loud?

② A: You seem to be busy. Can I come in?

   B: Sure. I'm preparing for the dance contest, but it's not easy.

③ A: I think you are good at getting into the rhythm.

   B: I see. I'll talk to her with all my heart.

④ A: I am planning to go to Jejudo.

   B: That's cool. I used to live there.

⑤ A: I accidentally broke my mom's favorite plate.

   B: That's too bad. I think you should apologize to her sincerely.

[18~19] 다음 글을 읽고 물음에 답하시오.

While Kate was hurrying across the cafeteria, she accidentally bumped into Hojun. Some food on Hojun's tray fell on his jacket. Kate didn't apologize. Hojun felt bad. He thought, 'Why doesn't she say something? It would be nothing if she apologized right now.' This case shows that when an apology is necessary, (A)_____. A quick apology shows that you are thoughtful and take responsibility for your action. All you need to do is to say, "I'm sorry." Then, the hurt friend will think nothing of ⓐit and laugh ⓑit off.

18 위 글의 흐름으로 보아 빈칸 (A)에 들어가기에 가장 적절한 표현은? (3점)

① you should apologize at once
② your apology should be sincere
③ you should think about it carefully
④ you must not hurt his or her feeling
⑤ you had better talk with your parents

[20~26] 다음 글을 읽고 물음에 답하시오.

(가)_____. One day, Sunmin borrowed her sister's favorite book. Later, she lost it. Sunmin didn't apologize because she thought it was not important. She thought, 'We're sisters, after all.' ⓐSunmin's sister disliked the way Sunmin had treated her. How could her own sister (나)_____ her feelings? This was not the first time Sunmin hadn't apologized to her little sister.

ⓑPeople need to apologize when they do something wrong. This includes family members and the people who are close to you. People get hurt more easily when the hurt comes from a family member or a friend. We may think that they will let it go because they are close to us. ⓒ Remember, however, that small mistakes and no apology add up to big emotional wounds. This is especially true among family members and loved ones.

Have you ever heard of the saying, "No more apologies, no more chances"? ⓓPeople make mistakes, so let one mistake break a beautiful relationship. Do you want to apologize to someone? Try to do it now. ⓔA quick and sincere "I'm sorry" can solve many problems.

19 위 글의 밑줄 친 ⓐ와 ⓑ가 공통으로 가리키는 내용을 우리말로 쓰시오. (5점)

→ _____

20 위 글의 밑줄 친 ⓐ~ⓔ 중 흐름상 어색한 것은? (3점)

① ⓐ   ② ⓑ   ③ ⓒ
④ ⓓ   ⑤ ⓔ

21 위 글을 쓴 목적으로 가장 알맞은 것은? (2점)

① to advise

② to invite

③ to entertain

④ to welcome

⑤ to advertise

22 위 글의 내용상 빈칸 (가)에 들어갈 말로 가장 적절한 것은? (3점)

① People sometimes make mistakes.

② Do you want to apologize to someone?

③ When an apology is necessary, you don't have to.

④ People don't need to apologize when they do something wrong.

⑤ Apologies are necessary among family members and loved ones, too.

23 위 글의 내용상 빈칸 (나)에 알맞은 것은? (3점)

① treat

② ignore

③ respect

④ borrow

⑤ apologize

24 위 글의 내용과 일치하는 것은? (4점)

① 선민이의 여동생은 선민이가 가장 좋아하는 책을 빌렸다.

② 가족이나 사랑하는 사람들 사이에서는 굳이 사과할 필요는 없다.

③ 선민이의 여동생은 언니가 자신의 기분을 무시했다고 생각했다.

④ 선민이의 여동생이 언니에게 사과를 하지 않은 것은 이번이 처음이 아니다.

⑤ 선민이의 여동생은 자신이 책을 잃어버린 것이 중요하지 않다고 생각하였다.

25 위 글을 읽고 답할 수 있는 질문은? (4점)

① Where did Sunmin lose her sister's favorite book?

② Why didn't Sunmin apologize to her sister?

③ When did Sunmin borrow her sister's favorite book?

④ Is it necessary for Sunmin to apologize to her friend?

⑤ How many times didn't Sunmin apologize to her little sister?

26 위 글 마지막 문단의 내용을 요약할 때 빈칸에 들어갈 말로 가장 적절한 것은? (3점)

> When you make a mistake, it is important to _____ not to break a relationship. Also, your apology should be quick and sincere.

① have ② want ③ make

④ solve ⑤ apologize

Because we are human, we all make mistakes. It is not easy to get along with everyone all the time. ⓐSometimes we hurt people's feelings without intend to. Sometimes, we do something wrong and regret it later. When that happens, what should we do? We should apologize. Read the following case studies and learn three things about a proper apology.

When June tripped over a backpack and fell, ⓑ Mike found it funny and laughed. He took a picture and uploaded it on an SNS. June saw the picture and became angry. Mike said, with a laugh, "Sorry, June!" and deleted it. After (가)that, June felt even more hurt ⓒbecause of Mike's casual apology. (A)June은 Mike가 행동했던 방식이 마음에 들지 않았다. Mike seemed to think it was nothing serious.

What did you learn from this case? Yes. You guessed right. ⓓYou should be casual when you apologize. Apologizing is necessary to build good friendships. Saying you're sorry is more than just words. You need to show that you respect the other person and care about his or her feelings. If you truly want to make things right, ⓔbe sincerely in your apology. ⓕAs you apologize more sincere, the others will receive your apology better.

27 위 글의 밑줄 친 (가)that이 가리키는 말로 가장 적절한 것을 고르면? (3점)

① 가방에 걸려서 넘어진 일
② Mike가 June을 보고 웃은 일
③ Mike가 June의 사진을 찍은 일
④ Mike가 찍은 사진을 SNS에서 본 일
⑤ Mike가 웃으면서 June에게 사과한 일

28 위 글의 밑줄 친 ⓐ~ⓕ 중 문맥상 또는 어법상 쓰임이 적절하지 않은 것은 몇 개인가? (4점)

① 2개
② 3개
③ 4개
④ 5개
⑤ 6개

29 위 글을 읽고 답할 수 없는 질문은? (3점)

① Why is apologizing necessary?
② Why did June feel even more hurt?
③ What picture did Mike upload on an SNS?
④ What should we do when we do something wrong?
⑤ What are the three things about a proper apology?

30 위 글의 밑줄 친 (A)와 같은 의미가 되도록 주어진 〈조건〉에 맞게 영어 문장으로 쓰시오. (4점)

June은 Mike가 행동했던 방식이 마음에 들지 않았다.

조건
• 7단어로 쓸 것.
• like, act를 사용하고 필요시 형태를 바꿀 것.
• 관계부사를 사용할 것.

→ _____

◎ 선택형 문항의 답안은 컴퓨터용 수정 싸인펜을 사용
하여 OMR 답안지에 바르게 표기하시오.
◎ 서술형 문제는 답을 답안지에 반드시 검정 볼펜으
로 쓰시오.
◎ 총 30문항 100점 만점입니다. 문항별 배점은 각
문항에 표시되어 있습니다.

[대전 ○○중]

01 다음 빈칸에 들어갈 단어로 가장 알맞은 것은?　(3점)

> If someone or something is _____ to
> you, you can't easily recognize them.

① strange　　② easy
③ interesting　　④ useful
⑤ familiar

[대전 ○○중]

02 다음 영영 풀이에 해당하는 단어로 알맞은 것은?　(3점)

> the quality or skill that makes it possible for
> you to do something

① value　　② object
③ ability　　④ performance
⑤ subject

[대전 ○○중]

03 다음 빈칸에 들어갈 말로 어법상 알맞은 것은?　(3점)

> This art museum is worth _____.

① to visit　　② visit
③ have visited　　④ visiting
⑤ visits

[울산 ○○중]

04 다음 우리말을 바르게 영작한 것은?　(3점)

> 그 주제는 논의할 가치가 있다.

① The topic is worth discussing.
② Discussing about the topic is worth.
③ The topic is worth to discuss about.
④ To discuss about the topic is worth.
⑤ The topic is a worth topic to discuss.

[대전 ○○중]

05 다음 문장을 분사구문으로 바꿀 때, 빈칸에 들어갈 말로 알맞은
것은?　(4점)

> Because I failed the test, I had to stay after
> school.
> → _____ the test, I had to stay after
> school.

① Failed　　② Failing
③ Not failing　　④ Having failed
⑤ Being failed

[대전 ○○중]

06 다음 밑줄 친 부분을 뜻이 같도록 올바르게 고친 것은?　(3점)

> <u>Watching TV</u>, he couldn't hear his phone.

① While he was watched TV
② Because she was watching TV
③ When I was watching TV
④ While he was watching TV
⑤ When I watched TV

07 다음 문장을 분사구문으로 바꿀 때, 빈칸에 들어갈 말로 알맞은 것은? (3점)

> Since I felt sad, I stayed home.
> → _____ sad, I stayed home.

① Felt
② Being felt
③ Feeling
④ Having felt
⑤ Not feeling

09 다음 주어진 우리말과 일치하도록 어법에 맞게 바르게 쓴 학생만을 **모두** 고르면? (4점)

> ⓐ 지나: 더 이상 사과가 없으면 더 이상 기회도 없다.
>   → No more apologies, no more chances.
> ⓑ 수아: 그녀의 가족은 그 소식을 듣고 흥분했어.
>   → Her family was excited heard the news.
> ⓒ 현민: 너는 이 속담을 들어 본 적이 있니?
>   → Have you ever heard this saying?
> ⓓ 찬수: 그 아기는 미소를 지었고, 그것이 가족을 행복하게 했다.
>   → The baby smiled, that made her family happy.

① 찬수
② 수아, 찬수
③ 지나, 현민
④ 지나, 수아, 현민
⑤ 지나, 수아, 현민, 찬수

08 다음 빈칸에 들어갈 단어로 어법상 알맞은 것은? (3점)

> Books about history are worth _____.

① read
② reads
③ reading
④ to read
⑤ have read

10 다음 문장을 분사구문을 이용한 문장으로 바꿔 쓰시오. (문장 전체를 쓸 것.) (5점)

> (1) As I got vaccinated against COVID-19, I now feel safer than before.
> → _____

> (2) As it was sunny, she didn't take her umbrella with her.
> → _____

11 다음 문장 중 어법상이나 문맥상 <u>어색한</u> 것을 <u>모두</u> 고른 것은?

(6점)

ⓐ Books about world history are worth read.

ⓑ Do you know if Jinsu speaks English?

ⓒ I want to know whether you are working alone.

ⓓ The robotic fish looks like a real fish.

ⓔ She wishes she is a great inventor.

ⓕ Sam rides a bike to pollute the air.

ⓖ I wish I could speak every language.

ⓗ I think I've never seen that man before. He looks familiar.

ⓘ The room was plain and simple, with no decorations.

---

① ⓐ, ⓑ, ⓓ

② ⓐ, ⓔ, ⓕ, ⓗ

③ ⓐ, ⓕ, ⓘ

④ ⓑ, ⓓ, ⓗ, ⓘ

⑤ ⓒ, ⓖ, ⓗ, ⓘ

[12~13] 다음 대화를 읽고 물음에 답하시오.

B: Andy, you went to the art museum, didn't you?

A: Yes. They had a special Chagall exhibition.

B: How did you like it?

A: It was fantastic! (가)<u>나는 그의 그림들에 쓰인 색깔들과 그의 창의성에 매료되었어.</u>

B: No wonder. He was one of the greatest painters ever. What else did you see in the museum?

A: I went to a gift shop and saw things like umbrellas, cups, and backpacks. Famous works of art were printed on them.

B: Did you buy anything?

A: Yes. I bought this T-shirt. How do you like it?

B: It looks great on you.

A: Thank you.

* B: Bora, A: Andy

12 위 대화의 내용과 일치하지 <u>않는</u> 것은? (3점)

① Andy는 Chagall 특별 전시회를 관람했다.

② Bora는 Chagall이 역대 가장 위대한 화가들 중 한 명이었다고 말했다.

③ Andy는 기념품점에서 우산, 컵, 가방 등에 유명 예술 작품들을 그렸다.

④ Andy는 기념품점에서 티셔츠를 샀다.

⑤ Bora는 Andy가 산 티셔츠가 그에게 잘 어울린다고 했다.

13 위 대화의 밑줄 친 (가)와 같은 의미가 되도록 주어진 〈조건〉에 맞게 영어로 쓰시오. (4점)

조건
- 12단어로 쓸 것.
- fascinate를 사용할 것. (필요시 형태를 바꿀 것)

→ _____

14 다음 대화의 빈칸에 들어갈 표현으로 올바른 것은? (3점)

A: Wow, look at this artwork. It's beautiful. Don't you think so?
B: Yes. _____.

① I am fascinated by its colors.
② I has fascinated by its colors.
③ I have fascinated by their colors.
④ I am not fascinated by its colors.
⑤ I had not fascinated by their colors.

[15~16] 다음 대화를 읽고 물음에 답하시오.

B: Claire, _____ your art class?
G: It's great. I learn a lot in the class.
B: What do you like most about it?
G: I enjoy learning different drawing skills. What about you, Allen?
B: I also like the class. I learn good painting skills. I love painting with many colors.
G: Oh, I saw your work last time. I thought it was very creative.
B: Thanks. I practice a lot.

*B: Allen, G: Claire

15 위 대화의 빈칸에 들어갈 말로 가장 적절한 것은? (2점)

① when is
② isn't it
③ is there
④ how do you like
⑤ do you know about

16 위 대화의 내용과 가장 일치하는 것은? (3점)

① Claire is very creative in her drawing.
② Both Claire and Allen like the art class.
③ Allen thinks Claire needs more practice.
④ Allen likes painting mostly with bright colors.
⑤ Claire enjoys learning different painting skills.

Welcome to the Pop Art Exhibition! What do you see? Paintings of soup cans? Big cartoons? Do they look like artworks? (가)Probably not, but think again. They are all famous works of pop art.

(A) Pop is short for popular. (B) It began in the 1950s in America. Pop artists at that time wanted to create something fun and easy. (C) Instead of difficult traditional art works, they turned their eyes to popular culture. They used images from TV, comic books, magazines, and advertising. When people saw familiar images in art exhibitions, they found them refreshing. (D) Since then, pop art has become truly popular. People thought that art was too difficult to understand. (E) By using daily images and bright colors, pop artists changed (나)that thought.

[충북 ○○중]

18 위 글의 밑줄 친 (가)Probably not이 글에서 의미하는 바로 가장 적절한 것은? (4점)

① 아마 그것들이 유명하지 않아 보일 것이다.

② 아마 그것들이 예술 작품처럼 보이지 않을 것이다.

③ 아마 사람들은 그 예술 작품들을 이해할 수 없을 것이다.

④ 아마 사람들은 그 예술 작품들을 좋아하지 않을 것이다.

⑤ 아마 그것들이 대중적인 예술처럼 보이지 않을 것이다.

[대전 ○○중]

19 위 글의 내용과 일치하지 <u>않는</u> 것은? (3점)

① pop은 popular의 줄임말이다.

② pop art는 1950년대 미국에서 시작되었다.

③ 1950년대의 팝 아트 예술가들은 쉽고 재미있는 무언가를 만들고 싶었다.

④ 팝 아트 예술가들은 TV, 만화책, 잡지와 광고에 있는 이미지들을 사용했다.

⑤ 팝 아트는 대중들이 이해하기에는 너무 어려웠다.

[대전 ○○중]

17 위 글의 흐름으로 보아, 주어진 문장이 들어가기에 가장 적절한 곳은? (3점)

So pop art means popular art, or art for people.

① (A)　　　② (B)　　　③ (C)

④ (D)　　　⑤ (E)

[충북 ○○중]

20 위 글의 밑줄 친 (나)가 가리키는 의미로 가장 적절한 것은? (4점)

① 예술은 이해하기 어렵다.

② 팝 아트는 재미있다.

③ 예술은 화려하다.

④ 팝 아트는 깊이가 없는 예술이다.

⑤ 팝 아트는 모든 사람들을 위한 예술이다.

Claes Oldenburg is another pop artist who made art ⓐ_____. He made sculptures of everyday items, such as a hamburger, cookies, and a brush. In the beginning, he created soft sculptures. They were made of plastic, paper, and other soft materials. For example, he used cloth to make toilets. Later, he made huge sculptures of ⓑ_____ items, such as an ice cream cone. (가)Because he wanted everyone to enjoy his art, he set up his works in ⓒ_____ places. He also (A)_____ a store inside his studio to sell his works. For him, artistic works were fun goods for people.

Roy Lichtenstein used cartoons in his works. They were large and painted in lively colors. He even included speech balloons in his paintings. Back then, ⓓ_____ were not regarded as an art form. However, Roy Lichtenstein thought differently. He asked himself, 'Why are they not?' Then Roy Lichtenstein broke down the wall between ⓔ_____ and popular culture by adding cartoons to art.

[서울 강남구 ○○중]

22 위 글의 흐름상 빈칸 (A)에 들어갈 가장 알맞은 말은? (3점)

① ran

② failed

③ broke

④ closed

⑤ returned

[서울 강남구 ○○중]

21 위 글의 빈칸 ⓐ~ⓔ에 들어갈 말로 가장 적절하지 않은 것은?
(3점)

① ⓐ: fun

② ⓑ: daily

③ ⓒ: outdoor

④ ⓓ: objects

⑤ ⓔ: high art

[충북 ○○중]

23 위 글의 밑줄 친 (가)를 분사구문으로 바르게 바꾼 것은? (3점)

① Wanted him to enjoy his art

② Wanting him to enjoy his art

③ Wanting everyone enjoy his art

④ Wanted everyone to enjoy his art

⑤ Wanting everyone to enjoy his art

Lesson 8 Have Fun with Art! **47**

24 Roy Lichtenstein은 만화를 예술에 첨가해서 무엇을 했는가?

(3점)

① 만화 카페를 운영했다.

② 다양한 장르의 만화를 창조해 냈다.

③ 순수 예술과 대중문화 사이의 벽을 허물었다.

④ 순수 예술 작품을 야외에 설치하여 대중화시켰다.

⑤ 특별한 주제와 창의적인 생각으로 만화를 재창조해
냈다.

26 위 글을 읽고, 〈보기〉의 학생들 중 글의 내용에 대해 올바르게
설명하고 있는 학생은?

(4점)

보기

- 석형: Claes Oldenburg의 작품 활동 후반 작
품은 주로 천 같은 부드러운 소재들로 만들어
지곤 했지.
- 정원: Claes Oldenburg의 작품 활동 목적은
작품 활동 초반에서 후반으로 가면서 달라졌
어.
- 준완: Claes Oldenburg는 모든 사람들이 그
의 작품을 즐길 수 있도록 다양한 노력을 했던
것 같아.
- 익준: Claes Oldenburg의 작품 활동 후반 작
품을 즐기기 위해서는 그의 작업실을 방문해
야만 하는데, 같이 갈래?
- 송화: Claes Oldenburg가 야외 장소에 거대
한 조각품을 설치한 이유는 자신의 작품을 대
중들에게 팔기 위함이었어.

① 석형　　　② 정원　　　③ 준완

④ 익준　　　⑤ 송화

25 위 글의 내용과 가장 일치하는 것은?

(3점)

① Claes Oldenburg was a pop musician.

② Claes Oldenburg painted strange paintings in
the end.

③ Claes Oldenburg didn't want everyone to
enjoy his art.

④ Roy Lichtenstein used speech balloons in his
sculptures.

⑤ Roy Lichtenstein thought cartoons were
regarded as an art form.

[27~30] 다음 글을 읽고 물음에 답하시오.

(A)Using common images, pop art looks plain. In other words, it doesn't look artistic. But (가)it is still worth ⓐpaying attention to. Although it looks plain, it ⓑis filled meaning. Let's learn about some famous pop artists. They became famous for their special artistic ability. (나)They were able to change common objects into amazing art.

Andy Warhol ⓒis called the King of Pop Art. He found his subjects in magazines and stores. One of his famous works ⓓis made up of pictures of Marilyn Monroe, the American actor. Another work shows cans of soup. He made many copies of these works. Why did he make copies of his works? He wanted to show ⓔthat art is something you see every day.

27 위 글의 밑줄 친 ⓐ~ⓔ 중 어법상 <u>어색한</u> 것은? (2점)

① ⓐ　　　　② ⓑ　　　　③ ⓒ

④ ⓓ　　　　⑤ ⓔ

28 위 글의 밑줄 친 (가)it과 (나)They가 가리키는 것을 바르게 고른 것은? (3점)

	(가)it	(나)They
①	pop art	pop artists
②	pop art	images
③	meaning	images
④	attention	pop artists
⑤	attention	objects

29 위 글의 밑줄 친 (A)의 의미와 <u>다른</u> 것은? (4점)

① Though pop art uses common images, it looks plain.

② Since pop art uses common images, it looks plain.

③ As pop art uses common images, it looks plain.

④ Pop art uses common images, so it looks plain.

⑤ Because pop art uses common images, it looks plain.

30 위 글의 바로 뒤에 이어질 내용으로 가장 자연스러운 것은? (3점)

① 팝 아트의 장단점

② 팝 아트 작품의 가격 변동

③ 팝 아트 작가와 작품 소개

④ 팝 아트의 나라별 특이점

⑤ 팝 아트를 감상하는 올바른 자세

◎ 선택형 문항의 답안은 컴퓨터용 수정 싸인펜을 사용
하여 OMR 답안지에 바르게 표기하시오.
◎ 서술형 문제는 답을 답안지에 반드시 검정 볼펜으
로 쓰시오.
◎ 총 30문항 100점 만점입니다. 문항별 배점은 각
문항에 표시되어 있습니다.

[울산 ○○중]

01 다음 영영 풀이의 빈칸에 들어가기에 가장 알맞은 말은? (3점)

advertising: the activity of _____
people to buy products or services

① following
② displaying
③ respecting
④ supporting
⑤ persuading

[서울 강남구 ○○중]

02 다음 빈칸에 들어갈 말이 바르게 연결된 것은? (4점)

• Let's _____ with pop music.
• The teachers should _____ their
  students.
• The band members _____ the drums
  for the performance.

① have fun	care about	set up
② laugh off	get hurt	trip over
③ come true	add up	have fun
④ make copies	put aside	add up
⑤ add up	trip over	pick out

[대전 ○○중]

03 다음 영영 풀이에 해당하는 단어로 알맞은 것은? (3점)

the ability to think, reason, and understand
instead of doing things automatically

① value
② object
③ emotion
④ performance
⑤ intelligence

[대전 ○○중]

04 다음 문장을 분사구문으로 바꿀 때, 빈칸에 들어갈 말로 알맞은
것은? (3점)

Because he had a fever, he couldn't go to
work.
→ _____ a fever, he couldn't go to
　 work.

① Had
② Being had
③ Having
④ To have
⑤ Not having

[대전 ○○중]

05 다음 빈칸에 들어갈 말로 어법상 알맞은 것은? (2점)

The art gallery is worth _____.

① to watch
② watches
③ watched
④ watching
⑤ watch

06 다음 문장과 뜻이 같도록 바르게 바꿔 쓴 것은? (3점)

> Smiling brightly, she waved at me.

① When I smiled brightly, she waved at me.

② While I smiled brightly, she waved at me.

③ While she smiled brightly, she waved at me.

④ Because she smiles brightly, she waved at me.

⑤ When I was smiling brightly, she waved at me.

07 다음 중 어법상 올바른 문장은? (4점)

① Heard the news, the little girl cried.

② While sat on the bench, she had a sandwich.

③ Surprising at the news, I couldn't say anything.

④ Didn't seeing the police officer, he didn't run away.

⑤ Having walked a long way, he sat down to take some rest.

08 다음 중 우리말을 바르게 영작한 것은? (3점)

> John은 그녀의 손을 꽉 잡은 채로 걸어갔다.

① John walked, held her hand tight.

② John walked, holding her hand tight.

③ John was walking, held her hand tight.

④ John was walking, hold her hand tight.

⑤ John walked, not holding her hand tight.

09 다음 짝지어진 문장들의 의미가 같도록 빈칸에 알맞은 말을 쓰시오. (한 칸에 한 단어씩 쓸 것.) (6점)

> (1) This is the house he lives in.
> = This is the house _____ he lives.
> = This is the house _____ _____ he lives.

> (2) As it was fine, we went on a picnic.
> = _____ _____ fine, we went on a picnic.

10 다음 밑줄 친 우리말과 일치하도록 〈보기〉의 단어들을 모두 사용하여 〈조건〉에 맞게 완성하시오. (5점)

Last Saturday I went to my friend's house to watch a movie. The title of the movie was *My Son*. I watched it because my friend recommended it. I liked the story of the movie. The story was about a brave man who tried to find his son. The main character was John. He was played by the actor Roy Jones, who was fantastic. It was touching. 감정에 호소하는 그 장면들을 보는 동안 나는 감명을 받았습니다. The movie was a really good movie.

> **보기**
>
> move, emotional, watch, the

> **조건**
>
> • 7단어로 쓸 것.
> • 단어를 추가하거나 〈보기〉의 단어를 변형할 수 있음.

→ _____

11 다음 밑줄 친 ⓐ~ⓔ 중 대화의 흐름상 어색한 것은? (3점)

B: Sandy, you can listen to many kinds of music in this music library.
G: That's cool, Bob. ⓐCan I listen to classical music?
B: Sure. ⓑDo you like classical music?
G: Yes. Beethoven is one of my favorite musicians. How about you?
B: ⓒI like classical music more than pop music.
G: I see. ⓓWhat do you like most about pop music?
B: ⓔI'm really fascinated by its exciting rhythms.

*B: Boy, G: girl

① ⓐ ② ⓑ ③ ⓒ
④ ⓓ ⑤ ⓔ

12 다음 대화의 빈칸에 들어갈 말로 가장 알맞은 것은? (3점)

A: I heard you joined the drawing arts club.
B: I did. We get together every Wednesday.
A: _____
B: It's great. I learn many useful skills of drawing arts.

① How can I join?
② How do you do?
③ What should I do?
④ How do you like it?
⑤ What's your hobby?

13 다음 ⓐ~ⓔ 중 대화의 흐름상 <u>어색한</u> 것은? (3점)

> Bora: Andy, you went to the art museum, didn't you?
>
> Andy: Yes. They had a special Chagall exhibition.
>
> Bora: ⓐ<u>How was it</u>?
>
> Andy: It was fantastic! I was fascinated by the colors in his paintings and his creativity.
>
> Bora: ⓑ<u>No wonder</u>. He was one of the greatest painters ever. What else did you see in the museum?
>
> Andy: I went to a gift shop and saw things like umbrellas, cups, and backpacks. Famous works of art were printed on them.
>
> Bora: ⓒ<u>Did you buy anything?</u>
>
> Andy: Yes. I bought this T-shirt. ⓓ<u>What do you like?</u>
>
> Bora: ⓔ<u>It looks great on you.</u>
>
> Andy: Thank you.

① ⓐ   ② ⓑ   ③ ⓒ

④ ⓓ   ⑤ ⓔ

14 대화의 흐름으로 보아 주어진 문장이 들어가기에 가장 적절한 곳은? (3점)

> How do you like my umbrella?

> A: Which painting did you choose?
>
> B: I chose *On White II*. (ⓐ)
>
> A: What did you like most about the painting? (ⓑ)
>
> B: I was fascinated by the bright colors. (ⓒ)
>
> A: What did you design with the painting? (ⓓ)
>
> B: I designed an umbrella. (ⓔ)
>
> A: I think it's beautiful.

① ⓐ   ② ⓑ   ③ ⓒ

④ ⓓ   ⑤ ⓔ

15 다음 중 짝지어진 대화가 <u>어색한</u> 것은? (2점)

① A: Why don't we make a tower?

    B: Wonderful! Let's build a tower like the Leaning Tower of Pisa.

② A: The other day I watched a play, *A Love Story in the War*.

    B: Oh, how did you like the play?

③ A: Do you know the band called *the Brothers*?

    B: Oh, I've heard about them. The singer is famous.

④ A: Did you finish your art homework?

    B: Yes. I drew the face of my role model on a plate.

⑤ A: Who is your role model?

    B: Well, I drew myself surfing in the sea.

16 다음 주어진 문장에 이어지는 대화의 순서를 가장 적절하게 배열한 것은? (3점)

A: How did you like the festival?

(A) I was satisfied with the special guest. Do you know the band called *the BOB*?
(B) I have heard about them. The singer is famous.
(C) No wonder. I hope to enjoy it someday.
(D) Yes. His performance was great.

① (A)-(B)-(C)-(D)
② (A)-(B)-(D)-(C)
③ (C)-(B)-(A)-(D)
④ (D)-(A)-(C)-(B)
⑤ (D)-(C)-(B)-(A)

17 다음 글의 내용과 일치하는 것은? (2점)

Last Saturday I went to my friend's house to watch a movie. The title of the movie was *My Son*. I watched it because my friend recommended it. I liked the story of the movie. The story was about a brave man who tried to find his lost son. The main character was John. He was played by the actor Roy Jones, who was fantastic. It was touching. Watching the emotional scenes, I was moved.

① 화자는 지난주 목요일에 친구 집에 갔다.
② 화자는 친구에게 'My Son'이라는 영화를 추천했다.
③ 영화의 이야기는 사고를 당한 아들을 살리기 위해 애쓰는 한 남자에 대한 것이었다.
④ 영화 주인공의 이름은 'John'이고 'Roy Jones'라는 배우가 그 역할을 연기했다.
⑤ 특수 효과를 이용한 장면들을 보면서 화자는 감동을 받았다.

[18~21] 다음 글을 읽고 물음에 답하시오.

Pop is short for popular. So pop art means popular art, or art for people. It began in the 1950s in America. Pop artists at that time wanted to create something fun and easy. (A)_____ difficult traditional art works, ⓐthey turned their eyes to popular culture. They used images from TV, comic books, magazines, and advertising. When people saw familiar images in art exhibitions, ⓑthey found ⓒthem refreshing. Since then, pop art has become truly popular. People thought that art was too difficult to understand. By using daily images and bright colors, pop artists changed ⓓthat thought.

[서울 강남구 ○○중]

18 위 글의 밑줄 친 ⓐ~ⓓ가 가리키는 것을 찾아 정확하게 적으시오. (6점)

ⓐ: _____

ⓑ: _____

ⓒ: _____

ⓓ: _____

[서울 강남구 ○○중]

19 위 글의 (A)에 들어갈 가장 알맞은 말은? (3점)

① For

② With

③ Through

④ Although

⑤ Instead of

[서울 강남구 ○○중]

20 위 글의 내용과 가장 일치하지 <u>않는</u> 것은? (4점)

① Pop art is popular now.

② Pop artists used bright colors.

③ Pop artists used daily images.

④ Pop art began in the 1950s in America.

⑤ Pop artists turned their eyes to difficult traditional art works.

[경기 ○○중]

21 위 글에서 언급되지 않은 것은? (3점)

① What does pop art mean?

② What kinds of images did pop artists use?

③ What did people think about art at that time?

④ Where and when did the traditional art start?

⑤ Who changed people's idea about art?

Claes Oldenburg is another pop artist who made art fun. He made sculptures of everyday items, such as a hamburger, cookies, and a brush. In the beginning, he created soft sculptures. They were made of plastic, paper, and other soft materials. (A)_____, he used cloth to make toilets. Later, he made huge sculptures of daily items, such as an ice cream cone. (가)_____, he set up his works in outdoor places. He also ran a store inside his studio (B)to sell his works. For him, artistic works were fun goods for people.

[충북 ○○중]

22 위 글의 빈칸 (A)에 들어갈 말로 가장 적절한 것은? (3점)

① However
② Therefore
③ For example
④ In addition
⑤ On the other hand

[충북 ○○중]

23 위 글의 밑줄 친 (B)와 용법이 <u>다른</u> 것은? (3점)

① It is possible <u>to pass</u> the exam this year.
② Brian will search on the Internet <u>to do</u> his homework.
③ We drive to the country <u>to relax</u>.
④ She learned math <u>to help</u> her child.
⑤ I went to the bank <u>to get</u> some cash.

[충북 ○○중]

24 위 글의 흐름상 〈보기〉의 ⓐ~ⓔ 중 빈칸 (가)에 들어갈 수 있는 것의 개수는? (4점)

ⓐ Wanting everyone to enjoy his art
ⓑ When he wants everyone to enjoy his art
ⓒ As he wanted everyone to enjoy his art
ⓓ Although he wanted everyone to enjoy his art
ⓔ Because he wants everyone to enjoy his art

① 1개   ② 2개   ③ 3개
④ 4개   ⑤ 5개

[충북 ○○중]

25 위 글의 내용과 일치하지 <u>않는</u> 대화를 고르면? (4점)

① A: How did Claes Oldenburg make art?
   B: He made it fun.
② A: Why did Claes Oldenburg set up his works in outdoor places?
   B: Because he wanted to sell a lot of his works.
③ A: What did Claes Oldenburg use to make toilets?
   B: He used cloth to make toilets.
④ A: What did he think about artistic works?
   B: He thought they were fun goods for people.
⑤ A: In the beginning, what kinds of materials were Claes Oldenburg's sculptures made of?
   B: They were made of plastic, paper, and other soft materials.

26 Claes Oldenburg는 왜 그의 작품들을 야외에 설치했는가?

(2점)

① 설치 비용을 줄이기 위해서
② 실내에 설치하기에는 공간이 좁아서
③ 야외에 설치하는 것이 더 간편하기 때문에
④ 모든 사람이 그의 예술을 즐기기를 원했기 때문에
⑤ 여러 예술가들과 공동으로 작품을 만들었기 때문에

[27~30] 다음 글을 읽고 물음에 답하시오.

Using common images, pop art looks plain. (A) But it is still worth paying attention to. (B) Although it looks plain, it is filled with meaning. Let's learn about some famous pop artists. (C) They became famous for their special artistic ability. They were able to change common objects into amazing art.

Andy Warhol is called the King of Pop Art. He found his subjects in magazines and stores. (D) One of his famous works is (가)_____ pictures of Marilyn Monroe, the American actor. (E) Another work shows cans of soup. He made many copies of these works. Why did he make copies of his works? He wanted to show that art is something you see every day.

27 위 글의 흐름으로 보아, 주어진 문장이 들어가기에 가장 적절한 곳은? (3점)

In other words, it doesn't look artistic.

① (A)   ② (B)   ③ (C)
④ (D)   ⑤ (E)

28 위 글의 빈칸 (가)에 들어갈 말로 가장 적절한 것은? (3점)

① made up of
② surprised at
③ interested in
④ confused by
⑤ satisfied with

29 위 글에서 다음 영영 풀이에 해당하는 단어를 고르면? (3점)

objects made out of stone, wood, clay, etc. by an artist

① artists   ② subjects
③ copies   ④ sculptures
⑤ toilets

30 위 글에 대한 언급으로 옳지 <u>않은</u> 것은? (4점)

① Some pop artists had their special artistic ability, which could make them become famous.
② Common objects could be changed into art by pop artists.
③ Marilyn Monroe was an American actor.
④ We can't know why Andy Warhol made copies of his works.
⑤ Pop art is so meaningful that paying attention to it is worthy.

◎ 선택형 문항의 답안은 컴퓨터용 수정 싸인펜을 사용하여 OMR 답안지에 바르게 표기하시오.

◎ 서술형 문제는 답을 답안지에 반드시 검정 볼펜으로 쓰시오.

◎ 총 30문항 100점 만점입니다. 문항별 배점은 각 문항에 표시되어 있습니다.

[경기 ○○중]

01 다음 영영 풀이에 해당하는 단어로 가장 적절한 것은? (3점)

> to make water, air, or land dirty

① spread

② cost

③ pollute

④ afford

⑤ remove

[울산 ○○중]

02 다음 중 단어의 영영 풀이가 틀린 것은? (3점)

① afford : to be able to do something

② success : the achievement of an aim or a purpose

③ pollute : to make water, air, land, etc. dirty

④ fair : a small private event where goods are bought and sold

⑤ headband : a narrow strip of material worn around the head

[경기 ○○중]

03 다음 영영 풀이에 해당하는 단어로 알맞은 것은? (4점)

> to move or take something away from a place

① hit

② filter

③ place

④ remove

⑤ realize

[대전 ○○중]

04 다음 빈칸에 쓸 수 없는 것은? (3점)

> After a while, I checked the water, and it looked _____ clearer.

① much

② still

③ even

④ far

⑤ very

[대전 ○○중]

05 다음 중 어법상 어색한 것은? (4점)

① I am not sure whether the baby is hungry or sad.

② I wondered how could he solve the problem.

③ I don't know whether he has a bike or not.

④ I need to know how much the pencil is.

⑤ I was wondering what it was.

06 다음 ⓐ~ⓔ 중 어법상 옳은 것은 모두 몇 개인가? (5점)

> ⓐ I don't know when he come back.
> ⓑ Do you think what his father does?
> ⓒ I wonder whether you ate the snacks.
> ⓓ Who do you believe broke the window?
> ⓔ Can you tell me when she did left there?
> ⓕ Do you know if he is coming to the field trip?

① 1개   ② 2개   ③ 3개
④ 4개   ⑤ 5개

07 다음 짝지어진 두 문장의 의미가 같은 것은? (4점)

① I am sorry that my puppy is sick.
= I wish my puppy were not sick.

② I am sorry that I can't ride a bike.
= I wish I can ride a bike.

③ In fact, I didn't go to bed early last night.
= I wish I went to bed early last night.

④ Actually he didn't let me use his drone.
= I wish he lets me use his drone.

⑤ In fact, Jack doesn't know my phone number.
= I wish Jack knows my phone number.

08 다음 중 문장의 해석이 적절한 것은? (2점)

① Do you know if Peter likes baseball?
→ 만약 Peter가 야구를 좋아한다면 너는 그걸 내게 말해 줄래?

② I wonder if Jenny loves taking pictures.
→ 나는 Jenny가 사진을 찍으러 갈 것인지 궁금하다.

③ Nobody knows if it is going to rain tomorrow.
→ 내일 비가 올 것인지 아무도 모른다.

④ I don't know whether Korea will win the match.
→ 나는 한국이 언제 그 경기에서 이길지 모른다.

⑤ Everyone wonders if he will be late for the meeting.
→ 모든 사람은 그가 회의에 올 것인지 궁금해한다.

09 다음 중 어법이나 문맥상 자연스럽지 못한 문장은? (4점)

① The girl hit in the idea to use corn cobs.

② The water around us was seriously polluted.

③ I picked up some dried cobs along the road.

④ He wondered how he could solve this problem.

⑤ The filtering system can clean up all the lakes not only in my village but also in other areas.

10 다음 글에서 Tony의 상황을 가장 잘 표현한 문장은? (3점)

> Tony really wants to join the school soccer team, but he can't join because he is not good at sports.

① If I were you, I could fly to the moon.

② I wish I could join the soccer team.

③ I show off as if I won the rival.

④ But for waiting, I couldn't get an autograph of Son Heung-min.

⑤ Without your help, I couldn't become a millionaire.

11 다음 대화의 빈칸에 알맞은 말을 주어진 단어를 바르게 배열하여 완성하시오. (3점)

> A: The baby is crying. Is the baby hungry or sick?
> B: I'm not sure. I wonder (is / baby / why / crying / the). So, I don't know what to do for the baby.

→ _____

[12~13] 다음 대화를 읽고 물음에 답하시오.

> B: I'm planning to visit my uncle in Mexico.
> G: What are you going to do there, Mike?
> B: I'll spend most of my time at his house because he has a big swimming pool.
> G: That's great. Can you swim well?
> B: No, _____. So I'll have fun with a water walking ball instead.
> G: A water walking ball? What is that?
> B: It's a large ball. We go inside it and walk on the water.
> G: That must be fun.

12 위 대화의 빈칸에 들어갈 표현으로 옳은 것은? (4점)

① I wish I can, but I can't.

② I wish I could, but I can't.

③ I wished I can, but I can't.

④ I wish I could, but I couldn't.

⑤ I wished I could, but I couldn't.

13 위 대화를 읽고 답할 수 없는 질문은? (3점)

① Can Mike swim well?

② What is a water walking ball?

③ Where does Mike's uncle live?

④ Who is Mike going to play with?

⑤ What is Mike planning to do at his uncle's?

[14~16] 다음 대화를 읽고 물음에 답하시오.

Bora: What are you doing, Jessie?
Jessie: I'm drawing Dr. Rebecca, my favorite superhero.
Bora: Wow, that's great.
Jessie: Thanks. I want to read people's minds like her.
Bora: Ⓐ(Can she control ⓐthem, too?)
Jessie: Yes. She can control your mind if she wants to.
Bora: That's very cool.
Jessie: What about you? Do you also have any favorite superheroes?
Bora: Sure. I love Sky X. I want to fly like him.
Jessie: I like him, too. He can even breathe in space.
Bora: Yes. He can do anything in space.

15 위 대화의 ⓐthem이 가리키는 것을 우리말로 쓰시오.　(3점)

→ _____

16 위 대화의 괄호 Ⓐ의 문장을 주어진 단어를 활용하여 같은 뜻의 문장으로 바꿔 쓰시오.　(4점)

to, it, possible, for, is

→ _____

14 위 대화의 내용과 일치하지 <u>않는</u> 것은?　(3점)

① Jessie는 지금 그림을 그리고 있다.
② Dr. Rebecca는 Jessie가 가장 좋아하는 슈퍼 영웅이다.
③ Dr. Rebecca는 사람들의 마음을 읽을 수 있다.
④ Sky X는 우주에서 숨을 쉴 수 있지만 날 수는 없다.
⑤ Jessie도 Bora처럼 Sky X를 좋아한다.

17 다음 대화를 통해 Tony에 대해 알 수 있는 것은?　(3점)

Tony: Can you play the guitar?
Yujin: Yes, I can. What about you?
Tony: I wish I could.

① 기타를 배웠다.
② 기타를 배울 것이다.
③ 현재 기타를 못 친다.
④ 기타를 배우는 중이다.
⑤ 현재 기타를 아주 잘 친다.

18 다음 글의 바로 뒤에 이어질 내용으로 가장 자연스러운 것은?

(2점)

> Who are the people who change the world? Do you think you are so young that you can't be one of these people? In the following stories you will meet three teenagers who used their ideas to make the world a better place.

① 세상을 더 나은 곳으로 만든 위인들

② 자신의 아이디어로 세상을 더 나은 곳으로 만드는 방법

③ 자신들의 아이디어로 세상을 더 나은 곳으로 만든 10대들

④ 전 세계적으로 도움을 필요로 하는 10대들

⑤ 도움을 필요로 하는 사람들에게 도움을 주는 방법

[19~21] 다음 글을 읽고 물음에 답하시오.

> As a young girl ⓐliving in the countryside in India, I often found that the water around us was ⓑseriously polluting. I wondered ⓒhow could I solve this problem. Then I hit on the idea to use corn cobs. Useless corn cobs were everywhere in my village. I thought that the small holes in the corn cobs could filter dirty matter ⓓout of the polluting water.
>
> One day, I picked up some dried cobs along the road, washed them, and placed them in a bowl of dirty water. After a while, I checked the water, and it looked much clearer. Then, (가)나는 농부들로부터 모은 옥수수 속대를 이용하여 여과 장치를 만들었다. My system removed 70 to 80 percent of the dirty matter from the water. I hope my filtering system can clean up all the lakes not only in my village ⓔbut also other areas.
>
> ※I=Lalita Prasida

19 위 글의 밑줄 친 ⓐ~ⓔ 중에서 어법상 바르게 쓰인 것은? (3점)

① ⓐ   ② ⓑ   ③ ⓒ

④ ⓓ   ⑤ ⓔ

20 위 글의 Lalita가 여과 장치를 만들었을 때 이용한 것은? (3점)

① She used corn that she had bought in the market.

② She used plastic cups that she had collected.

③ She used corn cobs that she had collected from farmers.

④ She used corn cobs that she had bought in the market.

⑤ She used plastic cups that she had received from her neighbor.

[22~25] 다음 글을 읽고 물음에 답하시오.

'Why can't many girls in Africa go to school ⓐas I can? I wish (가)_____, too.' I had this ⓑthought when I was twelve. I realized that their families couldn't afford it. I wondered if I could do something for those girls. Then I had an idea. For my birthday, I ⓒasked my parents to buy me a sewing machine. They bought me one, and I learned how to make headbands for myself. I created ten headbands and sold them at my school. Soon, I raised enough money to send one girl in Africa to school. I couldn't stop (나)there.

I started a business to help girls in Africa who couldn't go to school. Thanks to the success of my business, I can pay the school fees for many poor girls in countries like Kenya and Uganda to go to school. I also pay for their textbooks, uniforms, and pencils.

Isn't it amazing? My advice to you is to just do something. When you see a need, act. Start small, ⓓtaking little steps. Your warm heart can change ⓔlives.

※I=Mary Grace Henry

21 위 글의 밑줄 친 (가)의 우리말과 같은 의미가 되도록 〈조건〉에 맞게 영작하시오. (5점)

(가)나는 농부들로부터 모은 옥수수 속대를 이용하여 여과 장치를 만들었다.

조건

• 14단어로 쓸 것.
• 분사구문을 이용할 것.
• 관계대명사를 이용할 것.
• collect, build를 사용할 것. (필요하면 어형을 변형할 것.)

→ _____

22 위 글의 밑줄 친 ⓐ~ⓔ의 단어와 같은 의미로 쓰인 것은?(2개) (4점)

① ⓐ: <u>As</u> we go up the mountain, we feel colder.
② ⓑ: After much <u>thought</u>, she decided to give a hand to the man.
③ ⓒ: Did she <u>ask</u> you about the accident?
④ ⓓ: I'll <u>take</u> the grey jacket.
⑤ ⓔ: He started a new <u>life</u>.

23 위 글의 흐름상 빈칸 (가)에 들어갈 알맞은 말을 5단어를 이용하여 완성하시오. (5점)

→ _____

24 위 글의 Mary가 그녀의 학교에서 판매한 것은? (2점)

① pencils
② uniforms
③ headbands
④ birthday cakes
⑤ a sewing machine

25 위 글의 밑줄 친 (나)가 의미하는 것으로 가장 적절한 것은? (3점)

① 머리띠를 만들어 학교에서 팔기
② 머리띠 만드는 법을 스스로 배우기
③ 아프리카의 한 소녀를 학교에 보낼 수 있는 돈 모으기
④ 아프리카의 빈곤층을 돕기 위한 돈 모으기
⑤ 혼자서 머리띠를 만들어서 팔기

[26~30] 다음 글을 읽고 물음에 답하시오.

One day, when I was fourteen, I came across a little girl at a science fair. She had a robotic hand that could only open and close. I was surprised that the hand had cost her 80,000 dollars! 'I wish she (가)_____ a better robotic hand,' I thought to myself. (A) With that, I started to make a much cheaper and better robotic hand.

(B) After many failures, finally, by using 3D printing technology, I was able to make a useful robotic hand for the price of only 300 dollars. (C) I decided to share the designs and software for my 3D robotic hand with others for free. (D) No one person can change the world, but we can build a better world by working together. (E) (나)<u>Two heads are better than one.</u>

※I=Easton LaChappelle

26 위 글의 빈칸 (가)에 들어갈 말로 가장 적절한 것은? (2점)

① had

② has

③ will have

④ has had

⑤ is having

27 위 글의 흐름으로 보아, 주어진 문장이 들어가기에 가장 적절한 곳은? (3점)

> Maybe someone can take what I have done and do something useful with it.

① (A)   ② (B)   ③ (C)

④ (D)   ⑤ (E)

28 위 글의 밑줄 친 속담 (나)가 문맥 속에서 의미하는 것은? (3점)

① 무소식이 희소식이니 기다려야 한다.

② 살면서 한 번쯤은 운이 좋은 날이 있다.

③ 우리는 함께 일함으로써 더 나은 세상을 만들 수 있다.

④ 일을 지시하는 사람이 많으면 되는 일도 그르치게 된다.

⑤ 행동 뒤에 일어날 법한 결과를 생각하지 않고 행동하면 안 된다.

29 위 글을 읽고 답할 수 없는 것은? (4점)

① Who did Easton meet at a science fair when he was fourteen?

② What was Easton surprised about when he went to the science fair at the age of 14?

③ What did Easton decide to do with his 3D robotic hand?

④ How can we build a better world?

⑤ Why was the girl's robotic hand so expensive?

30 위 글의 내용과 일치하지 않는 것은? (3점)

① Easton은 열네 살에 과학 박람회에서 어린 소녀를 우연히 만났다.

② 소녀는 단지 펴고 오므릴 수만 있는 로봇 손을 착용하고 있었다.

③ 소녀는 그녀의 로봇 손에 8만 달러를 지불했다.

④ Easton은 3D 프린트 기술을 사용해서 유용한 로봇 손을 만들었다.

⑤ Easton은 그의 3D 로봇 손의 디자인과 소프트웨어를 다른 사람들에게 저렴하게 판매하기로 결심했다.

MEMO

정답 및 해설

Lesson 5 (중간)

01 ⑤	**02** ⑤	**03** ④	**04** ③	**05** ①	**06** ②

07 so that he could catch the first train to Seoul   **08** ④

09 ①	**10** ⑤	**11** disappointed not to be invited		**12** ①
13 ②	**14** ①	**15** ③	**16** ③	**17** ④	**18** ②	**19** ⑤	**20** ⑤
21 ①	**22** ③	**23** ①	**24** ⑤	**25** ③	**26** ②	**27** ⑤	**28** ②
29 ①	**30** ⑤				

01 '어느 동아리에도 속해 있지 않다면 너는 우리의 동아리에 가입할 수 있어.'라는 말로 보아, 빈칸이 있는 문장은 'Do you belong to any clubs?(너는 어느 동아리에 속해 있니?)'라는 질문이 적절하다.

02 ⑤ nation flag → national flag로 고쳐야 한다.

03 sacrifice: 희생; 희생하다

04 ④ can → could로 고쳐야 어법상 적절한 문장이 된다.

05 ① have never traveled → had never traveled로 고쳐야 어법상 적절한 문장이 된다.

06 과거의 특정 시점을 기준으로 그보다 더 이전에 일어난 일이 그 시점까지 영향을 미치는 경우 혹은 과거의 특정 시점보다 앞서 일어난 일을 나타낼 경우에 과거완료 시제인 'had+p.p.'를 쓸 수 있다.

07 so that이 이끄는 절은 목적을 나타내어 '~하기 위해서, ~하도록'이라는 의미를 나타낸다. so that이 이끄는 절의 동사는 can, may와 함께 주로 쓰인다.

08 A가 "넌 윤동주를 알고 있지, 그렇지 않니?"라고 질문하자, 이에 B가 "그는 한국이 일본의 지배하에 있을 때 많은 아름다운 시를 썼어."라고 대답했다. 따라서 빈칸에 들어갈 말로 ④ I've heard his name.(그의 이름을 들어 본 적이 있어.)가 적절하다.

09 "그 미술관은 틀림없이 흥미로울 거야."라는 A의 말에 대해 "응. 어서 그곳을 방문하고 싶어!"라는 B의 대답은 흐름상 가장 자연스럽다.

10 "노래 대회에 대한 조언 정말 고마워."라는 감사의 응답으로 ⑤ I can't thank you enough.(뭐라고 감사의 말씀을 드려야 할지 모르겠네요.)는 적절하지 않다.

11 '주어+be동사+감정형용사+to부정사구'의 순서로 쓴다. to부정사구에는 감정의 원인이 되는 내용을 쓰고, to부정사의 부정은 to부정사 앞에 not을 붙여 부정형을 만든다.

12 수원 화성은 (사람들에 의해) 지어졌으므로 was built가 알맞다.

13 수원 화성은 사람들을 보호하기 위해 지어졌으며, 정조의 명을 받은 정약용의 감독 하에 건설되었다고 언급되어 있다.

14 ①은 부사적 용법 중 목적을 나타내고 나머지는 모두 감정의 원인을 나타낸다.

15 "그 미술관은 틀림없이 흥미로울 거야."라는 A의 말에 "응, 난 미술에 관심 없어."라는 B의 대답은 흐름상 자연스럽지 않다.

16 Andy와 보라는 일본 식민지 시대에 살았던 시인 윤동주에 대해서 이야기하고 있다. (C)She led the March 1st Movement in Cheonan.(그녀는 천안에서 3.1 운동을 이끌었어.)는 문맥상 적절하지 않다.

17 보라는 Andy에게 윤동주 박물관에 갈 건데 같이 가자고 제안하자, Andy는 승낙했고, 언제 갈 건데 묻자, 보라는 다음 주 토요일에 갈 거고 윤동주 박물관은 경복궁 근처에 있다고 답한다. 따라서 ④번이 대화의 내용과 일치한다.

18 위 글에서 김구는 그의 인생 대부분을 일본 지배로부터 한국의 독립을 위해 싸우면서 보냈다고 언급되어 있다. 따라서 ⓑ dependence(의존)가 아니라 independence(독립)로 고치는 것이 문맥상 적절하다.

19 Kim Koo formed the secret organization in 1931 to fight against Japan. Lee Bongchang and Yun Bonggil belonged to the group.이라고 언급되어 있다.

20 두 번째 문단에 따르면, 김구는 대한민국 임시 정부에 합류하였고 후에 주석이 되었다('There he joined the Government of the Republic of Korea and later became its president.')고 언급되어 있다.

21 위 글에서 김구는 '위대한 국가적 영웅'(ⓐ)으로 한국의 독립을 위해(ⓓ) 싸웠다. 또한 1900년대에 학교를 세워 젊은이들을 교육했으며(ⓑ), 1919년에 대한민국 임시정부에 합류했으며 후에 주석이 되었다고(ⓒ) 언급되어 있다.

22 ⓐ worn → wearing / ⓔ have been → had been으로 고쳐야 어법상 적절한 문장이 된다.

23 윤봉길 의사의 "제 시계는 새것이지만, 더 이상 필요하지 않습니다."라는 말은 문맥상 자신은 조국의 독립을 위해 죽을 준비가 되어 있어서 더 이상 필요 없다는 뜻이다.

24 위 글에서는 ⑤ '김구는 중국 상하이로 간 후에 무엇을 했나요?'에 대해서는 언급된 바 없다.

25 두 번째 문단에 'After completing the tour of the museum, we moved to the tombs of the three heroes, Lee Bongchang, Yun Bonggil, and Baek Jeonggi.'라고 언급되어 있다.

26 김구 선생은 일본에 대항하기 위해 비밀 조직을 결성했다는 의미가 자연스러우므로, ⓑfor는 against(~에 저항하여)로 고치는 것이 적절하다.

27 '그렇게 함으로써, 그는 세 명의 의사에 대한 깊은 애정과 존경을 보여 주었다.'라는 문장이 들어가기에 가장 적절한 곳은 김구 선생

이 일본에 있던 세 의사의 시신을 한국으로 가져왔다고 이야기하고 있는 (E)이다.

28 문맥상 윤봉길 의사의 시계가 새것이었고 김구의 시계는 오래된 것이었는데, 윤봉길 의사는 김구 선생에게 시계를 바꾸자고 이야기하면서 자신은 독립을 위해 죽을 준비가 되었기 때문에 더 이상 새 시계가 필요 없다고 한다. 따라서 김구의 시계는 (가), (마)이고, 윤봉길 의사의 시계는 (나), (다), (라)이다.

29 위 글에서 ① '김구가 한인 애국단 사진을 찍었다.'는 내용은 언급된 바 없다.

30 위 글에서 화자는 자신의 소원이 무엇보다도 조국의 독립이라고 여러 번 말함으로써 조국의 독립을 강조하고 있다. 따라서 화자의 심경으로 가장 적절한 것은 ⑤ determined(단단히 결심한)이다.

Lesson 6 (중간)

1회

> **01** ① **02** ③ **03** ② **04** ⑤ **05** ③ **06** ①
> **07** I suggest we learn **08** ① **09** ⑤ **10** ② **11** ③ **12** ④
> **13** What would[will] you recommend that I take? **14** ③
> **15** ⑤ **16** ② **17** ④ **18** Being the symbol of the nation
> **19** don't become confused when someone uses the word kiwi, which has several meanings
> **20** ⑤ **21** ④ **22** ⑤ **23** ③ **24** ② **25** ① **26** ⑤ **27** ②
> **28** ③ **29** ③, ⑤ **30** ②

01 '특정한 지역에서 본래부터 살았던 사람이나 동물'이라는 영영 풀이가 가리키는 것은 ① native(토착민, 토종)이다.

02 (A) all year round: 일년 내내
(B) native: 태어난 곳의
(C) rival: 경쟁자, 경쟁 상대

03 come to one's mind: 생각이 떠오르다 / be known as ~ : ~로 알려져 있다

04 B는 장래에 대해 걱정하면서 무엇을 해야 할지와 무슨 일을 할 수 있을지 모르겠다고 말하고 있다. 따라서 이에 대한 A의 반응으로 ⑤ I don't think you should visit career centers.(나는 네가 직업 센터를 방문해서는 안 된다고 생각해.)는 적절하지 않다.

05 첫 번째 문장은 계속적 용법의 관계대명사가 들어갈 자리이다. 선행사가 a teacher이므로 who를 쓴다. 계속적 용법에서는 관계대명사 that은 쓰지 않는다. 두 번째 문장은 선행사가 watch이므로 which나 that을 쓸 수 있다.

06 ①은 '그가 다리를 다친 것이 나를 우울하게 했다'는 의미의 문장이다. 따라서 who를 which로 고쳐야 어법상 적절한 문장이 된다.

07 "I suggest ~."는 "난 ~를 제안해."라는 뜻으로 상대방에게 제안을 하는 표현이다. "Why don't you ~?", "What about ~?",

"How about ~?" 등으로 바꿔 쓸 수 있다.

08 ①은 일반적인 형용사이고, 나머지는 감정을 나타내는 형용사들이다.

09 ⑤는 '그가 다리를 다친 것이 나를 슬프게 했다'는 의미의 문장이다. 이때 쓰인 which는 앞 문장 전체를 받고 나머지 which는 모두 선행사를 받는다.

10 B가 작년에 방문했던 여행지와 그곳이 너무 훌륭했다고 말하고 있다. 따라서 빈칸에 들어갈 A의 말로 가장 적절한 것은 ② Let's share travel experiences.(여행 경험을 공유하자.)이다.

11 ⓒ have → has / ⓓ because of → because로 고쳐야 어법상 적절한 문장이 된다.

12 여학생이 미국인 친구가 포트럭 저녁 식사에 자기를 초대했다고 말한다. 이에 남학생이 여학생에게 저녁 식사에서 같이 먹을 음식을 가져가야 한다고 충고한다(C). 여학생은 무엇을 가져가야 하는지 추천해 달라고 묻자(A), 이에 남학생이 한국 음식인 김밥을 가져가라고 제안(B)하는 순서가 되는 것이 흐름상 가장 자연스럽다.

13 '당신은 무엇을 ～하기를 추천하나요?'는 What would[will] you recommend ～?로 쓸 수 있다. that I (should) take: 가져가야 할지

14 세라는 영국 요리인 피시앤칩스를 만들고 싶다고 했다. 이에 Brian은 피시앤칩스가 어떻게 생겼는지 묻고 세라의 피시앤칩스에 대한 이야기를 듣고 "That sounds interesting."이라고 했다.

15 (A)에는 홍콩이 멋지다고 하는 것으로 보아, 홍콩 방문이 기대된다는 I'm looking forward to our visit.라는 말이 들어가는 것이 적절하고, (B)에는 B가 A에게 무엇을 해야 할지 의견을 묻고 A가 빅토리아 피크에 관해서 이야기하고 있으므로 빅토리아 피크에 방문할 것을 제안하는 I suggest we visit Victoria Peak.라는 말이 들어가는 것이 적절하다.

16 "I suggest you ～."는 "난 네가 ～할 것을 제안해."라는 뜻으로 상대방에게 제안을 하는 표현이다. "Why don't you ～?", "What about ～?", "How about ～?" 등으로 바꿔 쓸 수 있다.

17 ④ How long has Andy lived in Philadelphia?(Andy는 필라델피아에서 얼마나 오래 살았는가?)에 대해서는 언급된 바 없다.

18 분사구문은 「접속사+주어+동사」로 이루어진 부사절을 분사를 포함하는 부사구로 표현한 것으로 시간, 이유나 원인, 조건 등을 나타낸다. 분사구문은 접속사와 주어를 생략하고 동사원형에 -ing를 붙여 만든다.

19 관계대명사 that은 계속적 용법으로 사용되지 않는다. 선행사가 the word kiwi이므로 that을 which로 고치는 것이 적절하다.

20 '당신은 마오리 마을을 방문하고 마오리 문화를 경험할 수 있습니다'라는 문장이 들어가기에 가장 적절한 곳은 '여러 지역에 마오리 마을이 있다.'는 문장 다음인 (E)에 오는 것이 적절하다.

21 ⓐ live on: ~에서 살다

ⓑ at: ~에서

ⓒ in English: 영어로

22 ⑤ How do visitors feel when they say "kia ora" to the Maori?(방문자들이 마오리 사람들에게 "kia ora"라고 말할 때 어떤 기분이 드는가?)에 대해서는 언급된 바 없다.

23 마오리족은 뉴질랜드의 원주민이다.('The Maori are the native people of New Zealand.')라고 언급되어 있다.

24 ⓑ wild → wildly로 고쳐야 어법상 적절한 문장이 된다.

25 (A)matches는 '경기'라는 뜻의 명사로 사용되었다.

② 성냥 ③ 짝, (잘 어울리는) 한 쌍 ④ 일치하다 ⑤ 어울리다

26 위 글에 따르면, 뉴질랜드 사람들은 중요한 행사에서 haka를 춘다고 하면서 뉴질랜드의 국가대표 럭비 팀 선수들이 시합 전에 하카를 춘다고 예를 들고 있다. 따라서 빈칸에 들어갈 말로 가장 적절한 것은 ⑤ For example(예를 들어)이다.

27 위 글에 따르면, 전쟁 춤으로 haka를 추기 시작했다('The Maori people, who you've already heard about, started doing the haka as a war dance.')라고 언급되어 있다.

28 (A) be amazed by ~: ~에 (깜짝) 놀라다

(B) with: ~를 가진, ~이 있는

29 선행사가 사람이 아닌 mountains이므로 관계대명사 who는 올 수 없다. 「접속사+대명사」는 제한적 용법에는 쓰이지 않는다.

30 위 글에 따르면, 뉴질랜드는 북섬과 남섬이라는 두 개의 주요한 섬이 있다.('New Zealand has two main islands, the South Island and the North Island.)라고 언급되어 있다.

Lesson 6 (중간)

01 ③ **02** ④ **03** ①

04 (1) plaid pattern (2) all my heart (3) run out of
(4) is worth investing

05 ⑤ **06** ① **07** ⑤ **08** ① **09** ① **10** ③ **11** ⑤ **12** ④

13 ① **14** ② **15** ⑤ **16** ① **17** ⑤ **18** ④ **19** ① **20** ⑤

21 ② **22** ⑤ **23** ①, ②, ③ **24** ④, ⑤ **25** ① **26** ⑤

27 ⑤ **28** ④

29 (1) 1년 내내 눈으로 덮인 많은 산들이 있다.
(2) 많은 온천과 호수, 초원 지역이 있다.

30 ②

01 '~에 대해 고마워하다', '어떤 것의 중요성을 이해하다'라는 영영 풀이가 가리키는 것은 ③ appreciate(고마워하다, 진가를 알아보다)이다.

02 '특정한 아이디어 또는 품질을 표현하거나 나타내는 행동, 대상, 이벤트 등'을 뜻하는 것은 ④ symbol(상징)이다.

03 '같은 지역에서 또는 같은 것을 위해 경쟁하거나 싸우는 사람'이라는 영영 풀이가 가리키는 것은 ① rival(라이벌, 경쟁자)이다.

04 (1) plaid pattern: 격자무늬
(2) with all one's heart: 진심으로
(3) run out of: ~가 다 떨어지다, 바닥나다
(4) be worth -ing: ~할 가치가 있다

05 ① how is the machine operated → how the machine operates / ② the way how → the way 또는 how / ③ the more deep → the deeper / ④ the day when I went to the hospital on → the day when I went to the hospital 또는 the day on which I went to the hospital로 고쳐야 어법상 적절한 문장이 된다.

06 ①은 '그가 팔을 다친 것이 나를 슬프게 했다.'는 의미의 문장이다. 이때 쓰인 관계대명사 which는 앞 문장 전체를 받는다. 나머지는 모두 선행사를 받는다.

07 관계대명사의 계속적 용법은 관계대명사를 이용해 추가적인 정보를 제공하는 역할을 한다. 선행사가 사람일 경우엔 who를, 사물일 때는 which를 사용한다. 반드시 관계대명사 앞에 콤마(,)를 붙인다. 관계대명사 that은 계속적 용법으로 쓰지 않는 것에 주의한다.

08 B의 질문에 G는 "피시앤칩스는 감자튀김을 곁들인 튀긴 생선이야."라고 답했다. 따라서 빈칸에 들어갈 말로 가장 적절한 것은 ① What does it look like?(그것은 어떻게 생겼니?)이다.

09 관계대명사절이 선행사에 대한 부연 설명을 할 때 관계대명사의 계속적 용법을 사용한다. 선행사가 사람이면 who를, 사물이거나 문장 전체일 때는 which를 사용한다.

10 (A) 선행사가 The kiwi이므로 관계대명사 which가 적절하다.
(B) 선행사가 a Maori village이므로 관계대명사 which가 적절하다. (C) 선행사가 people이므로 관계대명사는 who가 적절하다.

11 potluck party는 '초대받은 모든 사람들이 음식을 나누어 먹는 파티'이다.

12 ⓐ few → a few / ⓑ Most famous → The most famous / ⓒ which 삭제 또는 which filled → which is filled / ⓔ you visited → you (should) visit로 고쳐야 어법상 적절한 문장이 된다.

13 세호는 필라델피아에 갈 것인데 Jessie와 Andy에게 조언을 구하고 있다. 따라서 ① Seho has been to the Independence Hall before.(세호는 전에 독립 기념관에 가 본 적 있다.)라는 내용은 위 대화의 내용과 일치하지 않는다.

14 "피시앤칩스를 먹고 싶다."라는 A의 말에 대해 "그건 내가 제일 좋아하는 거야. 그건 어떻게 생겼니?"라는 B의 대답은 흐름상 자연스럽지 않다.

15 "Let's talk about ~."은 "~에 대해서 이야기해 보자."라는 의미

의 문장으로, 대화의 주제를 소개할 때 쓸 수 있는 표현이다. ⑤ Can I get your advice on ~?은 "~에 대해 당신의 조언을 구할 수 있을까요?"라는 의미의 문장이다.

16 knee length: 무릎 길이

17 많은 사람들이 재충전을 위해 아일랜드를 방문한다고 언급되어 있다. 따라서 ⓔ how to visit Ireland(아일랜드에 가는 방법)는 the reason people visit Ireland(사람들이 아일랜드를 방문하는 이유)가 적절하다.

18 '예를 들어, 뉴질랜드의 국가 대표 럭비 팀 선수들은 매 경기 전에 하카를 춘다.'라는 문장이 들어가기에 가장 적절한 곳은 뉴질랜드 사람들이 스포츠 경기나 결혼식 혹은 중요한 행사에서 하카를 춘다는 문장 다음인 (D)에 오는 것이 적절하다.

19 ⓐ scary: 무서운
ⓑ scare: 겁주다, 겁먹게 하다
ⓒ scared: 무서워하는, 겁먹은

20 ⓔIt은 인사말인 "kia ora"를 가리킨다. 나머지는 모두 마오리족을 가리킨다.

21 위 글에 따르면, 마오리족은 뉴질랜드의 원주민으로, 유럽인들이 도착하기 오래 전에 뉴질랜드에 살러 왔다.('They went to live on the islands long before Europeans arrived.')고 언급되어 있다.

22 ⑤는 to부정사의 용법 중 형용사적 용법으로 쓰였고, (A)와 나머지는 모두 감정의 원인을 나타내는 부사적 용법으로 쓰였다.

23 위 글에 따르면, 키위라는 단어는 과일과 새 그리고 국민이라고 언급되어 있다.

24 관계대명사의 계속적 용법은 관계대명사를 이용해 추가적인 정보를 제공하는 역할을 한다. 선행사가 사람일 경우엔 who를, 사물일 때는 which를 쓴다. 반드시 관계대명사 앞에 콤마(,)를 쓰며, 해석은 자연스럽게 순차적으로 한다. 관계대명사 that은 계속적 용법으로 쓰지 않는다.

25 (A) come to one's mind: 생각이 떠오르다 / (B) a couple of: 두서너 개의 / (C) be known as: ~로 알려져 있다

26 위 글에서는 키위라는 단어가 가진 여러 의미에 대해서 설명하고 있다. 따라서 위 글의 제목으로 가장 적절한 것은 ⑤ What Does the Word Kiwi Mean in New Zealand?(뉴질랜드에서 키위라는 단어는 무슨 의미를 갖고 있는가?)이다.

27 Kiwi is also the name of one of New Zealand's native birds.(키위는 또한 뉴질랜드의 토종 새들 중 하나의 이름이다.)라고 언급되어 있다.

28 ⓓhave made → have been made로 고쳐야 어법상 적절한 문장이 된다.

29 위 글에 따르면, 남섬은 'there are mountains which are covered with snow all year round.'로, 북섬은 'there are

many hot springs, lakes, and areas with green grass.'라고 언급되어 있다.

30 위 글은 뉴질랜드가 자연의 아름다움을 간직한 곳이고 뉴질랜드에 있는 두 개 섬의 특징에 대해서 설명하고 있다. 따라서 위 글의 제목으로 가장 적절한 것은 ② New Zealand's Fantastic Natural Environment(뉴질랜드의 환상적인 자연 환경)이다.

Lesson 7 (기말) 1회

01 ④	02 ②	03 ④	04 ①	05 ④	06 ⑤	07 ③

08 Jason shows how he repairs his car.   **09** ②

10 (A) 방법 / (B) 그것이 내가 그 어려운 문제를 푼 방법이다.

11 ②	12 ④	13 ③	14 ③	15 ②	16 ②	17 ④	18 ⑤
19 ④	20 ⑤	21 ①	22 ②	23 ⑤	24 ③	25 ①	26 ③
27 ①	28 ④	29 ②	30 ⑤				

01 hurt와 wound는 '상처', '부상'이라는 뜻을 가진 단어들로 유의어 관계이다. thoughtful과 considerate는 '사려 깊은'이라는 뜻을 가진 단어들이다.

02 ⓐ regret: 후회하다
ⓑ casual: 무심한
ⓒ wound: 상처; 상처를 입히다
ⓓ accidentally: 뜻하지 않게, 우연히
ⓔ advertising: 광고

03 ④proper는 '적절한, 올바른'이라는 뜻을 가진 형용사이다.

04 ② where → which 또는 that / ③ the way which → the way 또는 the way in which / ④ the reason which → the reason why / ⑤ where → when으로 고쳐야 어법상 적절한 문장이 된다.

05 '~하면 할수록, 더 …하다'라는 표현은 「The+비교급+주어+동사 ~, the+비교급+주어+동사 …」의 어순으로 쓴다. 따라서 주어진 단어들을 배열하면, 'The more sincere your apology is, the better it will be received.'가 된다.

06 ① how he plants a tree in → how he plants a tree / ② where we visited at → where we visited / ③ in where → in which 또는 where / ④ what → why로 고쳐야 어법상 적절한 문장이 된다.

07 '어떻게 ~하는지'는 「how+주어+동사」의 형태로 쓴다. 의문사절은 문장 내에서 주어, 목적어, 보어로 쓰일 수 있다.

08 관계부사 how와 the way는 같이 쓸 수 없으므로 how를 쓸 땐 선행사 the way를 생략한다. 선행사 the way를 쓸 땐 관계부사 how를 생략한다.

09 ⓑ failing → to fail / ⓓ where → which 또는 that / ⓕ

where → which 또는 where the artist was born in → where the artist was born / ⓖ that → which / ⓗ The famous → The more famous / ⓘ which I liked it very much → which I liked very much / ⓙ the better you will have photos → the better photos you will have로 고쳐야 어법상 적절한 문장이 된다.

10 방법을 나타내는 관계부사에서 the way how라는 표현은 쓰이지 않으며, the way 또는 how로 쓴다.

11 "난 실수로 엄마가 가장 좋아하는 접시를 깼어."라는 A의 말에 "넌 의사에게 진찰을 받을 수 있어."라는 B의 대답은 흐름상 자연스럽지 않다.

12 부가의문문은 상대방의 동의를 구하거나 사실을 확인하기 위해 평서문 끝에 짧게 붙이는 의문문이다. (A) 앞 문장이 긍정문일 때는 부정의 부가의문문으로, 앞 문장이 부정문일 때는 긍정의 부가의문문으로 쓴다. 따라서 haven't you가 어법상 적절하다. / (B) be busy -ing: ~하느라 바쁘다 / (C) 사람의 성격이나 태도를 나타낼 때 의미상의 주어로 'of+목적격'을 사용한다.

13 Jessie는 Andy의 도움 요청을 거절하지 않는다(ⓐ). Jessie는 Amy의 핸드폰 케이스가 부서졌다고 말하면서 핸드폰 케이스를 추천해 준다(ⓓ). 두 달 전, Andy가 다리를 다쳤기 때문에 Amy가 Andy를 도와주었다고(ⓔ) 언급되어 있다.

14 위 대화에서 A가 B에게 소리를 줄여 달라고 요청하자, B는 그러겠다고 대답했다. 따라서 빈칸에 들어갈 말로 가장 적절한 것은 ③ turn it down(소리를 줄이다)이다.

15 ⓑ was used to → used to / ⓒ tell → telling으로 고쳐야 어법상 적절한 문장이 된다.

16 위 대화에 따르면, Dustin은 섬의 어느 곳에서나 한라산을 볼 수 있다.(You can see the mountain from everywhere on the island.)고 언급했다.

17 (A), ④는 가주어 It / ①, ③은 인칭대명사 It[it] / ②, ⑤는 비인칭 주어이다.

18 hurt people's feelings: 사람들의 감정을 상하게 하다
without+(동)명사: ~하지 않고 / intend to: ~할 의도이다

19 Read the following case studies and learn three things about a proper apology.(다음 사례 연구들을 읽고, 올바른 사과에 관한 세 가지를 알아보자.)라고 언급되어 있다. 따라서 위 글 다음에 이어질 내용은 ④ Three things about a proper apology(올바른 사과에 관한 세 가지)이다.

20 위 글에서는 가족이나 가까운 사이에도 사과를 해야 한다.('People need to apologize when they do something wrong. This includes family members and the people who are close to you.)라고 언급되어 있다.

21 (A) borrow: 빌리다

(B) ignore: 무시하다
(C) close: 가까운, 친밀한

22 'let+목적어+동사원형' 어순이므로 ⓑlet go it → let it go로 고쳐야 한다.

23 (A)와 ⑤는 명사로 쓰였고, 나머지는 모두 동사로 쓰였다.

24 마지막 문단에서 '더 이상 사과하지 않는다면 더 이상의 기회도 없다.(No more apologies, no more chances.)'라고 언급되어 있다.

25 위 글에서는 빠르고 진심이 담긴 사과가 많은 문제를 해결할 수 있다고 언급했다. 따라서 빈칸 (가)에 들어갈 말로 가장 적절한 것은 ① Try to do it right now(지금 바로 사과를 해라.)이다.

26 ⓒ bumped up → bumped into(~에 부딪히다)로 고쳐야 어법상 적절한 문장이 된다.

27 June은 Mike의 건성의 사과 때문에 더욱 상처를 받았다고 한다. 따라서 ① casual(무심한, 건성의)이 적절하다.

28 위 글에서는 사과가 필요할 때 즉시 사과를 해야 한다.(when an apology is necessary, you should apologize at once.)고 언급되어 있다.

29 동명사 Saying ~(~라고 말하는 것)으로 시작하는 구를 이용해 주어를 만들 수 있다. 따라서 ② Saying you're sorry is more than just words.가 적절하다. 동명사나 to부정사구 주어는 단수 취급한다.

30 위 글에서는 ⑤ What do you need to do after saying "I'm sorry"?(미안하다고 말한 후에는 당신은 무엇을 해야 하는가?)에 대해서는 언급된 바 없다.

Lesson 7 (기말) 〔2회〕

```
01 ②  02 ①  03 ⑤  04 ⑤  05 ①, ④
06 Do you mind telling me    07 ③  08 ②  09 ②  10 ①
11 ③  12 ④  13 ③  14 ⑤  15 ②  16 ⑤  17 ③  18 ①
19 Kate가 호준이와 부딪힌 일    20 ④  21 ①  22 ⑤  23 ②
24 ③  25 ②  26 ⑤  27 ⑦  28 ③  29 ⑤
30 June didn't like how Mike had acted.
```

01 '당신이 한 일 또는 할 수 없었던 일에 대해서 아쉬움을 느끼다'라는 영영 풀이가 가리키는 것은 ② regret(후회하다)이다.

02 (A) regret: 후회하다 (B) casual clothes: 평상복

03 (A) accidentally: 우연히, 뜻하지 않게
(B) sincere: 진실된
(C) apology: 사과
(D) care about: ~에 마음을 쓰다, ~에 관심을 가지다

04 ① the more kind → the kinder / ② More you read books

→ The more books you read / ③ the good seat → the better seat / ④ The hard → The harder로 고쳐야 어법상 적절한 문장이 된다.

05 ② the way how → the way 또는 how / ③ How happened the accident → How the accident happened / ⑤ how did his uncle fix → how his uncle fixed로 고쳐야 어법상 적절한 문장이 된다.

06 "Do you mind ~?"는 "~을 해 줄래요?"라는 뜻으로 상대방에게 요청할 때 사용하는 표현이다. 동사 mind는 '꺼리다'라는 뜻을 갖고 있다.

07 선행사가 the house로 장소이므로 관계부사 where를 쓴다. 관계부사 where는 '전치사(in[on, at])+관계대명사(which)'로 바꿔 쓸 수 있지만 '전치사+that'으로는 바꿔 쓸 수 없다.

08 ⓑ lower → the lower / ⓓ the most → the more / ⓔ the more fresher → the fresher로 고쳐야 어법상 적절한 문장이 된다.

09 ① how live people → how people live / ③ how had she earned → how she had earned / ④ she how could → how she could / ⑤ how will we get → how we will get으로 고쳐야 어법상 적절한 문장이 된다.

10 ⓒ the reason for why → the reason why / ⓓ How happened the accident → How the accident happened / ⓔ which → how 또는 the way / ⑧ The more expensive you buy a computer, the more you can use programs → The more expensive computer you buy, the more programs you can use로 고쳐야 어법상 적절한 문장이 된다.

11 "Do you mind ~?"는 "~을 해 줄래요?"라는 뜻으로 상대방에게 요청할 때 사용하는 표현이다. 동사 mind는 '꺼리다'라는 뜻을 갖고 있으므로 이에 대한 대답으로 요청에 수락할 때에는 No, I don't. / No, not at all. 등을, 거절할 때에는 Yes, I do. / I'm sorry, but ~ 등을 쓴다.

12 '~하면 할수록, 더 …하다'라는 표현은 「The+비교급+주어+동사 ~, the+비교급+주어+동사 …」의 어순으로 쓴다.

13 위 대화에 따르면, Amy는 작년에 댄스 경연 대회에 나갔고, 올해 댄스 경연 대회에 나가는 민수에게 충고를 해 주고 있다.

14 appreciate: 감사해하다, 고마워하다

15 "창문 좀 열어 줄래?"라는 A의 질문에 "응, 알았어. 난 추워. 밖에는 바람이 너무 많이 불어."라는 B의 대답은 흐름상 자연스럽지 않다.

16 남학생은 제주도에 가는 수희에게 해변 방문하기, 한라산 등산하기 그리고 생선회 먹는 것을 추천해 주고 있다.

17 "네가 리듬을 잘 탄다고 생각해."라는 A의 말에 "그렇구나. 진심을 다해서 그녀와 얘기해 볼게."라는 B의 대답은 흐름상 자연스럽

18 이 글은 Kate가 호준이와 부딪혀 호준이의 재킷이 더러워졌는데도 그녀는 호준이에게 사과를 하지 않은 사례를 들면서 사과의 필요성에 대해 설명하고 있으므로, 사과가 필요할 땐 즉시 사과를 해야 한다는 내용이 들어가는 가장 것이 적절하다.

19 it은 kate가 우연히 호준이와 부딪힌 일을 가리킨다.

20 ⓓ so let one mistake break → but don't let one mistake break로 고쳐야 흐름상 자연스러운 문장이 된다.

21 위 글은 선민이와 그녀의 여동생의 사례를 통해서 잘못을 했을 때는 가족 구성원이나 가까운 친구 사이일지라도 빠르고 진실한 사과를 하라는 충고의 글이다.

22 선민이와 선민이 여동생의 사례를 들어서 가족 구성원이나 가까운 사람, 친구 사이일지라도 빠르고 진실한 사과를 하라는 글이므로 ⑤ Apologies are necessary among family members and loved ones, too.가 절절하다.

23 위 글에 따르면, 선민이는 책을 빌렸지만 잃어버렸고 그 책을 빌려준 여동생에게 사과하지 않았다. 따라서 빈칸 (나)에는 ② ignore가 적절하다.

24 Sunmin's sister disliked the way Sunmin had treated her. How could her own sister ignore her feelings?라고 언급되어 있다.

25 Sunmin didn't apologize because she thought it was not important. She thought, 'We're sisters, after all.'이라고 언급되어 있다.

26 마지막 문단은 실수를 했을 때에는 아름다운 관계를 깨뜨리지 말고 빠르고 진실한 사과를 하라는 글이다. 따라서 빈칸에 들어갈 말로 가장 적절한 것은 ④ apologize(사과하다)이다.

27 (가)that은 'Mike said, with a laugh, "Sorry. June!"'을 가리킨다.

28 ⓐ intend to → intending to / ⓓ casual → sincere / ⓔ be sincerely → be sincere / ⓕ As you apologize more sincere, the others will receive your apology better. → As you apologize more sincerely, others will receive your apology better로 고쳐야 어법상 적절한 문장이 된다.

29 위 글에서는 ⑤ What are the three things about a proper apology?(올바른 사과에 대한 세 가지는 무엇인가?)에 대해서는 한 가지 사례만 언급되어 있다.

30 선행사가 방법(the way)을 나타낼 때는 관계부사 how를 사용한다. 관계부사 how는 the way와 함께 쓰지 않는다.

Lesson 8 (기말)

1회

01 ① **02** ③ **03** ④ **04** ① **05** ② **06** ④ **07** ③ **08** ③
09 ③

10 (1) Having gotten vaccinated against COVID-19, I now feel safer than before.
(2) It being sunny, she didn't take her umbrella with her.

11 ② **12** ③

13 I was fascinated by the colors in his paintings and his creativity.

14 ① **15** ④ **16** ② **17** ② **18** ② **19** ⑤ **20** ① **21** ④
22 ① **23** ⑤ **24** ③ **25** ⑤ **26** ③ **27** ② **28** ① **29** ①
30 ③

01 strange: 낯선

02 '당신이 어떤 것을 하는 걸 가능하게 해 주는 자질 또는 기술'이라는 영영 풀이가 가리키는 것은 ③ ability(능력)이다.

03 be worth -ing: ~할 가치가 있다

04 be worth -ing: ~할 가치가 있다

05 분사구문은 「접속사+주어+동사」로 이루어진 부사절을 분사를 포함하는 부사구로 표현한 것으로 시간, 이유나 원인, 조건 등을 나타낸다. 분사구문은 접속사와 주어를 생략하고 동사원형에 ~ing를 붙여 만든다.

06 분사구문을 부사절로 바꿀 경우, 분사구문의 의미에 따라 부사절의 접속사가 달라진다. 위 문장은 '그가 TV를 보는 동안, 그는 전화기 소리를 들을 수 없었다.'라는 의미의 문장이다. 따라서 ④ While he was watching이 가장 적절하다.

07 분사구문은 「접속사+주어+동사」로 이루어진 부사절을 분사를 포함하는 부사구로 표현한 것으로 시간, 이유나 원인, 조건 등을 나타낸다. 분사구문은 접속사와 주어를 생략하고 동사원형에 ~ing를 붙여 만든다.

08 be worth -ing: ~할 가치가 있다

09 ⓑ heard → to hear / ⓓ that → which로 고쳐야 어법상 적절한 문장이 된다.

10 (1) 종속절의 시제가 주절의 시제보다 하나 앞선 시제이면 「having + 과거분사」로 바꾼다.
(2) 부사절의 주어와 주절의 주어가 다를 때에는 부사절의 주어를 생략하지 않는다.

11 ⓐ read → reading / ⓔ is → were[was] / ⓕ to pollute → not to pollute / ⓗ familiar → strange로 고쳐야 어법상이나 문맥상 적절한 문장이 된다.

12 Andy는 'I went to a gift shop and saw things like umbrellas, cups, and backpacks. Famous works of art were printed on them.'이라고 말했다.

13 be fascinated by: ~에 매료되다

14 A가 "이 예술 작품 좀 봐. 아름답다. 그렇게 생각하지 않니?"라고 질문하자, 이에 대한 B의 대답으로 ① I am fascinated by its colors.(나는 그것의 색깔에 반했어.)가 적절하다.

15 "How do you like ~?"는 "~이 어떤가요?"라는 뜻으로 상대방에게 만족이나 불만족을 묻는 표현이다.

16 위 대화에 따르면, Claire와 Allen은 모두 미술 수업이 마음에 든다고 했다.

17 '그래서 팝 아트는 대중적인 예술 또는 사람들을 위한 예술을 의미한다.'라는 문장은 'Pop is short for popular.(Pop은 대중적인(popular)이라는 단어의 줄임말이다.)'라는 문장 다음인 (B)에 들어가는 것이 가장 적절하다.

18 Probably not은 앞 문장 전체를 부정하는 의미로 사용되었다. 이 문장은 'They probably don't look like art works.'라는 의미이다.

19 위 글에 따르면, 팝 아트는 전통적인 예술 작품과는 달리 쉽고 신선했다고 언급되어 있다.

20 People thought that art was too difficult to understand.(사람들은 예술이 너무 어려워서 이해할 수 없었다고 생각했다.)를 가리킨다.

21 ⓓ에는 문맥상 objects(물건)가 아니라 cartoons가 들어가는 것이 자연스럽다.

22 팝 아트 예술가인 Claes Oldenburg가 그의 작품을 팔기 위해 그의 작업실에서 상점을 운영했다는 내용이다. 따라서 ① ran(운영했다)가 들어가는 것이 적절하다.

23 분사구문은 「접속사+주어+동사」로 이루어진 부사절을 분사를 포함하는 부사구로 표현한 것으로 시간, 이유나 원인, 조건 등을 나타낸다. 분사구문은 접속사와 주어를 생략하고 동사원형에 ~ing를 붙여 만든다.

24 마지막 문단에 'Then Roy Lichtenstein broke down the wall between high art and popular culture by adding cartoons to art.'라고 언급되어 있다.

25 Back then, cartoons were not regarded as an art form. However, Roy Lichtenstein thought differently.(그 당시 만화는 예술의 형태로 간주되지 않았다. 하지만 Roy Lichtenstein은 다르게 생각했다.)라고 언급되어 있다.

26 위 글에 따르면, 'Because he wanted everyone to enjoy his art, he set up his works in outdoor places.'라고 언급되어 있다.

27 ⓑ is filled → is filled with로 고쳐야 어법상 적절한 문장이 된다.

28 (가)it은 pop art를 가리킨다.
(나)They는 pop artists를 가리킨다.

29 (A)Using common images, pop art looks plain.은 분사구문이 쓰인 문장으로, '흔한 이미지를 사용하기 때문에 평범해 보인다.'라고 해석할 수 있다.

30 첫 번째 문단에서 Let's learn about some famous pop artists.(몇 명의 유명한 팝 아트 예술가들에 대해서 알아보자.)라고 언급되어 있다. 첫 번째로 Andy Warhol의 작가와 작품이 소개되었다. 따라서 이어서 나머지 작가와 작품 소개가 이어지는 것이 자연스럽다.

Lesson 8 (기말)

01 ⑤ **02** ① **03** ⑤ **04** ③ **05** ④ **06** ③ **07** ⑤ **08** ②
09 (1) where, in which (2) It being
10 Watching the emotional scenes, I was moved.
11 ③ **12** ④ **13** ④ **14** ⑤ **15** ⑤ **16** ② **17** ④
18 ⓐ: pop artists ⓑ: people ⓒ: familiar images
    ⓓ: People thought that art was too difficult to understand.
19 ⑤ **20** ⑤ **21** ④ **22** ③ **23** ① **24** ② **25** ② **26** ④
27 ① **28** ① **29** ④ **30** ④

01 advertising(광고)은 '사람들에게 제품이나 서비스를 구매하도록 설득하는 활동'이므로 persuading이 적절하다.

02 have fun: 재미있게 놀다
care about: ~에게 관심을 가지다
set up: 설치하다

03 '어떤 일을 자동적으로 하는 대신에 생각하고, 추론하고, 이해하는 능력'이라는 영영 풀이가 가리키는 것은 ⑤ intelligence(지성, 지능)이다.

04 분사구문은 「접속사+주어+동사」로 이루어진 부사절을 분사를 포함하는 부사구로 표현한 것으로 시간, 이유나 원인, 조건 등을 나타낸다. 분사구문은 접속사와 주어를 생략하고 동사원형에 ~ing를 붙여 만든다.

05 be worth -ing: ~할 가치가 있다

06 분사구문을 부사절로 바꿀 경우, 분사구문의 의미에 따라 부사절의 접속사가 달라진다. 위 문장은 '그녀는 밝게 웃으면서 나에게 손을 흔들었다.'라는 의미의 문장이다.

07 ① Heard → Hearing / ② sat → sitting / ③ Surprising → Surprised / ④ Didn't seeing → Not seeing으로 고쳐야 어법상 적절한 문장이 된다.

08 분사구문을 만드는 방법은 접속사절에서 접속사를 없애고, 반복되는 주어를 뺀다. 부사절과 주절의 시제가 같을 때에는 부사절의 동사를 현재분사(동사원형+-ing)로 바꾼다.

09 (1) 선행사가 the house로 장소이므로 관계부사 where를 쓴다.

관계부사 where는 '전치사+관계대명사(which)'로 바꿔 쓸 수 있다. (2) 분사구문을 만들 때, 부사절의 주어와 주절의 주어가 다를 경우엔 부사절의 주어를 생략하지 않는다.

10 분사구문은 「접속사+주어+동사」로 이루어진 부사절을 분사를 포함하는 부사구로 표현한 것으로 시간, 이유나 원인, 조건 등을 나타낸다. 분사구문은 접속사와 주어를 생략하고 동사원형에 -ing를 붙여 만든다. 따라서 주어진 우리말을 'Watching the emotional scenes, I was moved.'로 영작할 수 있다.

11 위 대화에 따르면, 여학생은 남학생에게 대중음악의 좋은 점이 무엇이냐고 묻고, 남학생은 신나는 리듬에 매력을 느낀다라고 대답하고 있다. 따라서 ⓒI like pop music more than classical music.(난 클래식 음악보다 대중음악을 더 좋아해.)로 고쳐야 문맥상 자연스럽다.

12 A의 질문에 B는 "아주 좋아. 유용한 소묘 기술들을 많이 배워."라고 답했다. 따라서 빈칸에 들어갈 A의 말로 가장 적절한 것은 ④ How do you like it?(그거 어떠니?)이다.

13 Andy의 질문에 보라는 "네게 잘 어울린다."라고 대답했다. 따라서 ⓓ를 "How do you like it?"으로 고치는 것이 문맥상 자연스럽다.

14 "How do you like ~?"는 "~이 어떤가요?"라는 뜻으로 상대방에게 만족이나 불만족을 묻는 표현이다. 따라서 "How do you like my umbrella?"가 들어가기에 가장 적절한 곳은 A가 "아름답다고 생각해."라고 대답한 곳 앞인 ⓔ이다.

15 "네 롤 모델은 누구니?"라는 A의 질문에 "난 바다에서 서핑하는 나 자신을 그렸어."라는 B의 대답은 흐름상 자연스럽지 않다.

16 A가 축제가 어땠냐고 묻자, B는 특별 초청 가수가 마음에 들었다고 답하면서, BOB라는 밴드를 아는지 물어본다(A). A는 그 밴드에 대해서 들어 본 적이 있다고 대답한다(B). B가 그 가수의 공연이 대단했다고 말하자(D), A가 자신도 언젠가 즐기고 싶다고 (C) 말하는 순서로 이어지는 것이 흐름상 가장 자연스럽다.

17 The main character was John. He was played by the actor Roy Jones, who was fantastic.이라고 언급되어 있다.

18 ⓐ they는 앞서 언급된 복수 명사 pop artists를 가리킨다. / ⓑ they는 부사절의 주어인 'people'을 가리킨다. / ⓒthem은 familiar images를 가리킨다. / ⓓthat thought는 앞 문장에서 언급된 '사람들은 예술이 너무 어려워서 이해할 수 없다고 생각했다.'는 내용을 가리킨다.

19 팝 아트 예술가들은 재미있고 쉬운 것을 만들고 싶어 한다고 언급했고, 반대로 어려운 전통 예술 작품 대신에 대중문화로 눈을 돌렸다는 흐름이 자연스러우므로, 빈칸에는 instead of(~ 대신에)가 들어가는 것이 적절하다.

20 Instead of difficult traditional art works, they turned their eyes to popular culture.(어려운 전통 예술 작품 대신에

그들은 대중문화로 눈을 돌렸다.)라고 언급되어 있다.

21 위 글에서는 ④ Where and when did the traditional art start?(전통 예술은 언제 어디에서 시작되었는가?)에 대해서는 언급된 바 없다.

22 Claes Oldenburg는 일상의 물건을 재료로, 특히 초기에는 부드러운 재료를 이용해 조각품을 만들었다. 그 예로, 변기를 만들기 위해 천을 이용했다고 한다. 따라서 빈칸에 들어갈 말로 가장 적절한 것은 ③ For example(예를 들어)이다.

23 (B)to sell은 to부정사의 부사적 용법으로 사용되었다. ①to pass는 명사적 용법이다.

24 빈칸 (가)에는 문맥상 '그는 모든 사람들이 그의 예술을 즐기기를 원했기 때문에'라는 내용이 들어가는 것이 적절하다. 따라서 ⓐ, ⓒ 문장이 문맥상 적절하다.

25 위 글에 따르면, Claes Oldenburg가 그의 작품을 야외에 설치한 이유는 모든 사람들이 그의 예술을 즐기기를 원했기 때문이라고 언급되어 있다.

26 위 글에 따르면, Claes Oldenburg가 그의 작품을 야외에 설치한 이유는 모든 사람들이 그의 예술 작품을 즐기기를 원했기 때문이라고 언급되어 있다.

27 '다시 말해서, 그것은 예술적으로 보이지 않는다.'라는 문장은 '팝아트는 흔한 이미지를 사용하기 때문에 평범해 보인다.'는 문장 다음인 (A)에 오는 것이 적절하다.

28 be made up of ~: ~로 구성되어 있다

29 '화가가 돌이나 나무, 진흙 등으로 만든 물건들'이라는 영영 풀이가 가리키는 것은 ④ sculptures(조각품들)이다.

30 위 글에 따르면, Andy Warhol이 그의 작품의 복사본들을 만든 이유는 '예술이 누구나 매일 보는 것임을 보여 주고 싶었기 때문이다.'(Why did he make copies of his works? He wanted to show that art is something you see every day.)라고 언급되어 있다.

Lesson 9 (기말) **1회**

> **01** ③ **02** ④ **03** ④ **04** ⑤ **05** ② **06** ③ **07** ① **08** ③
> **09** ① **10** ② **11** why the baby is crying **12** ② **13** ④
> **14** ④ **15** 사람들의 마음
> **16** Is it possible for her to control them, too?
> **17** ③ **18** ③ **19** ① **20** ③
> **21** using corn cobs that[which] I had collected from farmers, I built a filtering system
> **22** ②, ⑤ **23** they could go to school **24** ③ **25** ③
> **26** ① **27** ④ **28** ③ **29** ⑤ **30** ⑤

01 '물, 공기 또는 땅을 더럽게 만들다'라는 영영 풀이가 가리키는 것은 ③pollute(오염시키다)이다.

02 fair는 '박람회'라는 뜻으로 물건을 사거나 제품에 관한 정보를 얻는 대규모 행사를 의미한다.

03 '뭔가를 어떤 곳에서 옮기거나 없애다'라는 영영 풀이가 가리키는 것은 ④ remove(치우다, 제거하다)이다.

04 비교급을 강조할 때는 비교급 앞에 much, still, even, far, a lot 등의 부사를 쓰며 '…보다 훨씬 더 ~한'이라는 의미를 갖는다. very는 원급의 형용사(또는 부사)를 수식하며, 비교급은 수식하지 않는다.

05 ② how could he solve → how he could solve로 고쳐야 어법상 적절한 문장이 된다.

06 ⓐ he come → he will come / ⓑ Do you think what his father does? → What do you think his father does? / ⓔ did left → left로 고쳐야 어법상 적절한 문장이 된다.

07 ② can → could / ③ went to bed → had gone to bed / ④ lets → had let / ⑤ knows → knew로 고쳐야 어법상 적절한 문장이 된다.

08 ① 만약 Peter가 야구를 좋아한다면 너는 그걸 내게 말해 줄래? → 너는 Peter가 야구를 좋아하는지 아니? / ② 사진을 찍으러 갈 것인지 → 사진을 찍는 걸 좋아하는지 / ④ 언제 그 경기에서 이길지 → 그 경기에서 이길지 / ⑤ 그가 회의에 올 것인지 → 그가 회의에 늦을 것인지로 고쳐야 어법상 적절한 문장이 된다.

09 ① hit in the idea → hit on the idea로 고쳐야 어법상 적절한 문장이 된다.

10 현재 사실에 반대되는 소망 또는 현재 사실에 대한 유감을 나타낼 때는 'I wish+주어+동사의 과거형'을 쓴다.

11 간접의문문의 어순은 '의문사+주어+동사 ~' 순으로 쓴다.

12 현재 사실에 반대되는 소망 또는 현재 사실에 대한 유감을 나타낼 때는 'I wish+주어+동사의 과거형'을 쓴다. 여학생이 수영을 잘할 수 있는지 묻자, 남학생은 아니라고 답하면서 대신에 물 위를 걷는 공을 가지고 재미있게 보낼 거야.라고 했으므로 빈칸에는 "I wish I could (swim well), but I can't.(잘할 수 있으면 좋을 텐데, 그러지 못해.)"가 가장 적절하다.

13 위 대화에서는 ④ Who is Mike going to play with?(Mike는 누구와 함께 놀 것인가?)에 대해서는 언급된 바 없다.

14 위 대화에 따르면, Sky X는 우주에서 무엇이든 할 수 있다.("He can do anything in space.")라고 언급되어 있다.

15 인칭대명사 them은 앞 문장에 나온 people's mind(사람들의 마음)를 가리킨다.

16 Ⓐ는 "그녀가 그것(사람들의 마음)도 통제할 수 있니?"라는 의미의 문장이다. 따라서 Is it possible for her to control them, too?로 바꿔 쓸 수 있다.

17 유진의 질문에 "I wish I could.(나는 할 수 있으면 좋을 텐데.)"라고 답했다. 'I wish+가정법 과거 ~'는 현재 사실에 반대되는 소망 또는 현재 사실에 대한 유감을 나타내므로, Tony는 현재 기타를 못 친다.가 적절하다.

18 In the following stories you will meet three teenagers who used their ideas to make the world a better place.(다음 이야기들에서 여러분은 세상을 더 나은 곳으로 만들기 위해 자신들의 아이디어를 사용한 세 명의 십 대들을 만날 겁니다.)라고 언급되어 있다.

19 ⓑ seriously polluting → seriously polluted / ⓒ how could I solve this problem → how I could solve this problem / ⓓ out of the polluting water → out of the polluted water / ⓔ but also other areas → but also in other areas로 고쳐야 어법상 적절한 문장이 된다.

20 위 글에 따르면, 그녀는 농부들로부터 모은 옥수수 속대를 이용하여 여과 장치를 만들었다고 언급되어 있다.

21 여과 장치를 만든(built) 것보다 옥수수 속대를 모은 것이 더 이전의 일이기 때문에 과거완료시제인 had collected를 쓴다. using corn cobs: 옥수수 속대를 이용해서, corn cobs that[which] I had collected from farmers: 내가 농부로부터 모은 옥수수 속대, 여과 장치: a filtering system

22 ⓐ as: ~처럼, ~함에 따라
ⓒ ask: 요청하다, 묻다
ⓓ take a step: 조치를 취하다, take: 선택하다, 사다

23 자신이 학교에 갈 수 있는 것처럼 아프리카의 많은 소녀들도 학교에 갈 수 있으면 좋겠다는 소망을 나타내는 내용이 자연스러우므로 'I wish they could go to school. too.'가 적절하다.

24 I created ten headbands and sold them at my school.이라고 언급되어 있다.

25 밑줄 친 (나)there는 'I raised enough money to send one girl in Africa to school.'을 의미한다.

26 'I wish+주어+동사의 과거형 ~'은 '~하면 좋을 텐데.'라는 의미로 현재 사실과 반대되는 일을 소망하는 표현인다.

27 주어진 문장의 what I have done은 디자인과 소프트웨어를 공유하는 것을 의미하므로 (D)에 오는 것이 적절하다.

28 밑줄 친 (나)의 속담은 '두 사람의 지혜가 한 사람의 지혜보다 낫다'라는 뜻으로, 앞 문장의 'we can build a better world by working together.'를 의미한다.

29 위 글에서는 ⑤ Why was the girl's robotic hand so expensive?(그 소녀의 로봇 손은 왜 그렇게 비쌌는가?)에 대해서는 언급된 바 없다.

30 Easton은 자신이 만든 디자인과 소프트웨어를 다른 사람들과 무료로 공유하기로 결심했다.('I decided to share the designs and software for my 3D robotic hand with others for free.').라고 언급했다.

적중 1◌◌ + 특별부록

Plan B

우리학교
최신기출

시사·박준언 교과서를 배우는

학교 시험문제 분석 · 모음 · 해설집

전국단위 학교 시험문제 수집 및 분석
출제 빈도가 높은 문제 위주로 선별
문제 풀이에 필요한 상세한 해설

중3-2
영어

시사 · 박준언

값 6,000원